SINGLE ACTION SIXGUNS

John Taffin

ECHO POINT BOOKS & MEDIA, LLC
BRATTLEBORO, VERMONT

Published by Echo Point Books & Media
Brattleboro, Vermont
www.EchoPointBooks.com

All rights reserved.
Neither this work nor any portions thereof may be reproduced, stored in a retrieval system, or transmitted in any capacity without written permission from the publisher.

CAUTION: Technical data presented here, particularly technical data on handloading and on firearms adjustment and alteration, inevitably reflects individual experience with particular equipment and components under specific circumstances the reader cannot duplicate exactly. Such data presentations therefore should be used for guidance only and with caution. Echo Point Books & Media accepts no responsibility for results obtained using these data.

Copyright © 2005, 2018 by John Taffin

Single Action Sixguns
ISBN: 978-1-63561-691-0 (casebound)
978-1-64837-252-0 (paperback)

Interior Designed by Elizabeth Krogwold
Edited by Dan Shideler

Cover design by Fajar Wahyu

Cover art: Colt SAA ca. 45 factory engraved by Cuno Helfricht, circa 1893, courtesy of Hmaag / Wikimedia;
Background wood boards texture by Daria Yakovleva, courtesy of pixabay

–Dedication–

IN MEMORY OF

RON ELERICK,

THE KILTED PREACHER

—Foreword—

The year 1939 was an auspicious time for the entertainment business here in the USA. Some of the all-time best movies were released including *Gone With The Wind, Stagecoach, The Wizard of Oz,* and *Jesse James*. If your idea of entertainment ran more to shooting sixguns than seeing them shot on film, May 2, 1939, was also an auspicious date in your life, for on this date a Mrs. Augustin Taffin of Barberton, Ohio, brought forth a new son, wrapped him in Hoppe's uncut swaddling patches, and laid him in a manger disguised as a rifle rest. His father named him John August Taffin after grandfather Jean Augusta. Little did the Taffin family realize their world would be turned upside down as young John's father was killed less than a year later.

John was a sharp lad who did well in school, ending up with a master's degree in mathematics, which he used to teach in the public schools for over 30 years. (Many a casual young boy became a serious student when he discovered he had a teacher who shared the love of shooting and hunting. But I digress.) As a lad John had chosen Theodore Roosevelt as his idea of a hero, which gives us an excellent clue as to the character of John Taffin. Young John also was exposed to western movies, where he developed the love for the single action revolvers that are the focus of the book you are about to read.

While John became a mathematics teacher by trade, you could also make the claim he simultaneously earned a Ph.D. degree in sixgunology. There is no one I know with a broader base of knowledge about single actions in all their nuances than John. From the Colt cap & ball revolvers to the Colt Single Action Army, to the Remington 1875 and 1890, to the Great Western SAA revolvers, to the Ruger line of single action sixguns, to the ultra-modern Freedom Arms revolvers, John has tested them all.

As I write these words right after the Shootists Holiday 2004, I have not read the book you are holding in your hands. If it is half as good as John Taffin's first three books, it will still be twice as good and twice as detailed as any book on single action sixguns ever written. These words do NOT disparage Elmer Keith's *Sixguns* written half a century ago, for John's experience with single action sixguns now far exceeds that of Elmer Keith, whom all sixgunners, John included, see as our Patron Saint. Keith was indeed the inspiration for all of our modern big-bore sixguns. John picked up the torch and has carried it through four books on the subject, not to mention hundreds of articles dealing with sixguns almost exclusively.

So my friends, my heart pounds in anticipation of reading the book you are holding. I have been shooting for 53 years now and John's books thrill me every time I pick one up. This one will be a doozy too, mark my words.

Terry Murbach
Black Hills, Dakota Territory
June 2004

Contents

Introduction—Single Action: The Perfect Sixgun?..6

PART I: THE FIRST SINGLE ACTION SIXGUNS
In The Beginning 8
The S&W Models #1, #2, and #3 15
The Smith & Wesson Schofield 22
The Remington "Top-Straps" 27
The Colt Cartridge Conversions 33
The Colt Single Action Army First Generation 38
The Colt Bisley Model and Flat-Top Targets...............................49

PART II: ONE MAN'S INFLUENCE
The Single Action Sixguns of Elmer Keith.................................54
The Texas Longhorn Arms Improved Number Five 63
The Texas Longhorn Arms Flat-Top Target and South Texas Army............69

PART III: THE POST WAR SINGLE ACTIONS
The Colt Single Action Army Second Generation 77
The Colt Single Action Army Third Generation 84
The Colt New Frontier 91
The Great Western Single Action 96
United States Firearms Single Actions 104

PART IV: THE MODERNIZATION OF THE SINGLE ACTION SIXGUN
The Ruger Single-Six 111
The Ruger Flat-Top 118
The Ruger Old Model 125
The Ruger New Model 129
The Ruger Bisley Model 134
The Ruger Vaquero 139
The Ruger Hunter Model.. 145
The Ruger Old Army 150
The Freedom Arms Model 83 155
The Freedom Arms Model 97 163
The Mini-Guns 170
The Maxi-Guns 175

PART V: REPLICA SINGLE ACTION SIXGUNS
The Percussion Sixguns 189
The Single Action Replicas 190

PART VI: CUSTOMIZING SINGLE ACTION SIXGUNS
Peacemaker Specialists...195
Customizing The Single Action Army 203
Customizing The Old Model Ruger 211
Customizing The New Model Ruger 224
Single Action Grips and Grip Frames 235

PART VII: USING THE SINGLE ACTION SIXGUN
Tips For Handling Single Actions..252
Single Actions For Defensive Use? 262
Long Range Single Action Sixguns..271
Single Action Sixguns and Auxiliary Cylinders.......................279
Hunting With the Single Action Sixgun.................................. 286
Single Action Sixgun Games..293
Perfect Packin' Pistols Single Action Style................................301

PART VIII: SINGLE ACTION SIXGUN LOADS AND LEATHER
Single Action Sixgun Leather... 307
Crafting Your Own Single Action Leather 319
Single Action Sixgun Loads 325

–Introduction–

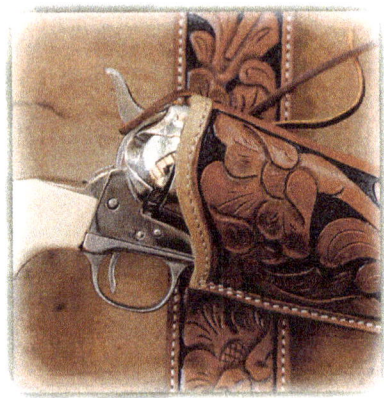

Pick up a large seashell and hear the ocean; pick up a single action and hear and feel history. Just holding an old Colt single action conjures up visions of the Earps and Doc Holliday at the O.K. Corral, Theodore Roosevelt in the Dakotas, and Lt. George Patton with Black Jack Pershing in Mexico. We can hear bugles in the afternoon, smell bacon and beans cooking over a campfire, feel the dust from the hooves of a thousand cattle, and taste steak and a big slab of apple pie washed down with hot coffee at the Irma Hotel. A sixth sense takes over and Matt Dillon, Paladin, Rooster Cogburn, all become real.

Look at a single action and see the beauty of the upswept hammer, the worn walnut stocks, the wear on the metal and bluing from a thousand trips in and out of a holster. See the classic lines any artist would call perfect. Run fingers over the metal, feel the bevels at the end of the cylinder and ejector rod housing, feel the sharp edges of the flutes, and the smooth radius at the top of the back strap where it meets the hammer. Feast and enjoy.

The feelings and emotions don't end with an old Colt. That old Single-Six .22 plays back memories of good friends and Saturday afternoons; a 1950s Colt .45 and I'm back in the Fast Draw contests that captured our imagination so well; a Flat-Top Ruger 44 Magnum brings back those first hunting trips; a Ruger 357 Maximum and I'm back shooting silhouettes; a Freedom Arms .454 and Africa returns; another Freedom Arms, this time a 44 Magnum, and I'm in Texas sitting in a deer blind waiting for the sun to come up, or slugging through waist deep snow up an Idaho mountain after a cougar; and that Texas Longhorn Arms 44 Special and I'm back hunting feral pigs. Imagination is a wonderful thing, but it takes something to trigger it, and nothing is better than a single action.

The single action revolver is a throwback. It should have been replaced in the last quarter of the nineteenth century with the double action revolver. It wasn't. The dawning of the twentieth century and the semi-automatics that came with it should have buried the single action forever. They didn't. Just when everyone thought the single action was dead and buried and never to be seen again, a miracle happened to save it. In the late 1940s and early 1950s it was television and the B western movies creating a demand for the Colt and Ruger single actions. By the late 1950s, the miracle was Fast Draw, then came Long Range Silhouetting, Handgun Hunting, and Cowboy Action Shooting, every one of which created a demand for quality single actions.

Even if none of these had occurred the single action would have survived. It is the coyote of the firearms industry: whatever the situation, it adapts. It just plain works for everything – hiking, hunting, camping, sixgun games, even self-defense; it is the best canvas ever made for the firearms engraver. Someone as mechanically challenged as I am can take one apart and put it back together with no parts left over and everything

The historical clock is turned back to the early 1870s with a pair of Cimarron 44 Colt Open-Tops with Buffalo Brothers Mexican Eagle grips and period-style leather by Rawhide Walt Ostin.

in the right place. It carries perfectly and easily on the hip, stows easily and handily under a bedroll beside a campfire, feels so comfortably at home in the hand, and shoots where it points. Whether chambered in .22 rimfire, the latest 500 Magnum, or anything in between, it is dependable, trustworthy, and accurate. There are very few man-made things in this world that can be called perfect; the single action comes as close as anything else.

This work should not be approached as an encyclopedia of single actions. It is not; it is a pure and simple love story. In the following pages I hope to share just a small portion of my nearly life-long love affair with the single action sixgun.

Good Shootin' and God Bless!
John Taffin
Boise, Idaho

DISCLAIMER: All loading data contained herein should be used with caution. The author is responsible only for that ammunition he personally assembles for use in his particular firearms. Because we have no control over your loading practices, nor the firearms you may choose for the use of such loads, neither the author, editor, publisher, nor manufacturers of components has any responsibility for the use of any reloading data found in these pages.

–Chapter 1–

IN THE BEGINNING

In the beginning, Sam Colt created the revolver, the single action sixgun. Perhaps we had better qualify that to say Sam created the first practical working revolver. The story goes that young Colt shipped out of Boston as a cabin boy and during his spare time watched the ship's wheel rotate and be locked into a desired position. That set similar wheels turning in Sam's mind and he soon whittled a working model out of wood of what he thought a revolver should be. It wouldn't surprise me to find out at the time he thought, "I hope no one ever calls my revolver a wheelgun." Well, I can at least imagine so!

In reality, by the time teenage Sam came up with his idea, the revolver was at least 150 years old as there is a six-shot, flintlock revolver in the armory of the Tower of London dating back to the late 1600s. Sam may not have invented the revolver; however, he made it work, he made it practical, he made it portable, and he made it affordable, and in doing all this he became known as The Man Who Made All Men Equal. We could also say Sam Colt, more than anyone else, was responsible for the Age of the Gunfighter. The first real gunfighter's weapon remains one of the finest handlin' sixguns ever, the .36-caliber 1851 Colt Navy. With its easy-packin' portability, it ushered in the era of the shootist. However, this was not Colt's first revolver, that distinction going to the five-shot, folding-trigger Paterson of 1836.

A decade later, after the bankruptcy of Colt's company and the start of war with Mexico, the out-of-production .36 Paterson was followed by the powerful but cumbersome Walkers and Dragoons. Hollywood notwithstanding, these big .44s were so heavy they were not carried in holsters but saddle scabbards. The sixgunner had to be on horseback to have easy access to his sixguns; however the advent of the 1851 Navy brought a sixgun easily capable of being carried readily accessible in a hip holster. Just before the dawn of the Civil War, the power of the Dragoons and Walkers was combined with the portability of the Navy as the 1860 Army arrived. Not quite as powerful as the Dragoons and Walkers of the 1840s, and not quite as small as the 1851 Navy, it was, however, in .44 caliber, and almost as easy to pack as the .36 Navy. By this time the revolver stage was solidly set for a long line of easy to carry, big bore single action sixguns. Colt was not the only choice as Remington in fact beat the 1860 Colt by two years with the introduction of their .44 caliber Model 1858. Both of the new .44s would see extensive service with the Army of the Potomac.

Sam Colt, who died in 1862, did not live to see the dawning of the era of cartridge-firing big-bore single actions. A decade after his death the planets must have lined up right as 1873 was a banner year for great firearms. Winchester introduced their first center-fire lever action, the Model of 1873 chambered in 44 WCF; the single-shot 1873 Trapdoor was introduced in 45-70 Government; and one of the greatest

In the beginning Taffin started with a pair of 7-1/2-inch Colt single action .45s carried in a double rig by Ray Howser of the Pony Express Sport Shop. The year is 1957.

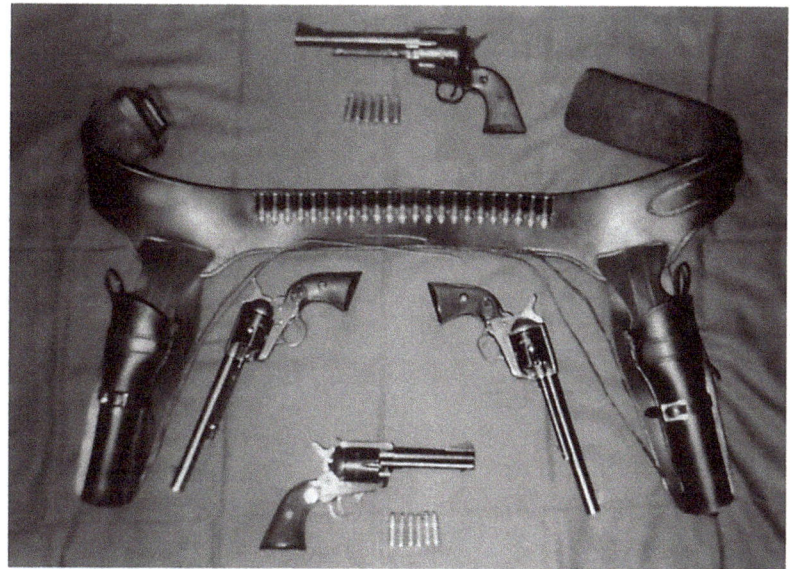

Taffin's single action sixguns from 1957: a 6-1/2-inch Ruger 44 Magnum Blackhawk; a 4-5/8-inch Ruger 357 Magnum Blackhawk; First and Second Generation 7-1/2-inch Colt Single Action .45s; and a Ray Howser double fast draw rig.

sixguns ever (I would not argue with anyone who called it *the* greatest sixgun ever) was also introduced at the same time. The Colt Single Action Army still exists, having gone through three production generations and being produced almost continuously except from 1941 to 1956 and for a short time in the 1970s. It has also been copied and modified by some manufacturers and certainly served to inspire others. In the last half-century single actions patterned after the great Colt Single Action Army have been offered by such companies as Great Western, Ruger, Seville, Abilene, Freedom Arms, Texas Longhorn Arms, Interarms, and United States Firearms. Foreign manufacturers such as Armi San Marco, Pietta, and Uberti have produced Italian replicas imported by American Western Arms, Cimarron, EMF, Navy Arms, and Taylor's & Co., while Herter's, Hawes, and EAA have all offered German-made big bore sixguns. Even Beretta and Taurus, long known for semi-automatics and double action revolvers, are now offering traditionally styled single action sixguns.

The first Colt Single Action Army, officially known as the Model P and affectionately as the Peacemaker, was offered in the now equally legendary 45 Colt. Those first single actions were designed at the bequest of the United States military for use by the cavalry and were originally offered with a Cavalry Model barrel length of 7-1/2 inches to duplicate the feel of the 1860 Army they would replace. The other standard barrel lengths soon offered were the 5-1/2-inch Artillery Model and one of the finest balanced sixguns, perhaps the finest, the 4-3/4-inch Civilian Model.

The practical working single action is almost two centuries old, having arrived on the scene in 1836 and then being improved in 1847, 1851, 1860, and finally in 1873, when it became basically the fine sixgun still existing today. Experts expected it to die with the coming of double action sixguns from Colt and Smith & Wesson in the 1870s and 1880s. It did not. It should have died in 1899 with the coming of the Smith & Wesson K-frame double action, as slick-handlin' a sixgun as one is likely to find. It did not. It should have been buried by the advent of the 1907 N-frame big bore sixgun from Smith & Wesson. It did not. By 1911 the 45 ACP-chambered Government Model, a gun designed to give the power of the 1873 45 Colt in a "modern" gun, should have made everyone forget the single action. The single action remained. It is a survivor.

Some very famous men who had every opportunity to choose a 1911 or a double action sixgun did otherwise. In 1916, before heading into Mexico after Pancho Villa, a young Army Lieutenant picked up a fully-engraved, nickel-plated, ivory-gripped .45 in El Paso. This was not a 1911 Government Model but a Single Action Army. That sixgun became famous as it was seen in many photographs taken of General Patton in World War Two. It survives today in the West Point Museum complete with S. D. Myres leather rig and two notches in the grip from the Mexican campaign.

The career of the infamous team of Bonnie and Clyde was stopped by former Texas Ranger Frank Hamer, whose favorite sixgun was "Old Lucky," a 45 Colt Single Action Army. Hamer was a real hero, a true "one riot, one Ranger" type of lawman. It was Hamer who said if he couldn't get it done with five rounds in his 45 Colt he was "guilty of sloppy peace officering." He got it done.

The single action still survives in this day of many superb double action revolvers and semi-automatics. Is

Single Action Sixguns | 9

Chapter 1 | In The Beginning

Summer 1967: Taffin shooting the Ruger Super Blackhawk 44 Magnum in the Payette National Forest.

"Personally, I like any handgun that looks good, feels good, and shoots good but first and foremost I am, always have been, and always will be a single action sixgunner."

the person who packs a single action at a great disadvantage? In the vast majority of cases I do not believe so. I pack a single action often, almost always when the hardware is packed openly, and even when I am testing a double action or semi-automatic, I more often than not will be wearing a single action. They just seem to holster and pack so much more easily than other types. The first shot is fast, though subsequent shots may be slower, but the big bore single action can be depended upon to deliver five shots from a gun whose balance and portability have never been equaled. In the areas I frequent the most, the mountains, forests, foothills and deserts of Idaho, the chance of needing anything other than a big bore single action is virtually nil. The single action suits me just fine.

Yes, packin' a single action with roots going back to the nineteenth century in this the first decade of the twenty-first century may be looked upon by some as operating with not quite a full deck and being controlled more by tradition than practicality. Given my choice, however, as to a single action sixgun or a high capacity nine I would pick the single action every time. I am not a peace officer, and God bless those who are, but if I had to go forth into the big city jungles every working day I would prefer a 100% reliable semi-automatic such as my Clark Custom Combat Commander .45 or at the very least a Smith & Wesson K-frame .357 or big bore N-frame. But I am not, so I remain perfectly comfortable with a single action sixgun.

My modest collection of personal sixguns as well as handguns on loan for testing and evaluation contains all types: single actions, double action sixguns, and both single action and double action semi-automatics. Stacked up against any of these the Single Action Army is a classic pure and simple, heading a list that also includes the Colt 1911

By 1956, Taffin, still a teenager, had three single actions that could easily have served him the rest of his shootin' life: Ruger's .22 Single-Six and 357 and 44 Magnum Blackhawks.

Government Model and Python; the Ruger Flat-Top and Super Blackhawk; and the original S&W 357 Magnum, 44 Magnum, and the answer to the peace officer's dream, the Combat Magnum of the 1950s. Personally, I like any handgun that looks good, feels good, and shoots good but first and foremost I am, always have been, and always will be a single action sixgunner.

From my first Colts in 38-40 and 45 Colt, through the .22 Single-Six and .357 and .44 Ruger Flat-Tops of the 1950s, through the Freedom Arms and Texas Longhorn Arms sixguns first arriving in the 1980s, to the New Model Rugers and USFA Single Actions of today, I'll take single actions. In the beginning, my revolver shootin' beginning, my first sixgun purchased was a single action. It was 1956, I was a teenager, and the sixgun was a Ruger .22 Single-Six. Fast-forward nearly 50 years and my latest sixgun is a USFA 7-1/2-inch 44 Special Flat-Top Target.

Why does the single action remain so popular to sixgun connoisseurs and countless thousands of shooters like me? Why do so many one-handgun owners who want a gun for plinking, a gun for the possible home defense, a gun for the car when traveling, a gun for packin' on the hip while roaming desert, foothills, forests, and mountains, pick a single action? Why do many shooters pass over the double actions and semi-automatics to buy an old-fashioned single action? The answer is simply because it suits his or her needs perfectly.

Single action sixguns take me back to the first date with the young blonde teenage girl that would become my wife four months later. Our first trip together in my '53 Merc was taken to Boyle's Gun Shop to pick up my custom Ojala rig. She knew what to expect from then on, but I can't believe she ever suspected that we would both be so involved in firearms in general and single action sixguns in particular over our now 46 years together. From our first times together she has shot with me and we were especially careful to shoot together as she was expecting each of our three kids. They say unborn children can hear music and the type of music played determines what they will prefer later. If this true they could also certainly hear gunfire and be pointed in the right direction gun-wise even before being born.

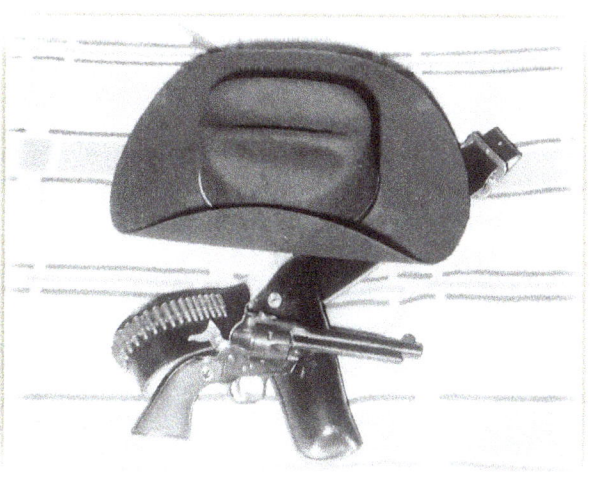

The author's first handgun – first revolver – first single action sixgun – was a Flat-Gate Ruger Single-Six .22 with a George Lawrence #120 Keith holster and belt, purchased in 1956.

Single Action Sixguns

Chapter 1 | In The Beginning

Great single action sixguns used in the 1950s: the Colt 1860 Army, Colt Single Action 44 Special, and S&W New Model #3 belonged to a shooting buddy; the 7-1/2-inch Colt 45s and the Ruger Blackhawks were Taffin's working single actions in 1957.

An expecting mother, Dot Taffin, takes a break from shooting single action sixguns in the summer of 1960.

Taffin shoots Ruger's 44 Magnum Blackhawk purchased new in 1957.

Whether this is true or not is debatable but we didn't take any chances. We shot single action sixguns.

One of the first negatives pointed out about single actions is that they are slow to load and unload. Frank Hamer would say you should not need any more than five rounds anyway, and anyone must confess there is no way to reload a single action as fast as a double action with a speedloader or the fastest of all reloads, the magazine-fed autoloader. However, when the autoloader's magazines are empty everything is reversed. The single action is much faster to load and reload than it is to fill the semi-auto's magazine. An accomplished single action sixgunner can actually reload faster than the average non-speedloader-using double action shooter – especially if the double action shooter is careless and finds himself with an empty case stuck under the extractor star. Empties can be ejected from a spinning single action cylinder pretty fast and those nose-heavy big bore rounds drop back in with no effort. Thell Reed is almost as fast doing this as Jerry Miculek is speed loading his double action. Almost.

The single action has always been considered far more likely to break than other types of actions. Both Colt and Colt-style replica single actions with leaf springs are prone to breakage when it comes to bolt and hand springs. Both of these are fairly easy to replace, but in a gun that is properly tuned they rarely break. They can also be rather easily replaced with coil springs and wire springs. Bill Ruger not only made the single action affordable for the average shooter; he also modernized it in 1953 with his all coil spring-driven Single-Six. With today's New Model Ruger and Freedom Arms revolvers, we have single actions that are virtually indestructible.

There are those who will try to tell us single actions are not as accurate as double actions or semi-automatics. A good gun is a good gun and after nearly a half-century of shooting virtually every type of repeating handgun I can say accuracy is a result of quality gun-building, not

The author getting ready to buckle on his Arvo Ojala rig and 7-1/2-inch Colt single action .45 for some fast draw practice in 1960.

Summer of 1960: the author shooting Ruger's .44 Blackhawk. Leather is the George Lawrence #120 Keith. Both sixgun and holster are still in use today. The belt has shrunk.

a certain type of action. But what about long hammer falls and heavy triggers? Most new handguns, whether single action, double action, or semi-automatic, require a trigger and action job as they come from the factory. If one doesn't wish to spend the extra dollars to have a single action perfectly tuned with a three-pound creep-free trigger and a lighter though still reliable mainspring then the answer is simply to get used to it. The human body is amazingly adaptable.

The single action is an inherently strong design. In fact, until the advent of the Ruger Redhawk and Super Redhawk, and now the Smith & Wesson Model 500, no double action could even come close to handling the pressures possible in many single action sixguns. The newer model single actions have massive frames coupled with a cylinder that is anchored solidly both front and rear, requiring an awful lot of shooting to get out of alignment. When I consider the thousands of heavy loads I have personally run through my 10-inch Freedom Arms 454 Casull, even I, a true single action connoisseur, stand in awe at the strength of this fine revolver. Coupled with the strength of the modern single actions from Ruger and Freedom Arms is the ability to pack this strength in such a practical and portable package. The Ruger Redhawks and Super Redhawks are very strong revolvers, but they are nowhere near as portable or as easy to holster as the single actions.

Whatever caliber is chosen, one of the great assets of the single action is grip shape. The single action grip is the finest ever devised to fit the most hands, but it is not universal. For my hands, the traditional Colt grip shape is perfect for calibers up to heavy 44 Special and 45 Colt loads. We are talking 250-grain bullets at 900 to 1100, possibly even 1200, feet per second. Go beyond these loads and recoil becomes a problem even for me with the Colt grip shape. Ruger addressed this problem by introducing the Super Blackhawk grip frame in 1959. For some reason it just never worked well for me. The Bisley Model introduced nearly three decades later does.

There's something almost spiritual about the single action. Did Sam Colt have some special help in coming up with that first practical single action? Did

Single Action Sixguns | 13

Chapter 1 | In The Beginning

> "There are qualities inherent in a good single action that cause soul, spirit, and heart to be stirred."

William Mason actually design the Colt Single Action Army or did he go to sleep one night only to wake up the next morning and find the plans had mysteriously appeared on his desk? Could the single action actually have come from the mind of mere mortals? It doesn't seem so to me. There are qualities inherent in a good single action that cause soul, spirit, and heart to be stirred. If one's emotions are not quickened by the feel and genuine great looks of a Colt Single Action Army, a Freedom Arms Model 83, a Texas Longhorn Arms Number Five, a Ruger Flat-Top or Bisley, something is definitely lacking in one's life.

It is quite difficult to explain all of this to anyone who doesn't understand. Pick up a single action, thumb back that big hammer, rotate the cylinder, and if you do not feel the dust of a Texas cattle drive, hear the sounds of the saloons along the Main Street of Dodge City, smell bacon and coffee on an open fire in the mountains of Montana, something is not connected. Take the next step. Fire that first shot and feel the gentle recoil of a 44 Special or 45 Colt, or experience the power of a 44 Magnum or 454 Casull. From that moment on you will either be a true lover of single actions or all hope is lost.

My Smith & Wesson and Colt double actions and semi-automatics will not be given up; they are normally the first choice when carrying concealed, but as I head for the desert, foothills, forests, or mountains, it is quite likely I will be packin' a single action. It may say Colt, Freedom Arms, Ruger or Texas Longhorn Arms on the barrel. Whatever the maker, a single action is made for the outdoors. When I head out, chances are extremely high it will be a single action that goes with me. A good single action sixgun, plenty of ammo, food, water, sleeping bag, and a companion fit to ride the river with are all I need to head for the hills and experience real life.

Single action sixguns build memories. Taffin looks back and thinks of a half century of shootin' single action sixguns.

–Chapter 2–

THE SMITH & WESSON MODELS #1, #2, AND #3

In 2007 Smith & Wesson will celebrate their 150th anniversary as the first American manufacturer of a revolver firing cartridge ammunition. That first revolver, arriving in 1857 and using fixed ammunition – a bullet and powder in a cartridge case as opposed to powder, ball, and cap – was the Smith & Wesson Model #1, a spur trigger, seven-shot single action, tip-up chambered in 22 Short. These little guns were hinged at the top of the frame in front of the hammer, the barrel and top strap actually tipping up to allow the removal of the cylinder for loading and unloading. They arrived just at the right time and S&W tip-up handguns would prove to be quite popular as hideout guns during the Civil War. The continued popularity of the Model #1 22 Short is evidenced by the fact it would be made in three variations with a total of more than one-quarter million being produced from 1857 to 1881.

S&W's first revolver was the seven-shot Model 1 .22 of 1857, shown with an early 32 S&W top break.

Whether in the nineteenth century or the twenty-first century, a 22 Short is not considered an adequate defensive choice, so Smith & Wesson's slight step up in power was the Model #1-1/2 chambered in 32 rimfire. By the time this little five-shot revolver had arrived at its third issue, it would be chambered in 32 Rimfire Long. More than 100,000 S&W .32s would be manufactured from 1865 to 1875. Certainly neither the .22 nor .32 versions of the Smith & Wesson single action were very powerful; however, they were very easy to conceal in pocket, sleeve, muff, or purse. This ensured relatively heavy sales.

Two styles of S&W single actions, the .22 tip-up, bottom, and the .32 centerfire top break.

In 1861, the slightly larger Model #2, a six-shot 32 Rimfire Long, arrived in time to see quite a bit of use during the Civil War. No military contracts were forthcoming, but it still found its way under the tunics and on the belts of many soldiers. More than 75,000 were manufactured when production ceased in 1874. Smith & Wesson's final tip-up revolver would be the Model #3 four-shot Pocket Pistol chambered in 41 Rimfire. This is an extremely rare single action with only 50 having been manufactured in 1867. Perhaps even the 41 Rimfire was too much for the hinge at the top frame. Something larger and better loomed over the horizon.

Single Action Sixguns | 15

Chapter 2 | The Smith & Wesson Models #1, 1-1/2, #2, and #3

The spur on the trigger guard of the Model #3 Russian helps steady the sixgun for more accurate shooting.

Before the arrival of the 41 Rimfire #3 in 1867, even before the outbreak of hostilities in the 1861, Smith & Wesson had planned to bring out a big bore revolver, but because of the Civil War those plans were necessarily put on hold until the late 1860s. Smith & Wesson held the Rollin White patent for a drilled-through cylinder to accept fixed ammunition, but they needed two more additional patents for the first big bore Model #3 revolver.

Model Numbers 1, 1-1/2, and 2 were all small-caliber revolvers hinged at the back top portion of the frame, a very weak design, and the cylinder had to be removed for loading and unloading. In order to offer a larger caliber in a more convenient form, Smith & Wesson needed both the W.C. Dodge and C. A. King patents. The former provided for a design that locked at the top of the back portion of the frame and pivoted on the barrel portion at the lower part of the front portion of the frame. This was to be combined with King's invention of simultaneous ejection of spent cartridges. Smith & Wesson was able to purchase both of these patents and in the 1869 produced the Smith & Wesson Model #3 "American" .44-caliber six-shot revolver, the first true big-bore cartridge-firing six-shooter.

There were several other improvements added to the American. For the first time cartridge cases were made of brass instead of copper and the cases were centerfire instead of rimfire. The 44 Smith & Wesson American cartridge was loaded with 25 grains of black powder under a 218-gr. bullet with a muzzle velocity of 650 fps. It gained a reputation for accuracy to 50 yards.

Suddenly all percussion pistols were made obsolete by this new weapon that was such a major improvement over both the cap-and-ball revolvers and single shot pistols of the time. Sam Colt introduced the first practical single action sixgun in 1836 but it would be Smith & Wesson who took the lead in manufacturing the first cartridge-firing big-bore single action sixgun. In December of 1870, the U.S. Government ordered 1,000 S&W Americans for military use. Once the cavalry managed to acquire the 44 Americans, Smith & Wesson soon began to receive orders from around the country. Consider the situation in the early 1870s. The Civil War had been over for five years and the country was looking westward. This meant the main concern for the U.S. Cavalry would be Indians and lawless elements scattered around the frontier. Most cavalry units were still armed with 1860 Army revolvers.

I can well imagine many who appreciated the excellent (for its time) 1860 percussion sixgun would see immediately what a great step forward the .44 American actually was. The 1860 Colt was a magnificent revolver

Taffin takes a break from shootin' an original S&W Model #3 Russian and dreams of the way it used to be.

Part I

and the best available during the Civil War; however, loading the Colt was a relatively slow process requiring a measured amount of powder being placed in the front of each chamber and then a round ball placed in the chamber and seated solidly over the powder charge using the rammer under the barrel. After all chambers were loaded, the percussion caps would then be placed on the nipples at the back of the cylinder. Once that sixgun was empty, a relatively long length of time would be required for reloading. This time would seem like eons during a battle. The great advantage of the Smith & Wesson .44 was its ease and rapidity of loading and unloading. As the lock at the back top of the frame was unlatched, the barrel swung down, empties were automatically ejected, and six new rounds would be loaded in the cylinder. The barrel then swung up, relocking the action. All of this could be accomplished in a few seconds, even faster than a modern swing-out cylindered revolver. I certainly know what my sixgun choice would have been in 1870.

Smith & Wesson had wisely placed sample revolvers in the right hands. General Gorloff, the Russian military attaché, was in the United States to order rifles from Colt and received an S&W American from Smith & Wesson. This resulted in an order for 20,000 S&W Americans by the Russian government in 1871. Six months later the Russian Grand Duke Alexis would visit Smith & Wesson and be presented with a fully engraved, pearl-stocked American before going west to hunt buffalo with two notable western figures, Buffalo Bill and George Armstrong Custer. That revolver was valued at over $400 in 1872. Consider its value in today's dollars!

From 1861 to 1865, Smith & Wesson was on solid financial footing producing hideaway guns for use during the war. However, when the hostilities ceased, the demand for the little tip-up pocket pistols took a major dip, resulting in a corresponding major financial setback due to decreased production after the Civil War. The Russian contract was a needed financial boost for Smith and Wesson, but the Russians asked for changes to the American including its ammunition. In fact, the Russians made several improvements to the S&W Model #3 American revolver as well as to its ammunition. For greater shooting comfort the square stock and grip frame of the American were rounded and diminished in diameter, a lanyard ring was added to the butt for security, a "knuckle" was added to the back strap to keep the grip from shifting in the hand when fired, and the 8-inch barrel was cut to a more convenient 6-1/2 inches. It was definitely a different revolver by the time the Russians got through with it.

However, it is concerning the ammunition that the Russians contributed the most. The S&W Model #3 was available chambered in either 44 Henry Rimfire or 44 Smith & Wesson American. The 44 S&W American cartridge, while of centerfire design, was very similar to the .22 rimfire ammunition still being used today. That is, the bullet was of the heel type with the base of the bullet smaller than the diameter of the rest of the bullet and fitting neatly inside the cartridge case. This resulted in both the bullet and the cartridge case having the same outside diameter. The Russians came up with better ideas that turned out to be great improvements. The bullet was made of uniform diameter, the lubrication

This original Model #3 Russian dates back to 1874, the 44 Russian cartridge to 1871.

Chapter 2 | The Smith & Wesson Models #1, 1-1/2, #2, and #3

The evolution of the S&W 44 single action is shown from top left clockwise: Model #3 American (1870), a pair of Model #3 Russians (1871), and the New Model #3 (1878).

was placed in grooves in the bullet that were inside the cartridge case, and the cartridge case was crimped into a crimping groove on the bullet. The powder charge was reduced to 23 grains, the bullet weight was increased to 246 grains, and the result was the magnificent 44 Russian, the father of the 44 Special and the grandfather of the 44 Magnum.

Even though the bullet weight was increased and the powder charge was decreased, the muzzle velocity actually went up 100 fps to 750 fps and the muzzle energy was increased from 200 to 316 ft. lbs. The 44 Russian also proved to be a superbly accurate cartridge. Even today 44 Russians fired in 44 Special and 44 Magnum cylinders often outshoot their descendants in the accuracy department.

Smith & Wesson also produced top-break pocket pistols beginning with the Model #1-1/2 32 S&W centerfire single action. Nearly 100,000 of these spur-trigger five-shooters where made from 1878 to 1892. There were three basic versions of the Model #2 .38 top-break five-shot single actions. The first two versions, both with spur triggers, were produced from 1876 to 1891, with more than 125,000 being manufactured. The final 38 S&W-chambered single action top-break, the Model 1891, would be offered with a standard trigger and trigger guard from 1891 to 1911 with more than 25,000 being produced.

Add these small-caliber top-break Smith & Wessons to the tip-up models and we have a total of just under three-quarters of a million pocket pistol-sized single actions produced by Smith & Wesson from 1857 to 1911. Add the more than 250,000 Model #3 single actions and we have over 1,000,000 single actions being produced by S&W in a half century. That is a lot of single actions by anyone's standards.

Production of Smith & Wesson big bore single action revolvers lasted from 1870 to 1912 with four basic models: the Americans (1870-1874), the Russians (1873-1878), the Schofields (1875-1877), and the New Model No. Threes (1878-1912). The Americans were made in 44 S&W American, a few in .44 rimfire, and of course the Russian contract guns in 44 Russian; the Schofields only in 45 S&W; and the Russians only in 44 Russian except for a few chambered in 44 rimfire. For the most part the New Model #3s were 44 Russians with a few scattered among 16 other chamberings from 32 S&W up to 455 Mark II.

There are three major variations of the Russian Model. The First Model Russian is basically the 44 American chambered in 44 Russian. Approximately 20,000 of these were manufactured for the Russian Government. The Second Model Russian contained most of the changes noted previously in addition to a spur being added to the trigger guard. Why that spur was put there is still a matter of contention. Was it to prevent the revolver from slipping when placed in the waistband? Pictures exist with Russian soldiers carrying the New Model Russian in a sash around the waist with the spur hooked over the top of the sash.

Perhaps the spur was added to parry a saber thrust? Perhaps. I neither carry the 44 Russian in a sash nor have I had to block any saber thrusts lately so I will go with

Taffin finds the Model #3 Russian was designed more for accuracy than for gunfightin' speed.

a third possibility: I believe the Russians did not have a gunfighter mentality but rather placed a high premium on accurate shooting. The use of the spur on the bottom of the trigger guard results in a very secure and steady hold by simply placing the middle finger around the spur when shooting. Slightly over 85,000 of these spur-equipped Second Model Russians were manufactured by Smith & Wesson.

Finally we come to the Third Model Russian, also known as the New Model Russian as well as the Model #3 Russian. This version has a smaller ejector rod housing than the Second Model. Approximately 61,000 were made. When the New Model Russian evolved into the New Model #3 in 1878, Smith & Wesson had reached the epitome of their single action revolvers.

Several years ago, when returning from the Linebaugh Seminar and Winchester Gun Show in Cody, Wyoming, my wife and I stopped in Idaho Falls for a break. She spotted a quilt store, while I went down the street to a local gun store. It proved to be a great stopping and shopping place. When I left the gun shop I came out with my first single action Smith &Wesson, a New Model Russian dated 1874. The finish was mostly gone, but the barrel was in good shape and it locked up and functioned very well, certainly well enough to allow it to be safely shot with black powder loads only.

Affordable Model #3 Russians in good shooting shape are not all that easy to find. However, Navy Arms offers a shooting replica of the New Model Russian chambered in the historic 44 Russian cartridge. The Navy Arms New Model Russian, or Model 3 Russian, is a faithful copy of the original complete with what are probably the tiniest sights ever placed upon a big bore sixgun, requiring intense concentration for me to achieve small groups on paper.

We earlier mentioned the spur on the bottom of the trigger guard, which steadies the sixgun during deliberate fire. This is one of those good news/bad news propositions. When I place my middle finger on the spur the first shot is very easy to control but my thumb will not reach the hammer to cock it for subsequent shots. If I bypass the spur there is no problem reaching the hammer. For the utmost in accuracy I use the spur; for fast one-handed shooting, I do not.

The Navy Arms New Model Russian is finished overall in a deep blue-black finish set off with a case colored hammer, trigger guard, and locking latch. The factory stocks are smooth European – not quite to my taste, so my personal Navy Arms New Model Russian has been fitted with Ultra Ivory grips from Eagle Grips. Ultra Ivory, while a synthetic material, is just about as close as one can get

> "For the utmost in accuracy I use the spur; for fast one-handed shooting, I do not."

Single Action Sixguns | 19

Chapter 2 | The Smith & Wesson Models #1, 1-1/2, #2, and #3

The Navy Arms Model #3 Russian is a faithful copy of the original Model #3 Russian; this example, top, dates back to 1874.

to real ivory without shelling out ivory-price dollars. The milky white color is there, the grain is there, and the warm feeling is also there. They provide a good contrast to the dark blue finish of the New Model Russian.

Colt ceased production of the Colt Single Action Army in 1941 with the word that it would never be produced again, but "never say never" applies here as 15 years later it was back. As a teenager in 1957 I spent a month's take-home pay to buy the first brand-new Second Generation Colt Single Action Army to arrive at the local gun shop. It was a 7-1/2-inch 45 Colt and I have been a devotee of 7-1/2-inch single actions ever since. Right after buying my first new Colt I discovered I had a neighbor who also loved single actions. He was quite a bit older than I was and his single action sixguns were all of the pre-war type. Even though by this time I had the above-mentioned new Colt – plus a 7-1/2-inch First Generation mate for it and three Ruger single actions (.22 Single-Six and 357 Magnum and 44 Magnum Blackhawks) – I found his three older single actions fascinating.

First was a Colt single action that had been expertly converted to a 7-1/2-inch 44 Special and customized further with an 1860 Colt backstrap, trigger guard, and grip. It had only fired one load since being built: the Keith 44 Special load. The 1860 parts had come from his second sixgun, a .44 1860 Colt cap-and-ball which now had the single action grip parts.

The third sixgun was the most intriguing to me. It was also a .44, but not a Colt. It was a S&W New Model #3 44 Russian. Up to that time I had always thought Smith & Wesson made double action sixguns only. After all, what movie cowboy hero ever carried a Smith & Wesson? After seeing this single action Smith & Wesson I began to watch more closely to see if I could really spot any hero using a Smith & Wesson. Robert Culp as Texas Ranger Hoby Gilman not only carried a Smith & Wesson in the TV series *Trackdown* but also used one in the movie *Hannie Caulder*. Just yesterday I watched Gary Cooper in *Along Came Jones* and he is carrying a Smith & Wesson single action when shot by bad guy Dan Duryea. Tonight I saw Tyrone Power as Jesse James carry a S&W Model #3 in a shoulder holster with a 7-1/2-inch Colt on one side, the Smith on the other. Even Wyatt Earp often carried a Smith & Wesson, as did Kurt Russell in the movie *Tombstone*.

That Smith & Wesson single action sixgun certainly did not have the marvelous balance of its Colt counterpart. Even as a teenager relatively lacking in gun knowledge, however, I could recognize that this was truly a marvelous piece of engineering. The Colt Single Action Army was, always has been, and always will be a real workhorse. The Smith & Wesson New Model #3 on the other hand is a true thoroughbred. In actuality, the S&W was a sixgun engineered for smokeless powder at a time when all cartridges were loaded with black powder.

In 1878, the Model #3 Russian evolved into the New Model #3, S&W's finest single action.

By this I do not mean smokeless powder should be used in any of these old sixguns with their questionable metals and heat-treating, but rather the machining and tolerances used in their manufacture were so precise they were easily fouled and would work very sluggishly after only a few rounds of blackpowder loads.

After seeing my first S&W single action more than 45 years ago I have wanted a 44 Russian-chambered Smith & Wesson New Model #3. Unlike the New Model Russian we do not, at least as this is written, have a replica New Model #3. My dream came true this past year when my wife came into some money unexpectedly and graciously shared it with me with the wonderful words, "Is there any gun you'd like to buy?" It just so happened one of the local gun shops had just taken in a New Model #3 in excellent condition. Dot did a little bargaining and it became mine. I am every bit as fascinated with it now as I was back in the 1950s. Both this New Model #3 and the earlier-mentioned original New Model Russian are used only with black powder loads. They are much too valuable to take a chance on ruining them using smokeless powder. Even though the last completed Smith & Wesson single action did not leave the factory until just before the beginning of World War I, all frames were actually manufactured during the black powder age.

Until very recently if one wanted 44 Russian brass it was necessary either to trim back 44 Special brass from 1.16" to .97" or search for original Russian brass. This case has not been generally available for more than 60 years, and all of it is of the relatively weak folded-head or balloon style that was originally used with black powder. I believe the manufacture of this brass stopped either just prior to or shortly after World War II.

Now thanks to Starline we have modern solid-head 44 Russian brass for the use of ammunition companies as well as reloaders. Black Hills was the first to offer modern 44 Russian ammunition with a 210-gr. load clocking right at 750 fps and capable of 1-1/2-inch groups at 50 feet with my hands and eyes. UltraMax now has a 44 Russian load that also shoots accurately at 80 fps less muzzle velocity. Ten-X offers a 44 Russian smokeless version chronographing the same as the Black Hills load, while their Black Powder Cartridge version is about 100 fps slower. Dies for reloading 44 Russian are available from RCBS. Unaltered 44 Special/44 Magnum dies will not work as their crimping and seating die is too long and the expander button reaches too far into the short Russian case, causing a bulge above the base.

Colt's run of First Generation Single Action Armies ran from 1873 to 1941 with approximately 357,000 units being manufactured while the big bore single actions from Smith & Wesson totaled around 264,000 sixguns from 1870 to 1912. Colt produced more single actions, but on the average Smith & Wesson produced more per year. If I had lived in the last quarter of the 19th-century I wonder which I would have chosen: a Colt Single Action Army or a Model #3 Smith & Wesson?

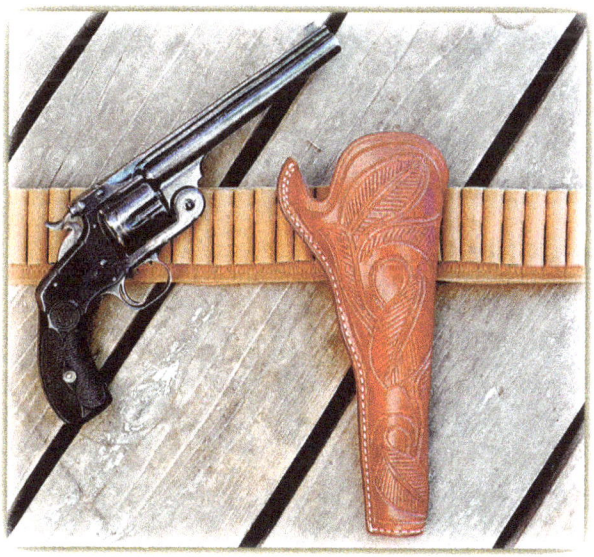

Some sixgunners on the frontier carried the S&W New Model #3 44 Russian, finding it to be a vast improvement over the Colt Single Action. Leather is by El Paso Saddlery.

Single Action Sixguns

–Chapter 3–

THE SMITH & WESSON SCHOFIELD

Maj. George Schofield, U.S. Army, redesigned the S&W Model #3 to make it easier to operate on horseback by locating the locking latch on the frame.

Smith & Wesson single actions of the 1870s: the 45 Schofield with the locking latch on the frame and the 44 Russian New Model #3 with the latch located on the barrel.

The advent of the large-caliber, cartridge-firing sixgun such as the Smith & Wesson Model #3 American caught Colt totally unawares. Sam Colt himself insisted shooters would always want to load their own ammunition using powder, ball, and cap. Sam died in 1862, however, and while his company continued to follow the path he had paved, Smith & Wesson went forward with its cartridge-firing sixguns, culminating with the introduction of that first big-bore sixgun, the American, in 1870. The United States Army, realizing that the then-standard issue Colt 1860 Army cap-n-ball sixguns were now definitely out of date, put out a call to all arms manufacturers to supply examples of new revolvers firing self-contained ammunition. Colt and Smith & Wesson both entered samples of their sixguns with Colt's being the 1871-72 Open-Top.

The powers that be at the United States Army rejected both arms for general service, but they did order 1000 Smith & Wesson Americans in 1870 and also told Colt to go back to the drawing board and come up with a sixgun with a top strap. When all the black powder smoke had cleared, the U.S. Army had adopted the stronger 45 Colt single action over the more sophisticated Smith & Wesson 44 American. The Colt was slower to unload than the automatically-ejecting Smith & Wesson, but it had three great advantages: 1) the 255-gr. 45 Colt with 40 grains of black powder was much more powerful than the 218-gr. .44 with less than 30 grains; 2) the newly designed Colt now had a solid frame as opposed to the top-break Smith & Wesson and the previously submitted 1871-72 Open-Top; and 3) the Colt Single Action Army passed tests requiring the firing of 200 rounds without thorough cleaning. It was necessary only to swab out the bore and keep shooting. The original load must have proven to be too much for most troopers as the powder charge was dropped from 40 grains to 30 grains so recruits could more easily handle the recoil. The civilian load was standardized at 35 grains of black powder under a 255-gr. lead bullet.

While the Smith & Wesson American had a great advantage in ease of unloading and reloading, it also required two hands to operate the latch on the top of the barrel. Major George Schofield of the 10th Cavalry had a better idea and set about to improve the Smith &

The Schofield, as all Model #3s, featured a break-top action hinged at the bottom front of the frame and latched at the back top of the frame. On the Schofield, the latch was on the frame itself to allow for easier opening.

Wesson Model #3 top-break .44 to make it more suited for military use, especially on horseback. Schofield changed the Smith & Wesson latch from the back of barrel assembly to the main frame, allowing it to be pushed in with the thumb of the shooting hand rather than opened with the off hand. This provided for one-handed operation even while on horseback. In 1873, a test was set up placing the Schofield Model Smith & Wesson against the Colt Single Action Army. While mounted on a moving horse, the horseman had to empty the sixgun, remove six cartridges from his belt pouch, and reload.

It took 26 seconds to unload the Colt and it was then re-loaded in 60 seconds. The improved Smith & Wesson Schofield took two seconds to unload and it was re-loaded in 26 seconds. One minute is an awfully long time to reload, especially when being fired on! The S&W Schofield took only one-third as much time to unload and reload as the Colt. The Army was impressed to the point of ordering Schofields for field use, but they did not drop the Colt Single Action Army.

Both the Colt and the Smith & Wesson were chambered in .45 caliber, but the cylinder of the Schofield was shorter than that of the Colt and would not accept the full length 45 Colt cartridge. While the Colt could handle the Smith & Wesson ammunition (the 45 S&W), the Smith & Wesson would not chamber the longer 45 Colt. Cavalry units equipped with .45 Schofields received unusable 45 Colt ammunition too often, while those equipped with Colt Single Action Armies had no problem using the wrong ammunition if they were issued 45 S&W rounds.

How much of a problem was this? Enough that it was at least given as a reason for ultimately dropping the Schofields. They became government surplus in 1880 and many of the 7-inch Schofields had their barrels cut back to 5 inches, making them quite popular with Wells Fargo agents. It has also been theorized that the Schofield was dropped as Smith & Wesson had other guns to build for other markets and no longer wanted the Schofield contract.

To operate the Schofield for loading or unloading, the hammer is placed on half-cock, the thumb pushes on the barrel catch, the barrel is swung open and down, which causes the automatic ejector to eject all cases and then return to battery. To reload, the new cartridges are placed in the cylinder and the barrel is pivoted upward and latched tightly. Shooting the Schofield is also quite different from shooting a Colt Single Action in both feel and felt recoil. However, it is quite pleasant to shoot with black powder 45 Schofield loads, it balances well with the 7-inch barrel, and it has excellent pointability. The wide rear sight and narrow front blade combination are quite fast to pick up, though not as precise as other sights such as those found on the Colt.

As with all traditional single action sixguns, the best safety on the Schofield is the shooter and, as is true of any traditional single action, it should be carried with only five rounds chambered and the hammer resting on the remaining empty chamber at all times. The half-cock is not a safety and engaging it will allow the cylinder to

Once the action of any Model #3 – including the Schofield – was opened, cartridge cases were automatically ejected.

Single Action Sixguns | 23

Chapter 3 | The Smith & Wesson Schofield

Colt or Smith & Wesson? The choice would have been very difficult between this Schofield circa 1875 and Colt circa 1879.

In the last decade of the twentieth century the Schofield Model was resurrected both by Navy Arms and Smith & Wesson.

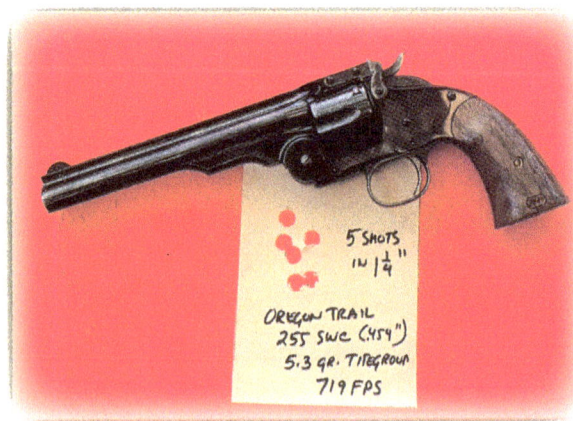

The Schofield is an accurate shooting .45 sixgun.

rotate, possibly bringing a live round under the hammer.

Gunfighters on both sides of the law carried Schofields and we definitely know that Schofield Number 366 belonged to Jesse James and may have been carried by the famous outlaw when Bob Ford, "that dirty little coward," shot him while his back was turned. (It is a tribute to the gunfighting ability of both Jesse and Bill Hickok that neither man's killer would face him head on.) Jesse apparently preferred both Colts and Smith & Wessons, as it is generally believed he carried both a Colt Peacemaker .45 and a Smith & Wesson .45 Schofield.

Thanks to the late Val Forgett, who is also responsible for the replica of the New Model Russian mentioned in the previous chapter, we now have access to a replica of the Smith & Wesson Model 1875 Schofield manufactured by Uberti and imported by Navy Arms. The Navy Arms is quite faithful to the original Schofield except the cylinder is longer and it is chambered, not for the original 45 S&W, but for the 45 Colt. First barrel lengths offered were 7 inches (Cavalry Models), followed by 5 inches (Wells Fargo Model) and 3 inches (Hideout Model). They are also now offered in 44-40 and 38 Special.

My first Schofield test gun, which I wound up purchasing, was a blued 7-inch Cavalry Model 45 Colt with smooth walnut stocks. The left grip bears the stamped mark of 1877 while both grips carry nineteenth-century martial inspection initials. The serial number, 54, is stamped on the butt. The blued finish of the Schofield is nicely set off with a case colored trigger guard, hammer, and latching system. Two screws hold the female part of the locking latch above the cylinder and when the rear screw is backed out, the latch can be

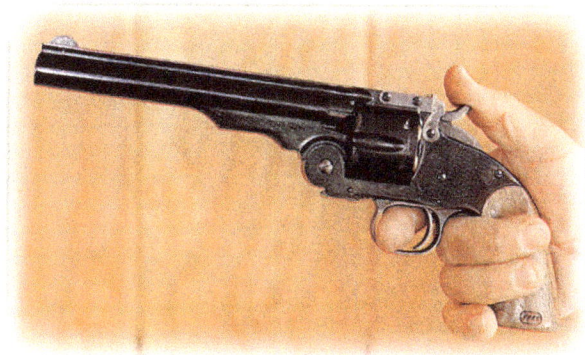

The Schofield grip frame allows easy access to the hammer.

The S&W Schofield fits the hand very well and is very comfortable to shoot.

lifted upwards allowing the cylinder to be removed. The overall finish, as we have come to expect from Uberti, is excellent and the fit is quite tight, so much so that black power loads with their attendant fouling are a problem just as they were with original Schofields. Unlike the original Schofield, however, this replica is safe to use with standard smokeless powder loads.

Sights consist of a half moon "German silver"-style front sight and a very wide rear "V" with a small "U" in the bottom of the "V." By centering the narrow front sight in the wide "V," I am able to get the Schofield to print to point of aim with 255-gr. bullets at 800 to 900 feet per second. This load is quite traditional in that it is assembled with the standard 45 Colt conical bullet, in this case one that happens to come from an old three-cavity Lachmiller #454255LC mold. This 255-gr. bullet over 8.0 grains of Unique also shoots into two inches and should be considered maximum. It is as far as I will go with the Schofield.

Black powder loads for the Schofield .45 are assembled with the same Lachmiller #454255LC bullet lubed with SPG lube. Both 30.0 grains of Goex FFFg and 34.0 grains of Elephant Brand FFFg are used with muzzle velocities of 829 and 786 feet per second respectively. These loads shoot exceptionally well in other 45 Colt sixguns but, as mentioned earlier, are a problem with the Schofield. That problem is not accuracy but rather the fact the Schofield is so tightly fitted that the cylinder begins to bind after a few shots. This could very well be one of the reasons the Colt was more popular on the Frontier than the Smith & Wesson and the Remington, which also reacts to black powder loads as does the Smith & Wesson. Both of the latter bind after a few shots, but the Colt just keeps shooting.

Shooting the Schofield gives me quite a different feel from shooting a Colt, probably because my hand has curled around Colt and Ruger Flat-Top grip frames for nearly a half century. I found the Schofield to be quite pleasant to shoot and with a little practice it could easily be handled as well as a Colt. With its automatic ejection of spent cartridges and easy to load cylinder, it could be quite a bit faster. It does balance well with the 7-inch barrel and also has excellent pointability, while the shorter 5-inch Wells Fargo Model rivals the 4-3/4-inch Colt as a gunfighter's top choice.

The original Smith & Wesson Schofield was produced only from 1875 to 1877 and in two versions. Approximately 3000 were manufactured in 1875. After the cylinder latch was improved, approximately 6000 were produced in 1876 and 1877, when production ceased. (The Navy Arms version incorporates the Second Model cylinder latch, while those that were offered by Cimarron have the First Model latch.) To celebrate the 125th Anniversary of the Schofield Model in 2000, Smith & Wesson offered the Schofield 2000, a completely new Schofield built on modern machinery from Smith & Wesson's Performance Center custom shop. The Schofield 2000 adhered to the old, original design as much as possible with today's considerations but included a frame-mounted firing pin. However, Smith & Wesson did retain the historically-correct cylinder that accepts only the shorter 45 S&W or 45 Schofield cartridge.

To build this new sixgun, Smith & Wesson not only discovered that all the original machinery was lost to history but that there were no original drawings still in existence. They found it necessary to work from an original Schofield Model borrowed from Smith Wesson historian and noted collector Roy Jinks. Smith & Wesson said of the re-introduction of the Schofield Model, "American firearms historians have come to recognize what Colonel Schofield had instinctively

Chapter 3 | The Smith & Wesson Schofield

The Smith & Wesson Performance Center offered the Model 2000 Schofield complete with presentation box for a short time.

understood the first time he held the Smith & Wesson Model 3 Schofield in his hand – it was the best revolver ever invented for the Horse Soldier. Now, 125 years later, Smith & Wesson reintroduces the Schofield. The Schofield Model of 2000 is a modern, top-break, single action from the Smith & Wesson Performance Center. It features the design concepts of the original Model 3 Schofield and incorporates the technical and engineering advantages the intervening 125 years have made possible. With its seven-inch barrel, bright blue finish, and walnut grips, the Schofield Model of 2000 is a modern classic."

The original Smith & Wesson Schofield was produced from 1875 to 1877 with fewer than 9000 guns being manufactured. The Model 2000 Smith & Wesson Schofield was also produced for only a short time ending in 2003. These were virtually hand built one at a time, with a retail price somewhere in the range of $1400. The original Schofield sold to civilians for $17.50.

As mentioned in the last chapter, I have often contemplated what I would have done had I lived in the 1870s and had to make a choice between a Smith & Wesson or a Colt Peacemaker. Many of those gunfighter types who lived in the last quarter of the nineteenth Century also faced the same dilemma. We do know that Jesse James, Wyatt Earp, and Bill Tilghman all carried both Smith & Wesson and Colt single action sixguns.

As with the Navy Arms New Model Russian discussed in Chapter 2, the Smith & Wesson Model 2000 deserves custom grips, and I again chose Eagle grips and their Ultra Ivory. Although it costs only about one-third as much as real ivory, one has to look very closely to determine whether or not it is the real thing. The craftsmen at Eagle expertly fitted a pair of Ultra Ivories to the Model 2000 and followed my wishes to decrease the thickness by about one-third. They not only look great, they feel exceptionally good.

A few years ago, just as with 44 Russian/44 Special, I had to make 45 Schofield brass by trimming 45 Colt cartridge cases to length. Now Starline offers excellent 45 Schofield brass, while Black Hills offers a 230-grain bulleted Schofield load clocking out at a mild-shooting 650 fps from the Smith & Wesson Model 2000. RCBS Cowboy dies are available to load both Colt and Schofield rounds.

After nearly a century of doing without big-bore Smith & Wesson single actions, we now have Navy Arms continuing to offer both the New Model Russian and the Schofield. Cimarron offered the Schofield for a while but have since dropped it. At least we saw a short run of Schofields from the original manufacturer. Dare we hope to see a New Model #3 soon?

–Chapter 4–

THE REMINGTON "TOP-STRAPS"

The year: 1862. Matthew Holden had just celebrated his seventeenth birthday. He had been saving his money all summer and now it was time to buy his first sixgun. Every week he went to town with Pa and would always look in the window of the gun shop, but he had decided never to go in and bother the gunsmith until he had money in his pocket. The time had come.

Excitedly Matt entered the shop and allowed a few seconds for his eyes to become accustomed to the light. He really didn't know what he wanted and didn't even know what was available. Pa was a shooter but it was always a rifle or shotgun to put meat on the table or scare something away that was bothering the stock.

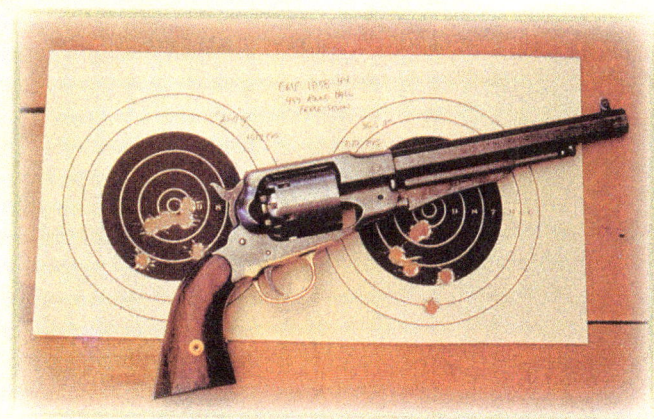

Did the original Remington percussion revolvers shoot as well as this replica from EMF?

It wasn't that Pa didn't hold with revolvers; after all, Matt knew Pa had given Ma a little five-shot .31 Colt that was always right there by Ma's bed, right beside her Bible. But this would be Matt's first time to ever even hold a revolver. Matt may not have known what he would find, but he knew it would have to be a pistol. He could always use one of Pa's long guns but he wanted his very own revolver that was easy to pack, powerful, and quick into action just in case. He expected to spend a lot of time on horseback exploring the country and whatever he chose would be his constant companion. It would have to ride well in a holster and feel good in hand. The first revolver he looked at just wouldn't do.

The gunsmith pulled a huge pistol from the display case explaining to young Matt it was a Colt Dragoon, and that it shot a .44 round ball faster than the mind could contemplate. He also assured him it was not only the most powerful revolver made but that there was no way it could ever be surpassed in power. Matt liked the sound of that, but once he picked up the Dragoon he realized its four-pound weight would not be practical for daily use. There was no way he could carry this sixgun all day on his slender frame. No, he needed something smaller.

The gunsmith reached back in the case and brought out just about the most beautiful thing Matt had ever seen. "Now this is more like it," he thought as he was handed a Colt 1851 Navy. It felt really good, balanced wonderfully well, and would certainly ride easy in leather, but Matt noticed the smaller hole in the barrel. It was a .36-caliber and Matt wasn't sure it would be enough. He remembered the bear Pa had shot when he was ten. Yes, he would need a bigger gun. Now if only there was a .44 that felt as good as this Colt .36.

The gunsmith said he had one gun left, explaining it was not a Colt but a new Remington. Matt handled the .44 Remington, and even though the grip was not quite as comfortable in his hands as the Colt Navy he felt better knowing it was a .44. It also had a more sturdy appearance and seemed to be very solid. The gunsmith pointed out to him this was due to the fact the Remington's mainframe and grip frame were all one-piece and it also had a top strap across the frame above the cylinder. That certainly made sense to even someone as young as Matthew Holden.

Yes, it would be the Remington. Matt had enough money to purchase the sixgun, powder, caps, lead, a bullet mold, and even a Slim Jim holster and wide belt. Matt had worked very hard that summer and now he was being rewarded. Little did he know what the not-very-distant future held for so many young boys all over the country. In just a very few short months he would be wearing that Remington when he joined the Union Army.

Single Action Sixguns | 27

Chapter 4 | The Remington "Top-Straps"

Today's Remington shooters have a choice of the antique version from EMF or a standard blued 1858 from Navy Arms.

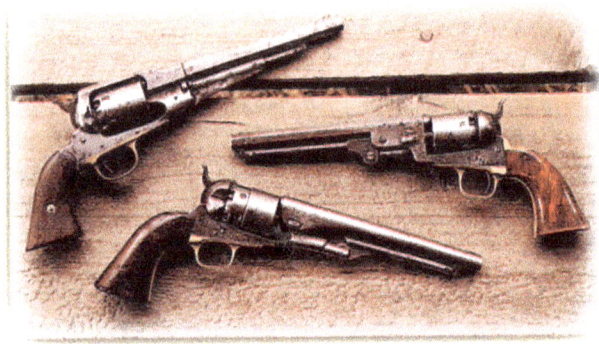

Original percussion sixguns from the middle of the 19th-century, the Remington 44 and Colt's 1851 Navy and 1860 Army, provided the sixgunner of that time period with a difficult choice.

Original sixguns from the 1860s? No, these antiqued 1858 Remington and 1860 Army are from EMF and Cimarron.

The Remington was available both as an 8-inch .44 New Model Army and a 7-1/2-inch .36 Navy Model. Percussion Colts were more readily available and in a greater profusion of models but the Remington cap-n-ball sixgun had several advantages over the Colt. The frame of the Remington was solid with a barrel that was permanently screwed into the frame while the Colt sixguns were all open-topped with removable barrels that were held in place by two small pins at the bottom of the front of the frame and a wedge pin that entered the barrel assembly from the side. A town marshal using his Colt to smack a hard-headed cantankerous drunk on Saturday night would surely bend his gun but the solidly-built Remington would be no worse for wear.

The Remington also had a better sighting arrangement with a rear sight that was a hog wallow through the top of the frame mated up with an easy-to-see front sight. The Colt carried a brass front sight while the rear sight was a notch in the cocked hammer. The Colt did have two great advantages. Most pistoleros found it to be quicker from leather and slightly faster to handle with its easier to reach hammer and more comfortable grip, and it also would shoot longer without jamming from fouling. However, no less a legend than Buffalo Bill Cody said his Remington never failed him.

When I first started visiting gun shops and then attended my first gun show in 1956 I found it was very easy to find Colt single actions, both the 1873 Peacemaker as well as various cap and ball sixguns, but I rarely saw any Smith & Wesson or Remington single actions. Perhaps

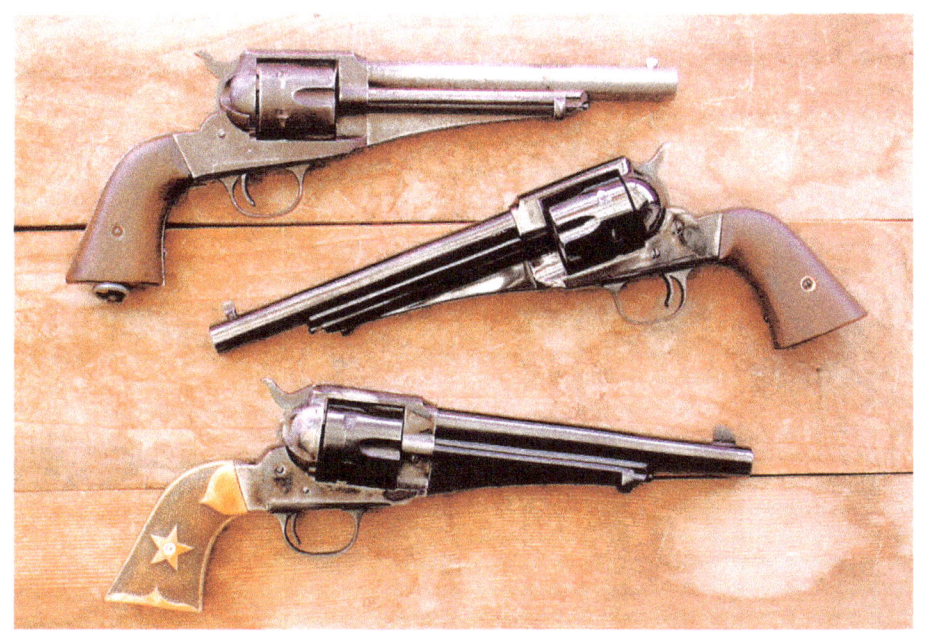

More than 125 years of Remington 1875 history is represented by an original Model 1875, a Hartford Armory Model 1875, and an EMF Model 1875.

they were there, and just perhaps my eyes had been trained by who knows how many B westerns, first in the movies and then by many hours of the new medium of television, to see Colts above all else. My first single actions, after my original Ruger .22 Single-Six, were Colts, thus beginning a lifelong appreciation for the Peacemaker, or Model P. I mentioned earlier the dilemma I would have faced in the nineteenth century if I had to choose between a Smith & Wesson or Colt. That choice would have been even more difficult by factoring in a single action from Remington.

Remington single actions have always been rather scarce. One of the great advantages of the Colt was not only the fact that it was made for a longer period of time – 1873 to 1941 – compared to the Remington's production run of 1874 to 1896. The Colt won the numbers game with 350,000 produced as opposed to the Remington's 30,000. Colts were also chambered for cartridges that for the most part were still available not only in the 1950s but even today. The top three cartridges found in First Generation Colts are 45 Colt, 44-40, and 38-40, while many of the Remingtons were chambered in the obsolete 44 Remington. To make matters worse, more than one-half of the Remingtons produced originally went to the Egyptian Government.

My first encounter with a Remington of any kind was a replica 1858 percussion Remington revolver by Navy Arms. It didn't take long to notice the cramped (for my hand) grip frame on that 1858. Over the years I have added several Remington 1875 replicas to my collection of shooting sixguns, but they have not seemed to feel as good in the hand as my Colts.

From the very beginning, when compared to the Colts, Remingtons have been an inherently stronger design. Where Colt used three parts – mainframe, backstrap, and triggerguard – bolted together, Remington forged a one-piece steel housing incorporating the mainframe and grip frame with no screws to loosen while shooting. Unlike the open-top design of Sam Colt's percussion revolvers, the early Remingtons had a solid top strap, which the United States military insisted that Colt adopt for their Single Action Army. It is quite obvious to me that someone at Colt took a good look at the Remington percussion revolvers before the 1871-72 Open-Top evolved into the Colt Single Action Army in 1873. Is also obvious that Remington engineers then looked back at the Colt of 1873 before the first Remington cartridge-firing revolvers arrived in 1874.

When we compare the percussion revolvers from Remington and Colt we find them to be quite different. This dissimilarity is also found when examining cartridge-firing single actions from Colt and Smith & Wesson. They are quite different as to look, feel, and operation. However, when we come to the Colt Model of 1873 and the Remington Model 1875 we find them to be quite similar in appearance except for the web found under the barrel of the Remington. In fact, when Hollywood wanted the sixgun used in the movie to be a Remington they simply added a pot metal-style Remington web under the barrel of the Colt. If one looks at close-up pictures of Westerns using Remingtons it is easy to see how crudely these webs are attached.

Was the purpose of the web simply to give a distinctive appearance? Was it there just to carry on the look of the .44 Remington percussion revolvers? Was it designed as an aid for easy holstering? Did the Remington engineers think it provided extra strength? Whatever the reason it is the one distinctive characteristic of the Remington 1875 when compared to

Chapter 4 | The Remington "Top-Straps"

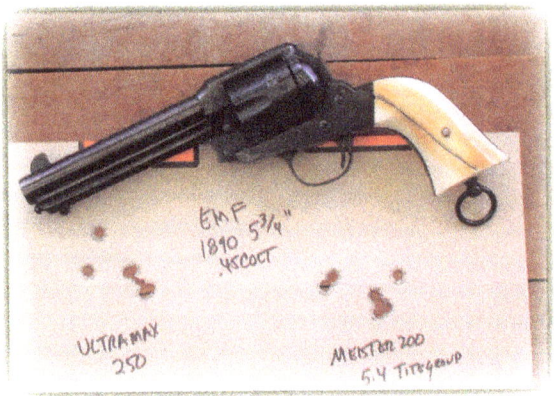

The Model 1890 Remington from EMF, here equipped with Buffalo Brothers grips, is also an excellent shooter.

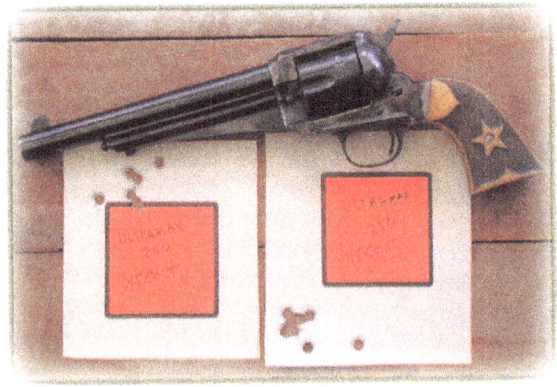

EMF's replica of the Model 1875 Remington is an excellent-shooting sixgun. Grips are by Buffalo Brothers.

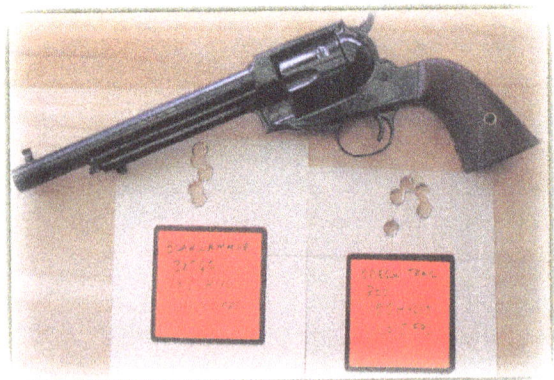

Hartford Armory's New Model 1890 handles heavy-bullet 45 Colt loads with ease and accurately.

the Colt Peacemaker. The first few hundred Remington 1875s were chambered in 46 Remington, but this was soon change to 44 Remington with approximately 16,000 being manufactured by 1878, most of which went to the Egyptian Government. All of these were 7-1/2-inch sixguns with a pinched post front sight and lanyard ring. In addition to the web, the cylinder pin of the Remington sixguns extended all the way to the end of the barrel rather than just to the front of the frame as with the Colts.

Somewhere between 2,000 and 4,000 Remington 1875s were produced over the next three years with a blade front sight, mostly without the lanyard ring and chambered in 44-40 and 45 Colt. Some minor changes were made in 1881 with between 4000 and 5000 being manufactured before the Model 1890 arrived. The last run, fewer than 1000, was chambered in 44-40 with 5-3/4-inch barrels. In 1883 approximately 1000 nickel-plated Model 1875s were purchased by the U.S. Government to arm the Indian Police. E. Remington & Sons suffered a bankruptcy in 1888, whereupon the company's name was changed to Remington Arms, under which brand a few "Model 1888" single actions were produced before the arrival of the Model 1890. The last of the Remington big-bore single actions were produced in 44-40 with fewer than 2000 being manufactured before production ceased in 1896.

Both 5-3/4- and 7-1/2-inch barrel lengths were offered in the Model 1890, which is easily distinguished from the Model 1875 by the lack of the full-length web under the barrel.

For several decades now, Uberti has been producing Remington replicas that have been marketed by Cimarron, EMF, and Navy Arms. I have considerable experience shooting both the 1875 and 1890 Models chambered in 44-40 and 45 Colt. I have never found these to be as easy to shoot as the Colt-style sixguns due to the shape of the grip, the angle of the hammer, and the heaviness of the mainspring. I simply cannot reach or cock the hammer on any of these Remington replicas as easily as I can on a Colt. One notable exception has been a 7-1/2-inch 45 Colt Model 1875 from EMF. This one seems to feel almost as good as a Colt in my hand and the hammer is very easy to reach. A subtle difference in size and angle, plus the fact it has been equipped with custom thin stocks by Buffalo Brothers, makes a big difference. In all of this time I have never had the privilege of handling, much less shooting, an original Remington. Now, thanks to Hartford Armory, the original Remington is back and I have not only been privileged to shoot these new sixguns but also to handle the original Remington 1875 used as their pattern.

The Hartford Armory offers both the Model 1875 and the Model 1890 chambered in 45 Colt.

Here in the first decade of the twenty-first century we have a new firearms manufacturer producing, not state-of-the-art semi-automatics, but rather original Remingtons, single action sixguns, which have not been seen for over 100 years. That new company is Hartford Armory and their first cartridge-firing efforts are high-quality Model 1875 and Model 1890 Remingtons made on thoroughly modern machinery using the finest American made 4130 and 4140 steels with forged, not cast, mainframes. To come up with these new Remington single actions, they very carefully measured and studied original Remingtons, not currently produced replicas, and they have deviated from the original design in only one way.

The original Remington cylinders were even shorter than those in the Colt SAA, and many of the modern 45 Colt rounds are deliberately made long enough to preclude their being used in Colts or replica Remingtons. The new Remingtons from Hartford Armory have cylinders approximately 1/8-inch longer than the originals in order to be able to handle currently-manufactured 45 Colt ammunition. Colt Single Actions, replicas thereof, and replicas of Remingtons are not strong enough to handle +P or heavy-duty 45 Colt hunting loads. Hartford Armory proclaims that this newest offering is not only true to the original design of the Remingtons but that it is also strong enough to handle any modern factory 45 Colt ammunition. It is in fact strong enough that by the time you read this it will be available in 44 Magnum with an extra cylinder in 44-40 if so desired.

I have been privileged to spend time with four Hartford Armory Remingtons, three Model 1890s and one Model 1875, all chambered in 45 Colt. These four sixguns were tested with everything from 200-gr. 45 Colt Cowboy loads at 700 fps all the way up to 265-gr. jacketed bullets at 1350 fps and 340 grain bullets at 1230 fps. The last two loads are normally the heaviest loads I use in a 45 Colt Ruger Blackhawk, which means, unlike the Colt or any of its replicas, this Remington handles the same 45 Colt loads that, until now, I felt safe shooting only in a Ruger Blackhawk.

The Colt Single Action Army grip frame or the modification of such, the XR3-RED frame found on the Blackhawk, are not the most comfortable for shooting heavy 45 Colt loads. In the process of testing these Remingtons and shooting these heavier loads I found the Remington grip frame to be much better suited to the shooting of heavy loads than the old original Colt-style.

Single Action Sixguns | 31

Chapter 4 | The Remington "Top-Straps"

Two 7-1/2-inch Remington Models from Hartford Armory, the 1875 (bottom) and the 1890 (top) are to be offered in 44 Magnum as well as 45 Colt.

When the Italians first started producing the Remington replicas, they changed the grip shape and hammer angle just enough to make it harder for me to reach the hammer spur. In comparing an original Model 1875 and these replicas I could see more room on the original between the back of the trigger guard and the front strap. The same original dimension has been incorporated into the Hartford Armory Models 1875 and 1890 and this, combined with the original shape, of the back strap makes all the difference when shooting heavy loads.

I consider the grip frame of the Colt, Colt-style, and standard Ruger Blackhawk comfortable in my hand with 250-gr. bullets up to the 900 to 1100 fps range, perhaps even 1200 fps. With the Remington, the comfort ceiling is raised considerably due to the fact the back strap is slightly straighter and comes up higher much like the design found on the original Colt Bisley Model, the current Freedom Arms guns, and the Ruger Bisley Model. Here we have had a better-designed grip frame for heavy loads since 1874 and it has been lost until now.

The Hartford Armory Remington comes from the factory with an incredibly smooth action, an easy to reach and operate hammer, and a trigger pull of 2-3/4 pounds on the 7-1/2-inch Model 1890 I spent the most time with. Each Hartford Armory Remington also features a beautifully polished blue finish, with a casehardened hammer and loading gate being used on production models, just as they were on the originals.

Until now the only single action I knew of that could be guaranteed to be fitted tightly has been a Freedom Arms. The Hartford Armory Remingtons are fitted just as closely, with cylinder lockup being absolutely tight with no movement side-to-side or front to back. The barrel cylinder gap on the 7-1/2-inch Model 1890 will not accept the smallest feeler gauge I have, which is .002". Cylinder-to-barrel alignment is so precise that the forcing cone angle is only two degrees. Larry Black, CEO of Hartford Armory, says, "a funnel is not needed when the cylinder and barrel line up properly." Tolerances on cylinder chambers are held tightly with chamber throats being a uniform .451".

Both the Model 1875 and 1890 Hartford Remingtons are fitted with pinched post front sights that I found quite easy to see. With the strength and accuracy afforded by these new Hartford Armory sixguns, they can do double duty as hunting handguns. To this end Hartford Armory has already solved the problem of various loads hitting to differing points of impact by offering a screw in front sight available in different heights with a special wrench for removal and installation.

Once in a great while progress can actually be wonderful. The original Remingtons have been gone for over 100 years. Now they are back, they are better, they are totally American-made, and they are suited to the handling of 44 Magnum and heavy duty 45 Colt loads. The wait was worth it!

–Chapter 5–

THE COLT CARTRIDGE CONVERSIONS

In the 1860s Smith & Wesson had planned a top-break .44-caliber sixgun firing fixed ammunition, but the project was tabled until after the war. Smith & Wesson had already been producing tip-up revolvers, that is, revolvers that were hinged at the frame in front of the hammer and unlocked at the bottom of the frame in front of the cylinder, thus allowing the muzzle to actually tip up in order to remove the cylinder for loading and unloading. This relatively weak design worked with the .22 and .32 rimfire cartridges for which the guns were chambered, but for more powerful cartridges a stronger design was necessary. The result was the beginning of Smith & Wesson's Model #3 revolvers, which where hinged at the front of the bottom part of the frame and unlatched at the top of the frame in front of the hammer. These were the first Smith & Wesson break-tops.

These four .44 sixguns led the way to the .45 Colt Single Action Army. They are, in replica form, the 1860 Army, Richards conversion, Richards-Mason conversion, and the 1871-72 Open Top.

The first big bore cartridge-firing sixgun manufactured with a bored-through cylinder was the 44 S&W American of 1870. It was first chambered in 44 Henry, the same ammunition as used in the Henry Model 1860 and Winchester Model 1866 leverguns. The United States Army, equipped with 1860 Colt cap-n-ball sixguns since the Civil War, decreed that the cartridge be changed to a .44-caliber centerfire, the 44 S&W. Three years before Colt introduced their first sixgun firing fixed ammunition, Smith & Wesson received a military contract for 1000 six-shot, top-break American revolvers using centerfire cartridges.

Smith & Wesson held the Rollin White patent for bored-through cylinders. Until S&W began using this patent, revolvers were of the percussion type that were loaded from the front of the cylinder with powder and ball. The first manufactured big bore sixgun with a bored-through cylinder was the Smith & Wesson of 1870. However, two years earlier Smith & Wesson had agreed to allow Remington to convert some of Remington's New Model .44s to a cartridge – the .46 rimfire – in a bored-through cylinder. More than 4000 of these converted Remingtons pre-dated Smith & Wesson's American.

Smith & Wesson had produced the first cartridge-firing revolver, the Model #1 .22, in 1857. Sam Colt strongly believed shooters would always prefer percussion revolvers. After the arrival of that first cartridge-firing Smith & Wesson, Colt would go on to produce the 1860 Army

Chapter 5 | The Colt Cartridge Conversions

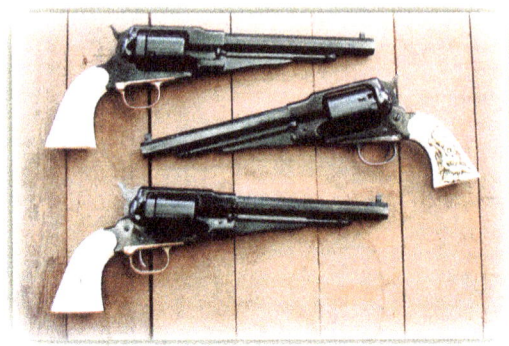

A standard model 1858 Remington percussion revolver is flanked by a pair of 1858 Remington with Kirst .45 Cartridge Konversion Cylinders, making them capable of handling standard 45 Colt loads. Custom grips are by Buffalo Brothers.

The historical clock is turned back to the early 1870s with a pair of Cimarron 44 Colt Open-Tops with Buffalo Brothers Mexican Eagle grips and period-style leather by Rawhide Walt Ostin.

The Colt 1871-72 Open-Top lives again in replica form from Cimarron. The matched pair of 44 Colts are fitted with Mexican Eagle grips from Buffalo Brothers, while the 45 Schofield-chambered Open-Top is fitted with a Tiffany style grip by John Adams.

.44, the 1861 Navy .36, and the 1862 Police Model .36. Even though Sam Colt died in 1862, Colt continued to concentrate on percussion revolvers – as well they might since they had a large government contract for the 1860 Army. However, after that Civil War it was obvious that the cartridge-firing sixgun handwriting was on the wall.

During the late 1860's the Thuer Conversion was performed on approximately 5000 Colt cap-n-ball sixguns. Remington had agreed to pay a royalty to Smith & Wesson to use bored-through cylinders, and either Colt would not or Smith & Wesson never asked. So Colt still had to get around the Rollin White patent held by Smith & Wesson. What is very strange is the fact that White had worked for Colt before going to Smith & Wesson, which means Colt could have had the first chance at the patent. Then again, maybe they didn't want it. Thuer's invention altered the cylinder of percussion revolvers to allow a tapered cartridge to be inserted from the front end. It was not tremendously successful.

Colt had thousands of parts on hand and the U.S. Army had thousands of percussion sixguns. Richards' patent was used by Colt to convert cap-n-ball sixguns to the new fixed ammunition style. Colts with the Richards Conversion are easily recognized by the ejector rod extending past the back of the ejector rod housing about one inch. Remington conversions are also encountered as the backs of cylinders of both Remington and Colts were cut off and a new section, a backplate, was fitted to the cylinders. Sometimes a completely new cylinder was built to accept rimfire cartridges.

In 1872, Colt introduced their first big bore cartridge-firing sixgun: an open-top frame, .44 rimfire-chambered sixgun that looked much like the basic 1860 Army cap-n-ball. When the Army announced testing to adopt a new revolver in 1872, Colt's entry was the 1871-72 Open-Top chambered in 44 Colt. The Army was not satisfied, telling Colt they wanted two major changes: the caliber increased to .45 and a frame with a solid top strap. Colt engineers, William Mason in particular, went back to the drawing board with the result being one of the all-time great sixguns, the Model of 1873, the Model P, the legendary Colt Single Action Army. Had it not been for the United States Army we may never have seen the Peacemaker. It took some time and several missteps but when they did it, they finally did it right. The classic sixgun of all sixguns, the Single Action Army is still in production as an original Colt by Colt, by United States Firearms, and also by several Italian manufacturers.

The cartridge conversions are a short-term but most important part of sixgun history, spanning the time frame from Colt's 1851 Navy and 1860 Army percussion revolvers to the Single Action Army. In the early days of movies, especially those made between the two World Wars, it is

Today's shooters can convert an 1851 Navy .36 to 38 Long Colt/38 Special by using the Kirst Cartridge Konversion Cylinder. Note the cutout in the recoil shield to allow loading without removing the cylinder.

not uncommon to often see original Henry rifles and Remington revolvers along with Colt single actions. Several of the higher budget westerns of the 1930s and 1940s strived to be historically correct, but most of the B westerns used Colts and Winchester lever actions no matter what time the setting of the story happened to be. (How many movies have been made with Winchester 94s made to look like Henry Models by simply removing the forearm?) With the profusion of Italian replicas of almost every revolver and lever action rifle from the nineteenth century, technical directors of movies can now more easily be historically correct. More and more movies, especially those made for television, are using not only Colts when appropriate but are also using Remingtons, Smith & Wessons, and cartridge conversions if the story happens to take place after the Civil War and before the advent of the Peacemaker.

The original Colt Cartridge Conversions, built mostly on 1851 Navy .36s and 1860 Army .44s, were chambered for the 38 Long Colt and 44 Colt cartridges that used a heel type bullet, that is, a bullet whose base was smaller in diameter than the rest of the bullet. This resulted in a bullet that was the same diameter as the outside of the case, much like today's .22 rimfire rounds. One has to stand in awe of the genius of the gun makers of 150 years ago when these cartridge conversions are examined. The cylinders had to be altered or replaced by a cylinder with a loading gate and new breech face and a rear sight built into the top. Quite often, instead of being done by the factory, conversions were performed by the local gunsmith or blacksmith, and they did it routinely without electricity or modern machinery. A forge and a file were basically all they had.

Charles Richards was an assistant factory superintendent at Colt and was awarded three major patents for breech loading firearms including the Richards Conversion of 1871. Existing cap and ball cylinders, such as those of the 1860 Army, were cut off at the back to allow the installation of a conversion ring that would accept cartridges: "My invention relates to that kind of revolver which has a chambered breech or cylinder. It has for its object to provide a compact and cheap form of this kind of arm, which shall be fitted for the convenient use of a flanged metallic cartridge, and it is particularly useful as furnishing a means of converting of a revolver constructed and intended for loose ammunition into one adapted for that kind of metallic cartridges which are loaded into the chambers from the rear."

To complete the conversion, the rammer for seating round balls over the powder charge was removed from beneath the barrel and replaced by an ejector rod and housing on the right side for removing spent cartridges. A loading gate at the rear of the cylinder swung open for loading and unloading. Many 1860 Army Models were returned to the factory to be converted, both from civilians and the U.S. Army, and others were produced as new sixguns at the factory. Among the various conversions, First Model Richards conversions are recognized by the rear sight on the conversion ring and an ejector rod housing that stops about one inch in front of the face of the cylinder.

With the arrival of the Second Model Richards conversions, the conversion ring, hammer, and loading gate were all improved, and the rear sight was moved from the top of the conversion ring back to the V-notch cut in the hammer as found in the original 1860 Army

Chapter 5 | The Colt Cartridge Conversions

Cimarron offers both the 1860 44 Colt and 1851 38 Long Colt/38 Special in the Richards-Mason Conversion. Custom grips are by Dustin Linebaugh and Buffalo Brothers.

cap and ball revolvers. The Richards Conversion was about to become the Richards-Mason Conversion. William Mason was superintendent of the armory at Colt from the mid-1860s until the early 1880s when he moved over to Winchester. He would be responsible for the improvements on the Richards Conversion, the 1871-72 Open-Top, and of course the Colt Single Action Army.

While Richards conversions were obviously alterations on 1860 Army Models, the Richards-Mason provided a completely new barrel with a provision for a longer ejector rod housing. They are easily distinguished from the Richards conversions by the web shape under the barrel, as it is boxier with a completely different profile. Most importantly, the Richards-Mason Conversion has a regular cylinder with no conversion ring. For more in depth information about Colt and Remington Conversions, I highly recommend *A Study of Colt Conversions* by R. Bruce McDowell, K-P Books, 1997. It is an invaluable resource for anyone interested in old Colts.

The one drawback to the Richards-Mason conversion compared to the First Model Richards is the placement of the rear sight. Without the conversion ring, the rear sight could not be mounted there so the less desirable path of placing it back on the hammer was taken. When Mason redesigned the Richards-Mason Conversion to become the 1871-72 Open-Top, the rear sight was placed on the barrel, and when the U.S. Army nudged him into coming up with something better after the Army trials of 1872, the result was the Colt single action with a Remington-style top strap and the hog wallow rear sight that could not get out of alignment.

Single action sixgun history would not be complete without the cartridge conversions. They are the bridge from Colt's percussion revolvers to the Colt Single Action Army, the legendary Peacemaker. As we have mentioned, for decades western movies featured Colt Single Action Armies, no matter whether the time frame was correct, almost exclusively. Once in a great while, a Smith & Wesson or Remington would show up but these instances were very rare. Now it is not at all unusual to see cartridge conversions in recently made movies such as *Crossfire Trail* or *Last Stand at Saber River* as moviemakers strive for more authenticity. Original cartridge conversions were real workin' sixguns and those remaining from the 1860s and 1870s show evidence of being well used. Those who spent hard-earned dollars to convert their cap and ball sixguns did not suddenly discard them when the Colt Single Action Army arrived. Today we live in a throw-away society in which money has very little value. It was quite different 140 years ago. Dollars did not come easy and firearms had to last. The conversions performed on cap and ball revolvers gave the owners of these sixguns a great return for the money invested.

The Richards conversion was performed on revolvers returned to the factory and percussion revolvers already on hand in Colt's inventory. Some 1860 Army Models were assembled as Richards conversions without ever being made into percussion revolvers. The Richards-Mason conversions were more encompassing, being performed on 1851 Navy, 1860 Army, and 1861 Navy percussion parts in factory inventory, as well as such revolvers returned to the factory for conversion. Also small frame conversions were done on the various

Colt pocket pistols. These conversions were performed throughout the 1870s as .36 and .44 percussion revolvers were too valuable to scrap simply because the Colt Single Action Army had arrived. Richards conversions on the 1860 Army were still in use by the military in the 1880s. From the very beginning 1860 conversions used a .44 centerfire cartridge while the Navy Models used both 38 Short and 38 Long in rimfire and centerfire versions.

Most cartridge conversions were used hard and for a long period of time. Even if one finds conversions in good shooting condition, they normally command collector prices as well as being chambered for ammunition no longer available. Thanks to the replica industry, shooters can now enjoy this period sixgun as Colt cartridge conversions are being offered by Cimarron in both an 1851 Navy and 1860 Army version. Cimarron originally offered both the Richards and Richards-Mason Conversions, but the former is no longer available. Unlike the originals, these sixguns are for reasonable smokeless powder loads and black powder loads rather than for black powder only.

As we have noted, the original Colt Cartridge Conversions were chambered for rounds that used a heel type bullet. To keep things simpler for today's shooters, the Cimarron cartridge conversions take an easier path. The 1851 Navy is chambered for standard 38 Special loads or 38 Long Colt loads, the latter of which are available from Black Hills Ammunition.

The 1860 Army conversion required the resurrection of an old cartridge, the 44 Colt, in modern form. Today's 44 Colt is simply the 44 Special trimmed back from 1.16" to approximately 1.10", and since the diameter of the cylinder of the 1860 Army is too small to accept six 44 Special rims, the rims are also trimmed. Properly headstamped 44 Colt brass is available from Starline.

For loading the 44 Colt, 44 Special dies can be used if they are short enough to neck-expand and crimp. If they don't, the bottom of each die can be trimmed accordingly. Today's .44 dies, most of which are designed to handle both 44 Special and 44 Magnum, will probably be too long for the 44 Colt. An easier way is to order 44 Russian dies from RCBS. This setup handles both 44 Colt and 44 Russian. The standard shellholder for the 44 Russian/44 Special/44 Magnum works but is larger than the necessary for the rims of the 44 Colt. A 30-30 shellholder works fine, however.

The original loading for the 44 Colt was 28 grains of black powder. In modern solid head brass, I use 25 grains by volume measure of Goex FFg, FFFg, Cartridge, and Hodgdon's black powder substitute Pyrodex in both the P and Select grades. Both the 38 and 44 Colt cartridge conversions are used with smokeless loads and black powder handloads. The 1851 Navy in .38 caliber binds up quickly with black powder but can be kept running fairly smoothly using black powder substitutes such as Pyrodex and Triple Seven. Seventeen grains of Pyrodex P in 38 Long Colt brass from Starline averages 860 fps and shoots into 2 inches at 50 feet. This is right in there with today's 38 Special loadings. My bullet choice for the 38 Long Colt is Lyman's #358212 150-gr. round-nose lubed with Lyman's Black Powder Gold. Magnum primers such as the CCI #550 are always used with black powder loads.

Cimarron's 1860 44 Colt cartridge conversion handles both factory and smokeless powder loads well and as an extra added bonus, no problems are encountered with black powder loads in the 44 Colt. RCBS's #44-200 FN 44-40 bullet lubed with Lyman Black Powder Gold and seated over 25.0 grains of Goex FFg yields a muzzle velocity of 770 fps and a five-shot group of 1-1/4 inches. The same amount of Pyrodex Select, by volume, raises the muzzle velocity to 839 fps for a group of 1-7/8 inches.

With little or no change, the grip frame of the 1851 Navy eventually became that of the Colt SAA, while the 1860 Army conversion carries the longer and more comfortable grip originally found on the 1860 Army. Original Colt Cartridge Conversions were available with either grip frame. Thousands of Colt percussion revolvers were produced from 1851 until Smith & Wesson introduced their first big bore cartridge firing sixgun in 1870, which was soon followed by the Colt Single Action Army in 1873.

When these two newer guns arrived most of the first guns went to fill military contracts. Even if a civilian had the money and wanted to buy one of the new revolvers, they were not immediately available. It would only be natural for the owner of a cap-n-ball sixgun shooter to advance to a cartridge-firing revolver by going the conversion route. At an age when money was very hard to come by and a brand-new sixgun might cost $15 or $20, it was possible to have a sixgun converted for just a few dollars.

In this day and age when money seems to flow so easily we sometimes forget this was not always the case. If we need something immediately we have only to reach for the plastic card in our wallet. Things were not so easy on the frontier. Cartridge conversions were very sound, economically speaking. They definitely filled a need.

–Chapter 6–

THE COLT SINGLE ACTION ARMY FIRST GENERATION

In the last chapter we talked of William Mason and his contribution to the design and manufacturer of Colt cartridge conversions. Mason did not stop with his improvement to the Richards conversion. As soon as the design was completed, Mason set about working on the Open-Top. While the Thuer, Richards, and Richards-Mason were true conversions on existing cap and ball revolvers or built from parts at the factory, the 1871-72 Open-Top was Colt's first big-bore single action cartridge-firing revolver, as it was not a conversion but a totally new design with new parts that do not interchange with the percussion models or their conversions.

All original Open-Tops were made in .44 rimfire. When the 1871-72 was submitted to the Army for testing and potential adoption, the request came back for a stronger gun in a more powerful chambering. That turned out to be one of the best requests in firearms history. The Army wanted a stronger sixgun and the result was the solid-frame Colt Single Action Army, still in .44 rimfire. The U.S. Army made one further request: a larger caliber in centerfire. That request turned out to be the stuff legends are made of. We cannot credit Samuel Colt with the design as he had died years earlier; instead it came from William Mason. So it happened that in 1873 one of the greatest sixguns ever was introduced. Maybe the greatest of them all.

The prototype may have been in .44 rimfire (some authorities say 44 Russian) but Serial Number 1 of the first Colt Single Action Army was offered in the now equally legendary 45 Colt. Basically designed for the military market, the SAA was offered in a barrel length of 7-1/2 inches to duplicate the feel of the 1851 Navy and 1860 Army. It had one-piece walnut stocks and a blued finish except for the frame and hammer, which were case hardened and colored.

The one drawback to the Richards-Mason conversion compared to the First Model Richards had been the placement of the rear sight. Without the conversion ring, the rear sight could not be mounted there so the less desirable path of placing it back on the hammer was taken. When Mason redesigned the Richards-Mason conversion to become the 1871-72 Open-Top, the rear sight was placed on the barrel, and when the U.S. Army encouraged Colt to come up with something better than the Open-Top after the Army trials of 1872, the result was the Colt single action with a Remington-style top strap and the hog wallow rear sight that could not get out of alignment.

The earliest Open-Tops had the 1851 Navy grip frame, but this was switched to the 1860 Army grip frame after about 100 Open-Tops were manufactured. In both cases the standard stock was one-piece walnut. Production of the Open-Top had begun in 1872 and proved to

The right hat, an early First Generation Colt single action, and a little imagination are all it takes to transport the author back to the nineteenth century.

The leather from Navy Arms is relatively new, but these old Colts served on the frontier: a 7-1/2-inch 44-40 Frontier Six Shooter circa 1879 and a 7-1/2-inch 45 Colt from 1881.

be very short-lived. The Colt Single Action Army was adopted by the Army after tests in late 1872, and the first order for 8000 Single Action Army Models was placed in the summer of 1873. Even though the Open-Tops were fitted with 1860 Army grip frames and stocks, the Single Action Army came standard with the older 1851 Navy grip frame and stocks. The advent of the Single Action Army ended the production of the 1871-72 Open-Top, but cartridge conversions continued to be produced as long as parts were available, well into the 1880s. Slightly more than 5000 Open-Tops had been produced before being replaced by the now legendary Model P.

The new Army cartridge used a 255-gr. conical bullet over a full 40 grains of black powder, and although the first 45 Colt single actions went to the United States Army for use on the frontier to replace the 1860 Army percussion models, it would not be long before the Model P would be offered to, and become a favorite of, the civilian market as well. The new sixgun spawned such sayings as "God Created Men But Sam Colt Made 'em Equal" and "Be Not Afraid of Any Man No Matter What His Size. When Danger Threatens Call On Me And I Will Equalize."

There were other sixguns to be sure. Thousands of earlier Colt 1851 and 1860 Models, as well as Remington 1858s in both .36 and .44 caliber, were still in service, along with cartridge-firing Smith & Wesson and Merwin & Hulbert sixguns. However, if a man could afford it and find one, the number one sixgun was definitely the Colt Single Action Army. Sixguns such as the Smith & Wesson and Merwin & Hulbert were beautifully made but they were fragile when compared to the solid-frame Colt and did not handle the fouling of black powder as well. Cylinders would soon bind, causing difficult rotation, while the Colt just kept working. The springs of the Colt were prone to breakage but they were easily replaced by anyone with a screwdriver. It took very little gunsmithing or engineering knowledge to repair a Colt Single Action Army on the frontier. Many old Colts have been found that were fixed

This is a beautiful example of a First Generation Colt with honest wear and no abuse. Gordon Marts' photo of his 38-40.

Single Action Sixguns | 39

Chapter 6 | The Colt Single Action Army 1st Generation

The four most popular calibers in the First Generation Colt Single Actions were 45 Colt, 44-40, 38-40, and 32-20.

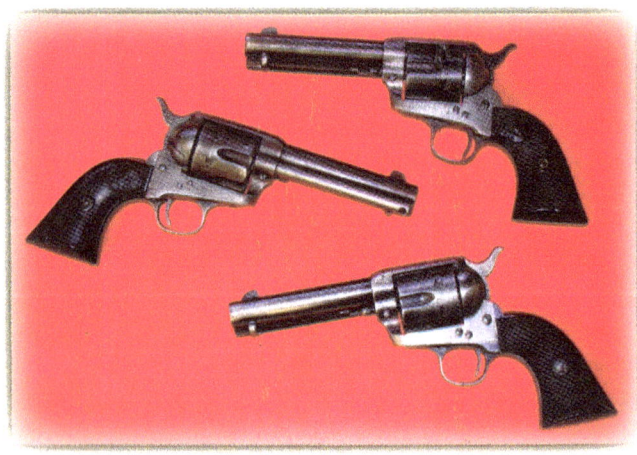

All three of these First Generation Colts were chambered in Winchester centerfire cartridges: 44-40, 38-40, and 32-20 as companions to the 1873 and 1892 leverguns.

with frontier engineering such as springs made out of corset stays and front sights made from coins. As mechanically challenged as I am, I can still keep a Colt running.

By 1877, the Colt Peacemaker was chambered in 44 W.C.F. (Winchester Center Fire) or 44-40 as a companion piece to the 1873 Winchester lever gun. The 44-40 carried the same 40 grains of black powder as the 45 Colt but with a flatter shooting 200-grain bullet. All 44-40 Colt single actions were marked "FRONTIER SIX SHOOTER" rather than a caliber marking on the left side of the barrel. In the 1880s, the second '73 Winchester chambering was added with the 38-40 or 38 W.C. F. This time the same powder charge of 40 grains propelled a 180-grain bullet. These three chamberings – 45 Colt (150,683 manufactured), 44-40 (64,489), and 38-40 (38,240) – accounted for the about 80 percent of the total sales of the First Generation Colt Single Action Army models produced from 1873 to 1941. More than 30 calibers appear in the other 20 percent with only two other chamberings gaining five-digit status. These are the third WCF cartridge, the 32-20 at 29,812 units, and the 41 Long Colt at 16,402. These figures are only for the numbers of standard Model Ps, not variations thereof.

A look through most books dealing with old Colts will show that the 45 Colt and 44-40 were the choice of many well-known shooters with only a few exceptions who preferred the 38-40. A 1930s Texas Ranger by the name of William E. Cooper carried a beautiful Cole Agee-engraved 5-1/2-inch 38-40; one of Tom Mix's favorite sixguns was a stag handled 7-1/2-inch 38-40 Single Action Army; and want to guess what John Wayne carried in his B westerns? Yes, it was a 5-1/2-inch 38-40 Colt Single Action Army.

My first shooting experience was not with the 45 Colt or 44-40 but rather the 38-40. As a teenager, I purchased a 4-3/4-inch 38-40 Colt Single Action Army in excellent shape. After adding a Lawrence Gunslinger outfit in black basketweave finish and handmade one-piece walnut stocks, I thought I was quite the sixgunner. Truth was the 60-year old Colt cost me two weeks' pay and the holster and belt another week's, so

A century of use does not show on this 1904 Colt Frontier Six Shooter. It has been totally tuned and stocked with wooly mammoth ivory by Jim Martin. Photo courtesy of Richard Talacek.

Gunsmith Jim Martin's favorite caliber is 44-40, as is this beautiful example from 1913 fitted with stag stocks by Martin. Photo courtesy of Richard Talacek.

I could barely afford to shoot more than a few rounds at a time in those pre-reloading days. When I did shoot it I practiced with a maximum fast draw using live ammunition. Thankfully I never had an accident but as I heard about several people shooting themselves in the leg, I stopped cocking the hammer before I had the sixgun out and leveled on the intended target.

Two double-action sixgun chamberings that would become most popular after World War II, the 357 Magnum and 44 Special, are rarely found in First Generation Colt Single Action Armies with only 628 and 507 having been produced in each chambering, respectively. Many of the 357s were put together hurriedly and sent across the Atlantic to take part in the Battle of Britain. Another rare chambering is the 44 Russian, but it becomes quite confusing to monitor the number of each caliber being produced as company records list 169 chamberings in 44 S&W and 357 in 44 Russian. Were they the same? Also, of the 507 44 Specials, at least some were marked both 44 Special and 44 Russian on the barrel. No sixgun in history has ever been chambered in more cartridges than the Single Action Army. Other chamberings included the English 476, 455, and 450 Eley, 45 ACP, 44 German, 38 Special, 38 Colt, 32 Colt, and 22 rimfire.

The original barrel length of the Model P was 7-1/2 inches, but both Artillery 5-1/2- and Civilian 4-3/4-inch barrels were offered as standard. Colt did offer other barrel lengths at extra prices, and those longer than 7-1/2 inches in length, especially 10 inches or longer, have come to be known as Buntline Specials. Now we can argue from now until breakfast about whether Ned Buntline really presented five long-barreled 45-caliber Colts to five Dodge City lawmen, two of whom were Wyatt Earp and Bat Masterson. Company records do not show that five sixguns were ordered, but company records are not always complete. A good case can be made either way and when we get through providing all the details and evidence, we can go out for a real Western breakfast, being no closer to the truth than when we started.

These things we do know: Colt provided any barrel length above standard on special order including

Chapter 6 | The Colt Single Action Army 1ˢᵗ Generation

This old Colt saw service in Mexico and has now been totally tuned, re-barreled and re-cylindered by Jim Martin. Photo courtesy of Richard Talacek.

some 16-inch sixguns with ladder-style adjustable rear sights. During the run of Second Generation Colts, a 12-inch Buntline was offered. Cimarron currently catalogs the Model P Buntline, which is a duplicate of the Buntline Special used by Kurt Russell in his memorable performance as Wyatt Earp in the 1990 movie *Tombstone*.

Watching the movie closely, we see that the Buntline Special used has a 10-inch barrel, not the standard 12-inch length of the Second Generation sixguns. Also, when Russell as Wyatt removes his special Colt from its presentation box we see the medallion inlaid in the right hand stock. This is also carried out in Cimarron's version as the badge-shaped shield containing the inscription, "WYATT EARP PEACEMAKER/From the Grateful People of Dodge City, Apr 8 1878." Notice there is no mention of Ned Buntline. Balancewise, the 12-inch sixguns are a little muzzle heavy, but I find that feeling lacking with the 10-inch barrel. It just seems to hang on target.

Approximately two dozen genuine long-barreled Buntline Specials have been authenticated with three of them being 44-40s and the rest 45s. At the other end of the spectrum, Colt also offered shorter barrels without ejector rod assemblies. These have been called both Sheriff's Models and Storekeeper's Models. Colt simply recorded them as being without ejector rod assemblies. I can't imagine any sheriff using a sixgun that would be a problem to reload because of the lack of the ejector rod, but there it is. Authentic Storekeeper's Models do not have the hole drilled in the barrel for the ejector rod assembly screw, nor do they have the offset hole on the right side of the frame to accept the end of the ejector rod assembly. Barrel lengths from 3 inches to 7-1/2 inches are known to exist with something over 1000 having been authenticated.

Lawmen and outlaws alike were connected to the Colt Single Action Army in the late decades of the 19th century and the early years of the twentieth century: Jesse James, Wyatt Earp, Bat Masterson, Cole Younger, Pancho Villa, Buffalo Bill, Bill Tilghman, and so on. The Colt single action was a particular favorite of the Texas Rangers until many, but not all, discovered the .45 Government Model automatic in 45 ACP.

As we mentioned in Chapter 1, in 1916 a young Army lieutenant was about to enter his first campaign heading into Mexico in pursuit of Pancho Villa under Blackjack Pershing. This was five years after the Army had adopted the Government Model .45 and more than 25 years since the Colt Single Action Army had been officially replaced. But Lt. George S. Patton rode into Mexico wearing a 4-3/4-inch 45 Colt Single Action Army, fully engraved and fitted with ivory grips carved in the Mexican Eagle pattern on the left side with the initials GSP intertwined on the right grip. Twenty-five

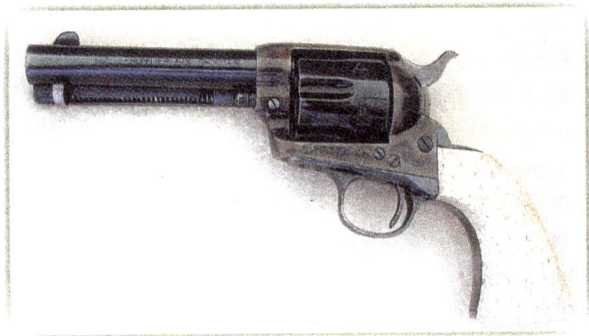

This beautiful Colt Frontier Six Shooter from 1901 is fitted with whalebone stocks by Jim Martin. Photo courtesy of Richard Talacek.

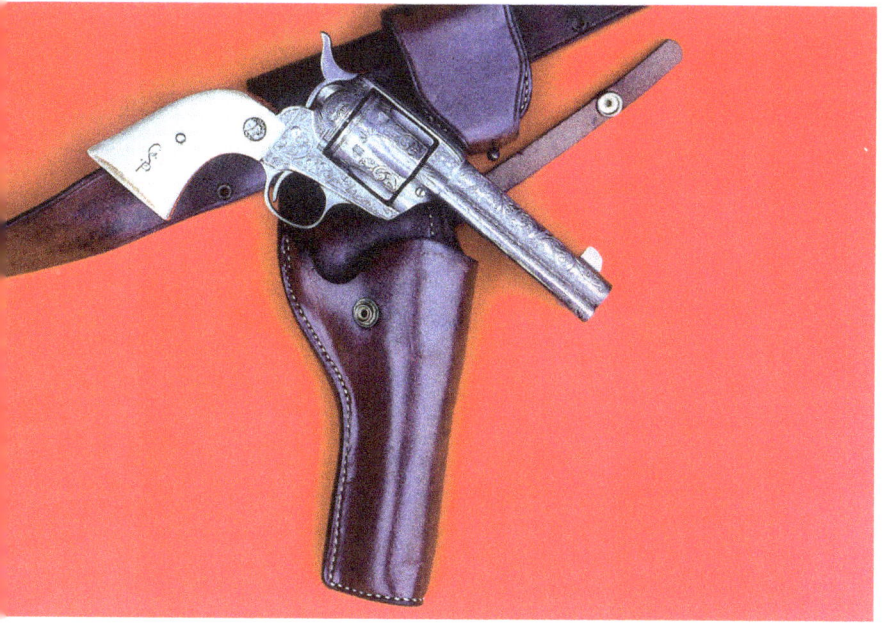

Perhaps the most famous Colt single action in existence is this fully engraved, ivory stocked, nickel plated 4-3/4-inch 45 Colt purchased by then Lieut. George Patton before going into Mexico with Blackjack Pershing in 1917. It became world-famous on the hip of General Patton in WWII and was carried by "Ol' Blood & Guts" in a holster by S.D. Myers.

years later, General George S. Patton would still be wearing this same Colt as he led his troops into battle in World War II. It is probably the most easily recognized Colt single action in existence.

There has been much erroneous information circulated about Patton and his pair of Colt Single Action Army .45s. First, there was no pair. Patton had one Single Action Army as described above. His other revolver was a registered Smith & Wesson 357 Magnum, plain blue, 3-1/2 inches, with ivory stocks bearing his initials on the right grip panel. Yet lore has it that Patton carried two Colts. The truth is that Patton sometimes wore his Colt on his left, sometimes on his right. He also switched the big S&W N-frame from hip to hip as the spirit moved him on any given day. So, when one photograph showed him wearing his ornate Colt on one hip and another photo showed him wearing a similar gun on his other hip, many people assumed he wore two matched Colts. He didn't.

What is significant is the fact that Patton held onto his Colt Single Action Army as a badge of authority even though it was considered obsolete by many experts. Another war hero to hang onto his Colt Single Action Army was General Skinny Wainright, survivor of the Battle of Corregidor in World War II's Pacific Theatre. Just before World War II, former Texas Ranger Frank Hamer led the capture of Bonnie and Clyde. Hamer's gun of choice was "Old Lucky," his Colt Single Action Army .45. These and other high-profile soldiers and lawmen continued to carry the Colt long after it was "obsolete."

By 1941 three things combined to kill the Colt Single Action Army. First, sales had plummeted over the years as the sixgunning public had discovered double-action 38 Specials and semi-automatic 45 ACPs. Old machinery, some dating back to the 1870s, was wearing out. What remained of the demand for the Colt Single Action was smothered by the onset of World War II and its production demands for desperately-needed war materiel.

Major Charles Askins said it best at the passing of the Colt Single Action Army: "Many an eye was dampened when the startling news was broadcast that Colt would discontinue manufacture of the grand Old Peacemaker." An era had come to an end.

"Another war hero to hang onto his Colt Single Action Army was General Skinny Wainright, survivor of the Battle of Corregidor in World War II's Pacific Theatre."

Chapter 6 | The Colt Single Action Army 1st Generation

The 1881 US-marked 45 Colt, top, needed total restoration to compensate for poor treatment in the past; the 1879 Frontier Six Shooter 44-40 should not and will not be touched but rather left as an example of Colt history.

These three First Generation Colts were only a phone call away and did not even come close to melting a credit card. Each was picked up for less than the cost of a new Colt Single Action Army. From top: a 1902 4-3/4-inch 32-20, an 1879 7-1/2-inch 44-40, and a 1917 4-3/4-inch 45 Colt.

During the late 1950s First Generation Single Action Armies were very easy to find at reasonable prices starting with my $90 4-3/4-inch 38-40. I say reasonable, but everything is relative. I went to work in 1956 for 90 cents an hour. In those years I also had a $35 Storekeeper's Model 41 Long Colt, a 12-inch-barreled 38 Special, and 7-1/2-inch 45 Colt. I was foolish enough to let them slip through my fingers. The 41 Long Colt was not in the best of shape, but it was a true Storekeeper's Model and I wish I still had it. Today it is common to find Model Ps in the same condition as my original 38-40 selling for $5000 and up. My quest now is for shooting-condition Colt Single Actions at my current definition of reasonable prices. I have managed to come up with seven shooting-condition Colts for a total outlay of $6400 or an average of just over $900 per sixgun. Compare that to the cost of a new Colt or even some of the replicas.

There are several ways to find these old sixguns, but I have a great advantage as the readers of both *Guns* and *American Handgunner* know of my desires. Other possibilities are searching websites, gun shows, and gun shops, but both patience and diligence are required, and in the case of the Internet, it pays to know your seller well.

It can be especially fruitful to let the local gun shop owners know of guns that would be of special interest. A few years ago I received a call from a reader telling me of three First Generations for sale through a local dealer in Oregon. I called the gun shop for information and was told they were a 7-1/2-inch Frontier Six-Shooter circa 1879, a 4-3/4-inch 32-20 from 1902, and a 4-3/4-inch 45 Colt dating back to 1917. All three were described in working order with very little finish left.

I reached in my wallet to make sure the plastic card was there and made a bid of $3000 for all three. He said he would get back to me. He called back later that day to inform me he had a higher bid, so I went to $3600. He said they were mine, but I still had inspection privileges. That was Friday afternoon. I drove over Monday morning and found three single actions all in shooting condition just as advertised. The Frontier Six-Shooter, which turned out to be all original including the one-piece walnut stocks, needed a new trigger; the 32-20 was fine as it was, and I decided the 45 Colt needed to be rebuilt.

The World War I era 45 had an excellent bore and chambers, several pits and scratches on the surface, black eagle grips slightly warped, and a cylinder that was a little loose. It needed several parts to return it to the first-class shooting shape when it left the factory. I found it shot to point of aim so there was no problem there, but a new bolt and hand were needed for tightening and tuning, the base pin needed to be replaced as did the base pin latch, and all the exterior screws needed to be replaced as the old ones had the typical buggered screwheads. With a gun this old, for continued reliability, it is wise to replace all springs. So this sixgun went off to Peacemaker Specialists to be totally rebuilt.

It had been stored in leather for over 50 years resulting in a finish not in the best of shape. There was still plenty of bluing in protected parts, but there was some discoloration in other places. Peacemaker Specialists as well as several others specializing in old sixguns do not think it is ethical to refinish an old sixgun that has never been re-finished but rather prefer to leave

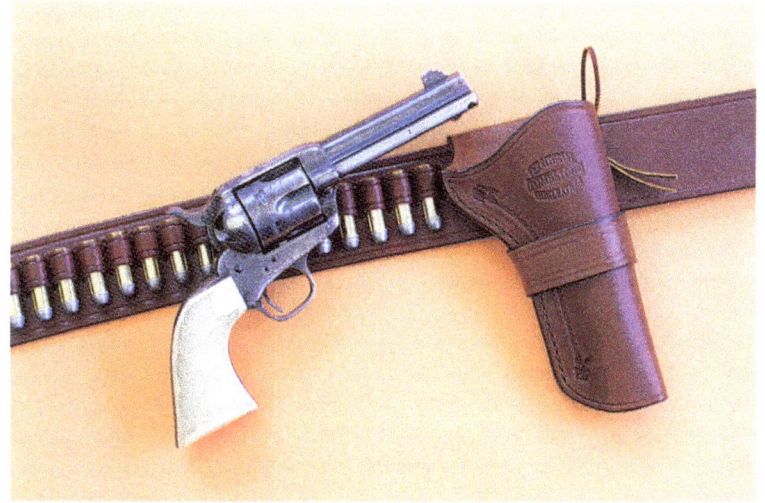

The new leather is from San Pedro Saddlery, but the 1917 Colt 45 has been totally restored on the inside only and fitted with old ivory stocks.

it in its original state. This is exactly what was done with the only major change on the exterior that of replacing the old black eagle grips with a set of aged, one-piece, fleur-de-lis carved ivory grips. This 45 Colt looks as genuinely old as it is, but when it comes to functioning, it is as perfect as a Colt single action can be and is in fact now ready for service to several generations of my family.

About five years ago I was talking to a friend who had been selling a collection of sixguns and rifles for the widow of his friend. There had originally been 41 guns for sale and all were gone except one, one apparently no one else wanted. When I heard it was a Colt SingleAction my palms started to sweat, my heart beat little faster, and I was prepared to hear about an old sixgun way out of my price range. "How much will you offer for an old Colt?" he asked me. "Depends upon the condition," I responded.

Don't let the finish fool you! Except for looks, and thanks to Peacemaker Specialists, this old 45 Colt is in perfect working order and expertly stocked with ivory in the fleur-de-lis pattern.

"Well," my friend said, "it's old, it's rusty, pitted, just not in very good shape." So that's why it remained the last gun to be sold. "Well," I answered, "if the frame is okay, I would pay $300 just to get the frame for a re-build." "If you will go $300," my friend said, "it's yours and I can call the selling of these guns a finished project." With that I agreed to purchase a Colt sight unseen and we went off to get the one last remaining firearm out of the back of the near-empty safe, a poor old sixgun that no one else wanted.

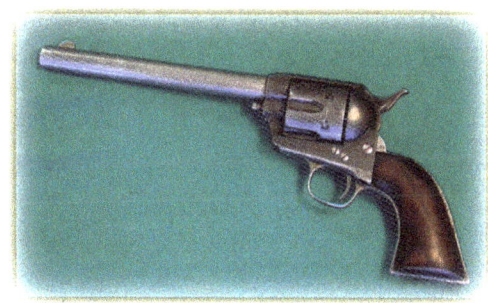

Most restorers will not refinish an old Colt that has not been refinished before. This before picture shows a sixgun with shrunken stocks, old and crude rebluing, rust in some areas, and what appears to be pipe wrench marks on the barrel.

I picked up the old Colt. It was a 7-1/2-inch Single Action Army with no caliber marking on the barrel; a very poor and very old-looking re-blue mixed in with patches of rust; one-piece wooden stocks that had shrunk considerably; and a barrel with scratches appearing to be from the teeth of a wrench or jaws of a vise as someone tried to remove or tighten it. The old Colt seemed to function okay, certainly much better than it looked. The top of the loading gate where it met the frame shared one-half of a circular dent with the frame and I tried to envision it as a mark made by a nineteenth-century bullet. Whatever the cause, it would require extensive welding to fix it. So much for a bargain frame! I discovered mismatched numbers when comparing the serial numbers on the frame, trigger guard, and butt.

Single Action Sixguns | 45

Chapter 6 | The Colt Single Action Army 1st Generation

The same sixgun after total restoration by Larry Larsen looks as good or better than when it left the factory in 1881.

The main serial number really caused my heart to take a leap, as this was a true "One of One Thousand" since the last three digits of the serial number were all zeroes. When one considers the fact that fewer than 358,000 Colt Single Actions were made from 1873 to 1941 at least as to serial numbers this would be a relatively rare sixgun. Then the impossible happened. There on the left side of the frame were two small letters that simply said US. Could it really be? Could this old mistreated relic be an authentic US Cavalry sixgun? Could I be so fortunate as to have found a piece of Frontier history for $300? If it really was authentic, why didn't someone else buy it much earlier? I decided to say nothing until authenticating or disproving the fact of whether or not it was a true US Cavalry Single Action Army.

It was packed up and sent off to John Kopec for inspection and possible authentication. Kopec lettered it as a true US-marked Colt issued in 1881. He was even able to tell me where it was originally issued. As with many single actions going through the government armory, parts were often separated with different containers for barrels, cylinders, frames, and grip frames. When the sixguns were re-assembled no attempt was made to reunite all original parts, hence the mixed serial numbers.

I was offered $1200 for the parts, so I decided to remit the difference between the actual purchase price and authentication expenses and the true value to the seller. That still gave me a good bargain and I felt better about the whole deal. My conscience remained clear.

So now what to do? Keep it for photos and occasional shooting? Sell it? Restore it? Since it had been re-blued once before it was definitely a candidate for restoration, a task that would require considerable work to bring it back the way it was in 1881.

The decision was made for total restoration and it was turned over to Larry Larsen, who specializes in restoring old Colts. This would prove to be one of his greatest challenges. Rust damage was removed from the cylinder, a small spot weld had to be repaired, the original hammer and trigger were welded and re-cut to allow perfect timing and lockup, a new black powder-style base pin was installed, and all screws and the base pin were fire-blued. Rust was removed from the trigger guard without removing the serial number or inspector's mark and both sides of the trigger guard were properly beveled to meet the frame sharply.

The butt had become rounded and worn; this was flat sanded and contoured correctly and a new serial number was cut, one that would assure no intention to faking this as an authentic and all original US Colt. To replace the shrunken original stocks, new one-piece walnut stocks were installed with the correct cartouches and inspector's marks. All rust was removed from the cylinder, the flutes were polished and beveled, and the barrel was polished to remove rust and scratches while still maintaining all original markings. The tip of the ejector housing was beveled and the correct black powder ejector rod was installed, complete with round bullseye head.

The entire sixgun, except for the mainframe and hammer, which were re-case hardened by Color Case Company, was properly and period-correctly re-blued, and necessary restamping was performed by Dave Lanara. The final result is a beautiful example of what a Cavalry Model Colt Single Action Army looked like in the last quarter of the nineteenth century. Add up all the money invested for the original purchase, the authentication, the extra money paid to the seller due to the true value, and the restoration and I was out of pocket well under $2000. I wouldn't sell it for twice that much.

One day I received a call from Shapel's Gun Shop informing me of a young fellow there with some sixguns for sale I would probably be interested in. When I arrived I found a young man who was selling his grandfather's old Winchesters and Colt single actions from around the turn of the century. There was a pair of 4-3/4-inch 32-20s and another pair each marked "COLT FRONTIER SIX-SHOOTER," which identified them as 44-40s. All four of these were also obviously everyday working sixguns as the finish was virtually non-existent, but the lettering was sharp and clear on all the guns and very few of the old screws showed any serious damage to their slots.

Looking at the serial numbers of the 44-40s, I found one to be in the black powder range and the other very early smokeless. Pulling the cylinders, I found the oldest gun did have some pitting in the barrel while the smokeless barrel was in excellent shape. Both cylinders locked up tight with a minimum of endplay and side-to-side movement for sixguns that were over 100 years old. I asked the young man how much he wanted for the pair of Frontier Six-Shooters and he mentioned a price that I felt was a little too high, especially for both of them. A counteroffer was made and accepted. I had two of Grandpa's sixguns, having paid $1000 each once again using plastic. I thought he was wrong for selling his grandfather's guns, and I was wrong for not buying the 32-20s as well. I did not want to spend $4000 at one time. However, writing from the comfort of historical perspective, I realize that by now the bill would have long been paid and I would have two more Colt Single Actions.

It did not take much to bring both these 44-40s into shooting shape. Both sixguns were taken apart carefully, all parts were soaked in carburetor cleaner to remove who knows how many years of accumulated dirt, and then everything was given a coat of Tetra Gun Grease before reassembling. For the black powder sixgun, all endplay was taken out of the cylinder with a couple of Power Custom end shims and the front trigger guard screw was replaced. When I put the works back together, I found I had a sixgun with a very smooth action. The second sixgun, from 1902, received the same treatment with the same results: a very smooth action. They built them that way 100 years ago. It was necessary to replace the mainspring on the latter gun as the one it had was much too heavy for my tastes. Even though one was made for black powder and the other for smokeless, both sixguns are now used with black powder loads exclusively, just to keep things simple.

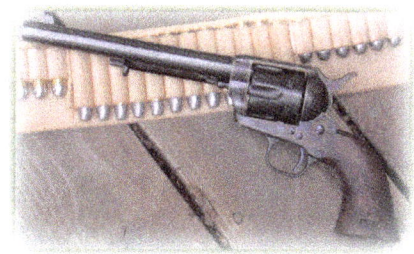

Original US-marked Colt was rescued from the bone pile and totally restored by Larry Larsen.

Original stocks from 1881? No, this restoration has been fitted with period-correct stocks including the cartouche.

Color Case Company did the restoration work on the mainframe and hammer of this 1881 Colt 45.

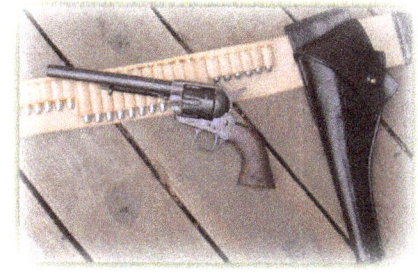

Another picture of the original US-marked cavalry Colt from 1881, totally restored by Larry Larsen with a period-correct belt and holster by El Paso Saddlery.

Chapter 6 | The Colt Single Action Army 1st Generation

Three generations of 7-1/2-inch Colt Single Actions chambered in 44 Special. The First Generation example, left, was originally chambered in 32-20; the Second Generation example with Eagle's Ultra Ivory stocks, center, was originally a 38 Special; while the Third Generation 44 Special is original. Expert conversions by Peacemaker Specialists.

One final Colt single action sixgun also came as a result of a call from Shapel's. This time a fellow had a reblued 4-3/4-inch 32-20 with exceptionally nice one-piece walnut stocks for sale for $500. I did not hesitate at all on this one. It was sent off to Eddie Janis at Peacemaker Specialists along with a 7-1/2-inch Second Generation 44 Special barrel and instructions to turn it into a first-class 44. Janis rechambered a 357 Magnum cylinder, fitted it and a barrel to the old frame, performed one of his Saddle Tramp action and trigger jobs, and once again the result was an excellent shooting sixgun in perfect working shape for less than the cost of a new Colt Single Action Army.

The only sour note to this story has to do with the take-off 32-20 barrel and cylinder. A fellow from Canada traveling on his old Harley up to the Arctic Circle and then south into the United States stopped to spend a couple days with me. I gave him the barrel and cylinder to restore an old Colt. I had offered to mail them to him, but he felt it was easier to just to take them back with him to Canada. They were confiscated at the border. That was more than five years ago and he is still trying to get them back. These were just parts, a barrel and cylinder, but they were confiscated just the same! Times have certainly changed since the first Colt Single Action Army arrived in 1873.

First Generation Colt Single Actions have a mystique all their own. This is definitely one of those "if you understand, no explanation is necessary; if you do not understand, no explanation is possible" situations. These old sixguns either stir wonderful emotions and feelings and heart, mind, soul, and spirit, or they don't. For me they definitely do it as no other sixguns ever have or ever will. They are also some of the finest built firearms ever produced. The early Second Generation Colts came close, very close, but toward the end of that run some of the guns produced were far removed from the original quality. The Third Generation Colts do not even come close to First Generation single actions. However, at least they are genuine Colts, and no other sixguns can make that claim.

Many excellent books have been written on the Colt single action, but for excellent pictures covering all their attributes and subtle variations, as well as detailed information about calibers and production dates, I highly recommend *A Study of the Colt Single Action Army Revolver* by Graham, Kopec, and Moore (1976). John Parson's little book *The Peacemaker and Its Rivals* (1949) gives a short history of the Model P, production figures by years and by calibers, and serial numbers sorted by year. Both books are out of print, but a search at www.abebooks.com or www.rayrilingarmsbooks.com normally turns up any shooting book I am trying to find.

–Chapter 7–

THE BISLEY AND FLAT-TOP TARGETS

By the late 1870s, for all practical purposes, the buffalo were gone. Once the buffalo disappeared, the Indian could no longer exist as he had for many centuries as the buffalo provided both food and shelter, with every part of those magnificent shaggy beasts being used. Once the herds were wiped out, the Indian's world was gone and it would not be long until reservations were a way of life.

With the frontier era pretty well over, men began to look at sixguns for recreational purposes as well as self-defense. Target shooting became widespread with well-known men such as Walter Winans setting nearly unbelievable records using the Smith & Wesson New Model #3 chambered in 44 Russian. Winans, whose reputation was made shooting single action revolvers as few others were able to do before or since, would say in 1920, "The revolver is obsolete." He should have known better.

If they were original they would be too valuable to shoot, but these replica single action and Bisley Model Flat-Top 45 Colt Target Models allow affordable shooting of nineteenth-century style target pistols.

Originally the Colt Single Action Army was, just as its name implies, adopted by the United States Cavalry in 1873. Fifteen years later it was time for Colt to introduce a variation on the Model P. As a teenager I spent much of my time hanging around the most interesting place I could find, the local gun shop and shooting range. When the owner suffered a fire in part of his shop and was faced with months of trying to salvage parts and equipment I was more than happy to work with him in the reclaiming operations.

One day as we were cleaning some parts a fellow came in with three handguns for sale. "Will you give me $65 for these three guns?" he asked. One was a Colt Single Action; the other two were old break-tops, their manufacturer long lost from my memory. At a time when one could have a pre-war Colt Single Action in excellent condition for around $90, the purchase was made even though the Colt exhibited no original finish.

By this time I was fairly familiar with sixguns but this Colt was a little different. The sights were not standard but rather a movable rear much like that found on the my original .22 Ruger Single-Six, that is, it moved in a dovetail for adjusting windage while the front sight was adjustable by loosening a screw and moving it up and down. The

Chapter 7 | The Bisley Model & Flat-Top Targets

top strap was also wider and thicker. That night, as I was reading about Colt Single Actions in the latest issue of *GUNS QUARTERLY*, I came across this same mysterious model of the Colt Single Action Army. It was not a standard model but a rare target model known as the Flat-Top Target.

The caliber marking on the barrel of the gun brought into the gun shop was 44 S&W. Colt records showed that Colt produced 51 Flat-Tops in 44 S&W and 51 Flat-Tops in 44 Russian. Many current researchers believe these were all the same, so therefore there were actually 102 Flat-Tops made in 44 Russian. The Colt Single Action Flat-Top Target Model was produced from 1888 to 1895 as Colt's offering for bullseye shooters. Some Flat-Tops were assembled from existing frames after 1895 and there exists one Flat-Top Target Model in 44 Special, a caliber which did not exist until 1907 or 1908. It has been my good fortune to handle this very special Special, which belonged to Elmer Keith. The 44 Russian was the target cartridge of the day, and Flat-Tops are also found in the English chamberings of .450 and .455 along with some 20 others.

Some of the Flat-Top Target Models were fitted with extra long grips that filled in under the butt of the standard Single Action Army grip frame to give target shooters better control of the sixgun. I have not seen or heard of any Flat-Top Target Models being fitted with the 1860 Army grip frame, which to me would have made perfect sense. The Flat-Top was officially dropped in 1894 as it was modified to become the Bisley Target Model. In England it was advertised as "Colt's New '95 Model, .455 Cal. Army And Target Revolver In One. Takes the standard service cartridge. No pistol shoots more accurately, quickly, or is as durable in construction. Every pistol guaranteed. Everyone should try it before buying a military, match, or frontier revolver."

The sighting system for the Bisley remained the same as that of the Colt Flat-Top Target Model, but with a wide hammer and trigger added. To make the sixgun more adaptable to target shooting, the grip shape was radically changed. The frame was slightly altered to ride about 1/8-inch higher in the back. The grip frame was given a smooth curve that went right to the top of the back strap and also was curved higher behind the trigger guard. This allowed the grip to nestle deeper in the hand for stability while target shooting. The grip shape of the Single Action Army was designed, either purposely or accidentally, to help tame the felt recoil of big bore cartridges by allowing the sixgun to roll naturally in the hand. (I would guess accidentally, as the grip frame first appeared on the 36-caliber Model 1851 Navy, which exhibited very minimal felt recoil.) The Bisley grip frame was introduced to stabilize the sixgun and keep it from shifting in the hand during target shooting.

The Bisley Target Model lasted for less than 20 years, the last one being shipped around 1913. Both the Colt Single Action Flat-Top and Bisley disappeared before World War I. Since the Bisley was originally designed as a target sixgun for competition at the English town of that name, the most popular caliber in the Bisley Target Model was the British 455 Eley, followed by the 32-20 and 38-40. In the Single Action Flat-Top Target Model the number one chambering was not 44 Russian or even 45 Colt, but the easy-shooting 38 Colt. There was a good reason for its popularity. It had virtually no felt recoil and if current-production 38 Long Colt ammunition from Black Hills is any indication, it was exceptionally accurate.

The next three top chamberings in the Single Action Flat-Top were the 45 Colt, .22 rimfire and 41 Long Colt. Target Models are very rare and not easily found. It isn't often that one walks into a gunshop as that one did 50 years ago. The true value of that .44-caliber Flat-Top Target Model in the late '50s was more like $700; imagine its value today. Today Target Models definitely demand collector prices. Very high prices. Of the total Colt single action production prior to World War II of nearly 357,000 sixguns, fewer than 1000 each were Single Action and Bisley Target Models, 917 for the Single Action and 976 for the Bisley.

Even if one could a find Flat-Top Single Action or Bisley Target Model, it would certainly be too valuable to be an everyday shooting sixgun. Thanks to Cimarron, however, we can at least capture the flavor of the original

The obvious differences in the Colt Single Action Army and the Bisley Model are seen here to be grip frame, hammer, and trigger.

Classic Colt 38-40 sixguns include 4-3/4-inch SAA, 7-1/2-inch SAA with lanyard ring, and 5-1/2-inch Bisley Model. Photo courtesy of Gordon Marts.

Flat-Tops as both models are now offered as replicas manufactured by Uberti with a 7-1/2-inch model of each in 45 Colt chambering. Originally, only 100 45s were made in the Single Action Target model by Colt and 97 in the Bisley style in this caliber. Now thanks to these replicas anyone can own and shoot a 45 Target Model Colt.

The Bisley Model started out as a target pistol, but it did not stay that way. Colt recognized a demand from shooters for a standard, fixed-sight Model P with the Bisley Model hammer, trigger, and grip frame. For me, and probably for most shooters, the original Colt Single Action has better balance and is faster from leather than the Bisley. The Colt single action grip frame is also considered to be the best for shooting as it rolls naturally in the hand upon recoil, which in turn places the thumb in the proper place for fast recocking of the hammer. However, once that recoil increases past a certain point, the rolling of the grip frame in the hand becomes a liability and often allows the hammer to dig into the back of the hand. This is why the standard grip frame did not last very long on the Ruger 44 Magnum Blackhawk. For most shooters, the Bisley Model grip frame does a much better job of handling big recoil than the original single action style.

I first became acquainted with the Bisley Model in the early days of *GUNS* magazine in the 1950s in the form of two excellent articles authored by a grand old gentleman by the name of Walter Rogers. His second article praised Bill Ruger for offering such great single action sixguns in magnum calibers, but it was his first article that featured the sixgun he had carried most of his life. Rogers was born about the time of the legendary gunfight at the OK Corral and spent his lifetime as a cowboy, forest ranger, and outdoorsman. His firearms of choice, naturally, were a Winchester lever action rifle in 25-35 and a Colt Single Action.

That first article is titled "Take Your Time Fast" and featured his fast leather and a special single action. Rogers' Colt was not your ordinary Model P. In fact it was not a Model P at all but rather a Bisley Model. For much of his life Rogers carried that Bisley 45 in a homemade holster on a companion homemade combination cartridge and money belt. His sixgun was not 100% Bisley as the hammer spur had been modified to have the same shape as the Colt Single Action Army. One often encounters old Colt Single Action Army Models with Bisley-style hammers; Rogers reversed it by using a Bisley Model with a standard single action hammer. It worked for him.

The old Bisley Model often found favor with those who had short thumbs for whom the hammer was more easily reached than on the Single Action Army. Photo courtesy of Gordon Marts.

Single Action Sixguns | 51

Chapter 7 | The Bisley Model & Flat-Top Targets

Many an old cowboy found the Bisley Model perfectly adequate as his every day packin' pistol.

This shot-out Bisley Model 44-40 has been given a new lease on life with a 44 Special barrel and cylinder. Maple stocks are by BluMagnum.

Another fan of the Colt Bisley and contemporary of Rogers was the saddle and holster maker to the Hollywood stars, Ed Bohlin. Bohlin had short fingers and preferred the low-riding hammer of the Bisley to the standard Colt Single Action Army. If one watches carefully it is often possible to notice a Bisley riding in the holster of many a 1930s good guy or bad guy "B" movie cowboy. Buck Jones often carried a Bisley Model, as did Andy Clyde, who portrayed California Carlson in the Hopalong Cassidy series. Even Charles Bronson used a pair of Bisleys as he starred with Yul Brynner in the movie about Pancho Villa.

At about the same time I found my first Bisley in a gun shop. It was a 4-3/4-inch .45 refinished with a gold plated cylinder and barrel and the balance of the gun in nickel. Grips were imitation stag. Altogether it was quite gaudy looking. However, the price was quite reasonable and I've always regretted not buying it at the time.

The first Bisleys were true target models, at least as much as possible in the 1890s, with adjustable front and rear sights quite crude by today's standards but much more conducive to target shooting than the fixed sights usually encountered on a Colt Single Action Army. Colt determined that shooters wanted standard Bisley models and within two years of the introduction of the Bisley Target Model, it was fitted with the standard sighting system of the Colt Single Action Army while maintaining the newer Bisley grip shape, hammer, and trigger. All of these are marked (BISLEY MODEL) followed by the caliber designation on their barrels, except those found in 44-40, which are also marked with "COLT FRONTIER SIX SHOOTER," just the same as the standard Colt Single Action Army in 44-40.

As with the Colt Single Action Army, barrel lengths were standardized with more than half of them being 4-3/4 inches and the balance almost evenly split between 5-1/2 and 7-1/2 inches, and with a very few also being made without ejector rod assemblies. These are extremely rare with fewer than a dozen known and are an example of striking the proverbial gold should one be found. There are no examples known of any Buntline Special Bisleys.

By 1912, sales of the Colt single action in general were on the decline and the Bisley was dropped from the Colt catalog. For the next several years Bisleys would still be produced from inventory parts on hand. In its short life of less than 20 years, the Bisley was serial numbered along with the standard Colt Single Action production. The most popular calibers in the Colt Single Action, in order of preference, were 45 Colt, 44-40, 38-40, 32-20, and 41 Long Colt. With the Bisley the order changed radically with the 32-20 first, followed by the 38-40, then the 45 Colt, 44-40, and 41 Long Colt. Of the 356,629 single actions produced before production ended in 1941, a total of 44,350 were Bisley Models while 310,386 were standard Single Action Army Models.

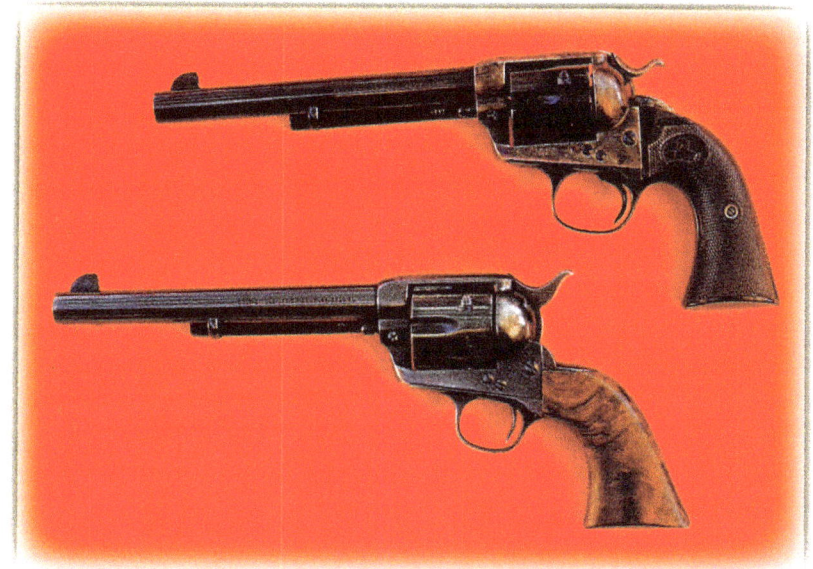

For less than a cost of a new Colt, these two century-old examples were purchased and rebuilt. They are now 7-1/2-inch 44 Specials fitted with Second Generation barrels. The Bisley Model with a Christy cylinder has been re-finished by Hamilton Bowen, while the Single Action Army has been rebuilt and tuned by Peacemaker Specialists with new parts including a rechambered 357 Magnum cylinder.

Thirty years ago it was possible to pick up Bisley Models quite reasonably, certainly less than a comparable Single Action Army, and I managed to pick up two poorly re-finished 44-40 Bisley Models with equally poor barrels for less than $200 each, both of which have long since been rebuilt into 44 Specials with new barrels and cylinders. One by Hamilton Bowen has a 7-1/2-inch barrel and has been totally refinished as original including the casehardened frame and hammer. It is not only a most attractive sixgun but an excellent shooter when using the Christy 44 Special cylinder with Specials or 44 Russians, or slipping in the original 44-40 cylinder. I once ran 50 rounds of black powder 44 Russians through this Bisley Model with all rounds cutting one hole at 25 yards.

My other rebuilt Bisley Model is a nickel-plated 4-3/4-inch sixgun with a 44 Special Colt cylinder and a Douglas barrel all done by Trapper Gun. This is another very attractive sixgun, especially with its genuine stag grips. It also rides easy in a holster and is really not all that difficult to use for fast work, but I can see why Walter Rogers preferred the standard hammer for this type of application. I think of him every time I shoot it.

The Bisley Model has been gone since before World War I, but its tradition lives on in replicas offered by both Cimarron and EMF and also in the grip frames found on both the Freedom Arms Model 83 and the Ruger Bisley Model. Neither grip is a copy of the original, but both are similar. The Bisley Model was also used by Harold Croft and Elmer Keith for building some very special single action sixguns, as we shall see in the next chapter.

Three Generations of Colt single actions are represented here with the Bisley Model only been made during the First Generation production run.

A full century separates these two Colts: a Bisley Model rebuilt into 44 Special, and a current production Third Generation 44-40 Single Action Army.

Single Action Sixguns | 53

–Chapter 8–

THE SINGLE ACTION SIXGUNS OF ELMER KEITH

Elmer Keith relaxes on the back porch of his Salmon, Idaho home in the 1950s with his 7-1/2-inch 44 Special Colt SAA and George Lawrence holster.

He lived a life most of us can only dream of. Born in Missouri in 1899, he and his family moved to Montana six years later, and he grew up around former outlaws, lawmen, buffalo hunters, and Indian fighters. His life spanned the time from the Civil War veterans and gunfighters of the frontier to the more modern age of handgunning. His teachers had survived the bloodiest war in our nation's history and had seen the great herds of buffalos and the cow towns that helped build the West. He was Elmer Keith, and there will never be another like him when it comes to one man's influence on firearms in general and single action sixguns, the 44 Special, and the 44 Magnum in particular.

As a young boy Keith was in a terrible fire that left him scarred and crippled and likely to die young. His hands were in particularly bad shape, charred and fused by the fire to his forearms. His parents would not countenance such a disability, so they filled him with Old Granddad to dull the pain, broke his useless fire-grafted hands away from his arms, spread his fingers, and using tallow-filled gloves nailed to a board, persuaded the boy's hands to heal in a normal position.

Not only would Keith live four score and more years, he would gain complete use of his hands and become an expert shot with rifle, shotgun, and his beloved sixgun. As a young cowboy he was described as a "snake with a sixgun." He himself said that he buckled on his single action sixgun every day as naturally as one pulled on one's pants. That good habit would serve to save his life more than once.

Keith's was a great life but also one that was laced with tragedy. He survived not one but two terrible fires. He admitted later searching for the man that started the hotel fire that crippled him as a child. With his ever-present sixgun on hip, his search proved unsuccessful and he would later admit that he was glad he had not found the arsonist.

In his early years in Montana and Idaho, Keith was a bronc buster and cowboy. He never made it past the eighth grade but he was smart enough to marry a schoolmarm. He and his beloved Lorraine spent much of their life on the Salmon River in Idaho far from town, living on a ranch with no modern conveniences of any kind. What we call "roughing it" for perhaps a few days' vacation each year was his daily life. Lorraine had to be tough as she had to spend many months alone in the backcountry with the kids while Keith was off guiding hunters, an avocation that helped the struggling family survive in those dark depression days. It was a hard-fought existence at best. One of the great tragedies of Keith's life occurred at this time, when an outbreak of flu took his young daughter and left him so sick he could not even get out of bed to attend her funeral.

In the 1950s, Elmer and Lorraine Keith moved into the town of Salmon, Idaho, and Keith continued to fill out his life writing for *Guns*, *Guns & Ammo*, and *The American Rifleman*, as well as authoring several books and answering hundreds of letters per month from readers all over the world. His writing career began quite by accident.

In 1925, an event occurred that would change the course of Keith's life completely and establish him as one of the most famous gunwriters of all time. It was the Fourth of July and like most young cowboys, Keith decided to celebrate the birth of this great country by firing his sixgun into the air: "I started to celebrate the morning of the Fourth. Picked up an old .45 S.A. Army 5-1/2 inch loaded with 40 grains bulk by my Ideal measure and 258 grain Ideal bullet, stepped out on an upstairs porch and turned the old gun at a 45 degree angle and started shooting. When the gun rose from recoil of my first cartridge I unconsciously hooked my thumb over the hammer spur and thus cocked gun as it recovered from the recoil. When I turned the next one loose I was almost deafened by the report and saw a little flash of flame. My hand automatically cocked gun and snapped again but no report. I stopped then knowing that something was wrong. The upper half of three chambers was gone. Also one cartridge and half of another case. Also the top strap over cylinder. My ears were ringing otherwise I was all O.K." (*American Rifleman*, August, 1925)

As far as I know this quotation is from the first article written by Elmer Keith. He would go on to a gunwriting career lasting nearly 60 years, publishing hundreds of articles on sixguns, rifles, and shotguns in addition to 10 major books including *Sixgun Cartridges and Loads* (1936), *Sixguns* (1955), and his autobiography *Hell, I Was There!* (1979). The first gives major insights into Keith's early experiments with sixguns, the second is the sixgunner's bible, and the latter is definitely a fascinating account of an outdoor life in the early part of this century. Be warned! The latter is one of those can't-put-down books that, once started, will push all other activity to the background.

Keith was born intelligent, and he learned as he lived. (The above-referenced .45 sixgun was not his first blow-up. Another .45, loaded with 300-grain 45-70 rifle bullets, had let go on him some time previously.) The gun described in the 1925 *American Rifleman* article had been loaded with oversized 260-gr. .458" bullets, and the combination of these oversized, soft bullets and compressed, crushed black powder resulted in an explosion not unlike what would have occurred with a like charge of Bullseye. (All this is known only because Keith sent the gun and remaining shells to gunwriter Chauncey Thomas for an autopsy.)

This time Keith learned! Realizing that the relatively thin chamber walls of the 45 Colt cylinder couldn't withstand his hot-rodding, he turned to the 44 Special. In these days of nearly instant communication and rapid-fire spreading of knowledge, it may be hard for us to believe but in 1925, when he wrote about his latest blow-up, Keith had never even seen a 44 Special!

The 44 Special first saw the light of day in the 1908 Smith & Wesson New Century or Triple-Lock. Colt followed a few years later, in 1913, with Single Action Army models that carried the barrel inscription "RUSSIAN AND S&W SPECIAL .44," the 44 Special being simply an elongated 44 Russian. More than 10 years later Keith had still not come upon what would become his beloved 44 Special, and all of Keith's early experimentations were probably with well-worn black powder Colt .45s. It is not surprising that the .45s blew. It was time for Keith to look for a cartridge that would give him the power he wanted in a sixgun with a greater safety factor. That cartridge would prove to be the 44 Special.

Then came a meeting of two notable sixgunners: "Even in 1928, "Keith wrote, "when Harold Croft of Philadelphia visited me for a month at my little ranch in Durkee, Oregon, he told me frankly, when I met him at the station, that everyone he knew in the revolver clubs in the East had asked him to find out if the long range sixgun work I had written of was true; all firmly believing it was not. Croft witnessed my hitting a four-foot square target at 700 yards with every sixgun save one of the suitcase-full he brought along, before said gun was empty. The one exception was a 2" barreled .45 Colt 'slip' gun, which due to its extremely high trajectory, required eleven shots before I finally dropped one through the target – and that was finally accomplished by aiming at a small sage brush on top of the mountain behind the target over 3/4 mile away. Croft also witnessed my killing several jack rabbits at from 125 to 150 yards, as well as hitting one eagle *[definitely written in a different time! – JT]* at 200 yards, with .44 Special S.A. Colts." (*American Rifleman*, May, 1939)

Croft, described by Keith as a gun crank and collector, hit it off with the cowboy famously. Croft was a dedicated sixgunner and designer and brought four special

Chapter 8 | The Single Action Sixguns of Elmer Keith

Croft's M2, originally a lightweight 45 Colt, was also converted to 44 Special after Croft's visit with Elmer Keith.

Harold Croft's M1 converted to 44 Special and fitted with ivory stocks.

Note the beautiful engraving, long-range front sight, and special base pin on Keith's #5 SAA.

Keith's long-range front sight presented a clear flat sight picture and was pinned and fitted to a barrel band.

lightweight sixguns along to show to and shoot with Keith. These were all built on Colt single actions and Bisleys and basically designed primarily as lightweight self-defense single actions. These four sixguns were numbered 1, 2, 3, and 4; more on these shortly.

Keith liked the sixguns that Croft had designed and saw real possibilities with Croft's designs, not in a lightweight pocket sixgun but as a full-size single action 44 Special sixgun: "Needless to say, after playing with Croft's guns awhile I decided to have one of my S.A.A. guns worked over to incorporate some of Croft's improvements, with few ideas of my own thrown in." The result was the famous Number 5 Single Action pictured in many of Keith's articles over the next 30 years as well as in *Sixguns*.

Keith wrote about the Number 5 44 Special in the April, 1929 issue of *The American Rifleman* in an article titled "The Last Word." The Number 5 was truly the last word in sixguns for nearly 60 years until the coming of the Freedom Arms Casull, the Texas Longhorn Arms Improved Number Five, and the custom revolvers of Hamilton Bowen, John Linebaugh, Jim Stroh, and Andy Horvath.

Keith's Number 5 was basically a Colt single action with a Bisley backstrap and a Single Action Army front strap. Grips were ivory, barrel length was 5-1/2 inches, sights were fully adjustable, the base pin was over-size, and the cylinder pin catch was a masterful design that operated on the lever principle.

Keith had learned his lesson well concerning heavy loads in the 45 Colt and the paper-thin cylinder walls of the Colt Single Action Army. That is why the last word in caliber selection was the 44 Special. "It has been quite recently that I have changed from .45 Colt to .44 Special caliber for my 6-guns, for a number of reasons. For one thing, I have found it much easier to obtain good, reliable, accurate reloading tools for the .44 than for the .45 Colt. The bore diameter of the Colt's .44 Special guns does not vary to anything like the extent of the .45 Colt. I have seen .45 Colt guns with groove and cylinder diameters measuring only .450, which with a heavy load is very apt to scrap the old Peacemaker. Remember, the .45 Colt has been built for over half a century, and several different generations have bored the various guns; so it is it any wonder that guns of various ages vary in bore diameter?

"If a man wishes the most powerful handgun," Keith continued, "and still wishes to use only factory ammunition, then the .45 Colt is the one best bet, with Remington black-power loads. However, if he wishes to

In the late 1920s this was The Last Word in single action sixguns: Elmer Keith's #5 SAA 44 Special.

reload, then the .44 Special is the best of them all. The walls of the cylinder in the .44 are thicker than in the .45, also the rear end of the barrel; and the .44 will stand more pressure with safety than the .45. The .44 Special is more accurate and can be safely loaded to give equal or often better velocity that the .45 Colt with the same weight bullets. I am all through with heavy smokeless loads in the .45 Colt."

For the next 30 years the 44 Special would be Keith's cartridge. His favorite load was a 250-gr. hard-cast bullet of his design over a heavy dose of #80 powder, soon to be replaced by the then-new 2400. His load with the latter powder was 18.5 grains in balloon-head brass. When the modern solid brass appeared in the 1950s, Keith's standard load was lowered to 17.0 grains of 2400. Both of these loads are HEAVY and should be used with caution and only in heavy-framed modern 44 Special sixguns such as the Colt Single Action Army or New Frontier or the Smith & Wesson Model 24. Velocity is around 1,200 feet per second.

Not only did Keith define the last word in sixguns with his single action 44 Special, he also designed a new bullet to wring out the best accuracy and greatest power from his souped-up cartridge: "After fooling with different bullets in the 6-gun for years, and carefully noting their effects on game and their grouping on target, I have finally designed what I honestly believe to be the best all around bullet in existence. I drafted this bullet for the .44 Special to go with my No. 5 gun. I found that to suit the target shooter a bullet must be long and heavy, with correct balance; and must be extremely accurate. Last, but not least, it must cut a clean hole in the target. To be extremely accurate at long range it must have some taper at the point and have a long bearing surface on the lands. It must provide space for plenty of lubricant. The base band must be wide to insure accuracy. There must be a wide band of groove diameter in front of the crimping groove to snugly ride the throat of the cylinder and insure perfect lining up of the cartridge in the chamber. The bullet must have a good crimping groove to properly hold it in the case against recoil."

Keith's bullet was, and is, as famous as his love for the 44 Special. His loads with the Keith bullet were used all over the world by the forerunners of today's handgun hunters. Today, almost all semi-wadcutter bullets are automatically referred to as a Keith bullet. They are not! Keith was very disappointed to see the mould makers change the design of his bullet to allow for easier casting. To be a true Keith bullet a semi-wadcutter must have a long, flat nose and have three equal-sized bands of full caliber, one at the base, one between the lube groove and crimping groove, and one ahead of the crimping groove. The lube groove must be square cornered and hold plenty of lube, and the crimping groove must be cut at the proper angle. The closest designs I know of today are those molds offered by RCBS and NEI.

From 1929 until the early 1950s, Keith considered the 44 Special the King of Sixguns. He asked ammunition manufacturers to bring out his load with a 250-grain bullet at 1200 feet per second. All of them were afraid of liability problems and the possibility of blowing up an old sixgun. Keith suggested that a longer-than-standard

Single Action Sixguns

Chapter 8 | The Single Action Sixguns of Elmer Keith

44 Special case – a 44 Special Magnum as it were – would provide more power but could not be chambered in ancient sixguns. His idea seemed to fall on deaf ears. Then, in 1953, Keith visited both the Smith & Wesson and Remington factories and received somewhat of a promise that Remington would develop the ammunition for any sixgun Smith & Wesson would manufacture. For their part, Smith & Wesson promised to build a sixgun that would handle any load that Remington would devise.

Keith returned to Salmon, Idaho and heard no more until the end of 1955. He then received a call that told him his dream had come true and that he would soon receive one of the first of the new Smith & Wesson 44 Magnums along with Remington ammunition. Keith asked for a powerful loading of the 44 Special at 1200 feet per second. He received a 44 Magnum loading of over 1500 feet per second. His 44 Special sixguns were retired, and Keith would spend the rest of his sixgun shooting life, until his stroke in 1981, with his beloved 44 Magnum. For most of his remaining years his sixgun of choice would be 4-inch S&W 44 Magnum, although he regarded Ruger's single action Super Blackhawk 44 Magnum as the ideal hunting sixgun.

Keith died in 1984 after spending his last years confined to bed in a nursing home after a debilitating stroke. It was a terrible way to leave this earth for a man who lived the life he lived. All of us who love big-bore sixguns and the great sixguns and cartridges we have today owe a great debt of gratitude to the grand old man of sixgunning. (I'm somewhat of a romantic and I often send a few salutary rounds downrange for Elmer Keith or Skeeter Skelton and a few other lesser-known sixgunners who have been part of my life.)

It was only natural that the Colt single action in 44 Special would be Elmer Keith's favorite sixgun from the 1920s until the 1950s. After all, he was a cowboy. Over the years Keith always featured his sixguns in his articles, and as a teenager I purchased a copy of *Sixguns*, published in 1955, subsequently spending many hours carefully studying the pictures of his many custom sixguns. My habit had been to haunt the newsstands looking for magazines having anything about handguns. Now everything important, at least to me, was available in one book. Other teenagers were interested in the new rock and roll music, movies, and fast cars. My passion was sixguns.

Keith's book covered everything: long range shooting, gun fighting, double action shooting, quick draw, holsters, trick shooting, and reloading. I read and re-read *Sixguns* until my first copy was dog-eared and needed replacing. The pictures of the beautiful sixguns were referred to over and over again with the impossible hope that someday I too would own such guns. After I met Keith for the first time, he supplied me with a list of all of his old sixgun articles from *The American Rifleman* and I was able to add all of those to my file.

Keith was not satisfied with stock factory sixguns and enlisted the help of some of the top gunsmiths and engravers in the country to customize his. Little did I realize that someday I would have the pleasure of handling all of his famous sixguns, and, in fact, unloading many that had been loaded since before his stroke. I could scarcely believe it!

> "Other teenagers were interested in the new rock and roll music, movies, and fast cars. My passion was sixguns."

Keith carried his 4-3/4-inch 45 Colt and 7-1/2-inch 44 Special in full floral carved leather by George Lawrence.

There before me were all the famous sixguns I had read about and seen pictured over the last 30 years. All of the famous single action Colts and Rugers, and the double action Smith & Wessons – they were all there, plus the leather he had also made famous: the Lawrence #34 DA holster, and the #120 Keith SA holster, and even the Bohlin quickdraw rig that he designed in the '60s.

On page 103 of *Sixguns* appears a photo of four beautiful Colt single actions owned by Keith. All four of these are still part of the Keith Collection and display two unique characteristics: the obvious quality of the custom work performed on three of them and the varying stages of use each had received. The four single action Colts, all 44 Specials, include 1) a King short action job with 7-1/2-inch barrel; 2) an original, one-of-a-kind 7-1/2-inch Flat-Top Target; 3) the Number 5 SA Colt, an extensively customized 5-1/2-inch Flat-Top Target Model with a special grip made by combining a Bisley backstrap and Colt SAA trigger guard; and 4) a 5-1/2-inch Flat-Top Target with a Keith-designed folding three leaf rear sight.

Colt number 1 was an obvious favorite as it showed the most use. This short-action 44 Special has ivory grips with a steer head carved on the right grip, a wide hammer, a Smith & Wesson type rear sight, and a front sight held on by a barrel band. Even though the sixgun shows extensive blue wear, it is still quite tight. Since the ivory grips have a Colt medallion inset in them, I assume that they are original Colt manufactured stocks.

Colt number 2 is the only known 44 Special Colt SA Target Model to ever leave the Hartford factory. Its finish is all blue with "eagle-style" hard rubber grips. It also shows much use.

Keith's fourth Colt was another Flat-Top Target made up by Neal Houchins with special one-piece rosewood grips made by Pachmayr. This was Keith's long-range sixgun and it has a folding rear sight with three different blades for different ranges. With its a dull blue it is certainly an everyday workin' sixgun. Except for the long-range rear sight, this Colt looks a great deal like the original Ruger Flat-Top Blackhawks.

Colt number 3 was the one written up as "The Last Word" in the April, 1929 issue of *American Rifleman*. This sixgun is so special it deserves some further explanation.

Modern examples of single action sixgun customizing really began with the aforementioned Harold Croft of Pennsylvania. Croft had read the early articles of a very young Elmer Keith writing in the *American Rifleman* in the mid-1920s. He was so fascinated by Keith's first efforts that he packed a suitcase full of the sixguns referred to by Keith in his *American Rifleman* article and took the train all the way west across the continent. He wound up at Keith's little cow ranch in Durkee, Oregon. At the time, Keith and Croft were definitely not on the same page, with Croft stressing lightweight pocket pistols built on SAA and Bisley platforms while Keith was more interested in full-sized single actions for long-range shooting and everyday packing. They came together in a remarkable way.

Croft was an idea man, not a gunsmith, with his thoughts carried out by M.R.F. Sedgley and Neal Houchins. Sedgley did all the radical framework and Houchins the sights, stocks, and action work. Croft showed up at Keith's ranch with four featherweight .45s, all specially numbered. Numbers M1 and M3 were on

Chapter 8 | The Single Action Sixguns of Elmer Keith

Keith carried his #5 SAA 44 Special in the #120 Keith holster by George Lawrence. Keith obviously believed life was too short to spend it with an ugly gun or ugly leather.

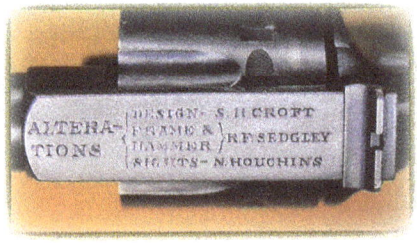

The top strap of M1 contains all the particulars about the custom work performed, a most fitting historical record in steel.

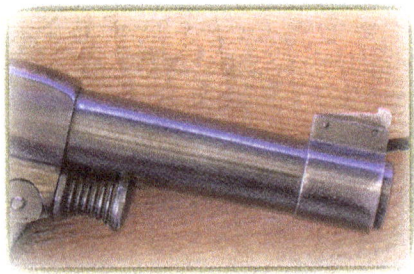

From this close-up of Croft's M2 it's easy to see where Keith got the idea for the base pin and barrel band front sight for his #5 SAA.

the SAA frame while M2 and M4 started out as Bisleys. To produce the featherweights, the recoil shield was hollowed out, the ejector rod was removed, the frame narrowed down in front of the trigger guard, and the loading gate hollowed out. At the same time all of this was accomplished, the frames were also flat-topped and fitted with adjustable sights. All of the Croft Featherweights weighed between 30 and 32 ounces and were written up in the *American Rifleman* in 1928.

Croft obviously had a tremendous effect on Keith. One year later Keith unveiled his idea of the perfect sixgun. Although his was a full-sized sixgun, he obviously incorporated many of Croft's ideas including the flat-topped frame, adjustable sights, and the modified grip frame with the custom work on his sixgun being carried out by Sedgley, Houchins and J.D. O'Meara. Keith called his new sixgun the #5 SAA as it had been patterned after Croft's numbers 1 to 4. On the reverse side of the coin, Keith also had a special effect on Croft. Remember, Croft's sixguns were all .45s, while Keith's #5 was a 44 Special. I've been able to handle Keith's #5 SAA, but wouldn't it also be something to find the Croft sixguns?

A few years ago I received a call from a widow in Montana who was looking for some information about a revolver belonging to her husband. She said it had been purchased by her husband through a classified ad in *The American Rifleman* in 1948 from a man named Croft. That revolver turned out to be M2. As it turned out, soon it would be reunited with one of its brethren.

Not many years later, I was contacted by Sam Reed concerning a custom sixgun that had been in his family for about 30 years. He mentioned Sedgley and Croft, and I really got interested, and for good reason: M1 had been found. So now we had M1 and M2.

In addition to the wonderful custom work, there are two very interesting things about these revolvers. We have said that Keith also had a special effect on Croft. Both sixguns have been converted from 45 Colt to Keith's special caliber, the 44 Special. Both guns are also dated identically: "May 13 1925" and "April 5 1927."

In his book *Sixguns* Keith says Croft visited him in 1928, but he must be off a year as the article on the Croft sixguns appeared in a 1928 issue of the *Rifleman*, meaning Croft must have visited him in 1927. You don't do any comfortable sixgun shooting in Eastern Oregon/Western Idaho in January and February. I'm guessing the newer date on the sixguns reflects the visit to Keith, while the older date is the original completion date. This, however, is only a calculated guess.

There is something else very noticeable about M1. The cylinder has 12 bolt notches. Why 12 notches with only six chambers? There is no safety on a Colt Single Action Army except that of letting the hammer down on an empty chamber. Croft solved this by placing extra notches on the cylinder allowing it to be locked in place with the hammer down between two loaded rounds, making it perfectly safe to carry with six rounds.

All of these custom improvements were passed along to Colt, but none of them was followed except the flat-topping of the frame and the adjustable sights found on the New Frontier that appeared more than three decades later.

Gordon Marts of New Mexico duplicated the #5 grip frame for the author by modifying a Bisley backstrap and fitting a single action grip frame and trigger to this Bisley model 44 Special. Custom grips are also by Marts.

Keith was highly interested in Croft's sixguns except that his desire was for a greatly improved full-sized revolver that would eventually become his favorite single action and one he carried for nearly 30 years. Keith says of his revolver, which became No. 5, "My friend O'Meara is now working over a Bisley, and fitting S.A.A. guard and front strap. He is also bending the Bisley back strap to the S.A. Army angle. His grip will extend about one-eighth inch higher at base of hammer, due to the difference in the frames of the Bisley and S.A. Army; but it should be very similar to the grip of this No. 3 Featherweight. No. 3 has a hammer with something similar to that of No. 1 and I believe made from a regular S.A. hammer, with piece attached to conform with the Bisley in shape and to fill the large cut in the Bisley back strap. The mainspring is like that of the regular S.A. Army, and does not engage a stirrup as in the case of the Bisley....

Here again we can see the beautiful engraving on Keith's #5 as well as the adjustable rear sight and modified Bisley hammer.

"For the ideal heavy belt 6-gun I believe that a 5-1/2-inch Bisley or S.A. Army, fitted with flat-top frame and sights like those of No. 1 or No. 4, with Bisley backstrap and S.A. Army front strap and guard, Bisley hammer and trigger, ejector left on, and with Croft's base-pin catch and a tool-steel pin with a large head similar to, though shorter than, the one on No. 4, and with the frame left full weight, would be the ideal gun for this country and for the hills in general." (*The American Rifleman*, September, 1928)

Six months later in the April, 1929 issue of *The American Riflemen* Keith unveiled "The Last Word." As the title indicates, he felt the No. 5 was the finest single action sixgun it was possible to build. All three gunsmiths – Sedgley, Houchins, and O'Meara – contributed to his new 5-1/2-inch No. 5 44 Special. This highly customized Colt featured adjustable sights with interchangeable front blades, special base pin and base pin catch, flat-topped frame fully engraved and fitted with ivory stocks, and the No. 5 grip frame.

The No. 5 sixgun began Keith's three-decade promotion of heavy loads in the 44 Special that would eventually result in the 44 Magnum. This was also the sixgun for which Keith designed the #429421 bullet. At the same time, his call for an improvement in sixgun powders would soon be followed with the introduction of Hercules 2400. That bullet

Three of Keith's favorite ivory stocked custom Colt single actions included a 7-1/2-inch 44 Special with King short action, custom hammer, and adjustable sights; same modifications on a 4-3/4-inch 45 Colt; and the 5-1/2-inch #5 SAA.

Single Action Sixguns | 61

Chapter 8 | The Single Action Sixguns of Elmer Keith

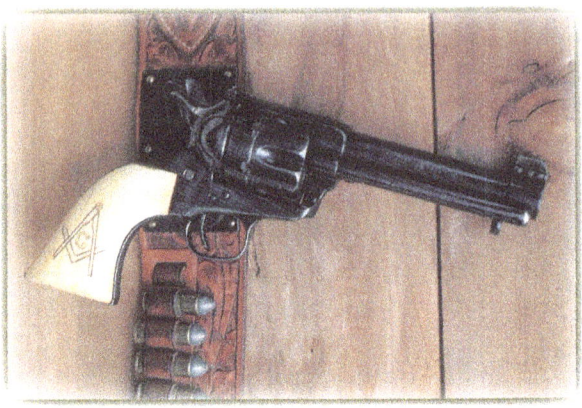

Keith also carried his 45 Colt SAA in a Bridgeport Rig consisting of a special stud on the hammer screw and a metal plate on the belt. The sixgun swung freely and was always ready for instant use.

The special stud on the hammer screw of Keith's 45 SAA is easily seen here and also the metal plate of the Bridgeport Rig that accepted it.

One of Keith's favorite long-range sixguns was this 7-1/2-inch Colt 44 Special with King short action, custom hammer, and adjustable rear sight. Notice that the front sight is on a barrel band.

and that powder would be associated with Keith from 1929 on with the 44 Special and then the 44 Magnum. Keith died in 1984, but it is a rare sixgunner who cannot identify the Keith Load when it comes to both the 44 Special and the 44 Magnum.

Although Elmer adopted the 44 Special in 1927, he did not completely abandon the 45 Colt single action. A 45 Colt single action is pictured on page 102 of *Sixguns*, a 4-3/4-inch-barrelled model with S&W-type adjustable rear sight and barrel band front sight. Before the advent of the 44 Magnum, Keith always said that if he had to depend on factory ammunition his choice would be the 45 Colt.

This 45 Colt, with a wide hammer spur, is also interesting in that it has a special stud on the left side of the gun that replaced the hammer screw. The stud fitted on a clip fastened to the belt so the gun can swing on the clip without a holster, ready for instant use. Keith is pictured using this Colt on page 167 of *Sixguns*. The sixgun shows extensive blue wear and I am guessing that Keith carried it a lot on the quick-draw belt clip.

These five single actions were obvious favorites and were probably used heavily for about thirty years, that is, until the advent of the 44 Magnum. In the 1950s, Keith carried a 4-inch 1950 Target Smith & Wesson 44 Special as his favorite sixgun, soon to be replaced by the same basic gun but chambered for the 44 Magnum. Three single action Rugers were also favorites of Keith: a standard 7-1/2-inch Super Blackhawk with beautiful custom fancy grained wood stocks and two Old Model Ruger Blackhawks, one in 45 Colt and the other chambered for 41 Magnum. Both of these were fitted with brass Super Blackhawk grip frames and custom wood stocks. The Dragoon-styled Super Blackhawk was Keith's top choice for a 44 Magnum single action sixgun.

On the sixtieth anniversary of the Keith #5 SAA, a new sixgun emerged, the Improved Number Five. We'll take a look at in the next chapter.

–Chapter 9–

THE TEXAS LONGHORN ARMS IMPROVED NUMBER FIVE

After Elmer Keith had his completed #5 SAA 44 Special, he commented at the time that "To my notion this is the finest and best Colt in existence . . . and the gun is quickly aimed and fired. The gun is a natural pointer to anyone used to the SAA. . . . For general excellence of grip, balance, sights, trigger and hammer, I do not think this gun can be improved upon." Everything Keith mentioned – grip, balance, sights, trigger, and hammer – would definitely be very difficult to improve. This sixgun sits in the hand so sweetly and points and shoots equally well. It was, as Keith called it, The Last Word when it came to single action sixgun perfection.

It is not as fancy as Keith's #5 SAA and is a 45 Colt instead of a 44 Special, but this TLA Improved Number Five with Dall sheep horn stocks by Roy Fishpaw is hard to beat for good looks and great performance.

After spending a year shooting his new sixgun, Keith felt that the #5 SAA was fine enough to be fully engraved, and the walrus ivory stocks, which had shrunk, were replaced with carved elephant ivory. Elmer's son Ted informed me the #5 SAA sixgun was used so much by his father it had been re-blued twice.

That was in the late 1920s. Keith went on to become probably the most respected and most widely-read gun writer of all time. His influence can be seen not only in the 44 Magnum, which came about as a direct result of his 30 years of shooting and writing about the 44 Special, but also in the Keith bullet, a term which has wrongly become synonymous with semi-wadcutter sixgun bullets; Keith loads for 44 Special, 45 Colt, 38/44, 357 Magnum, 41 Magnum and 44 Magnum; and also in the Keith holster, cataloged by Lawrence as #120, but again a term that has become synonymous with a high-riding, no-nonsense, western-style holster.

In the 1960s Bill Grover entered the single action scene. In 1964, Keith sent young gunsmith Bill Grover an autographed copy of *Sixguns*. Grover, as so many of us young sixgunners did, held Keith in high esteem at the hero level. Grover was fascinated by the #5 SAA pictured and described in Keith's book and spent as much time studying the pictures of Keith's single action sixguns as I did. In 1981, Grover moved from gunsmith to gunmaker as his company, Texas Longhorn Arms, began producing right-handed single actions; that is, the loading gate and ejector rod were on the left side of TLA single actions, allowing a right-handed sixgunner to keep the gun in his right hand as it is loaded and unloaded with the left hand. Grover claims that Sam Colt

Single Action Sixguns

Chapter 9 | The Texas Longhorn Arms Improved Number Five

was obviously left-handed or he would not have made his single actions backwards. Of course Sam Colt died more than 10 years before the advent of the Colt Single Action Army; however, all of his percussion pistols were set up for left handers, that is, switched to the left hand for capping with percussion caps. If you are from Texas, as Grover is, you can call sixguns pistols, or "ma pistols," as he calls his sixguns in a thick Texas accent.

In 1927, Elmer Keith set out to make the finest possible single action sixgun. Grover was so captivated by the #5 SAA pictured and described in Keith's book he tried numerous times to duplicate the old gun without success. In 1986, at the SHOT Show, Grover met Dan Love of Arthur, Iowa. Love had the detailed pattern for the grip of the #5 SAA as drawn for him by Keith himself when Love visited Keith in 1971. Love contacted Ted Keith and received numerous black and white photos of the #5 SAA and, along with the photos, the Keith family gave permission for Grover to build the Improved Number Five as long as it did not contain Elmer Keith's name, as that belonged to Smith & Wesson and their Elmer Keith Commemorative.

In the summer of 1986, Grover, using the black & white photos and the patterns from Dan Love, began in earnest to try once again to build the #5 SAA as the Improved Number Five. It was obvious he would need more help to perform all the operations that had been done by several gunsmiths in the 1920s on the original #5. I met with Grover in 1987 at the SHOT Show, as a number of like-minded individuals gathered at the Texas Longhorn Arms booth to discuss the Improved Number Five. The result was a trek to the Texas Longhorn Arms factory to work on the Improved Number Five.

Grover relates that in two weeks time, they had the first complete Improved Number Five gun made. Starting with a block of steel, machining parts, making workable patterns, spring, sights, and screws, and countless other items took all the men's time. Those present and working on the project were Bill Oakes from Lancaster, Kentucky; Dan Love from Arthur, Iowa; Bill Konig, a renowned grip maker from Centerville, Tennessee; and Robert Luna from Pleak, Texas, a very fine hand polisher. Grover headed up the operation, planning what each would be doing, with all work and design being done in the Texas Longhorn Arms factory. Starting with ideas only, they developed a prototype, moving from paper to steel to finished product in two weeks. As Bill says, that is quite an accomplishment. It took the entire crew working together to get it out in such short order.

Bill Grover had set out not to copy the Keith #5 SAA but to really improve on it while retaining the original flavor. He succeeded in producing a real salute to Elmer Keith, the undisputed Dean of the Sixgunners. The grip straps, grip contour, base pin, and lever latch are all identical to those on Elmer's original #5 SAA. I have handled both sixguns at the same time and, when it comes to the grip frame, the original #5 and the Improved Number Five feel and look the same. The lever latch, other than being a mirror image of the Improved Number Five, is also identical.

Grover himself machined the frame and cylinder. While they were being fitted and polished, Glenn Foley of Alice, Texas made the barrel. Grip maker Bill Konig worked with Dan Love and Grover to come up with a two-piece grip that actually appeared to be of one piece as on the original Colts. This newest one-piece-type grip was ingeniously fitted to the Improved Number Five with no screw holes going through either side. This one-piece look gives the gun a clean, uncluttered look. While accomplishing all this, Grover sought out master machinist and designer Keith DeHart for assistance with the base pin and lever latch. DeHart was shown what was needed along with the drawings from Dan Love and the pictures that Ted Keith had sent. It was pointed out that they had to make the assembly in reverse as the new right-handed single actions were the mirror image of the Colts and the original #5 SAA. DeHart duplicated the #5 base pin locking lever to perfection in reverse.

What then are the improvements that make up the Improved Number Five? Keith said his #5 SAA could not be improved on when he wrote it up as the Last Word; however, things change over a 60-year period. Some things Grover kept the same; others he definitely improved. The new lockwork consists of all music-wire coil springs. A round trigger guard as found on the pre-war Colts is used. The trigger itself is rounded like a shotgun trigger and sets back in the utmost rear of the trigger guard, moving only very slightly when the gun is cocked. The low, wide hammer spur is designed for easy reach and is checkered with plenty of room in front of the checkering so the thumb can "roll" with the hammer as it is being cocked. This allows for fast and easy cocking both from the leather and for deliberate shooting at targets or game.

The vast majority of Improved Number Fives where chambered in 44 Magnum and 45 Colt with 5-1/2-inch barrels. This one has been custom stocked by Roy Fishpaw.

Since the loading gate and ejector rod are on the left side, a right-handed shooter can load, shoot, empty, and reload without ever taking the gun out of his right hand. As a single action sixgunner for nearly 50 years, I've always placed the sixgun in my left hand for loading and unloading. This is unnecessary with the Improved Number Five, but I find myself still doing it. A half-century of habit is hard to overcome.

The three-tiered front sight on the Improved Number Five was designed by Grover to provide two distinct sighting points, allowing the sixgunner who still has good eyes to hold at different points for short and long range shooting. To match the front sight, the rear sight is fully adjustable and of the old Micro Sight style with the rounded front found on the early Flat-Top Ruger Blackhawks. The top strap is a heavy, wide flat-top style also. The firing pin is of the rebounding style, frame-mounted rather than on the hammer itself to better handle heavy loads – a style first used on production single actions by Ruger and Great Western in the 1950s.

The entire Improved Number Five is made of 4140 certified aircraft steel. The cylinder is double heat-treated to ensure strength, and both the cylinder and the frame are larger and stronger than the original #5 SAA. Keith chose the best cartridge for his #5 SAA, the 44 Special. If Keith were alive today, Grover is sure he would opt for the 44 Magnum, so the Improved Number Five is chambered thusly.

The first Improved Number Five was serial number K1. Subsequent sixguns were to be serial numbered through K1200. The K stands for Keith and only 1200 of these were planned. Mine is K44. Grover's original idea was to make the Improved Number Five in 44 Magnum only. When he asked my advice as to caliber, I responded that I did not think Elmer would mind at all if the new Number Five were available to sixgunners in 44 Magnum, 45 Colt, 44 Special, and even 41 Magnum. Thus the TLA Number Five is found in 44 Magnum and 45 Colt and (rarely) in 41 Magnum.

> "As a single action sixgunner for nearly 50 years, I've always placed the sixgun in my left hand for loading and unloading."

Single Action Sixguns

Chapter 9 | The Texas Longhorn Arms Improved Number Five

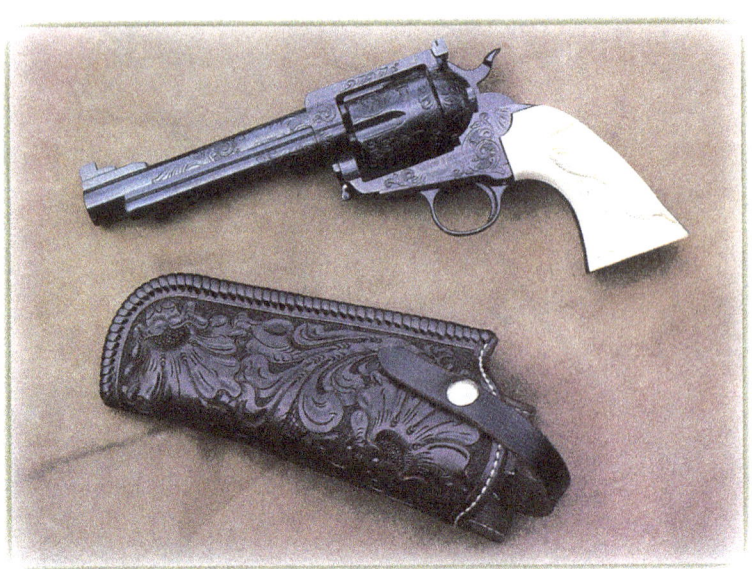

Grover's personal Number Five has been fully engraved and ivory stocked in the Keith style and is completed with floral-carved Lawrence #120 Keith holster.

Elmer Keith's original 44 Special #5 SAA compared to a standard-production 44 Magnum Improved Number Five by Texas Longhorn Arms.

The Improved Number Five is very easy to handle with its Keith-style grip and low-riding wide hammer.

When shooting that first Improved Number Five, I was able to get groups in the one-inch neighborhood, both with 20.0 grains of 2400 and the Keith bullet at 1300+ fps, and also with 22.0 grains of #2400 and the Lyman #429244 Thompson gas check bullet clocking out at 1500+ fps. The Improved Number Five is an extremely well built sixgun and should give a lifetime of service. Keith knew what he was doing when he incorporated the ideas of Harold Croft and the skills of J.D. O'Meara to come up with the #5 single action grip. With a physique on the small side, Keith had very small hands, so the grip frame is designed to keep felt recoil to a minimum. Although originally designed to handle the recoil of 250-gr. bullets at 1100 to 1200 fps, the gun also does a creditable job in handling 250s at a full 1500 fps.

Like the original Keith #5 SAA, the Improved Number Five by Texas Longhorn Arms has a standard 5-1/2-inch barrel with a very few being made with 7-1/2-inch barrels. The 5-1/2-inch barrel length is a good compromise between the easy-packin' 4-3/4-inch and the easier shootin' 7-1/2-inch length. Keith felt he had the best possible single action in his original #5 SAA; I think he would have liked Grover's Improved Model.

Grover sent me the original Improved Number Five serial number 1 for testing in 1988. Not only was I able to test this Number Five but I also compared it to the original. Keith died in 1984 but I was able to meet with Elmer's son Ted and photograph the two sixguns side-by-side and also hold one in each hand. As I expected, the grips felt the same. There's no doubt that the grip frame of the No. 5 inspired Bill Ruger to build the Bisley Model Ruger. However, the Ruger Bisley grip frame is much larger than the Keith design as Elmer had smaller than normal hands. Because of the size of the No. 5 grip frame I have found one's grip must remain very consistent to shoot it accurately.

The Improved Number Five from Texas Longhorn Arms managed to retain the flavor of the original while being stronger and replacing Keith's favorite cartridge of the 1920s through 1950s with his choice from 1955 on, the 44 Magnum. Even with its larger frame and cylinder,

Typical groups fired at 25 yards exhibit the accuracy of the TLA Improved Number Five 44 Magnum in Taffin's hands.

the TLA Number Five still maintains Colt-style balance rather than seeming overly large. In comparing the Keith No. 5 with the Grover Improved Number Five, we find a mix of identical features and improved features. The former includes the grip frame, the cylinder base pin latch release, and a 5-1/2-inch barrel. Differences include the right hand/left hand features already described; the one-piece style grip; a larger frame with a double heat-treated cylinder; the 44 Magnum chambering; the use of 4140 aircraft steel, coil springs, rounded trigger guard, frame-mounted firing pin, improved adjustable sights, and a larger ejector rod head; and the absence of frame screws protruding from the left side of the sixgun. I certainly call all of this improvement.

As mentioned, Grover's original plans were to build 1200 Improved Number Fives in .44 Magnum with 5-1/2-inch barrels. After testing the original I ordered serial number K44, which I now have, and also purchased an identical Improved Number Five chambered in 45 Colt. The plan of 1200 44 Magnums never materialized, and neither did the 1000 each of the West Texas Flat Top Target and South Texas Army. In addition to the standard guns there were a few fully factory engraved models and a few stainless-steel Number Fives built by Grover. On several hunting trips together he also showed me special guns with folding leaf express style sights. Texas Longhorn Arms offered a unique product in an uphill battle. They were never able to keep up with orders and were undercapitalized, factors that led to the closing of their doors in 1998. Today all TLA sixguns can be viewed as collector's items; however, mine remain working collectibles.

Test-Firing the Texas Longhorn Arms Improved Number Five 5-1/2-inch 44 Magnum

BULLET/LOAD	MV	5 SHOTS AT 25YDS
H&G 250 Keith/19.0 gr. #2400	1273	1-5/8"
H&G 250 Keith/19.5 gr. H4227	1109	1-1/2"
Lyman #431244GC/24.0 gr. H4227	1395	1-5/8"
Lyman #431244GC/21.5 gr. AA#9	1403	1-1/2"
Lyman #431244GC/25.0 gr. WW296	1434	1-5/8"
RCBS #44-300FN/21.5 gr. WW296	1365	1-7/8"
Hornady 240 XTP/25.0 gr. WW296	1543	1-1/4"
BRP #295.429/21.5 GR. WW296	1378	1-1/2"
BRP #295.429/21.5 GR. WW296	1378	1-1/2"
RCBS #44-300/21.5 GR. WW296	1365	1-7/8"
Black Hills 240 JHP Factory Load	1293	1-3/4"

Chapter 9 | The Texas Longhorn Arms Improved Number Five

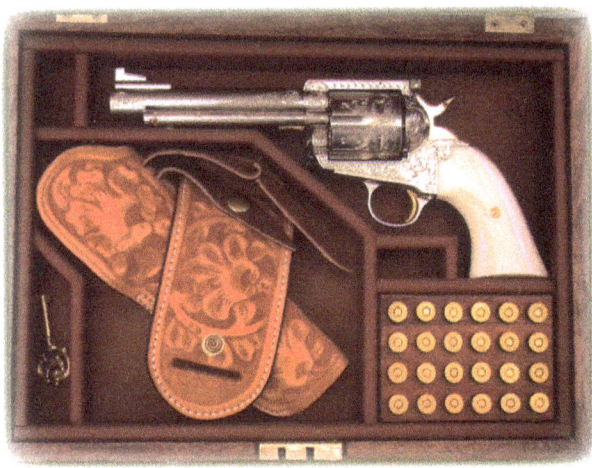

One of the finest Improved Number Fives in existence. The ivory stocks are by Roy Fishpaw, engraving by Terry Wallace, leather by the Ted Blocker, presentation box by Gordon Marts, and plating by The Gold Line Co. The project was put together by Al DiPrima on a sixgun donated by Bill Grover.

Bill Grover used his Number Five for hunting, taking this nice Texas whitetail on the YO Ranch.

Bill Grover commissioned several Number Fives with engraving and custom stocks, but one of the finest custom Number Fives in existence was finished after TLA closed their doors. Al DiPrima of Impact Custom Arms wanted to do something to pay back the firearms industry for all the pleasure he has derived in his shooting life. It would take eight years of work and planning on the part of several individuals, but the results were well worth the time and effort involved. Bill Grover donated a 44 Magnum Improved Number Five to start the project. This sixgun was then sent to Ken Kelly at Mag-Na-Port for porting and a custom inverted muzzle crown. DiPrima then contacted Terry Wallace of Vallejo, California, who is well-known for engraving work on high-grade rifles and shotguns, to do the engraving. Working in between the projects that paid his bills, Wallace spent five years completing the engraving.

The engraved Improved Number Five was then sent to The Gold Line Co. in Wolcott, Connecticut for finishing in nickel with gold accents. Master gripmaker Roy Fishpaw of Lynchburg, Virginia supplied the ivory stocks and Don Brown of Ted Blocker Holsters supplied a beautifully carved Texas Hi Ride holster. (For anyone looking for the best in sixgun stocks or quality leather, both of these men are highly recommended.) A high-quality classic sixgun deserves a special resting place and Gordon Marts of Santa Fe New Mexico crafted a nineteenth century-style fitted case of Madagascar mahogany. In addition to providing security for the Improved Number Five, this locking case also holds the custom holster and 24 rounds of 44 Magnum ammunition.

Elmer Keith's original #5 SAA was fully engraved and fitted with ivory stocks. The one-of-a-kind Improved Number Five commissioned by Al DiPrima is a fitting tribute to the legendary sixgunner. In accordance with DiPrima's original intention to give something back to the shooting sports, the custom Grover Number Five was sold for $9000 and the money placed in The Shootists Building Fund for a future building at the Whittington Center in Raton, New Mexico.

Bill Grover never got over the closing of Texas Longhorn Arms; it broke him physically. He died in October 2004 and is greatly missed.

–Chapter 10–

THE TEXAS LONGHORN ARMS FLAT-TOP TARGET & SOUTH TEXAS ARMY

"Sam Colt was left-handed – that's why the Colt Single Action has the loading gate on the right side!" This is one of the first things I heard from Bill Grover as I met him for the first time at the 1987 Shootists Holiday. I didn't have the heart to tell him that Sam Colt died in 1862 and probably had nothing to do with the design of the 1873 Colt, the famed .45 Peacemaker.

Even if Sam didn't design the Colt, Grover's point is well taken. The Colt Single Action is definitely made for a left-hander. I know that I personally always load and unload my single action Colts, Rugers, etc., by switching them to my left hand. Bill Grover took care of what he considered a mistake of history by offering his line of Texas Longhorn Arms single actions made for right-handers. By reversing the Colt and placing the ejector rod and loading gate on the left side, it is natural for a right-hander to open the loading gate with his right thumb, and eject empties and load new rounds with the left hand, the sixgun never leaving the right hand. Natural it may be, but it is hard for this shooter to break a 50-year habit.

Standard production Texas Longhorn Arms .44s included the Improved Number Five, West Texas Flat-Top Target, and South Texas Army, all shown here with the Improved Number Five in 45 Colt with custom stocks by Roy Fishpaw and one of the last #120 Keith holsters by George Lawrence.

In addition to the Improved Number Five of the last chapter, Bill Grover first offered his "right-handed" single actions in three standard models: the West Texas Flat-Top Target, which – just as the name implies – is a target-sighted single action sixgun; the South Texas Army, a fixed sighted single action that looks quite a bit like a mirror image of a standard Colt SAA; and the Texas Border Special, a 4-inch-barreled Sheriff's or Storekeeper's model.

Each Texas Longhorn Arms sixgun is marked "One of One Thousand" as there were to be only 1000 of each made during the initial production. My first test Texas Border Special was serial numbered B-44 to match its 44 Magnum chambering. All three models were available in blue, blue with a case-hardened frame, nitre blue, nitre blue with a case hardened frame, or antique nickel finish and chambered for 32-20, 357 Magnum, 44 Special, 44 Magnum, 45 Colt, or any other center-fire sixgun chambering desired.

What made the Texas Longhorn Arms sixguns different from the Colts, other than the obvious moving of ejector rod and loading gate to the left side? I spent a few hours back in the 1980s with Bill Grover

The TLA Flat-Top Target with 44 Special Keith loads was used by Taffin to take these two huge feral pigs in northern Oregon.

Single Action Sixguns | 69

Chapter 10 | The Texas Longhorn Arms Flat-Top Target & South Texas Army

The Improved Number Five, top, contains numerous custom features, while the South Texas Army is a standard, fixed-sight single action sixgun.

asking the same question and it was an absolute pleasure to see his eyes light up. Here was a man who really cared about building a top quality sixgun.

What then made the TLA sixgun worth its then $1500 retail price tag? Each sixgun was completely fabricated of 4140 steel, with coil springs throughout and a spring-loaded firing pin set in the frame. The cylinder locked into place with a precisely-fitted locking bolt. Grover maintained that a properly-timed TLA sixgun would stay properly timed if it was handled correctly. This means no line around the cylinder from the drag of the locking bolt.

For better aesthetics, a number of cosmetic features were added to the Texas Longhorn Arms single actions. All trigger guards were rounded with the trigger also rounded and set far back in the trigger guard and contoured like a shotgun trigger. The three frame screws do not protrude all the way through the frame, leaving the left side of the sixgun clean for engraving. Also, all screw slots line up together, a feature that takes a great deal of careful fitting.

As with the early Colts, Grover fitted each of his sixguns with one-piece grips of walnut or fancy woods. At The Shootists Holiday in 1987, he had samples with ivory, curly maple, and pecan. Grover took special care to see the grips fitted correctly, both on the gun and in the hand. No slab-sided feeling here. The grips were curved in the right places and felt as though they belonged in the hand.

Each TLA sixgun was fitted with a large base pin, something custom gunsmiths have done for years on Colt SAAs, and the pin was held in place with a screw at the front of frame rather than the spring loaded "modern" set up which fails so often with heavy loads. For better handling, the grip straps on the West Texas Flat-top Target and The South Texas Army were extended by 3/16 of an inch, allowing more room for the little finger. I really appreciated this feature! Each sixgun was fitted with a low, wide hammer, deeply cut in front of the spur to allow for ease of cocking with no need to change the grip. Tolerances were kept very close with barrel/cylinder gaps held at .0015" to .002", and the serial numbers were are all hand stamped with original Colt-style stamps.

Originally I had my choice of two guns for extended testing after shooting both at the Shootists Holiday: a 5-1/2-inch South Texas Army in 45 Colt and a 4-inch Texas Border Special in 44 Magnum. I chose the 44 Magnum for a number of reasons. I was fascinated with the round-butted, easy carrying big bore sixgun; I've always wanted a 44 Magnum in a Colt Single Action; and most importantly, the little Border Special shot closer to point of aim without filing down the front sight than the 45 Colt South Texas Army. I do file the sights on my guns but not on borrowed test guns.

Shooting a 44 Magnum in a short-barreled, 38-ounce sixgun is normally not a very pleasant experience. Since the barrel was marked ".44 CALIBRE," I re-checked with Bill Grover specifically to make sure that it was really intended to fire full-house 44 Magnums and not just 44 Specials. Loading the cylinder for the first time with factory 44 Magnums, I prepared myself for an unpleasant experience and as the little sixgun went off I was pleasantly surprised to experience no pain. The little .44 really roared and bucked, but it did not punish.

The reason for this lack of pain was the Texas Border Special's round-butted grip. This was long before they became popular on Ruger Vaqueros and custom sixguns. Such a grip frame not only makes a sixgun easier to conceal, it takes the sting out of 44 Magnum loads. This was a no-nonsense, defensive single action sixgun on which no one would be afraid to bet one's life. It packed very easily in a hip holster or even behind the belt. The specially-designed hammer made cocking for the first shot very fast and easy to get to for repeat shots, although I would think a 250-gr. bullet at around 900 fps would be much better as a defensive proposition than a full-house 44 Magnum.

As you may have noticed, single action sixguns are my passion – with great single action sixguns being my consuming passion – and if the single action sixgun just

Three great 7-1/2-inch single action hunting sixguns compared: the Ruger Old Model, Colt New Frontier, and the West Texas Flat-Top Target.

happens to be chambered for the 44 Special, so much the better. The 44 Special first saw the light of day in 1907 and the Colt Single Sction, the reigning and only single action of the day, was soon offered in 44 Special. However, only a little over one tenth of one percent of all the pre-war Colt Single Actions were chambered in 44 Special. There were enough of them around, however, for Elmer Keith, Gordon Boser, John Lachuk and others to experiment with throughout the 1930s, 1940s, and 1950s. These pioneers eventually developed loads that gave 1200+ feet per second with a 250-gr. Keith bullet, which outperformed the 357 Magnum, then the hottest factory cartridge available, by a considerable margin.

By the mid-1950s, both Colt and Great Western were producing traditional single actions and both offered 44 Special chamberings, but guns thus chambered were rare. I've seen only one 44 Special Great Western and fortunately it was reasonably priced. Both of my original Second Generation Colt single action 44 Specials were acquired before they became collector's items, a circumstance for which my checkbook and I are very grateful. I once winced at paying $125 for a Second Generation Colt Single Action in 44 Special. Now they are running $1500 to $2000 or more.

Beginning in 1962, the adjustable-sighted Colt New Frontier was offered as a modernized version of the earlier Flat-Top Target single action. Few Second Generation New Frontiers in 44 Special were ever produced – and even fewer Third Generations by the time the model was discontinued in 1984. The era of the traditionally-styled 44 Special single action with adjustable sights was over.

Or was it? About that time, Bill Grover let me borrow his personal 44 Special West Texas Flat-Top Target with a 7-1/2-inch barrel. After much arm-twisting, and given the fact that he desperately needed to put a new front porch on his place, Grover agreed to sell me the revolver. The era of the target-sighted 44 Special single action was back. At least for me.

Bill Grover was not just a fine gunsmith but a master gunmaker as well. I do believe his Flat-Top Target was his finest effort. It was certainly love for me at first sight and definitely at first firing. When I had finally caught Grover at the right time, he not only agreed to sell me the Flat-Top but also offered to fit it with two more cylinders, one in 44 Magnum and the other in 44-40. I agreed to meet Bill in Texas for a hunting trip and take three animals, one with each cylinder.

For the 44 Magnum I chose 240gr. Remington jacketed hollowpoints over 20.0 grains of 2400. Not full-house loads, these would not be suited for really big game but should be fine for a Corsican sheep or Catalina

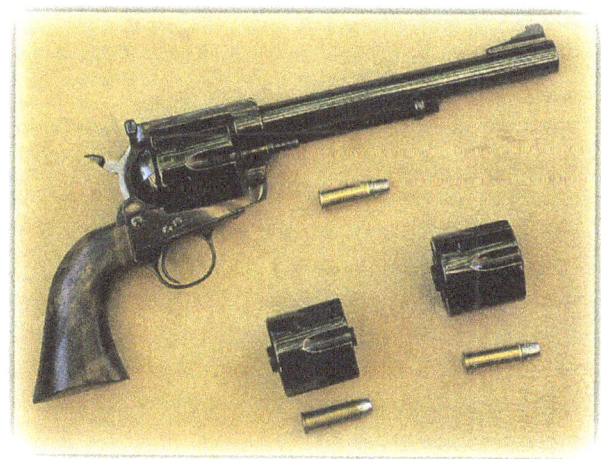

A most versatile hunting handgun is the West Texas Flat-Top Target with three cylinders chambered in 44 Special, 44-40, and 44 Magnum.

Single Action Sixguns | 71

Chapter 10 | The Texas Longhorn Arms Flat-Top Target & South Texas Army

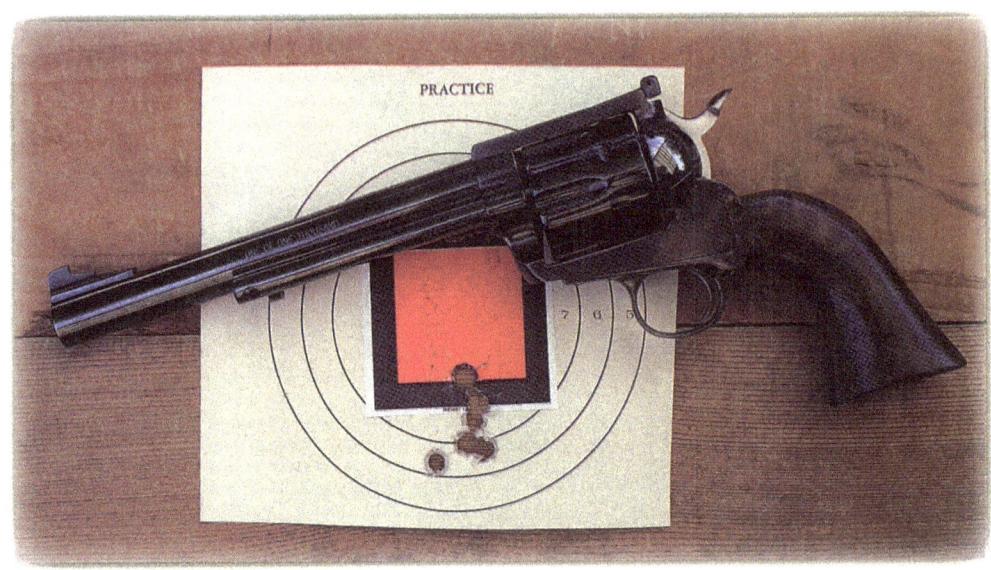

The excellent accuracy of the West Texas Flat-Top Target is obvious.

goat at close range. The 44-40 was loaded with the Speer 225-gr. pure lead hollow point in a copper cup over 10.0 grains of Unique, and for the 44 Special, the then-new Hornady 200-grain XTP was loaded over 18.5 grains of 2400. These loads are not necessarily recommended for any other sixguns but this one. I found that the 44-40 load and the 44 Magnum were dead on with the rear sight bottomed out, and three fourths of a turn up brought the lighter 44 Special bullet to point of aim.

When the Texas Longhorn Arms West Texas Flat-Top Target came back from Bill's shop with all three cylinders, Grover also included one of his Texas High Rider Holster systems. The High Rider worked with any single action sixgun and was especially handy with 7-1/2-inch barrel lengths. It was designed to be worn high either strong side or cross draw and consisted of a holster proper and a belt slide. The holster could be removed simply by unsnapping it and lifting it out of the belt slide.

Our Shootists Spring Sixgun Safari was held on the ranch of my dear friend Frank Pulkrabek outside of Kerrville, Texas. (A few short years later Frank was killed by a drunk driver as he was taking hunters back to the San Antonio Airport. I still miss him.) At the beginning of our hunt I slipped the 44-40 cylinder into the TLA .44, placed the 44 Special cylinder in a sock tied to my belt, and headed out. We had not been out fifteen minutes when I spotted a Merino ram with a large blood patch on his throat and nose. The guide said we had to kill it, so up came the 44-40 and down went the ram. I had the first animal in my quest for three critters with the same sixgun but different chamberings. (It later turned out that the ram had been wounded that morning when a bullet aimed at one animal went all the way through its intended target and clipped him. None of the other hunters knew he had been hit, as Merinos have about three inches of heavy wool and it takes a long time for them to show blood.)

Changing cylinders, I let the guide take care of the Merino and went hiking after some other animals. After spending an hour chasing goats back and forth through the trees and brush, I finally got a shot at a wide-horned catalina/angora and the 44 Special did its job. His horns measured 40 inches wide and he made a beautiful snow white mount. Now I had to hike back to the jeep, and pick up the 44 Magnum cylinder.

There was a big black and white spotted, long-haired catalina on the ranch, and that old billy was plenty smart, running me up and down the canyon for the next three hours until I finally figured out what was going on. Grover was with me now and I asked him to give me time to get back on top so he could come through the bottom to drive the billy up to me.

At 6 p.m., I was hidden in some trees waiting for that old black and white billy. Around 6:30, here he came. I knew I was perfectly hidden, but he looked right at me! Curiosity got the best of him and he stepped out of the group of several goats to get a better look. At 75 yards the Remington 44 Magnum did its work cleanly and quickly. The third animal of the desired trio had been taken with the three-in-one 44 WCF/Special/Magnum Texas Longhorn Arms sixgun.

The West Texas Flat-Top Target as offered by Texas Longhorn Arms had a 7-1/2-inch barrel and weighed in at 45 ounces. The grip frame was Colt Single Action style, although slightly longer, with one-piece stocks of figured walnut. There are single action stocks and there are single action stocks; some feel like a piece of 2x4. The TLA stocks were perfectly, and I do mean perfectly, shaped, with all the curves and flares in the right place. There are many single action stocks being offered but very few makers really understand how a single action stock is supposed to feel. This one was right!

The trigger guard was smaller and rounder than found on most Colt Single Actions and the shotgun style trigger sat far back in the rear of the trigger guard. The hammer was wide and checkered and deep enough in the front to allow the thumb to slip naturally when cocking. Sights were fully adjustable with a melted Micro-style set at the rear of the flat-top frame. The rear sight was mated with a Patridge front sight giving the sharp black sight picture that I prefer for most sixgun applications. The finish was a highly-polished deep blue-black and all metal-to-metal and metal-to-wood fit was excellent.

The action and lockwork of the Flat-Top Target incorporated music wire coil springs in every application. Operation was smooth and positive, and the cylinder locked up tight with any of the three cylinders in place. Grover not only built them right but also built them tight. In fact, I ran into trouble in the beginning because Grover built the 44-40 cylinder using Winchester brass and I loaded my original rounds with Remington brass. We then found out that Remington brass has thicker heads and would not fit the tight dimensions and tolerances of the extra Flat-Top Target cylinder as Grover built it.

Taffin shooting the TLA West Texas Flat-Top Target 44 Special.

Test-Firing the TLA 7-1/2-inch Flat-Top Target 44-40

Brass for the 44-40 is very thin and cylinder walls of Colt single actions in 44-40 are as thin as those chambered for the 45 Colt – after all, the 44-40 is basically a 45 Colt necked down to .44. The following loads are for use only in the Texas Longhorn Arms West Texas Flat-Top Target or similar sized large-frame single actions. Groups for all loads were shot at 25 yards and clocked over a PACT chronograph.

LOAD	MV	GROUP
Speer 225 HP/10.0 gr. Unique	1154	1-/8"
Hornady 200 XTP/20.0 gr. IMR4227	1047	1-5/8"
Hornady 200 XTP/18.5 gr. H4227	1060	1-3/4"
Hornady 200 XTP/17.5 gr. 2400	1153	1-1/4"
Hornady 200 XTP/18.5 gr. 2400	1262	1-1/4"
Hornady 200 XTP/10.0 gr. Unique	1149	1-1/8"
Sierra 180 JHP/10.0 gr. Unique	1115	1"
Lyman #42798/10.0 gr. Unique	1144	2-1/2"

Chapter 10 | The Texas Longhorn Arms Flat-Top Target & South Texas Army

Test-Firing the TLA 7-1/2-inch Flat-Top Target 44 Special

The 44 Special, the original chambering of the TLA Flat-Top Target, is very dear to my heart, soul, and spirit. I am often asked what I would choose if I could only have one sixgun. That would be a terrible situation to be in, but if pressed I tend to lean toward either a Colt New Frontier 44 Special with 7-1/2-inch barrel or an original Ruger Blackhawk Flat-Top 44 Magnum, also with a 7-1/2-inch barrel. Now I have the best of both worlds with not only a first-class 44 Special and 44 Magnum but also a 44-40 cylinder thrown in for good measure! Not only is the 44 Special Flat-Top Target a fine-shooting sixgun with many loads, it is spectacular with the Keith load of a 250-gr. hard cast bullet over 17.0 grains of 2400.

LOAD	MV	GROUP
Oklahoma Ammunition 215 SWC	1067	1-1/2"
Speer 240 SP/16.3 gr. 2400	1270	1"
Speer 225 HP/16.3 gr. 2400	1348	2-1/2"
Hornady 240 XTP/ 17.0 gr. 2400	1485	1-1/4"
Hornady 200 XTP/18.5 gr. 2400	1376	1-1/4"
RCBS KT SWC/17.0 gr. 2400	1379	7/8"
RCBS KT SWC/7.5 gr. Unique	1023	2-3/8"

Test-Firing the TLA 7-1/2-inch Flat-Top Target 44 Magnum

The crowning glory of the Texas Longhorn Arms West Texas Flat-Top Target is the 44 Magnum. Here we not only have a sixgun that shoots both 44-40s and 44 Specials into one inch, but it does the same thing with the 44 Magnum. I was happy with the 44-40 shooting one-inch groups with Hornady XTPs and Speer and Sierra hollow points; I was overjoyed with the 44 Special doing the same thing with both Speer 240-gr. jacketed hollow points and hard-cast Keith bullets. What then do you think I felt when the 44 Magnum, loaded with Lyman's #431244GC bullet over 21.5 grains of AA#9 at 1436 feet per second, out-shot both the 44-40 and the 44 Special?
Note: "FL" denotes factory load.

LOAD	MV	GROUP
Oklahoma Ammunition 240 JHP FL	1453	2"
Oklahoma Ammunition 240 JSWC FL	1376	1-1/4"
Remington 240 JHP FL	1489	1-1/8"
Winchester 240 JHP FL	1493	1-1/2"
Winchester 250 SXT Black Talon FL	1416	1-3/4"
Black Hills 240 JHP-XTP FL	1345	1-1/2"
Black Hills 300 JHP-XTP FL	1200	1-1/2"
Bull-X 240 SWC/8.5 gr. Unique	1209	1-1/8"
NEI 260 KT/10.0 gr. Unique	1216	2-1/4"
BRP 295 KT/10.0 gr. Unique	1157	1-3/4"
BRP 295 KT/21.5 gr. WW296	1395	1-1/8"
Lyman #431244GC/24.0 gr. H4227	1423	1-1/2"
Lyman #431244GC/21.5 gr. AA#9	1436	3/4"
Lyman #431244GC/25.0 gr. WW296	1473	1-1/2"
RCBS #44-300FN/21.5 gr. WW296	1402	1-1/4"
Hornady 240 XTP/25.0 gr. WW296	1559	1-1/8"

Test-Firing the TLA 7-1/2-inch Flat-Top Target 44 Russian

Since those first three cylinders were fitted to my West Texas Flat-Top Target, I have returned it to Texas Longhorn Arms for a fourth cylinder in 44 Russian, the original .44 chambering found in Smith & Wesson's #3 single actions. The Russian and Winchester centerfire .44s were contemporaries and the Special and Magnum just naturally followed the Russian, so it seemed quite an appropriate thing to do. Then when Black Hills and Starline resurrected the 44 Colt it seemed natural to add a fifth .44 cylinder. Unfortunately, the best laid plans of mice and men really do oft-times go astray and the doors of Texas Longhorn Arms closed before the 44 Colt cylinder could become reality.

LOAD	MV	GROUP
Oregon Trail 225/4.0 gr. Red Dot	828	1-3/8"
Oregon Trail 225/4.0 gr. TiteGroup	800	1-1/4"
Oregon Trail 225/4.0 gr. WW231	818	1-1/2"

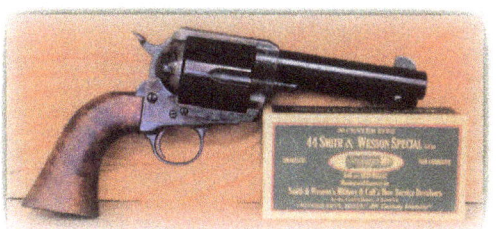

Grover's alternative to the Colt Single Action Army was the Right-handed South Texas Army with a longer grip frame.

A very few South Texas Army Models were made in stainless steel (top).

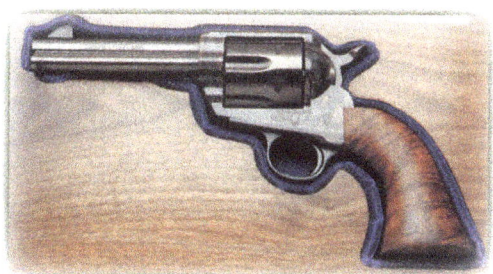

Texas Longhorn Arms presented this South Texas Army to George Bush when he was governor of Texas.

Test-Firing the TLA 4-3/4-inch South Texas Army in 44 Special

Grover's other right-handed single action was the South Texas Army with fixed sights, a barrel length of 4-3/4 inches, and most chambered in .44 or 45 Colt. Unlike the TLA West Texas Flat-Top Target, my South Texas Army has only one cylinder, that being in 44 Special. Everything we have said about the Flat-Top Target is also true of the South Texas Army except that it has Colt Single Action Army-style fixed sights. Both of these sixguns have grip frames much closer to the 1860 Army than the 1873 Army. The former grip has a slightly different angle, being a little straighter than that found on the Colt Single Action Army, and it is also longer, allowing room for the little finger. Texas Longhorn Arms grip frames are exceptionally comfortable when shooting heavy loads.

LOAD	MV	GROUP
Black Hills 240 SWC	825	1-1/2"
Bull-X 240 SWC/5.5 gr. 452AA	860	2-3/8"
Bull-X 240 SWC/6.5 gr. 452AA	966	2-1/2"
Bull-X 240 SWC/11.0 gr. HS-7	997	1-5/8"
Bull-X 240 SWC/7.5 gr. Unique	968	1-3/8"
Hornady 240 SWC/6.0 gr. Unique	803	1-7/8"
Speer 225 JHP/8.0 gr. Unique	1083	2-1/8"
SPeer 240 SWC/6.0 gr. Unique	823	1-1/2"
BRP 245 Keith/6.0 gr. Unique	895	1-3/4"
BRP 245 Keith/7.5 gr. Unique	1030	1-3/4"
Lyman #429421/7.5 gr. Unique	929	2-1/2"
Lyman #429360/7.5 gr. Unique	968	1-3/8"
Lyman #429215GC / 8.5 gr. Unique	1139	1-5/8"

Chapter 10 | The Texas Longhorn Arms Flat-Top Target & South Texas Army

Texas Longhorn Arms offered four standard models: the West Texas Flat-Top Target, the Improved Number Five, the South Texas Army, and the Border Special.

> "I never like trying to identify 'my favorite sixgun,' but my favorite type has long been a 7-1/2-inch adjustable sighted big bore single action."

Grover's original plans were to build 1200 Improved Number Fives in 44 Magnum with 5-1/2-inch barrels. After testing the original, I ordered serial number K44, which I now have, and also purchased an identical Improved Number Five chambered in 45 Colt. The plan of 1200 44 Magnums never materialized, nor did the 1000 each of the West Texas Flat Top Target and South Texas Army.

In addition to his Texas Longhorn Arms models, Grover also built a few other custom guns. Two of these for me were both 44 Specials using Ruger Old Model frames. One of these is a 7-1/2-inch with custom fancy walnut grips by Charles Able and the other a 4-3/4-inch Packin' Pistol with a Colt Single Action grip frame fitted with one-piece ivory grips by BluMagnum. The long-barreled sixgun is serial number JT1. The Packin' Pistol 44 Special is one of seven. The first, SS1, was for Skeeter Skelton; mine is SS4. SS2 belongs to Bart Skelton; Bob Baer has SS3; Jim Wilson, SS5; Terry Murbach, SS6; and Grover kept SS7. There will be no more. Both of these sixguns fit in my very special sixguns category.

I never like trying to identify "my favorite sixgun," but my favorite type has long been a 7-1/2-inch adjustable sighted big bore single action. The TLA West Texas Flat-Top Target and custom 44 Special on an Old Model Ruger frame are very special sixguns in my "favorites" category.

While they can still be found occasionally at gun shops, shows, and auction sites, we will probably never see the production of Texas Longhorn Arms sixguns again. It would be wonderful if someone with plenty of financial resources would underwrite the return of the Improved Number Five, the South Texas Army, the West Texas Flat-Top Target, and the Border Special. I can at least hope. Now that Bill Grover has left us, it would be a fitting tribute to him to have his sixguns returned to production.

–Chapter 11–

THE SECOND GENERATION COLT SINGLE ACTION ARMY

My life has been blessed in many ways, not the least of which was the privilege of growing up in the Fabulous Fifties. Wedged in between the end of the Korean War and the psychedelic '60s and then Vietnam, the 1950s allowed kids to be kids. Music was still music, and the gathering place was the local drive-in with real french fries hand-cut from real potatoes, great burgers that came from corn-fed beef, and chocolate shakes as thick as fresh concrete.

The 1950s were also the greatest decade of the twentieth century for firearms development. Just in handguns alone, the 1950s brought us some of the best sixguns ever produced. From Smith & Wesson came the 1950 Target in 44 Special and 45 ACP, as well as fixed sighted versions of both; the Highway Patrolman 357 Magnum; the 1955 Target 45 ACP; the Combat Magnum 357; and the original 44 Magnum. Ruger arrived in 1949 with their semi-automatic .22 pistol and then followed with great single actions, the 22 Single-Six in 1953, the 357 Blackhawk in 1955, the 44 Magnum Blackhawk in 1956, and the 44 Super Blackhawk in 1959. Great Western also entered the sixgunnin' stage in 1954 with the first replica of the Colt Single Action Army.

Over at Hartford, Colt introduced the .357 Magnum (actually the name of the revolver, not just its chambering), followed up by the Python in 1955. More importantly for single action sixgunners, something major was about to happen. Production of the Colt Single Action Army ceased with the start of World War II with no plans to resume production. More than a third of a million Colt Single Actions had been manufactured from 1873 to 1940, with production peaking in 1902 at 18,000 units, followed by 1907 with 16,000 coming out of Hartford. That was the last year for production figures to reach five digits, and 1929 saw the last four-digit number with 1400. The Depression kicked in and by 1935 and 1936 production figures equaled 100 each. They went up to 700 in '37, back down to 500 in '38 and a meager 400 in the year I arrived upon this planet, 1939. There was a final surge in 1940 of 859 units with more than 500 going to help defend Britain in World War II.

In all probability, Colt was more than ready to cease production of both the New Service double action revolver and the Single Action Army. Machinery was wearing out, sales were down, and those having money during the Depression years were more apt to turn to the

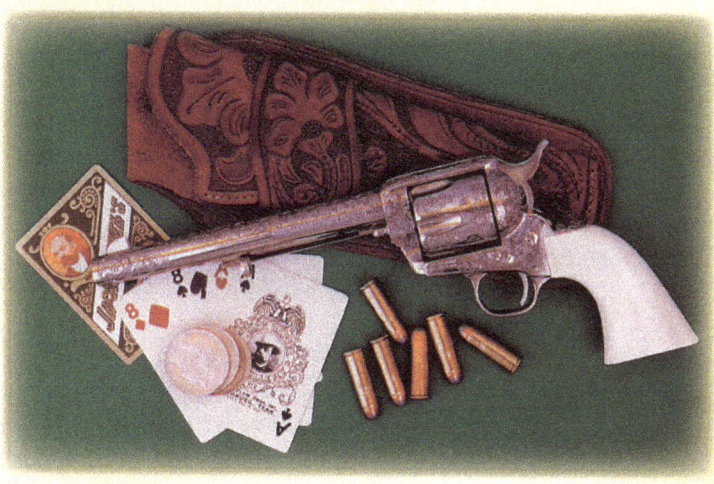

Bill Maims did the engraving; Larry Larsen did all the rest of the custom work including stocking with one-piece ivories on this Second Generation Colt Single Action Army.

Chapter 11 | The Colt Single Action Army 2nd Generation

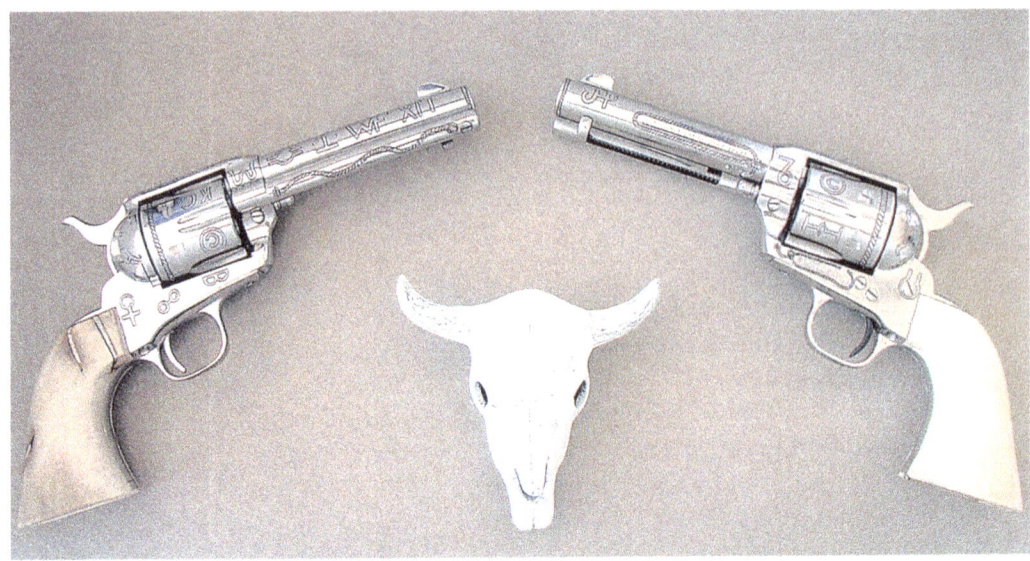

Authentic cattle brands, one-piece custom stocks by Jim Martin, and nickel plating all come together to provide two exceptionally attractive Second Generation Colt Single Actions. Picture courtesy of Richard Talacek.

relatively new Smith & Wesson 357 Magnum or even switch from revolvers to the semi-automatic 1911. By 1941 the Colt Single Action Army was dead and buried and never to be seen again, or so both Colt and just about everyone else thought. The single action was considered totally obsolete, a relic of the frontier. There were no more Indian Wars, cattle drives, gunfighters. . . . The West had been tamed, at least officially.

However, history rarely ever follows a straight path. The path began to deviate in the early 1950s for one reason: television. A brand new company, Great Western, had started making a replica Single Action Army in California with their Frontier Model in 38 Special, 357 Magnum, 44 Special, and 45 Colt in 1954. The first issue of *GUNS* magazine arrived in January 1955 with a pair of single actions on the front cover of that premiere issue.

The single action was back as the arrival of TV resulted in a whole new generation discovering B Western movies and the Single Action Army. Hopalong Cassidy, Gene Autry, and Roy Rogers found their careers totally revived. Tim McCoy, Buck Jones, Bob Steele, the Durango Kid, Wild Bill Elliott and many more were, as Gene Autry's theme song said, *Back in the Saddle Again*. Great Western and *GUNS* were off and running.

Even before the Great Western arrived, a young Bill Ruger saw the possibility of a modern single action with virtually unbreakable springs and introduced the .22 Single-Six in 1953. The sixgun itself was slightly scaled down in size from a Colt Single Action but the grip frame was a dead ringer for the old Colt Model P. Perhaps the Ruger Single-Six was the inspiration for Great Western to bring back a full-sized Single Action Army one year later. TV had a great influence on shooters and the shooting public wanted the authentic Colt Single Action Army. When production ceased in 1940, the selling price had been around $40 at a time when the Smith & Wesson .357 Magnum was selling for $65. Smith could not keep up with the demand; Colt sales had plummeted. People always want what they can't have, and the lack of real Colts began to drive up the price. By the 1950s, used Colts had topped the $100 mark.

We had the Ruger Single-Six and the Great Western, but what of the Colt Single Action Army? Many shooters and collectors tried to prevail on Colt to resurrect the SAA after World War II, and while Colt did offer barrels and cylinders, mostly in 45 Colt and 38 Special, they had no plans to resurrect the Model P. The powers-that-be at Colt reasoned they would have to charge at least $100 for a new Colt Single Action Army and they just didn't believe anyone would be willing to pay that price. However, the fact that used prices had risen to that level began to put things into a more positive perspective for the return of the Single Action Army. The Colt was dead and buried, never to rise again, when that first issue of *GUNS* hit the stands in January 1955. The situation was about to change.

Tombstone was billed as "the town too tough to die"; the Colt Single Action Army was simply the gun too good to die. The rebirth of the SAA occurred in 1956 when single action sixgunners got their wish and the Second Generation of Colt Single Actions began. First introduced in 45 Colt and 38 Special in 7-1/2- and 5-1/2-inch barrel lengths, the new Colt Single Action was later offered in 357 Magnum and 44 Special. A 4-3/4-

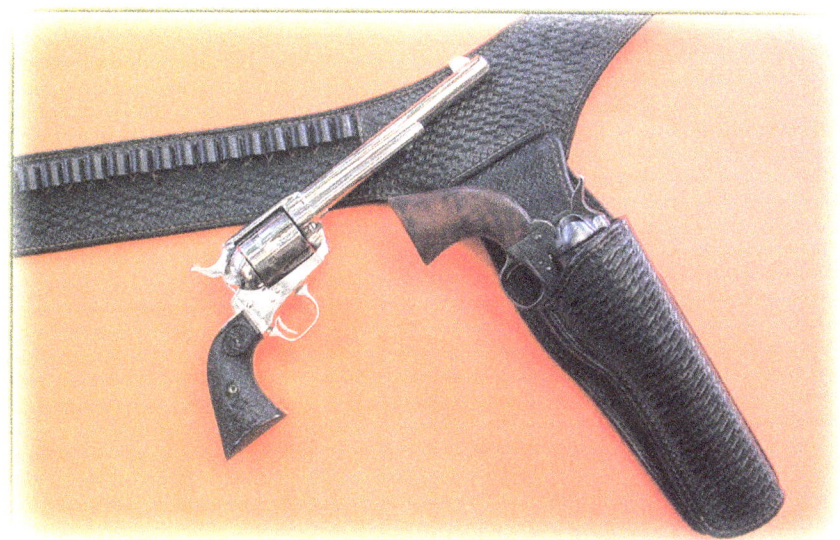

Taffin used this Arvo Ojala rig for Fast Draw in the 1950s-1960s. Colt single actions pictured are chambered in 45 Colt.

inch barrel length was also added to the line. For some unknown reason, all the other calibers were made in all three standard barrel lengths, but the 44 Special was never made in the 4-3/4-inch length during the Second Generation run.

My first Second Generation Colt Single Action Army was the first one I saw at Boyle's Gun Shop. It was a 7-1/2-inch 45 Colt with a retail price tag of $125. I already had a First Generation 4-3/4-inch 38-40 from around the end of the nineteenth century and no money. There was no such thing as plastic cards, and who would give a teenager credit? Boyle's would. They simply kept an index card with your name on it to track purchases and payments: nothing to sign, no interest payments. My name was put on a card and I had my first brand new Colt. To this day, almost 50 years later, I have never been without a running gun bill.

I had been in ecstasy when I purchased my first sixgun, the .22 Ruger Single-Six, one year earlier. I moved up a notch with the 38-40, and then soared even higher with this new 45 Colt with the same 7-1/2-inch barrel length used by TV pistoleros Matt Dillon, Paladin, Chris Colt, and Clay Hollister. What was interesting to me about these four characters is the fact they used sixguns rarely seen in the old Western movies. Silver screen cowboys almost always used 4-3/4-inch and 5-1/2-inch single actions, but TV had opted for the more authentic barrel lengths used throughout the 1870s and into the 1880s.

Not too long I found that first 45 Colt, the brand new sport of Fast Draw arrived on the national scene, and I acquired a second 7-1/2-inch 45, this one a First Generation example. A double fast draw rig was ordered from the Pony Express Shop in California, and I began spending most of my non-working hours drawing, spinning, and dropping those Colts back into their respective holsters. When I started I had marks where the spinning barrels contacted the insides of my arms, but not only did I learn the tricks but actually got pretty good at them. The only other gun trick I ever learned, or even tried to learn, was the Road Agent's Spin. This trick is performed by pretending to surrender one's single action by offering it butt first and then spinning it with the finger in the trigger guard so it turns over and comes up into a cocked-hammer firing position in the hand. I got pretty good at that also with either one or two 7-1/2-inch Colts.

This well-used Second Generation 7-1/2-inch 44 Special was one of the favorite Fast Draw sixguns of Jim Martin. Photo courtesy of Richard Talacek.

Single Action Sixguns | 79

Chapter 11 | The Colt Single Action Army 2nd Generation

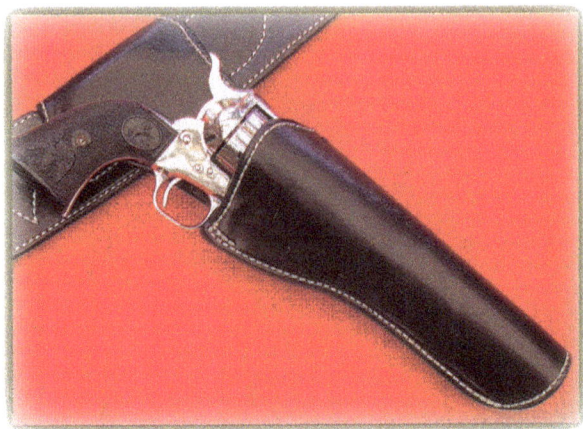

The only 44-40 Second Generation Single Action Army is the Peacemaker Centennial 7-1/2-inch nickel-plated Frontier Six-Shooter here shown in a 1960s style Andy Anderson Gunfighter rig perfectly crafted by Rawhide Walt Ostin.

General Patton did not like them, but many peace officers did – mother of pearl grips, that is. This Second Generation 45 Colt wears Eagle Grips mother of pearls favored by Tom Threepersons. The leather is an exact copy of Threepersons' holster by Rawhide Walt Ostin.

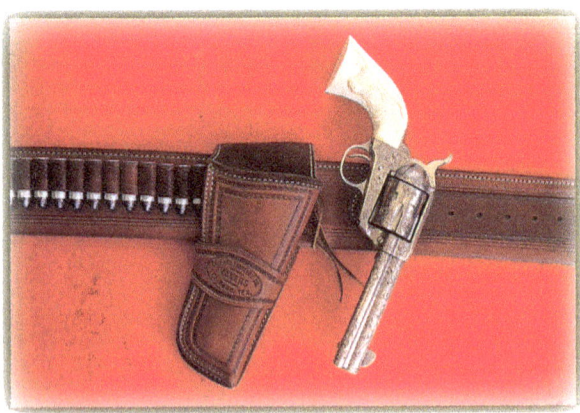

This Second Generation single action in 45 Colt has been engraved and plated by Jim Riggs and ivory stocked by Paul Persinger. Leather is El Paso Saddlery's #1930 Austin.

When organized Fast Draw hit my area I joined the Green Valley Rebels and ordered a single Arvo Ojala holster and belt, black basket weave, for the 7-1/2-inch Colt. That Ojala rig is special for several reasons, not the least of which is the fact that I picked it up from Boyle's Gun Shop during my first date with my eventual wife in late 1958. I still have the Ojala rig and Diamond Dot, but the 45 Colt had to go in the early 1960s to help pay for college tuition and also to feed the three hungry kids we had by then. Those were tough times, but they did serve to strengthen us and bring us even closer together, and the lost Colt has been replaced many times over the ensuing 40 years.

Second Generation production didn't even approach that of the First Generation guns – neither in years made, chamberings offered, nor total guns produced. According to two excellent publications for students of the Second Generation Single Action Army, Don Wilkersons' book *The Post-War Colt Single Action Army* (1978), and George Garton's *Colt's SAA Post War Models* (1979), serial numbers started in 1956 with 0001SA and ended in 1974 in the 73,300SA range. The SA suffix was used to distinguish Second Generation single actions from First Generations. All production figures cited in the remainder of this chapter come from these two books, both of which are high on the sixgunner's list of must-have publications. Another highly recommended, must-have book covering all Colt Model P generations as well as their repair, rebuilding, and restoration is Jerry Kuhnhausen's *The Colt Single Action Revolvers: A Shop Manual* (2001). This book is filled with hundreds of drawings depicting everything about the function and specifications of all Colt SAA parts. Even if one never works on a Colt, the information contained in this book is still invaluable.

The Second Generation Colt Single Action, as mentioned, arrived in 1956 in two chamberings, 38 Special and 45 Colt, with the standard Colt case-hardened frame in barrel lengths of 5-1/2 and 7-1/2 inches. One year later the 4-3/4-inch barrel arrived in both chamberings, and a nickel-plated finish option was offered. The 44 Special was made available for 5-1/2- and 7-1/2-inch models. In 1960, the 357 Magnum chambering was introduced, a move which led to the dropping of the 38 Special chambering in 1963. Three years later, in 1966, the 44 Special was dropped. Then until 1974, when production ceased, only the 45 Colt and 357 Magnum were offered.

Wilkerson offers the following production figures. A total of 11,710 38 Specials were produced in all standard barrel lengths and both blue and nickel; however, nickel-plated 38s are very rare with a total of just over 500 having been produced. Switching to the 45 Colt we find 37,000 produced in all barrel lengths with approximately seven percent being nickel-plated. Since the advent of Cowboy Action Shooting, prices of Second Generation Colts have taken a decided upswing with a 4-3/4-inch 45 in excellent condition now demanding $2500 or more. There were 7200 4-3/4-inch .45s produced, with approximately 20 percent being nickel-plated.

Colt Single Action Army Models chambered in 44 Special are quite rare in the Second Generation run though far outdistancing the slightly more than 500 produced in the First Generation period. My wife bought me one of those original First Generation 44 Specials, but when we saw how rare it was we decided it needed to be in a special collection. We traded it to a collector for all our money back plus a 45 Colt New Frontier and a Second Generation 5-1/2-inch 44 Special in excellent condition. So we wound up with two Colt Single Actions without any outlay of money. I still have both of these great single actions, but in retrospect I wish I had held on to that rare 44 Special. Only 2230 Second Generation 44 Specials were made and only in the two standard barrel lengths of 5-1/2 and 7-1/2 inches with only 170 of these being nickel-plated. The 357 Magnum

Three generations of Single Action .44s, from top: Third and Second Generation 44 Specials and First Generation 44-40.

was second only to the 45 Colt in numbers produced, with 17,375 made in all three barrel lengths with just over two percent being nickel-plated.

The Buntline Special, offered in any barrel length during the First Generation run, became available in 1957 in .45 caliber only and with a standard 12-inch barrel length only. Four thousand were produced in the blue/case-hardened finish, but the nickel-plated version is very rare with a total of only 65 leaving the factory. The rarest Second Generation Colt is the 3-inch ejectorless Sheriff's Model in 45 Colt with just over 500 being offered as a special run commissioned by Centennial Arms. I well remember one sitting on the shelf at the gun shop for very long time with a price of $139.95. I didn't have that kind of money during my college years; in fact I don't think I could have come up with the 95 cents. In retrospect I wish I had borrowed the money and bought that Sheriff's Model.

The Sheriff's Model was the beginning of thousands upon thousands of specially serial numbered Second Generation commemorative issues. It would take several pages just to list all of these, but the ones I find the most significant are the 1873-1973 Peacemaker Centennial special sixguns. These are some of the finest revolvers ever produced by Colt, which is not always

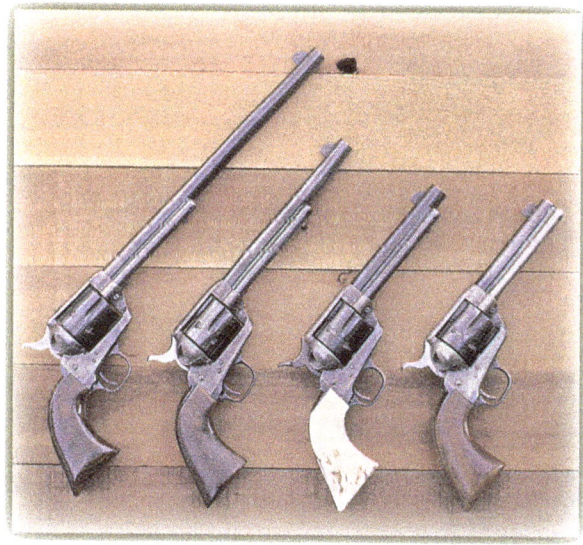

In addition to Second Generation standard barrel lengths of 4-3/4, 5-1/2, and 7-1/2 inches, Colt also offered the 12-inch Buntline chambered in 45 Colt.

Single Action Sixguns | 81

Chapter 11 | The Colt Single Action Army 2nd Generation

The only 44-40 offered during the Second Generation run was the Peacemaker Centennial 7-1/2-inch nickel-plated Frontier Six Shooter in 1973.

The companion sixgun in the Peacemaker Centennial set was a 7-1/2-inch US-marked 45 Colt cavalry pistol. The original one-piece walnut stocks on this example were replaced with ivory stocks by Roy Fishpaw.

Taffin shooting the Peacemaker Centennial 7-1/2-inch 44-40; holstered sixgun is the other half of the mismatched pair, the 7-1/2-inch US Cavalry 45 Colt.

true of most commemoratives. The Peacemaker Centennials were offered with a 7-1/2-inch US-marked 45 Colt finished in the original military blue/case-hardened frame and hammer and a companion 7-1/2-inch Frontier Six-Shooter, nickel-plated and chambered in 44-40. Five hundred sets were offered with both sixguns in special presentation boxes, as well as 1500 of each sold individually. About 12 years ago I walked up and down the aisles of the Reno Gun Show thinking about buying a cased set of both Peacemaker Centennial Models. I even had the plastic card in my hand but I just didn't do it. Two years ago I found an identical set on the Internet for the same price. This time I did not hesitate. These are beautifully finished and fitted sixguns and as far as I know the only 44-40 offered in the Second Generation run.

To compete with Ruger's .22 Single-Six, Colt began offering a .22 single action in 1957 known as the Frontier Scout. These were first offered with

During the run of Second Generation Colts, the 22 New Frontier was offered as an alternative to the Ruger Single-Six. It could not compete and disappeared from production.

4-3/4-inch barrels and then expanded to include a 9-1/2-inch Buntline Scout .22 in 1960. All of these featured the standard Colt Single Action Army fixed sights. All-blue and nickel-plated versions were offered as well as some chambered in 22 Magnum. The Scout was dropped in 1970 and replaced by a fixed-sighted Peacemaker and an adjustable-sighted New Frontier. Unlike the Scouts, these featured the case-hardened frame of the standard Colt Single Action Army. They were offered in barrel lengths of 4-3/4, 6, and 7-1/2 inches. These were quite beautifully finished and excellent shooting revolvers, but they never could compete with the Ruger Single-Six. They are found in both a 22 Long Rifle version as well as two-cylinder models with both the standard 22 and also a 22 Magnum cylinder. Production ended in 1976.

The Second Generation Colt Single Action Army models are some of the finest Colts ever produced, especially the earlier ones. As the machinery started wearing out Colt still produced the Model P and the buyer is advised to carefully inspect those made in the last two years of production, 1973 and 1974, beginning at serial number 65000SA. This is not to say that these were below par but is rather a warning that some slipped through that were not quite up to expected Colt standards. Even these can be brought back to near-perfection by a competent gunsmith.

> "The Peacemaker Centennials were offered with a 7-1/2-inch US-marked 45 Colt finished in the original military blue/case-hardened frame and hammer and a companion 7-1/2-inch Frontier Six-Shooter, nickel-plated and chambered in 44-40."

Single Action Sixguns

–Chapter 12–

THE THIRD GENERATION COLT SINGLE ACTION ARMY

By the 1970s Colt's tooling was once again wearing out, and the Colt Single Action was again pronounced dead in 1974. However, this time Colt did not say it would never be resurrected. Return it did in 1976 with the Third Generation of the Colt Single Action Army. Changes occurred, most of which were ill-advised.

First was the match-up of the hand and the cylinder. The hand design was changed for easier assembly and the cylinder no longer had a full-length bushing but a button bushing at the front end. Very recently, Colt has rethought this change, and all currently produced Third Generation Single Actions now once again contain a full-length cylinder bushing. Also, with the advent of the latest generation of Model Ps, shooters have had a choice of the original black powder-style screw in the front of the frame to hold the cylinder pin or a spring loaded catch, a change that occurred long before World War I.

Third Generations with all three standard barrel lengths and chambered in 45 Colt and 44-40.

The strangest change in moving from Second Generation to Third Generation was the change in the barrel threads going from 20 threads to the inch to 24 threads to the inch. With thousands of First Generation sixguns out there being prime candidates for new parts, why in the world would Colt change the hand, cylinder, and especially the barrel threads? A Third Generation barrel can be fitted to a First or Second Generation, but it is strictly a one-time occurrence as the new barrel is basically being re-threaded as it is installed. It is unfortunate that whoever was in charge of this project didn't really appreciate and understand the Single Action Army and its mystique.

The first Third Generations also suffered a change in the hammer outline, resulting in a profile with a very poorly-executed flat look. However, this has also been changed to give the hammer profile a more rounded and pleasing look. The frame of the first Third Generations was very square and extended too far back, but this, too, has been corrected.

The Third Generation run has been a back-and-forth affair, coming and going, a standard production and then a Custom Shop offering. Things now seem to have settled down, and not only is the SAA a standard production item but Colt is also doing a very good

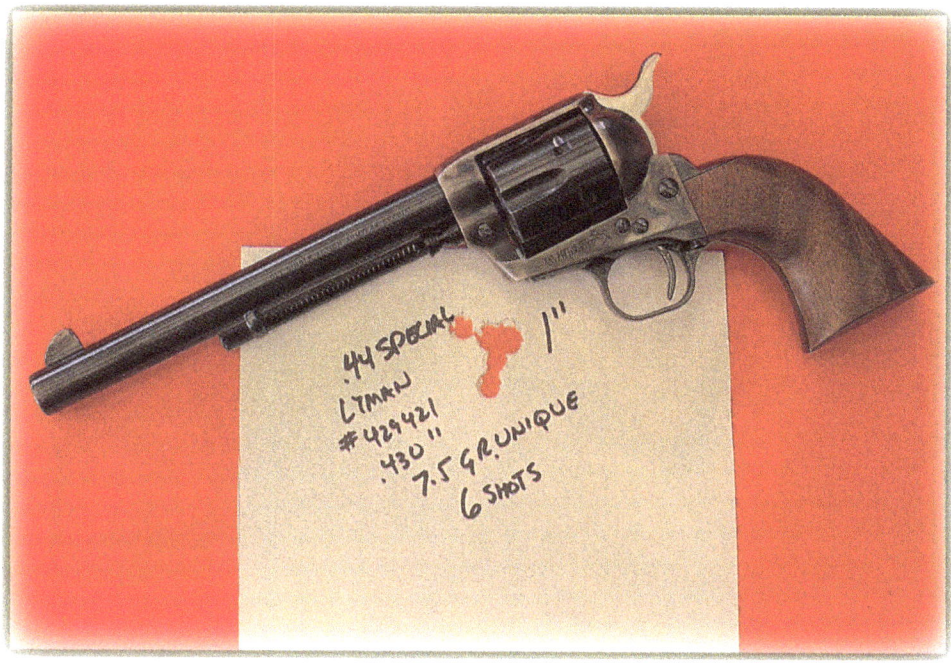

Tom Sargis tuned and stocked this good-shooting 44 Special Third Generation with one-piece walnut stocks.

job of fitting and finishing. It would be difficult for any untrained eye to see the difference existing between the three generations. Believe it or not, an experienced sixgunner is able to feel that difference just by handling and cocking the action.

The surest way to tell is by serial numbers. All First Generation single actions have numbers only in their serial numbers, and most will have six digits; Second Generation sixguns have an SA at the end of the serial number, which will run lower than 80,000SA; and Third Generations began with 80,000SA. If the S or A or both are anywhere except at the end it is a Third Generation Colt.

The first run of Third Generation Colt Single Actions lasted into the late 1980s when the market was flooded with all types of variations as to finish and barrel length (and often second-rate examples) before the production was to cease again, for the third time. These Third Generation Colt Single Actions were produced in 45 Colt, 44 Special, 44-40, and 357 Magnum. The Second Generation run had ended at approximately serial number 73,300SA, but when the Third Generation appeared there was a gap in the serial numbers and they began at number 80,000SA. When Third Generation production hit serial number 99,999SA, the SA was then placed in front of the number.

Colt dropped the 44 Special from their Second Generation single actions in the mid-1960s, and it is no small thanks to Skeeter Skelton that we got the 44 Special back in the Third Generation Single Action Army. He led the way in persuading Colt to do this, and they later presented him with fully engraved, ivory stocked 4-3/4-inch 44 Special. Especially if one intends to use anything more than standard factory level loads, the 44 Special is much preferred over the 45 Colt, 44-40, and 38-40, all of which have much thinner cylinder walls than the Special.

To my way of thinking one of the best things about the Third Generation Colts is that for the first time since 1940, the Colt Single Action Army was once again made available in the "dash" cartridges: the 44-40, 38-40, and now even 32-20. Lest one think that the 38-40 is old and antiquated and fit only for the boneyard, consider that ballistically it is a dead ringer for that most modern of all semi-automatic catridges, the 1990s-born-and-bred 40 S&W as originally loaded. The ultra-modern, totally up-to-date 40 S&W used the same standard load as the 100+ year-old 38-40, which is a 180-grain bullet at about 900 to 1000 fps. In fact for my early reloading experiments with the 40 S&W I used cast bullets designed for 38 Winchester Centerfire

As a teenager, I purchased a 60-year-old 38-40 4-3/4-inch Colt Single Action Army in excellent shape and later added a Lawrence Gunslinger outfit in black basket weave finish and handmade one piece walnut stocks. I thought I was quite the sixgunner, but eventually the 38-40 moved on downstream. As I finished college and began to have a few more dollars coming in than going out, I looked for a replacement Colt SAA in 38-40, but none ever surfaced, at least not at a reasonable price.

Single Action Sixguns | 85

Chapter 12 | The Colt Single Action Army 3rd Generation

Colt's Third Generation 38-40 has been held to tight tolerances resulting in groups such as this one.

Both Colts and Great Westerns in 45 Colt, 44 Special, 44-40, and 357 Magnum were found over the years and purchased eagerly but no 38-40.

When I heard in the early 1990s that Colt would once again produce a 38-40 Single Action Army I could hardly believe it. Ruger had offered a special run of 38-40/10mm Blackhawk convertibles (a very accurate sixgun with either cylinder), and good shooting replicas had been offered, but would we really have a genuine Colt Single Action 38-40 again? My emotions immediately went back 35 years; ever since I allowed that old 38-40 to get away I kept expecting to someday find one. Now someday was here. Finally, the Colt Single Action Army 38-40 was a reality in both blue and nickel finishes, and in 4-3/4- or 5-1/2-inch barrel lengths, with the 7-1/2-inch barrel arriving later. After 35 years I was again shooting a real Colt Single Action Army 38-40.

During the First Generation era of the Colt Single Action Army, buying a 38-40, whether it was a SAA or a double action New Service, was a real act of faith. Barrel grooves and chamber mouth diameters ran from tight to over-size and it was not uncommon to have a tight chamber and oversize bore or vice versa. The very good news is that Colt did it right with the Third Generation run. Both barrels and cylinder dimensions are tight. The chamber mouths on my gun run .399" to .400", and it is one of the tightest sixguns I have seen this side of Freedom Arms. Sloppy reloads need not apply for service. All primers must be seated flush or below and brass must be properly sized and crimped or it is no-go. The rounds simply will not fit the cylinder if they are less than perfect.

The 38-40 is a bottlenecked cartridge looking much like a 45 Colt necked down to .40-caliber; in spite of its name the 38 WCF is not a .38-caliber but a true .40-caliber. This is why 38-40 bullets work in the 40 S&W. Being a bottlenecked case, the 38-40 requires a standard sizing die and lubing of brass before sizing. I use Dillon's spray lube for all of my 38-40 reloading and use a Progressive RCBS Model 2000 press. The fact that the 45 Colt, 44-40, and 38-40 all fit the same shell holder on the Model 2000 and can handle the same powder charge makes it very easy to reload. It takes less than 10 seconds to change the die plate, and the powder measure stays with the press. It's only necessary to switch cartridge cases and bullets. For the 38-40, I use Starline brass with CCI #300 standard primers and have pretty much settled on 8.0 grains of Unique with an Oregon Trail 180-grain RNFP (lead round nose flat point) bullet as my standard load.

Shooting any fixed-sight single action for the first time can be a really frustrating experience. Quite often they will shoot away from the sights and be off as to both windage and elevation. My new Colt Single Action Army 38-40 proved to be right on the money for windage and shot three inches low. A little careful filing on the front sight raised the elevation, bringing point of aim and point of impact to the same spot. The original sights on the First Generation sixguns consisted of a very shallow rear sight mated up with an inverted-V front sight. If one had good eyesight, the tip of the front sight could be matched up with the top of the rear V and very precise shooting could be performed. Somewhere along the line, the rear sight became a square notch but

Selected Loads for the Colt Third Generation Single Action Army 38-40 4-3/4-inch

LOAD	MV	5 SHOTS/25 YARDS
Lyman #401043 180 gr. 8.0 gr. Unique	1022	1-1/8"
Same bullet with 9.2 gr. Unique	1065	2"
Same bullet with 10.0 gr. Unique	1235	2"
Same bullet with 5.8 gr. Bullseye	864	1-3/8"
Same bullet with 6.5 gr. WW452AA	983	1-1/4"

the front sight is still tapered toward the top, resulting in a strange sight picture with the front sight not filling the rear sightfully.

When the SAA became a Custom Shop only offering, the chamberings were 44-40 and 45 Colt only; the 44 Special and 357 Magnum were dropped. The third chambering became the 38-40.

All three chamberings were custom-cataloged with a Royal Blue finish mated with the case-hardened frame made famous by Colt or a full bright nickel finish. An extra nice custom touch was the nickel-plated Colt with bright blued screws on frame, backstrap, and trigger guard. For some strange reason known only to Colt, all three chamberings were first available with 4-3/4- and 5-1/2-inch barrels but only the 45 Colt was offered with a 7-1/2-inch barrel.

The 44-40s I have encountered all have chamber throats of .430"; however some .44 bullets of this size will not fit the chambers. My rule of thumb is to use the largest bullet that can be easily seated in the chamber. In the past this has been difficult unless one was a bullet caster; however, commercially-cast .44 bullets are now available in weights from 180 to 225 grains. I prefer the latter for use in the 44-40. They are offered sized .427", .429", and .430", making it an easy task to tailor loads to a certain sixgun.

Colt has not been careful enough in chambering their 45 Colt cylinders. Some chamber throats are as oversized as .460"; the ideal is .452", and the Third Generation .45s I have encountered run 457" to 458". For most of my loading of standard .45 loads for use in Colt or replicas, I prefer .454" bullets. Throats should never be oversized as a reamer cuts smaller holes, not bigger, as it wears. Oversized throats simply mean the reamer was too large to start with. It doesn't do any good to replace the oversized cylinder with another Third Generation .45 cylinder. It would probably have the same malady. The only answer seems to be having a competent gunsmith re-chamber a 357 Magnum cylinder to a tight 45 Colt.

It may look like an antique, but this is a Third Generation 44-40 totally tuned and antiqued by Peacemaker Specialists.

Single Action Sixguns

Chapter 12 | The Colt Single Action Army 3rd Generation

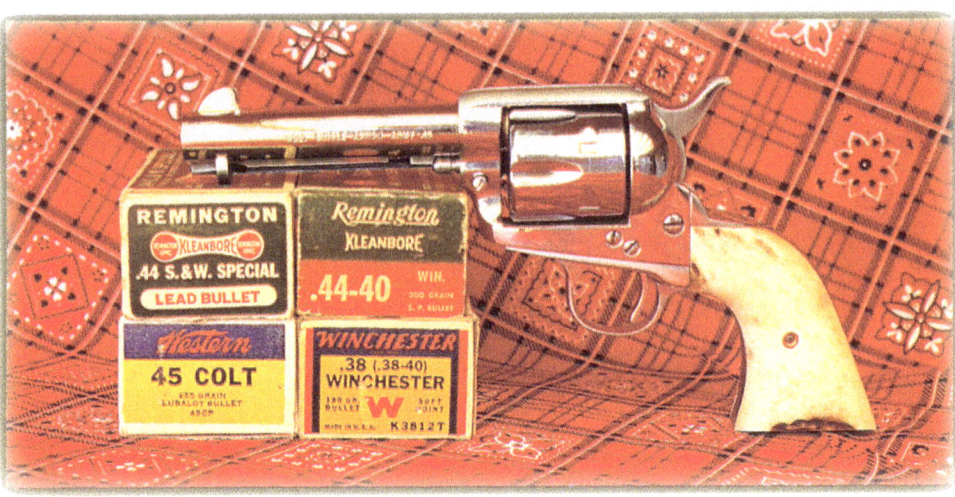

In the late 1980s and early 1990s, the Third Generation Colt was offered in blue/case colored or nickel plating with a 4-3/4-inch barrel with a choice of 45 Colt, 44-40, 38-40, and 44 Special.

The Colt Single Action Army is no longer a Custom Shop offering but rather a standard production item; the price has been dropped significantly twice in the last few years bringing it down to the $1200 range. It is now offered in all three barrel lengths; blued and case-hardened or nickel-plated finishes; and in six caliber offerings: 45 Colt, 44-40, 38-40, 357 Magnum, 38 Special, and even in 32-20, another chambering which had not been seen since before World War II. The latest word from Colt is the offering of one more chambering, the rebirth of the 44 Special. All Third Generation 44 Specials I have measured have .430" to .431" chamber throats, making them just about perfect for today's jacketed or commercial cast bullets of .430" in diameter.

Permit me here to repeat once again something I said about the Colt Single Action Army 20 years ago. Pick up a Colt Single Action and you will discover true sixgun quality. The aesthetic value of the Colt SAA cannot be approached by any other handgun. If your soul, spirit, and heart are not touched by the feel and genuine great looks of the Colt Single Action Army, something is wrong. Slowly cock the hammer and listen. As the big hammer moves past the safety notch, one hears a distinct "C"; the hammer continues past the half cock and an audible "O" registers. As the hand pushes against the ratchet on the back of the cylinder, one who listens carefully will hear an "L"; and finally as the hammer and trigger come together in the firing mode, a definite "T" sounds.

If you are not emotionally affected by the graceful lines of the big bore Colt, you are on dangerous ground, my friend. You have crossed over the line from enjoying fine handguns as works of art into the drab world of viewing them as working tools such as computers or claw hammers. If this is true, it is time to slow down, quit taking life so seriously, and enjoy the finer things once again.

If you find yourself in such as state as just described, head for the nearest Colt Single Action Army. Pick it up and if you are sincere in wanting to be helped, run your fingers along its sensuous shape and you will feel the dust of a thousand cattle in your nostrils, you will smell bacon sizzling in a pan over an open fire, you will hear a piano tinkling from the Long Branch – why, you may even envision yourself back 100-plus years pinning on a star. The old Colt will do that to one whose heart is in tune.

In addition to the standard model single actions, Colt also offered Third Generation Sheriff's Models in 44-40, and a convertible 44-40/44 Special, in both blue

The classic single action, a 4-3/4-inch nickel-plated Third Generation Colt 45 with stag stocks. Leather is El Paso's Duke rig.

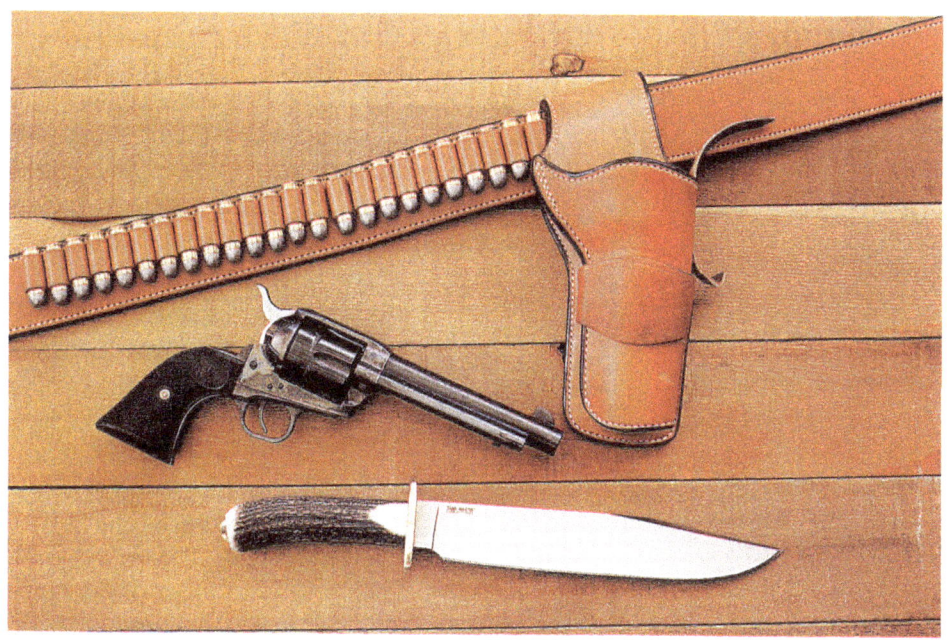

The Colt Cowboy was offered for a while as an alternative to the Ruger Vaquero. It could not compete and it is now gone from production.

and nickel finishes with 3-inch barrels. At the other end of the spectrum, we had the Buntline Special offered in nickel-plated 44 Special and 44-40 and both nickel-plated and blue/case-hardened finishes chambered in 45 Colt.

To compete with the Ruger Vaquero and to also gain a share of the market of cowboy action shooters, the Colt Cowboy was unveiled at the Colt booth at the 1998 SHOT Show. I must admit I was totally underwhelmed. When I first saw it I went directly to the Colt rep to ask if it was made in Germany; they assured me it was All-American made. But it did not look, feel, or smell like a Colt. It did say COLT on the barrel. Colt went back to the drawing board and made a few changes to have the Colt Cowboy look much more like a real Colt. They didn't quite make it.

The Cowboy sold for about 35 to 40 percent of the price of a new Colt Single Action so there were major differences, not the least of which is the transfer bar safety. However, unlike the Ruger Vaquero, opening the loading gate on the Colt Cowboy does not free the cylinder. Just as with the Colt Single Action Army, the hammer must still be placed on the half cock notch to be able to rotate the cylinder just as it has been in Colt sixguns since 1836 and Single Action Armies since 1873.

For a gun selling for so much less than the genuine Colt Single Action Army, one should certainly expect differences in fit and finish. The case-colored frame on the sample I examined was not as vivid colorwise as that found on the genuine Single Action Army, being somewhere in between that found on the Ruger Vaquero and the original Colt sixgun. The fitting of the grip frame to main frame was not quite as good as that found on the current Single Action Army, and the hard rubber Second Generation-style grip without the eagle found on Third Generation grips was slightly undersize for the grip frame. The grip frame was not quite square where it met the main frame behind the trigger guard. Cylinder lock-up was tight with very little play from side to side or fore and aft when the hammer was cocked.

The barrel/cylinder gap was very tight and would not accept the .002" feeler gauge I had on hand. As revealed by the Hornady digital caliper, the Colt Cowboy's cylinder was slightly larger than that of the Colt SAA with the diameter being 1.677" compared to the Single Action Army size of 1.654". However, lengthwise both cylinders are the same size at 1.610". For size comparisons, the Ruger Vaquero goes 1.737" and 1.703" respectively.

It may not have been a Colt Single Action Army, but the Colt Cowboy did shoot very well. Using my standard everyday 45 Colt load of a 250-gr. round-nosed flat point bullet from Oregon Trail over 8.0 grains of Unique gave a muzzle velocity of 855 fps. This load pretty much duplicates the original black powder loading with groups at a cowboy shooting distance of 50 feet resulting in five of six holes touching and measuring 7/8 of an inch. No one could complain about this. Shooting the Colt Cowboy was enhanced by the fact the sights were very easy to see with a square notch rear mated with a front sight that is only slightly tapered from top to bottom.

The Colt Cowboy sold for more than a Vaquero or Italian replica, somewhere in the neighborhood of $500

Single Action Sixguns | 89

Chapter 12 | The Colt Single Action Army 3rd Generation

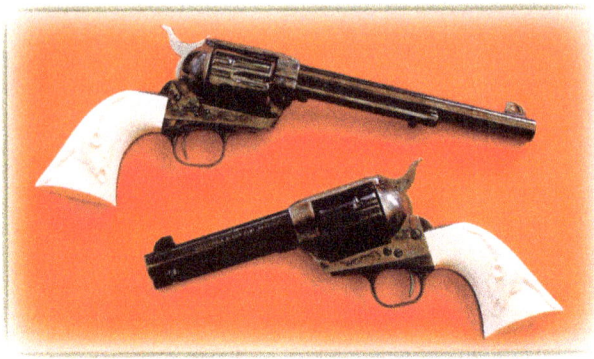

Two Third Generation Colt single actions, a 7-1/2-inch 45 Colt and a 4-3/4-inch 44 Special, have both been beautifully enhanced with carved ivory stocks by Paul Persinger.

No single action sixgun is more deserving of engraving than a Colt. These Third Generation single actions, a 38-40 and a 44-40, are both engraved by Dale Miller. Custom stocks are Eagle's Ultra Ivory and bighorn sheep by Paul Persinger.

No Colt single actions are more valued by Taffin than these Third Generation .45s that belonged to Ron Elerick, The Kilted Preacher. Carved custom stocks are by Kirk Ratejesak.

to $600. The Ruger Vaquero is larger and stronger for those who want to use full power loads, while the Italian replicas duplicate fairly well the original Colt Single Action Army. This alone doomed the Colt Cowboy from the very beginning. For the price of a Cowboy, one got a sixgun with the same grip feel as an SAA, balance and appearance almost the same as a 5-1/2-inch Single Action Army 45, and even the legend "Colt's Patent F. A. Mfg. Co." on the barrel. For all of this, it never quite connected with shooters and is now gone from the Colt catalog. Perhaps Colt would have been better off trying to produce the best possible Single Action Army at the lowest possible price.

I have mentioned the fact that Third Generation Colt Single Actions are not the equal of the First and Second Generation versions, and I have been accumulating the Model P since purchasing that first one nearly 50 years ago. Strangely enough, when I survey my Colts I find I have more Third Generations than either First or Seconds, most of them tuned by specialists such as Bob Munden, Tom Sargis, Eddie Janis of Peacemaker Specialists, and Shapels Gun Shop. They have been stocked with ivory by Paul Persinger, Ultra Ivory by Eagle Grips, exotic woods by BluMagnum, and black micarta by Charles Able. A pair of 4-3/4-inch Third Generations, a nickel-plated 44-40 and a blued 38-40, both bear the talented and skillful engraving of Dale Miller.

My first Third Generation Single Action was the newly-introduced 7-1/2-inch 44 Special in 1978. I still have it. The last one purchased was also a 7-1/2-inch, this one a 44-40. Two of my most special sixguns are Third Generations, both 45s, a 5-1/2-inch with the standard blue/case-hardened finish and the other a nickel-plated 7-1/2-inch version. What makes these extra special is the fact they belonged to my dear friend and Brother, Ron Elerick, the Kilted Preacher. Ron, all 6'10" of him, was an evangelist, a very different kind of evangelist, as he walked where angels fear to tread. Ron ministered to outlaw bikers. He definitely looked the part and rode a Harley all over the country spreading the Word. I miss him terribly, but these two Colts keep me connected to him.

–Chapter 13–

THE COLT NEW FRONTIER

My wife Dot and I were traveling from Freedom Arms on our way to Yellowstone, stopping over to spend the night in Jackson, Wyoming. The next morning, looking for a place to eat before hitting the road, we ran into a bunch of other folks doing the same thing with the result being a line stretching out to the boardwalk. Standing in line to eat when there are so many restaurants in this country is one of my least favorite things to do.

Dot said, "Why don't you go over to the gunstore and look around while I keep our place. I'll get the table." Across the street to the Bitter Root Trading Company I went to spend my waiting time looking through the racks of old Winchester and Marlin leverguns, Sharps rifles and carbines, and then over to the pistol case to look at the Colt single actions and Bisley Models. By the time I got to the end of the showcase, a sixgun on the bottom shelf caught my eye. It also caught my checkbook. When I returned to my wife at the breakfast table, I had a small package under my arm. It contained a beautiful 7-1/2-inch Colt New Frontier 44 Special.

When the Fabulous Fifties ended, it was the beginning of a new era, one that some called a breath of fresh air. Little did we know what would soon be coming in the 1960s. For now, we had a young dynamic president to replace the grandfatherly Ike. To honor the new president and the new spirit of optimism that swept the land, one firearms company decided to bring out a new sixgun. In late 1961, Colt introduced its New Frontier model in honor of John F. Kennedy's ringing declaration, "We stand at the edge of a New Frontier. . . ." Within two years, rifle shots would ring out in Dallas, Camelot would be gone, and a specially engraved New Frontier would never be presented to JFK.

Our country's innocence was gone, never to return, but the Colt New Frontier would remain in production for the next two decades. Colt flat-topped the frame of the Single Action Army, added an adjustable rear sight mated with a radically sloping ramp-style front sight, and thus invented one of the most beautiful sixguns to ever come from the Hartford factory. Just as with the Colt Single Action Army on which the New Frontier was based, the new sixgun carried a deep blue finish on its barrel, cylinder, and grip frame topped off with beautifully mottled colors on its case-hardened main frame.

In the production of the First Generation Colt Single Action Army sixguns from 1873 to 1940, a few target models, both Single Action Army and Bisley, were produced. They incorporated a slightly

Taffin's favorite type of sixgun is a 7-1/2-inch single action with the New Frontier being high on the list.

Chapter 13 | The Colt New Frontier

Whether in the homemade rig, top, or El Paso's Tom Threepersons, bottom, the 44 Special New Frontier, bottom, is almost as versatile as the Ruger 44 Magnum Flat-Top. It packs easy and is well-suited for hunting.

flat-topped frame, a rear sight windage-adjustable by drifting and locking in place, and a front sight that could be adjusted up and down. During the 1920s, Elmer Keith tried to interest Colt in modernizing the Colt by flat-topping the frame and adding fully adjustable sights. He even offered the loan of his custom sixguns including his famous #5 SAA but Colt would not listen.

Had Colt been more open-minded, Ruger may never have gained a foothold. Keith's #5 SAA, built in the mid-1920s, was a 5-1/2-inch single action chambered in the favorite cartridge of the day (at least for reloaders), the 44 Special. The grip frame of the #5 SAA was created by mating a Bisley back strap with a Single Action Army trigger guard. Its influence today can be seen in the Freedom Arms and Ruger Bisley revolvers. The frame was flat-topped and carried a fully adjustable rear sight mated with a post front sight with a bead. Keith called it The Last Word as he considered it the finest possible sixgun. It was definitely the last word in single actions in the 1920s.

Finally, in 1962 Colt caught on and rolled out the New Frontier, which was as close to Keith's #5 as that company would ever get. A Colt Single Action Army in that year cost a relatively expensive $125, while the New Frontier was $140. This at the same time when 357 and 44 Magnum Ruger Blackhawks were going for less than $100 and the superbly crafted and blued Super Blackhawk in .44 Magnum was selling for $116.

Our local store had a New Frontier 44 Special that I drooled over quite often but with college tuition, three hungry kids, and a wife who stayed home with them, there was no way. Had I been able to look into the future, I would somehow have borrowed the money and bought the Colt. Today it would be worth no less than ten times the original price.

The Colt New Frontier began with serial number 3000NF. That first gun stayed in the Colt plant. The last of the Second Generation New Frontiers was in the 72XXNF serial number range, which translates to a total of slightly more than 4000 New Frontiers manufactured from 1961 to 1974. Four chamberings were offered in this first run of these Colt Flat-Top Target sixguns: 45 Colt, 38 Special, 357 Magnum, and 44 Special.

According to Colt expert Don Wilkerson, the 38 Special is the rarest chambering, followed by the 44 Special. Wilkerson gives the following production figures for the Second Generation New Frontiers. Fewer than 100 .45 New Frontier Buntlines were also produced.

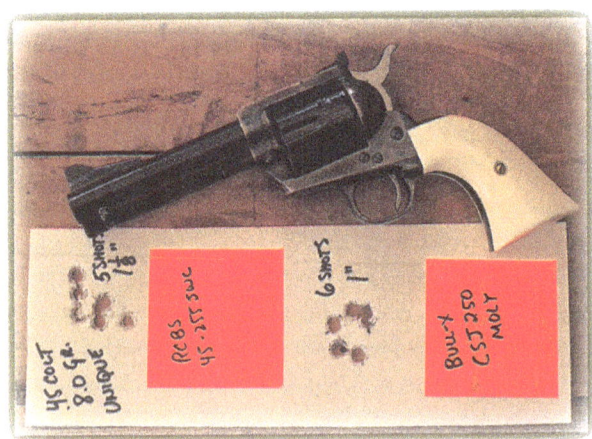

Whether using home cast or commercial cast bullets, this 45 Colt New Frontier delivers.

92 Part 3

New Frontier Production By Barrel Length (Second Generation)

CALIBER	4-3/4"	5-1/2"	7-1/2"
.38 Special	0	39	10
.44 Special	0	120	135
.45 Colt	85	520	1,020
.357 Magnum	78	795	1,305

In 1978, the New Frontier went back into production with the Third Generation Colt Single Action Army. Serial Numbers began at 01001NF, using five digits instead of four. In the last and, according to Colt, final run of New Frontiers, chamberings were 45 Colt, 357 Magnum, 44 Special, and 44-40. All of the Second Generation New Frontiers were standardized with a finish of bright blue except for the casehardened frame. Third Generation New Frontiers can be found in full blue and nickel finishes and included nickel-plated Buntline New Frontiers in 45 Colt, 44 Special, and 44-40. The 44-40 was available in the short barrel length of 4-3/4 inches but I do not believe any 44 Specials were offered in this length.

Wilkerson gives the following figures for Third Generation New Frontiers:

New Frontier Production By Barrel Length (Third Generation)

CALIBER	4-3/4"	5-1/2"	7-1/2"
45 Colt	1,106	57	7,407
44 Special	0	783	2,761
44-40	519	0	1,046
357 Magnum	0	0	509

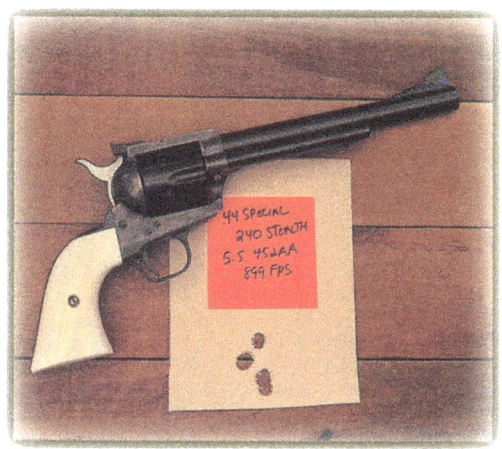

A Third Generation 44 Special New Frontier shoots like a target pistol.

This 45 Colt New Frontier performs admirably with Oregon Trail Bullet Company's 255-grain SWC.

All Third Generation figures are for blue/case-hardened models except the 357 Magnum, which was offered only in a nickel-plated version. Approximately 25 blued 44 Special New Frontiers were produced, as well as 60 in 45 Colt, all with 7-1/2-inch barrels. Production of the New Frontier ended in 1982, with a small number being assembled in 1983, and an even smaller number, 66, in 1984 before they disappeared altogether.

Take a very close look at any Third Generation New Frontier before buying. Some of the later ones were hastily thrown together and will require some expert gunsmithing to bring them up to standard. My Breakfast Special – the Third Generation New Frontier 44 Special purchased before

Chapter 13 | The Colt New Frontier

The two best New Frontiers for hunting are the 7-1/2-inch 45 Colt or 44 Special.

bacon, toast, and hashbrowns in Jackson – was dropped off at Munden Enterprises before ever being fired. Bob Munden performed his action magic, replacing springs and smoothing the action. Then it was off to his gripmaker, Mike Wallace. I asked to be surprised as to choice of wood, and I certainly was – breathtakingly so. When the 44 Special arrived back here in Idaho it wore heart-stopping one-piece grips of walnut that fit my hand perfectly. Wallace is part of a select group of men who understand what single action grip-making is all about.

The Colt New Frontiers maintain the beautiful looks, feel, and balance of the Colt Single action Army with the added advantage of adjustable sights. It is a rare fixed sighted sixgun that shoots to point of aim and when it does it is normally for only one load. The New Frontier's sights allows for any reasonable load to be dialed in. The New Frontier makes an excellent hunting sixgun, especially with a 7-1/2-inch barreled 45 Colt or 44 Special, and it will get the job done up close on deer and black bear-sized game. They are not Magnums, but the 45 Colt will easily handle loads using 260-gr. Keith style bullets at 1000 to 1150 feet per second, while the 44 Special uses the same style bullets of 250 grains at 1200 to 1250 feet per second.

Jacketed bullets are normally an expensive and unnecessary option with the 45 Colt and 44 Special at these muzzle velocities, but Speer still catalogs their original "jacketed" .44 bullets that consist of a copper cup with a lead core. These are offered both as 225-gr. hollow points and 240-gr. flat points with the former getting the nod for 44 Special use at 1100 feet per second. I would like to see the same design offered in .45 caliber. The short-barreled New Frontiers in both .44 and .45 caliber make excellent packin' pistols, easy to carry and relatively lightweight when compared to 454 Casulls and Ruger 44 Magnums. With heavy 44 Special and 45 Colt loads, one can handle anything up close except the big bears.

I can only think of two easy improvements to the New Frontier that could have been done by Colt. First, as with almost all sixguns, they cry for custom grips. I cannot understand why Colt would produce such a beautiful sixgun, and then fit it with stocks made out of some of the plainest walnut available. I wish they had also used a different front sight with a flat black post front sight instead of the glare-gathering sloping ramp front sight. The Colt high front sight does go well with one of my favorite sixgun shooting pastimes, namely long range shooting at small rocks on yonder hill. The secret to this style of long range shooting is not holding

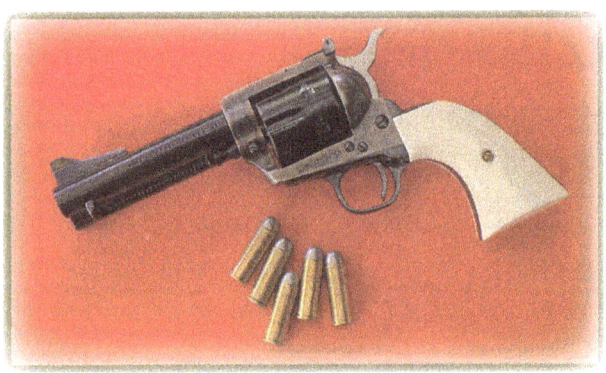

A 4-3/4-inch Colt New Frontier chambered in 45 Colt is a top candidate for the title of Perfect Packin' Pistol.

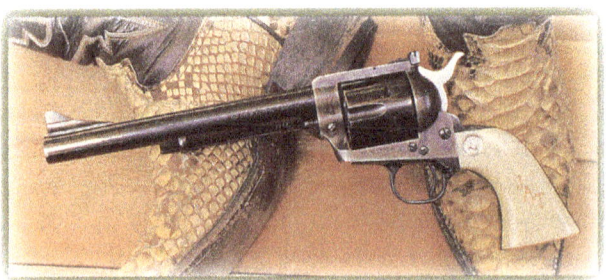

Not only does it have the classic look, but the New Frontier is also fitted with adjustable sights, making it much better suited to hunting and long range shooting.

over as one does with a scope sighted rifle or pistol, but simply holding up enough front sight with the intended target perched on top. This is only for fun shooting at inanimate objects, not for hunting! Misses don't count on the former, but they can be really messy on the latter.

Loading for the Colt New Frontier for me at least is normally pretty traditional. I see no advantage, actually a disadvantage, in using jacketed bullets in the non-magnum big bore New Frontiers except for the above mentioned .44 225-gr. hollow point by Speer. I say this because pressures with jacketed bullets are higher than I like for the desired velocities. The 44 Special and 45 Colt beg for cast bullets and are at their best with hard-cast, Keith semi-wadcutter bullets.

Today, Third Generation Single Action Armies are cataloged in 45 Colt, 44-40, 44 Special, 38-40, 357 Magnum, 38 Special, and 32-20, but Colt says New Frontiers are gone forever. For now, New Frontiers seem to be readily available at gun shows and the really good news is that they are not regarded as highly by collectors as the Single Action Army, so prices are usually quite a bit lower: several hundred dollars lower in my area. Perhaps someday Colt may consider it reasonable to return the New Frontier in a modernized form with coil springs. The frame and cylinder are too small for a 44 Magnum, but it would make a dandy 41 Magnum in addition to 357 Magnum, 44-40, 38-40, 32-20, and of course, 45 Colt and 44 Special.

A pair of exceptional shooting 44 Special sixguns: Second and Third Generation New Frontiers.

Selected Loads for the Colt New Frontier 44 Special

BULLET	LOAD	BARREL LENGTH	MV
Lyman #429421	7.5 gr. Unique	5-1/2"	964
RCBS #44-250KT	7.5 gr. Unique	5-1/2"	1014
RCBS #44-250KT	17.0 gr. 2400	5-1/2"	1154
RCBS #44-250KT	7.5 gr. Unique	7-1/2"	1067
RCBS #44-250KT	17.0 gr. 2400	7-1/2"	1208

Selected Loads For the Colt New Frontier .45 Colt

BULLET	LOAD	BARREL LENGTH	MV
Lyman #454424	18.5 gr. 2400	5-1/2"	1151
Lyman #454424	20.0 gr. H4227	5-1/2"	1040
H&G Keith	8.0 gr. Unique	5-1/2"	920
H&G Keith	9.0 gr. Unique	5-1/2"	982
H&G Keith	10.0 gr. Unique	5-1/2"	1,032
Lyman #454424	18.5 gr. 2400	7-1/2"	1165
Lyman #454424	20.0 gr. H4227	7-1/2"	1085
H&G Keith	8.0 gr. Unique	7-1/2"	981
H&G Keith	9.0 gr. Unique	7-1/2"	1000
H&G Keith	10.0 gr. Unique	7-1/2"	1090

–Chapter 14–

THE GREAT WESTERN SINGLE ACTION

The Great Western Single action sixgun was introduced to the shooting public on the front cover of the first issue of *GUNS* magazine in January, 1955.

I've said it often but it still bears repeating. The 1950s had to be just about the greatest time ever for growing up. We were not disadvantaged with 150-channel TVs, cell phones, VCRs, computers, electronic games, or adults who thought they had to show us how to organize and then coach us so we could play football and baseball. Drugs were prescriptions from Doc Reeder's Drug Store. Outside was for continuous activity; inside was for eating and sleeping. Mom still stayed home and cooked three meals a day, seven days a week. We never had to go out to eat and couldn't have afforded it if we had wanted to do so. Until McDonalds started to show up, I don't know of anyone who ever "went out to eat" except for gathering at the local drive-in during high school days.

We did have one great disadvantage – and it is the only one I can think of – and that was a relative lack of information available on firearms, especially handguns. There were virtually no gun magazines yet in the early 1950s. The outdoor magazines rarely published anything about handguns; in fact the only magazine that did, and certainly not often enough, was *American Riflemen*. Paperback books had started to show up from such publishers as Trend and for 75 cents one could have *The Complete Book of Handguns*; even though it was "complete," a new copy came out just about every year.

Then it happened. It was the dead of winter, late December, 1954, and I had gone downtown to see a movie – a western of course – and stopped in at the newsstand. There it was. I had to blink to make sure it was real. I know my heart skipped a beat. Maybe two. There on the rack was a new magazine called *GUNS* and it was dated January, 1955.

At the time, I was a junior in high school and reading every book I could find about guns and hunting. We had a great school librarian in those pre-PC days, and I made frequent trips to town just to check out the newsstands for any gun publications. My search for knowledge had been rewarded. *GUNS* was only the first and over the next few years would be followed by *GUNS & AMMO*, beginning as a quarterly in 1958; *GUN WORLD*, 1960; and *SHOOTING TIMES*, which started life as a newspaper in the early 1960s.

Jim Martin also stocked this 357 Atomic Great Western. The short-lived Atomic was a pre-357 Magnum+P. Photo courtesy of Richard Talacek.

Now we had real gun magazines with articles about handguns in general and single action sixguns in particular. During the first year of publication, GUNS carried an article titled "A Six-Shooter For TV Cowboys." Just about every B western movie made saw the good guys and bad guys alike packin' Colt single actions. But this six-shooter for TV cowboys was not a Colt. The Colt single action had been manufactured from 1873 to 1941 with no major design changes; however, production ceased in 1941 after nearly 360,000 Model P's had been made in something over 30 different chamberings with the most popular being 45 Colt, 44-40, 38-40, and 32-20. Colt's official stance was that the Colt Single Action Army was dead and buried, never to be seen again. Sales had been going down for years and they saw no need to resurrect the Single action Army after the war.

Then a strange phenomenon occurred. In the late 1940s television began to appear around the country. There wasn't much to fill the TV time in those days, and all I vividly remember are old B Westerns and wrestling. There were so many western movies that they soon spawned western TV shows on a regular weekly basis. Viewers wanted single action revolvers like those they saw on television, and two companies answered the call. A young gunmaker had introduced a .22 semi-automatic pistol in 1949 that was reliable, accurate, and relatively low-priced. This was Bill Ruger's first production arm, and four years later, in 1953, one of the all-time great successes in revolverdom arrived with the Ruger .22 Single-Six. Ruger's .22 is basically a copy of a Colt Single Action Army with a smaller frame and coil springs, but the grip frame remained Colt-sized. It was an immediate success and remains tremendously popular more than a half-century later.

Meanwhile at the other end of the country, another gun company was founded: Great Western Arms Co. of Los Angeles. Bill Wilson, president and one of three founders, had contacted Colt in 1953 and was assured they had no plans to resurrect the Colt Single Action Army. Shooters wanted real Colts and they couldn't get them, so Great Western stepped into the void. The Great Western looked so much like a Colt Single action Army that they actually used real Colts in the early advertising. In fact, some of the Great Western parts came from Colt. Great Western became the "Six-Shooter for TV Cowboys."

Great Western began in 1954 and I saw the first ads when I was a junior in high school, which was also 1954. I do recall keeping a Great Western catalog in my English book to help me get through that last period of the day as the clock hands moved oh so slowly headed for 3:15 and dismissal. Great Western presented John Wayne with an early matched pair, fully engraved with ivory grips. It is believed The Duke used these Great Westerns in his last, and what many say is his best, movie, *The Shootist*. The picture of the Duke with his Great Westerns was in my history book. It got me through to lunch.

In the late 1950s I bought my first Great Western single action. I had great luck with the Ruger Single-Six .22 so I purchased a used Great Western .22. That turned out to be a mistake. The 5-1/2-inch .22 proved to be a really poor-shooting sixgun and was definitely out of time. I can't say if it came from the factory that way or if it had been abused. Thirty-five years later I picked up two more 5-1/2-inch Great Western .22s that have proven to be excellent shooters, and they are also favorites with the grandkids.

Chapter 14 | The Great Western Single Action

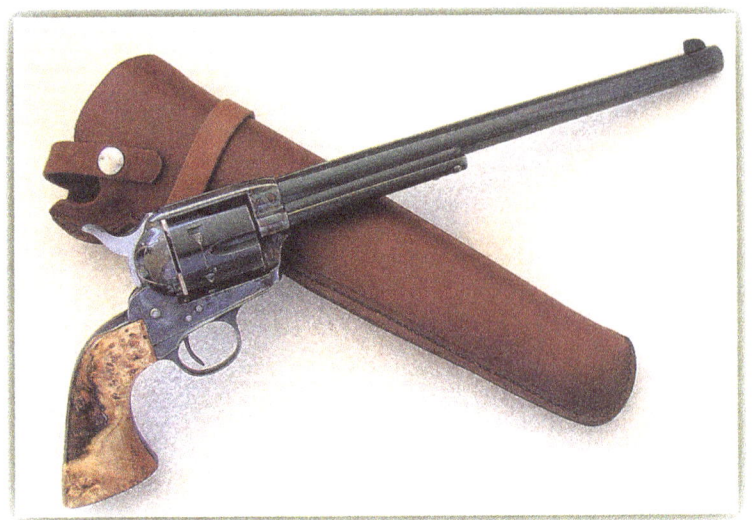

Great Western Buntline Specials are also very rare. This Buntline is from the collection of Jim Martin, who stocked it with fiddleback maple. Photo courtesy of Richard Talacek.

Elmer Keith in the first chapter of his book *Sixguns* (1955) commented that the sample Great Western single action that he had received was "very poorly timed, fitted, and showed a total lack of final inspection. The hand was a trifle short, the bolt spring did not have enough bend to lock the bolt with any certainty, the mainspring was twice as strong as necessary and the trigger pull about three times as heavy as needed." Maybe the same guy made his test gun and my .22. Later in his book Elmer was able to report: "We are happy to report that Great Western has really gotten on the ball and is now cooking on all four burners. They overhauled their design and inspection departments, put in some gunsmiths who knew the score and are now turning out first-class single action copies. We have one in 4 3/4-inch 44 Special and it is a very fine single action in every way, perfectly timed, sighted, and very accurate. It has performed perfectly with factory loads and our heavy handloads and is very accurate at extreme ranges, the real test of any sixgun."

Great Western sixguns were totally American-made and are not to be confused with the Hawes Single actions, which came later. Hy Hunter was an early distributor of Great Westerns, as was EMF, and Hunter also later brought in the German made J.P.Sauer & Sohn Hawes versions. I have no idea how many Great Western Single actions were manufactured in the less than 10 years they were in business. It was not unusual to find them at bargain prices 10 years ago, but the prices have tripled and quadrupled since then. They are also not all that commonly found at gun shows anymore.

At first glance, Great Western single actions look identical to Colt single actions with subtle differences in the hammer profile and shape of the trigger guard. They show up on many TV Westerns and are easy to spot when the hammer is cocked. Colts have the firing pin on the hammer, while Great Westerns have a frame-mounted firing pin such as that introduced by the old Christy Gun Works and picked up by Bill Ruger for use in all of his single actions. Unlike Rugers, the Great Westerns have sort of an upside down L-shaped hammer. However, Great Western could be ordered with Colt hammers.

Great Westerns were made in the three standard barrel lengths of 4-3/4, 5-1/2, and 7-1/2 inches plus a 12-1/2-inch Buntline Special. The standard model was a 5-1/2-inch 45 Colt that sold for $99.50 in 1960 at a time when the resurrected Colt Single Action Army .45 had a price tag of $125. There was a slight additional charge for other calibers and barrel lengths. In addition to 45 Colt and .22, the Great Western was offered in 38 Special, 44 Special, 357 Magnum, 357 Atomic, and 44 Magnum. The "Atomic" was simply a heavily loaded 357 Magnum, and believe it or not, the 44 Magnum was on the standard Colt-sized mainframe. I have heard rumors to the effect that a 44-40 was also offered and I do know they did make some examples chambered in 22 Hornet.

Great Western also offered both pearl and ivory grips, engraving, nickel plating, and even the installation of adjustable target sights. The Deputy Model was a 4-inch-barreled version with a full-length barrel rib, adjustable sights, deluxe blue finish, and walnut stocks instead of the standard issue B-Western type imitation stags. The Deputy was offered in .22, 38 Special, 357 Magnum, and possibly 44 Special.

The Great Western not only arrived at the time the TV Western was king, but it also profited by the Fast Draw sport that arose. For those that participated, Great Western offered a specially tuned 4-3/4-inch 45 with a brass backstrap and trigger guard. It was popular enough that they soon offered a "Professional Fast Draw Model" in all calibers and barrel lengths. A copy of the Remington Double Derringer was also offered chambered in either 38 S&W or 38 Special.

The Great Western Cap and Ball Revolver looked much like the Old Army that came from Ruger in the early 70's but without the top strap.

Most of the parts of the Great Western single action are interchangeable with the Colt Single Action Army except for the hammer and the screws for the hammer, trigger, and bolt. The threads on these three screws were changed to help prevent them from loosening as the gun was fired. Two years after the Great Western was introduced, Colt brought back the Single Action Army and, no matter how good the quality had become, Great Western's fate was sealed. In their advertising Great Western gave a whole list of reasons for selecting their single action instead of another brand, which at this time was Colt.

The reasons offered were these: Great Westerns were made of 4130 chrome molybdenum steel, the same as used for stress parts in aircraft and guided missiles. Barrels were made of medium carbon steel of the finest quality, their manufacture overseen by the man formerly in charge of producing Weatherby barrels. Cylinders were made of SAE 4140 chrome molybdenum steel heat-treated to a tensile strength of 185,000 pounds per square inch. (Overloads in the 45 Colt have gone as high as 100,000 pounds psi.) Both the bolt and trigger were improved over the original and were guaranteed for 20 years (unfortunately the company did not last half that long!). A frame-mounted firing pin was used. Stocks were imitation stag designed to resist warping.

Late model actions were carefully fitted and assembled with the smoothest and softest actions ever incorporated into a single action revolver. Mainsprings were designed for easier cocking. The sear and bolt spring, which often failed in original guns, have been specially heat-treated and guaranteed for 50,000 movements. There were no aluminum cast parts. Great Western offered a larger variety of finishes – including mirror blue, case hardened frame, chrome, nickel, gold, silver, or combinations thereof – than any other manufacturer. Great Westerns were also the only single actions offered in a variety of barrel lengths and in all popular calibers. Front sights were purposely tall to allow for individual sighting in, and adjustable sights were also available. The hammer was made of SAE 6150 chrome vanadium steel, giving greater strength and wear resistance than any other.

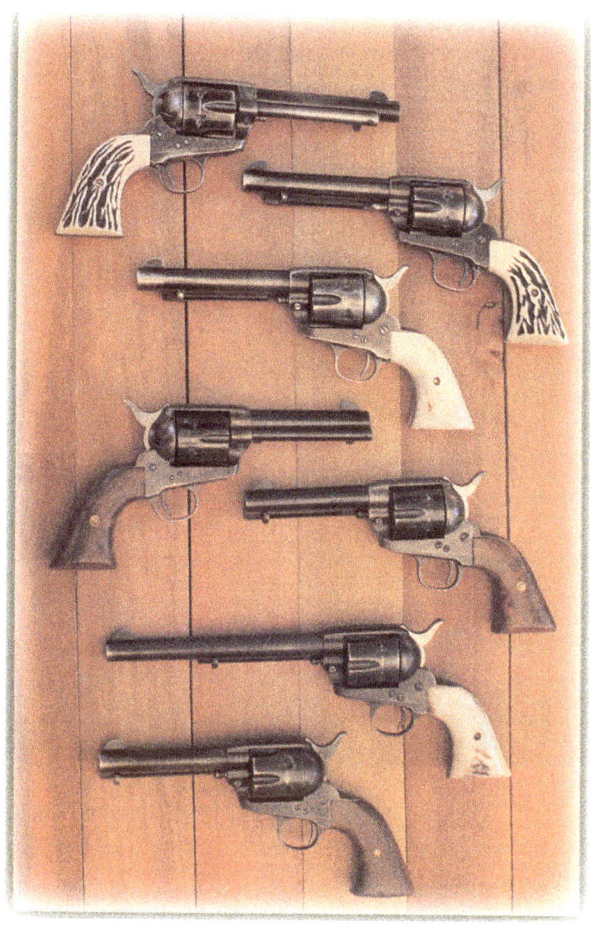

Standard Great Westerns were offered in 4-3/4-, 5-1/2-, and 7-1/2-inch barrel lengths and are shown here chambered in 45 Colt, 44 Special, 38 Special, 357 Atomic, 44 Magnum, and 22 Long Rifle.

Thus sayeth the advertising copy, anyway. Of course, much of this is hype, and I have owned or fired approximately one dozen Great Westerns over the past 40 years and I have never had a spring fail or a part break. I cannot say that about Colt single actions or current replicas. I have purchased Great Westerns with broken parts, whether from use or abuse I do not know, but one 44 Magnum had a broken firing pin (cost $7.50 to fix), and a chrome-plated 4-3/4-inch 45 Colt was found with a split forcing cone. I replaced the barrel with a nickel-plated Colt barrel and it's been giving service now for another 10 years.

An attempt has been made to write a book about Great Western, but the author gave up after running into too many dead ends. Noted fast draw shooter, technical director, and gun-spinning expert Jim Martin shared with me the fact he used to buy Great Westerns in kit form. These were offered substantially lower than

Single Action Sixguns | 99

Chapter 14 | The Great Western Single Action

Taffin shooting a real Saturday Night Special, a Great Western built to celebrate *Gunsmoke*.

> "The first sixgun to really catch my eye, it was a 7-1/2-incher in relatively poor shape. What really caught my eye was the fact the barrel was marked .44 SPECIAL, and these are very rare."

the finished product, and Martin would pick up a kit, fit and finish it, sell it, and then do it all over again for pocket money. About six months ago I got a letter from one David Davis who was in the Air Force in 1955 and was able to order Great Westerns through the PX. His original requisition dated December 1955 saw him purchase three great Westerns: a 38 Derringer, a 7-1/2-inch 22 Long Rifle, and a 7-1/2-inch 357 Atomic, all for the grand total of $181.50.

That figure makes us long for those days, but when Davis got out of the Air Force he went to work for Great Western as a machinist for $1.25 per hour while gunsmiths received $2.00. To put this into perspective I went to work unloading freight in 1956 for 90 cents an hour. Davis also remembers when they tested the first 44 Magnum, the bullet went through the backstop and headed who knows where. I have never seen one of the Great Western cap and ball revolvers, but Davis did and purchased one of the prototypes.

My latest Great Western was purchased just a couple years ago at one of our local gun shows. I had only been inside for a few minutes when I spotted it on the first table, in the second aisle. The first sixgun to really catch my eye, it was a 7-1/2-incher in relatively poor shape. What really caught my eye was the fact the barrel was marked .44 SPECIAL, and these are very rare. The original grips were long gone and replaced by a set of ill-fitting Flat-Top Ruger Blackhawk stocks. Even though the finish was well worn, the $125 price tag was very attractive for a sixgun to be used in a rebuild project. The cylinder pin would not budge when the spring loaded catch was pressed and my fingers grasped the head of the base pin. So I asked the two men manning the table to please pull the base pin while I looked around a few more aisles.

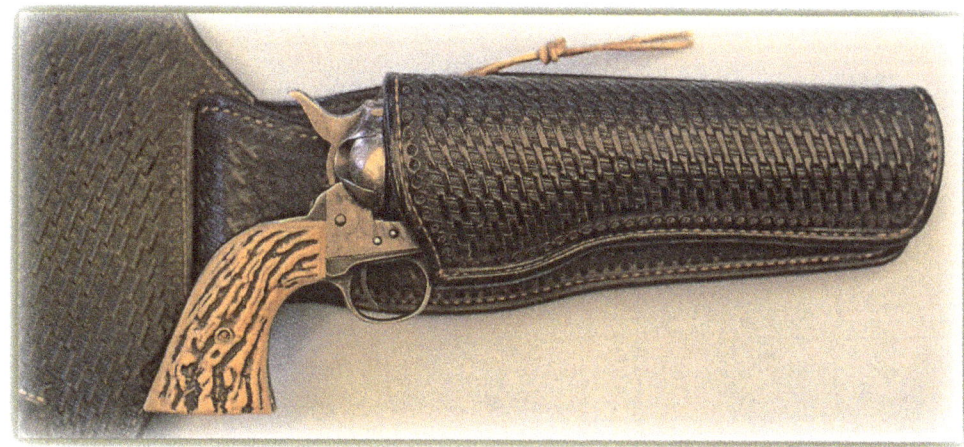

Matt Dillon's 7-1/2-inch 45 Colt single action was carried in a plain tan Arvo Ojala Hollywood Fast Draw Rig; Taffin chose black basket weave.

Returning a half-hour later I found the gun was no longer on the table as it had been set aside so they could work on getting the base pin out. I assured the sellers I would buy the gun and be back again shortly. Returning later I found they had sold the gun, even though I had told them I would take it, because the other guy was willing to take it without pulling the pin. Now there were hundreds of people in the gun show but I realized there was only one other person in that entire gun show beside myself who would be interested in such a project gun. I found friend and fellow writer Brian Pearce several aisles over; he smiled and opened his coat to show me the Great Western stuffed in his belt.

They had told him I had decided not to take the Great Western, so when he heard the real story he offered to sell it to me on the spot. He was caught in the middle but it certainly wasn't his fault. There was a reason the pin was never pulled, and Brian spent several hours working on getting the cylinder pin out by dismantling the gun and driving it out from the rear. When he got it out, removed the cylinder and looked at the barrel, he found it was totally destroyed by the use of black powder without proper cleaning – and although the barrel was marked 44 Special, the cylinder would accept a 45 Colt. What we had here was a movie prop gun that would accept blackpowder "5-in-1" blanks. Who knows but what some famous TV or movie Western star had used it extensively.

Now that we knew what we really had, Pearce offered to sell it to me again if I wanted to use it as a project gun. I did as I had some special plans for that particular Great Western. In September 1955 during my last year in high school a new type of TV Western arrived with a relatively unknown actor in the lead. John Wayne was originally picked for the part but turned it down and instead introduced that first episode with James Arness as Marshall Matt Dillon. Virtually everyone watched Matt, Kitty, Chester, and Doc and various other characters from Dodge City every Saturday night. That western was, of course, *Gunsmoke*.

Matt used a 7-1/2-inch 45 Colt single action and eventually one of the new Arvo Ojala Hollywood Fast Draw holsters. In fact, he gunned down Arvo Ojala in the opening of each episode with this rig for several years. In 1957 I purchased my first 7-1/2-inch Colt single action 45 Colt, and then one year later custom ordered an Arvo Ojala rig. Matt went for plain brown, but I decided on black basket weave. *Gunsmoke* ran for several decades and now, thanks to videotapes and cable TV, is still seen virtually every day in virtually every part of the country. Since this Great Western had been a movie gun, I decided to rebuild this old single action to honor Marshall Dillon and all the other characters of *Gunsmoke*.

All-new internal parts were ordered from Brownells. A search through my parts box revealed a

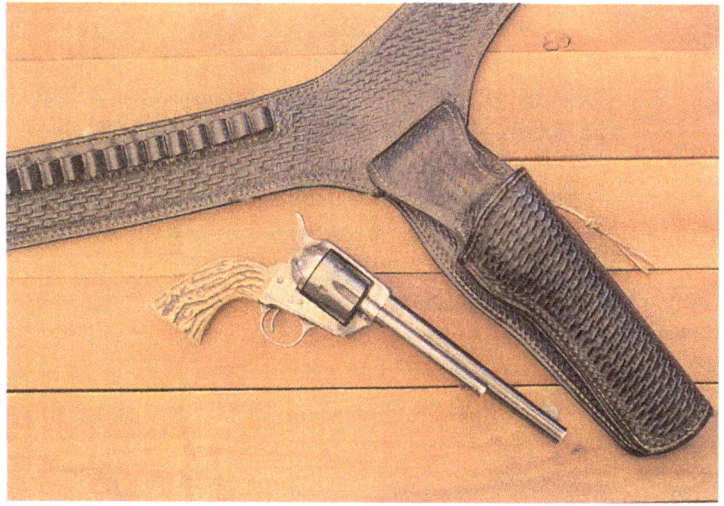

Both the 7-1/2-inch Great Western and the Arvo Ojala date back to the late 1950s.

Single Action Sixguns | 101

Chapter 14 | The Great Western Single Action

One never knows what to expect when rebuilding an old sixgun; results such as this with the Great Western .45 are very gratifying.

Colt single action cylinder chambered in 45 Colt along with the real treasure needed to complete the project. More than 30 years ago I spent $5 at a gun show for a used 7-1/2-inch 45 Colt Great Western barrel. It is a most unusual barrel as it is tapered somewhat and lighter than most .45 barrels, but it is properly marked and has been in my shop for three decades ever since, waiting for the right project. The right project had finally arrived.

What was left of the Great Western sixgun along with new parts was taken to Mike Rainey, then resident gunsmith at Shapel's. He put everything together, tuned the action, and even shimmed under the back of the collar button base pin bushing of the Third Generation Colt cylinder to adapt it to the slightly longer frame of the Great Western. The resulting sixgun turned out to be more than could have been hoped for. Not only does it function smoothly – it also shoots! Using 8.0 grains of Unique under a Oregon Trail 255-gr. bullet or RCBS's #45-270 bullet over 17.0 grains of XMR 5744, or just about any other combination, results in five-shot groups right at one inch.

Only one thing was needed to complete this project and that was the proper grips. I was contacted at just the right time by a reader who knew that I semi-collected plastic stag grips such as those found on the original Great Westerns and also made by both Fitz and Franzite for virtually every other revolver well into the 1950s. I threw these grips away in the 50s but go even as high as $5 for a pair now, and I have installed some on Italian replicas to make them resemble B movie sixguns. I never pay more than $5 for a pair of these grips; free is even better. However, the reader said he had a beautiful pair in perfect shape that I could have for $15 postpaid. So I relented and I am happy I did so, as what I got was not the typical hollow plastic stag grips, but rather solid, heavy-duty, plastic stag grips as found on many movie guns prior to World War II. In fact, Tom Mix had such a pair on his 7-1/2-inch 38-40 Colt single action. These stags now reside on my real Saturday Night Special.

Gone, long gone, are the days when network TV entertained us with the likes of *Gunsmoke*; *Have Gun, Will Travel*; *Bonanza*; *Maverick*; *Cheyenne*; and dozens of other bits of Western Americana. Network TV really has become the Vast Wasteland of Newton Minow's prediction. However, my real Saturday Night Special continues to bring back many pleasant memories of a most enjoyable time of my life.

The first issue of *GUNS* in January, 1955 featured a cased set of a pair of Great Westerns chambered in 45 Colt with 4-3/4-inch barrels. Unlike most Great Westerns with frame-mounted firing pins, these guns, which have no caliber markings on the barrels, have Colt-style hammers with the firing pin on the hammer. Since they are very early production sixguns, their serial numbers are GW183 and GW184. They are not case-colored and their frames and ejector rod housings have the same plum purple color found on many early Ruger loading gates.

Thanks to publisher Tom von Rosen and editor Jeff John of *GUNS*, it was my recent pleasure to be able to actually hold and shoot these historic sixguns. The 50-year old Great Westerns were not as bad as the one described by Keith, but close! It was time to correct this situation and I received permission from *GUNS* to have these sixguns brought to perfection by the previously mentioned long-time single action gunsmith, fast draw shooter, trick shooter, and instructor of movie cowboys on the use of the single action sixgun, Jim Martin. Sixgun #184 was as it left the factory except for the fact nearly all the screw heads were buggered, as were those on the #183, and it simply needed the screws replaced and the touch of a master tunesmith. Companion #183 was an entirely different matter. Who knows how many people had handled this sixgun over the past half century? Those that did apparently knew nothing about

Cased sets of Great Westerns are very rare. This pair of 45s was presented to the founder of **GUNS** magazine in 1954 and each is inscribed on the backstrap "To George von Rosen from Hy Hunter."

how a single action works and #183 had paid the price. It would not cock. I dismantled it and to see what the problem was and found someone had filed through the full cock notch on the hammer resulting in the hole for the stud on the hand being filed through also. No wonder it wouldn't cock! Both Great Westerns were shipped off to Jim Martin. Little did he know what be would really getting into as #183 turned out to be a major challenge.

I quote from Martin: "Serial #183 is the one I had all the problems with. Most of the parts that were in it were wrong, and the top radius of the bolt was out of line with the approaches and the locking slot on both guns. That's why the scratches are where they are. The parts I used in #183 include an AWA hand, Colt bolt and sear and bolt spring.

"The trigger is a Colt but had to be extended and a half cock notch was moved down to allow the bolt to clear the cylinder in the half cock position. The full cock notch was repaired, the hammer cam was repaired so that the bolt would fall at the start of the approach instead of where it was falling before.

"Trying to get all these modified parts to time together is where I ran into all the problems. The area in the front of frame under where the sear and bolt spring is screwed in had to be reduced so that the bolt side of the spring would have enough pressure to make the bolt fall. I tried every make of spring I had here and none of them would work without modification. Evidently it wasn't right from the beginning, which would explain some of the damage that was done to the gun. I used an AWA pre-lightened mainspring in #184 and a Wolff spring in #183. This was easier and less expensive than using two Colt springs plus the grinding and polishing on them to make them lighter. Anyway, they are a whole lot better than they were."

If Jim Martin had been the head gunsmith for Great Western way back when, perhaps they would still be in business. These two early sixguns are now tuned and slicked the way a single action should be. As the hammer is cocked the parts all work together instead of fighting each other. Fifty years after I first saw those Great Western cover sixguns, I actually got to shoot them and shoot they do! Using Black Hills 45 Colt 250-gr. RNFP loads at 775 fps resulted in #183 placing six shots into 1-1/8 inches at 50 feet and #184 going 1-3/8 inches at the same distance. Considering that they were short-barreled sixguns having tiny little V-notch rear sights and very slim blade fronts, I would settle for that anytime.

If Great Western had started with the proper gunsmithing, and if they had modernized instead of copying the Colt single action, and if Colt had not resumed production of the Single Action Army and if Ruger had not introduced the adjustable-sighted coil-spring operated 357 Blackhawk, maybe Great Western would still be around. Maybe.

Single Action Sixguns | 103

Chapter 15

UNITED STATES FIREARMS SINGLE ACTION SIXGUNS

Real treasures are very hard to find, especially when it comes to yard sales. How many times have I heard of great gun bargains being found at yard sales? One of our acquaintances several years ago bought an old belt with a funny-looking metal plate on it. That funny plate was a Bridgeport Rig (see picture in Chapter 8) worth several hundred dollars – and that is not the end of the story. The old belt was a money belt and had several gold coins stashed inside it for who knows how many generations. The total cost for this treasure was $3! That's the good news; the bad news is one has to wade through hundreds of yard and garage sales to find anything. That equates to working for very cheap wages.

I don't do yard or garage sales. However, until I could no long take the constant liberal slant and spin of our local paper, it was my regular habit to read the "Guns For Sale" section in the morning paper's want ads as well as attend all the local gun shows. Reading the paper took very little time, and even if one buys nothing at a gun show, it is always a pleasant experience to visit with other shooters. By checking the paper and gun shows, I expected to find at least one special sixgun per year. It may be a like-new Ruger 357 Flat-Top or Old Model Blackhawk, or perhaps even an inexpensive specimen for re-building into a 41 Special, 44 Special, 44-40, or 38-40, or perhaps even a Colt Single Action, as I found in the early 1970s under an ad which read simply, "Colt Single Action .44 and Old Belt and Holster."

The address given in that particular ad was a trailer park just outside of town, and I was rewarded by finding a First Generation 7-1/2-inch Single Action with an old cartridge belt and holster just as advertised. As I handled the Colt I felt everything all sixgunners do when their spirit and soul come in contact with such a beautiful sixgun. Except for minor pitting on the top strap, the .44 sixgun was in excellent shape mechanically and the case coloring had turned a beautifully aged gray. The left side of the barrel was marked "RUSSIAN AND S&W SPECIAL 44," dating it between 1913 and 1929 and making it one of the rarest of the First Generation Single Actions.

The sad part was I knew I could not afford the price of $450. Sadly, I reluctantly thanked the man for his time and left. My excitement was obvious as I told my wife all about the Colt .44 when I arrived back at home. Then the unexpected occurred. I had become so excited over the .44 sixgun, I forgot to stop at the local boot repair shop; and since she was going out to do some shopping anyway I asked her to pick up my boots. When she returned home she handed me the boots with a slight smile on her face. As I took the boots I realized they felt a few pounds heavier than normal. In the left boot was the Colt! She had gone out on her own and purchased the 44 Special – a most special sixgun, and definitely a most special wife.

After doing a little research on the Colt and finding out more about its rarity, we decided it belonged to a collector, not a shooter such as me. So we traded it for all of our money back plus two Colt shooting sixguns, a Second Generation 5-1/2-inch 44 Special and a 7-1/2-inch 45 New Frontier. I still have both of these Colts and that Special is really special, but I wish I still had the other one also. Over the next two decades I would never see another Colt Single Action like that one, and I still haven't.

By the early 1990s several manufacturers and importers were offering replicas of the Colt Single Action. The first sixguns dating back the 1970s shot OK but with their brass grip frames they were not very authentic. During the 1980s that started to change as replicas came closer in appearance to the sixguns used in the nineteenth century. Finally at a SHOT Show in the early 1990s, I found a single action with the Russian and S&W Special marking, beautifully finished with deep bluing and very vivid case colors. This was a brand-new sixgun, a replica single action from a new company then known as United States Patent Firearms Manufacturing Company. USPFA's sixguns were Italian replicas, but they were not only fitted and finished in this country – the work was done in the old Colt Armory!

At that time USPFA was a relatively new company that had taken over the old manufacturing facility of the Colt Patent Firearms Co. In keeping with the move into this historic facility, USPFA's catalog was printed in the 1870s style and language, advertising "Holster, Belt, And Pocket Pistols, Revolving Carbines, & Single Action, Central Fire, Army, Six Shot, Revolving Pistols. Also The Old Armoury Custom Shop, Ornamental Engraving & Special Guns Made To Order. All Of Our Work Is Guaranteed Highest Standard Attained."

In talking with the USPFA folks at the SHOT show, arrangements were made to examine their sixguns in depth. To this end, three sixguns were ordered for testing and evaluation. One was a blued and case-colored 7-1/2-inch RUSSIAN AND S&W SPECIAL 44. The other two were to be in 45 Colt and 44-40 with one a 4-3/4-inch barrel, the other 5-1/2-inch, and one to be nickel finished. In a short time I received the 44 Special, a 5-1/2-inch nickeled 45 Colt, and a 4-3/4-inch 44-40 finished with the same beautiful blue and case colors as the 44 Special. All three sixguns were fitted up tightly with little or no perceptible cylinder movement either fore, aft, or side-to-side. All were of the 1870s black powder style with a bullseye ejector rod head and a screw through the front of the frame to secure the cylinder pin.

The serial number was found in three places, in 1870s style, on front of the trigger guard behind the front screw, on the bottom of the frame in front of the trigger guard, and also on the butt. Above each serial number was the letter P. Since these sixguns were still technically imports, the hammers carried the government-mandated safeties as found on all Uberti centerfire single action sixguns.

All of these sixguns proved to be excellent shooters, but USPFA was not satisfied with offering Italian replicas; that was only the starting point. Their goal was a completely American-made sixgun of all American-made parts. The goal was not immediately attained, but it was approached in steps with each one, such as using American barrels and cylinders with Italian frames, bringing them closer to meeting the goal. In the process their name was changed to USFA for United States Firearms. What we now have is just about the finest traditional factory-built single action sixgun I have ever seen; and unlike other replicas, this one is all-American. It is no longer just assembled in this country with imported parts but is entirely, 100 percent made in America.

There are those who think that writers get specially-selected guns, so two USFA single action sixguns were ordered through regular dealer channels and paid for up front, so they were definitely not specially-selected samples. In fact they were custom-built after they were ordered, as are most USFA sixguns, and came through with consecutive serial numbers. The sixguns ordered were a classic single action, a 45 Colt with a 4-3/4-inch barrel, while the second sixgun was a 38-40 with a 7-1/2-inch barrel.

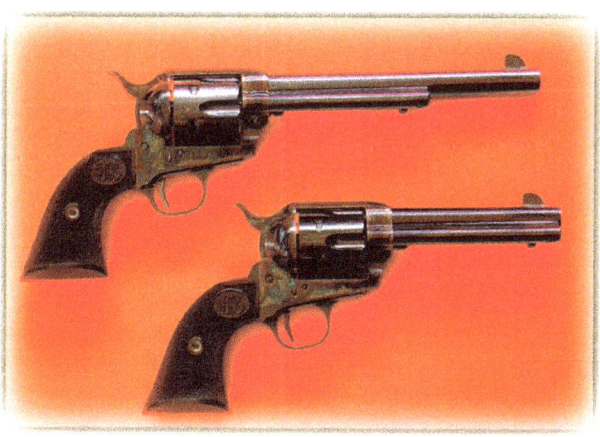

Two beautifully fitted and finished sixguns from USFA, a 7-1/2-inch 38-40 and a 4-3/4-inch 45 Colt. All that is needed to complete the picture is to fit Eagle's Ultra Ivory stocks.

Single Action Sixguns | 105

Chapter 15 | United States Firearms' Single Action Sixguns

USFA single actions are beautifully finished with case-hardened frame and trigger.

It did not take long to realize these were sixguns done right. Most single actions need some work to either tune them or fit them enough to satisfy someone who has been shooting single actions as long as I have. That does not mean to say they are not usable out of the box but rather they often need such work performed as trigger pulls reduced, actions smoothed out, cylinders tightened, and grips fitted properly. Not so with these sixguns. The main frame and the hammer were beautifully case colored, while the balance of each sixgun was finished in a deep, dark color. Grips furnished as standard were checkered hard rubber with a "US" molded into the top part of the grip.

One of the first things I normally do with any sixgun is fit it with personally chosen custom stocks, usually preferring ivory, stag, or some exotic wood. On pure looks alone, the USFA Single Action Army sixguns definitely need replaced, but the grips are so perfectly fitted to the frame and feel so good in the hand that I am very hesitant to change them. The Eagle Ultra Ivory grip panels are sitting on my desk right now and they will be replaced, but I'm in no hurry. If one looks at the grips on most single action sixguns, the fitting leaves a lot to be desired, but not so here. These grips have been fitted to the grip frame on a factory-built revolver as carefully as custom grips by the master grip makers.

One of the things I always look for in the fitting and finishing of a single action sixgun is the radiusing of the lower part of the back of the hammer and the two "ears" formed by the back strap where it screws into the mainframe on both sides of the hammer. A well-made single action will exhibit a smooth mating of the contours of all three. USFA sixguns are very nearly perfect in this area and the same careful fitting can also be found where the top of the face of the hammer meets the top strap. The fit of the trigger guard to the bottom of the mainframe is so perfectly done one can run a finger over the area and not feel where one part begins and the other ends. The same is true where the back strap meets the mainframe. The front of the ejector rod housing as well as the cylinder are both beveled, which not only looks good and feels good but also provides for easier holstering.

A sixgun can look good and feel good, but these are only two legs of a three-legged stool; it must also shoot well. Two critical measurements predict how well it will shoot and how much care was taken in the assembling of these sixguns: chamber throat diameters and trigger pulls. Both USFA sixguns receive a perfect grade of 100 percent. I have seen chamber throats on 45 Colts as small as .449" and as large as .460". All six chambers on the 45 Colt from USFA measure a uniform and perfect .452". The 38-40 is also uniform and correct

A picture right out of the 1920s: a USFA 5-1/2-inch single action marked "COLT AND S&W SPECIAL 38" and an S.D. Myres holster and belt.

at .400". Trigger pulls on both sixguns are exactly as I prefer, being set at three pounds. Cylinders lock up tight both in the hammer down and hammer-cocked position. In fact, when the hammer is cocked, the cylinders on either sixgun are as tight as those found on the single action by which all others are judged, the Freedom Arms revolver. These sixguns are simply built right.

Shooters have a choice in rear sights of a V-notch or square rear sight; Vs are more historically accurate and for young eyes; square notches are more practical for my more mature eyes. The square rear notch is perfectly filled in by a front sight that also has a square profile rather than tapering to the top. USFA sixguns can be ordered with a choice of a spring-loaded cross pin or screw in black powder style cylinder base pin latch. I went with the more modern spring-loaded version.

Fixed-sight sixguns do not always shoot to point of aim. Point of aim depends on the load used, how one sees the sights, and how one grips the sixguns. The ideal is a sixgun that shoots right on for windage and a little low so the front sight can be filed down to bring the preferred load right to point of aim. Both the sixguns tested were dead on for windage with most of my loads, my grip, and my eyes. The 38-40 shot anywhere from one to three inches low and can be easily filed to hit point of aim with one particular bullet weight and load. Caution is necessary here as one must be careful to not only use the right load when filing the front sight but also to shoot as one normally expects to shoot. For me, I will get three different points of elevation depending upon whether I am resting the sixgun on sandbags, resting only my hands, or shooting offhand. The difference can be several inches.

The 45 Colt is just about perfect as it is. Not only is it dead on for windage, but it also shoots most of my 45 Colt loads right to point of aim for elevation. There's no reason to touch the front sight blade with a file. I can't remember ever experiencing a traditional single action in the nearly five decades I have been shooting them that came as perfectly sighted and timed and with perfectly-fitting grips and perfect trigger pull. The only possible way I can see to improve a USFA sixgun is by spending some time polishing the interior parts with a stone to give that buttery-slick feel to the action.

With the way these sixguns were put together I expected them to shoot very well and that is exactly what occurred. Both the 45 Colt and the 38-40 exhibited several five-shot groups at 50 feet that were one inch or less. My most used loads with these two calibers are 8.0 grains of Unique under 250- to 255- and 180-grain

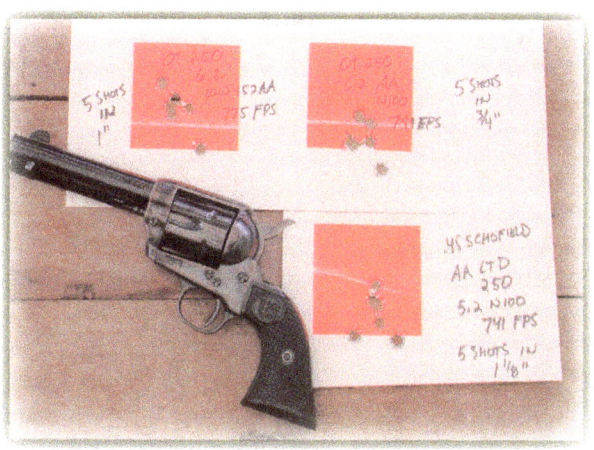

The term "keeper" can definitely be applied to this USFA 4-3/4-inch 45 Colt.

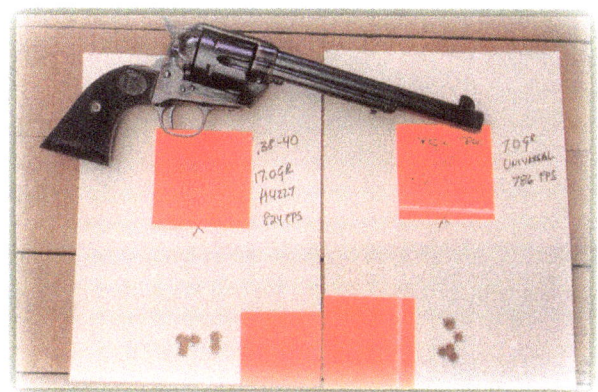

Maybe the 38-40 shoots better, but then again Taffin might just shoot longer barrels better. Whatever the case, this is superb performance from a single action and with a little file work the groups will be brought right to point of aim.

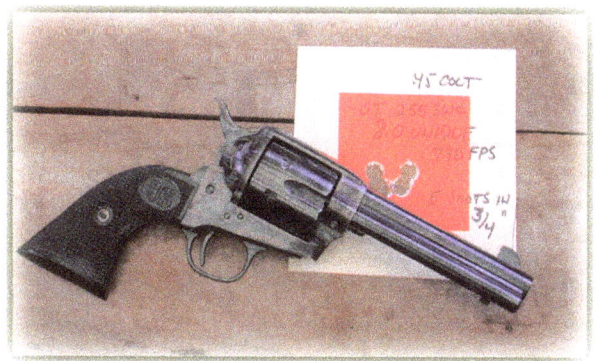

This 4-3/4-inch United States Firearms 45 Colt exhibited excellent accuracy and shot right to point of aim out of the box.

Single Action Sixguns | 107

Chapter 15 | United States Firearms' Single Action Sixguns

bullets respectively. These two calibers, as well as the 44-40, are loaded on the RCBS Model 2000 progressive press. This is very convenient as all three use the same shell plate and by using the same powder charge it takes me all of 10 to 20 seconds to remove one die plate and substitute another. With both the 45 Colt and 38-40 loads using Unique, group size was under one inch. Considering the fact I no longer see the sights as clearly as I once did, this is remarkable performance from these two sixguns

Neither the 45 Colt nor the 38-40 chambered in traditional Single Action Army sixguns should ever be "magnumized" but, rather, both should be kept at reasonable muzzle velocities. To gain the greatest slap-down power with these two cartridges in Single Action Army sixguns I prefer two very special bullets with wide, flat noses. For the 45 Colt, the choice is RCBS's #45-270 SWC, a Keith-style bullet that weighs out at 281 grains cast 20:1 lead and tin. With 8.0 grains of Unique, this bullet whips up only around 800 fps from a 4-3/4-inch barrel, but with this heavy a bullet I'd say that's plenty for most applications. With the 38-40, I go with the Gordon Boser-designed Lyman #401452 he came up with more than 60 years ago for his wildcat 401 Special. In Starline's 38-40 brass, with 8.0 grains of Unique from the 7-1/2-inch barrel of the USFA single action sixgun, this load clocks out well over 1000 fps and shoots into one inch at 50 feet. One cannot ask for more from the old 38 Winchester Centerfire.

The Rodeo by USFA is the same sixgun as the single action but it's finished in a matte blue.

Selected Loads For USFA Single Actions

4-3/4-inch, 45 Colt

BULLET/LOAD	MV	5 SHOTS AT 50 FT.
Oregon Trail 255/8.0 gr. Unique	798	3/4"
Oregon Trail 255/6.0 gr. Red Dot	810	1 1/4"
Oregon Trail 255/7.2 gr. WW231	797	1 3/4"
Oregon Trail 255/18.5 gr. H4227	855	1 1/2"
Oregon Trail 250/6.2 gr. WW452AA	775	1"
Oregon Trail 250/6.2 gr. AAN100	799	3/4"
RCBS #45-270/8.0 gr. Unique	783	1-3/4"

7-1/2-inch, 38-40 Winchester (38 WCF)

BULLET/LOAD	MV	5 SHOTS AT 50 FT.
Black Hills 180 RNFP	999	1"
Oregon Trail 180/8.0 gr. True Blue	844	1 3/8"
Oregon Trail 180/17.0 gr. H4227	824	7/8"
Oregon Trail 180/7.0 gr. WW231	883	1 3/8"
Meister 180/8.0 gr. Unique	960	7/8"
Lyman #401452/8.0 gr. Unique	1034	1"

The standard chambering for USFA single actions is 45 Colt, but other choices include 32 WCF (32-20), 41 Long Colt, 38 Special, 38 WCF (38-40), 44 WCF (44-40), 45 ACP, 44 Russian, and 44 Special. The latter can be marked "RUSSIAN AND S&W SPECIAL 44" as were Colt single actions until 1929. The 44 Russian cartridge arrived in 1871, the longer 44 Special in 1908.

The USFA Custom Shop also offers a full blue or nickel finish; walnut, pearl, or ivory stocks; and special engraving from names all the way up to full coverage scroll engraving. For those placing function over form, USFA also offers the Rodeo in both 38 Special and 45 Colt. The less expensive Rodeo is the same basic sixgun as the Single Action Army but it comes with bead-blasted satin blue finish instead of the beautiful finish of the standard revolver.

United States Firearms single actions are not what you would call inexpensive. These revolvers are not assembly line mass-produced, and either USFA has excellent machinery producing perfect parts or it takes a lot of hand fitting to produce a single action sixgun of this quality. However they have managed to keep the suggested retail price just about halfway between a quality replica and a Third Generation Colt.

Remembering the old Colt SAA bearing the designation "RUSSIAN AND S&W SPECIAL 44" that my wife bought for me, I ordered not one but two USFA sixguns with 7-1/2-inch barrels and identical markings. These USFAs are beautiful 44 Special sixguns, made as well or better as any of the First Generation Colts, finely finished, tight with no cylinder play either front to back or side to side, and they shoot as good as they look. Every thing positive said about the 45 Colt and 38-40 USFA single actions also applies to the 44 Special versions. My only decision now is what caliber or version to order next.

Great 44 Special sixguns and genuine Keith bullets belong together. I have molds from Lyman, RCBS, and NEI, all casting Keith bullets that are very close to Keith's original design. However, for those who do not cast, Lynn Halstead of Dry Creek Bullet Works offers a 255-grain Keith that clocks out at just over 900 fps over 7.5 grains of Unique, making an excellent everyday working load for the USFA 44 Special.

USFA single actions have beautifullu case-colored frames and cylinders.

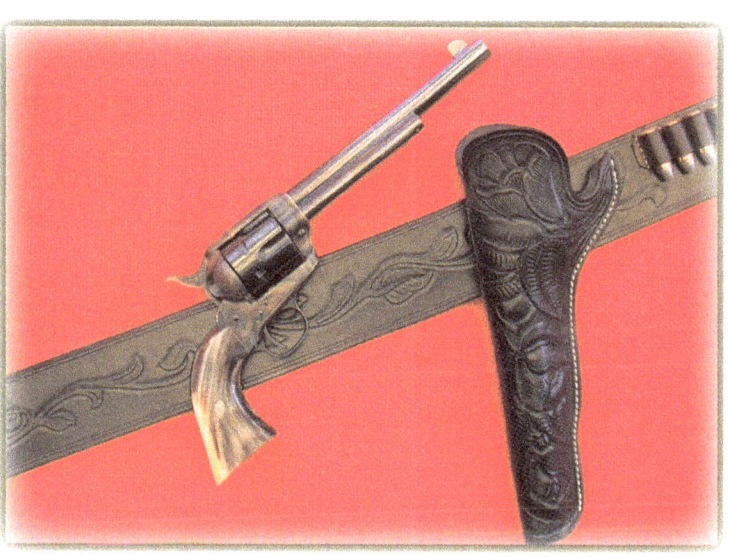

Be still my heart! USFA 7-1/2-inch 44 Special, desert bighorn sheep grips by Roy Fishpaw and leather by Rawhide Walt Ostin.

Chapter 15 | United States Firearms' Single Action Sixguns

These are probably two of the finest 44 Special single actions ever factory produced, both by USFA: a full-blue 7-1/2-inch Flat-Top Target and a blued/case-colored 7-1/2-inch single action. The beautiful grips are desert bighorn sheep by Roy Fishpaw.

Selected Loads for USFA Single Actions in 44 Special

44 Special 7-1/2-inch Single Action

LOAD	MV	5 SHOTS/50 FT.
Oregon Trail 240 SWC/6.0 gr. Unique	770	1-1/4"
Oregon Trail 240 SWC/5.0 gr. Bullseye	798	1-1/4"
Oregon Trail 240 SWC/5.5 gr. WW452AA	870	3/4"
Oregon Trail 240 SWC/8.0 gr. Universal	993	1-1/2"
Oregon Trail 240 SWC/7.0 gr. Unique	925	1-3/8"
Dry Creek 255KT/7.5 gr. Unique	905	1-3/8"
Lyman #429421/7.5 gr. Unique	975	1-3/4"
Lyman #429215GC/7.2 gr. Unique	1015	1-1/4"
RCBS 250KT/7.5 gr. Unique	999	1"

44 Special Flat-Top Target 7-1/2-inch

LOAD	MV	5 SHOTS/20 YDS
Oregon Trail 240 SWC/5.0 gr. Bullseye	858	1-1/4"
Oregon Trail 240 SWC/5.5 gr. WW452AA	873	1-3/8"
Oregon Trail 240 SWC/8.0 gr. Universal	1092	2"
Lyman #42924215C/7.5 gr. Unique	1048	1-3/8"
Winchester 240RNFP	769	1-1/4"
Federal 200 SWCLHP	1014	3/4"
Blazer 200 Gold Dot JHP	1028	5/8"
Speer 200 Gold Dot JHP	908	1-1/8"

–Chapter 16–

THE RUGER SINGLE-SIX

That wonderful year, 1956! Ike was in the White House, and I was looking forward to graduation and freedom from studies – and also to having a job that would supply enough money to buy my first gun. A paper route through high school kept me in clothes and spending money and also allowed me to give my mother one week's pay per month.

Graduation finally arrived and I invited the most beautiful woman I could find out for hamburgs, fries, and a milkshake at the local drive-in after the graduation ceremony. I got a lot of looks from others that night but then again I have never been one to follow the crowd. My grandmother and I had a wonderful time. Girls are everywhere but grandmothers only come two to a customer.

I would have had a double date had my paternal grandmother not passed away while I was a freshman. Grandma never had much as far as this world's goods go, but her heart was even bigger than her 4'10" stature might indicate and she felt 10 feet tall that night. I think some of the guys were jealous when they realized they could have done the same thing and had a special evening with a special person instead of being stuck with their airhead dates.

Taffin started his shooting life with the Marlin Mountie and the Ruger Single-Six.

Myself, I had just turned 17 and would soon have a real job and be able to buy my own rifle. The money would be no problem and in those wonderful days one only had to be 16 to buy a gun but 21 to vote. Wise men realized the vote was more dangerous than the gun. There were no guns in my house. My father, who did have guns, had died in an automobile accident before I reached my first birthday and the guns disappeared. Even my mother did not know who took them.

Mom was a widow at age 19 in the days when government help and its attendant interference rarely existed. In late 1942 Mom remarried and my step-dad promptly went off to war. I was not very old but I still remember that dreadful morning when we received that terse telegram that said Missing In Action. It would be over a year before we knew if he was dead or alive as he spent the remainder of the war in a POW camp after being wounded in action. When my step-dad came home he had the usual liberated war trophies including a Luger and a P-38 that were promptly sold after he was released from the veterans' hospital. The money was desperately needed. Guns were not to be in our house. My step-dad had seen enough of guns.

Chapter 16 | The Ruger Single-Six

When I purchased my first gun, my step-dad hit the roof. When I brought home the second one he only went as high as the ceiling. By the time of the third one, he wanted me to show my gun collection to everyone who came to the house and everything was O.K. It was quite a decision as to what that first gun would be. I had grown up reading the likes of Jack O'Connor and Elmer Keith but on my ninety-cent an hour wages, the first gun would have to be a .22, a .22 rifle. My uncle had taught me how to shoot using both .22 rifles and pistols, but I wanted a rifle, a real good-looking, swell-feeling rifle. That left only one choice in my young eyes. A Marlin Mountie.

If memory serves me right, that Marlin .22 cost me two weeks' take home pay. It was worth every penny. I don't believe I have been any more enthralled with any new gun, rifle or sixgun, single-shot or semi-automatic, in the last five decades than I was with that Marlin .22. Saturdays were always spent with a couple of boxes of .22s, good friends, and that wonderful little lever gun. For me the smell of powder smoke and Hoppe's #9 were a whole lot more appealing in those days than the smell of perfume.

(That would change in a few years, but only for a short time. My courtship with Dot lasted a little over three months. It is the only time in my life that my guns gathered dust. Fortunately for me the girl I picked has been totally supporting of my love for good guns.)

I now had a grand .22 rifle. It was soon paid for and it became time to add a companion piece, a good .22 sixgun. According to an ad in the *American Rifleman*, a young fellow on the East Coast was making a reputation as a gun builder with a semi-automatic .22 that sold for less than one week's pay. But his new design beckoned even more. At $57.25 it would take some time to pay for but it was a sixgun, a single-action sixgun – a sixgun that looked much like the sixguns that I had seen on the screen from the front row as I watched so many times on a Saturday afternoon.

No one knew it at the time, but when that small ad appeared in the pages of the *American Riflemen*, a firearms dynasty was beginning. William Ruger, with financial backing from his partner Alexander Sturm, had begun offering a Luger-looking .22 semi-automatic pistol in 1949. Using what were then modern manufacturing methods, Bill Ruger was able to offer his standard .22 semi-auto for the incredibly low price of $37.50. Ruger's pistol took on the much more expensive Colt Woodsman, and shooters soon found that these little .22s coming from the Red Barn in Connecticut would actually outshoot the more expensive target grade pistols. The beginning may have been modest, but Ruger was on its way to becoming a major factor in the firearms industry.

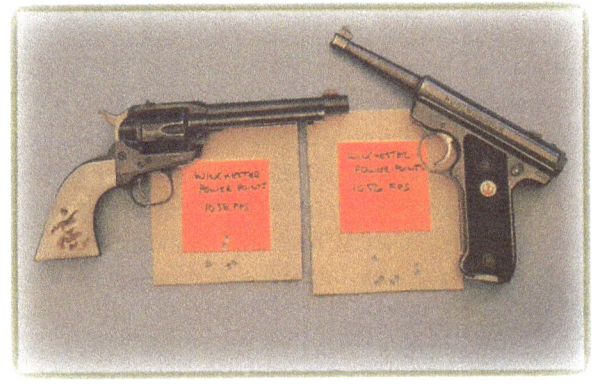

These very early Ruger .22s, a Single-Six and a Mark I, still shoot.

One of the reasons Ruger has had such a positive effect both as to styles of firearms as well as manufacturing methods is the simple fact that Ruger has always tried to produce the types of firearms that average shooters wanted at blue-collar prices. Bill Ruger not only had an uncanny ability to perceive what shooters really wanted; he also had a great appreciation for history.

In the early 1950's, the Colt Single Action Army had a great history behind it with the emphasis on "behind." Colt had stopped manufacturing the Model P in 1940 with no thought of ever producing it again. In fact, with the coming of the modern double action revolver and the 1911 semi automatic pistol, both of

Spurred on by the success of his Mark I .22 introduced in 1949 and inspired by the Colt Single Action Army, Bill Ruger modernized the single action sixgun with the .22 Single-Six in 1953.

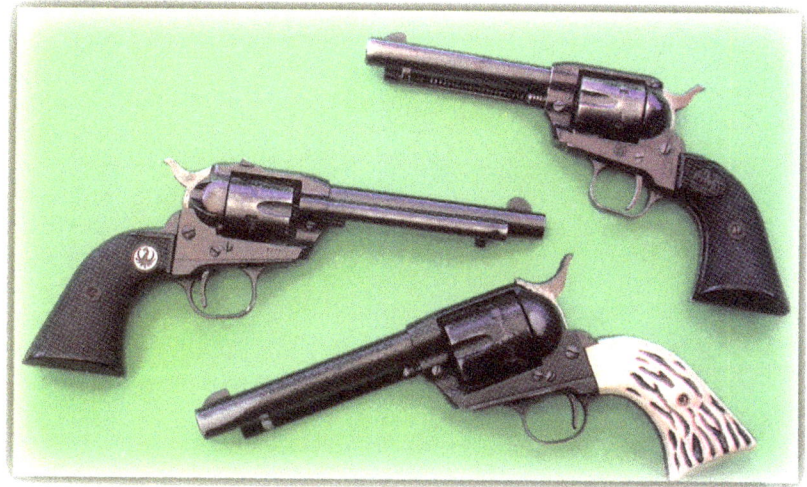

Both Colt with its .22 Scout and Great Western with its .22 Frontier tried to compete with the Ruger Single-Six. They could not.

which predated World War I, the Colt Single Action Army was in reality dead long before the funeral was held on the eve of World War II.

However, history does not always ride a straight freeway but rather has a habit of taking strange twists and turns. The single action sixgun may have been dead and buried in 1941 but it was not going to stay that way. Television, which started to appear in the late 1940s, was pretty widespread by the early 1950s. Our family was poor as poor could be, but by 1950 we had a black and white television sitting in the corner cranking out hour after hour of old B Western movies from the 1930s. The quality of both movies and TV was pretty mediocre, but nevertheless they created a demand for single action sixguns. Bill Ruger knew if he built a quality .22 semi-automatic pistol, it would sell. Now four years later he applied the same principle to the single action sixgun.

Ruger was savvy enough to bring out a sixgun that operated and felt like a Colt Single Action Army, but rather than chambering it for an expensive-to-shoot centerfire cartridge, he instead scaled down everything but the grip frame to .22 size. The grip frame was virtually identical to that of the Colt Single Action. Although the new Single-Six was a traditional single action with a flat loading gate that opened to reveal the cylinder chambers to insert cartridges and an ejector rod for shuckin' empties, the lockwork was redesigned to use coil springs, eliminating the breakage-prone flat springs of the Colt. The action was so strong that when a Single-Six was hooked up to a machine that continuously cocked and dry-fired the gun at a display at that year's NRA Show, the machine broke. The gun didn't. Bill Ruger now had a second winner on his hands.

During the 1920s and 1930s Elmer Keith had written several articles for the *American Rifleman* highlighting improved and custom single action sixguns. As Bill Ruger arrived at the Ruger Single-Six, he sent a letter to Keith telling him all about the new revolver and also how much Keith's articles had influenced him, especially "Sixgun Improvements," which appeared in June, 1932. Another article by Keith on long-range shooting shows a custom Colt Single Action Army bearing a striking resemblance to Ruger's soon-to-be Super Blackhawk.

That first Ruger .22 Single-Six was purchased with my own money as a teenager in those wonderful bygone days. As mentioned earlier, one only had to be 16 to purchase any firearm, and kids and guns were very rarely ever a problem. Those early days shooting that wonderful little single action .22 with the accompanying smell of Hoppe's #9 after each shooting session stirred deep

Taffin's oldest grandson, John Christopher, shooting the Bisley Model Single-Six.

Ruger .22s are made for kids of all ages: grandson Brian John, age nine years, shooting the Vaquero-styled Single-Six.

Single Action Sixguns | 113

Chapter 16 | The Ruger Single-Six

The Old Model Ruger .22 was offered with both short and long barrels as well as an auxiliary .22 Magnum cylinder.

emotions and sent me on the path to a lifelong enjoyment of single action sixguns. That .22 was the first Ruger single action I ever owned, but it was only the beginning. I feel I have grown up with Ruger sixguns. In fact, in the 1950s there was a very popular TV show entitled *You Are There* that treated historic events as if they were happening before the TV cameras with reporters interviewing famous characters from the past. With Ruger single actions I feel very much as if I have been there almost from the very beginning.

Ruger's .22 Single-Six joined my modest (now up to two) gun battery along with a plain black Lawrence #120 Keith holster and matching cartridge belt. I was in heaven with two great .22s and time to enjoy them. I would hate to count the number of jackrabbits and other varmints that have fallen to those .22s over the years, nor how many cans, rocks, and dirt clods have met their fate since 1956. An early advertisement for the Ruger Single-Six .22 featured a drawing of a hand holding a Single-Six superimposed over a rattlesnake. Shooters got the message: this was definitely an outdoorsman's sixgun.

Whether with fixed or adjustable sights, the .22 Single-Six has been the .22 by which all other revolvers have been judged for over 50 years. Extra cylinder is chambered in .22 Magnum.

The original .22 Single-Six would be produced from 1953 to 1962, at least officially. However, only 50 were produced in 1953, followed by more than 10,000 in 1954. By the time I purchased mine in 1956, the total production had reached well over 50,000. The early sixguns had a flat loading gate, a 5-1/2-inch barrel, a flat-top frame with the rear sight in a dovetail to allow for windage adjustment, and a Colt-style front sight. The sight picture presented by the Single-Six was actually better than that found on the Colt as the rear notch was a square matching up well with a non-tapered front sight. In 1957, the Single-Six received a real contoured loading

Looking at this early advertising for the Single-Six, there is no doubt this .22 was designed with the outdoorsman in mind.

In 2003, to celebrate the 50th Anniversary of the Ruger Single-Six, Ruger offered the New Model Anniversary .22, here shown with an original Flat-Gate Single-Six.

gate in place of the original flat gate. The original barrel length was soon joined by lengths of 4-5/8, 6-1/2, and 9-1/2 inches as well as convertible models with two cylinders chambered in 22 Long Rifle and 22 Winchester Rimfire Magnum.

In the late 1950s Ruger also produced some lightweight 4-5/8-inch Single-Sixes with alloy frames. Some had alloy cylinders while others were fitted with steel cylinders. An engraved Single-Six was also offered at the then-staggering price of $150.50. A wise man would have purchased as many as he could find. As far as I know none of these Single-Sixes in the first decade of production was fitted with adjustable sights. That would come in the next decade.

From 1963 to 1973 we have the second generation of Ruger Single-Sixes offered in both the original sight configuration, as well as the Super Single-Six with fully adjustable sights. Most of these were produced as convertible models and mostly with 5-1/2- and 6-1/2-inch barrel lengths. In addition to offering a .22 Single-Six with fully adjustable sights, Ruger also made another change that is either inconsequential or of great concern, depending upon one's viewpoint of what a single action sixgun grip frame should feel like. The first decade of Single-Sixes had for all practical purposes a grip frame that was a dead ringer for the Colt Single Action Army. This was one of its great assets. In 1963, someone in their infinite wisdom changed the grip frame ever so slightly, resulting in more knuckle room behind the trigger guard. For my hands and my shooting spirit I wish it had never been done.

Taffin's Granddaughter Laura Seals shooting the Ruger 32 Magnum Single-Six.

Elyse Panzella and Laura Seals, Taffin's granddaughters, after an enjoyable session shooting Rugers.

Single Action Sixguns | 115

Chapter 16 | The Ruger Single-Six

A 1950s .22 Single-Six with one the latest Single-Sixes, a stainless steel 32 Magnum.

The second generation, or Old Model, Single-Six would also last for one decade before being replaced by the New Model line of Ruger single actions. Until this time all single action revolvers were safe only when carried with the hammer down on an empty chamber. Some exceptions where cap and ball revolvers, including Ruger's Old Army, with a notch between cylinders allowing a safe resting place for the hammer even though the cylinder was fully loaded. All New Model Rugers are easily distinguished by a mainframe having two pins instead of three screws. In fact the Single-Sixes produced from 1953 to 1973 are often characterized as "Three Screw" Rugers with approximately one-half million being produced.

The New Model was, and is, safe to carry with a fully-loaded cylinder because the hammer never rests on the primer of the cartridge case. Instead, a transfer bar is fitted. When the hammer is cocked this bar slides into place between the hammer and the firing pin. Once the sixgun is fired, it retreats and the hammer no longer contacts the frame-mounted firing pin. I was one who was not happy at the time with this change in the standard single action. However, after more than 30 years of its being used I am convinced it has prevented countless numbers of negligent discharges. In the old days virtually everyone knew how a traditional single action revolver should be treated; today, too many folks simply would not take the time to learn. They can thank Bill Ruger for simplifying matters for them.

By 1974 Ruger New Model Single-Sixes received a new look with the addition of a stainless steel version. Whether the Ruger Single-Six is one of the original flat-gates, the contoured gate model, the Old Model, or New Model, or even if it is blue or stainless, Ruger Single-Sixes have provided a half-century, and well over one million examples, of the near perfect outdoorsman's .22. It was made for rough use with nary a whimper. Even those found with most of the finish gone still have the near indestructible action Ruger is known for.

In 1984, Ruger took another excellent step in chambering the Single-Six for the then-new 32 H&R Magnum. My early experiments with fully loaded 32 Magnums using jacketed hollowpoint bullets resulted in explosive results when shooting past-dated cans of split pea soup at 25 yards. The green spots on my red Bronco and also on myself proved to me this was no toy. Twenty years later, a third chambering would be offered in the Single-Six New Model: the 17 HMR, thus giving Single-Six shooters a very flat-shooting varmint load. The first two decades of Single-Six production resulted in one-half million sixguns, and this figure was doubled over the next two decades. In all probability total production of Single-Sixes is now somewhere around 1.5 million. I call that quite a success story and a real tribute to the vision of Bill Ruger.

Today Ruger offers both fixed-sight and adjustable-sight Single-Sixes with both the standard grip frame and the Bisley model style grip. New Model Ruger Single-Sixes do not have the same feel as the Old Model Single-Six. They also are not as smooth in operation, nor do they have the same Colt single action grip frame as they did until 1963. The Ruger Bisley model grip frame is actually a great improvement, especially on the hard-

The Ruger Single-Six is now also offered in 17 HMR.

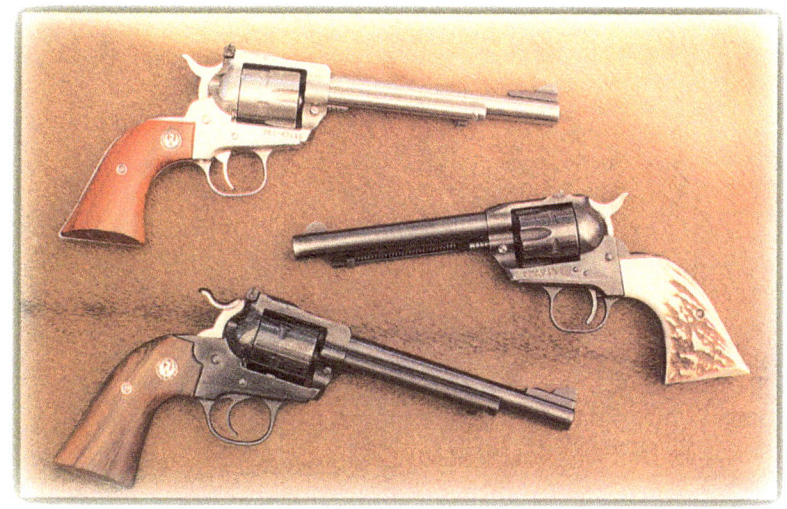

A half-century separates the original .22 Single-Six, center, from the currently-produced stainless steel Single-Six and the Bisley model Single-Six.

kicking centerfire models. The New Model .22s will shoot rings around my old Single-Six! They flat-out shoot good, exceptionally so.

Both of Ruger's .22 sixguns, the New Model Single-Six and the New Model Bisley, will do in a pinch for paper punching Bullseye style. I am not a Bullseye shooter by any stretch of the imagination. However, with both of these Single-Sixes, I can stand on my hind feet and keep all the shots in the black on a standard target at 25 yards.

With all the loads tested through both .22 Rugers at 25 yards, all the groups were 1-1/2 inches or less for five shots from a rest. They really go wild with Winchester's .22 offerings, with groups averaging 7/8 of an inch with Winchester's Power Points, SX, and Wildcat loads. This from a single action un-tuned and out of the box in my hands, using my original eyes. I wonder what someone who could really shoot would get from these little sixguns? My old Single-Six is a fine shooter; the New Models are simply better!

Someday my original Marlin Mountie and Single-Six will go to one of my grandsons and hopefully, the new .22 Marlin Model 39 and Ruger New Model Single-Sixes in my workin' gun battery will go to one of my grandkids' grandkids. I pray they will live in a world that will allow them the same enjoyment that I have had.

After the death of Tom Ruger, and thanks to the urgings of Terry Murbach, Bill Ruger commissioned 53 Shootists Bisley .22s made in stainless steel.

Selected Loads for the Ruger New Model .22 ingle-Six

	BISLEY MODEL 6-1/2"		STAINLESS STEEL 6-1/2"	
	MV	GROUP*	MV	GROUP*
CCI Blazer	986	1-1/2"	1065	1-1/4"
CCI MiniMag HP	993	1-1/4"	1019	1-1/8"
CCI SGB	959	1-1/8"	977	1-1/4"
CCI Stinger	1188	1-1/2"	1201	1-1/2"
Federal HP	984	1"	979	1-1/2"
Remington Yellow Jacket	1045	1-1/8"	1122	1-1/2"
Winchester PowerPoint	933	7/8"	1051	7/8"
Winchester SX	961	1"	999	7/8"
Winchester Wildcat	988	7/8"	972	7/8"

*Five of six shots at 25 yards.

Single Action Sixguns

–Chapter 17–

THE RUGER FLAT-TOP

The .357 Flat-Top Blackhawk was standardized with 4-5/8-inch and 6-1/2-inch barrels with the 10-inch length being very rare. Original stocks were checkered rubber and then changed to walnut.

Ruger did not remain with .22 production exclusively for very long. The Single-Six just begged to be made into a full-sized single action for the big bores of the time, the 44 Special and the 45 Colt. Ruger again showed his astuteness by passing over the big bores and offering what has been a most popular centerfire sixgun chambering for many decades, the 357 Magnum. By 1955, the Single-Six was scaled up to full size and had gained excellent adjustable sights and a flattening of the top of the frame that would give the revolver the nickname the Flat-Top. Elmer Keith reported at the time that the first Blackhawk would soon be offered in both 44 Special and 45 Colt. Other developments were happening that would change this.

"God Bless Bill Ruger for putting Magnum rounds in single action workin' guns!" I remember reading this quote in the middle '50s in an article in *GUNS* magazine. The piece was written by an old cowboy, trapper, ranger, etc., one Walter Rogers. This really impressed me as Rogers had carried Colt Single Actions all of his life, mainly a 4-3/4-inch 45 Colt Bisley model with a standard Single Action hammer. Now, in his later years, Ruger had given him a nearly perfect single action, the .357 Blackhawk. After packin' Colts for so many years, Rogers found tremendous improvements in the then-new big-bore single action Ruger. The Ruger had virtually unbreakable coil spring, and excellent adjustable sights made up of a Micro that set low in the wide flat top strap.

Ruger's 357 Magnum was announced while I was senior in high school and just one year before I purchased my .22 Single-Six. Just over 1700 were made that first year with a total production of over 43,000 by the time production ended. What a magnificent single action this was. I had yet to see one in 1955, but one of the outdoor magazines of the time carried a life-size picture of the new Blackhawk, which became the #1 pin-up on the sloping ceiling of my bedroom. It was the first thing I saw when I awoke and the last thing I saw before going to sleep. It would be two years before I would ever see the real thing.

To come up with the .357 Blackhawk, Ruger went to a full-size single action with a cylinder the same size as the Colt. However, instead of trying to replicate the Colt Single Action Army, Ruger enlarged and flattened the top strap and added a fully adjustable Micro rear sight

The original Ruger Flat-Tops, the .22 Single-Six of 1953, the .357 Blackhawk of 1955, and the .44 Blackhawk of 1956. Who could ask for anything more?

matched up with a front sight of the quick draw style on a ramp base. In doing so, Bill Ruger was tremendously influenced by the earlier writings of Elmer Keith. The same virtually unbreakable lockwork found in the .22 Single-Six was also present in the Blackhawk, and as with the Single-Six, the Blackhawk's grips were also Colt-style, that is, checkered black rubber.

The first Ruger Blackhawk arrived just in time to find its way into the pages of the 1955 edition of Elmer Keith's monumental work, *Sixguns*. Keith said, "When Ruger first mentioned bringing out his now famous Single Six, incorporating all coil springs and a new type rebounding firing pin, we urged him to bring out a larger version as to frame, barrel, and cylinder, for the most popular big cartridges, .357 mag, .44 Spl. and .45 Colt. We also criticized his .22 caliber Single Six, suggesting that the flat top be left a full flat top frame and the rear sight be fitted back at the extreme rear-end and adjustable for both windage and elevation.

"We recommended a sloping ramp-type front sight with its highest point near the muzzle to give maximum sight radius. We also asked for an improved thumb piece on the extractor rod, which we will get, and a wide Bisley-type hammer and wide trigger, not in view at this writing…. The first production, against our wishes, is to be in .357 caliber and we expect it will be sometime before he can get into production of larger calibers. For the shooter, be he plinker, peace officer, cow-poke or hunter, this new Ruger is a good well-made arm. Colt collectors may prefer the original old peacemaker but any shooter who wants to have first-class target sights combined in a really modern arm with all the improvements including the rebounding separate firing pin will find the new Ruger Blackhawk the finest single action revolver manufactured to date. Aside from the few minor improvements we have mentioned and which we will no doubt get in the final production run, it is the best commercially made gun we have yet tested in single action….

"The frame of this Ruger closely follows the design Harold Croft and myself dreamed up 30 years ago, except that the top strap is even thicker and heavier, and does not extend to the rear quite as far... We would have preferred a slightly larger frame and a cylinder a bit larger in diameter, especially for the .45 Colt cartridge, but this 357 Ruger is one honey of a gun and amply heavy for .357 and .44 Special and will give standard chamber wall thickness if Bill ever chambers it for the .45 Colt…. Bill Ruger has a far better single action than has ever come out of the Colt factory."

Skeeter Skelton was also a great fan of the Ruger .357 Blackhawk: "I recall a day in early 1956 when I saw my first one. That was when, with a few simple precautions, a man could display his guns in racks and on the walls of his house without serious fear of thievery. This one hung behind glass in a huge, peg board-walled gun room of Dewey Hicks, an Amarillo home builder and owner of possibly the largest collection of guns, especially antique handguns in that part of West Texas. . . . This new Ruger .357 looked good. It seemed an excellent idea to have an adjustable-sighted single action in the powerful chambering. . . . It looked and felt like a customized Colt, with a thick, wide flat topstrap, inset with the steel Micro rear sight. Its 4-5/8-inch barrel was somewhat muzzle heavy, partially due to its steel ejector rod housing, which was not changed to aluminum for years. I liked it very much. . . .

Chapter 17 | The Ruger Flat-Top

Ruger's 10-inch 357 and 44 Magnum Flat-Tops compared to Colt's 12-inch Buntline Special 45 Colt. Wyatt Earp may have preferred the latter, but sixgun hunters would favor the adjustable sights and magnum chamberings of the Blackhawks.

"Over the years I owned and used a succession of Ruger .357s with 4-5/8-and 6-1/2-inch barrels, taking a great deal of game up to javelina size with them. I bought one of the seldom seen .357 Flattop Blackhawks with a factory 10-inch barrel from a friend. He could shoot it very well but couldn't find a comfortable way to carry it. I had the barrel cut to 7-1/2 inches, which was never a standard factory length for the .357 Blackhawk, and had the nicest-carrying Ruger I've ever owned." (*Shooting Times*, March, 1977)

If ever a handgun was designed with the outdoorsman in mind, it was the Ruger .357 Blackhawk. These first centerfire sixguns from Ruger were virtually indestructible, fitted with rugged adjustable sights, carried an easy packin' 4-5/8-inch barrel, and were chambered in the most powerful cartridge available in 1955. I was in for a rude awakening the first time I fired the .357 Blackhawk. It was on a Sunday afternoon and I got belted twice. I had been used to shooting the .22 Single-Six by curling my little finger under the butt and resting on whatever was available. After one shot from the .357 Magnum and the ensuing sharp rap on my finger as the Blackhawk recoiled, I was immediately cured of that habit.

Ruger .357 and .44 Blackhawks are shown with some of the early advertising in the 1950s.

In those days there was no such thing as ear protectors – at least I never saw any – and the horrendous muzzle blast from the .357 penetrated all the way to my brain but apparently not far enough. My ears were still ringing on Thursday and yet I continued to practice unprotected sixgunning. I pay the price today with one dead ear and the other operating at about 25 percent. It would be at least 10 years before I started wearing ear protectors and I'm very fortunate today not to suffer from tinnitus. No firearm, except in an emergency or possibly a hunting situation, should ever be fired without ear protection.

My 4-5/8-inch .357 Blackhawk was a three-digit serial number example and certainly served me well. For my use I made myself a belt and holster; cast bullets over my long-suffering mother's stove, often splashing little pieces of lead on her refrigerator; and using 38 Special brass, assembled loads with 13.5 grains of Hercules 2400. My bullets of choice, both from Lyman molds, were the Elmer Keith-designed 168-gr. #358429 and Ray Thompson's gaschecked 156-gr. #358156. The latter has two crimping grooves, with the top groove normally used for 357 Magnum brass, and the bottom for 38 Special loads. I still use both bullets today. My bullets were molded one at a time in Lyman single cavity molds, and since 38 Special brass was easy to obtain at bargain basement prices, more often than not the Blackhawk was loaded with heavy 38 Specials. It was a great sixgun, and being the stupid teenager that I was, I showed my appreciation by selling it. Not once, but twice. I sold it, got it back, and sold it again. It is a miracle that any of us survive our too often brainless teenage years.

The standard Packin' Pistol barrel length was soon joined by the 6-1/2-inch barrel 357 Blackhawk and before the end of the 1950s, the rarest .357 Blackhawk appeared:

Ruger .357 Flat-Tops are excellent shooters.

the 10-incher. Several years ago at a local gun show I spotted a Flat-Top, as these original .357 Blackhawks are now called, in a batch of revolvers placed in somewhat of a pile on the table. As I started to remove some of the other sixguns so I could get to the one I really wanted to see, I soon realized the barrel stretched through most of that pile. What I had found was the seldom-seen 10-inch .357 Magnum Blackhawk mentioned by Skeeter. I wrote the check as quickly as I could, and then found that it was even rarer than I had imagined as it was one of only 50 of approximately 1000 10-inch .357 Blackhawks made with eight-groove rifling.

The finish was well worn, and the front sight was too low. It has now been fitted with a Patridge front sight of the proper height and re-blued. Had it been in excellent shape to begin with I would have left it alone, but this was a shooting sixgun, not a collector's piece. For some unknown reason, Ruger has never offered the .357 Blackhawk in the 7-1/2-inch length.

The 357 Magnum Blackhawk Flat-Top version has a special place in my heart for several reasons. It was the first new centerfire single action I had ever purchased. In between my Ruger Single-Six and the .357 Blackhawk came a beautiful 4-3/4-inch Colt Single Action Army, circa 1900, chambered in 38-40, but it was the .357 Blackhawk that not only really taught me to shoot but was also the main vehicle for my learning about reloading and bullet casting.

Meanwhile over at Smith & Wesson in 1955, engineers were working on chambering a new Magnum. For more than 30 years, Keith had been calling for his 44 Special loading to be offered commercially. The powers that be were afraid Keith's 44 Special load of a 250-grain bullet at 1200 feet per second would strain older sixguns, so they decided to build an entirely new gun for a new cartridge. Smith & Wesson and Remington teamed up to give us the 44 Magnum cartridge, a load that upped Keith's loading to an unprecedented 1500 feet per second.

The original 44 Magnum cartridge was more than Keith had envisioned and definitely more cartridge than Bill Ruger realized at the time. His company rechambered three .357 Blackhawks to the new 44 Magnum, fitted them with 4-5/8-, 5-1/2-, and 7-1/2-inch barrels, and displayed them at the NRA Show. Keith told Ruger that the cylinders and frames, the same size as those of the Colt Single Action, were too small for the 44 Magnum. Further testing proved him right. After one of the converted sixguns blew, Ruger lengthened the frame from 3.313" to 3.438" and increased the cylinder length from 1.604" to 1.749". The result in 1956 was the .44 Blackhawk.

In some parts of the country, the Ruger .44 actually hit the shelves before the Smith & Wesson 44 Magnum. That was in 1956 and the Smith & Wesson, beautifully finished and with a magnificently smooth action and trigger pull, sold for $140; the Ruger, not quite so nicely finished, sold for $96. With the advent of the new big-bore Smith & Wesson 44 Magnum, Ruger was able to jump on the project very quickly. The following story may or may not be true, but if it is not, it is one of those that should be:

The story goes that a Ruger employee found an empty 44 Magnum cartridge case in the dumpster behind Remington. (Maybe so, but what in the world was he doing rummaging through Remington's trash?) A more likely story is that one of Bill Ruger's friends from either Remington or Smith & Wesson secretly delivered a bag of a 44 Magnum brass to Bill Ruger one night. This story sounds more plausible, but then again it may also fall into the myth category. Anyhow, soon after Ruger got hold of a 44 Magnum case, the Ruger 44 Blackhawk was introduced.

It really doesn't get much better than this! Lyman's #429421 over 10.0 grains of Unique in a 7-1/2-inch .44 Blackhawk.

Single Action Sixguns | 121

Chapter 17 | The Ruger Single-Six

Most Ruger 44 Magnum Flat-Top Blackhawks are found with 6-1/2-inch barrels, but they are occasionally found with 10-inch and 7-1/2-inch barrels. All the 44 Magnums came with walnut stocks. The extra fancy grips on the 10-inch model really are factory grips.

Ruger never catalogued a short-barreled 44 Magnum Flat-Top, so Taffin made his own. Starting with a 6-1/2-inch Blackhawk, the barrel was cut to 4-3/4 inches and a stainless steel Old Army grip frame was added, fitted with Circassian walnut grips by Roy Fishpaw.

Made for rugged outdoor use and handgun hunting: Ruger's 7-1/2-inch Super Blackhawk with Flat-Top grip frame, and 7-1/2-inch 44 Magnum Blackhawk.

Skeeter Skelton was an early fan of the new Ruger .44 Blackhawk. "In 1960, I took a hiatus from law-enforcement to go into the cattle business. I foolishly sold many of my best guns. Still a trader, I dropped into Bud Maffett's gunshop in Clovis, New Mexico, and spied a standard model flattop Ruger 44 Magnum with an unusual 7 1/2-inch barrel. I have always preferred the early flattop Ruger to the more massive Super Blackhawk, so when Bud priced this one – the first I had seen with the longer than standard 6-1/2-inch barrel – at $50, I snapped it up. Although I owned several 44 Magnums of various types, this old flattop is still my favorite. I've taken a great deal of game with it and trust it implicitly." (*Shooting Times*, August, 1978)

I spent a lot of time, and money, in my local gunshop in those days so it was there that I found the first Ruger 44 Magnum Blackhawk in my area. It had a four-digit serial number, 6-1/2-inch barrel, and kicked like 44 mules all at once. Previously I had fired the S&W 44 Magnum and thought the recoil was bad. But it only kicked; the Ruger went well beyond the kick stage. Upon firing my first full-house load from the Ruger .44, the barrel was pointing skyward and the hammer dug a hole in the back of my hand that rapidly turned red, blood red. It took a lot of learning on my part to handle Ruger's first 44 Magnum, but it eventually became one of my favorites.

The original barrel was cut to 4-5/8 inches. I carried the gun for many years over many miles of desert, sagebrush, foothills, forest and mountains of Idaho in a George Lawrence #120 Keith holster. Later, when I needed that barrel for a 44 Special project, the Flat-Top 44 was sent back to Ruger and re-barreled to 7-1/2 inches as it remains today. I was also fortunate to find an original 7-1/2-inch Flat-Top .44 in the early 1970s, but instead of Skeeter's $50 price I had to go $147, which was still a tremendous bargain. At about the same time I also found a 10-inch .44 Flat-Top for the incredible price of $125.

Ruger's Flat-Top Blackhawks, as these original Magnums have come to be called, would be offered only for a relatively short time. The .357 Blackhawk, first offered with a 4-5/8-inch barrel, was soon joined by a 6-1/2-inch version and a very rare 10-inch length. It would be manufactured from 1955 to 1962. The 44 Magnum Blackhawk that arrived one year later would also be offered in two very rare versions with 7-1/2- and 10-inch barrel lengths. Its production also ended in 1962. Ruger collectors say there never was a 4-5/8-inch factory produced .44 Blackhawk, but Elmer Keith relates in *Sixguns* (1961, second edition) how he was presented with one in this short length by Bill Ruger in 1956.

The Blackhawk was an instant and ongoing success although the original Flat-Tops were made only until 1963. Production of the .357 Blackhawk reached approximately 43,000 units by the time it ceased in 1962. The 44 Magnum's 6-1/2-inch barrel length was the most common (approximately 27,000 produced); the 10-inch length was rare (1,500 produced) and the 7-1/2-inch rarer still (1,000). By 1957 I had acquired all three single actions offered by Ruger: the .22 Single-Six, the .357 Magnum Blackhawk, and the .44 Magnum Blackhawk. Had I never advanced past that point I would still have enjoyed nearly five decades of enjoyable sixgun shooting.

Selected Loads for the 4-5/8-inch Ruger .357 Flat-Top, 38 Special Brass

BULLET/LOAD	MV	5 SHOTS/25 YDS
RCBS #38-150 KT/11.0 gr. 2400	1111	2-1/4"
RCBS #38-150KT/13.5 gr. 2400	1370	2-1/2"
Lyman #358156/13.5 gr. 2400	1356	1-1/4"
Lyman #358156/13.5 gr. 2400	1329	1-3/4"

Selected Loads for the 6-1/2-inch Ruger .357 Flat-Top, 38 Special Brass

BULLET/LOAD	MV	5 SHOTS/25 YDS
RCBS #38-150 KT/11.0 gr. 2400	1111	2-1/4"
RCBS #38-150KT/13.5 gr. 2400	1419	2"
Lyman #358156/13.5 2400	1396	2-1/4"

Selected Loads for the 10-inch Ruger .357 Flat-Top, 38 Special Brass

BULLET/LOAD	MV	5 SHOTS/25 YDS
Lyman #358156/13.5 gr. 2400	1432	7/8"

Selected Loads for the 4-5/8-inch Ruger .357 Flat-Top, 357 Magnum Brass

BULLET/LOAD	MV	5 SHOTS/25 YDS
Lyman #358156 / 14.0 gr. 2400	1359	2-1/2"
Lyman #358156 / 15.0 gr. 2400	1386	1-5/8"
Lyman #358156 / 16.0 gr. 2400	1467	2-1/8"

Selected Loads for the 6-1/2-inch 44 Magnum Blackhawk Flat-Top

BULLET/LOAD	MV	5 SHOTS/25 YDS
Lyman #429421/10.0 gr. Unique	1192	1"
Lyman #429421/18.5 gr. 2400	1355	2-1/2"
BRP 295SWCGC/10.0 gr. Unique	1164	1-3/8"
RCBS #44-300SWC/16.3 gr. 2400	1155	2-1/4"

Chapter 17 | The Ruger Flat-Top

Selected Loads for the 7-1/2-inch 44 Magnum Blackhawk Flat-Top

BULLET/LOAD	MV	5 SHOTS/25 YDS
Lyman #429421/10.0 gr. Unique	1187	3/4"
Lyman #429421/18.5 gr. 2400	1389	2"
Lyman #429421/22.0 gr. 2400	1519	2-3/4"
Lyman #431244GC/22.0 gr. 2400	1528	2-1/2"
BRP 295SWCGC/10.0 gr. Unique	1170	1"
RCBS #44-300 SWC/16.3 gr. 2400	1164	1-3/8"

Selected Loads for the 10-inch 44 Magnum Blackhawk Flat-Top

BULLET/LOAD	MV	5 SHOTS/25 YDS
Lyman #429421/10.0 gr. Unique	1203	2-7/8"
BRP 295SWCGC/10.0 gr. Unique	1173	1-1/8"
RCBS #44-300 SWC/16.3 gr. 2400	1198	1-5/8"

Taffin with one of his favorite single action sixguns, a 7-1/2-inch Ruger Flat-Top .44 Blackhawk.

It has been 50 years since the first Ruger Blackhawk arrived, and I could easily spend the rest of my outdoor life with these easy-packin' and good-shootin' Ruger single actions. The loading of a 250- to 300-gr. hard-cast bullet over 10.0 grains of Unique is a tack-driver in most Ruger 44 Magnum single actions and at 1150 to 1200 feet per second in a long-barreled sixgun, it will certainly handle most sixgun chores quite nicely.

2005 marks the 50th anniversary of the original centerfire Ruger, the 357 Magnum. To celebrate this historic milestone Ruger is offering a Fiftieth Anniversary Model of the original Flat-Top. Since 1972 all Ruger 357 Blackhawks have been built on the same size frame as the 44 Magnum instead of the smaller frame used on the 357 from 1955 to 1972. Instead of taking the easy way and simply marking the current production 357 Blackhawk as a special anniversary model, Ruger is instead going back to their roots and downsizing the 357 Blackhawk to the original Colt SAA-size frame.

In addition to the smaller size, compared to current New Models, the Fiftieth Anniversary 357 Blackhawk will also have a flat-topped frame, Micro adjustable-rear sight, checkered hard rubber grips with a black eagle medallion, a grip frame identical to the original XR3 version, and a 4-5/8-inch length barrel just as on the original. The only basic difference between this Anniversary Model and the original will be the transfer bar action. Scheduled for production only in 2005, we can hope Ruger decides to make it a standard production model offered not only in .357 but also in 44 Special and in barrel lengths of 4-5/8, 5-1/2, and 7-1/2 inches; I would even like to see it offered in a 10-inch version.

–Chapter 18–

THE RUGER OLD MODEL

To help better control the felt recoil of the single action 44 Magnum, Bill Ruger reached back into history once again and fitted his 44 with a modified Colt First Dragoon grip frame. Both original Blackhawks had aluminum alloy Colt single action-size grip frames. The new Blackhawk, the Super Blackhawk of 1959, now had the longer grip frame with a square back trigger guard, the rear sight with the now familiar ears on both sides, and the 7-1/2-inch barrel as standard. The Super Blackhawk has been, and remains, one of the #1 handgun bargains of all time. It is excellent for hunting, and is one case where the purchaser actually gets more than he pays for.

The Ruger Super Blackhawk is one of the all-time classic single actions and is preferred for handgun hunting by three generations of shooters.

In the 1961 edition of Elmer Keith's *Sixguns*, Keith relates his part in the advent of the Super Blackhawk. Speaking of the original .44 Flat-Top, Keith says, "It proved to be a very fine single-action .44 Magnum, but I still was not satisfied. The new gun was very accurate and handled the big load perfectly, but the extractor button was inadequate, and the rear sight still wiggled around when raised out of its mortise. I filed down the front sight until it shot perfectly at 50 yards with the rear sight down in its mortise. The trigger guard also rapped the second finger for some shooters, so they kicked about this. Others want a larger and longer grip. I asked Bill to redesign the gun and bring it out with the old, square-back, second Dragoon grip, with ample length of grip and also ample room for the second figure behind the guard. Also I asked for a Bisley-type hammer spur sharply checkered and a wide-grooved trigger instead of the narrow, old Single Six trigger; also for a larger extractor button, and that the flutes of the cylinder be eliminated leaving it straight sided and thus stronger.

In 1959 the Ruger .44 Magnum Super Blackhawk was offered as an improvement to the .44 Flat-Top Blackhawk. Both are excellent hunting handguns especially with 7-1/2-inch barrels. Leather is by Taffin and Bianchi.

"He sent me the first prototype, and it was a great improvement over any single-action cartridge gun that I had ever seen or used and we took it into elk country that fall. It accounted for four elk with clean kills. The barrel was 7-1/2" and he had greatly improved the rear sight by extending the top of the frame in a flange on both sides of the rear sight so it could not move sideways when raised. The hammer was Bisley-type all right, but needed sharper checkering and also needed to be cut down deeper just in front of the knurled or checked portion.

Single Action Sixguns | 125

Chapter 18 | The Ruger Old Model

A half-century of 44 Magnum Blackhawks from Ruger is represented by the Flat-Top, the Super Blackhawk, and the Hunter Model.

"The trigger and grip were perfect and the heavy unfluted cylinder was another great improvement…. This second prototype I have is in every respect by far the finest single-action sixgun I have ever owned. It is wonderfully accurate and handles any and all factory loads perfectly, as well as having a cylinder of ample length for my handloads, and is one of the most comfortable .44 Magnums to fire I have ever used. I wanted to name it the Dragoon Ruger, but Bill has called it the Super Blackhawk, in my opinion a helluva name for a fine gun of this type and caliber."

Skeeter Skelton saw it differently: "The Super Blackhawk .44, coming along in 1959, is the most finally finished of any Ruger handgun. It replaces the standard, alloy grip frame with one of steel – an idea I like. The Super was the first Ruger sixgun to feature raised shoulders on the top strap to protect the rear sight when it is fully elevated – another well-considered change and one that has since been adopted on all Ruger single actions with adjustable sights.

"I have always found the old Colt single action grip, a carryover from the 1851 Navy, to be more comfortable than that of any other handgun. The original .357 and .44 Blackhawks were exactly the same shape, and the current Ruger production which comes with a grip sprung farther to the rear, leaving more room between the front strap and trigger guard, is no improvement for my hand.

"The square back trigger guard on the Super Blackhawk was ill-advised and is a design that was discarded by Colt more than a hundred years ago. Since its lower rear corner protrudes more to the rear than a guard of standard, rounded proportions would, I failed to understand the claims that it is less likely to rap knuckles in recoil.

"The wide trigger of the Super is a definite aid in controlling let-off. The low, wide hammer spur, for me, manipulates less easily than the old longhorn type that copies the Colt. The unfluted cylinder of the Super adds recoil-dampening weight, and is said to be stronger

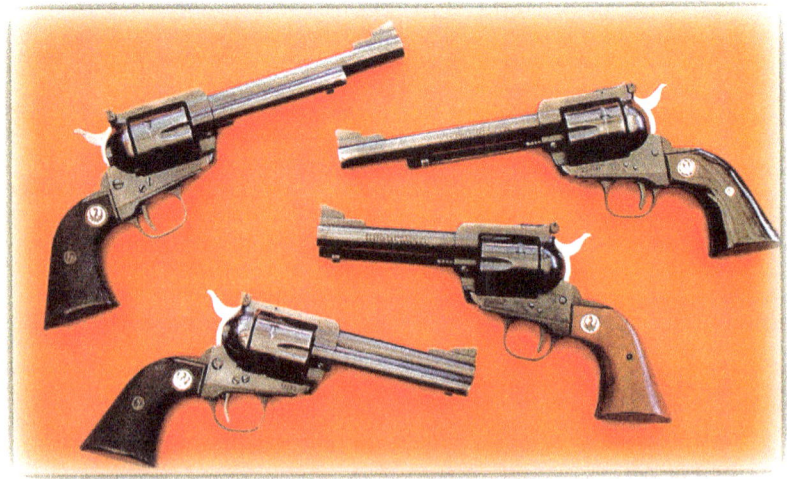

Both the Flat-Top 357 Blackhawk and the Old Model Blackhawk were offered with 4-5/8-inch and 6-1/2-inch barrels. The Old Models on the right no longer have the flat top frame nor is the grip frame the same size and shape as that of the Colt Single Action.

than the older-fluted style, but my standard .44, now a discontinued model, has digested thousands of the heaviest of loads without a whimper, and is noticeably more comfortable to pack around than my Super.

"Yep, I have both, keeping this Super model because of its prestige value. But I prefer to carry the obsolete standard .44 Blackhawk, and would be the first customer for an all steel, fancy finished renovation of this good gun." (*Shooting Times*, March 1969)

I am more inclined to agree with Skeeter than with Elmer. The Dragoon-style square-backed trigger guard of the Super Blackhawk nails the knuckle of the middle finger on my shooting hand. Neither do I accept the passing of the Colt-style grip frame of the original Single-Six and Flat-Tops. For me at least, with 250- to 260-gr. bullets at muzzle velocities of 1100 to 1200, possibly 1250, fps, the old Single Action Army grip frame remains the best. I have searched gun shows and been contacted by readers with the original XR3 grip frames for sale. These have been installed on several Old Model Rugers that came with the "improved" XR3-RED grip frame. Two extra XR3 grip frames complete with grips now reside in my parts box awaiting attachment to the next Old Model sixgun. With heavier loads, the answer again for me personally is neither the Super Blackhawk nor the "the improved" Old Model grip frame, but rather the Bisley Model which appeared in the mid-1980s.

In 1962, the Flat-Top Blackhawks were phased out and what is now known as the Old Model Rugers arrived. The 44 Magnum Blackhawk disappeared altogether. Even though its place had basically been taken three years earlier by the Super Blackhawk, they were both produced side-by-side until 1962. Two major changes occurred with a switch from the Flat-Top to the Old Model Rugers. The top strap received the same protective ears around the rear sight as the Super Blackhawk and, as mentioned, the grip frame was changed to allow more room between the back of the trigger guard and the front strap. No more Colt Single Action Army grip frame feel. No more Flat-Top profile. The steel ejector housing of the Flat-Tops was now changed to alloy on the Old Models. Such is progress.

The .44 Blackhawk was gone, but the 357 Magnum (4-5/8- and 6-1/2-inch barrels) was soon joined by the then-new 41 Magnum (4-5/8- and 6-1/2-inch barrels) and 30 Carbine (7-1/2-inch barrel). Then one hot summer day while attending graduate school in Montana I wandered into a gun shop and found a brand-new Ruger Blackhawk, the first chambered in 45 Colt. For the first time we now had a sixgun strong enough

Ruger .357 Blackhawks such as the Old Models are the top choice for thousands of single action shooters.

Changes in top strap profile can easily be seen when comparing this pair of Old Model .357 Blackhawks to the Flat-Top version at the bottom.

The 45 Colt literally became a new cartridge in the early 1970s with the introduction of the 7-1/2-inch Ruger Old Model Blackhawk in 45 Colt.

Chapter 18 | The Ruger Old Model

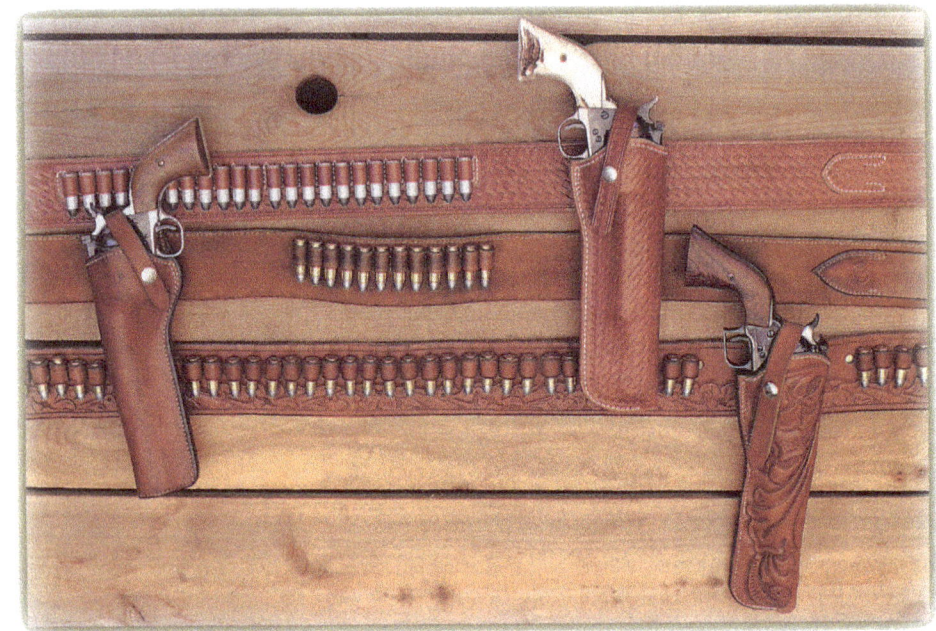

Excellent sixgun/leather combinations for handgun hunting: Old Model 45 Colt and Flat-Top 44 Magnums in leather by Lawrence, Bianchi, and Taffin.

Old Model Rugers with 4-5/8-inch barrels, whether the ivory stocked 45 Colt or the 41 Magnum with stag grips, make excellent perfect Packin' Pistol candidates.

Ruger's .45 Blackhawk is capable of handling heavier loads than the Colt New Frontier 45 Colt.

to at least start to explore the real potential of the then nearly 100-year-old 45 Colt cartridge. For my use I settled on a load for the 7-1/2-inch 45 Colt Blackhawk using a 300-gr. hard-cast bullet over 21.5 gr. of either H110 or WW296 for an even 1200 fps. A new era in big-bore sixgunning had arrived.

The 41 Magnum arrived on the scene in 1964 and the Old Model Blackhawk was soon chambered in the new Magnum caliber. While only two centerfire calibers, the 357 and 44 Magnums, had been produced in the Flat-Top, the Old Model Ruger Single Actions would be available in 357 Magnum, 30 Carbine, 41 Magnum, and finally just a couple of years before the series ended in 1973, the 45 Colt. Some dual cylinder models were available in 357/9MM and 45 Colt/45 ACP. The 357 Magnum and 41 Magnums, strangely enough, were manufactured only with 4-5/8- and 6-1/2-inch barrel lengths, while the 30 Carbine and 45 Colt came with the more desirable, at least to this sixgunner, 7-1/2-inch barrel. The 45 Colt was also offered with the shorter 4-5/8-inch barrel length.

Ruger's 41 Magnum single action sixguns were very scarce for many years with only one being available, the Ruger Blackhawk. Anyone ever owning more than two sixguns dreams of building that near-perfect sixgun. A few years back I located a new Old Model .41 Ruger with a 4-5/8-inch barrel at a local gunshow at a bargain price. It shot well so a Stainless Old Army grip frame that had been in my parts box for more than a decade was fitted to it along with my last blued steel ejector rod

Ruger's .45 Blackhawk Convertible allows the shooter to use 45 Colt or 45 ACP ammunition simply by changing cylinders.

housing. Then it went off the Roy Fishpaw for a pair of his Circassian walnut grips that are guaranteed to make your mouth water. The extra weight of the steel parts helped reduce felt recoil; the grips made it handle better as well as look better. The little .41 single action will handle just about any situation short of the big bears.

Ruger did what Colt would not do and brought out a modern .45 single action. These guns will take much heavier loads than the ancient Colt design but some have overdone it. It is not a 44 Magnum. And with its light weight, as compared to a Colt single action, it is a real kicker with heavier loads.

The Ruger .45 Blackhawk was the first 45 Colt that could utilize the case capacity of the 45 Colt cartridge efficiently. And it is at its best with the big 300-gr. bullets from BRP, NEI, or RCBS. Again, it is not a 44 Magnum. The .44 will easily do 1300 to 1400 feet per second with 300-gr. bullets; the 45 Colt is better suited to 1100 to 1200 fps with the same weight bullets.

Selected Loads for the 7-1/2-inch 45 Colt Old Model Blackhawk

BULLET/LOAD	MV	5 SHOTS/25 YDS.
Lyman #454424/20.0 gr. H4227	1086	1-1/4"
Lyman #454424/18.5 gr. 2400	1255	1-3/4"
BRP 295SWCGC/21.5 gr. WW296	1245	1-1/2"

Selected Loads for the 4-5/8-inch 41 Magnum Old Model Blackhawk

BULLET/LOAD	MV	5 SHOTS/25 YDS.
Lyman #410459/19.5 gr. 2400	1472	1-7/8"
Lyman #410459/7.0 gr. WW231	1023	1-3/8"

The .44 Super Blackhawk is a natural for hunting and general outdoor use. It is very popular in the mountains and desert areas as it is virtually indestructible when used with common sense. The standard barrel length for the Old Model Super Blackhawk is 7-1/2-inch with a very few being made in 6-1/2-inch (leftover .44 Blackhawk barrels?) and two being made in the 10-inch length.

Selected Loads for the 7-1/2-inch Old Model Super Blackhawk

BULLET/LOAD	MV	5 SHOTS/25 YDS.
Lyman #429421/10.0 gr. Unique	1233	1-3/4"
Lyman #429421/18.5 gr. 2400	1382	1-3/4"
BRP 295SWCGC/10.0 gr. Unique	1183	1-1/2"
RCBS #44-300 SWC/16.3 GR. 2400	1199	1-3/4"

–Chapter 19–

THE RUGER NEW MODEL

Ruger 44 Magnum Packin' Pistols include, from the top, Mag-Na-Port custom Super Blackhawk, stainless-steel New Model, and custom Flat-Top, all with 4-5/8-inch barrels.

The Ruger .357 Blackhawk has been offered in three versions (from left): the original Flat-Top, 1955; the Old Model, 1963; and the New Model, 1973.

The decade of the 1950s was tremendously important as far as sixguns were concerned. From Colt came the 357 Magnum Python (1955) and the reintroduction of the Colt Single Action Army (1956). Smith & Wesson gave the world the 1950 and 1955 Target Models, the Highway Patrolman (1954), the Combat Magnum (1955), and in 1956, the 44 Magnum. The relatively new company of Sturm, Ruger was not to be outdone, introducing four single action sixguns: the .22 Single-Six (1953), the .357 Blackhawk (1955), the .44 Blackhawk (1956), and their crowning glory in 1959, the 44 Magnum Super Blackhawk.

We were still an innocent society in the 1950s. Music was still music, cars still looked like cars should, movies did not have to be rated, and the average person still felt he was in control. Then came the 1960s and everything turned upside down and radicals took charge.

By the 1970s we were ruled by trial lawyers who combined with individuals who had performed stupid acts of negligence, but it was no longer their fault as personal responsibility went out the window. The situation remains the same today, only worse.

Ruger knew something had to be done to head off what should have been worthless lawsuits, which had turned instead into cash cows for trial lawyers and "victims." The Old Model Ruger Blackhawk had lasted only one decade when they were replaced with the New Models with a transfer bar safety in 1973. Prior to this, all single actions of the Colt-style lockwork could be carried safely only if the hammer were allowed to rest on an empty chamber. Now with the New Model Rugers, a single action sixgun could be safely carried with all chambers loaded. At the time, I did not like to see the old guns replaced and I still look for the old-style sixguns in gun shops and gun shows. However, in retrospect I can see the transfer bar has prevented perhaps an innumerable number of negligent discharges.

130   Part 4

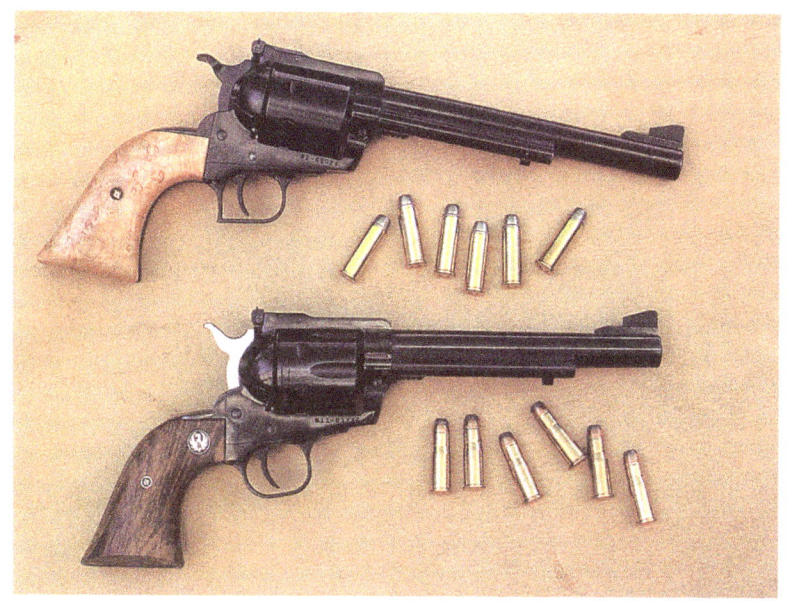

The Ruger Super Blackhawk became the New Model in 1973, while the special run New Model 38-40 was offered only in 1990.

Our resident Ruger single action experts, Elmer Keith and Skeeter Skelton, saw things through different eyes. Keith writing in *Guns & Ammo* in October, 1973 had particular praise for the New Model Super Blackhawk. "The action is a safe one and a great improvement over all the older Ruger and Colt single-actions…. All told, I consider this New Model Super Blackhawk one of the best-engineered and safest single-action sixguns ever produced."

Skeeter Skelton was also lavish in his praise:

"Later Bill Ruger abandoned the Blackhawk's excellent, time-tried, well-loved design and in doing so came up with what is undoubtedly the safest, most rugged single action made to date. Called the New Model Blackhawk, it was first introduced in .22 caliber in 1972, with the .357 Blackhawk following in 1973. Externally the new models are virtually indistinguishable from their earlier counterparts, but the internal mechanisms are vastly altered….

"Fully loaded with six rounds, with the hammer down over a live round, this revolver cannot be made to discharge by the heaviest of blows on the hammer spur. The changes are due to an entirely new locking system and incorporated trigger-actuated transfer bar…. Some users, veterans of the old-style locking system, have had to make a conscious effort to accustom themselves to the new manner of loading. It takes only a little practice in the beginning and is no problem that all. And it does allow you that one extra shot." (*Shooting Times*, March, 1977)

Up until the advent of the New Model Ruger, all single actions were handled the same way. The hammer was put on half cock, the loading gate was opened, and the cylinder could be rotated to allow removal of fired cartridge cases and the insertion of five new rounds. I was taught in 1956 to load one round, skip the next chamber, load four more rounds, carefully cock the hammer all the way back, and then also carefully let the hammer down on an empty chamber. This all changed with the coming of the New Model. It had no half cock on the hammer. To load or unload, the loading gate is opened, allowing the cylinder to rotate while the hammer remained in place fully forward. Once the cylinder was loaded, the loading gate was closed, and the New Model was safe to carry fully loaded with six rounds.

With the coming of the New Models, the 357 Magnum was now chambered in the full .44-size frame instead of the Colt Single Action-size frame of the Flat-Tops and Old Models. In 1974, stainless-steel Blackhawks began to appear beginning with the best-selling 357 Magnum. When long-range silhouetting spread across the country in the late 1970s and early

Tough sixguns for everyday use are Ruger's New Model Packin' Pistols including stainless-steel Blackhawks in 357 Magnum, 44 Magnum, and 45 Colt.

Single Action Sixguns | 131

Chapter 19 | The Ruger New Model

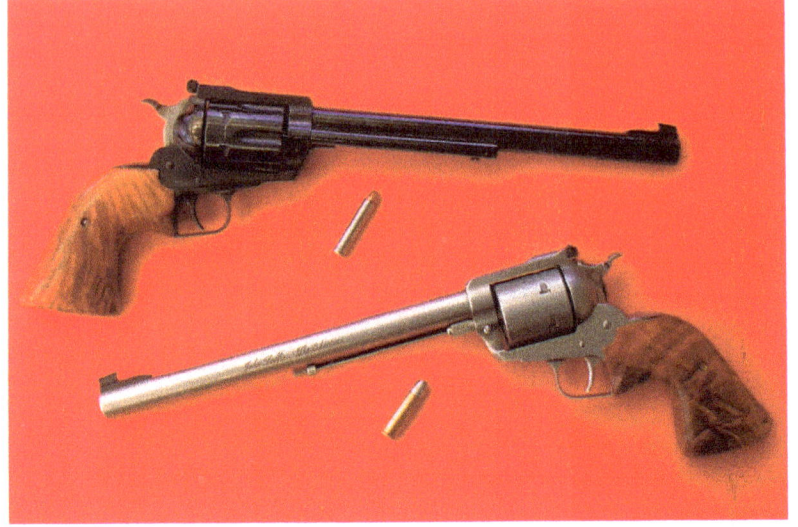

Two of the finest long-range Ruger single action sixguns are the 10-1/2-inch 357 Maximum, top, and 10-1/2-inch stainless-steel 44 Magnum, bottom. Custom stocks are by BluMagnum.

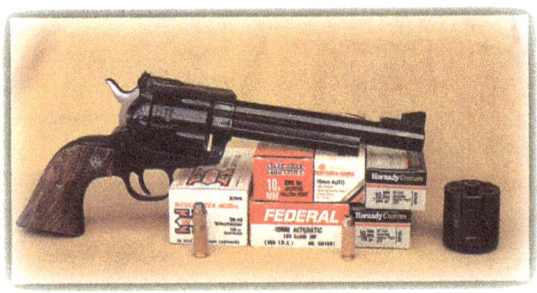

The Ruger New Model 38-40/10mm Convertible, a Buckeye Sports Limited Edition in 1990, has proven to be exceptionally accurate in both chamberings.

High on the list of great shooting 38-40s is this limited edition Ruger New Model fitted with a Belt Mountain base pin, stainless-steel Vaquero grip frame, and red stag stocks by Roger Warmuskerken.

1980s, Ruger answered the call for sixguns better suited for knocking over long-range steel in several ways. First came the 10-1/2-inch 44 Magnum Super Blackhawk, which became an early single action favorite with the long-rangers. Both my wife and I used this model in revolver category for several years. When the stainless-steel version appeared, I no longer needed to hold on to the blued versions, so they became custom sixguns. One is now a custom five-shot 45 Colt by Jim Stroh and the other a six-shot 44 Magnum by David Clements. Both wear 5-1/2-inch barrels and Bisley Model grip frames, hammers, and triggers.

The 10-1/2-inch stainless steel New Model Super Blackhawk is certainly one of the most accurate and easy shooting 44 Magnums I have ever encountered. The combination of the long barrel and BluMagnum walnut stocks that fill in behind the trigger guard help greatly to tame the powerful cartridge. I think enough of mine that I had Gary Reeder fancy it up a might and also inscribe the barrel in script with "John Taffin, The Shootists." I expect to keep it a long time and then pass it on to one of the grandkids.

A second sixgun for long-range silhouetters was the 357 Maximum. For this gun, the Super Blackhawk frame and cylinder were both lengthened to accept a cartridge .30" longer than the standard .357 Magnum. When loaded properly, that is, with 180- to 200-gr. bullets at 357 Magnum muzzle velocities, it was superbly accurate with plenty of knockdown power on stubborn rams. Those who did not understand it tried to turn it into a "357 Swift" with lighter bullets at higher velocities and then blamed the gun when it would not cooperate. Top straps eroded when used with the wrong ammunition, light jacketed bullets actually came apart, and some writers who did not understand the concept served to bring about its demise. It is unfortunate that such a grand sixgun died because of a lack of understanding.

Selected Loads for the 10-1/2-inch Stainless Steel New Model Super Blackhawk

BULLET/LOAD	MV	5 SHOTS/25 YDS.
Lyman #429421/10.0 gr. Unique	1264	1-1/2"
Lyman #429421/18.5 gr. 2400	1470	1"
BRP 295SWCGC/21.5 gr. WW296	1471	1"

The Super Blackhawk has always been a great favorite with big game hunters, and remained so with the New Model version, perhaps even more so. New calibers came with the New Model Blackhawk design. In addition to the calibers of the Old Model, Ruger now brought out special editions in 30 Carbine/32 Magnum/32-20; 38-40/10MM; 44 Magnum/44-40 to name some of recent years. The Super Blackhawk is now offered in short barrel lengths with standard Blackhawk steel grip frames.

Ruger single actions are not perfect. Most need the actions slicked up and the trigger pulls lightened. Economics and liability both preclude the offering of super-smooth actions and 3-lb. trigger pulls. One simple trick that works on the New Models is to remove one leg of the trigger spring from its pin on the grip frame to lighten the trigger pull considerably. Simply remove the grip and pop off one leg with a small screwdriver.

Ruger offers a conversion of all of their Old Model designs to the new transfer bar safety at no charge. All of the old parts are returned with the conversion on each customer's gun. This is a desired change for old sixguns with worn parts or those that may be handled by shooters who are not familiar with the safety problems of the old style action. It is not generally known, but Ruger will also reblue older Rugers at the same time for a very reasonable price. I've had two .357s done and the blue jobs are better than those on the new guns. They also refinish the aluminum grip frames at the same time.

It may have been old-time sixgunner Walter Rogers who first said "Bless Bill Ruger for putting Magnum calibers in real workin' sixguns" in print but he has been joined by thousands of shooters over the last five decades who have had the same feeling. Bill Ruger caught the mood of sixgunners in 1953, and Ruger has continued to offer "real workin' sixguns" ever since.

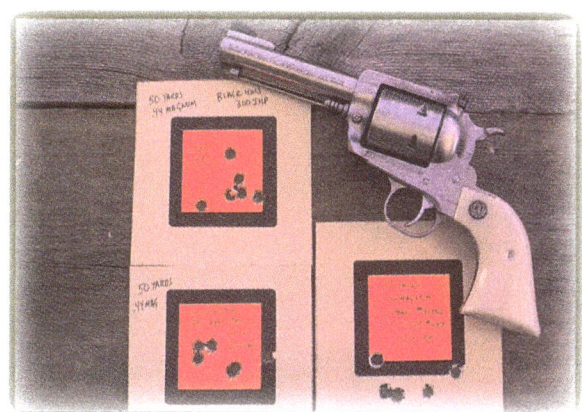

Ruger 4-5/8-inch stainless-steel New Model Blackhawks are all excellent shooters whether in 44 Magnum, or . . .

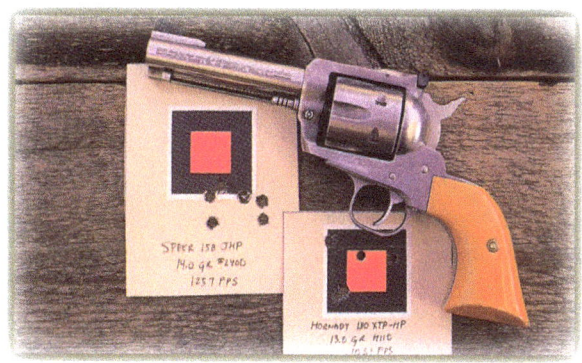

357 Magnum, or . . .

45 Colt.

Single Action Sixguns

–Chapter 20–

THE RUGER BISLEY MODEL

Just before the turn of the nineteenth century into the twentieth, target shooting had become quite popular using both Colt and Smith & Wesson single action sixguns. In 1895, to accommodate the paper punchers, Colt modified the grip frame of their standard Single Action Army to produce a target version known as the Bisley model. (See Chapter 7.) The grip frame was much longer and came up higher in the back and also behind the trigger guard to give a completely different feel; in fact, it wasn't so much a gunfighter grip as it was a more secure and deliberate feeling target grip. Ninety years later, Ruger set out to perform the same modification on their Super Blackhawk.

Ruger's Bisley model grip frame is not a copy of the Colt Bisley grip frame. The Ruger Bisley grip frame does not come up as high behind the trigger guard and the front strap is much straighter, avoiding the ladle shape of the Colt. The result is a grip frame that actually handles recoil much better than either a standard single action grip or the original Colt Bisley model grip frame. This is what Keith hoped to achieve with his grip shape back in the 1920s and has been carried out to near perfection by Ruger.

When Elmer Keith designed his version of the perfect sixgun in the late 1920s he combined the front strap of a standard Colt Single Action with a modified backstrap from the Bisley. His goal was to maintain the excellent feel of the Colt grip as to the area of the front strap and behind the trigger guard while also raising the backstrap higher to better control felt recoil and prevent the sixgun from rotating backwards in the hand when using heavy loads. The result was the #5 SAA. (See Chapter 8.)

When Bill Ruger wisely decided to offer a Bisley grip frame on his Super Blackhawk, he did not use either the original Colt style or the Keith but rather came up with a marvel of engineering that makes it possible to control the heaviest loads practical in a sixgun. In fact, its use is absolutely necessary to even come close to handling some loads such as the 500 Maximum that are way beyond practicality in a sixgun.

When Ruger brought out their Bisley model in 1985, they labeled it as a target version of the Super Blackhawk. Instead of using target loads, most Bisley fanciers go to the opposite extreme, using hard-cast bullets at high-end velocities. Without the Bisley grip frame, most of us could not handle these heavy loads.

Ruger's 44 Magnum single action sixguns evolved over three decades beginning with the .44 Blackhawk in 1956, right; the Super Blackhawk, 1959, center; and the Bisley Model, left, in 1985.

I am one who has never liked the Super Blackhawk grip frame or the Old Model Ruger grip frame (XR3-RED), also found on the New Models, as much as the original Colt SAA style found on the Ruger Flat-Tops (XR3). I was therefore happy to see the introduction of the Bisley Ruger, as this grip frame is near perfect for my hand. To me it feels much like the Freedom Arms single action grip and, although it's a bit larger, much like the original Keith #5 SAA grip that is also found on the Texas Longhorn Arms Improved Number Five. One thing about the Bisley grip, there seems to be no middle of the road: a shooter either loves it or hates it. I definitely like the Bisley grip frame. It changes the felt recoil for me and avoids the knuckle-dusting of the Super Blackhawk frame. I do get pinched on the trigger finger by the tip of the radically curved trigger, but this can easily be taken care of by shortening and straightening the trigger.

Custom gunsmiths have adopted the Bisley Ruger as the best candidate for conversions to their really hard-kickin' five-shot single action Rugers chambered in 475 and 500 Linebaugh. The frame size of the Bisley is the same as that of the Blackhawk or Super Blackhawk, but the grip frame handles the recoil of the big cartridges much better than the others. I know I could not even come close to handling the felt recoil of either the 500 Linebaugh or the 445 SuperMag in a single action sixgun without the Bisley Model grip frame.

When the Bisley Model arrived in 1985 it was greeted as both an improvement and a throwback that should never have been. One gun writer called it the solution to a problem that never existed, while another one called it the best single action grip ever devised and the only one to use for heavy recoiling sixguns. I decided to see for myself by using three 7-1/2-inch 45 Colt Rugers, all with steel grip frames. One was the new Bisley. Another was a New Model fitted with the Super Blackhawk grip frame. The third was an Old Model with an Old Army stainless steel grip frame. All were equipped with smooth wood grips and all were fired with the same load, Lyman's #454424 Keith bullet over 21.5 grains of 2400. This load in 45 Colt duplicates the 44 Magnum and is for use only in heavy-framed 45 Colt sixguns such as the Ruger or Freedom Arms Model 83.

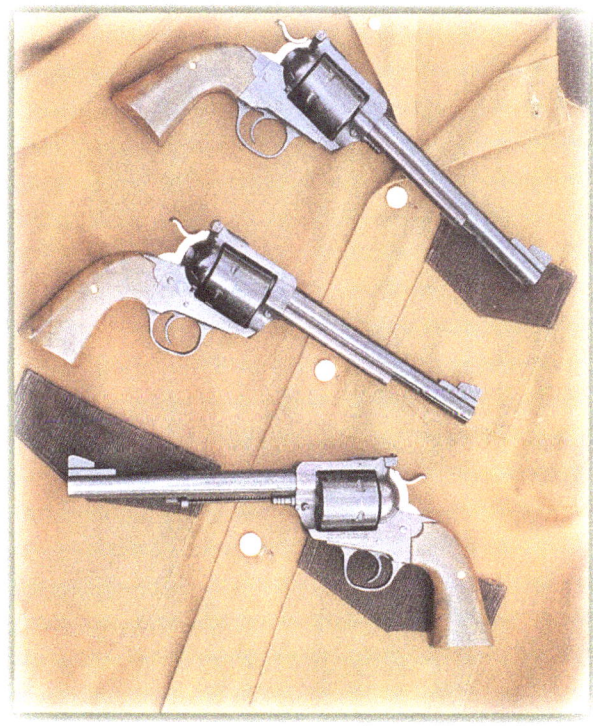

Over the past 20 years the Bisley Model has been offered in the big-bore chamberings of 45 Colt, 44 Magnum, and 41 Magnum. Custom stocks are by Charles Able.

Single Action Sixguns | 135

Chapter 20 | The Ruger Bisley Model

The Bisley Model 357 Magnum does an excellent job of reducing felt recoil even with the heaviest Magnum loads.

Muzzle velocity of the Old Model clocked out at 1430 fps and the top of my trigger finger was rapped solidly as the sixgun came back in recoil. The New Model Super Blackhawk chronographed at 1398 fps and this time rapped me solidly both in the palm and on the knuckle. The Bisley's velocity figure was slightly slower at 1380 fps with the felt recoil being a heavy push in the palm of my hand. There is no doubt in my mind the Bisley grip frame does the best job of absorbing recoil of the three Ruger grip frames tested. However, a new problem arose as the testing proceeded with heavy loads above 1200 fps: my trigger finger starting getting rapped on the bottom. The curved tip of the Bisley trigger was catching the bottom of my trigger finger and actually bruised it during a long session of firing heavy loads. As mentioned, this can easily be corrected by straightening the overly curved trigger. A person with a less fleshy trigger finger should have no problem that all.

Ruger's Bisley Model 41 Magnum is a top choice for deer hunting; Taffin took this Texas whitetail buck using Lyman's 220-gr. #410459KT and 19.5 grains of 2400.

I quickly made two changes to the Bisley .45. I do not like aluminum ejector rod housings or warning labels on barrels. The alloy housing was replaced with a steel version and the barrel was replaced with a pre-warning 7-1/2-inch New Model 45 Colt barrel. Finally the grip frame, as well as subsequent grip frames from 357 Magnum, 41 Magnum, and 44 Magnum Bisleys, were all shipped to Charles Able to be fitted with fancy walnut stocks. To this day the Bisley is cataloged only with a 7-1/2-inch barrel and offered in 45 Colt, 357 Magnum, and 44 Magnum, but only occasionally and sparingly in 41 Magnum. Special small quantity runs have also been offered through Ruger distributors in stainless steel with 5-1/2-inch barrels and chambered in 45 Colt, 44 Magnum, and 41 Magnum. The Single-Six framed Bisley has been offered with fixed sights in both a 22 Long Rifle/22 Magnum and a 32 Magnum version.

The Ruger Bisleys have proven themselves to be well built, strong, nice-shooting sixguns. In fact these revolvers seem to be put together with more care than normal. I purchased two Bisleys when they first came out, one in 45 Colt and the other in 41 Magnum. One was purchased locally and the other through a distributor. The barrel/cylinder gaps on them are .002" and .003" respectively; two subsequent Bisleys in 44 Magnum and 357 Magnum go .001" and .002". This is exceptional for revolvers in the Bisley price range.

The 357 Ruger Bisley is about as comfortable a shooting 357 Magnum as one is likely to encounter. Many sixgunners are bothered by recoil even in 357s and this sixgun will be of tremendous help for them. I see no point in anyone trying to shoot any sixgun that is more powerful than they can handle, and if the bottom line is a .357, this one can be loaded heavily and still not bother anyone. For nearly 50 years my favorite standard weight cast bullet for the 357 Magnum has been the Lyman #358156 gas check designed by Ray Thompson. This is an excellent performer in the .357 Bisley over 15.5 grains of 2400 for a muzzle velocity of 1587 fps, a figure that is no doubt aided by the tight barrel/cylinder gap.

The 41 Magnum is a grand cartridge but has never had much respect except from true connoisseurs. Ruger began chambering the 41 Magnum in their Old Model Blackhawk in 1964 and carried it over to the New Model in 1973 with 4-5/8- and 6-1/2-inch barrel lengths. For some reason it was never offered with a 7-1/2-inch barrel, the length I prefer for most shooting, hunting, and long-range use. This situation was corrected in the Bisley and results in the 41 Magnum's really coming alive. I have found it to be exceptionally flat shooting and accurate out to several hundred yards. The 41 Magnum Bisley has become a real favorite. I especially like the way this sixgun shoots with Lyman's #410459 220 grain cast bullet over 19.5 grains of 2400. Velocity is around 1500 fps. While the 41 has never been as popular as its bigger brother, it is a fine cartridge in its own right, and the Ruger 4l Magnum Bisley is probably the most pleasant of all 41 Magnums to shoot except the mammoth Dan Wesson 41.

Ruger has been making .44s for a long time and they have made a lot of really good ones. My favorite has always been the classic .44 Flat-Top. The Bisley comes real close to edging out the Flat-Top as my choice of the best 44 Magnum. All it would take would be for Ruger to remove the warning stamping on the barrel and finishing everything off with a really top-quality blue job.

It is no problem achieving a full 1500 fps with the 44 Magnum using 250-gr. cast bullets in the Ruger Bisley, and brass extracts easily. Both the 250-gr. Keith and the Lyman-Thompson #431244GC are excellent performers in the .44; 21.0 grains of 2400 is a little milder than the normal "standard" load of 22.0 grains but still gives 1400+ fps. BRP's 295-gr. Keith SWCGC, (NEI's #295.429) is an excellent heavyweight bullet, performing well in the Ruger Bisley .44 over 21.5 grains of WW296 or H110 for around 1350 fps; and the same bullet over 10.0 grains of Unique gives around 1150 and is very pleasant shooting and accurate.

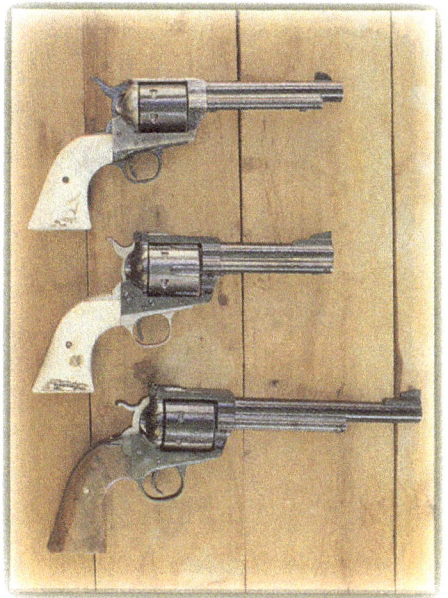

Three levels of comfortable shooting with the 45 Colt: the Colt Single Action Army for standard loads, the short-barreled Blackhawk for 1200 fps loads, and the Ruger Bisley for 300-gr. bulleted loads.

Jacketed bullets and Hodgdon's Li'l Gun give excellent results in the Ruger Bisley in 45 Colt.

Single Action Sixguns | 137

Chapter 20 | The Ruger Bisley Model

These standard model 45 Colt Model Blackhawks were turned into Bisleys by adding a Bisley grip frame, hammer, and trigger. Custom stocks are by Scott Kolar and Lett Manufacturing.

Ruger gave new life to the 45 Colt when it first chambered the oldest of the big bore cartridges 35 years ago. For the first time it was possible to safely load the 45 Colt to 1200 fps or more. When used with common sense, the Ruger Bisley makes a fine heavy-duty 45 Colt. I like 21.0 grains of 2400 with a 260-gr. cast bullet for around 1300 fps. One of my favorite bullet/load combinations in the Bisley .45 is NEI's 300-gr. #310.451 Keith-style bullet over 21.5 grains of WW296 for 1200 fps. Definitely not a 44 Magnum heavyweight load but a respectable load that does not give excessive recoil and certainly more than adequate for any deer or black bear. Sierra, Hornady, and Speer all make jacketed hollow points for the 45 Colt at 240-, 250-, and 260-gr. weights respectively. While they are wasted in the Colt Single Action, they're perfect for the Bisley 45 Colt and will give around 1250 fps when coupled with 25.0 grains of H110 or WW296.

The 357 Magnum Bisley Model is such a favorite of mine that I picked up a spare New Model 9mm cylinder and shipped both sixgun and extra cylinder off to Gary Reeder. Reeder chambered the 9mm cylinder to his 356 GNR, which is the 41 Magnum necked down to 357. Stag grips were fitted and polished smooth, the sharp corners at the toe and the butt of the grip frame were slightly rounded and the entire sixgun was finished in high polish blue with gold embellishments. That result is a very good-looking and good-shooting sixgun.

The Bisley Model is so popular that Ruger and Brownells now offer a conversion kit consisting of a Bisley grip frame, hammer, trigger, and stocks for converting any Blackhawk to the Bisley Model. I simply switched parts between two Bisley Vaqueros and two 4-5/8-inch .45 Blackhawk New Models, one in blue and the other in stainless, resulting in two excellent candidates for the category of Perfect Packin' Pistol. The switching of parts was quite painless, requiring no fitting and a pleasant evening's work. It is not quite so easy starting with new parts, grip frame, hammer, and trigger that have never been installed on a sixgun. Going this route will probably require some fitting and polishing, but the end results are well worth the effort. Bill Ruger has been responsible for a number of excellent sixguns; the Bisley is one of the best.

An example of how beautiful a Bisley Model can be made. Gary Reeder slightly rounded the corners of the butt, finished the entire gun in a high polish blue, and added gold embellishments.

—Chapter 21—

THE RUGER VAQUERO

In the earlier chapters we have seen how readily and eagerly gun writers of the time accepted Bill Ruger's single action sixguns. In comparing them to Colt Single Action Army models it was often said the Ruger Blackhawk was a better single action sixgun than the old Colt Model P. That argument still continues today, and the problem with the argument all comes down to whether one is arguing from the head or from the heart. There is no doubt any Ruger Blackhawk is stronger than any Colt Single Action ever produced. Ruger wins that one. On the other hand speaking from pure aesthetics, anyone must surely admit, at least artistically speaking, that the Colt has classic lines the Ruger has never achieved, at least until now. I sat in Bill Ruger's office in the early 1990s as he showed me the new single action sixgun Ruger was about to unveil – but let us back up a bit and see how we got there.

The ancestry of the Vaquero, all 7-1/2-inch sixguns: Flat-Top Blackhawk, Super Blackhawk, Bisley Model, and the Vaquero.

Once I purchased my first Ruger I could not help comparing it to the classic Colt Single Action Army. The .22 Ruger Single-Six looked much like a Colt and felt much like a Colt with two great advantages: it was virtually indestructible and exceptionally inexpensive to feed. That was the great reality of this little sixgun and perhaps even more important, at least to me, was the fact that it began my deep and enduring love affair with the single action sixgun.

The first centerfire Ruger, the 357 Magnum Blackhawk, became readily available in my area about this time and while it did not have the beautiful esthetically flowing lines of the Colt it was close and even superior in one all-important way. At the time, pre-war Colt Single Actions were plentiful and cost about the same as one would pay for a new Ruger or Smith & Wesson Highway Patrolman. By the time I had 50+-year-old 38 Special, 45 Colt and 41 Long Colt Single Action Armies added to my first 38-40, I soon discovered that 50-year-old Colt springs broke, especially hand and bolt springs, and Ruger coil springs did not. Even new Colts that were not properly tuned placed undue stress on hand and bolt springs, causing their premature demise.

It did not take me long to realize the ideal situation would be a Colt Single Action Army with Ruger lockwork. That of course never happened. But 35 years later we came almighty close. The sixgun Bill Ruger had on his desk to show me in the early 1990s was a totally

Single Action Sixguns | 139

Chapter 21 | The Ruger Vaquero

These early 7-1/2-inch stainless-steel Ruger Vaqueros in 45 Colt have been used in many cowboy action shooting matches by Taffin with both smokeless and black powder loads. The leather is by The Leather Arsenal.

A pair of genuine stag stocks really dresses up a Vaquero.

The very first Vaqueros were blued and case colored and chambered in 45 Colt with 7-1/2-inch barrels.

different style of Ruger single action. Until that time every Ruger Blackhawk had fully adjustable sights; even the original .22 Single-Six had a rear sight adjustable for windage by drifting it right or left in its dovetail slot. In the late 1970s and early 1980s, a new shooting game arrived – cowboy action shooting. This sport required four traditionally-styled firearms – a levergun, a shotgun, and two sixguns – all of which had to be originally manufactured prior to 1899 or replicas thereof.

As the sport spread across the country, a special dispensation was given to allow the use of Ruger Blackhawks shooting in the Modern Class, but they were not allowed in the Traditional Class, which required two sixguns with fixed sights such as those found on the Colt Single Action Army. Ruger saw a large market and decided to fill it. Credit Bill Ruger for taking a giant backward step forward and offering a twentieth-century sixgun with a real nineteenth-century look. Traditional single actions are normally thought of as having case-colored frames, and although a few early Single-Sixes were finished with a case-colored frame, they were never offered to the public. Ruger "de-horned" the Blackhawk and case-colored the main frame, making it look very much like the original Colt Single Action. The Vaquero had arrived.

After a history of making sixguns spanning nearly four decades, the fixed-sight Vaquero might seem like anything but progress at first glance. After all, the Blackhawks had been delivering superior service for four decades because they had excellent adjustable sights. Beginning with the 357 Magnum, then the 44 Magnum, the 41 Magnum, the 30 Carbine, and the 45 Colt, all Blackhawks have come equipped with the familiar massive top strap fitted with an adjustable rear sight.

The Vaquero, as the name implies, is a throwback to the "B" western movies of the 1930s and 1940s. It was designed to conjure up in the Old West in every sixgunner's mind. Ruger does not make very many marketing errors. Cowboy action shooting was big 15 years ago when the decision was made to go with the Vaquero and is even larger now with more than 70,000 members in the main governing body, SASS (Single Action Shooting Society). I wouldn't be surprised to find there are at least that many who also participate in local matches without being members of SASS. Cowboy action shooting is based on the enjoyment of the guns and clothes from the last quarter of the nineteenth century, and thanks to Ruger and the introduction of the Vaquero, aficionados could have an authentic-looking single action sixgun with virtually unbreakable lockwork and a transfer bar, making it perfectly safe to carry loaded with six rounds. This last item is very important as many of those taking part in cowboy action shooting are not experienced shooters but rather brand-new to the shooting sports. The Vaquero provides the safest possible single action sixgun for their use.

The first Vaquero was offered in the 7-1/2-inch Cavalry barrel length only and only in 45 Colt. At the time, the authenticity of its looks and chambering made it the preferred cowboy action shooting model. This is why the first chambering in the Vaquero was not the 44, 41 or 357 Magnum but the 125-year-old 45 Colt. The first gun was a 7-1/2-inch blued and case-colored .45, but the demand was so great for this new/old sixgun that Ruger added the two standard Colt Single Action Army barrel lengths of the 4-3/4-inch Civilian or Gunfighter's Model (in Ruger's case this length is 4-5/8 inches) and the 5-1/2-inch Artillery Model, all in blue with a case-colored frame. Then came stainless steel models in 45 Colt, 44 Magnum and, at least for a short while, in 44-40.

As we have pointed out, when the Vaquero first arrived the most popular caliber for cowboy action shooting was the old 45 Colt. It is still popular, but there is one large contingent of cowboy action shooters who are driven largely by the need to shoot as quickly as possible with minimum recoil. This need resulted in a call for a medium bore cartridge in large frame sixguns. For these shooters, the answer has been light-loaded 38 Specials in the 357 Magnum Vaquero, a situation I find hard to understand. Today less than five percent of the Vaqueros sold have 7-1/2-inch barrels, and at least in the matches I have seen there are a lot more .38/.357 than 45 Colt sixguns.

One of the great selling points of Blackhawks for all these years is the fact that its sights were fully adjustable and whatever the load, within reason, and however one held the sixgun or saw the sights, they could be adjusted to match point of aim with point of impact. Since the Vaqueros are fixed-sighted guns, it could become a real problem getting a gun that shoots to point of aim. Ruger has taken care of this problem as the front sight blade is generously high to allow each individual sixgunner to adjust his/her sights by judicious filing for the particular load and hold he/she prefers. My first 45 Vaquero shot three inches low with 300-grain bullets and twelve inches low with 225-gr. bullets. It was dialed in to hit point of aim with 255-gr. bullets at 850 to 950 fps.

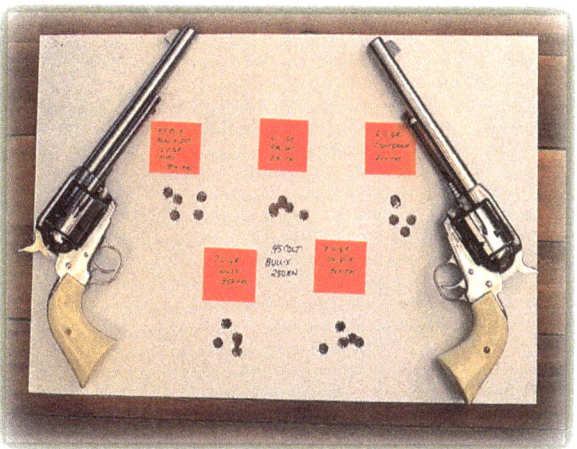

Vaqueros will definitely shoot!

These 4-5/8-inch Vaqueros with carved ivory polymer grips by Bob Leskovec effectively conjure up visions of the Old West.

Stainless steel Vaqueros and Kirkpatrick leather are a good, authentic-looking combination for cowboy action shooting. One holster and one sixgun also make a good choice for just plain woods bumming.

Single Action Sixguns | 141

Chapter 21 | The Ruger Vaquero

Ruger's Vaquero is offered in stainless steel and blue/case colored finishes, and in three standard barrel lengths: 4-5/8, 5-1/2, and 7-1/2 inches.

The standard Vaquero has now been joined by the Bisley Vaquero. Many shooters prefer the felt recoil dampening effect of the Bisley grip frame.

The Vaquero, in either blue/case-colored or stainless steel, and especially in the shorter barrel lengths, has become tremendously popular with cowboy action shooters. In fact, at the last local match I attended more than 80 percent of the competitors were using Vaqueros. There's an extra added bonus with the traditionally-styled Ruger: the stainless steel version of the Vaquero strikes me as the near-perfect outdoorsman's sixgun, especially for a packer or guide or woods bum who wants a strong, dependable sixgun that will shoot one load to the preferred point of aim with no worries about adjustable sights getting out of whack. A 4-5/8-inch 45 Colt or 44 Magnum adjusted to hit point of aim with 300-gr. bullets at 1250 fps in the .44 or around 1100 fps in the .45 is an excellent shooting, easy to pack big bore sixgun. Some Vaqueros have even been converted to five-shot 500 Linebaugh, giving an extremely powerful but lightweight, easy to pack, go-anywhere sixgun. Recoil? Don't even ask!

Sizewise the Vaquero is slightly larger than the Colt Single Action Army (for now). A close look at a 7-1/2-inch Vaquero in 45 Colt reveals a sixgun that at 43 ounces is 10 percent heavier than its counterpart from Hartford, a similarly barreled Colt Single Action Army. The flat-top frame is contoured and rounded off very nicely to provide a western style single action look, and the traditional hog wallow style rear sight sets high enough that one can sight down the top of a Vaquero without cocking the hammer. The rear sight does not extend all the way to the back of the frame but rather stops about five-sixteenths of an inch in front of the hammer face resulting in a dished out area that gives a flat sight picture. I find blackening this area with spray-on sight black helped my groups immensely.

The front sight of the Vaquero is shaped like a traditional Colt Single Action front sight and with a height of 3/8 of an inch affords plenty of latitude for filing. It is also shaped to provide a flat black sight picture. The grip frame is Blackhawk style and size and is steel rather than the alloy found on most Blackhawks since 1955. The firing pin is frame mounted as on all Ruger Blackhawks and the Vaquero has a transfer bar single action. This means it is loaded by opening the loading gate, which then allows the cylinder to rotate for loading or unloading with the hammer down.

The frame of the Vaquero is case-colored, not case-hardened. The colors are somewhat subdued and show up best in certain lighting, but they are nowhere near as bright as those found on most Colt Single Actions or Colt-style replicas. Holding a Colt Single Action Army in one hand and a Ruger Vaquero in the other really emphasizes the difference. There are two other major

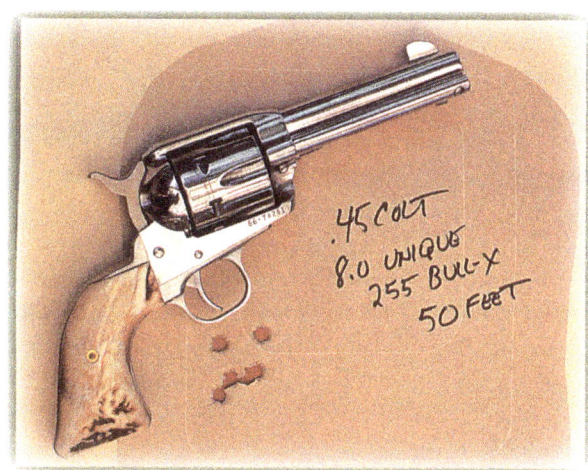

Suitable for self-defense? This stainless-steel .45 Vaquero will do the job.

differences with the Vaquero compared to the Colt, those being the fact the Vaquero is every bit as strong as the Blackhawk from which it descended and also the great difference in price when compared to the Colt. And therein lies the great popularity of the Ruger Blackhawks whether they be standard Blackhawks, Super Blackhawks, or Vaqueros. They are priced within reach of any sixgunner. The legacy of Bill Ruger is not just great shootin' sixguns, but truly affordable, great-shooting sixguns.

Shooting the Vaquero is pure single action pleasure. It is safe to carry fully loaded with six rounds. That is not important to those of us who were raised with old style single actions and know how to handle them but it is tremendously important to new shooters. I do not change very easily so I must admit I treat all single action sixguns the same. Yes, I normally still load five rounds even in true six-shot sixguns; and even though the Vaquero is safe fully loaded with six rounds, cowboy action shooting rules allow only five rounds and the hammer down on an empty chamber, even in New Model Rugers.

Currently Vaqueros are usually seen in the two shorter barrel lengths with the choice of blue/case-colored or stainless steel finish and chambered in 45 Colt, 44 Magnum, or 357 Magnum. The Vaquero is also now available in a Bisley version in the same chamberings and finishes but with the Bisley grip frame, hammer, and trigger; and it has even been offered in a Sheriff's Model style with a 3-1/2-inch barrel and birds head grip. Some special-issue Vaqueros have been offered through Ruger distributors as 38-40/40 S&W and 45 Colt/45 ACP convertible models with dual cylinders.

By the time this book is printed, Ruger is scheduled to introduce two new single action sixguns. One will be the Fiftieth Anniversary Model of the Blackhawk chambered in .357 with a New Model Flat-Top frame the same size as the original Blackhawk frame; and to follow up with this model, a newer Vaquero will be offered with an original Blackhawk/Colt single action-sized frame. First sixguns will be chambered in 357 Magnum and 45 Colt.

Is the Vaquero a hunting handgun? I prefer adjustable sights, but if one chooses one hunting load and files in the sights to hit to point of aim, and if the chambering chosen is 45 Colt or 44 Magnum, yes it could be. What about the Vaquero for defensive use? Again with the proper load, yes. A short-barreled Vaquero or Sheriff's Model in 357 Magnum (very heavy to pack all day in this chambering), 44 Magnum or 45 Colt could be a very effective defense gun. A better choice would be the newer, smaller, lighter Vaquero.

I am a great fan of the Colt Single Action Army; that is no secret. But I am also a great fan of the Vaquero. It has the same ability to conjure up visions in my mind's eye as the Colt. When I hold a Vaquero I am 10 years old again and sitting in the front row of the Allen Theater watching a double feature. It may be Roy, or Gene, or Hoppy; it doesn't matter. My soul is stirred, my spirit is kindled, my heart beats a little faster; a good single action will do that. Colt Single Actions and Vaqueros conjure up great visions from our historical past: bacon frying over a campfire during a drizzling rain in the

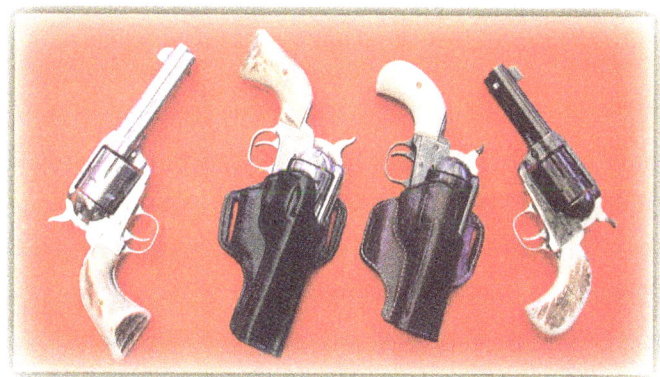

Vaqueros set up for defensive use include stainless-steel 45 Colt and 44-40 by Dave Lauck with shortened barrels, slightly rounded butts, and tuned actions; also two "Sheriff's Models," also in 45 Colt and 44-40, built by David Clements using Qualite' Pistol & Revolver bird's-head grip frames. The excellent concealable leather is by Rawhide Walt Ostin and the red stag grips are by Roger Warmuskerken.

Single Action Sixguns | 143

Chapter 21 | The Ruger Vaquero

The new, smaller-frame Vaquero of 2005.

mountains, the smell of powder smoke from Tombstone or Dodge City, trail dust from thousands of longhorn cattle walking north, bugles in the afternoon.... Each time one is picked up the same images emerge.

As this book was finished, word was received that Ruger was revamping the Vaquero. Since its introduction the Vaquero has been made on the standard Ruger 44 Magnum frame, making it not only larger but also heavier than traditional styled single actions such as the Colt single action and replicas thereof.

The current Vaquero will be replaced by the New Vaquero, which will be about 7/8 the size of the original, or about the same size as the Colt SAA and replicas.

In addition to downsizing it, Ruger is also making several other changes to the Vaquero. The hammer shape has been changed to make it both easier to reach and also to look more like a traditional single action army hammer; the grip frame shape reverts back to the original XR3 used on Ruger Blackhawks from 1955 to 1972; grips are checkered hard rubber with an impressed Ruger eagle medallion; and for easy loading and unloading, the action has been slightly modified so each chamber lines up with the loading gate opening and the ejector rod.

The New Vaquero will be fitted with an internal lock that can be accessed only by removing the right grip panel. This lock is found below the mainspring strut and when locked into place with a special key from Ruger the mainspring is blocked and the hammer cannot be cocked. Chamberings for the New Vaquero will be 357 Magnum and 45 Colt. Both calibers will be offered with 4-5/8- and 5-1/2-inch barrels with the 45 Colt also available with a 7-1/2-inch barrel. Shooters will have a choice of either stainless steel or blued/case colored New Vaqueros. The New Vaqueros I have handled, a 4-5/8-inch blue 357 and a 5-1/2-inch stainless steel 45 Colt, both seem to be smoother and tighter than standard Vaqueros and both came with 3-5/8-lb. trigger pulls.

Some have already raised concerns about those who would try to use heavy 45 Colt loads in the New Vaquero, as many shooters do in the older large-frame Blackhawks. However, Ruger has never recommended anything other than standard, SAAMI-level 45 Colt factory loads in their sixguns. Many reloading manuals have a separate section for 45 Colt loads for the Ruger and T/C Contender, but every one I have consulted says "For Ruger Blackhawk Only," not the Vaquero. The original Vaquero has been extremely popular with sixgunners; I expect the New Vaquero to be even more so as it will be lighter, smaller, and easier to pack all day. I will be more than happy to use standard 45 Colt loads only in the New Vaquero and recommend that all others do the same.

With the Vaquero, the bacon smell is a little lighter, the trail dust a little fainter, but it is there. The Spirit of the Old West lives on with the Vaquero.

Taffin shooting one of the short-barreled Vaqueros; he is thinking of Roy, Gene, and Hoppy.

–Chapter 22–

THE RUGER HUNTER MODEL

In 1935 the newly introduced 357 Magnum was written up with dire warnings as to its recoil and muzzle energy. It was, of course, at that time the most powerful handgun ever produced, with its muzzle velocity more than 500 fps higher than any 44 Special or 45 Colt factory load. Today, very few experienced handgun shooters consider the 357 Magnum to be all that powerful or intimidating. The change in attitude came about 20 years later with the introduction of the 44 Magnum that drove the same weight bullets found in the 44 Special and 45 Colt at the muzzle velocity of the 357 Magnum. The 44 Magnum kicked! Hard!

Today we have the situation in which the 44 Magnum has been tremendously overshadowed by the 454 Casull, the 475 and 500 Linebaughs, and the latest big bore sixgun cartridge, the 500 S&W Magnum. These are special-purpose handguns exhibiting tremendous recoil well above the level of the 44 Magnum, but this does not change the fact that the 44 Magnum in standard weight sixguns kicks as hard now as it did in 1956. Those of us who were in on the advent of the 44 Magnum had a lot of learning to do and a great deal of experience to go through to be able to handle the new powerhouse.

Nearly a half-century of handgun hunting progress from Ruger: the Super Blackhawk, 1959; the Bisley model, 1985; the Hunter model, 1992; and the Bisley model, 2004. Excellent hunting handguns all.

The original Smith & Wesson 44 Magnum sixgun was nothing more than an especially heat-treated S&W 1950 Target 44 Special fitted with a full-length cylinder and a bull barrel, which increased the weight from 39 to 48 ounces. It still recoiled heavily. Elmer Keith said it was no worse than a 38 Chief's Special while Major Hatcher said it felt like being hit in the palm of the hand with a baseball bat. That was the Smith & Wesson. The Ruger Blackhawk was even worse – in fact it was such a thumper that Ruger decided to increase its weight and in 1959 brought out the now classic Super Blackhawk. For more recoil-reducing weight, a non-fluted cylinder was used and the grip frame was increased in size from the Colt single action style to the Colt dragoon style and made of steel rather than a lightweight alloy as on the Flat-Top.

Ruger has always managed to price their sixguns to appeal to the average shooter. In 1956, A Ruger Blackhawk cost less than 70 percent of the $140 price tag of the Smith 44 Magnum. When the

Single Action Sixguns | 145

Chapter 22 | The Ruger Hunter Model

Ruger's greatest bargain when it comes to a single action hunting handgun is not only accurate, but it handles today's heavy hunting loads.

Super Blackhawk came out in 1959, it was a highly polished specimen in a wooden case for $120, and this improved model Blackhawk won acceptance from .44 shooters immediately. It still cost less than the Smith, even with the improvements, and many sixgunners felt that its recoil was less because of its grip design. When Dirty Harry arrived and everyone had to have a Smith & Wesson 44 Magnum, many shooters soon discovered the Ruger Super Blackhawk was not only significantly less expensive, it was usually available.

The 1956 44 Magnum Flat-Top Blackhawk evolved into the Super Blackhawk of 1959, which then became the New Model Blackhawk in 1973, followed by the Bisley Blackhawk, a Super Blackhawk with a Bisley grip frame, in 1985. The first three were never chambered in anything except the 44 Magnum, but the 357 Magnum, 41 Magnum, and 45 Colt chamberings of the standard Blackhawk line were added to the Bisley, along with the 44 Magnum.

The Super Blackhawk has been one of the real workhorses of the handgunning world. Ruger, early in the silhouetting game, brought back the long-barreled .44 by offering a 10-1/2-inch 44 Magnum for the long-range shooters. Approximately 1000 of the original .44 Flat-Top Blackhawks had been made with 10-inch barrels. These were a favorite of some handgun hunters in the late 1950s and early 1960s, and I carried one for several seasons in a Goerg shoulder holster. The newer long-barreled Super Blackhawk became a favorite of silhouetters and hunters alike.

The Super Blackhawk and its companion, the Bisley, are two of the greatest sixgun bargains available today in 44 Magnum chambering and are the hands-down favorite of those seeking reliability, accuracy, and economy in a 44 Magnum hunting handgun. I am one who has never liked the way the Super Blackhawk grip frame bites the knuckle on my middle finger and so hailed the introduction of the Bisley Ruger as the grip frame near-perfect for my hand. With the .44 Blackhawk, the Super Blackhawk, the Super Blackhawk New Model, and the Bisley .44 Blackhawk, one would expect Ruger's .44 Magnum evolution to be complete.

Ruger did not think so. Just as the Blackhawk became the Super Blackhawk to add weight and controllability for 44 Magnum sixgunners of the 1950s and the Bisley grip was adopted to help control felt recoil in the 1980s, the Super Blackhawk was once again given a facelift in the 1990s. The result was the Super Blackhawk Hunter model.

Two major changes were made to the Super Blackhawk to turn it into a Hunter model. The square-backed trigger guard found on the Super Blackhawk since 1959 was discarded. The grip frame was still Super Blackhawk size and although the trigger guard was rounded, grips from the Super Blackhawk and Hunter Model were interchangeable. In addition to rounding the trigger guard of the grip frame, Ruger also changed the grip material. Instead of smooth wood as found on the Super Blackhawk, the Hunter comes with factory laminated camo finished grips.

Ruger added recoil-reducing weight to the original .44 Blackhawk in 1959 by adopting a longer barrel, non-fluted cylinder, and a larger steel grip frame. To take the next step up to the Hunter model, the Super Blackhawk was made heavier by the use of a heavy ribbed barrel, bringing the weight of the Super Blackhawk up from 48 ounces to 53 ounces. That extra five ounces really makes a difference with today's heavily-loaded hunting ammunition for the 44 Magnum. I definitely find the Hunter Model much more comfortable to shoot than a standard Super Blackhawk. The adding of the combination of a rounded trigger guard and a heavy barrel certainly works much better for handling felt recoil for me when shooting long strings of heavy-loaded .44s.

In earlier chapters we mentioned how Bill Ruger had expressed to Elmer Keith the fact he had been influenced by Keith's writing about custom single actions in the pages of the *American Rifleman* prior to World War II. As I looked at the Hunter Model Super Blackhawk I had a feeling I had seen this gun before, long before Ruger started advertising it. My feeling was proved definitely correct when I found a picture of a Pachmayr custom Colt Single Action in a 1939 Elmer Keith article that, while not a dead-ringer for the Ruger, certainly looks like its paternal grandfather. That old Colt had the same wide hammer and ribbed barrel profile as one finds on this new Ruger of more than a half-century later.

Besides the added weight, the Ruger Hunter model also has many other desirable features such as a smooth trigger, which should be required equipment on all hard-kickin' magnums; a wide hammer for easy cocking; a long ejector rod and housing as originally supplied on the Ruger 357 Maximum for easy, positive removal of spent cases; an interchangeable front sight system comparable to those of the GP-100 and Redhawk double action sixguns; and of course the aforementioned heavy-ribbed barrel.

The weight-adding one-half inch wide ribbed barrel is also scalloped to accept a pair of Ruger rings for mounting a scope on the Hunter model. I normally use a 2X or 4X Leupold LER scope as I have had excellent service out of Leupold scopes for many years. Ruger's mounting the scope on the barrel rib instead of the frame results in the scope mounted far enough forward the hammer is easily reached in front of the rear lens of the scope instead of under it. Any handgun hunter who has tried to wedge his thumb in between the top of the

> "I normally use a 2X or 4X Leupold LER scope as I have had excellent service out of Leupold scopes for many years."

Ruger Hunter models are most versatile, offering the use of a scope or iron sights almost instantaneously.

Chapter 22 | The Ruger Hunter Model

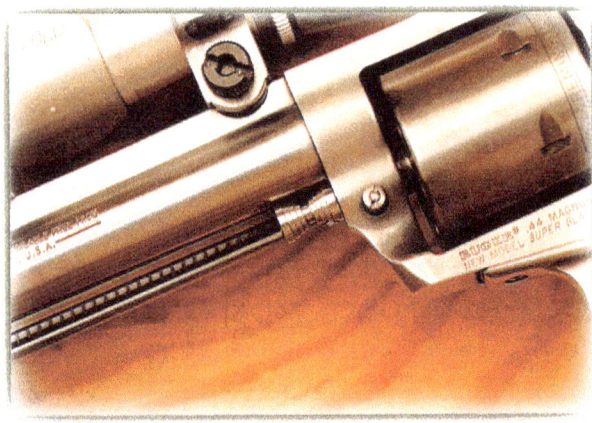

Two things can be seen very easily here: one of the Ruger scope rings attached to the Hunter model barrel, and the Belt Mountain base pin.

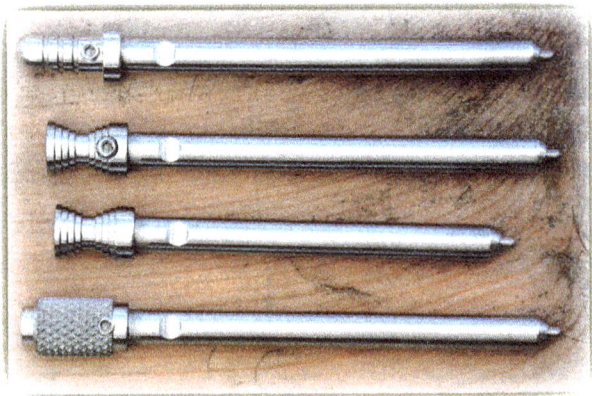

An easy way to customize a single action and tighten up the cylinder is the addition of a Belt Mountain base pin offered in several versions including the standard model, the #5, and large knurled head. With their locking arrangement, they are a necessity for hard-kicking single action sixguns.

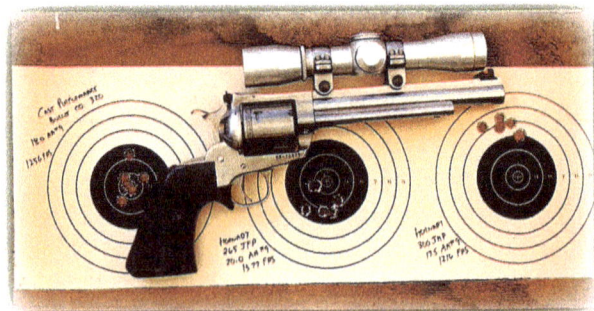

Yes, the Hunter model 44 Magnum shoots very well.

hammer and bottom of the scope while trying not to spook a trophy buck standing within shooting distance will especially appreciate this feature.

When it was first offered in 1992, the Ruger Hunter model was available only in 44 Magnum in stainless steel with a 7-1/2-inch barrel. I hoped to see a 10-inch model as well as 4-5/8-inch and 5-1/2-inch barrel lengths for use as easier shooting packin' pistols. I also wanted to see it chambered in 357 Magnum, 41 Magnum, and 45 Colt, and with the Bisley grip frame.

In addition to all the improvements in morphing the Super Blackhawk into the Hunter model, the only other thing needed is the addition of a slightly larger-diameter Belt Mountain base pin with a locking screw to keep it in place. Kelye Schlepp of Belt Mountain saw a niche and filled it perfectly. Kelye now offers a full line of base pins for nearly every single action sixgun, and these base pins actually perform three functions. First, they have a locking screw to hold the base pin securely under recoil; second, most base pins offered by Belt Mountain have a larger, easier to grasp head to make removal easy; and finally, all Belt Mountain pins are slightly larger in diameter, which serves to take some of the looseness out of the cylinder/base pin connection.

Once in awhile it will be necessary to turn down the base pin slightly to fit the center hole in the factory cylinder or frame, but I have not experienced this using Belt Mountain base pins in Colts, Colt-style replicas, or Ruger single actions. Belt Mountain offers several designs of base pin heads from original factory configuration to shorter models to allow for longer travel of the ejector rod head. My two favorites are the large knurled style and the Number Five. The latter is named for its similarity to the base pin found on Elmer Keith's #5 SAA created in the late 1920s. With the addition of the aforementioned Leupold scope, nothing else needs to be done to make this Ruger ready for hunting. The Ruger Hunter has proven to be an exceptionally accurate sixgun out of the box. My personal standard for a great shooting sixgun is five-shot groups of one inch at 25 yards. Garrett's 320-gr. hard cast hunting load clocks 1300 fps and shoots into 5/8 of an inch at 25 yards, while their 310-gr. SWC hunting load at 1270 fps puts all five shots in 1-3/8 inches at 50 yards. Excellent results. RCBS's #44-300 SWC bullet over 21.5 grains of H110 clocks out at 1200 fps with five shots in 1-1/4 inches at 50 yards. Again, these are excellent results.

The Hunter model is built for heavy-duty outdoor use.

I'm still looking for a 10-inch Hunter model as well as other factory chamberings. Nothing yet, although I do believe there were some special Ruger distributor offerings of the Hunter model in 45 Colt. What we have received within the last two years are two more Hunter models. Most shooters, myself included, prefer the Ruger Bisley grip frame for big bore Magnum sixguns. Ruger now offers the Bisley Hunter model, stainless steel, 44 Magnum, 7-1/2-inch barrel and with the Bisley grip frame, hammer, and trigger. This is without a doubt the finest big bore hunting handgun ever offered by Ruger.

Recently, Ruger corrected what I would consider a 50-year mistake. In all the time Ruger has produced .22 Single-Sixes they have never offered my favorite barrel length of 7-1/2 inches. When it comes to big-game hunting handguns at relatively low prices, we had the Super Blackhawk Hunter and the Bisley Hunter both chambered in .44 Magnum and both with 7-1/2-inch barrels, but what about the small game and varmint hunter? Ruger has covered both situations and is now offering the .22 Single-Six Hunter model, all stainless steel, with adjustable sights, a heavy ribbed 7-1/2-inch barrel set up to accept Ruger scope rings, and an auxiliary .22 Magnum cylinder. This is simply one great little sixgun, but I am torn between keeping it scoped or available with iron sights as it not only works extremely well for hunting varmints and small game, but it is also very well suited for plinking.

Whether the quest is varmints, small game, or big game, the easily scoped Ruger Hunter Models in 22 LR, 22 Magnum, or 44 Magnum will handle the task nicely.

The .22 Hunter model I tested performed equally well with either cylinder. Federal's American Eagle .22 HPs clocked out at 1058 fps and placed five shots in 3/4 inch at 25 yards, while with the Magnum cylinder in place, Federal's .22 Winchester Magnum HPs did 1527 fps with a five-shot group of 3/4 inch at the same distance. I am perfectly satisfied with the Single-Six Hunter version as a convertible model chambered in 22 Long Rifle/22 Magnum, but for those whose tastes are more exotic, it is also offered in 17 HMR. I hope Ruger also brings it out with the Bisley grip frame.

For the beginning handgun hunter, or the seasoned veteran, I know of no better first choice, all things considered, than a Ruger Hunter model. Once again Ruger has done a masterful job of filling a niche.

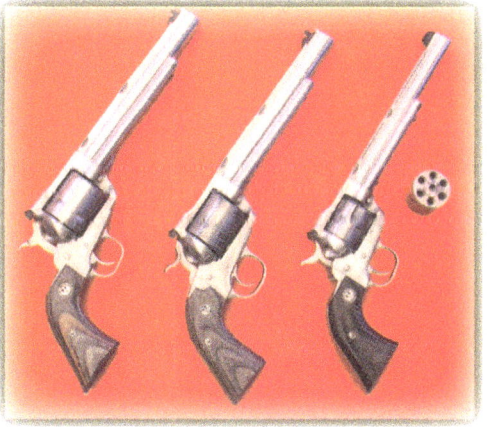

Ruger's complete lineup of Hunter Models includes the Super Blackhawk 44 Magnum, the Bisley Model Hunter 44 Magnum, and the 22 Convertible Single-Six Hunter model.

Single Action Sixguns

–Chapter 23–

THE RUGER OLD ARMY

The widespread use of cartridge-firing sixguns from Colt, Remington, and Smith & Wesson in the 1870s soon resulted in the end of production of percussion revolvers, and, for the most part, their use. As the cap-and-ball system became obsolete, many percussion revolvers were converted to fire cartridges.

The original percussion era may have ended, but another would begin a century later. Today there may be more cap and ball revolvers in use than there were in the nineteenth century. Thanks to some forward-thinking individuals including the late Val Forgett of Navy Arms, we now have replicas of most nineteenth-century percussion revolvers at our disposal. Bill Ruger was also a black powder enthusiast, and his appreciation of the Remington pocket revolver can be seen in the little .22 Bearcat. When Ruger decided to offer shooters a percussion revolver, he looked to the past for inspiration, but he did not want a copy or a replica. Ruger would introduce a completely new design.

Ruger's Blackhawk is known for its exceptional strength, and Bill Ruger wanted any percussion revolver bearing his name to be a strong as the Super Blackhawk and at least as accurate. There would be no thought given to a design such as the open-top style offered by Colt from 1836 to 1862; instead Ruger's cap and ball revolver would have a the top strap just as found on their Blackhawks.

Some black powder shooters simply like the Old Army! Photo courtesy of Victor Spearman.

Ruger's twentieth-century version of the nineteenth-century percussion revolver was based upon the Old Model Rugers produced from 1963-1972, and the Old Army – as the new percussion revolver would be known – used the same basic action and grip frame as found on all Ruger single actions. It would also incorporate coil mainspring, hand spring, and bolt spring.

The loading lever, rammer, and base pin of the Old Army are linked together and held in place by one large screw that is easily locked or unlocked by using a coin. It exerts the best leverage in seating the ball over the powder of any percussion revolver ever produced, and the Old Army also has an excellent locking latch under the barrel to secure the loading lever. I have never had the loading lever come loose under recoil in shooting any Old Army.

The Old Army was first produced in 1972 and until recently was available only as a 7-1/2-inch blued or stainless steel version with adjustable sights. It is very popular not only for general shooting but is also a proven winner at the firing line in black powder matches. I purchased one of the very early stainless steel Old Army revolvers as that finish makes cleanup after shooting black powder or a black powder

The Ruger Old Army is offered in stainless-steel and in both adjustable sighted, here shown with a Super Blackhawk grip frame, and a fixed-sighted version.

substitute so much easier. That revolver has been in use for over three decades now and is just as good as ever. The nipples have had to be replaced several times but it still performs better than I can.

When I had my 1960s 7-1/2-inch Super Blackhawk's barrel cut to a more convenient-to-pack 4-5/8 inches and finished with a stainless steel-type coating, I found the Super Blackhawk grip frame was larger than I needed on this smallish 44 Magnum, so I simply swapped grip frames and triggers with the Old Army. The handling qualities of both revolvers were greatly enhanced.

The Old Army is one percussion revolver that can be carried safely with six rounds as there are safety recesses between each chamber for resting the hammer. They should always be used unless the hammer is resting upon an empty chamber. Stainless steel nipples are set deeply into the cylinder to help prevent fragments from fired caps falling into the mechanism or behind the cylinder, thus causing a jam. This has never occurred with any Old Army revolver I have used. The Old Army is also the only percussion revolver that can be dry fired as the hammer nose is designed to clear the nipples by .005". The Old Army also bears the distinction of being the only Ruger single action that still has the old-style mechanism of the Flat-Top and Old Model Blackhawks rather than the New Model transfer bar.

Ruger proof-tested the prototype Old Army by seating a round ball on top of the cylinder full of Bullseye. If such a test were tried using a cartridge case and bullet in almost any revolver results would normally be disastrous. The Old Army held, but it should be fired only with black powder or black powder substitutes and never with smokeless powder.

With a tremendous popularity rise in cowboy action shooting especially in the decade of the 1990s, Ruger saw a market for a traditionally styled percussion revolver for the competition, which does not allow adjustable sights. The basic Old Army stayed the same except for the Vaquero treatment. That is, the adjustable rear sight was removed, the top strap rounded and given the old-style hog wallow rear sight groove, and the ramp front sight was replaced by a traditional blade. Those who prefer to stay authentic use replicas of such early percussion revolvers as the Colt 1851 Navy or 1860 Army or the Remington New Model Army; those who want the best possible percussion revolver when it comes to function and accuracy (and also easy cleanup) go with the Ruger fixed-sighted Old Army. As with the original adjustable sighted Old Army, this version was first also available in both blued and stainless finishes with a 7–1/2-inch barrel.

After more than three decades of producing only 7-1/2-inch Old Army models, Ruger is now offering a fixed-sighted, stainless steel or blue, 5-1/2-inch Old Army. The only basic difference, other than barrel length, from the original long-barrel versions is the fact that the loading lever mechanism cannot be removed without unscrewing the catch from the bottom of the barrel. Standard grips on the 5-1/2-inch Old Army are imitation ivory with the Ruger Eagle medallion.

Shooting black powder does become a little messy and my hands tend to get a little slippery whether using a Thompson lubed wad between powder and ball or placing lube (Crisco, in my case) on top of the seated ball. This

The Old Army shoots as accurately with Triple Seven as any cartridge firing revolver.

Single Action Sixguns | 151

Chapter 23 | The Ruger Old Army

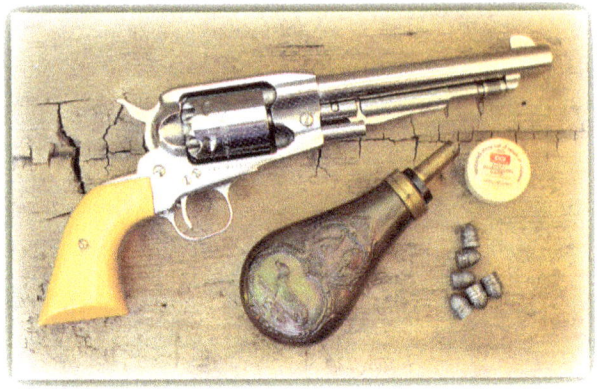

Powder, round balls and percussion caps are all that is needed for a pleasant afternoon shooting of the Ruger Old Army.

The latest Old Army versions from Ruger: easy handling, accurate shooting, stainless-steel 5-1/2-inch models with Eagle's Gunfighter grips.

For use in cowboy action shooting matches, Bob Mernickle offers this excellent rig for the 5-1/2-inch Old Army.

situation did not suit the slippery ivory grips, so they were replaced with checkered buffalo horn Gunfighter stocks from Eagle. The dark horn color provides a nice contrast to the stainless steel finish, while the checkering prevents the overly slick feeling and the Gunfighter style shelf at the top of the grip panel provides extra security and prevents the revolver from shifting in the hand while fired. This could be a concern with a heavy-recoiling 44 Magnum, but even the heaviest black powder loads in the Old Army exhibit no more recoil than a +P 38 Special.

I prefer to shoot the Old Army with a full-house load using 35 or 40 grains of black powder or black powder substitute by volume measure. A Thompson lubed wad is seated over the powder, and then a Speer .457" round ball is rammed home. The extra leverage of the loading lever of the 7-1/2-inch Old Army is really appreciated when using this much powder; the shorter lever on the 5-1/2-inch Old Army is much more difficult to use. Bill Cleghorn of Hillsboro, Oregon solved this problem by sending along a clever little extension that slips over the end of the shorter loading lever. Works great. After all chambers are loaded, then and only then are CCI #11 percussion caps placed on the nipples and the hammer let down in one of the safety notches if I am loading six rounds.

Even with the short barrel of the 5-1/2-inch Old Army, muzzle velocities are right up there. With 40.0 grains (by volume) of Goex FFFg, Muzzle velocity is 900 fps; 40.0 gr. of Pyrodex P is just under 1,000 fps; while a full-house loading of Hodgdon's Triple-7 FFFg gives even higher velocities in excess of 1,100 fps.

Thanks to Taylor's & Co. and R&D, Ruger Old Armies can easily be changed into cartridge-firing sixguns. Taylor's is now offering R&D conversion cylinders chambered in 45 Colt to fit the Ruger Old Army. These are available in both blue and nickel finishes. The latter matches up very nicely with the Ruger Old Army stainless steel. In order to use these conversion cylinders, one removes the original cylinder and uses the same base pin that is part of the Old Army loading lever with the new cylinder. The R&D comes with a back plate with six firing pins, safety notches between chambers, and a locating pin in the back of the cylinder which mates up with a corresponding hole in the conversion ring/back plate.

To load, the back plate is removed, cartridges are placed in the cylinder, the back plate is replaced, and the cylinder is carefully placed in the Old Army frame and the base pin is returned. To unload, it is necessary to remove the cylinder, take off the back plate, and remove the cartridges. If they do not fall out by gravity, it is handy to have some kind of a rod or a wooden dowel to tap them out from the front of cylinder. One of the rings around the firing pins is a different color so it is easy to see which chamber is empty if one loads only five rounds. For extra added convenience, Belt Mountain is now offering a special large knurled base pin to fit the Old Army when used with these cylinders. The entire factory loading assembly and base pin are removed, set aside, and replaced by the Belt Mountain pin. This makes removal of the empty cartridge cylinder and the return of the loaded cylinder much easier.

Taylor & Co.'s R&D drop-in cylinders converts 5-1/2-inch Old Armies into accurate-shooting 45 Colt sixguns.

The Taylor & Co.'s R&D cylinder consists of two pieces: the cylinder proper and the backplate.

Selected Loads For the 7-1/2-inch Ruger Old Army

Speer .457" Round Ball / Speer #11 Magnum Percussion Cap / Thompson Wad

Load	MV	5 Shots/ 50 Ft.
30.0 gr. Goex FFg	680	1-1/4"
35.0 gr. Goex FFg	816	1"
40.0 gr. Goex FFg	870	1-5/8"
30.0 gr. Goex FFFg	868	1-1/8"
40.0 gr. Goex FFFg	959	1-3/4"
30.0 gr. Goex CTG	693	1"
35.0 gr. Goex CTG	746	1"
40.0 gr. Goex CTG	920	1-1/2"
35.0 gr. Pyrodex P*	967	3/4"
30.0 gr. Pyrodex Select	651	1-1/4"
35.0 gr. Pyrodex Select	797	3/4"
40.0 gr. Pyrodex Select	1045	1-3/8"
*Favorite Match Load		

Single Action Sixguns

Chapter 23 | The Ruger Old Army

Selected Loads For the 5-1/2-inch Old Army

Speer .457" Round Ball / CCI #11 Percussion Cap / Thompson Wad

LOAD	MV	5 SHOTS/50 FT.
35.0 gr. Triple-7 FFF	925	1-3/8"
40.0 gr. Triple-7 FFFg	1130	1-3/4"
35.0 gr. Pyrodex P	740	1-7/8"
40.0 gr. Pyrodex P	983	2"
35.0 gr. Goex FFFg	854	1-3/4"
40.0 gr. Goex FFFg	898	1-3/8"

45 Colt With Taylor's R&D Cylinder

BULLET/LOAD	MV	5 SHOTS/50 FT.
AA Ltd 255 Conical/7.0 gr. HP-38	795	1-1/2"
AA Ltd 255 Conical/9.5 HS-6	643	1-5/8"
AA Ltd #504 250 RNFP/9.5 HS-6	601	1"
AA Ltd #504 250 RNFP/30.0 Triple-7	783	1-3/8"
Black Dawge 235 SPG/35.0 CTG	692	1-1/4"
Black Dawge 235 SPG/35.0 Swiss FFFg	920	1-1/2"
Oregon Trail 250 RNFP/7.0 gr. HP-38	673	1-1/4"
Oregon Trail 250 RNFP/9.5 gr. HS-6	608	1-1/2"
Oregon Trail 250 RNFP/6.0 gr. Red Dot	863	1-1/2"
Lyman #454190/33.0 gr. CTG	640	1-1/2"
Black Dawge 250 BP	983	1-5/8"
Cor-Bon 250 BP	644	1-1/2"
Wind River 250 BP	706	1-1/2"
Black Hills Black Hills 250RNFP	716	1-1/2"
PMC 250RNFP	724	1-1/4"
Ultramax 250RNFP	770	7/8"
Ultramax 200RNFP	739	1-1/8"
3-D 255 RNFP	638	1-3/8"
4W 200 RNFP	673	1-1/2"
4W 250 RNFP	668	1-1/2"
Ten-X 250 RNFP	786	1-1/2"

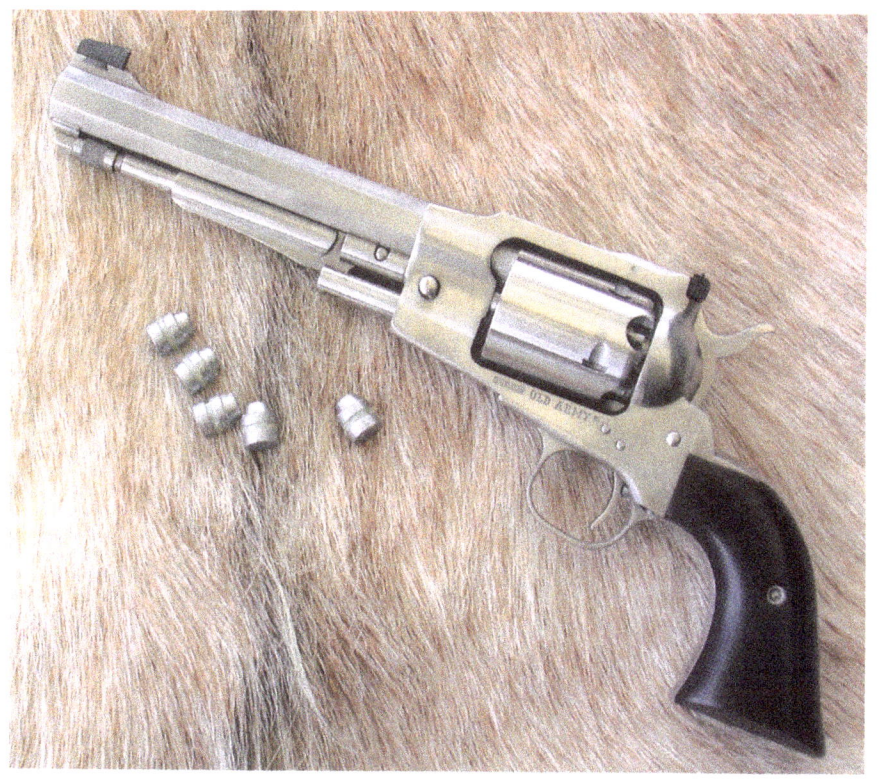

For those wishing to hunt with the Old Army, David Clements offers a five-shot .50-caliber conversion on the Old Army.

I often hear from shooters who plan on using the Old Army for hunting. A realistic look at the performance of the Old Army reveals we are basically shooting a +P 38 Special, which is certainly not to be considered very seriously for hunting anything above small game. There is, however, a great answer for those who desire to use the Old Army for hunting. Gunsmith David Clements offers a custom five-shot 50 caliber Old Army, which is definitely serious enough for handgun hunting. Using a Speer .490" round ball, CCI's #11 Magnum Percussion Cap, and a .50 Ox Yoke Wad, 50 grains (by volume) of Triple-Seven FFg results in a muzzle velocity of 1175 fps; 50 grains Triple-Seven FFFg, 1350 fps; and 50 grains of Pyrodex P clocks out at 1110 fps. The Clements Custom .50 Ruger Old Army can also be used with a 250-grain SPG-lubed .50-caliber bullet with 45 grains of Triple-Seven FFFg at 1140 fps, and with the same charge of Pyrodex P at 1105 fps. Now we have some serious hunting loads for the Old Army.

Thanks to replicas, shooters may have a choice of almost every percussion sixgun ever offered by Colt or Remington or even some of the lesser-known makers. However, without a doubt, the Ruger Old Army is the finest cap and ball sixgun ever offered, anywhere, any time.

The five-shot .50-caliber conversion cylinder by David Clements compared to the standard six-shot Ruger Old Army cylinder.

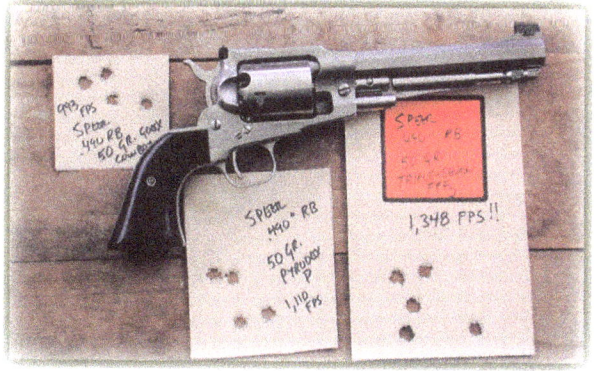

This .50-caliber sixgun by David Clements is ready to go hunting.

Single Action Sixguns | 155

–Chapter 24–

THE FREEDOM ARMS MODEL 83

In 1957, I purchased the first Second Generation Colt Single Action Army to arrive in my area. It was my first 45 Colt sixgun. At that time the myth of weak 45 Colt brass was widespread, and even to some extent continues today thanks to some writers who have kept it alive. I forgive their ignorance. Perhaps there is some justification for the "weak" label, as original 45 Colt brass was of the balloon head style with a very small rim. In my early days of reloading I never had a case come apart, but that thin little rim more than once pulled out of the shell holder. I can assure everyone that brass manufacturers do not separate their facilities into weak and strong sections. These same manufacturers use the same high-quality materials and manufacturing techniques for 45 Colt as they do for 44 Magnum. Sectioning both cases will prove this to be true.

In the early 1950s there was one man who certainly did not believe the "weak" label attached to the 45 Colt. In fact he was using the 45 Colt for his experiments with high velocity sixgun ammunition. At that time 45 Colt brass had just become available with solid head construction, while 44 Special brass was still of the balloon head style. This young Utah gunsmith had a dream and a goal. The dream was to achieve 1800 fps with a 230-grain bullet in a standard-size sixgun while the goal was to do it safely. Had Dick Casull listened to the experts of the time the 454 Casull would never have arrived and Freedom Arms would not be celebrating nearly 25 years of building the world's finest single action sixguns.

Casull began experimenting with his 45 Magnum even before the 44 Magnum arrived. He was quite limited in what revolver he could use for his special loads in that the only one suitable was the Colt Single Action, as Ruger's much stronger Blackhawk was still several years into the future. The Colt SAA is a beautifully balanced, easy-packin', easy-shootin' sixgun, but Colt cylinders are almost paper-thin in 45 Colt chambering. The SAA is built for standard loads equivalent to the original black powder loads with pressures that are relatively low. Casull discovered very early that the 45 Colt cylinder would not even come close to holding what he was trying to achieve as he bulged many cylinders in the early stages. With heavier loads, cylinders burst and top straps blew.

If a conventional six-shot cylinder was just not strong enough to contain the pressures he was working with, the obvious answer would be a five-shot cylinder that would give greater strength and more metal between chambers. By using 4140 steel and five-shot cylinders made as large as possible and still fit the frame window of the Colt Single Action, Casull achieved 1300 feet per second with a 230-gr. .45 hard-cast bullet. Not enough. He then turned to special heat-treating and in

Doesn't this look like fun? Taffin Shooting the 4-3/4-inch Freedom Arms .454 with full-house loads using 340-gr. bullets.

Dick Casull's personal 12-inch Freedom Arms .454 and two of his early experimental sixguns.

1954, using a Colt single action .45 with an oversized five-shot cylinder, Casull hit 1550 fps with 250-gr. bullets. Remember, this was two years before the 44 Magnum appeared, and his results were 100 fps faster with 10 grains heavier bullet than the factory-loaded 44 Magnum of 1956.

Casull had the power but he was concerned about the margin of safety, so in 1957 he decided to build his own single action frame. Using 4140 steel for the frame and 4150 steel for the cylinder, the first 454 Magnum was created. In the early 1960s reports of Dick Casull and his 45 Magnum started showing up in gun magazines. At the time, Casull was also converting Ruger Super Blackhawks to five-shot .45s.

Several attempts were made to turn his dream sixgun into a production revolver. This would not be realized until Dick Casull and Wayne Baker came together. In March 1979 Baker and Casull began Freedom Arms, producing .22 mini-guns. Four years later in October, 1983 the first factory-built five-shot 454 Casull left the Freedom Arms factory located in the Star Valley area of Freedom, Wyoming. The 454 Casull revolver was now reality, but it would be several years before it was widely accepted by the general shooting public.

This was also about the same time I was getting serious about a writing career. Long-range silhouetting took up much of my time, and I had been writing for two club journals, Elgin Gates' *The Silhouette* and *The Sixgunner* of Handgun Hunters International. Relatively speaking, very few people in the industry knew who I was or where I was coming from. I decided to call Wayne Baker and found a most personable man who was willing to trust me with one of his expensive revolvers. He sent me a 10-inch Premier Grade .454 that was soon outfitted with silhouette sights. I used it for the long-range game, switched to standard sights or a scope for hunting, and also fired thousands of heavy test loads through my first, but not last, .454.

Along the way I was able to introduce several other writers to the wonders of the .454. This test gun was subsequently purchased and today remains as tight as the day it left the factory. My first article on the 454 Casull appeared in *American Handgunner* in 1986. That article definitely helped to begin my writing career with *American Handgunner*. The art department did an exceptional job in laying out the first published extensive handloading information for the .454 and those pages were tacked up in reloading rooms all over the country.

From the very beginning the Freedom Arms .454 revolver, now known as the Model 83, has been built to exacting tolerances. Cylinders are line bored, that is, locked into the frame so a pilot hole can be drilled to form each chamber, which should be locked into precise alignment with the barrel in any sixgun for top accuracy. Freedom Arms revolvers are not assembled by reaching into a box or bin and taking out the cylinder, the frame, and the barrel and putting them together. They are in fact hand-fitted from the very beginning of mating one particular cylinder to one particular barrel and frame. Many other manufacturers' firearms are built to a certain price level; Freedom Arms does it the opposite way, that is, they build the best possible revolver that

Dick Casull in front of his Freedom, Wyoming home with his 12-inch .454.

Single Action Sixguns | 157

Chapter 24 | The Freedom Arms Model 83

Taffin's friend and fellow Shootist Al DiPrima with an Alaskan brown bear taken with the Freedom Arms .454.

How well do single action sixguns shoot the 45 ACP? Check out the target on the right shot with a 45 ACP cylinder in the Freedom Arms Model 83.

their machinery and craftsmen are capable of achieving and then set the price. That price is high, but Freedom Arms makes no apology for it and it is a rare purchaser of a Freedom Arms revolver who would say it is not worth the price. I have yet to find such an individual.

No one ever expected to see a production revolver that would be more powerful than the 44 Magnum and to also be able to do it in such a portable package. Consider this: standard factory loading of the 44 Magnum in the 1980s was a 240-gr. bullet at around 1400 fps. Factory ammunition for the Freedom Arms five-shot 454 Casull revolver consisted of a bullet with a hard lead core and a heavy .032" copper jacket. Using my 10-inch .454 revolver the factory 260-gr. load clocked out at 1884 fps, and the 300 at 1690 fps. Using H110 I was able to duplicate both loads using the factory jacketed bullets. Dick Casull also designed two gas-check cast bullet molds especially for use in the Freedom Arms .454. With my handloads, the 260 clocks out at 1986 fps, while the 300 breaks 1800 fps. This is with 34.0 and 32.0 gr. of H110 respectively. J.D. Jones designed a special 340-gr. flat-nosed cast bullet that also achieves 1800 fps using 32.0 gr. of H110 in the same 10-inch revolver. Recoil? Up to that time it was worst I had ever experienced.

Times were tough for Freedom Arms in those early days. It was not easy to convince even most gun writers that the .454 was something they even needed to look at, which helped even more to make the Casull a tough sell for several years. Finally the word did get out and the .454 became a favorite choice of serious big game hunters. However, Freedom Arms wisely realized that some diversification was necessary

Not only does Freedom Arms offer the finest single action revolvers ever built, but they also offer Taffin's favorite shoulder holster for scoped single actions.

as everyone did not need or even want the power of the .454, and yet many shooters had the desire to own such a masterpiece of revolver engineering and manufacturing. In February 1986 Freedom Arms offered their first Model 83 chambered in 45 Colt, followed one month later by the 44 Magnum.

The Freedom Arms 44 Magnum maintained the same five-shot cylinder and line-boring operation as its older brother, resulting in as-near-as-possible perfect barrel/cylinder/frame alignment. This made it nearly perfect for long-range silhouetting, and once the infamous price ceiling rule was reversed it became a favorite on the firing line and very quickly the revolver of choice of the top shooters. As with the .454 Model 83, the specially designed grip of the 44 Magnum minimizes felt recoil as much as possible.

In the 1980s I used both the .454 and 44 Magnum 10-inch Freedom Arms Model 83s, set up with silhouette sights, for competition. When hunting season arrived, the .454 received a change of sights for the field. I have since added two more Freedom Arms Model 83s to my hunting battery, both with 7-1/2-inch barrels and fitted with scope sights. The .454 was my choice for Africa, but the 44 Magnum remains my most used hunting handgun, especially for whitetails. For game under 200 pounds I prefer the Black Hills 240-gr. jacketed hollow point as it is superbly accurate in my 7-1/2-inch 44 Magnum and normally drops everything immediately with lung shots.

One of my most memorable hunting experiences consisted of a long, steep, uphill climb in waist-deep snow after a mountain lion. For this outing, I carried a 6-inch iron-sighted .44 Model 83 in a shoulder holster. That mountain lion is now stretched out on a limb above my desk looking down even as I type this.

As silhouette shooters began to look more and more for the best possible revolver for competition, Freedom Arms stood ready to accommodate them. In January, 1991 the first five-shot 22 Long Rifle Model 83 (it was originally known as the Model 252) arrived and quickly became the revolver of choice with the .22 silhouette shooters. The test gun I had in .22 was so accurate I hesitated to publish the results knowing that many would find them hard to believe. It was no simple matter for a .22 to make silhouette weight when chambered in the large framed Freedom Arms Single

Taffin's Favorite Freedom Arms model 83 for deer-sized game: both 44 Magnums, one with a 6-inch barrel and the other 7-1/2-inch with Leupold scope. Exotic wood grips by Charles Able.

Chapter 24 | The Freedom Arms Model 83

Taffin took this 8-point Texas whitetail with the Freedom Arms 44 Magnum using Black Hills 240-grain JHP .44 load.

YO Ranch management buck taken at 125 yards with the Freedom Arms 44 Magnum and Black Hills 240-grain XTP-JHP load.

Idaho Leather offers their Model 44 shoulder holster for the Freedom Arms 6-inch 44 Magnum and a whole host of other sixguns. The design, material, and craftsmanship are all top-quality.

Action. The cylinder was shortened and the barrel extended back through the frame; the hammer also had four holes drilled completely through the side to help cut weight and improve lock time; and the 10-inch barrel was tapered from approximately .780" at the frame to .750" at the muzzle end. The result was a silhouette revolver that is one ounce under four pounds.

A big game rifle that will shoot into one inch with three shots at 100 yards is a joy; the Model 83 revolver will do it with a full cylinder of five shots. Both Winchester T22s and CCI MiniMag +Vs put five shots into 1 inch at 100 yards, closely followed by the CCI Pistol Match load at 1-1/8 inches and the PMC Match Rifle load at 1-1/4 inches. This is not from a heavy barreled target rifle but a revolver, a sixgun, with five separate holes that must each line up with the barrel. This is precisely why Freedom Arms are worth the cost.

One year later, in January, 1992, Freedom Arms added the 357 Magnum to the Model 83 line. Now silhouette shooters had a superbly accurate centerfire revolver with minimum recoil. To make the four-pound competition weight limit the .357 has a 9-inch barrel instead of the 10-inch barrel available on the .454, 44 Magnum, and 22LR Model 83s. Originally, as a follow-up to the 454 Casull and 252 Casull, the 357 was named the 353 Casull. Now it is simply the Model 83 357 Magnum. However, with the arrival of the 357 Magnum chambering in the Model 83, whole new vistas arrived for the original Magnum of the 1930s. How about 160-grain jacketed bullets at 1750 fps, 180-gr. jacketed bullets at 1650 fps, and 200-gr. jacketed bullets at 1500 fps? That is 400 fps faster than I can safely achieve with my pet 8-3/8-inch Smith & Wesson 357 Magnum. For several decades a standard heavy 357 Magnum loading has consisted of Lyman's #358156GC over 15.0 grains of 2400. From the 9-inch barreled Model 83 the muzzle velocity is 1640 fps with groups of 1-1/4 inches at 25 yards, 1-1/2 inches at 50 yards. Outstanding performance.

In December, 1993, Freedom Arms went really big-bore by chambering the Model 83 for the 50 Action Express. At the time it was dubbed the Model 555. The original 50 Action Express was designed by Evan Whildin and was chambered in a Desert Eagle that was a true fifty, that is, the groove diameter was .510" as were the bullets, and

Randy Smith, with a Freedom Arms 357 Magnum, and Guide Don McMinn with one of the finest blackbucks ever taken on the YO Ranch.

At 100 yards Hornady's 210-gr. XTP over 22.0 grains of Accurate Arms #9 for 1750 fps is unbelievable in its performance. The first three rounds fired from the Model 83 41 Magnum at 100 yards measured 7/8 of an inch. With the next five shots, three went into 5/8 inch, four into 1-1/4 inches, and all five were a most satisfying 1-1/2 inches at 100 yards. This is not only the most accurate 41 Magnum I have ever had in my hands: it is simply the most accurate centerfire revolver I have ever shot.

The final chapter, at least for now (there may be another big-bore chambering by the time you read this) on the Model 83 was written in April of 1999 with the arrival of the 475 Linebaugh. In 1996, Freedom Arms started experimenting with one of their Premier Grade five-shot revolvers chambered in 475 Linebaugh. It was my privilege then to fire the newest big bore but I was unable to share anything about it until they were ready to introduce it. The cylinder of the Freedom Arms features enclosed case rims so it was necessary to reduce the rim diameter of .475 cases made from 45-70 brass to fit the Freedom Arms cylinders. Naturally, Freedom Arms was reluctant to introduce their revolver in 475 Linebaugh until factory ammo was available.

Once Buffalo Bore began offering a factory load for the 475 Linebaugh having the necessary small rim, the 475 Linebaugh Freedom Arms revolver became a reality. With Buffalo Bore's loads, all assembled with hard-cast bullets, the 420-gr. LBT-LFN (Long Flat Nose) "light load" does 1000 feet per second from a 7-1/2-inch Freedom Arms 475 Linebaugh, while the full-

the bore diameter was .500". The ATF said no, semi-automatic handguns may not be more than one-half inch in barrel and bullet diameter. So barrels were shrunk in diameter, and bullets are now .500". This means the 50 AE cannot be loaded with the .510" bullets of the 500 Linebaugh. CCI's Lawman Factory 325 JSP clocks out of the 7-1/2-inch-barreled Model 83 50 AE at 1,342 fps, while my handload using the Speer 325 JHP does just a shade under 1500 fps with 21.0 grains of Blue Dot. For cast bullets I use BRP's 385-gr. LBT flat-nose over 32.5 grains of H110 for 1460 fps.

Freedom Arms had two more big bores to introduce in the Model 83 before the turn of the century. In December 1997, the Model 83 41 Magnum arrived first as the Model 654. As I discussed the 41 Magnum project with Randy Smith and Bob Baker of Freedom Arms in 1996, I opined that many factory 41 Magnums would not handle heavy bullets, bullets much over 220 grains, very accurately. The problem had to be barrel twist, so Freedom Arms addressed this with a barrel twist of 1:14. Heavyweight bullets that used to provide shotgun-style patterns at 50 yards now will shoot well in a 41 Magnum. Both the Cor-Bon 265-gr. Hard Cast and the Federal 250-gr. Hard Cast factory load designed for hunting will stay right at one inch at 50 yards. These loads are designed for the deepest possible penetration and achieve muzzle velocities of 1400 fps and 1300 fps respectively.

Not 25 yards, not even 50 yards, this group was shot with the Freedom Arms 41 Magnum at 100 yards. Taffin calls it the most accurate sixgun he has ever fired.

Single Action Sixguns | 161

Chapter 24 | The Freedom Arms Model 83

Freedom Arms entries for the title of Perfect Packin' Pistol, the 4-3/4-inch .454 and 4-3/4-inch 475 Linebaugh, both gripped with micarta.

house load with the same bullet achieves 1380 feet per second. With the 420-gr. WFN (Wide Flat Nose), muzzle velocity is 1330 feet per second.

Since the advent of the 475 Linebaugh in the Freedom Arms Model 83, Hornady and Ruger teamed up to produce the 480 Ruger, which is nothing more than a slightly shortened 475 Linebaugh. Buffalo Bore also offers factory-loaded 480 Ruger ammunition with a 420-gr. bullet at 1100 fps from a 7-1/2 barrel. Using this load in a 4-5/8-inch Freedom Arms Model 83 fitted with a 480 Ruger cylinder, I took a 1200-lb. bison in November 2000 with a broadside shot at 35 yards. Penetration was complete. In one side and out the other.

Wayne Baker, founder and first president of Freedom Arms, is now basically retired from that position, Dick Casull is out on his own with Casull Arms, and Freedom Arms is now under the charge of Wayne's son Bob Baker. I asked Bob if he had any plans for a special 25th Anniversary sixgun. He has already been thinking about this, so in a very few short years we will see a special Silver Anniversary revolver, possibly a pair in a fitted case. I'm looking forward to it.

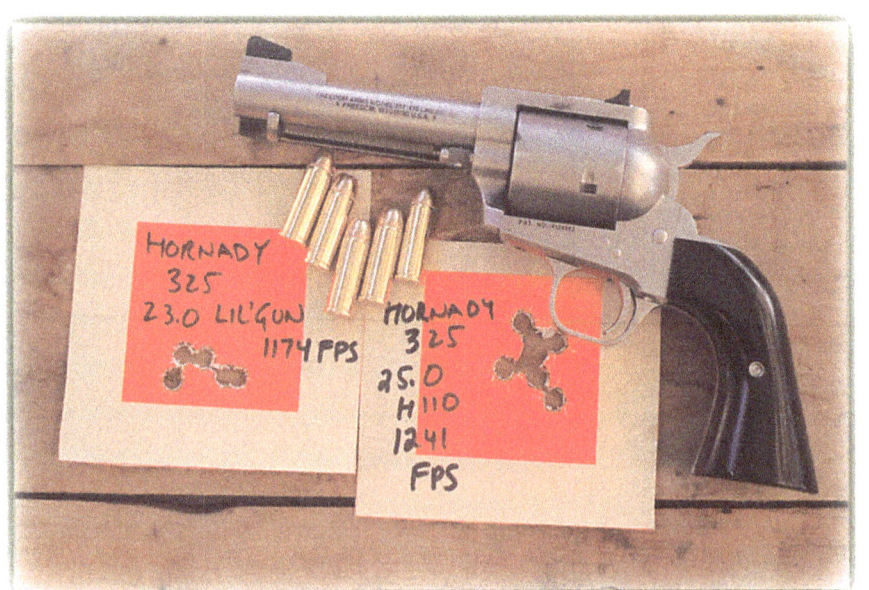

Easy shooting and accurate loads in the Freedom Arms 475 Linebaugh using 480 Ruger brass.

–Chapter 25–

THE FREEDOM ARMS MODEL 97

In 1997 the original Freedom Arms revolver, the large-framed Model 83, was joined by a new sixgun first known as the mid-frame but now appropriately known as the Model 97. The Model of 1997 is about 90 percent of the size of the Freedom Arms standard Model 83 and, as expected, is built to the same exacting tolerances and specifications as the original. It is slightly smaller than a Colt Single Action Army, and to me the grip frame feels much like that of the old Colt Bisley. The first Model 97 arrived not as the traditional Freedom Arms five-shooter but rather as a true sixgun chambered for six 357 Magnum rounds. Available with both adjustable sights and fixed sights, the Model 97 is available with standard barrel lengths of 4-1/4, 5-1/2, and 7-1/2 inches.

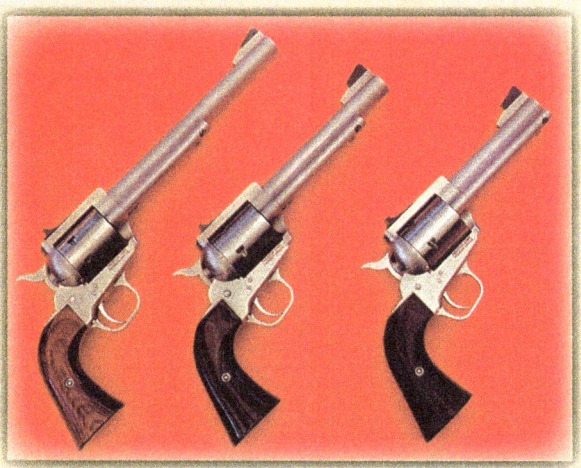

The Freedom Arms Model 97 is offered in three standard barrel lengths of 4-1/4, 5-1/2, and 7-1/2 inches.

The six-shot 357 Model 97 with fixed sights is aimed at the cowboy shooter and revolver fancier who wants the finest possible sixgun available but not necessarily the bulk or power that is afforded by a 454 Casull, 44 Magnum, or 475 chambering. The five-shot Freedom Arms model 83 revolver will take virtually any load assembled with the traditional magnum pistol powders such as 2400, H110, and WW296, with any weight bullet, and it'll beg for more. The Model 97 357 Magnum is designed to handle standard loads, but it is built to the same exact tolerances and specs as the big gun.

I had great plans for the first Model 97, a 7-1/2-inch adjustable-sighted version. Turkeys. For two years in a row I purchased the turkey hunt at the Idaho Wild Turkey Federation Banquet. I had the number one and number two guides from the state of Idaho on both hunts. We walked all over the mountains. We hid in blinds. We called. We got nothing. As I look back on it, two things jinxed me on these hunts. First, I dressed in camouflage; I do not like camouflage at all. I had the whole bit: pants, shirt, cap, even a face mask that caused me to hyperventilate. But the number one problem contributing to my non-success had to be the gun I was carrying. Idaho does not allow turkey hunting with a handgun so I had to carry a shotgun. I'm sure the gods of the hunt were not happy about this, as I am first and foremost a handgun hunter and I betrayed my first love.

Two 357 Magnums from Freedom Arms: the Model 83 has a five-shot cylinder while the smaller Model 97 has a six-shot cylinder. Obviously these two sixguns are built for different purposes.

If I were to get a turkey it would have to be with handgun, so I would have to go where this was possible.

Single Action Sixguns | 163

Chapter 25 | The Freedom Arms Model 97

Who needs a shotgun for turkeys? This Texas tom was taken on the Penn Baggett Ranch using a Freedom Arms 357 Magnum.

The answer was Texas, which allows the taking of turkeys with a handgun. At SHOT Show 1997 I talked with Texas rancher Penn Baggett of Trophy Heart Outfitters about a spring hunt and the possibility of using the newly unveiled Freedom Arms 357 Magnum sixgun for a gobbler. Three months later found me sitting in a blind on Penn's ranch in Crockett County, Texas, about an hour and a half before daylight.

As the dawning of the new day arrived I was watching a group of deer about 150 yards out across a creek when I happened to look down closer in front of me. I could not believe what I was seeing. I blinked to see it if it was real. I thought I was dreaming. There in front of me, not more than 50 yards away, was a big tom turkey! As I raised the sixgun and looked through the 4X LER Leupold scope, the gobbler looked straight at me. I lined the crosshairs up where the neck meets the body, then came down an inch or so to give myself some leeway and squeezed off a shot. The gobbler went down as if struck by the proverbial poleaxe. I could tell by the way he was

twitching he was not going anywhere. The jinx was over! I had my first but not last Texas turkey!

Before heading for what proved to finally be a successful hunt, I had sighted the Freedom Arms 357 in at 50 yards and test-fired it with 14 different loads. The most accurate load tested, Black Hills 125-gr. jacketed hollow points, clocked out at 1600 fps while clustering five shots into 5/8 of an inch at 50 yards. It was chosen to break the jinx. I walked off 49 paces to the downed bird, which figures out to 44 yards the way I step. The 125-grain jacketed hollow point had entered exactly where I held the crosshairs and functioned perfectly.

By August 1998, the second Model 97 was unveiled as a five-shot 45 Colt. This gave us a .45 slightly smaller than a Colt single action with the strength of the Ruger Blackhawk. To add to its versatility, an extra cylinder was available, chambered in 45 ACP.

My Holy Grail is a search for what I dub the Perfect Packin' Pistol. Of course, no such critter exists, which keeps the quest interesting as we get closer and closer to perfection. The Freedom Arms Model 97 45 Colt is about as close as we are going to come in a factory revolver; in fact it is the most compact single action 45 Colt ever factory produced. For 125 years the Colt Single Action Army in .45 Colt has been the best balanced sixgun ever offered to the single action sixgunners; the 45 Colt Model 97 from Freedom Arms is one ounce lighter than a 5-1/2-inch Colt SAA at 38 ounces, two ounces lighter than the same barrel length in the Colt New Frontier. It also has the same natural feel and pointability as the Colt. There all similarity ceases. The grip shape of the M97 is longer and straighter than the Colt SAA and could easily be argued to be an improvement over the finest grip shape ever devised, or discovered, by man.

Two more candidates from Freedom Arms for the Perfect Packin' Pistol title: 5-1/2-inch Model 97s chambered in 45 Colt and 44 Special.

Taffin is shown enjoying a relaxing day shooting the Model 97.

With its light weight, the Model 97 definitely does exhibit some recoil with 255-gr. bullets at 1000+ fps, and although it is not an unpleasant recoil, it is one that takes its toll when hundreds of rounds are fired in one session. Nothing like the punishment inflicted by the same amount of full-house .454s from the large-framed Model 83, but enough to leave some soreness in the shooting hand.

The Model 97 is a thoroughly modern sixgun made with stainless steel, factory custom hand fitted parts, extremely close tolerances, and a modern action with a transfer bar. Unlike the Model 83, which has a safety that must be engaged by placing the hammer in the safety notch, the Model 97 has an automatic safety that places a bar of steel between the hammer and the firing pin when it is lowered. Personally, I never put my trust in a sixgun with a safety that must be engaged but rather always carry such a sixgun with an empty chamber under the hammer. This includes the Colt Single Action, all replicas, Ruger Flat-Tops and Old Models, and the full size Freedom Arms Model 83. Out of habit, and even though it is equipped with a transfer bar safety that engages automatically, I usually carry the Ruger New Model with an empty under the hammer also. The five-shot Model 97 45 Colt will be safe to carry fully loaded with a round under the chamber but old habits are hard to break; I carry four.

It is easy to see the difference and size of the two Freedom Arms models, the .454 Model 83 compared to the 45 Colt Model 97.

The 45 Colt mid-frame Freedom Arms revolver with its five-shot cylinder allows more metal between chambers, almost 90 percent more than a Colt Single Action and, unlike the Colt with its near paper-thin walls, the Freedom Arms Model 97 has the cylinder bolt slots between the chambers rather than underneath them. In this respect, it resembles the large-frame Freedom Arms revolvers. In my sixgunning experience, this says the Freedom Arms Model 97 45 Colt mid-frame is stronger than a Colt Single Action or New Frontier but nowhere near the bank vault strength of the original Freedom Arms M83 454 Casull. Its five-shot cylinder in all probability places the 45 Colt Model 97 at the same strength level as the Ruger .45 Blackhawk, but I have no intention of using the heavy 45 Colt loads tailored for the Ruger in the Freedom Arms Model 97. My max loads for the .45 Blackhawk are 300-gr. hard cast bullets at 1100 to 1200 fps; for the Model 97 I will stay with 255-gr. bullets at around 1050 fps. None of my 300-gr. loads will fit the

Single Action Sixguns | 165

Chapter 25 | The Freedom Arms Model 97

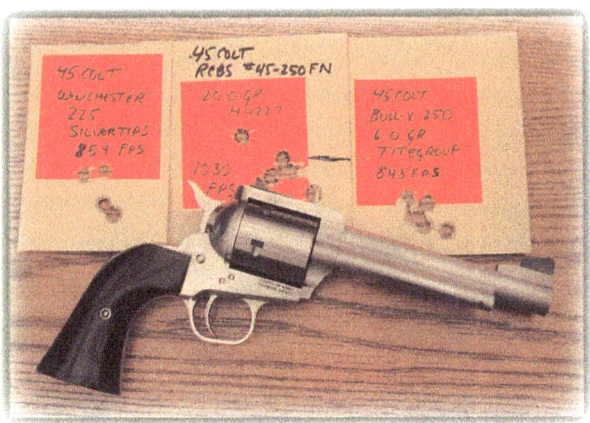

Typical groups fired with a Freedom Arms 45 Colt Model 97.

short cylinder, 93 percent as long as the Ruger, of the Model 97 anyway. When bullets are seated properly, they protrude through the front face of the cylinder, preventing cylinder rotation.

My favorite single action, my favorite sixgun in fact, is a big-bore with a 7-1/2-inch barrel. I started with a pair of 7-1/2-inch Colt Single Actions in Fast Draw as a teenager and the love of this style sixgun has stayed with me and has simply grown stronger and more dedicated over the years. When I was informed by Freedom Arms that the 45 Colt version of the Model 97 was to be available, I could have easily opted for the 7-1/2-inch length, but to maintain its easy packin' qualities, I went with a 5-1/2-inch barrel and to complete the picture ordered adjustable sights and black micarta grips. It is made even more versatile with the addition of the 45 ACP cylinder, allowing a whole range of target and defensive loads.

With its interchangeable front sight system on the adjustable-sighted models, the height of the front blade can be easily changed as one goes from 185-gr. jacketed hollow point 45 ACPs to 260-gr. hard-cast 45 Colt loads. The size of the Mid-Frame Model 97 45 Colt with adjustable sights allows it to be adapted to leather made for the Colt Single Action Army or Ruger Vaquero.

As with all adjustable sighted Freedom Arms sixguns, the Model 97 is easily scoped by removing the rear sight assembly and using a special Lovell combination base and ring set from Freedom Arms. The rear sight assembly of the Model 97 removes easily by loosening two screws. It is then lifted out of its recess in the top of the frame, revealing three drilled and tapped holes, and the mount is put in its place and snugged down.

Favorite loads assembled for the Model 97 45 Colt definitely include Hodgdon's H4227 and 250-gr. bullets.

With RCBS's 45-250FN, a deadringer for the original 45 Colt bullet of the 1870s, or Oregon Trail's 255-grain SWC, and 20.0 grains of H4227, muzzle velocity is 1000 fps and group size is right at one inch at a distance of 25 yards. If a 45 Colt sixgun doesn't shoot well with 18.5 to 20 grains of H4227 and a 255-gr. bullet, it probably will never work with anything.

Switching to the 45 ACP cylinder and using a Leupold 4X scope showed this 45/45ACP sixgun to be no slouch in the little brother department. With Winchester's 185-gr. FMC Match, four shots cut one ragged little hole at 25 yards that measured 3/8 of an inch. This from a revolver, a single action revolver, without moon clips.

The 41 Magnum arrived in a five-shot Model 97 in April, 2000. Friend Penn Baggett, who has hosted me on many a turkey, javelina, and whitetail hunt on his ranch outside of Ozona, Texas, pronounces the 41 Magnum Model 97 as the perfect ranch revolver. I can't argue with him. The 41 Magnum has never been received as a hunting round as readily as the 44 Magnum but I doubt there is a critter that walks in Texas that cannot be handled with the 41 Magnum. It certainly is more than adequate to handle deer- and black bear-sized game anywhere.

After the 41 Magnum, the Model 97 came out in 2002 as a six-shot 22 Long Rifle with extra cylinders offered in 22 Long Rifle Match and 22 Magnum rimfire. Several bricks of 22s, an assortment of semi-autos and revolvers chambered for the 22 Long Rifle, and four grandkids, were all loaded into the pick-up along with the Freedom Arms Model 97. I heard things like, "Gee, Papa, you can't miss with this one!" as my youngest grandson Brian shot a .22 mounted with a red dot scope.

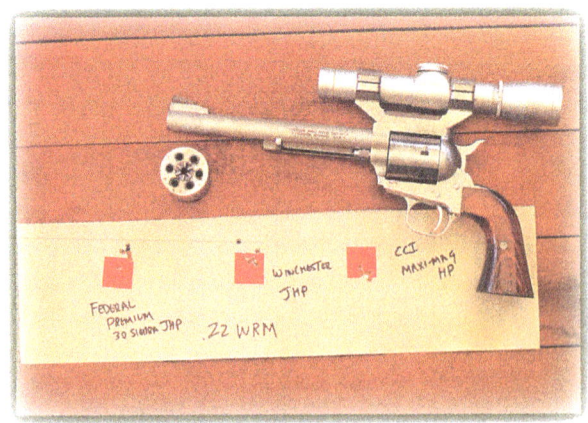

Is it possible for a .22 single action sixgun to shoot this well? Only if it is a Freedom Arms Model 97.

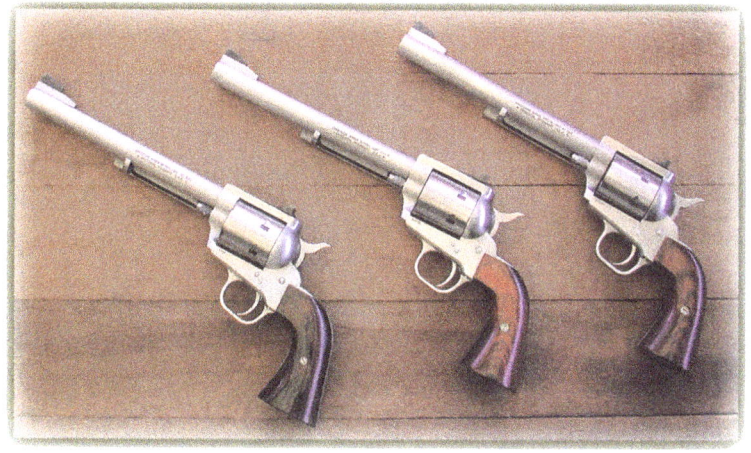

Freedom Arms Model 97s for the small game and varmint hunter: 7-1/2-inch adjustable-sighted models in 357 Magnum, 32 Magnum/32-20, and 22 Long Rifle/22 Magnum.

This was also the day Whitney, one of my granddaughters, discovered how much fun a .22 semi-automatic pistol can be. "Oh, Papa, it's an automatic and I'm afraid I will mess up!" I assured her there was nothing to worry about as long as she did exactly as instructed. When her fourth shot not only hit the bull's-eye, but the x-ring as well, we couldn't keep the magazines full fast enough for her. After shooting so many rounds so quickly through the semi-autos, she then also learned the great relaxing pleasure a single action sixgun can be. No, the Freedom Arms revolver cannot be fired as quickly as a semi-automatic, but it is a rare semi-auto that can shoot as well as this sixgun.

Not only did the grandkids have a great time shooting this .22 from Freedom Arms; so did granddad. So much so that I tested it with both iron sights and a 4X Leupold scope in place using 18 different 22 Long Rifle loadings and five versions of 22 Magnum Rimfire. To prevent shooters from getting the Long Rifle and Magnum cylinders confused, the back of the Magnum cylinder is clearly marked "22M" between two chambers. The performance of this Model 97 is nothing short of amazing. One thing that stands out to me is the fact with both cylinders, using either 22 Long Rifle or 22 Magnum rimfire ammunition in the same barrel, groups of less than one-third of an inch for five shots at 25 yards resulted. CCI's Mini-Mag hollow points, Remington's Yellow Jackets, and Winchester's high velocity hollow points all came in well under one-third of an inch with the 22 Long Rifle cylinder in place, while CCI's Maxi-Mag hollow points delivered the same results with the 22 Magnum cylinder in use. This type of performance puts the Model 97 way up at the top of the list for hunting of small game or varmints as it certainly has the built-in capability of head-shooting meat for the table.

Kids and guns and dogs still go together. Taffin's grandsons, Brian John, Jason Michael, and John Christopher with a Freedom Arms Model 97.

I've never been what one would call overly fond of the 22 Magnum as a revolver cartridge mainly due to the fact the convertible sixguns I have normally used worked well with 22 Long Rifle cartridges but were mediocre with the 22 Magnum cylinder in place or vice versa. Freedom Arms has changed all of that with their Model 97.

The 44 Special has definitely been chambered in some great sixguns. Most double action connoisseurs hold the original 44 Special in the highest esteem even to the point of labeling the old Triple-Lock

Taffin's grandson, Brian Panzella, then age nine, shooting the Freedom Arms Model 97.

Chapter 25 | The Freedom Arms Model 97

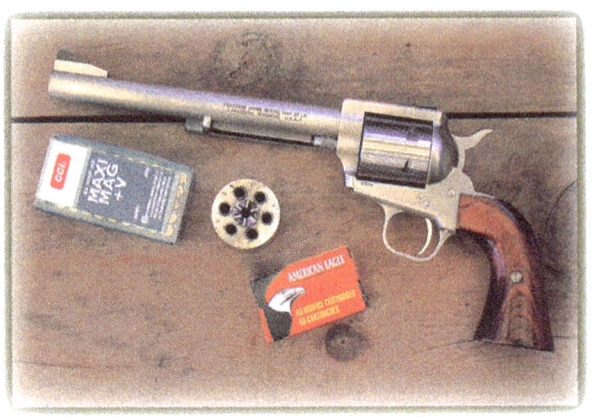

Whether used with the 22 Long Rifle or 22 Magnum cylinder in place, the Freedom Arms is probably the best-shooting .22 convertible revolver ever offered.

as the finest revolver ever built. It has had no equal, let alone a superior, in any other factory-produced 44 Special – until now. Currently, the 44 Special Model 97 introduced in 2002 is available only with adjustable sights. Personally I cannot see any reason to offer it any other way, with barrel lengths of 4-1/4-inch, 5-1/2-inch, and 7-1/2-inch, with the 5-1/2-inch version weighing in at 36.5 ounces on a postal scale. Standard grips furnished on the Model 97 are the same as the Model 83, the reddish colored impregnated hardwood grips with black micarta stocks available as an option. Black micarta really contrasts nicely with the stainless steel finish of any Freedom Arms sixgun.

My most-used standard load for the 44 Special for nearly 50 years has been the 250-gr. Keith hard-cast bullet over 7.5 grains of Unique. BRP's 245KT and Dry Creek's 245KT (the commercially-cast bullets that are closest to the original Keith design) clock out at 1016 fps and 951 fps respectively when shot over Doc Oehler's Model 35P chronograph. They put their four shots into 1-1/8 and 7/8 inches respectively at 25 yards. Switching to my home-cast Keith bullets from the molds marked NEI 260.429KT and RCBS #44-250KT resulted in muzzle velocities of 1002 fps and 961 fps, again respectively, with groups of 7/8 and 1-1/8 inches also. This 44 Special will definitely shoot. A load that falls into the same category as these is the RCBS Keith bullet over 17.0 grains of H4227 for 1002 fps and equally tight groups.

For whitetail deer and similar size animals, if I were forced to choose only one load for the 44 Special it would be Speer's 225-gr. jacketed hollow point over 16.0 grains of 2400 for 1240 fps and the exceptional accuracy of four shots into 5/8 of an inch. This bullet is not the normally-encountered jacketed hollow point but rather a copper cup with a lead core. This is just about the perfect jacketed bullet, along with the 240-gr. flat-nosed version from Speer, for the 44 Special.

Two other favorite bullets, this time of the hard-cast persuasion, are also included. The standard Keith load using RCBS's version clocks out at a sizzling 44 Special velocity of 1270 fps from the short-barrel Model 97. Switching over to Ray Thompson's design, Lyman's #431244GC, and using 17.5 grains of 2400 results in well over 1200 fps and shoots equally well. The Model 97 has a relatively short cylinder, but all these loads with the Keith bullet chamber with room to spare.

In 2003, the sixth chambering for the Model 97 arrived in the form of a 32 Magnum version with an extra 32-20 cylinder, and as expected from Freedom Arms, this little gun is also superbly accurate. Shooting with the 2X Leupold in place to remove as much human error as possible resulted in exceptionally small five-shot groups with either the 32 Magnum or 32-20 cylinder in place. Groups of well under one inch at 25 yards are commonplace.

The most accurate load in 32 Magnum proved to be Sierra's 90-gr. JHC over 10 grains of H110 for five shots in one-half inch and a muzzle velocity of 1260 fps, while the 32-20 shot best with Speer's 100-gr. JHP over 10.0 grains of 2400 for slightly under 1200 fps and five shots in five-eighths of an inch. There is no practical difference between one-half inch and five-eighths of an inch, nor between all the other groups that came in at three-quarters and seven-eighths of the inch. When groups of one-inch are considered "large," one gets some idea of what an excellent shooting sixgun this .32 from Freedom Arms really is.

The Freedom Arms Model 97 will fit in holsters made for the Colt Single Action Army such as this #1930 Austin from El Paso Saddlery.

The latest offering from Freedom Arms in the Model 97 is the newest rimfire magnum, the 17 HMR (Hornady Magnum Rimfire). It is the same basic sixgun as the .22 rimfire version with a slightly smaller hole in the barrel, and the 10-1/2-inch Model 97 17 HMR with a Redfield LER 4X scope in place has proven to be exceptionally accurate.

CCI's 17 HMR TNT HP clocks out at 2164 fps and places five shots into .595" at 25 yards, while Federal's 17 HMR TNT HP does 2304 fps and .307", and Remington's .17 HMR V Max comes in at 2276 fps and a group of .466". No matter what the label on the box, all 17 HMR ammunition comes out of the same CCI plant in Lewiston, Idaho, and it is all top quality.

At SHOT Show 2004, Freedom Arms unveiled the Round Butt. The first round-butted, short-barreled Model 97 was a 3-1/2-inch-barreled, fixed-sighted Model 97 in 45 Colt weighing exactly 32 ounces. That adds up to a heavy-duty 45 Colt that is about as easy to pack as one is going to be able to find. To come up with the Round Butt version, Freedom Arms rounds the heel of the butt only, leaving the toe intact. For my personal use I will put a very slight radius on the front toe.

Also for my use in the 3-1/2-inch M97 45 Colt I have settled on standard weight bullets in the 900 to 1000 fps range. These same loads will average 150 to 200 fps more in 7-1/2-inch sixguns, so they are not lightweight loads by any means. My #1 load of choice is a hard-cast 265-gr. WFNGC (wide flat-nosed gas check) from Cast Performance Bullet Company over 18.5 grains of 2400 for 975 fps. Using the same charge of 2400 for jacketed bullets finds Speer's 250-gr. Gold Dot at 935 fps and Barnes' 225-gr. XPB at 980 fps. One of these three loads will handle anything likely to be encountered when I am packing the little 45 Colt.

Freedom Arms' philosophy has been the same since they opened their doors in 1983. Instead of building to a price, they build the best possible sixgun and price it accordingly. A whole lot of satisfied sixgunners appreciate it.

Freedom Model 97 chambered in 32 Magnum with an auxiliary cylinder in 32-20 is both very easy shooting and superbly accurate.

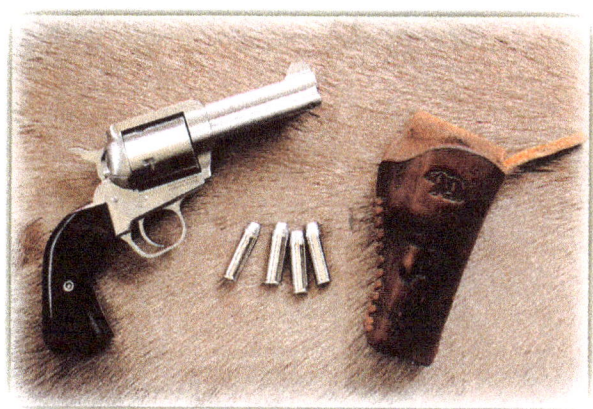

For easy packin' or defensive use with a single action sixgun, an excellent choice is the Freedom Arms Model 97 45 Colt with a 3-1/2-inch barrel and rounded butt. Leather is by Bob Baer.

Freedom Arms' latest Model 97 is chambered in 17 HMR.

–Chapter 26–

THE MINI-GUNS

If there is anything more enjoyable and at the same time simpler than shooting .22s at tin cans, charcoal briquets, golf balls (there really is a reason for them to exist!), or any other suitable safe target, I do not know what it is; plinking is the grandest of single action sixgun activities. If I could somehow capture the great enjoyment that we experienced as teenagers gathering together to shoot Marlin lever action .22s and the then-new Ruger Single-Sixes in the 1950s and spread it from one end of the country to the other, it would certainly have a most positive effect on people's attitudes and actions. We might even get rid of the great divide in this country between the red and blue zones of the political map.

The Bearcat was made for ease of carry when the going required a minimum of weight to be packed.

There are those who would have us believe times have changed to the point that kids and guns no longer go together. That is total nonsense. Kids and guns have always gone together, at least since the invention of the .22 and the advent of so many wonderful revolvers and semi-automatic pistols chambered in this most popular of all cartridges. That first .22, the S&W Model #1 of 1857, may have been originally designed as a hide-out gun but .22s are so much more today. There was a time when just about every father taught his sons weaponry beginning with a .22; that situation simply does not exist today, and fathers who live up to their responsibility in this area are in a small minority.

Even in this high-tech, high-speed, high-stress first decade of the twenty-first century, we can still hold on to the basic fact that kids and guns do go together when tied to proper teaching and supervision. Time spent with a kid shooting is an almost absolute guarantee that that child will not be a problem later on. Yes, kids and guns in general go together, and in particular kids and Rugers go together. Ruger has been making single actions .22s for a half-century now and I would hate to have to count the number of kids, now adults, who not only admit their first handgun was a .22 Ruger but also freely confess it is still one of their favorite sixguns.

My first revolver was a .22 Ruger Single-Six in the mid-1950s, and I have often spoken of the memories associated with it. By the time the 1970s arrived, my son was 10 years old and ready for his very own first revolver. It had to be a .22, it had to be a single action, and it had to be a Ruger. The bargain we struck together was I would pay half if he would save up the other half. It took him quite a few odd jobs to come up with his $20, but on his tenth birthday we walked into The Gunhaus and put down $39.50 for a brand-new Ruger Bearcat. The shop owner threw in a box of .22s, I fashioned a belt and holster, a friend made custom grips, and another generation was ready to enter the satisfying world of sixgunning. He still has that Bearcat, but his son, my grandson, already has designs on it. I never realized how much that Bearcat meant to him and his own memories associated with his first .22 until recently when I received a special letter from him on my birthday:

"Dear Dad: Your birthday was today. I have a hard time reconciling your age with my mental image of you. I remember clearly the young man in his late 20s and early 30s who took us to the Kings Table three nights a week making me take salad each time but also allowing an extra pudding once in a while. I felt very special and proud when I accompanied you to Bob Rice Ford to buy a new pickup truck and then on top of the world every time I was able to ride in the bed sitting on a wheel well and hanging on for dear life.

"I remember how excited I was, nearly trembling, when we went to the gun shop run by the short man with black horned-rim glasses and a noticeable limp to pick out my first handgun. I was ten years old, and as I invested my life savings, which was equally matched by you, probably pulled from that black leather wallet chained to your belt, to meet the price tag of the Ruger Bearcat. I was in awe of my new purchase. Imagine how I felt then when the gun shop owner leaned over and with a wink dropped a 50 count box of .22 shells in my hand and lifted a finger to his lips in a gesture that I knew meant I wasn't to tell anyone of his generosity. Later, when you made the belt and holster I voted myself the coolest kid in the world. And why wouldn't I be? I had a dad that could shoot better than anyone I knew, let me carry my sidearm like a real cowboy, molded his own bullets, and reloaded his own ammo.

"My friends couldn't believe stories about shooting big bore handguns. They were playing with chrome-plated cap guns worn in plastic holsters. They would fire a few caps until their pistols jammed and usually ended up popping caps on the sidewalk with a rock since that was a more reliable way to ensure the caps were properly exploded. My gun was real, the bullets were real, and the holster was real leather stitched by hand. Having my name carved in my belt truly completed the ensemble."

Memories such as this are definitely priceless! Non-shooters may find all this hard to understand, but if you are reading this book I expect you understand perfectly.

Ruger's Bearcat arrived on the .22 scene in 1958; call it the largest of the mini-guns. Unlike the Single-Six, the Bearcat features a one-piece grip frame/main frame combination, originally cast from aluminum alloy and later replaced by steel. The Bearcat has especially been popular with those who must consider weight important: backpackers, hikers, fishermen, smokejumpers, anyone who wants a lightweight .22 that carries unobtrusively.

When Ruger switched to New Model production with a transfer bar safety in both the Single-Six and Blackhawk series, they elected to drop the Bearcat rather than adding a transfer bar. The Bearcat was resurrected in 1993 and is now available in a stainless-steel version complete with a transfer bar safety, but unlike the Single-Six and the Blackhawk sixguns, the Bearcat features a half-cock notch on the hammer.

With the Bearcat being offered in stainless steel I decided to order another one with the idea of some of my grandkids being the testers as well as the "expert" panel that would pass judgment upon this little sixgun. Elyse Panzella, age 17; Laura Seals, age 16; and Brian John Panzella, age 9, joined me to test the newest Ruger single actions.

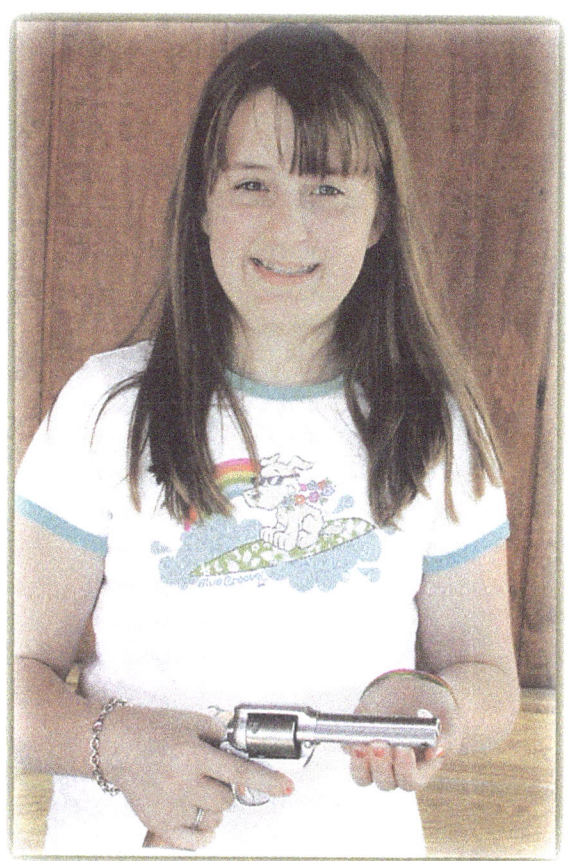

While the Bearcat was basically offered as a single action kit gun, one of its greatest assets is how easily it can be handled by young kids with small hands. Taffin's youngest granddaughter, Hannah, finds it suits her perfectly.

Single Action Sixguns | 171

Chapter 26 | The Mini-Guns

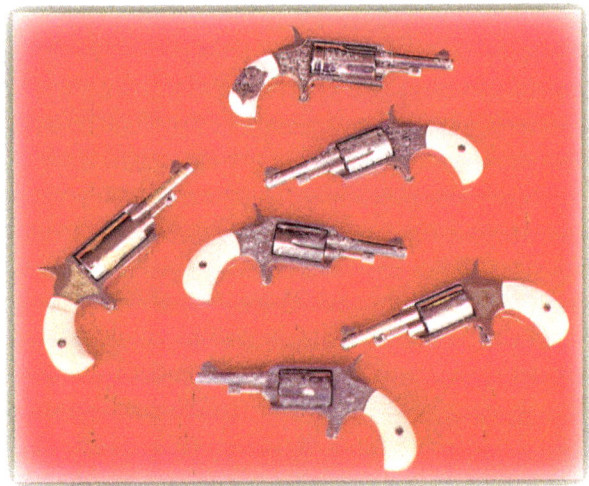

Freedom Arms offered a large selection of .22 mini-guns including those chambered for the 22 Magnum.

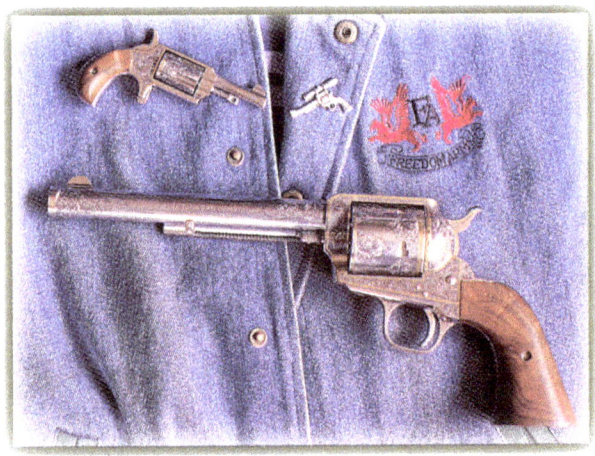

The small size of a Freedom Arms .22 mini-gun is easy to see when compared to a full-sized .454 single action sixgun.

The long and the short of the Ruger Bearcat from the talent of Bob Baer. Top gun is now a six-inch Field Pistol while the 2-inch "Sheriff's Model" with rounded butt was made on an early aluminum-framed gun. Photo courtesy of R. G. Baer.

The Bearcat has a very small grip frame that will fit the smallest of hands yet also works in my large, stubby-fingered hands. The newest Bearcat came with ill-fitting grips, but this was easily resolved when I remembered I still had the original grips from my son's Bearcat of 30+ years ago. Could they possibly fit? Not only did they fit the newer grip frame, they also matched up better than the current factory stocks.

The Bearcat's fixed sights are very close to being dead on for windage while shooting low with most ammunition, making it is an easy task to sight it in perfectly. There is quite a variation in the point in impact of various 22 Long Rifle loads, so it was necessary to make a choice before filing the front sight. My unsolicited advice to Ruger, as it has been for over 40 years, is to give us a Bearcat with adjustable sights. This little .22 is too sweet not to have the advantage of being able to be sighted in perfectly for whatever ammunition is chosen.

The Bearcat features satin finished stainless-steel construction with an aluminum alloy ejector rod housing (should be steel) and a non-fluted cylinder with engraving of both a bear and a cougar. No wonder his old Bearcat conjures up such images and pleasant memories for my son. With eight grandkids in the family, and several of them fast approaching a "gun of my own" category, I predict this little sixgun will be in the Taffin family for quite a while; my youngest granddaughter, Hannah, already has her eye on it. The Bearcat will spend many years traveling in backpacks, fishing tackle boxes, pockets, anywhere a small space is encountered that will accept this diminutive .22. The fact it is stainless steel requiring very little care means it will be a most valuable sixgun for years to come. Maybe someday one of my grandkids will take one of their grandkids shooting with this same .22 Bearcat.

The Bearcat may be small, but it is nowhere near the smallest of the .22 mini-guns. It may seem to be a strange admission coming from someone who has earned his living mostly from big bore sixguns but I will admit not only that I like .22s but that I have also carried a mini-gun everyday for many years. After all, they are single actions! No, I do not consider them ideal defensive propositions, but it certainly is comforting to have one in deep concealment on my person, and a whole lot of peace officers in this country feel the same way. The mini-guns are weapons you definitely hope you never need to use, but if you wind up in trouble they could very well be the difference between life and death.

Freedom Arms, well known today for their high-quality single action sixguns, actually began life

A unique offering from Freedom Arms was an assortment of belt buckles which were designed to hold one of their mini-guns.

producing mini-guns. In 1979, four years before the first Model 83 arrived, Freedom Arms was way at the other end of the spectrum offering very small four- and five-shot .22 pocket revolvers.

The beautifully made little mini-guns were originally offered in four versions: two four-shot .22 Magnums with 1- and 1-3/4-inch barrels, and the same barrel choice with shorter cylindered versions in 22 Long Rifle. They also offered a longer-barreled 22 Magnum Boot Gun to be carried just as the name implies and a solid brass belt buckle holding a short-barreled 22 Long Rifle mini-gun. Pressing a button on the buckle between the grip frame and the back of the spur trigger allowed the mini-gun to drop into the hand. For nearly two decades now I have carried one of the mini-guns in my shirt pocket, first a 22 Long Rifle version, and then a special 22 Magnum given to me by a special friend. Freedom Arms mini-guns are long out of production, but the mini-gun still exists.

North American Arms of Provo, Utah, has been producing exquisite .22 mini-guns since the 1980s in several versions. All versions are five-shooters. As with the Ruger Old Army and the original Remington percussion revolvers, these little guns also have a slot between chambers to accept the hammer. They are safely carried fully loaded with five rounds when the hammer is resting in one of these slots.

The cylinder pin is spring-loaded and when removed allows the cylinder to be taken out of frame, loaded, and replaced, after which the cylinder pin is also put back in place. This is not a fast operation to be sure, but then again these are not designed as primary defensive weapons but as last-ditch, save-your-hide little firearms. The 22 Short mini-gun weighs 4 ounces, the 22 LR mini-gun goes 4.5 ounces, and the .22 Mini-cap & ball comes in at 5.1 ounces with the .22 Super cap & ball at 7.2 ounces. All have 1-1/8-inch barrels except the latter, which is one-half inch longer.

I'm not sure why these little guns have front sights since there are no rear sights and they point-shoot extremely well anyway. Again, if they ever have to be used seriously it will be up close and sights will not be necessary. The 22 Short version fired with CCI's 22 Shorts gives a muzzle velocity of 642 fps while the Long Rifle version using standard velocity CCI long rifles with its heavier bullet comes in at 585 fps. At 10 feet both guns when point-shot hit right at point of aim, or perhaps we should say to point of point. At this close range there would be no problem putting a bullet exactly where one wanted it to go. Aside from this serious nature these little single actions sixguns are fun for popping beverage cans at close range.

As we mentioned earlier, cylinders must be removed for loading. When switching to the Companion percussion models, as they are named, I am reminded of the operation of the first successful revolvers, Samuel Colt's Paterson five-shooter, which also required that the cylinder be removed and a special tool used for loading. The Paterson soon received a built-in loading lever, but the mini-guns are too small for such an apparatus.

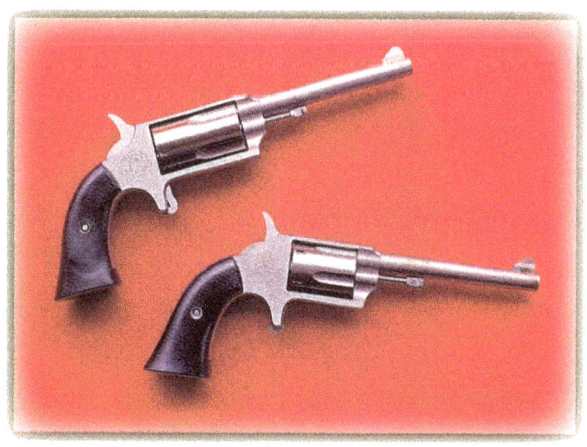

Freedom Arms Boot Guns were designed for just that, to be carried concealed in a boot top.

Single Action Sixguns | 173

Chapter 26 | The Mini-Guns

North American Arms .22 mini-guns are very easy to conceal and point shoot well.

When the cylinder of the black power gun is removed, a provided powder scoop holding the proper amount of black powder (2.5 grains for the Mini Companion and 4.0 grains for the Super Companion) is used to load each chamber; a 30-grain .22 bullet is then placed upon each chamber and seated with the special seating tool (a wooden dowel also works). Only then, after all chambers have been loaded with powder and bullet, are #11 percussion caps placed on each nipple and the cylinder replaced in the frame.

Specifications call for use of FFFFg black powder or Pyrodex. Using the latter the Mini-Companion gave a muzzle velocity of 234 fps while the Super-Companion came in at a whopping 320 fps. Powerhouses they are not. However, it's pleasant to spend an afternoon with cold drinks, sitting in the shade loading and shooting these little guns with friends and family. A pound of powder in the smaller gun will last for 3000 rounds while the larger gun gets only 1875 rounds from a pound of powder. With bullets at four dollars per hundred, cheaper in larger quantities, a little money makes for a whole lot of enjoyable flat-out fun shooting.

The price of so-called progress in this country has been very high. The simpler times are long gone. Kids can't take guns to school anymore to shoot on the way home; in fact if they even point their finger like a gun or even draw pictures of gun, as we did every day back in the late 1940s as we re-fought WWII, they will probably be suspended. May we never lose the connection between kids, guns, and dogs.

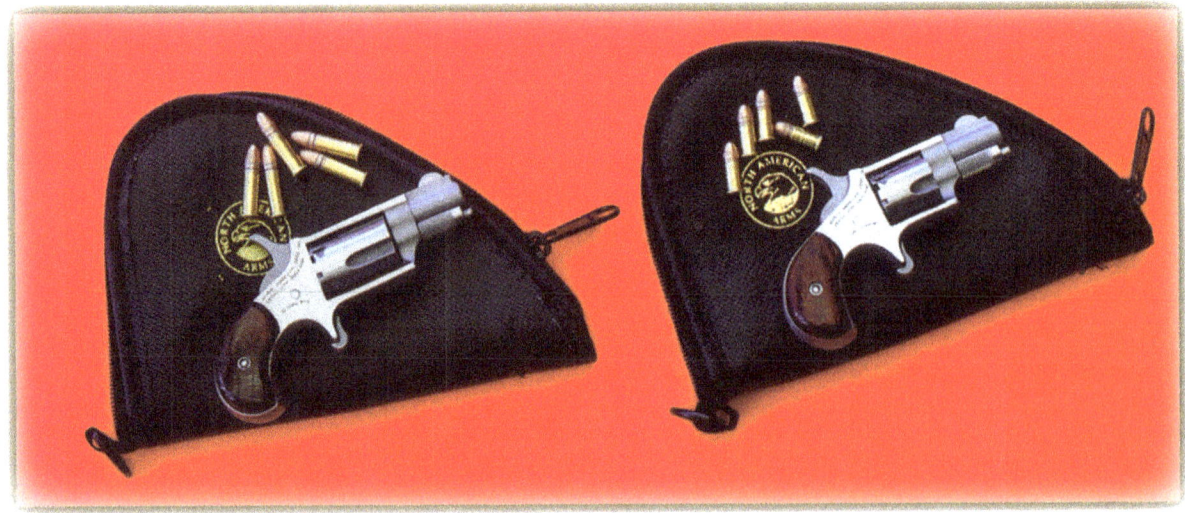

Shooters have until a choice of 22 Long Rifle or a 22 Short in the mini-guns from North American Arms.

–Chapter 27–

THE MAXI-GUNS

In his 1955 book *Sixguns*, Elmer Keith reported he had tried a revolver weighing five pounds and chambered for the 45-70 rifle cartridge: "It was accurate and the load was not at all unpleasant to shoot from the huge gun. However the gun was so crudely made it did not function worth a whoop and could not be recommended, but it proved such a gun is entirely possible." Sometime in the late 1950s or early 1960s two 45-70 revolvers were handmade in a joint effort by Clarence Bates of Arizona and Stu Brainard of Idaho. Brainard displayed his big revolver at local gun shows for many years until his death.

Now enter Earl Keller. In the mid-1970s, Keller started manufacturing the Century Model 100 revolver in 45-70. Keller died in 1986 after making slightly fewer than 400 of the big sixguns. I bought serial number 276, having received it eight years after placing the order! Elmer Keith had serial number 12. At the time of his death, Keller had requests and reserved serial numbers for more than 2500 more of the big 45-70's. Just before his death, Keller negotiated the sale of his company to Paul Majors, who produced 120 more revolvers in Keller's Evansville, Ind., plant before moving the entire operation to Greenfield, Ind.

The Ruger Super Blackhawk, which is normally thought of as a big sixgun, is literally dwarfed by the Century 45-70.

The Greenfield Centurys are manufactured using investment casting with a frame of 120,000-lb. tensile strength bronze and the barrels and cylinders of 4140 steel. This is a big revolver! Weighing in at six pounds, it dwarfs ordinary revolvers like the Colt Single Action or Ruger Super Blackhawk; and two hands are the norm in firing this big sixgun. Although the Century is huge, the grip frame is of the proper proportion and is quite comfortable. Recoil, rather than being a quick snap, is more like a large shove.

The Century is a traditional single action six-shot revolver, which means loading one cartridge at a time and ejecting one at a time. Its diameter is such my hand and fingers are stretched to capacity just to revolve it. There is a cross bolt safety for safely carrying six shots, but I do not use it as I much prefer to let the hammer down on an empty chamber, loading only five rounds. Sights are a fully adjustable Millett rear sight set into a massive flat-top frame. The front sight is a rifle ramp with a dovetail allowing different height and blade combinations, an excellent idea.

I've fired the .45-70 Century quite extensively, both the original Evansville model and the new Greenfield model. The Century has proven to be quite accurate at both 25-yard paper and random rocks out to 250 yards. Bringing out the big .45 is a guarantee of drawing a crowd at any public shooting range. My top bullet preference is the 405-gr. cast bullet from RCBS's #45-405FN mold.

Single Action Sixguns | 175

Chapter 27 | The Maxi-Guns

Gary Reeder offers his custom sixgun in the hard-kickin' – much worse than the S&W Model 500 – 500 S&W Magnum single action stretched-frame sixgun.

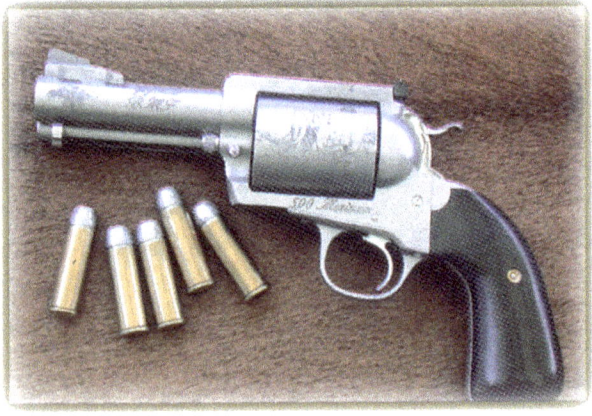

It packs easy but shoots H-E-AV-Y: Gary Reeder's 500 Maximum Packin' Pistol.

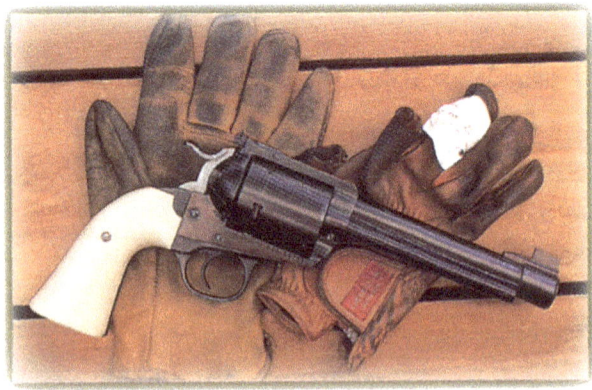

Why the gloves and taped knuckle? It's a 500 Linebaugh Long!

In addition to the Model 100 45-70, I have also tested two other Century sixguns, a Model 400 in 444 Marlin and a Model 500 in 50-70 Government. The Model 50-70 is appropriately dubbed "The Mother Load" and is so inscribed on the barrel. The Century has also been offered in 30-30 Winchester and 375 Winchester. Personally speaking, I can see no use for the 30-30, 375, or 444 chamberings in this big gun. It deserves better, namely the old 45-70 Government and 50-70 Government chamberings. The 444 Marlin cannot do anything that cannot be accomplished by the 44 Magnum and the 445 SuperMag in more compact sixguns, and the 30-30 and 375 are definitely in the light caliber category in this monster.

The Model 400 in 444 Marlin did perform well in the accuracy department, but I was surprised to find the factory 444 Marlin Remington 265-gr. load delivering less than 1500 feet per second, or about what a good 44 Magnum will do. The 444 Marlin is hampered by case capacity: too much, not too little. The case is so long that there is little room left for bullet seating in the Century chamber and 300-gr. bullets seated deep bulge the brass.

The real powerhouse of the Century sixguns is the old black powder 50-70 Government cartridge. It pre-dates the 45-70 and safely delivers over 1400 fps with a 525-gr. bullet! Century tells me they have regularly shot 450-gr. bullets to 1800 fps from the Mother Load. In looking for bullets for the biggest of the big, I came across the RCBS #50-515 FN mold and .512" sizer. With my alloy of three parts lead to four parts type metal, these dropped from the mold at 525 grains. Huge!

I do believe the 50-70 is actually more accurate than the 45-70 as all loads I tried printed excellent groups despite the fact that this gun kicks. Even though it weighs six pounds, recoil of full-house loads brings it rarin' right back, and care must be used when it is fired off sandbags not to get hit in the head or face. In spite of its reaction to heavy loads, the recoil is not punishing by any means – again just a large, heavy push. Loads for the 50-70 were assembled using the top grease groove rather than the crimping groove to give a little more case capacity, though I doubt it is needed. Even the top loads show no signs of excessive pressure on primers nor do fired cases have any stickiness tendency in the cylinder. The Century big sixes shoot well; the only question is how practical are they? The huge cylinders are at the outer limits of one's being able to physically turn them for loading and unloading and no one is going to fire a six pound revolver off-hand for very long. It may not be practical but it is different and a real attention-getter.

The 500 Linebaugh, top, is built on a standard Ruger frame while the 500 Maximum, bottom, requires the 357 Maximum frame as a platform.

In the 1980's John Linebaugh came forth with his two cartridges, the 500 using a 348 Winchester case and a 475 based on 45-70 brass, with both cases cut back to 1.400". Recoil was, and is, heavy with these really big sixguns built on Ruger New Model frames, and one would think the 475 and 500 Linebaughs would be the ultimate, the top, as far as we could go. Then along came the Linebaugh Longs, the 475 and 500 Maximums using the same basic brass as for the regular Linebaugh cartridges but at 1.610" length. Linebaugh used the only gun available for conversions to Linebaugh Long calibers: the out-of-production Ruger 357 stretched frame Maximum. As only a limited number of these sixguns are available and production has stopped, the conversion automatically became a more-expensive-than-usual affair as Ruger Maximums have acquired semi-collectible status and one usually has to pay at least $500 to get one to use as a platform for conversion. The Ruger Maximum may be gone, but Gary Reeder is now offering Maximum length frames on his custom sixguns, including one chambered for the S&W Magnum.

Gary uses very little of the Ruger Maximum except the frame, a new five-shot cylinder being fitted along with a new barrel. Ruger Bisley parts, namely grip frame, hammer and trigger, are fitted to the Ruger Maximum frame as the Bisley grip is the only grip that will handle the very heavy recoil of the big Maximums in full-house loadings. It's an expensive proposition. The frame of a Ruger Maximum and the needed Ruger Bisley parts will cost the would-be owner of a Linebaugh Long revolver at least $800 and that's before the required barrel, cylinder, and action work.

Something as simple as attaching the ejector rod housing so it will stay on becomes a real problem with these big guns. Even with his standard 475 and 500, Linebaugh prefers to build revolvers with a 6-inch barrel with a built-in barrel band that holds the front sight and also gives support to the ejector rod housing, thus preventing it from flying forward under the tremendous recoil generated by these five-shot guns. This is even more critical with the Linebaugh Longs. Even with their long cylinders these big guns balance well and pack easily, and one has to look twice to even notice that the cylinders are made to handle brass that is one third of an inch longer than normal.

My first shot through the 475 Linebaugh Long-chambered five-gun with moderate loads told me very quickly that I had my work cut out for me. These guns kick and kick hard. There is no way around it, or any way to make it sound any different. I have fired hundreds of rounds per day with 44 Magnum and 454 Casull and well over a hundred per day with both the 475 Linebaugh and the 500 Linebaugh. Not so with the 475 Linebaugh Long. I had just forty cases to work with and that was more than enough per shooting session.

Linebaugh's 475 Long uses Winchester 45-70 cases with the brass cut to 1.610" and loaded with .475-caliber bullets. Winchester brass is thin enough that it simply is a matter of trimming and loading with the proper dies, and the standard 475 Linebaugh dies work fine in loading the Linebaugh Long. These dies, as well as those for many wildcat rounds, are available from RCBS. The 475 Linebaugh Long will do 1550 fps with a 370- to 380-gr. cast bullet and 1500 fps with a 410-gr. bullet. Recoil is understandably fierce.

The 500 Linebaugh Long is right at the very edge, more likely over it, of manageability and only with tremendous concentration and strength can it be

The "small" 44 Magnum is shown for comparison with the 475 Linebaugh, 475 Maximum/Linebaugh Long, 500 Linebaugh, and 500 Linebaugh Long/Maximum.

Single Action Sixguns | 177

Chapter 27 | The Maxi-Guns

BFR's long-cylindered 45-70 compared with their standard-size sixgun, in this case chambered in 22 Hornet.

handled. Both the 475 and 500 Linebaugh Longs are only for those revolver shooters with vast experience shooting big bores. Very few handgunners will really be able to handle the recoil of this biggest of all big bores.

The recoil with the 500 Linebaugh Long in full-house loadings is H-E-A-V-Y, V-E-R-Y H-E-A-V-Y! A shooting glove is essential, and I used a Chimere with the lightly padded palm and then taped the knuckle of the middle finger on my shooting hand with several layers of adhesive tape. I also taped my trigger finger to avoid being cut by the bottom of the trigger. Even so, it takes a tremendous amount of concentration and expended strength to fire thirty to forty rounds of this biggest of all revolver cartridges that will still fit in a portable package. I have fired thousands upon thousands of the heaviest revolver cartridges over the years, but I found myself taking a tremendous beating from shooting the big 500 Linebaugh Long.

A full-house load for the 500 sends a 440-gr. bullet out at 1500 fps, and I repeat, recoil of the 500 Linebaugh Long is like nothing else ever experienced. The 475 Linebaugh revolver generates at least three times the recoil of a 44 Magnum, and the 500 Linebaugh Long/Maximum almost puts the 475 Linebaugh Long/Maximum in the mild class. Today it may be very difficult to find many custom sixgunsmiths willing to build either the 475 or 500 Linebaugh Long as they do not wish to test-fire them. Can't say I blame them. Smith & Wesson wisely came out with a sixgun weighing more than four pounds with their version of the 500 Maximum, the 500 S&W. Even so recoil is still horrendous with full-house loads.

After building the 475 and 500 Linebaugh Longs, John took a step backwards with a smaller Long caliber, the more practical 44 Linebaugh Long. Basically the same cartridge as the 445 SuperMag and the 44 Schafer Magnum before it, the 44 Linebaugh Long uses stronger brass made from 303 British or 30-40 Krag brass. The 44 Linebaugh Long goes way beyond the 44 Magnum and in the six-inch-barreled Custom Bisley/Maximum is, when compared to the Long 475 and 500, quite easy to handle. With 250- to 300-gr. 44 bullets, the 44 Linebaugh Long is a 1600 plus fps gun and makes an imminently practical packin' pistol with plenty of power for big game.

A few years back a company by the name of D-Max started exhibiting long-cylindered revolvers at the SHOT Show. Apparently, they were never able to turn out many of these revolvers, which appeared to be well made and, except for being crafted of stainless steel, were spitting images of the five-shot sixguns made by a custom gunsmith several years ago. In the 1980s, while at our local gunshop, Shapel's, I met a man from Utah who was building five-shot 45-70 sixguns by welding two Ruger frames together end-to-end to get the proper length for the rather long 45-70 cartridge, and then crafting five-shot cylinders for these elongated frames. Bill Wheeler has since succumbed to cancer and unless his partner, Neil Topping, is still building these guns, they are no more; however, this basic 45-70 is now being distributed by Magnum Research as the Biggest Finest Revolver (BFR).

Putting the 45-70 in a revolver is a real Catch-22 situation. To help tame recoil and give a true sixgun with a cylinder that holds six rounds requires enough mass to bring the weight up to six pounds as on the Century revolver. If one desires less weight and easier packin', the cylinder must be smaller as on the BFR 45-70 with its five-shot capacity and weight of four pounds, four and one-half ounces. This means that to gain portability, one

The largest sixgun available today, the BFR 500 S&W Magnum.

also gains more recoil. Recoil of the 45-70 Magnum Research BFR revolver is neither excessive nor punishing but it will get your attention and one best pay attention when shooting it, especially with 300-gr. bullets at more than 1600 fps.

To aid in controlling recoil, the BFR 45-70 is fitted with rubber grips that fill in behind the square-backed trigger guard, which is notorious as a knuckle-buster for many shooters when found on the Super Blackhawk. Since it is supplied with Uncle Mike's Rubber grips I found it necessary to wear Uncle Mike's shooting gloves, to keep the checkered rubber from gnawing on my palm and rubbing it raw or raising blisters. Checkering as found on these grips is fine for a few shots or hunting in foul weather, but not when firing a long string of test loads.

The BFR 45-70 is an all-stainless steel (except for the sights), five-shot, 10-inch-barrelled revolver that appears to me made of many parts that are also found on the Ruger Super Blackhawk. I would suspect that the castings for the BFR come from Pine Tree Castings, the same company that supplies Ruger, and at one time Wesson Firearms and Texas Longhorn Arms. The grip frame is definitely Ruger Super Blackhawk-size, and stag grips from my Ruger Super Blackhawk also fit the BFR perfectly. The alloy rear sight appears identical to that of the Ruger Super Blackhawk rear sight, while the front sight is different in that it is ramp-style with an orange face and a base that is held onto the barrel with an Allen screw. The grip frame is also secured to the main frame with Allen screws.

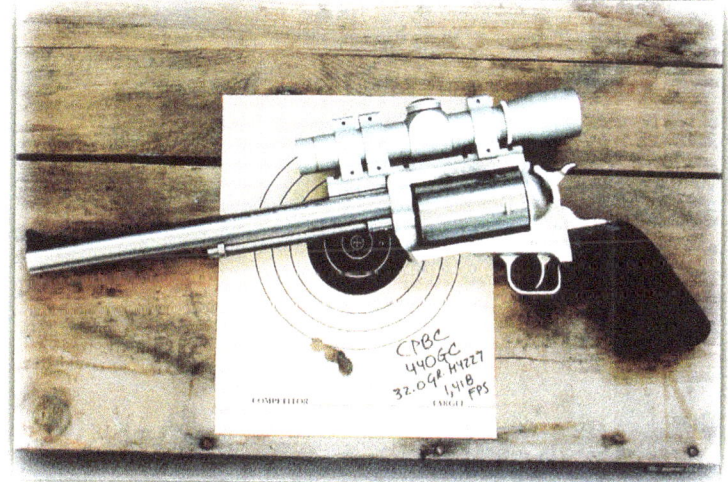

The BFR 500 S&W, with its extra long cylinder, may look ungainly but it does shoot well.

Unlike the Super Blackhawk, the BFR 45-70 has a feature that is usually only found on custom single actions, namely, the cylinder will rotate either clockwise or counterclockwise when the loading gate is opened. This is always helpful on hard-kickin' sixguns should a bullet jump the crimp, protrude from the case and the

Single Action Sixguns | 179

Chapter 27 | The Maxi-Guns

In addition to the long-cylindered maxi-guns, BFR also offers a superbly shooting, standard-sized 475 Linebaugh.

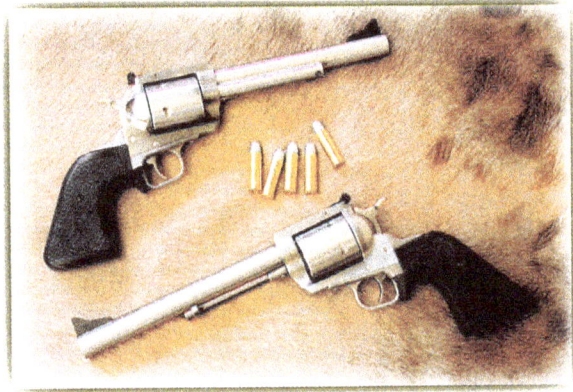

BFR also chambers their standard sized sixgun in 454 Casull.

This is a big revolver to be sure but not all that unwieldy. Its weight is only four ounces more than a Dan Wesson 44 Magnum with a 10-inch heavy barrel. It is packable and could easily be used for hunting. One can well imagine the penetration afforded on big game by a hard cast 500-gr. bullet! Whatever the use it is pressed into, it will definitely draw crowds wherever shooters gather. The BFR in the 45-70 version is offered with either a 7-1/2-inch or 10-inch barrel and in 444 Marlin or 45 Colt/.410.

Magnum Research is also offering the newest sixgun big bore cartridge, the 500 S&W Magnum, in the BFR revolver. The basic platform of the .500 is the long-cylindered 45-70 re-chambered and fitted with a 1:15 twist 10-1/2-inch barrel that is hand-lapped with cut rifling. At the front is a recessed crown, while at the back end of the barrel, barrel-to-cylinder gaps are held under .005". The huge five-shot cylinder is also free-wheeling. With the 500 Magnum being much shorter than the 45-70, the bullet has a long way to travel through the cylinder throat into the forcing cone and down the barrel. It certainly does not seem to affect the accuracy in any way.

The BFR 500 is constructed of stainless steel, with a soft, brushed finish. The grip frame is fitted with wraparound rubber grips, which were once again much appreciated when firing full house loads. The BFR features a fully adjustable rear sight mated up with a ramp front sight, but I ordered the test gun with a 2X Leupold LER pistol scope on an SSK base. It was not at all uncommon to have groups fired with the BFR 500 S&W Magnum be well under one inch at 25 yards. With the milder loads, and no anticipation of heavy recoil, some loads were in the one-half inch range.

The BFR is offered in two versions: the Short Cylinder chambered in 454 Casull and 480 Ruger/475 Linebaugh and the Long Cylinder offered in 444 Marlin, 450 Marlin, 45-70, and a special 45 Colt that

front of the cylinder, thus butting up against the back of the barrel keeping the cylinder from rotating forwards. With a free-wheeling cylinder, one simply rotates it backwards until the round in question comes in place to be removed with the ejector rod. The cylinder is the massive heart of this big revolver and measures 1.740" in diameter and 2.735" in length. A Ruger Super Blackhawk comes in at 1.730" and 1.701" for the same measurements respectively. The heavy bull barrel of the BFR 45-70 measures 10 inches in length and is a straight .850" from frame to muzzle end, while the Super Blackhawk tapers from .800" to .715" at the muzzle end.

BFR's 454 is a five-shot. It comes standard with a free-wheeling cylinder and Pachmayr grips.

United Sporting Arms offered an excellent long-cylindered sixgun chambered in both 357 and 375 SuperMag. These are all 375 SuperMags and were built in three different locations. Photo courtesy of Lee Martin.

also accepts 3-inch 410 shotgun shells. My test BFR came in 480 Ruger/475 Linebaugh with a 1-1/2-to-4X Burris mounted on an SSK T'SOB base, the most secure mounting system in the industry.

BFR revolvers are totally American-made with cut-rifled, hand-lapped, recessed muzzle-crowned barrels, tight tolerances, and soft brushed stainless steel finish and are normally equipped with an adjustable rear sight mated up with a front sight with interchangeable blades of differing heights. A full complement of 480 Ruger and 475 Linebaugh handloads, as well as factory 475 Linebaugh loads from Buffalo Bore, were fired through the BFR. It performed flawlessly with no malfunctions whatsoever and also proved to be superbly accurate. Six of the loads tested grouped four shots into 5/8 of an inch at 25 yards. That is excellent by anyone's standards.

In the early 1970s, United States Arms began production of the Abilene revolver, which was then turned over to Mossberg in the late 1970s. Production continued until around 1983. A similar sixgun, the Seville, continued to be manufactured by United States Arms. A stainless-steel version of the Seville was known as the El Dorado. The El Dorado preceded both the stainless steel Freedom Arms and the Ruger single actions.

A second split within the company saw United Sporting Arms of Arizona being formed. Whether in blue or stainless steel, the Arizona sixguns were all called Sevilles. They were offered in standard length cylinders chambered in such cartridges as 45 Colt, 44 Magnum, and 41 Magnum, while a stretched frame/cylinder version became very popular with long-range silhouette shooters when chambered in 357 or 375 Maximum. The Sevilles were capable of shooting loads with much higher velocities than either the Dan Wesson SuperMag or the Ruger Maximum. At one time I used a 10-1/2-inch United Sporting 375 Maximum/SuperMag for long-range silhouetting and found it to be exceptionally accurate and flat shooting. United Sporting Arms was quite innovative and even offered the 41 and 44 SuperMags before Dan Wesson. The Sevilles disappeared for good in the late 1990s.

In the early 1980s, Elgin Gates, president of the International Handgun Metallic Silhouette Association (IHMSA), lent me his personal 375 SuperMag. I eventually ordered my own 375, which turned out to be consecutively numbered to Gates'. In both cases they were exceptionally accurate long-range sixguns and up to that point the fastest shooting revolvers for the long-range game. When I stopped shooting silhouettes, the 375 SuperMag was traded off for a much more practical 7-1/2-inch Second Generation 357 Magnum New Frontier. I found a 4-3/4-inch 45 Colt New Frontier barrel, had the 357 cylinder tightly chambered to 45 Colt, and *voila!* I had a Personal Practical Perfect Packin' Pistol.

United Sporting Arms also built a few standard sized .454-chambered revolvers; the top sixgun is one of only five built with the IHMSA markings, while the bottom sixgun is a standard 357 Magnum. Photo courtesy of Lee Martin.

Chapter 28

THE PERCUSSION SIXGUNS

Colt replicas produced by such Italian firms as Armi San Marco, Pietta, and Uberti are available from such distributors as Cimarron, EMF, Navy Arms and Taylor's and Co. In addition, for a time Colt Blackpowder Arms, under license from Colt, produced both Second and Third Generation percussion sixguns by importing parts, then assembling and finishing them in this country. The fit and finish of these "Colts" was normally of higher quality than standard replicas from Italy, but they are definitely not real Colts. Percussion revolvers have come a long way since the 1960s and today's cap and ball sixguns are well made, well finished, with a great improvement found in the case colors and with well above average accuracy. In fact, with the right load they often rival modern revolvers when it comes to the latter. Colt-style cap and ball replica sixguns include the 1836 Paterson; 1847 Walker; First, Second, and Third Dragoons; both the 1851 and 1861 Navy; and the 1860 Army.

Sam Colt was born in 1814 and at the age of 16 found himself on board a ship bound from Boston to Calcutta. It is said that he got the idea for a revolving pistol by watching the ship's wheel. He was not the first to come up with the idea, but his 1836 Paterson was the first practical pistol using a revolving cylinder as well as percussion ignition. Sam Colt received a patent on the Paterson at the same time that Santa Ana was overrunning the defenders at the Alamo.

The Paterson was a five-shot 40-caliber revolver with a folding trigger and no trigger guard. More efficient than the single shot pistols they had been using, the Texas Rangers took to the long-barreled Texas Paterson immediately. In 1844 Texas Rangers Jack Hays, Sam Walker, and 14 others, all armed with Texas Patersons, fought more than eighty Comanches, killing 33 of them.

Today's replica Paterson can be had with or without a loading lever and in 36 caliber only. Due to the lack of a trigger guard and the fragile folding trigger, it feels quite strange at first, but consider it took the place of a single-shot pistol, greatly increasing firepower. It was the high capacity pistol of its day.

By 1845, Congress had annexed the Republic of Texas, making war with Mexico a foregone conclusion. Four years earlier, Colt had gone bankrupt and the needed supply of arms had dried up. As the Texas Rangers joined the regular Army in 1846, Sam Walker went East looking for volunteers and Colt revolvers. The two Sams, Colt and Walker, put their heads together and vastly improved the Paterson design.

The replica 1836 Colt Paterson is offered both with and without a loading lever just as were the originals.

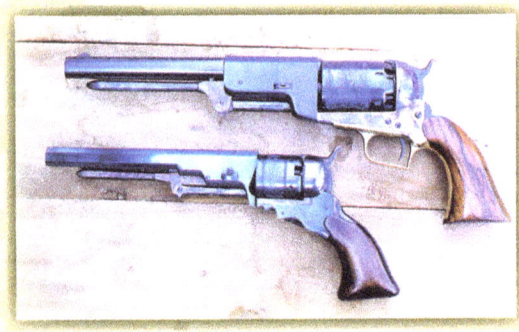

The 1847 Walker was a true fighting handgun and a great improvement over the much smaller Paterson.

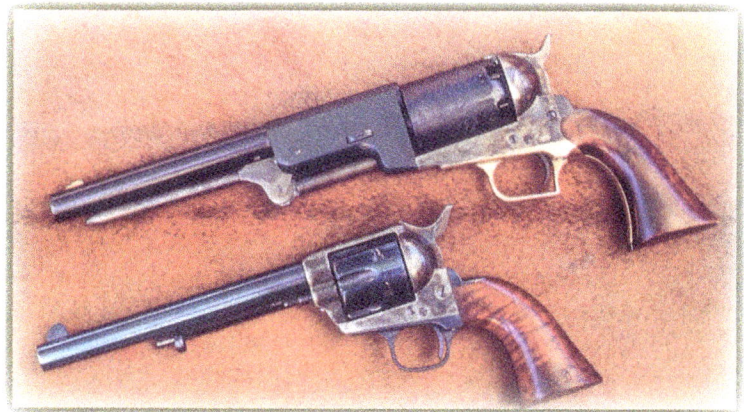

The Single Action Army may have been the "Big Iron On His Hip," but the Walker is much larger and weighed almost twice as much.

Gone was the fragile folding trigger. It was replaced by a stationary trigger surrounded by a trigger guard. The cylinder was enlarged to hold six .44-caliber chambers, all of which would accept up to 60 grains of black powder. However, there was a major problem. Colt had the design, but no money and no manufacturing facilities. The U.S. Government provided the funds with their orders for a thousand Walkers, and Eli Whitney Jr. provided the manufacturing facility. Thus this transitional model from the Paterson to the Dragoons is also known as the Whitneyville Walker Dragoon.

Sam Walker considered the sixgun that bore his name good for use on man or beast and effective as a common rifle at 200 yards. The Walkers were issued in pairs, and Col. Walker's arrived four days before he was killed as 250 Texicans battled 1600 Mexicans. The war was over in early 1848, leaving Sam Colt solidly entrenched as a firearms maker. The Walker had performed well, but it was a huge sixgun with a 9-inch barrel weighing more than four and a half pounds. It would soon be replaced by the Dragoons.

I tested a few Walkers with Goex FFFg and Pyrodex P with all loads measured by volume, not by weight. Walkers did their best work with 55 grains of Goex FFFg and a Speer .454" round ball lubed with a Thompson wad for a muzzle velocity of 1224 fps or 60 grains of Pyrodex P lubed with Crisco for 1109 fps. The mighty Walker remained the most powerful sixgun for almost 90 years, until 1935 and the arrival of the 357 Magnum dethroned it. Walkers are so heavy that they are very difficult to use one-handed, and I would be willing to bet that the first two-handed shooting with a sixgun was done by the first man to shoot a Walker. The replicas share a malady of the originals in that the loading lever often drops on recoil.

In 1848 Colt began replacing the Walker with the Dragoon series. The loading lever latch was improved, the barrel was shortened by one and one-half inches, the cylinder by one-fourth inch, and the grip shape improved, all resulting in the four-pound First Model Dragoon in 1848. One year later, the cylinder locking bolt and slots were changed from oval shape to rectangular shape and the Second Model Dragoon appeared. By 1851, the square-backed trigger guard, still found on the Ruger Super Blackhawk today, was dropped in favor of a rounded trigger guard and the Third Model Dragoon had arrived. A few of the original Third Models were made with an adjustable leaf rear sight, as are a few of the replicas. Originals with this sight are almost impossible to find.

One of the shortcomings of the Walker was the loading lever latch, which often released upon firing.

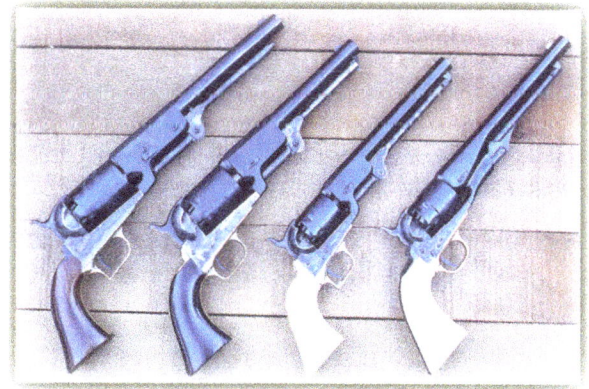

The great Colts of the percussion era: the Walker, Dragoon, 1851 Navy, and 1860 Army. With any one of these a sixgunner in the middle of the nineteenth century was well armed.

Single Action Sixguns | 183

Chapter 28 | The Percussion Sixguns

All percussion revolvers are used only with black powder or a black powder substitute such as Pyrodex, and all charges are measured by volume.

It takes a sturdy belt and holster to pack a Colt Dragoon; Taffin had to make his own.

A classic sixgun from the middle of the nineteenth century, the Third Model Dragoon.

The Third Model Dragoon, even at four pounds, is much easier to handle than the Walker but is about at the limit for both a holster pistol and a one-handed sixgun. The test model came from the Uberti factory and carries a brass backstrap and trigger guard with a case colored frame, hammer, and trigger. The one-piece walnut stocks are well fitted and comfortably shaped. The action is very smooth and tight. As with the Walker, a pin protrudes from the back of the cylinder between chambers, and a hole in the face of the hammer accepts this pin, allowing the hammer to be let down between chambers and the carrying of six shots safely. It shot exceptionally well with the best loads being a full 50 grains of Goex FFFg or the same volume of Pyrodex P under a Speer .454" round ball ignited by Speer #11 percussion caps. Muzzle velocities run 950 and 990 fps respectively.

Both the Walker and the various Dragoons were all deemed more than a little heavy for fast work from a holster but the advent of the 1851 Navy .36 changed all that. With the advent of this miniature Dragoon, a man was as dangerous with his sixgun in a properly designed holster as he was with the sixgun in his hand. Perhaps even more so, as any practiced sixgunner can draw and fire a single action sixgun faster than the average person can react. For the first time real speed from leather was possible. The age of the gunfighter had arrived.

The 1851 Navy has a 7-1/2-inch barrel, either round or octagonal, and is a very well balanced sixgun with one-piece walnut grips and case coloring on frame, hammer, and loading lever. Examples can be found with either a brass back strap and trigger guard and shotgun style gold bead front sight, or a silver plated back strap and trigger guard and a front sight that fits into a dovetail cut. These are mildly recoiling weapons with an 86-gr. round ball and 25 grains of Goex FFFg black powder producing 950 fps. All charges mentioned are of course by volume, not by weight, using a black powder measure. Quick to get into action, mild recoiling and accurate, the 1851 was a gunfighter's weapon. It was used to perfection by Wild Bill Hickok.

In 1860, on the eve of the War Between the States, Colt introduced his crowning glory, his finest percussion sixgun. The 1851 Navy was perfect for holster use but was rather small in caliber; with improved metallurgy would it be possible to place the power of the Dragoon in the sixgun the size of the 1851 Navy? Colt engineers went to work and the result was a sixgun only slightly larger than the 1851 Navy and slightly less powerful than the Dragoon. Basically, the Colt 1860 Army .44 carries a Dragoon-sized grip frame on a Navy main frame with a

The Colt 1851 Navy .36 combined with the Slim Jim holster made a gunfighter as dangerous with the sixgun on his hip as in his hand.

rebated cylinder larger at the front to be able to hold a full 40 grains of black powder under a 44-caliber ball. Barrel length is 8 inches, and the highest velocity I have recorded with the 1860 Army is only 35 fps slower than the Dragoon. This was accomplished with 15 grains less powder.

The 1860 Army was extremely popular with both the military and civilian population. During the Civil War, the United States Army ordered 130,000 1860s at $17.69 per unit. This would be the last full-sized big bore percussion revolver offered by Colt as the cartridge era was about to dawn. Smith & Wesson rolled out the first cartridge revolver in the 1850s, the Model 1 firing the 22 Short, and then went big-bore with the 44 American arriving in 1869. When the patent ran out for bored-through cylinders with cartridge ammunition, Colt added an ejector rod to their 1860, fitted it with a bored through cylinder, and offered both the Richards and Richards-Mason Conversions on both the 1851 Navy and 1860 Army.

In 1871 Colt's first big-bore cartridge-firing sixgun arrived: the 1871-1872 Open-Top. The 45-caliber Colt Single Action Army arrived in 1873 and the cap-n-ball era was pretty much over as far as manufacturing was concerned.

"During the Civil War, the United States Army ordered 130,000 1860s at $17.69 per unit."

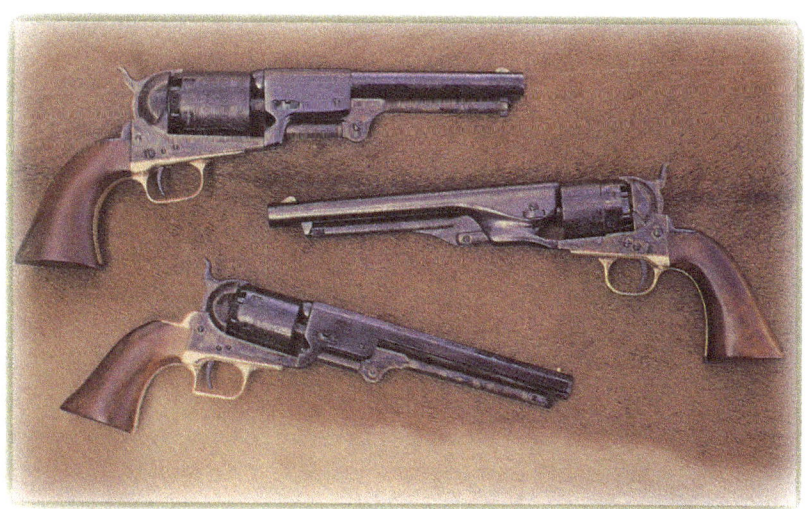

The Colts of the Civil War era included the Dragoon .44, Army .44, and the Navy .36.

Single Action Sixguns | 185

Chapter 28 | The Percussion Sixguns

The 44-caliber percussion sixguns of 1847 - 1860: from top left counterclockwise, the Walker, Dragoon, 1860 Army, and the Remington Army.

In 1861 Colt introduced their final six-shot, medium-bore, full-sized sixgun blending the size and 36-caliber of the 1851 Navy with the round barrel and streamlined loading lever of the 1860 Army. The result, the 1861 Navy, is probably the slickest-looking and easiest-handling of all the sixguns of the cap-n-ball era. During the period from 1848 to 1862, Colt developed several five-shot pocket pistols. The best of these, at least to my way of thinking, is the last cap-n-ball from the Colt factory, the 1862 36-caliber New Model Police: the Colt Detective Special of the nineteenth century. This trim little five-shooter was very popular as a concealment handgun. Grips on replicas are one-piece walnut; the frame, hammer, and loading lever are all case colored; and the action is tight with a somewhat heavy mainspring. The front sight is a very tiny shotgun style gold bead that makes this little gun shoot 18 inches high at 50 feet, but it was designed for very close-quarter work and does fine across card table distances.

Colt's 1847 Walker and First Model Dragoon had been a success, so Colt looked to providing easily carried, easily concealed revolvers. The first ones off the line were versions of the 1848 Colt Pocket Model .31, the Baby Dragoon. These were five-shot, 31-caliber revolvers in four barrel lengths: 3, 4, 5 and 6 inches. The first Pocket models did not have a loading lever as these were guns to be loaded at convenience by removing the cylinder, placing a powder charge and then either tapping a round ball into the chamber on top of the powder charge by using a rod of the proper size and a lightweight mallet, or by simply pushing the ball home by using the cylinder pin on the frame. This method of reloading may sound very slow, but the tiny revolvers were still an improvement over single-shot derringers. The replica 1848 has a 3-inch octagon barrel. Using a volume of 10 grains of powder allows one to shoot 700 rounds through one of these little guns with each pound of powder.

Downsizing at its ultimate: the .44 Dragoon and the .31 Baby Dragoon.

186 Part 4

Remington's .31 Pocket Pistol is about the same size as the Ruger Bearcat.

One year after introducing the Baby Dragoon, Colt introduced the improved 1849 Pocket Model, also a five-shot 31-caliber revolver. This new sixgun had a round instead of a square backed trigger guard, and a loading lever was attached under the barrel, thus allowing the cylinder to be charged without being removed from the revolver itself. Originally, the factory referred to this revolver as the Improved Model Pocket Pistol, but collectors now refer to it as the Model 1849. Several hundred thousand 1849s were made by Colt, and holding one of the replicas in hand certainly provides a great reason for their popularity. These little revolvers weighed around one and one-half pounds compared to the four and one-half pounds of a Walker or four pounds of the Dragoon.

Remington's excellent line-up of full size top-strap pistols was discussed in Chapter 4, but prior to the Civil War, Remington had a whole line of both single action and double action pocket revolvers. With the end of hostilities Remington introduced the New Model Pocket revolver. As with the above-mentioned Colt pocket models, this was also a five-shot 31-caliber revolver made for easy carry and concealment. It actually is smaller than the Colt pocket models, in fact about the size of a Ruger Bearcat. The solid, one-piece frame of the Remington New Model Pocket .31 is brass, while the cylinder and 3-inch barrel are blued. As tiny as this little revolver is, it still has a loading lever so it may be loaded without removing the cylinder.

The first high-capacity handgun goes all the way back to the Civil War with a revolver made for the Confederacy. In fact quite a few famous Confederate officers preferred the high-capacity sixgun known as the LeMat. Francois LeMat was born in France in 1821, making him a contemporary of Samuel Colt. He started out studying for the priesthood, but changed his path and became a doctor. He immigrated to the United States in 1843. His career shifts from medicine to theology to firearms reveal LeMat to have been a most talented and diverse individual. He held patents in several countries on such things as ships' salvage, harbor improvements, cannon ammunition, and revolvers. On a more peaceful note Dr. LeMat also held several patents on medical instruments.

In 1856 LeMat first patented his Grapeshot Revolver, a massive combination revolver that combined a nine-shot cylinder rotating around a central shotgun barrel. Just prior to the Civil War LeMat's revolver was ready for production and the governor of Louisiana made

With its nine-shot cylinder as well as a second barrel accepting shot or a larger ball, the LeMat was the first high-capacity sidearm. Note the lever on the hammer to change from the firing pin from the cylinder chambers to the shotgun barrel.

Single Action Sixguns | 187

Chapter 28 | The Percussion Sixguns

Two lesser-known percussion pistols available today in replica form are the .44 Rogers & Spencer and the .36 Spiller & Burr.

LeMat a colonel. LeMat had formed a partnership with his cousin by marriage, U.S. Army Major Pierre Gustave Toutant Beauregard. The partnership did not last very long, but Beauregard would carry the LeMat revolver as a general in the Confederate Army. Somewhere around 3,000 LeMat revolvers were produced in Paris during the Civil War.

As one would expect from its 10-shot capacity, the LeMat is a large revolver with a weight of 3-1/2 pounds, heavier than the Colt 1860 but lighter than the Colt Dragoon and Walker. It was made in several variations such as a rimfire and a Baby model. Today if one is in search of a shootable LeMat in good condition, a price tag in the $10,000 range should be expected. Pristine examples, of course, will bring much higher prices. Thanks to Navy Arms, modern examples of the LeMat revolver are available for today's shooters.

Navy Arms offers three modern percussion revolvers on the LeMat pattern, a Cavalry, an Army, and a Navy Model. All three are nine-plus-one shooters with the Cavalry Model having a spur trigger guard and swiveling lanyard ring, the Army Model with a round trigger guard and solid lanyard in the butt, and the Navy Model with the center lever on the back of the hammer to allow firing of the center barrel. The sixgun pictured is a LeMat Navy Model.

The Navy Arms LeMat revolver loads like any other percussion revolver. First, a measured amount of powder is poured in the front of the cylinder chamber and a round ball is placed on top of the powder charge and rammed home with the loading lever found on the left-hand side of the barrel. This is a very short-stroke lever so round balls cannot be seated very deeply. I followed this well-established procedure on my sample LeMat. Once the powder charge and round balls were placed in each cylinder, I used that age-old black powder wonder, Crisco, to seal the chambers. I used .451" round balls from Buffalo Bullet Company for the main part of the cylinder and a 65-caliber round ball in the center barrel. This center barrel may also be used as a shotgun. Only after all chambers were loaded and greased were the percussion caps, CCI #10, placed on the nipples.

Thirty grains' volume of Swiss 3F resulted in a muzzle velocity of 900 fps for the 45-caliber round balls. For me the LeMat is a two-handed proposition, as the angle of the grip frame is quite different from that of the standard Colt single action revolvers. The hammer is easy to reach and the spur is wide and flat, making it easy to cock. If you are old enough to remember the heyday of TV westerns in the late 1950s you should remember one series in which the hero carried a LeMat. Don Durant as Johnny Ringo was able to fast-draw the LeMat from a special, low-riding spring clip holster.

The Rogers & Spencer .44 was first known as the Freeman, as it was the result of an 1862 patent by one Austin Freeman. The first revolvers were manufactured by C.B. Hoard in Watertown, New York. At the same time, the company of Rogers & Spencer was manufacturing a

The 1847 Walker, at 4-1/2 pounds, is not the easiest revolver to shoot offhand.

revolver known as the Pettingill. This was a double action hammerless revolver, something neither the shooting public nor the government was ready to accept. Hoping for a government contract, Rogers & Spencer acquired the right to produce the Freeman under their name. From a double action hammerless revolver they went to a traditional single-action, six-shot revolver bearing some little resemblance to the Remington. The Navy Arms Rogers & Spencer is a solid frame revolver with a somewhat boxier appearance than the Remington.

The grip frame of the Rogers & Spencer is much larger at the bottom then either the Remington or the Colt, and the hammer is higher, suggesting that this revolver was intended more for target shooting than for combat. The replica Rogers & Spencer has an 8-inch octagon barrel, a rear sight channel cut in the top of the frame, and a front sight that is an inverted brass cone.

With the outbreak of the Civil War, the South found itself basically without arms manufacturers. Both the Colt and Remington factories were in the North and all of their revolvers went to the northern forces. The only way Johnny Reb could acquire a Colt or Remington was to capture one, so the South was forced to open new manufacturing plants. Since they were not concerned with infringing on existing patents, they freely borrowed existing designs. The Spiller & Burr is a copy of the Whitney revolver and looks much like the Remington .36 Navy. In addition to having to start from scratch in building manufacturing facilities, the South also had a problem with material acquisition. Anything and everything was melted down to be made into firearms. Because of a shortage of steel, the frame of the Spiller & Burr is made of brass. Who knows how many church bells became revolver frames?

The Spiller & Burr differs from the Remington in that the loading lever and cylinder pin are connected and the simple turning of a lever at the front of the frame allows both to be extracted from the frame, allowing the removal of the cylinder for cleaning. The Navy Arms replica of the Spiller & Burr has the requisite one piece main frame/grip frame of brass. The removable trigger guard is also brass while the rest of this well-made sixgun, including the octagon barrel, is blue. Sights are the traditional single action style cut in the top of the mainframe matched up with an inverted brass cone as the front sight.

Once again thanks to the manufacturers of replicas we not only have copies of most cartridge firing sixguns of the nineteenth century but percussion sixguns as well. It doesn't take much imagination fueled with black powder smoke to be transported back 150 years or more in spirit.

Single Action Sixguns | 189

–Chapter 29–

THE SINGLE ACTION REPLICAS

The first SAA replicas, the Great Westerns, were totally American-made and are not to be confused with the Hawes single actions that came later. Hy Hunter was an early distributor of Great Westerns, as was EMF, and he also later imported the German made J.P. Sauer & Sohn Hawes versions. Unlike the Great Western, which was Colt Single Action-size, the Hawes Western Marshall was larger, similar to the Ruger in strength and size. They are normally found in 45 Colt and 357 Magnum and can still be picked up at bargain prices. J.P Sauer also produced the Herter's line of PowerMag sixguns chambered in 44 Magnum, 357 Magnum, and 401 Herter's PowerMag. Herter's sold their PowerMag sixguns for $62 for the two magnums, and only $47 for the 401. A mail order firm, they were basically put out of business by the Gun Control Act of 1968. Herter's sixguns have an extremely large grip frame, but they are good, solid, very strong sixguns and they also can still be found at a bargain prices.

The German-made Hawes and Herter's sixguns may be gone, but Germany still sends us very strong and exceptionally reasonably priced sixguns through European American Armory (EAA). My trip to Germany to visit the manufacturing facilities is one that will never be forgotten. Arriving in Germany shortly after the Berlin Wall came down and the country was unified again, it was my good fortune to stand at the top of an abandoned guard tower on the East German border on our Independence Day. I do not think I really appreciated this country and the freedoms we have until that moment.

I was in Germany to visit the Weihrauch factory in the Bavarian area of Germany and to see EAA's Single Action Bounty Hunter being made. The Weihrauch family had been forced to flee East Germany when the Russians erected the wall, leaving their factory and home and coming to the Western side to start all over again. Now the second generation of Weihrauchs is producing single action sixguns. The old Weihrauch plant in what was formerly East Germany is still an abandoned building and stands as the perfect monument to the failure of communism.

EAA offers the Bounty Hunter in both blue and nickel finishes and chambered in 357 and 44 Magnum as well as 45 Colt.

The Bounty Hunter is a traditionally styled single action sixgun with a sight set-up consisting of a hog wallow through the top of the frame and a blade front sight. This set-up is easier for me to see than that found on most Colt Single Actions as a square sight picture is afforded. As one of the modern styled single actions, the Bounty Hunter is safe to carry with six shots, as an agreement with Ruger allows the use of a transfer bar although this sixgun maintains the typical Colt and Old Model Ruger style half-cock loading/unloading notch.

While I was in Mellrichstadt, arrangements were made to build a special German single action sixgun. An order was placed with the Weihrauch factory for a Bounty Hunter in the original single action caliber, 45 Colt, with an all-blue finish, an easy packin' 5-1/2-inch barrel, and one-piece walnut stocks. Hans Weihrauch suggested the special serial number JOHN 001 to commemorate my pleasurable trip to Germany. My Bounty Hunter weighs in at two pounds seven ounces and, being built on a 44 Magnum frame, is much stronger than a Colt Single Action. It is in fact in some measurements larger than the Ruger Vaquero. In addition to a 44 Magnum sized cylinder and frame, the Bounty Hunter has a Colt-style top strap. It is a quality single action sixgun at a very reasonable price.

Sometime after the demise of the Great Western sixgun and before the price of the Colt Single Action Army really began to escalate, Italian-made replicas began to arrive in this country. Those early examples were usually poorly finished, had brass grip frames, and only from a distance resembled the original Colt Single Action Army. They were found in many spaghetti Westerns made in the late 1960s and early 1970s and it always bothered me to see those brass grip frames on sixguns that were supposedly Colts.

Many of the replica sixguns have already been covered in previous chapters. All of these replicas came about because of an increased interest in Western history, brought about mainly due to the tremendous rise in popularity of cowboy action shooting, which in turn resulted in a demand for more authentically styled replicas. Companies such as Cimarron, EMF, and Navy Arms worked to convince the Italian gunmakers to turn out a more authentic replica. These and other importers today bring us truly authentic replicas.

One individual who has toiled for authentically styled replicas is Cimarron's Mike Harvey. I have been using and testing and reviewing Cimarron products since the very beginning and it is quite satisfying to track the improvement from the very first replicas. When visiting Cimarron in November 2002 to pick up a pair of Open-Tops, we also spent some time with Mike Harvey. At that time he talked about a stainless steel Model P and I felt it would certainly be welcomed as a large number of devotees to the Single Action Army would very much like to have their favorite sixgun in stainless steel.

Stainless steel, artistically speaking, will not take the place of beautiful case colors and deep blue, but it still remains very attractive and even more practical than nickel-plating, which can flake off. If stainless steel is scratched, it can easily be polished. Secondly, for an

Cimarron's latest offering of the Model P is a stainless-steel version, here shown with 7-1/2-inch barrel in 45 Colt with custom stocks from Buffalo Brothers.

Single Action Sixguns | 191

Chapter 29 | The Single Action Replicas

Cimarron offers their Model P in antique looking Original Finish, here seen on guns chambered in 45 Colt, top, and 44-40. The .45 has been fitted with an 1860 grip frame.

outdoor finish it is pretty hard to beat stainless steel. If the weather is bad, one worries about a blued sixgun; if the finish is stainless, simply wipe it off when returning home. The third reason is the most important to me. I like to shoot black powder loads, and although cleanup is not as tedious as some would have us believe, it still requires more care than when using smokeless powder loads. Stainless steel is not only easier to clean, it also makes it easier to see the places that remain to be cleaned.

Cimarron is now importing Uberti-manufactured stainless steel Model Ps in both 357 Magnum and 45 Colt in the three standard Single Action Army barrel lengths of 4-3/4, 5-1/2, and 7-1/2 inches. Not only are they being made in stainless steel, it is also a very nicely polished stainless steel imparting almost a nickel finish look. By now the Italians know how to make single actions and they have pretty much captured the proper look and feel of the Single Action Army. The stainless steel versions are just about the best work they have ever done.

I have been shooting a pair of 7-1/2-inch .45s the past several months. The grips on the stainless Model P are just about perfect as to shape and size and are well fitted to the frame. However the color and finish are just not quite right for my taste. This has become a moot point with me as most of my using sixguns are fitted with custom stocks. For this pair of 7-1/2-inch stainless steel Cimarrons I selected antique faux ivory stocks from Buffalo Brothers. Sixgun #57 has been fitted with stocks with a Longhorn steer skull on both sides, while a double Mexican Eagle decorates both panels of #58. The combination of polished stainless steel and antique ivory is most pleasing to the eye and the carving on the grips provides a comfortable non-slip surface for the hands.

I am fortunate to have an original Colt Frontier Six-Shooter, as the early Colts chambered in 44-40 were called, circa 1879, with one-piece stocks and a 7-1/2-inch barrel. The well-worn original finish of this Colt Frontier Six-Shooter was earned through over 100 years of service. The Original Finish offered on the Cimarron Model P, although brand-new, is a dead ringer for what little finish is left on the old Colt Six-Shooter. Cimarron's finish is not simply an in-the-white sixgun with no bluing. Instead it has age marks, blemishes, and even a small spot or to with a brownish patina look. The one-piece stocks are also appropriately stressed. The only two obvious things signifying the Cimarron Model P as anything other than an old Colt from the 1880s are the barrel marking of "44 W.C.F." instead of "COLT FRONTIER SIX-SHOOTER" and the fact that the stocks still have plenty of varnish intact. One other great difference is the condition of the bore. If only the old Colt could match the pristine bore of the Cimarron Model P.

This antiqued 44-40 raise images of its own. Horses tied at the hitching posts all along Main Street, a crowded saloon on Saturday night packed with cowboys from the neighboring ranches, a piano playing above the shouts and laughter, round tables packed with those who think they can actually beat the man dressed in black who shuffles the cards oh-so-effortlessly. A shot rings out and all other noise stops. "Somebody better get the Marshal!"

Without actually counting I would guess I have tested no fewer than 100 replica single actions over the past decade. I have yet to find one that could be called a poor shooter. In fact the vast majority of them are well above average, and this particular Cimarron sixgun is

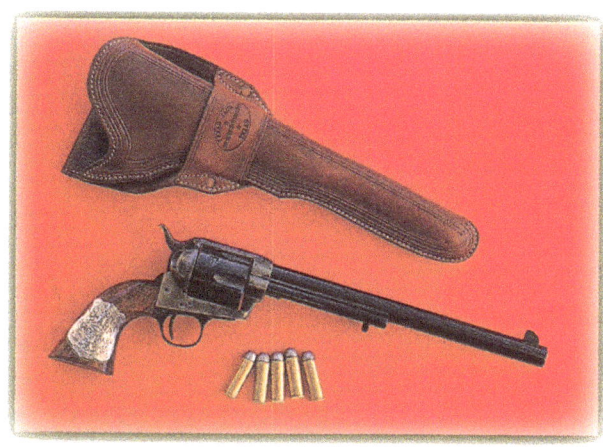

Cimarron offers this extremely good looking and good shooting Wyatt Earp .45.

about as good as they get. It shoots to point of aim with most loads as far as windage is concerned and about an inch low. A few file strokes will take care of the latter. Cimarron's Original Finish is offered in all calibers and barrel lengths.

Cimarron has another unique offering in their Wyatt Earp Model. The Cimarron Model P Buntline being offered is a duplicate of the Buntline Special used by Kurt Russell in his performance as Wyatt Earp in the 1993 movie *Tombstone*. Watching the movie closely, we see that the Buntline Special used has a 10-inch barrel, not the standard 12-inch length of the Second Generation sixguns. Also, when Russell as Wyatt removes his special Colt from its presentation box we see the medallion that is inlaid in the right hand stock. This is also carried out in Cimarron's version as the badge-shaped shield contains the inscription, "WYATT EARP PEACEMAKER, From the Grateful People of Dodge City, Apr 8 1878." Notice there is no mention of Ned Buntline.

Balancewise, the 12-inch sixguns are a little muzzle heavy, but I find that impression lacking with the 10-inch barrel. It just seems to hang on target. The Wyatt Earp Peacemaker, as is the above mentioned 44-40 Model P, is offered in the antique looking Original Finish, or the traditional blued barrel, ejector housing, cylinder, and grip frame, mated with a case-colored frame and hammer. Screws are furnished in the bright nitre blue finish rather than the traditional blue-black finish.

Shooters, be they cowboy action participants or simply those who appreciate nineteenth-century single action sixguns, now have a nearly full menu of sixguns to pick from. The Colt Cartridge Conversion, Open-Top, Model P, Bisley, and Flat-Top Target Model are all now replicated. Add in the Remington 1875 and 1890, S&W Schofield and Model #3 Russians, even "replicas" of single actions that never existed such as the Lightning and New Thunderer with their Colt 1877 Double Action style grip frame. The only sixguns missing are the S&W New Model #3 and the Merwin Hulbert. Dare we hope?

Cimarron's Model P Jr. has the same size grip frame as the Model P, but just about everything else is scaled-down. The balance of the gun is about the same size as a Ruger Single-Six, and actually it has same size frame as the Lightning. Unlike the Model P, the junior version has a frame-mounted firing pin. Although the cylinder is smaller, the Jr. is a true six-shooter. For younger shooters, or those who cannot handle much felt recoil, a Model P Jr. in .38 would be an excellent choice.

The Cimarron Lightning Model is patterned after the old double action Colt Lightning 38.

If one wishes to remain authentic, instead of 38 Specials he can simply load the gun with 38 Long Colts. The Model P Jr. is also available with a 3-1/2-inch barrel and makes a fine little sixgun when chambered in 32-20.

The Lightning is a replica of a single action sixgun that never existed, as is the New Thunderer. Colt's original Lightning and Thunderer were double action sixguns chambered in 38 Long Colt and 41 Long Colt respectively. Available with either a 4-3/4- or 3-1/2-inch barrel length and in blue/case colored or nickel finish, the New Thunderer mates a standard grip frame with a back strap that is a copy of the style found on the old

Single Action Sixguns | 193

Chapter 29 | The Single Action Replicas

The original Colt .41 Thunderer in the center is flanked by Cimarron's Lightning and New Thunderer, both with custom grips by Buffalo Brothers.

Importers of replicas have worked hard to produce authentic-looking sixguns such as this Model P 7-1/2-inch .45 from Cimarron and the 4-3/4-inch Peacekeeper .45 from AWA.

AWA's Peacekeeper is vastly improved in looks and handling with custom fancy wood stocks by Jim Martin. Photo courtesy of Richard Talacek.

Lightning and Thunderer Colt double action sixguns of the 1870's. This back strap carries a pronounced double action style hump that fares very well with the gun's relatively low recoiling cartridges, the 45 Colt and 44 Special. Grips are one-piece walnut either smooth or fine-line checkered.

Replicas have come a long way since the days of the spaghetti western. The late Val Forgett started the importation of percussion revolver replicas and worked several decades to provide shooters with many varied and authentically-styled nineteenth-century sixguns. Both Navy Arms and Cimarron, along with such other firms as Early & Modern Firearms and Taylor's & Co., continue to fill the needs and wants of shooters when it comes to high-quality replicas.

Although not replicas strictly speaking, two other lines of quality sixguns should be mentioned. At one time the Swiss manufacturer Hammerli offered a very high-quality single action sixgun known as the Virginian. This was offered in 357 Magnum and 45 Colt with a three-tone finish: a chrome-plated grip frame, a blue/case colored main frame, and the balance of the gun blued. They were the first single action revolvers to use a longer than normal base pin with two locking notches. Known as the Swissafe, the front notch caused the base pin to protrude far enough beyond the back to the frame to prevent the hammer from contacting the cartridge. It is still used on many replica sixguns.

These revolvers were imported by Interarms, and when their manufacture was switched to Interarms in Virginia, they became the Virginian Dragoons offered with both fixed and adjustable sights and either stainless-steel or blue/case colored finish. The Dragoons were exceptionally strong revolvers, the last of which were produced in 1984.

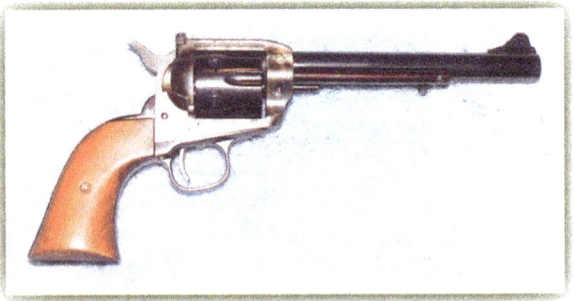

The Virginian Dragoon was in American-made, heavy-framed sixgun by Interarms and was offered in both fixed and adjustable sighted models.

–Chapter 30–

PEACEMAKER SPECIALISTS

The Colt Single Action Army was so superbly designed that is still exists today, more than 125 years after its introduction. More than one-half million have been produced, with even more replicas manufactured than the originals. The basic design goes back almost two centuries and yet it also still lives today in such modern guns as the Ruger Blackhawk and the Freedom Arms revolver. As good as it is, the Single Action Army – whether a First, Second, or Third Generation or a replica thereof – can be improved with a touch of a master's hand. This brings us to Peacemaker Specialists.

Eddie Janis' personal 45 Colt with aged ivory grips and Thad Rybka leather. Photo courtesy of Peacemaker Specialists.

Eddie Janis of Peacemaker Specialists specializes in Colt Peacemakers to the extent that he will not work on any other revolvers even though they may be replicas of this great old design. Peacemaker Specialists' work generally consists of fine-tuning Second and Third Generation Colts and rebuilding First Generation sixguns. The sixguns produced by Colt from 1873 to 1941 are normally found to be superb examples of the gunmaker's art in their original form. However, many were used hard over the course of their shooting lives; those that were used with black powder loads were not always cleaned properly; and some, whether intentionally or unintentionally, were often mistreated.

The early Second Generation Colts were also fine sixguns but lacked perfection, often being found with oversize chambers. As machinery began to wear the later sixguns slipped in quality. Many Third Generation revolvers also need help, the kind of help that Peacemaker Specialists is known for.

One of the biggest problems encountered with all generations of Single Action Armies is interior action parts that are well worn or were not very closely fitted in the first place. The cure requires hand-fitting of bolts and cylinder hands and precise handwork to have the bolt lock into its locking notch in the cylinder precisely at the time the hammer reaches its furthest backward travel and the hand has finished rotating the cylinder. For all of three of these events to coincide requires a master's touch with stone and file. This is a time-consuming operation that requires much patience. Janis carefully stones and files his Gunslinger Deluxe Action Job to perfection.

Single Action Sixguns | 195

Chapter 30 | Peacemaker Specialists

This First Generation 45 Colt from 1917 required a total interior re-build and fitting of fleur-de-lis ivories by Peacemaker Specialists. Leather is by San Pedro Saddlery.

> "The biggest problem with most Colt single actions is found in the barrel and cylinder."

Janis says of this operation: "Our priority in doing an action job is not to make the gun feel smooth and light. Our priority is to build a gun that is totally reliable by eliminating wear and parts breakage. By accomplishing this goal, the by-product is having a pistol that feels like it's running on ball bearings but locks up like a bank vault." Janis has worked on several of my Colts from all three generations and I can testify to the fact that everything he has said is absolutely true. The sixguns are virtually unbreakable, which is quite a bit to say about a sixgun that operates with flat springs, and feel remarkably smooth. Of course, Janis replaces all the original springs with his custom-made Gunfighter springs. I always enjoy handing one of my Peacemaker Specialists sixguns to someone who has a new Colt or replica and asking them to cock the hammer. The look on their face is always priceless.

The biggest problem with most Colt Single Actions is found in the barrel and cylinder. Many older guns will be found with pitted barrels and cylinders from black powder use while newer sixguns will often have oversized chambers. The correct dimension for a .45 Colt cylinder is a chamber mouth that measures .452", but sizes of .456" to .458" are common. To correct this, Janis normally re-chambers 357 Magnum cylinders to the proper 45 Colt dimension. Barrels that are pitted are replaced by Second Generation barrels on First and Second Generation sixguns, while Third Generation Colts normally have correct barrels that do not need to be replaced. When replacement barrels are installed, the lettering can also be re-cut with period correct style markings.

Even though Janis specializes in refinishing old Colt Single Actions and bringing them back to even better than new condition, he is such a purist and has such respect for the history associated with the old guns that he will not refinish an old Colt single action unless it has been previously refinished. He is not alone in this as many gunsmiths have such respect for the history of the old revolvers that they feel they must maintain the character this magnificent sixgun has earned over many decades. Such a sixgun was a particular 45 Colt manufactured in 1917. It had never been refinished, but most of the bluing and case coloring were long gone and it had several stains and some minor pitting from storage in an old holster for more than 50 years.

Peacemaker Specialist turned this gun show bargain sow's ear into a silk purse. A Third Generation 44-40, it was a hopeless case until Eddie Janis worked his magic, bringing it to perfection.

Neither Peacemaker Specialists nor I would destroy the integrity and purity of this grand old sixgun by refinishing it. It still shows age and use on the outside, but looks are somewhat deceiving as Janis totally rebuilt the interior, replacing necessary parts and performing his Gunslinger Deluxe Action Job. He also had on hand an old pair of one-piece ivory stocks carved in the fleur-de-lis pattern and these were expertly fitted. This beautiful sixgun maintains its integrity while still performing to perfection. The ivory stocks themselves are aged to the point they appear to have always been part of this sixgun.

Peacemaker Specialists saved me from one of the worst sixgun decisions I ever made, one in which I should have known better. I had been out all day in the cold and wet; I was tired, hungry, and in a hurry as the gun show was in its last hour when I arrived. Up and down the aisles I went looking for that all-elusive bargain that all show attendees are hoping to find. If there were any to start with they should have all been gone. I know that. Now.

I moved quickly, knowing that time was at a premium. Another mistake. About halfway through the show I spotted it, "it" being a Colt Single Action.

The price tag was low, too low, but I picked it up anyway. Attached to the $650 tag was a Third Generation 7-1/2-inch 44-40 at a time when new Colts were selling in the $1500 - 1600 price range. It looked to be a genuine $1000 savings. Of course at that price one would not expect a sixgun in new condition, but I had no idea what a bargain I was holding. The barrel and cylinder looked new, but the grip frame had mismatched numbers and the mainframe had some pitting and had obviously been re-finished. The dealer said it had gotten wet and he had to re-blue the frame and replace the barrel and cylinder.

That should have sent up the warning signals, but I wanted a bargain so badly I wasn't thinking straight. I was looking for a shooter, not a museum piece. It really didn't look all that bad, and the action felt good and smooth, so the check was written and I headed home. Little did I know what was ahead.

After a hot shower had refreshed me, I prepared for a relaxing evening enjoying my new treasure. The shower must have also cleared up my eyes as I began noticing things I hadn't spotted before. Even though the barrel was definitely brand new and Colt manufactured, the cylinder wasn't quite right. The backstrap had a notch at the bottom for a shoulder stock, while the trigger guard had a very early serial number from the 1870's. The mainframe somehow seemed thinner, and it turned out it was.

Figuring the inner parts could probably stand being cleaned and oiled, I dismantled my great bargain and soon discovered why it seemed so smooth. Both the bolt spring and handspring were handmade out of a piece of lightweight metal and would last about just long

Single Action Sixguns | 197

Chapter 30 | Peacemaker Specialists

enough to operate the action a few times. The cylinder was Italian, not Colt, and both the hand and bolt were on their last legs. Faced with a major re-building project, Monday morning found me at Shapel's looking for Colt parts. Fortunately they had a new Third Generation 44-40 Colt cylinder plus all the springs, the bolt, and the hand that I needed to fix my bargain Colt. By the time I returned home Peacemaker Specialists was open, and I put in a call to Eddie and explained what I had.

He would put in all the new parts and give it a Saddle Tramp action job. I had noticed the hammer notches were also just about gone so I told him they would need to be welded up and re-cut. This often needs to be done on old Colts, and even though this gun was a rather recent Third Generation example someone had totally abused the hammer.

The 44-40 sixgun and parts were on their way to Peacemaker Specialists within a few minutes of my hanging up the phone. When it arrived, Eddie looked it over carefully and called to inform me the problems were worse than I expected. The notches on the hammer could not be welded up and re-cut as someone has already tried that and botched the job. The hammer would have to be replaced. By now my bargain sixgun had become a perfect example of the proverbial rat hole sucking in money, but I was now in so deep I decided I might as well go all the way. If we were to do this right we would also have to find a replacement Colt back strap and trigger guard.

By now the only thing left of my bargain Colt was the mainframe, barrel, and ejector rod housing. The grips, while being original hard rubber Colt, were cut down to fit the slightly smaller Italian grip frame that had been attached, so they also would have to be replaced to fit the new grip frame that Janis had polished to mated perfection with the main frame. Since the frame, which we found out was definitely thinner as someone had polished it to get out some of the pits, already looked old I opted for Peacemaker Specialists antique look. Instead of a blued and case-colored new sixgun, I would have a brownish looking "old" sixgun that, much like the aforementioned 45 Colt from 1917, would actually be brand new on the inside and function as perfectly as a Colt single action can operate.

We still had not arrived. Before the project was finished it was discovered the ejector rod housing didn't fit properly and had to be replaced. Now I was down to a $650 mainframe and barrel! Somewhere there had to be a pony in this pile! I found it when Eddie sent the sixgun back for test firing before he re-finished it.

It shot wonderfully well, windage was perfect, and it placed 200-gr. .44 bullets in a tight little circle. At least it would shoot.

Before returning it to Peacemaker Specialists I found a pair of Third Generation Eagle grips in my parts box, attached them so they could be polished to the new grip frame, and sent everything back for the final step. Within a few weeks I had my sixgun back and it was a dandy. It looks like it is a 125-year old sixgun that has seen use but not abuse. When viewed in the sunlight the barrel and cylinder are very brown, not blue, and now the minor pits in the mainframe no longer look out of place. This sixgun looks as if it was carried in leather on a daily basis as its owner went about business on horseback in all types of weather. Functioning is perfect as expected when Janis does a re-building project and action job. But something was still wrong.

The grips! Brand new grips on a 125-year old sixgun just do not look right at all. They would have to be aged also. All I would need to do would be to sand them and take off the high spots and round off the horse and eagle emblem, perhaps smooth out the checkering. But how? The answer was found in a piece of mesh screen normally used to sand dry wall. It is pliable and can be cut into small pieces. It did a perfect job of adding years to the new grips. They even feel old with all the sharp edges gone. The final result is a Colt Single Action Army in my favorite 7-1/2-inch barrel length and with the great chambering of the frontier, the 44 Winchester Center Fire/44-40. It looks as if it could tell tales of cattle drives, and cow towns, and campfires, and shootouts, while only its owner knows for sure it is a product of the 1970s rather than the 1870s.

By the time this project was finished the cash register had rung repeatedly. With all the parts and the hand fitting I have more invested in this sixgun than the retail cost of a brand new Colt Single Action Army! However, the upside is the fact that this Colt Single Action Army is as perfect as it is humanly possible to make it and is definitely not your run of the mill sixgun found in many a holster. Considering everything I really do have a bargain!

I have a passion for single action sixguns that must regularly be fulfilled. It is never filled but most certainly is fulfilled often enough to keep me on an even keel. So when the phone rang one afternoon, I was elated to hear the words "Colt Single Action." Along with those three magic words guaranteed to lift the most despairing soul, my good friends at Shapel's passed on the information a fellow was in the gun shop with a Colt Single Action for

Both First and Second Generation 44 Special Colt single actions are rare; these two were converted from a First Generation 32-20 and a Second Generation 38 Special by Peacemaker Specialists.

sale. That, along with the phrase "at a good price," got my attention very quickly, and within a few moments I was at the gun shop that has proven to be a gold mine of sorts for uncovering so many great sixguns and leverguns in the past.

As I looked at the sixgun being offered for sale, I saw more than what was in my hands. I looked forward to what it could be. The old Colt was a 4-3/4-inch Single Action with a barrel marked .32 W.C.F. It had obviously been re-blued somewhere along the line after first being buffed improperly as so many old guns are. Perfect it may not have been, but the price was right, exceptionally so for a pre-war Colt single action. The deal was struck and I now had a poorly re-finished Colt complete with a pitted barrel – and one great redeeming feature, an exceptional pair of walnut stocks.

A look through the records of Colt single action serial numbers revealed this particular Colt was manufactured in 1907, the very same year Smith & Wesson introduced the first great N-frame double action sixgun, the New Century (aka Triple Lock), and the 44 Special cartridge. With the Colt bearing a serial number placing it in the company of the first 44 Special, it seemed natural that this sixgun would become a 44 Special. I had been saving a new Second Generation Colt 7-1/2-inch 44 Special barrel for years and it now seemed the time had arrived for building that special Colt.

As I discussed the re-building with Peacemaker Specialists, I decided to send along a less than perfect 44 Special cylinder, a 357 Magnum cylinder for re-chambering to 44 Special if necessary, and the original 32-20 cylinder, all to give Janis wide latitude in making the best possible choice for re-cylindering the old Colt. Several new parts were required: a new cylinder pin and bushing, a new mainspring, a few screws, and an ejector rod and spring. These were joined by the new 44 Special barrel. A 44 Special cylinder that Janis had on hand was exchanged for my 357 cylinder plus a few dollars.

Now came the major part of the work. The new cylinder and barrel were installed with minimum barrel clearance and the forcing cone cut to 11 degrees. An oversize cylinder bolt removed all play in the cylinder. Over nearly a century of use, both the trigger and hammer notches had worn considerably. These were both welded up and re-cut. In the process the action was tuned, the trigger pull set at 3-1/2 lbs., and all internal parts totally smoothed and de-burred in what Janis calls his Saddle Tramp Package. This was to be an everyday working gun so I did not opt for the Gunfighter Package with lighter springs and hand honed action.

First Generation Colts, those made from 1873 to 1941, generally have parts that interchange with Second Generation Colts made from 1956 to 1974, while Third Generations, from 1976 to the present with several interruptions, have different barrel threads, hands, and cylinder ratchets and bushings. Only recently has Colt gone back to the full-length cylinder pin bushing on their cylinders. Parts may interchange but pre-war rear sight notches, being of the very narrow "V" shape, do not mate up well with the thicker front sights on Second Generation barrels. Janis addressed this by milling out the rear sight to give a clear and square sight picture.

Chapter 30 | Peacemaker Specialists

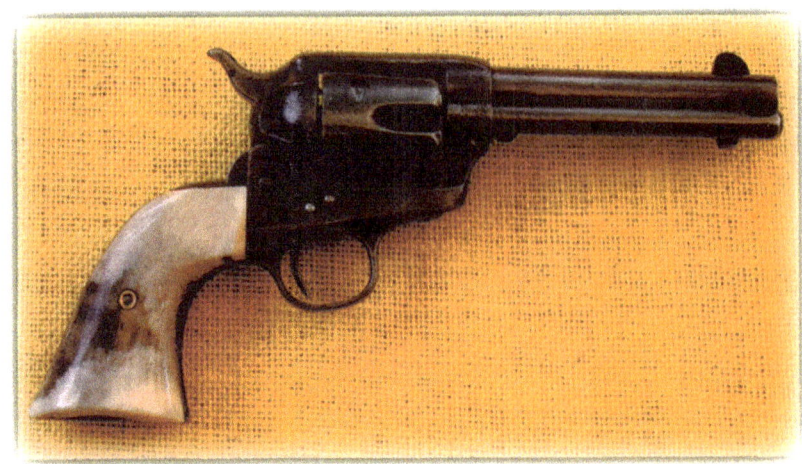

By fitting a new barrel and cylinder and antiquing them, this 1899 Colt .45 retains its hundred-year-old look, complete with bone grips by Peacemaker Specialists.

When the work was all finished, the original plan called for Peacemaker Specialists to return the .44 for test-firing before refinishing to a case-colored frame and hammer with the rest of the sixgun blued. Before this was done we wanted mainly to make sure the windage was correct, or more specifically to see if the sights matched up with my eyes and hold. To facilitate his sighting in of the 44 Special, I had supplied Janis with samples of my intended load for this sixgun, namely the 250-gr. Keith hard-cast bullet over 7.5 grains of Unique. This load clocks out at 950 to 1,000 fps from a 7-1/2-inch barrel.

When the 7-1/2-inch 44 Special arrived back home, I was more than pleasantly surprised with its looks. The new barrel and cylinder matched very well with the old re-blued frame giving it a certain amount of character, and the walnut stocks just seemed to belong on a 7-1/2-inch Colt 44 Special. However, a friend needed a pair of one-piece walnut stocks for his Colt, so they were replaced with Eagle's Ultra Ivory grips. Someday it may be re-finished; for now it suits me just fine. A 7-1/2-inch single action is just about my favorite sixgun when it comes to balance and easy shooting qualities, and this example is no exception. The action is smooth, there is no looseness, and the trigger pull is clean and crisp.

An 1899 Colt .45 with buffalo bone grips from Peacemaker Specialists matches up nicely with period-style leather by El Paso Saddlery.

Janis' favorite Colt Single Action Army appears to be the 45 Colt with a 4-3/4-inch barrel, and I recently had the opportunity to examine five examples of Janis' personal sixguns, all with the shorter barrel length. One would expect the owner of Peacemaker Specialists to have the best possible single actions and that is exactly what these five sixguns are. All have had the actions totally rebuilt with oversized parts and then tuned to perfection. All have new 357 Magnum cylinders properly rechambered to a correctly dimensioned 45 Colt. Of the five, three have also been fitted with new 45 Colt barrels, which have also been marked the way the original barrels were lettered. The sixguns are as follows:

A First Generation Single Action Army from 1899 with an exterior showing its 100+ years of use. However, rather than being refinished, the newly installed barrel, cylinder, and ejector tube have been antiqued to match the original parts. To add to its look of antiquity it has been expertly fitted with buffalo bone grips.

A perfect example of sixgun art is this 1903 Colt .45 rebuilt by Peacemaker Specialists and engraved by Charlie Baker.

A First Generation Single Action Army from 1903, absolutely one of the most beautiful Colts in existence. In addition to all the Peacemaker Specialists action, barrel, and cylinder work, this sixgun has been beautifully C-engraved in Helfricht style by the late Charlie Baker. It was then plated with antique silver; highlighted with fire blue screws, base pin, base pin latch, and trigger; and for the *piece-de-resistance*, fitted with one-piece ivory stocks carved with a horsehead.

A Second Generation Single Action Army from 1959, making it an early production example. In addition to all the action work, the 357 Magnum cylinder has been re-chambered to correct 45 Colt dimensions. Both the front edge of the cylinder and the ejector tube have been beveled in the 1880s style. To make this a perfect working sixgun, it has been fitted with oil finished one-piece walnut stocks; a sixgun from the mid-twentieth century with the look of the 1880s.

The fourth sixgun is dubbed The Last Frontier and is Peacemaker Specialists' beautiful rendition of a Colt New Frontier manufactured in 1970. The barrel and cylinder and both been replaced, oversized action parts have been fitted, the front sight has been stoned square and serrated, the rear sight has been replaced by an Elliason, and the plain-jane factory walnut stocks have been replaced by beautiful one-piece elephant ivories. Surely this is one of most beautiful New Frontiers in existence, and as all 4-3/4-inch New Frontiers chambered in 44 Special or 45 Colt, it ranks high on my list of Perfect Packin' Pistols.

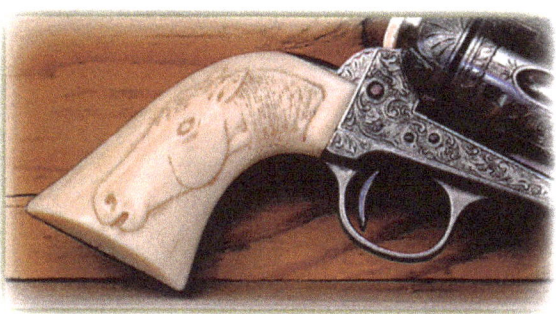

Helfricht C-style engraving graces this 45 Colt with custom ivory grips, the personal sixgun of Eddie Janis.

A Second Generation 45 Colt totally tuned and smoothed by Eddie Janis, fitted with one-piece walnut stocks and mated with a Derry Gallagher holster made from horsehide.

Single Action Sixguns | 201

Chapter 30 | Peacemaker Specialists

A classic among classics, the Colt Single Action .45 with one-piece walnut stocks all by Peacemaker Specialsits.

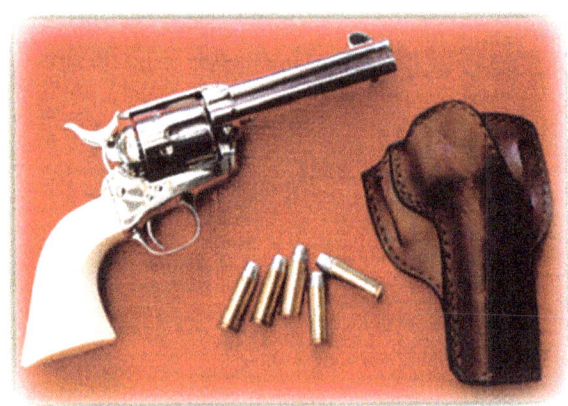

Colt's 4-3/4-inch New Frontier 45 Colt is an excellent Packin' Pistol made even more so my being totally tuned and fitted with one-piece ivories by Peacemaker Specialists.

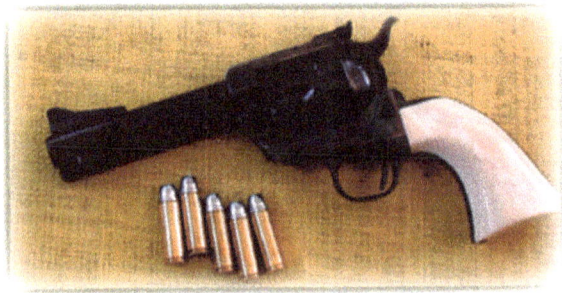

Many of the Third Generation Colts require special attention. This .45 has now been totally tuned and fitted with one-piece ivories by Peacemaker Specialists. Concealment leather is by Bob Mernickle.

The final example is one of a matched paired of consecutively serial-numbered Third Generation nickel-plated Colt Single Actions. This revolver has been set up for cowboy action shooting with an adjustable hammer stop, unloading funnel cut in the frame to facilitate speed loading, and bolt blocks installed to decrease both bolt twisting and cylinder side play during the hard usage that the sixguns often see during competition. All this is in addition to the Gunslinger Deluxe Action Job, and to make it more user friendly, sharp edges have been de-horned including those at the toe and heel of the grip frame, which now, incidentally, carries one-piece elephant ivory stocks.

Peacemaker Specialists now has a second division known as Peacemaker Parts. In addition to performing superb action jobs on Colt single actions as well as complete rebuilding, they also have all the necessary screws, several different styles of base pins, base pin bushings, firing pins, hands, bolts, all springs, and even bolt and trigger screws that are different in length to allow for the tapered frame.

In addition to all these newly manufactured parts, both First and Second Generation barrels and cylinders are available for most calibers and models, and eventually these may also be offered as newly manufactured parts. When I first started shooting it was not unusual to pick up Colt Single Actions for $40 or less and then re-build them using parts remaining from pre-war production. Both the low prices and old parts are gone, but it is still economically feasible to pick up an old Colt and, using Peacemaker Parts, put it back into excellent shooting shape.

–Chapter 31–

CUSTOMIZING THE COLT SINGLE ACTION

Single action sixgun. If you are a real sixgunner those words stir something deep within your soul. No handgun has ever captured the imagination and spirit of shooters as the single action in general and the Colt Single Action Army in particular. The Colt Single Action Army was just that, a revolver adopted by the U.S. Army in 1872 with the first production chambering being in 45 Colt. Now more than 130 years later the single action sixgun and the cartridge are stirring up emotions among those who cherish them both. Why?

The 45 Colt is certainly the most versatile of all sixgun cartridges. It started life as a black powder cartridge in 1873 with a payload of a 255-gr. bullet over 40.0 grains of black powder for a reported 850 fps. Modern brass, bullets, black powder, primers, and sixguns will better that by about 100 feet per second. The advent of the Ruger Blackhawk 45 Colt in the early 1970s gave sixgunners a .45 that would safely handle the same 255-gr. bullet, even a 300-gr. bullet, to a full 1200 feet per second.

Long before the Ruger, experimenters were hard at work. In the 1920s Elmer Keith was pushing the 45 Colt 'way beyond the limit of what the Colt sixguns could stand. In 1936, in his book *Sixgun Cartridges and Loads*, he actually published a load of 22.0 grains of 2400 using balloon head brass and 260-gr. bullets. THIS LOAD IS DANGEROUS! I have duplicated this load using balloon head brass and fired it in a bull-strong 454 Casull and it is definitely in the 44 Magnum category. No Colt single action was built for these pressures. I'm sure he turned more than one Colt into twisted and torn metal using this load. He later dropped back to 20.0 grains and then 18.5 when solid head brass appeared in the 1950s.

Today the 45 Colt is more popular than ever and it retains its versatility with a whole range of both factory and custom guns being offered. The 45 Colt, with loads at or below the original black powder loads of more than a century ago, is the most popular cartridge for purists and traditionalists taking part in cowboy action shooting, while

Fellow lovers of ivory-stocked single action sixguns and many other things, Theodore Roosevelt and the author meet. Painting by Graham Leggett.

Single Action Sixguns | 203

Chapter 31 | Customizing The Colt Single Action

Sometimes all a Colt needs to be personalized is stag stocks and leather such as this rig by Galco.

custom five-guns are offered that will snap at the heels of the 454 Casull and leave the 44 Magnum gasping for air. With the proper sixgun and load, the 45 Colt will handle anything that walks on this continent. Many a buffalo and grizzly bear fell to the old black powder-loaded 45 Colt but those were different times. Today, the old 45 Colt single action, especially in an adjustable sighted version such as the New Frontier, is a nearly perfect close range hunting sixgun and, worn in a properly designed holster, it is always ready should opportunity present itself in the form of deer, black bear, elk, or even moose.

In addition to the 45 Colt, the Colt Single Action and replicas thereof are mostly found chambered in 44-40, 44 Special, 38-40, 357 Magnum, and 32-20, while Rugers come with frames marked 357 Magnum, 44 Magnum, 45 Colt, and even 44-40. In addition to fully custom sixguns, there are numerous embellishments that can be added to already existing single actions turning them into truly personal custom sixguns. What follows in the next four chapters is a run-down of some of what can be done, what is available, and where to find it. I do not propose this as an exhaustive survey but rather offer it to provide information about the products and pistolsmiths that I have personally experienced for customizing and custom building the single action sixgun.

Fast draw shooter and single action sixgunsmith Jim Martin prefers 7-1/2-inch Colts, one-piece bone grips, and cattle brands as found on his personal Colt. Photo courtesy of Richard Talacek.

Once in a great while even though we are panning for water we actually find gold. Such was a situation I found myself in when cleaning out the basement of an older couple's house. Several loads of decades-accumulated junk filled the back of my pick-up for the trip to the local dump. However, there was gold among the trash. The old gentleman had been a long time life member of the NRA and most of the magazines from the 1920s to the 1950s were in that basement. They did not go to the dump!

I spent a long time going through those magazines, clipping sixgun articles. Most of them were by Elmer Keith, but there where others covering such topics as the 44 Special as well as customizing the Colt Single Action Army, including Gordon Boser's 401 Special. Many of these custom single actions had adjustable sights and there's no doubt in my mind that a young and new gunmaker by the name of Bill Ruger received much inspiration from looking at the pictures of these old classic custom Colts.

There are actually three categories of custom single actions. First there are the changes that any shooter can make to turn his sixgun into something that is personally his own. I'm not a mechanic, and if I can undertake these modifications, anybody can. Second, there are the changes such as re-barreling or re-chambering or both that require the skills of a good gunsmith. Third, and finally, there are the completely custom sixguns requiring custom-built cylinders and barrels. Larry "Missouri Cyclone" Crow of Competitive Edge Gun Works has an excellent series of videotapes including four of special interest to sixgunners. They are *The Colt SAA*, *Customizing the Colt SAA*, *The Ruger Vaquero*, and *Customizing the Ruger Vaquero*. The Ruger tapes apply to the Blackhawk as well. Larry is very thorough. These are easy to understand tapes and are also available on CD.

In my opinion, the Colt Single Action Army is so perfect that very little is required in the category of embellishments. I almost always fit my Colts with custom grips made to fit my hand and particular taste.

Fifty plus years ago one of the top Western music groups was Bob Wills and the Texas Playboys. Wills also appeared in several movies as a sidekick and musical interlude. Jim Martin built this Colt single action in his honor. Photo courtesy of Richard Talacek.

Grip makers offer grips of exotic woods, genuine stag, elegant ivory, even buffalo bone or ram's horn stocks. Single action stocks will be covered in depth in Chapter 34.

Colt Single Actions can easily be converted from other calibers to 45 Colt. Eddie Janis of Peacemaker Specialists (see the previous chapter) is a young man who truly appreciates Colt Single Actions and offers both .45 barrels and cylinders for upgrading Colts to 45 Colt be they First, Second, or Third Generation models. In addition, Janis can slick up an action and make it sing. A unique service offered by Janis is that of taking a perfectly finished, modern manufactured Third Generation Colt Single Action and turning it into one that appears to be a 100-year-old gunfight's pride by antiquing the finish and remarking the lettering.

Jim Martin can also super-slick up a single action be it Colt, Great Western, or replica. He specializes in sixguns and is a long-time single action gunsmith, fast draw shooter, trick shooter, and instructor of movie cowboys on the use of the single action sixgun. In the 1950s Great Western not only offered completed sixguns but kits as well. As a young man, Jim Martin purchased Great Western kits, assembled them and sold them, using the money to buy more kits. You can bet his guns had much better actions than the factory-finished guns.

One of the problems with Colt Single Actions, especially in 45 Colt, is over-sized chambers. I once started with a Second Generation Colt New Frontier in 357 Magnum chambering and sent it to John Linebaugh along with a 4-3/4-inch Second Generation New Frontier barrel in 45 Colt with instructions to make a tight 45 Colt with minimum tolerances. The result is an easy to pack .45, now equipped with factory ivories, that will cut one ragged hole at 25 yards with 260-gr. cast bullets over 20.0 grains of H4227 for 1000 feet per second muzzle velocity. It's a definite candidate for the Perfect Packin' Pistol title.

These Colt New Frontiers have been customized several ways. Starting life as 357 Magnums, their cylinders have been tightly re-chambered to 45 Colt; 4-3/4-inch 45 Colt barrels have been fitted with minimum barrel/cylinder gaps; custom ivory and stag grips have been fitted; actions have been tuned and tightened; and finally, all were matched up with El Paso Saddlery's #1930 Austin rigs in basket stamping and floral carving.

Single Action Sixguns | 205

Chapter 31 | Customizing The Colt Single Action

The first two custom Colt Single Actions by Hamilton Bowen: an 8-1/2-inch 32-20 with adjustable sights and a 5-1/2-inch 41 Special. Both will shoot one-hole groups at 25 yards.

Hamilton Bowen has built many really large, high-power single action sixguns, but he has strong traditional leanings and likes building sixguns shooting the older, milder cartridges as well as the 475 and 500 Linebaugh powerhouses. Two of his creations are the 50 Special and the 41 Special. I first shot the 41 Special in a Bowen Ruger Security Six at The Shootists Holiday in 1987. I liked the concept, so much so that I handed over a Colt Single Action to be made into a 5-1/2-inch-barreled 41 Special. My idea was a sixgun that would handle 200-gr. bullets at 900 to 1200 feet per second or about the same as heavy-loaded 44 Specials with 250-gr. bullets.

Bowen returned my Colt with a 5-1/2-inch Douglas barrel and custom 41 Special cylinder. Everything else is stock. In fact, except for the non-fluted cylinder, it looks like an ordinary Colt Single Action Army. But ordinary it is not, as it is one of the finest shooting single actions I have ever come across in a half-century love affair with the old thumb-buster. Brass for the mild 41 Special wildcat is easily made. Using an RCBS case trimmer set to 44 Special length and hooked up to a quarter-inch drill for power, and with my friend Joe Penner feeding the brass and yours truly running the drill, we were able to produce 125 41 Special cases in less than one-half hour. Trim, de-burr, load and shoot – that's all that is necessary for the 41 Special.

I keep the 41 Special loads in the Special range, staying below 1250 feet per second with 215- to 220-gr. bullets. Machine-cast 215-gr. SWC commercial bullets over 12.5 grains of 2400 cut one ragged hole at 25 yards from this fixed-sighted Colt. Velocity is 1063 feet per second: very mild and pleasant to shoot, and incredibly accurate. The 41 Special must be gaining in popularity as Midway now offers 41 Special brass of the proper length and properly head stamped.

Having wanted a quality 32-20 sixgun for years, I sent a second Colt Single Action Army to Hamilton to be made into a semi-long-range varmint pistol. For this sixgun an 8-1/2-inch barrel with a post front sight was mated up with an adjustable rear sight from a S&W N-frame. As expected, this sixgun also shoots superbly and is probably one of the most accurate 32-20s in existence. It had been previously re-blued, so Bowen case-colored the frame and corrected a Colt omission by also case-coloring the hammer.

Hamilton Bowen-built 32-20 is an excellent small game and varmint sixgun.

Two winning hands. Milt Morrison built Taffin's Toy by starting with a Bisley Model 44-40 and turning it into a nineteenth-century belly gun.

One of the slickest custom sixguns is offered by Milt Morrison of QPR on a replica Bisley model Single Action. To arrive at an easy to conceal defensive single action, Morrison removes the ejector rod housing and the ejector mount slot on the right side of the frame, welding and re-contouring the frame in the process. The standard Bisley grip frame is removed and replaced by a brass QPR bird's head grip frame adapted to a Colt-style mainframe. At the same time the original Bisley hammer is also changed from its link system to a roller system to work with the new mainspring. Of course, the entire action is tuned in the process and all cylinder end shake is removed.

The original barrel is discarded and replaced by a 2.5-inch .800" diameter barrel; the rear sight notch is changed from its V-shape to give a square picture; a new front sight is fitted; and the trigger is contoured to match the inside of the trigger guard. Finally, the mainframe is re-color-cased, the rest of the gun is finished in QPR's high luster Black Diamond blue, and an 18K gold band is inlaid around the cylinder. It is certainly one of the most beautiful and efficient single action belly guns in existence and one that any nineteenth century gambler, outlaw, or lawman would certainly have appreciated. Chambered in 44-40, it is potent but very easy to shoot and control thanks to the heavy barrel.

Taffin's Toy by Milt Morrison of QPR is easily concealable and easy to shoot.

Single Action Sixguns | 207

Chapter 31 | Customizing The Colt Single Action

Theodore Roosevelt is still an inspiration to many after nearly a century. This 7-1/2-inch Third Generation 44 Special was commissioned by Ken Durham to honor the great man, soldier, hunter, rancher, and the first cowboy in the White House.

Next to tuning and fitting custom grips, one of the best ways to customize such an already near-perfect sixgun as the Colt single action is to have it engraved. Two of the most famous single actions in existence are the fully engraved Colts of Theodore Roosevelt and General George S. Patton. Roosevelt's Colt was a 7-1/2-inch Frontier Six-Shooter 44-40 with full engraving, nickel plating, and ivory grips with "TR" carved into them. Carried in an equally fancy carved cross draw holster, the 44-40 was his constant companion on his ranch in the Dakota Badlands in the 1880s.

Young Lieutenant Patton chose a special sixgun before he joined Black Jack Pershing to pursue Pancho Villa in 1916. That sixgun was a Colt Single Action Army .45 with the "Gunfighter" length 4-3/4-inch barrel, fully engraved, and ivory grips with the initials "GSP" etched into them. There are two notches cut into the grips and we do know Patton had a "stand up on your feet and shoot it out" gun battle with *bandidos* while in Mexico. This sixgun, carried in a Myres Border Patrol holster, became his authority symbol in World War II.

The man Patton and Pershing were after was Pancho Villa, who also carried a Colt single action .45 with a 4-3/4-inch barrel and full nickel plating with extra fancy ivory grips featuring a carved steer head with gold horns and ruby eyes. Texas Rangers routinely carried fancy sixguns. Frank Hamer, the Ranger who came out of retirement to stop Bonnie and Clyde, is most known for carrying a plain vanilla 45 Colt Single Action that he called "Old Lucky." But Hamer also had his fancy sixgun, a fully engraved and ivory stocked Colt single action .45. Tom Threepersons, who designed the famous holster that still bears his name, packed a nickel-plated Colt .45 with pearl grips bearing the Colt factory medallion and a carved steer head.

A look through any museum or book of Colt firearms will reveal dozens of fancy firearms carried by peace officers and outlaws alike. It goes without saying that the stars of the "B" movies of the 1930s and 1940s such as Tom Mix, Buck Jones, and Tim McCoy all packed fancy sixguns across the silver screen. Even John Wayne, who also starred in "B" movies at the beginning of his long career, died in his final movie, *The Shootist*, packing a fully engraved .45 single action.

When I began to really become interested in sixguns as a teenager in the 1950s, Elmer Keith was the handgun writer. His book *Sixguns* was published in 1955, and my dog-eared copy opens almost automatically to the page showing his #5, a completely custom Colt Single Action 44 Special that Keith had built up in the 1920s. This was a sixgun! Chambered in the top caliber of the day, it was fully engraved and ivory stocked. I located an old copy of *the American Rifleman* from April 1929 and read the firsthand account of the building of the #5

Friend and Fellow Shootist Brian Pearce traveled to Elmer Keith's old homestead in Durkee, Oregon to shoot a pair of #5 SAAs re-created by Hamilton Bowen.

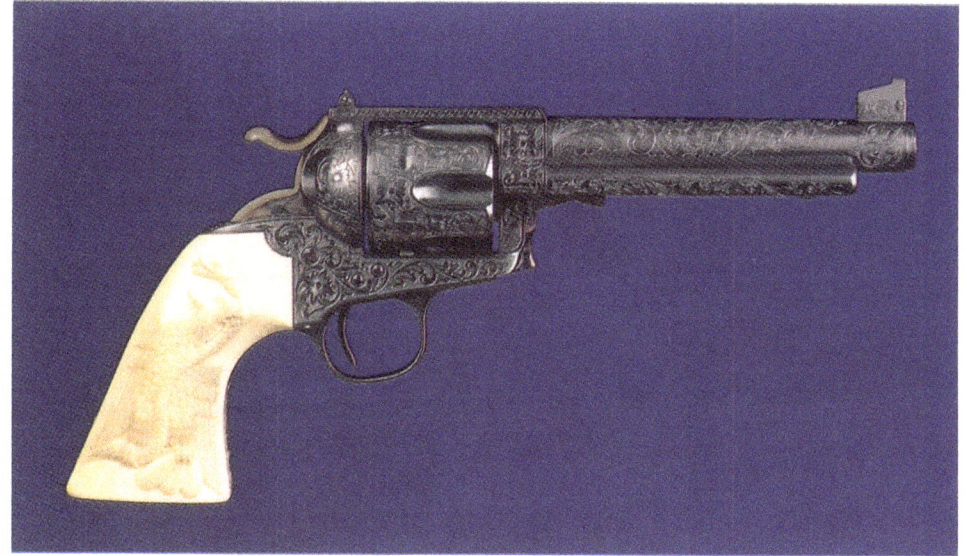

One of the most famous single actions in existence, at least among truly dedicated sixgunners, is Elmer Keith's #5 SAA 44 Special; this breathtaking re-creation of the #5 SAA was built by Hamilton Bowen on a USFA mainframe.

SAA, as Keith called it. The picture of the fully engraved sixgun in the article was even better than that found in the book and I dreamed of the day when I might have such a sixgun.

I already had a 4-3/4-inch .45 Colt with ivory grips by Charles Able that I had selected years earlier for engraving. This sixgun would be a shooter, not a piece to hide away, so I made sure it shot to point of aim with a favorite 45 Colt load. It took a slight bit of filing on the front sight to get the point of impact to point of aim and then the blued Colt with a case-hardened frame was sent south to Boerne, Texas to be engraved by Jim Riggs.

On this sixgun Riggs used a style that looks very much like pictures I have seen of sixguns that were engraved in the frontier period. The scrollwork is more subdued and a sunburst effect graces the loading gate and recoil shield. My name is also engraved on the backstrap so this sixgun will, in all probability, eventually go to my oldest grandson, who also bears my name. With its satin nickel finish and ivory stocks, this Colt Single Action Army is one that any single action sixgunner would like.

Do not make the mistake of thinking the cost of engraving is out of reach. Of course we are not talking museum high-grade presentation pieces here. I see no practical use for a sixgun that has taken hundreds, perhaps even thousands of hours to complete and is replete with 100 percent coverage of very intricate patterns. A sixgun such as this is highly valuable, strictly for show, and only for the rich.

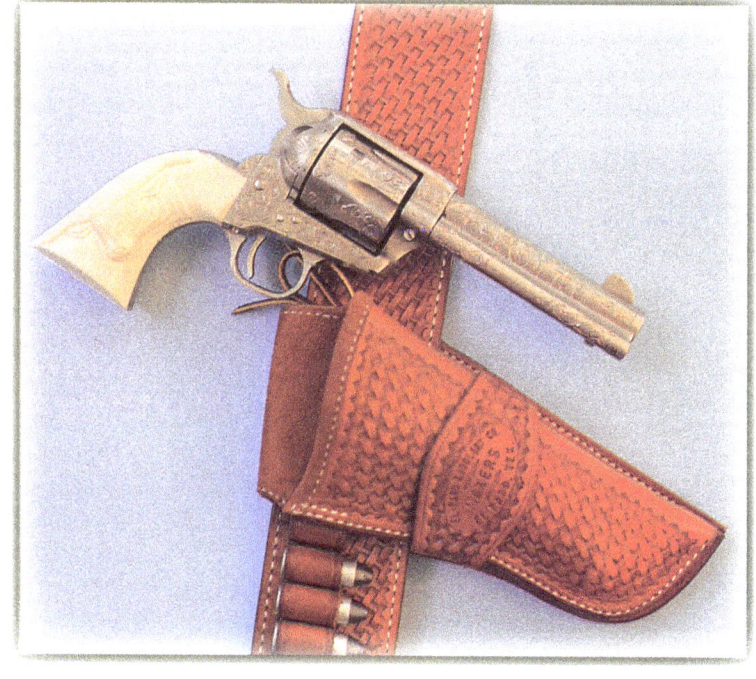

Jim Riggs-engraved Second Generation 45 Colt is beautiful but also serves as a working sixgun. Leather is by El Paso.

Single Action Sixguns | 209

Chapter 31 | Customizing The Colt Single Action

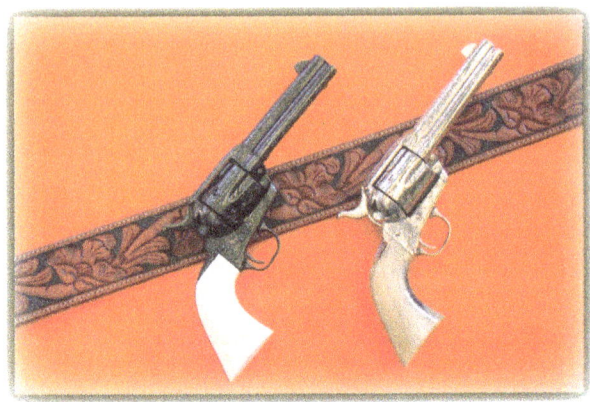

Engraving and custom grips turn classic Colt single actions into true works of art. Third Generation Colts, a blued 38-40 and a nickel-plated 44-40, were engraved by Dale Miller and fitted with Eagle Grips Ultra Ivory stocks and one-piece bighorn sheep grips by Paul Persinger.

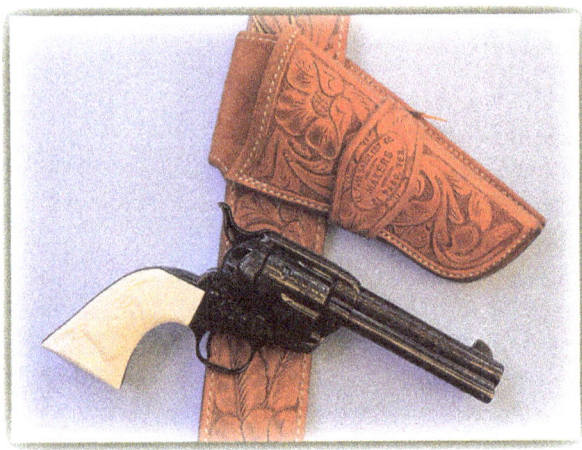

Colt Third Generation 4-3/4-inch 38-40 shoots so well it was deemed worthy of engraving by Dale Miller, Ultra Ivory grips by Eagle Grips, and leather by El Paso.

El Paso Saddlery's double rig carries this mis-matched pair, a blued 38-40 engraved by Dale Miller and a nickeled 45 Colt engraved by Jim Riggs.

My fancy guns are fancy working guns, but working guns nevertheless. They are carried in quality leather, and they are carried and shot routinely. A gun that isn't for shooting has little value for me. I do have three very limited run sixguns that are collector's items not for shooting. However, these have been given to my wife to put away as an investment for her "golden" (whoever came up with that misnomer?) years.

For less than the cost of a new sixgun, one can have a truly personal engraved firearm. It will look great and also still be a true working sidearm.

I place high importance on passing down special firearms to subsequent generations. One day I realized that I had only one engraved Colt Single Action but three grandsons. This had to be taken care of. So a nickel-plated Third Generation 4-3/4-inch 44-40 was sent off to Dale Miller for engraving. The nickel plating was stripped and Miller engraved the barrel, cylinder, and frame with tasteful scroll engraving, beautifully executed. The back strap has scrollwork at the top and bottom with enough room left in the middle to engrave my name should I so choose. The rounded part of the top of the backstrap as well as the recoil shield on both sides of the hammer are all engraved with a pattern of the sun coming up on a beautiful morning.

Eddie Janis of Peacemaker Specialists performed one of his Saddle Tramp action jobs on the revolver, and Milt Morrison of Qualite re-finished the sixgun in bright nickel. It now wears beautiful ram's horn grips by Paul Persinger, whose work is as perfect as it gets. The result is a fancy sixgun but still a workin' sixgun.

Two down, a 45 Colt and a 44-40, one to go. A third 4-3/4-inch Colt Single Action, a Third Generation 38-40 that had already had been tuned and also had proven to be an excellent shooter, was sent off to Dale Miller. Miller covered 3/4 of the 38-40 in scrollwork and then beautifully re-blued the entire gun, including the hammer (for some reason Colt stopped finishing hammers many years ago). Miller's work is absolutely beautiful and affordable. To finish off the project, Eagle Grips fitted the pair of one-piece Ultra Ivories with a steer head carved on the right grip panel.

For the past two decades I have been putting "things" away for my grandsons. Interesting books, special pictures, copies of my articles. The sixguns I have described are more than fancy firearms that fulfill a whim. They are my legacy to future generations.

Chapter 32

CUSTOMIZING THE OLD MODEL RUGER

The New Model Rugers have been used for building some of the most powerful sixguns in existence. Serious single action sixguns chambered in such powerful cartridges as 475 and 500 Linebaugh, 445 SuperMag, 475 and 500 Linebaugh Long, are all dubbed serious sixguns as they will handle the largest, toughest, meanest critters on earth. At the other end of the spectrum, we have the sensible single action sixguns. Those meant for daily packin', or plinkin', even defensive use or close range hunting. When the 357 Blackhawk was introduced in 1955, Ruger intended to next bring it out in both 44 Special and 45 Colt. Things don't always work out the way they should and the introduction of the newest magnum in 1956 resulted in a larger-framed Blackhawk in the 44 Magnum with the 45 Colt being chambered in the same basic sixgun 15 years later. The 44 Special, which would have been perfect for the original Colt Single Action-sized 357 Blackhawk, never materialized.

Each of these 7-1/2-inch Old Model Rugers has been customized simply by reverting back to the original Colt-style feel of the Flat-Top Rugers. The 30 Carbine, top left, and a pair and a spare of 45 Colt Blackhawks have all been fitted with XR3 grip frames and original grips.

Today several gunsmiths are specializing in custom Ruger single actions and especially the Flat-Top and Old Model 357 Blackhawks. In keeping with the spirit of the original Colt SAA, these Rugers are chambered for cartridges found in the old trooper. The original cylinder can be re-chambered for such cartridges as the 41 Special, 44 Special, 38-40, 44-40, and possibly 45 Colt, and even for a few of the old cartridges that have been resurrected thanks to cowboy action shooting, the 45 Schofield and 44 Russian.

If one's tastes should so dictate, semi-auto rounds such as the 45 ACP, 40 S&W, and 10mm can be chosen while new cylinders can be manufactured in such great cartridges as the 32-20. And there is nothing that says we cannot keep the original 357 Magnum chambering while adding custom touches such as a tuned action, new sights, and a case-colored frame. Some gunsmiths may be hesitant to re-chamber to 45 Colt as the Colt SAA and Ruger Blackhawk have been associated with heavily loaded cartridges for over three decades. For example, a 45 Colt on a Ruger 357 Three Screw frame is definitely for standard loads only as the Colt SAA-sized Flat-Top or Old Model will not handle heavy 45 Colt loads.

The Colt Single Action Army is so perfect as is that very little is required in the category of embellishments. I almost always fit my Colts with custom grips made to fit my hand and particular taste.

Chapter 32 | Customizing The Old Model Ruger

A Colt? No, this Old Model Ruger has been turned into a Colt-style 32-20 by Hamilton Bowen.

Grip makers offer grips of exotic woods, genuine stag, elegant ivory, even buffalo bone or ram's horn stocks. Sixguns from the Ruger stable require a few more touches other than grips. My tastes normally run heavily to the traditional, and that means I prefer the original grip frame as furnished on the Single-Six and .357 and .44 Blackhawks, introduced in the 1950s that perfectly duplicated the feel of the Colt Single Action Army. Unfortunately the Ruger grip frame was "improved" in 1963 and the feel was changed dramatically. My Old Model .45 Rugers, which were introduced some seven years later, all came with the improved grip frame and have now been fitted with the old Flat-Top grip frame that is easily identified by the interior XR-3 marking as opposed to the XR-3RED of the post-1963 guns.

For those preferring an all-steel Ruger Blackhawk, Old Models can be fitted with stainless steel grip frames from the Old Army while New Models will accept any New Model stainless steel grip frame. All blued Ruger Blackhawks come with alloy ejector tubes and these can be replaced with tubes from either Bowen Classic Arms or Qualite Pistol & Revolver. The addition of a steel ejector tube and grip frame helps to dampen felt recoil dramatically. A final touch is a high quality all-steel replacement rear sight now being offered by Bowen Classic Arms.

Most Rugers, be they of Old Model or New Model persuasion, have relatively heavy trigger pulls. New Models are the easiest to lighten by the non-gunsmithing shooter. Simply remove one grip panel and then use a small pick or screwdriver to remove the dogleg spring from its post at the top of the grip frame. This is one leg of the trigger return spring and the trigger will operate perfectly well, and lighter, with only one leg in place.

Old Model Rugers require a little more work and the assistance of another hand. With the grips removed, cock the hammer and place a small pin in the small hole at the base of the mainspring strut. This will keep the mainspring compressed as the grip frame is removed. Watch out for the handspring, which enters the mainframe through a small hole in the rear of the mainframe and is held in place by the top of the grip frame. After the grip frame is removed, remove the mainspring strut and then, with extreme care and wearing adequate eye protection, remove the pin slowly, allowing the mainspring to decompress and be removed. A vise will help.

Clip one coil from the mainspring, and with the aid of the above-mentioned third hand, compress the mainspring back on the strut, replace the pin, and re-assemble the sixgun. Remove only one coil at a time until the desired results are attained. Remember, if too many coils are removed they cannot be replaced. I have never found it necessary to remove more than two coils.

Hamilton Bowen of Bowen Classic Arms is well-known for really big sixguns, but he has another side – his favorite side, a kindler, gentler side. Even before the advent of the Colt-styled Ruger Vaquero, gunsmiths, both professional and home-style, were slimming the top strap of the Ruger Blackhawks, removing the adjustable sights, and welding and re-shaping the top of the frame to that of a a hog-wallow fixed-sight sixgun. My friend Jim Taylor did this many years ago to a Ruger .357 rescued from the bone yard; fast draw exhibition shooter Joe Bowman has used a pair Ruger .357 Blackhawks made to look like Colt Single Action Army .45s for years, and Bowen now offers the same conversion as a custom option on the Three Screw Ruger single actions.

At the 1993 Shootists Holiday, I was privileged to handle, examine, and, most importantly, shoot what has turned out to be in Hamilton Bowen's "favorite handgun of all times." It is his favorite for two reasons. First, it is a best-grade piece done by a gunsmith who thrives on perfection and looks to the past masters of the gunsmithing

The 357 Magnum Blackhawk was originally scheduled to be chambered in 44 Special. What Ruger did not do, Hamilton Bowen does: four of a kind 44 Special conversions on Old Model and Flat-Top .357 Blackhawks.

craft for inspiration; and secondly, it is chambered for that most pleasant-shooting sixgun cartridge, the ancient but certainly still viable 32-20 or 32 Winchester Center-Fire (32 WCF). I can certainly understand why this is the favorite handgun of a pistolsmith responsible for so many superb creations. Starting life as a standard Old Model .357 Ruger Blackhawk, this 32-20 has been fitted with a custom line-bored cylinder mated with a .32-caliber barrel. The cylinder has been chamfered in the old Colt blackpowder style, and the base pin is a custom job, oversized and mated perfectly with the cylinder. As with most of Bowen's single action conversions, this one contains an internal bearing block to eliminate the flexing of the cylinder bolt from side to side.

The barrel is a round Douglas barrel with a beautifully machined integral front sight base that has been dovetailed and fitted with a windage-adjustable post front sight. This mates with a rear sight that is a perfectly square notch cut into a frame that has been shaped to match the old Smith & Wesson fixed-sighted top straps or perhaps even those on the Remington cap-and-ball sixguns. The alloy ejector rod housing has been replaced with a steel housing that is held on by a screw that completely fills the hole and fits perfectly flush with the ejector rod housing.

Such a classic sixgun as this would have to be all steel, so the original Ruger aluminum grip frame had to go, being replaced by a Colt Single Action Army-style backstrap and trigger guard with a pair of Colt black Eagle grips filed to fit. A longtime standard bullet for the 32-20 has been Lyman's #311316, a 120-gr. flat-nosed gas-check design. As so often happens with sixguns, at least in my experience, Hodgdon's H4227 was the powder of choice giving 1-1/4-inch 25-yard groups with 12.0 grains for 1237 feet per second from the 4-5/8-inch barrel of the 32-20.

To my somewhat biased way of thinking, the most sensible of all single action sixguns is a good 44 Special. I decided to have a 44 Special Ruger made to my specifications after reading of such a conversion by Skeeter Skelton in the 1970s. Skeeter was responsible for a whole bunch of sixgunners finding new appreciation for the 44 Special. However, a number of mistakes were made with my first custom Ruger. I opted for a red insert front sight instead of an easier to see black front sight. At least black is much easier to see these days and a black post sight is the best of all.

The Ruger Old Model or Three Screw .357 was sent off to a gunsmith back East who re-chambered the cylinder to 44 Special and relined the original barrel. The lining would have worked fine but I believe he used a section of 444 Marlin barrel as the twist was very slow and my dream 44 Special would not shoot for the proverbial sour apples unless a full-house load of a 250-gr. bullet at 1200 feet per second was used. The barrel was discarded and replaced with a 4-5/8-inch barrel taken from my 44 Blackhawk, which was then returned to Ruger for a 7-1/2-inch barrel. (This was when Ruger still had Three Screw Super Blackhawk barrels available.) With the replaced barrel, the 44 Special shot fine, so the whole gun was then finished in bright blue and fitted with ivory grips.

For a number of years now I have been picking up any reasonably priced Ruger Flat-top or Old Model Blackhawk 357 encountered for the express purpose of having them made into 44 Specials. We are not talking about using collector-grade Blackhawks, some of which can still be found in unfired condition, but rather original Three Screw 357 Magnums, some of which have been in-service for four to five decades. The original Ruger .357 Blackhawks, as opposed to the New Model Blackhawks,

Single Action Sixguns | 213

Chapter 32 | Customizing The Old Model Ruger

Hamilton Bowen literally wrote the book on the custom revolver. It is highly recommended reading for an understanding of what really goes into building a custom sixgun.

were made on a smaller frame and make into lighter, trimmer sixguns than a Ruger 44 Magnum Super Blackhawk or 45 Colt Blackhawk. If one needs the power, the New Model Blackhawk in 44 Magnum or 45 Colt is the answer. If, however, one simply wants a sensible single action, a 44 Special conversion is a better answer.

Pictured are four 44 Special Blackhawk conversions and one 41 Special Blackhawk with case colored frame and hammer, all by Hamilton Bowen. Three of the .44s are on Flat-tops, one on an Old Model, and the .41 on a Flat-Top frame. The latter has to be one of the most beautiful single action sixguns in existence. Two of the .357 Flat-Tops are now a matched pair of 4-5/8-inch bright blue 44 Specials with stag grips. The third one had been rode hard and put up wet and although it was mechanically fine, the finish was pitted in places. This has been made into a real workin' 44 Special sixgun with a bead blasted finish and factory original walnut grips. It also carries a 4-5/8-inch barrel.

The final 44 Special conversion by Bowen on an Old Model frame is fitted with a 7-1/2-inch barrel, polished grip frame, and black micarta grips by Charles Able. This is a long range 44 Special and, like the other three, annually sees many hundreds of rounds consisting of hard-cast Keith 250-gr. semi-wadcutters over 7.5 grains of Unique as its standard load. This load goes right at 950 feet per second from the long-barreled 44 Special and shoots into 1-1/4 inches with Oregon Trail 240-gr. semi-wadcutters. The best load I have found for the 4-5/8-inch 44 Special Blackhawk is Speer's 225-gr. lead interior/copper cup exterior hollow point over 17.0 grains of Hodgdon's H4227 for a potent 1020 feet per second. It groups right at one inch.

About 20 years ago I saw an ad for 44 Special conversions by Andy Horvath. In talking with Horvath I soon learned that this was a man who loved sixguns in general and particularly single action 44 Specials. Wanting a very special 44 Special, I asked Horvath if he could do a round-butted, four-inch barreled .44 built on a Ruger .357 Three Screw Blackhawk, a real 44 Special packin' pistol. The answer came back affirmative, so off went a 6-1/2-inch .357 Three Screw Blackhawk,

Two of Taffin's very special Specials are these 7-1/2-inch .44 conversions by Hamilton Bowen and Bill Grover.

A beautiful pair of 44 Special conversions by Andy Horvath: the top sixgun features a 5-1/2-inch S&W ribbed barrel, case colored frame, and special hammer, while the bottom 4-inch round-butted sixgun has been fitted with a Super Blackhawk hammer and engraved by Tedd Adamovich.

a 7-1/2-inch Super Blackhawk barrel, and some special items I had been saving for just such a project. From my parts box, I pulled my last Ruger blued steel ejector rod housing and my last 1960s wide Super Blackhawk hammer.

For grips I sent a pair of Rosewood Ruger grips from an over-run of .22 Single-Six Colorado Centennial stocks in the 1970s. The result was a beautiful round-butted, 4-inch 44 Special. The bluing was deep and matched well with the grip frame that Horvath had polished and round-butted so it slipped into my hand perfectly. Horvath also jeweled the sides of the hammer and trigger and made a cylinder pin with a flat face to allow maximum ejector rod travel to fully extract empties. My Horvath Lil Ruger has now been engraved by grip-maker Tedd Adamovich and sometimes wears the round-butt grip frame and at other times a standard grip frame with ivory stocks. I was so pleased with this special 44 Special I took it to the first Shootists Holiday in 1986 and it was certainly well received among the knowledgeable sixgunners in attendance. In fact, one very well-known gunsmith of the day worked the action several times, turned it over in his hands repeatedly, and then looked up and said, "I have to get better." I felt that was very high praise for the work of Andy Horvath.

The word spread and other sixgunners opted for the same type of Lil Ruger sixgun from Andy in other chamberings such as 45 Colt and 41 Magnum. The 44 Special, along with several of these other L'il Guns built by Horvath, were featured in the September/October, 1990 issue of *American Handgunner* and the fire was lit around the country and even in Hollywood. Either Don Johnson or Mickey Rourke or both saw the article and wanted my little 44 Special for a movie they were doing. There was no way I was about to turn my Lil Gun loose but I did suggest that Andy Horvath be contacted and as a result he not only built guns for the movie but also made personal L'il Guns for both Johnson and Rourke. Horvath has been busy ever since!

Recently I have had the pleasure of working with one of Horvath's latest 44 Specials. Starting with a Flat-Top .357 Blackhawk, Andy re-chambered it to 44 Special, fitted it with a full-ribbed heavy

Even something as simple as a hammer can be a work of art. Check out this beautifully crafted hammer by Andy Horvath.

Chapter 32 | Customizing The Old Model Ruger

They don't get much nicer than this! Custom Ruger Old Model 44 Special #SS4 by Texas Longhorn Arms features a Colt grip frame with one-piece ivories by BluMagnum.

barrel with an undercut post front sight, re-contoured the front edge of the top strap to blend imperfectly with the ribbed barrel, then fitted it with a an abbreviated style #5 base pin. The finish is a deep, high polished blue set off perfectly by a case-hardened frame and hammer. The hammer is really something special as from the side view it has a very thin and curved profile while from the top the oval shaped wide spur has beautiful fine line checkering. It is a pleasure to cock this sixgun and feel the parts operate smoothly with each other. I've never been a big fan of the Super Blackhawk grip frame, but for this special 44 Andy fitted a modified Super Blackhawk grip frame which had been shortened and re-contoured on the back strap. This whole piece of sixgun artistry was then fitted with beautifully grained fancy walnut stocks perfectly contoured for my hand. It will be very difficult to send this sixgun back!

In the late 1980s I saw a very special 44 Special on a Ruger Old Model. The barrel was 4-5/8 inches in length, the grip frame was polished bright, and the grips were made from the horns of a bighorn sheep. This special sixgun was shown to me by Bart Skelton. It had belonged to his late dad Skeeter and now belonged to gunwriter John Wootters. That sixgun made my heart pound even further for other 44 Specials. Two Three Screw .357 Blackhawks went off to Bill Grover of Texas Longhorn Arms. Grover had been instrumental, along with Bob Baer, in building the "Skeeter Gun," as they called it. Its serial number was SS1 (or the complete story of this special 44 Special, see my previous book, *Big Bore Handguns*, by KP Books), and I have SS4. The second Skeeter Gun, SS2 in the series, is now in Bart Skelton's hands; Bob Baer has SS3; Bill Grover has SS5; friend and fellow writer Terry Murbach has SS6; and Sheriff Jim Wilson, also a good friend and fellow writer, has the last gun SS7. The Shootists held a special seven-gun salute and memorial service to Skeeter in 1992 and there will be no more 44 Specials built in this series.

Although all seven of us have SS sixguns they are all quite different, revealing the individual tastes of the owners. My particular SS4 started life as a 357 Magnum Ruger Flat-Top Blackhawk from the 1950s. Again, lest any collectors out there take me to task, it was not a collector's item as it had been re-blued at the factory. None of the other .357 Blackhawks used for conversions to .44 Special had anywhere near collector's item status either. In looking for convertible specimens, actions are important, finish is not. Grover and I put our heads together on this one. The cylinder has been tightly re-chambered to 44 Special to allow the use of .429" diameter bullets but kept to minimum dimensions for long case life. Barrel/cylinder gap was set at .0025". The Ruger XR3 grip frame and steel ejector housing were not discarded but put back for use on the other 44 Special Grover was building. In their place Grover fitted steel Colt parts, a Colt backstrap and trigger guard and a Colt ejector housing along with a Bullseye-headed ejector rod.

With the installation of the Colt backstrap and trigger guard, it was necessary to machine a special hanger to accept the Ruger mainspring and strut. Grover also replaced the trigger return spring with a new coil spring. The main purpose of a Colt back strap and trigger guard on a Ruger is to allow the installation of one-piece stocks, and this Ruger now wears ivories by BluMagnum. For sighting equipment, Grover installed

Taffin shooting the 7-1/2-inch 44 Special conversion built by Bill Grover of Texas Longhorn Arms on a Ruger 357 Magnum Old Model.

a Texas Longhorn Arms Improved Number Five front sight – bold, flat, and black – and a Number Five base pin with a large, easy to grasp head was also installed. The front of the cylinder was beveled as on the old Colts and the gun was engraved to read "SKEETER SKELTON .44 SPECIAL" on the left side of the barrel and "TEXAS LONGHORN ARMS INC, RICHMOND TEXAS" on the topstrap. Serial number is marked S.S.4 in the same three places as the original Colts.

The second 44 Special sixgun from Grover was built with a 7-1/2-inch barrel using a 10-1/2-inch Ruger Super Blackhawk barrel. The XR3 grip frame of SS4 now resides on this sixgun along with rosewood stocks. This long-range sixgun made to compliment the SS4 Packin' Pistol also wears a Number Five front sight and a Number Five base pin. Serial number is JT1 and it is also marked in three places as with the SS4 sixgun. Both of these 44 Special sixguns shoot my everyday working load of 7.5 grains under a 240-gr. SWC bullet superbly.

Ruger's Old Model Blackhawks, being Colt Single Action size, make excellent little guns; this 44 Special by Bob Baer was dubbed Baby by the maker.

Bob Baer was earlier mentioned as one of those who worked on Skeeter Skelton's 44 Special #SS1. For several years, he had been suggesting that I send him a proper sixgun for customizing. One Sunday morning before church I hit the gun show early before most of the vendors had opened their tables and was rewarded with a bargain basement-priced Old Model Three Screw .357 Ruger Blackhawk. It was sent off to Baer with instructions to simply build me a special gun, his choice of style and caliber. Having seen, handled, and shot many of Baer's creations from short barrels to long barrels, from round butts to lanyard rings, from .22s to .357s to .44s, with all kinds of artistic touches abounding, I certainly did not know what to do expect but I knew I would not be disappointed.

Single Action Sixguns | 217

Chapter 32 | Customizing The Old Model Ruger

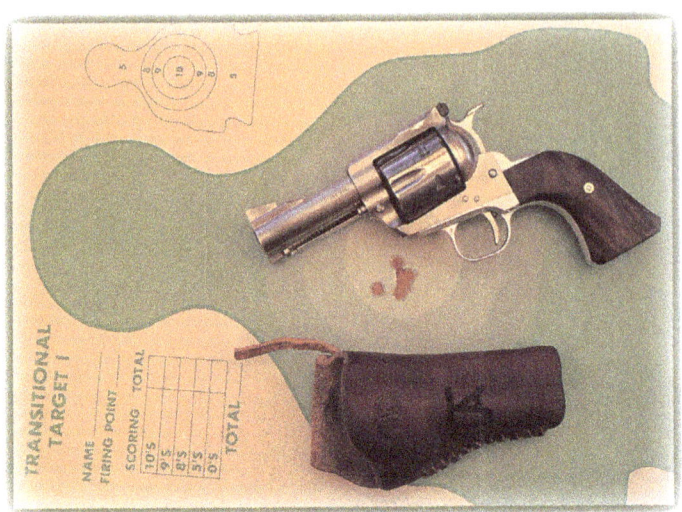

Bob Baer's Baby is not only easy to carry. It shoots, too.

Since Baer had a pretty good idea where my heart lies, the conversion turned out to be a 44 Special. The front and rear edge of the grip frame are both tapered to make it more comfortable in the hand with no sharp edges to emphasize recoil. Tedd Adamovich of BluMagnum made the fancy walnut grip blanks, which Baer then expertly fitted to the bright polished aluminum grip frame. The aluminum ejector rod housing is also polished bright while the rest of Baby, as Baer dubbed it, is finished in satin hard nickel plating. To aid in the project, gunsmith Keith DeHart expertly re-chambered the cylinder and furnished the 3-1/4-inch barrel. The total package is a very easy to pack 30 ounces.

Other special custom touches include a shortened base pin head and a thinned ejector rod head with a recess in the bottom of the ejector housing so the housing does not have to be removed to remove the base pin. The hammer spur has been slightly lowered, broadened, and checkered; the top strap has been tapered on both sides; and the front edges of the cylinder have been chamfered. One of the really special custom touches is a very slight offset placed at the back edge of each chamber so that one may remove fired cartridges with a thumbnail if so desired. Of course the entire action has been smoothed.

Sixguns are very personal and to identify this as my very personal sixgun, special markings on this 44 Special include my initials "JAT" on the front of the frame. In front of the trigger guard on the bottom of the frame, we find "RGB," and "01 SS SPL." The RGB is for Robert G. Baer, and the SS is for Skeeter Skelton who inspired us all so many ways. I was able to take Baby to Texas, and Bob and I broke it in shooting 250-gr. Keith bullets over 7.5 grains of Unique, all the while thinking of Skeeter.

Ben Forkin of Montana began his gunsmithing career the right way, working under Hamilton Bowen. That should tell you something about the quality of his work. Ben is a complete gunsmith working on single action and double action revolvers, semi-automatics, and bolt

Rugers, just as Colt single actions, benefit aesthetically with case colored frames and hammers. Top 44 Special conversion is by Andy Horvath, middle 41 Special by Hamilton Bowen, and bottom 44 Special by Ben Forkin.

Ben Forkin created this exquisite case-colored 44 Special conversion using a 44 Magnum Flat-Top barrel, Forkin front sight, and Bowen rear sight.

action rifles. He also does big-bore custom conversions on Marlin leverguns. When Ben and Kelye Schlep of Belt Mountain Base Pins stopped by my place after the 2003 Shootists Holiday, I could not resist sending an Old Model Ruger .357 back to Montana with him.

Except for the short-barrel conversions by Bob Baer and Andy Horvath, all of the custom Three Screw Blackhawks previously mentioned have 4-5/8- or 7-1/2-inch barrels. It was time for something different. I had just recently purchased a like-new 6-1/2-inch 44 Magnum Flat-Top barrel and it seemed like the perfect time to use it. We decided to do a 5-1/2-inch 44 Special complete with case hardened mainframe and hammer. Ben performed his usual action work: smoothing, tuning, and tightening; re-chambered the cylinder to 44 Special, cutting it to use .430" Keith bullets; cut the 44 Magnum barrel to the proper length, fitting it with a post front sight mated up with a Bowen adjustable rear sight; and finished off the package with one of Belt Mountain's #5 base pins.

In addition to the Ruger barrel I also had a Flat-Top XR3 grip frame, which Ben perfectly fitted to the Old Model frame. The original XR3 grip frame is the same size and shape as that found on the Colt Single Action Army and feels much better in my hand than the XR3-RED grip frame shape that is standard on the Old Model Ruger. A sixgun this nice deserves the original grip frame shape, and the end result is a most pleasing 44 Special capable of stirring soul and spirit and one that also shoots the standard 44 Special loading of a Keith bullet over 7.5 grains of Unique extremely well.

David Clements is another custom sixgunsmith building many big bore New Model conversions, but he also turns out some fine Three Screw special sixguns. Looking for something a little different? Consider this: an Old Model Ruger .357, an extra cylinder, and a 4-3/4-inch Colt 44-40 New Frontier barrel placed in Clements' skilled hands. The result is New Frontier lookalike 44 Special/44-40 sixgun. The custom stocks are by Larry Caudill of Albuquerque. Caudill specializes in custom rifle stocks and saves the left-over gun stock woods for custom sixgun grips. His work, like Clements', is superb.

Clements Custom Guns has come up with one of the most beautiful conversions of a Ruger to 45 Colt that I have ever seen. Starting with an original Flat-Top Blackhawk in 44 Magnum chambering, Clements re-

A dual-cylindered conversion by David Clements features 44 Special and 44-40 cylinders, 4-3/4-inch Colt New Frontier barrel, and custom stocks by Larry Caudill.

Single Action Sixguns | 219

Chapter 32 | Customizing The Old Model Ruger

Every Old Model conversion does not have to be a 44 Special. This 38-40 conversion by Larry Crow is not only beautifully styled but also shoots extremely well.

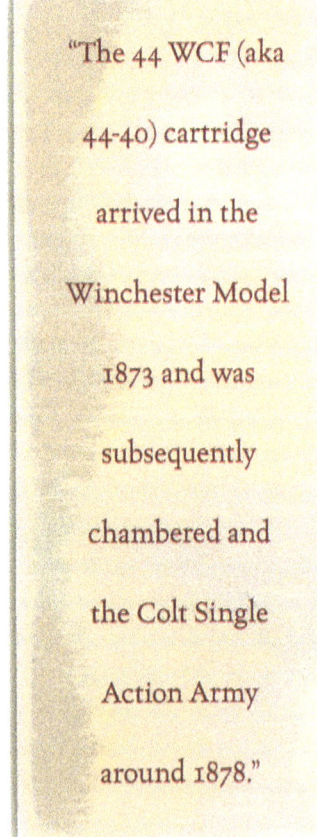

"The 44 WCF (aka 44-40) cartridge arrived in the Winchester Model 1873 and was subsequently chambered and the Colt Single Action Army around 1878."

chambered the cylinder, fitted a 5-1/2-inch barrel and ivory micarta stocks. The frame was case colored Colt-style and the balance of the sixgun was deeply blued, resulting in a most beautiful, good-shootin'.45 Colt that was very hard for this sixgunner to return.

The 44 WCF (aka 44-40) cartridge arrived in the Winchester Model 1873 and was subsequently chambered in the Colt Single Action Army around 1878. To come up with a cartridge a little flatter shooting than the 44 WCF, Winchester necked the cartridge to .40 caliber and for some reason decided to call it the 38 WCF, perhaps better known as the 38-40. It was also chambered in that Winchester Model '73 and then in the Colt Single Action Army in the 1880s. My first centerfire single action was a 38-40, so I was immediately drawn to the work of Larry Crow. Crow of Competitive Edge Gun Works is not only a gunsmith specializing in single actions, leverguns, and shotguns, but he also has a great set of video tapes covering gunsmithing and customizing Colts and Rugers as well as Marlins. Crow knows his way around traditional firearms. It just so happens his favorite cartridge is the 38-40. In addition to working on guns for others he also builds his own cowboy action shooting firearms and obviously uses them to good advantage as he is Missouri Cyclone, the current Missouri cowboy action State Champion. He, of course, used a pair of his own custom 38-40 New Model Rugers.

Crow's CAS sixguns are built on New Model Ruger Vaqueros, but the Three Screw Ruger .357 Blackhawk makes a dandy platform for building a standard-size 38-40. Two Old Model 357 Blackhawks have been converted to 38-40 by Crow. The shorter barrel version has a second cylinder chambered to .401 Herter Powermag, as both the 38-40 and the 401 use the same diameter bullet. In fact we could add the 40 S&W and 10mm to this list as well as the 41 Long Colt when the case is loaded with heel-type bullets. The 7-1/2-inch 38-40 Blackhawk is in my hands as I write this, and a beauty it is. The cylinder has been line-bored and re-chambered to a tight 38-40. Using a .401" Shilen barrel, Larry cut it to 7-1/2 inches, tapered it like a Colt SAA barrel,

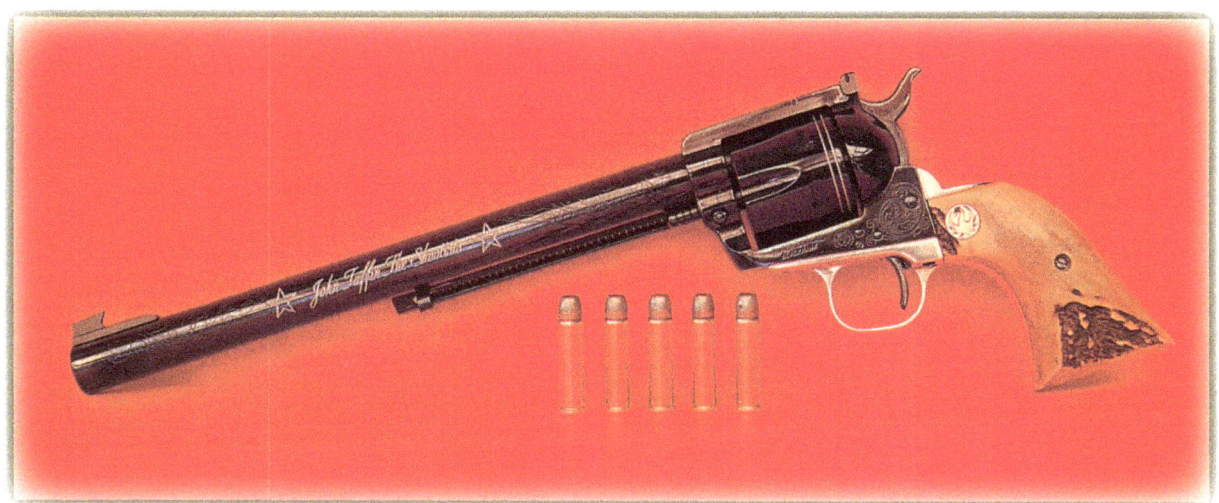

Taylor-Throated it, and then mated it to the frame with a very tight barrel/cylinder gap. The front sight is of the Colt New Frontier style mated up with a Bowen adjustable rear sight. Other niceties include a polished stainless-steel Colt-style two-piece grip frame from Power Custom and Belt Mountain's #5 base pin. The cylinder has also been fitted with a Power Custom bushing. Of course, the action has been tuned and tightening with all end shake and side-to-side movement eliminated with the fitting of an oversized cylinder bolt.

This custom Long Range Ruger 357 Magnum Flat-Top was re-barreled by Mike Rainey and then beautifully finished by Gary Reeder.

The finish is one of those "has to be seen to be believed" deluxe blue jobs. The Ruger was first polished and then finished Deluxe High Polish Blue. Then came the gold embellishments. On the left side of the barrel running the full-length of the ejector rod housing appears "CUSTOM BUILT FOR JOHN TAFFIN"; behind the front sight is the seal of the American Pistolsmiths Guild along with Larry Crow's signature; on the left side of the frame we have "Custom Ruger by Competitive Edge Gun Works"; and finally we have the caliber marking on the top of the barrel in front of the frame. I was most happy to see "38 W.C.F." instead of "38-40."

At one time Ruger, through one of their distributors, offered a 6-1/2 inch Blackhawk with two cylinders, one in 38-40 and the other in 10 mm. In recent times, the Vaquero was also offered in a convertible 38-40/40 S&W. In both cases the Rugers used were New Models, which means they were built on the 44 Magnum frame. These are super strong sixguns and I have run some very heavy loads through the 38-40 Blackhawk. However, I really prefer standard 38-40 loads and a standard-size sixgun such as my old circa 1900 Colt.

John Gallagher does the impossible, turning an Old Model .22 Single-Six into a five-shot 41 Special complete with his custom grips.

The Ruger .357 Blackhawk can also be customized without changing caliber. When a New Model 357 Maximum was used as a platform for a custom big-bore sixgun, the 10-1/2-inch bull barrel was placed in my parts box awaiting who knows what future project. At the time I did not really foresee any possible use for a long, heavy, 38-caliber

Single Action Sixguns | 221

Chapter 32 | Customizing The Old Model Ruger

barrel, at least not until I found a .357 Flat-Top Blackhawk at a gun show for less than $200! The finish was worn, and someone had made a mess of the front sight by trying to install a plastic insert that had long ago disappeared. However, it would make a perfect project gun at a most reasonable price.

Now that I had the economically purchased Flat-Top I had to decide what to do with it. The action was sound, but it was not really shootable because of the front sight. The thought came to me that it would make a perfect choice to match up with the 10-1/2-inch 357 Maximum barrel. With that in mind, I took the old Ruger, the Maximum barrel, a long ejector rod housing, and as a special touch a pair of original Ruger stag grips that a reader friend had so graciously supplied, all to Mike Rainey, resident gunsmith at Shapel's.

Rainey fitted the bull barrel to the little Ruger and also matched the stag grips to the Ruger frame. This was to be a one-load sixgun – that is, if my load of choice would work. I wanted to shoot only heavyweight cast bullets, expecting the bull barrel to dampen recoil, thereby placing this custom .357 into the pleasant shooting category. My load consisted of Cast Performance Bullet Co.'s 187-gr. hard cast gas check bullet over 13.0 grains of either WW296 or H110. Muzzle velocity was just a shade under 1300 fps, recoil was mild, and accuracy was excellent. It was now time to re-finish the 357 Magnum Long Range Ruger.

Gary Reeder is known for excellent re-finishing so my newest Long Range Ruger was sent off to Flagstaff to be high polish blued and fancied up a mite. Reeder polished the aluminum grip frame bright, put gold bands around the cylinder, and embellished the left side of the barrel with "John Taffin The Shootists" placing it in the Not-For-Sale

John Gallagher's 41 Special is not only easy to pack but shoots exceptionally well with three of the four shots in the same hole.

Whether with the 44-40 or 44 Special cylinder in place, this Ruger conversion with Colt barrel by David Clements shoots very well.

category to be saved for the fourth John Taffin, my eldest grandson. By the time he inherits it, it will hopefully have seen thousands of 187-gr. Cast Performance Bullet Co.'s bullets run down the barrel and should still be in excellent shape.

All of the conversions we have talked about have been done on the Colt-sized Three Screw .357s. There are two other ways to go: the 44 Magnum Blackhawk or Single-Six. Some choose the former for a tight-chambered 45 Colt, but it seems a waste to be to change it from its original 44 Magnum. Shoot 'em and enjoy 'em for what they are, the first truly big-bore Magnum. A common customizing over the decades is that of shortening a .44 Flat-Top or Three Screw Super Blackhawk to 4-5/8 inches and fitting a Old Army stainless steel grip frame. The Single-Six is such a small frame and cylinder, however, that we have very few choices. John Gallagher can turn an original Three Screw .22 Single-Six into a lightweight, easy to pack, five-shot 41 Special. It should go without saying these are for standard loads only.

For a conversion such as the 41 Special on a Single-Six one must start with a Three Screw model, as there is not enough room in the New Model to re-cut the loading gate area without cutting into the lock work. Gallagher's 41 Special has a 4-inch barrel, knurled locking base pin, full window cylinder with minimum barrel/cylinder gap, and a very trim Colt SAA style serrated front sight mated up with the windage adjustable rear sight. Stocks are of a beautiful light colored exotic wood with lots of grain.

This is about as small as one can get with a single action and still have a big bore sixgun. With 6.0 grains of Unique, Oregon Trail's 215-gr. SWC clocks out at 822 fps, while the Speer 200-gr. JHP does 855. That puts the Gallagher 41 Special in the same league as the 45 ACP. It may well be the ultimate single action trail gun.

If there is such a thing, I probably have too many custom Old Model Rugers, but then again I have eight grandkids. Only three of them are boys, but the girls also shoot. I guess I will keep looking for candidates for customizing.

Single Action Sixguns | 223

–Chapter 33–

CUSTOMIZING THE NEW MODEL RUGER

An assortment of 44 Special, 41 Magnum, and 45 Colt Lil Guns by Andy Horvath, any of which make excellent trail guns.

Ruger's Three Screw .357 Blackhawk, the original Flat-Top (1955-1962) and the Old Model (1963 - 1972) are excellent platforms for building Colt Single Action-size custom revolvers. With the coming of the New Models in 1973, Ruger not only made the single action simpler and safer for beginning shooters, but they also removed the standard-size single action .357 Blackhawk from production. Three Screw Rugers were built on three frames: the smallish .22 Single-Six, the standard sized .357 Blackhawk, and the large 44 Magnum frame. When the transition was made, the 357 Magnum moved up to be housed in the 44 Magnum frame. That is why very few 44 Specials are built on New Model frames as they would be the same size as the 44 Magnum. What would be the point?

The 44 Magnum-sized New Models have been used for building truly powerful, five-shot single actions chambered in such cartridges as heavy-duty 45 Colt, 454 Casull, 475 and 500 Linebaugh. The 357 Maximum frame has been used to build monster revolvers in 445 SuperMag and both the 475 and 500 Linebaugh Long/Maximum. We will look at some of these shortly, but first we'll check out the more pleasant shooting sixguns, the .22s and .32s that could easily be called single action kit guns or trail guns. These little revolvers carry easily in pocket, holster, tackle box, or even a kit bag, if such a thing still exists. A "kit gun" is a handgun compact enough to fit in the little bag made famous by the song from World War I: "Pack up your troubles in your old kit bag…" Today the term is applied to any small-framed, small-caliber revolver or semi-automatic.

In the previous chapter I described the short-barreled, round-butted 44 Special Lil Gun crafted by Andy Horvath. A few years later I had Horvath build me two more truly little Lil Guns. This time we started with a Ruger .22 Bisley Model and a 32 Magnum Single-Six. The same basic work that had been performed on the 44 Special transformed these two small frame Rugers into family heirlooms. In addition to the regular work I had Andy swap grip frames so I wound up with a custom .22 Single-Six and a Bisley Model .32. Both of these guns were written up in *American Handgunner* in the September/October, 1995 issue.

The .22 Single-Six was responsible for the greatest sixgun shot I ever made or ever will make. Shortly after these little Lil Guns appeared I found myself on a varmint hunt out of Jarbidge, Nevada. I was hunting with well-known writer Clair Rees and Rod Herrett of Herrett's Stocks. If I did not have them as witnesses I would not even dare to relate what happened.

We had tired of shooting with scope-sighted rifles and handguns and pulled out the iron-sighted .22s. Since the hunt was sponsored by Winchester, we all were shooting Winchester's .22 Power Point hollowpoint .22's. My .22 revolver was the .22 Single-Six from Andy Horvath. We were sitting on a slight hill overlooking a field with a dirt bank at the far end. Things had slowed down a mite so I asked them to spot for me while I shot at a little rock on that bank. I carefully aligned the sights, squeezed off a shot, and was told that it was just a little low. Holding up the front sight in the rear notch, perching the rock on top of the front sight, I slowly squeezed off the second shot and heard: "You hit it!"

When they put the range finder on it, the reading was 181 yards. I said, "Guys, I'm ready if a squeakie comes out on that bank." (A squeakie is a small ground squirrel.) Sure enough in just a few minutes, one came out. I lined up the sights the same as I had for the second shot on the rock, squeezed off, and nailed the squirrel. A lot of luck? Absolutely! Could I duplicate it? I doubt it! In fact, I learned long ago when a shot like this is made, the smart sixgunner immediately puts his sixgun away so there is no chance of being called upon to repeat such a performance. In fact I never fired that little .22 for the rest of the trip.

Three years ago I contacted Horvath once again with the idea of building a Trio of Trail Guns. Lil Guns designed for easy packin' in desert, foothills, woods, or mountains, they would also be sixguns that would be easily handled by any of my grandkids. Three Single-Six Rugers were thereafter sent off to Horvath at his Diagonal Road gunshop to have him perform his Lil Gun magic.

The two Ruger .22s shot so well as they were I was a little hesitant to have them reworked, but only a little. The New Model .22 Single-Six stainless steel, 6-1/2-inch barrel was cut to 4 inches along with a corresponding reduction in the length of the ejector tube and ejector rod. A new base pin was fitted with a larger but shorter head that is knurled for easy removal. The liability warning was removed from the left side of the barrel, and the stainless steel grip frame was rounded at the back of the butt. The sharp edge was removed from the toe of the butt. An extra nice touch was the checkering of the front of the ejector rod head. Factory ejector rod heads are very small, often allowing the finger to slip off while removing spent shells. The checkering prevents that. Instead of the factory grip panels I found a pair of light-colored grips panels in my parts box appearing to be of Goncala Alves that I felt would look good mated up with stainless steel. They did.

The second New Model .22 Single-Six differed from the first in that it was a Bisley Model and blued. All the same operations were performed on this Bisley Model, but the altering of the grip frame and polishing of the warning label from the left side of the barrel necessitated re-bluing, so the entire little .22 Bisley was refinished in a high polish bright blue. The grips supplied for this project had what appeared to be a lot of attractive grain and Andy's refinishing managed to bring it out beautifully.

The third New Model Single-Six was chambered in 32 H&R Magnum and also had a blue finish. This sixgun was found used at

Taffin's nine-year-old grandson, Brian Panzella, gave high marks to the Andy Horvath .22 Single-Six.

Chapter 33 | Customizing The New Model Ruger

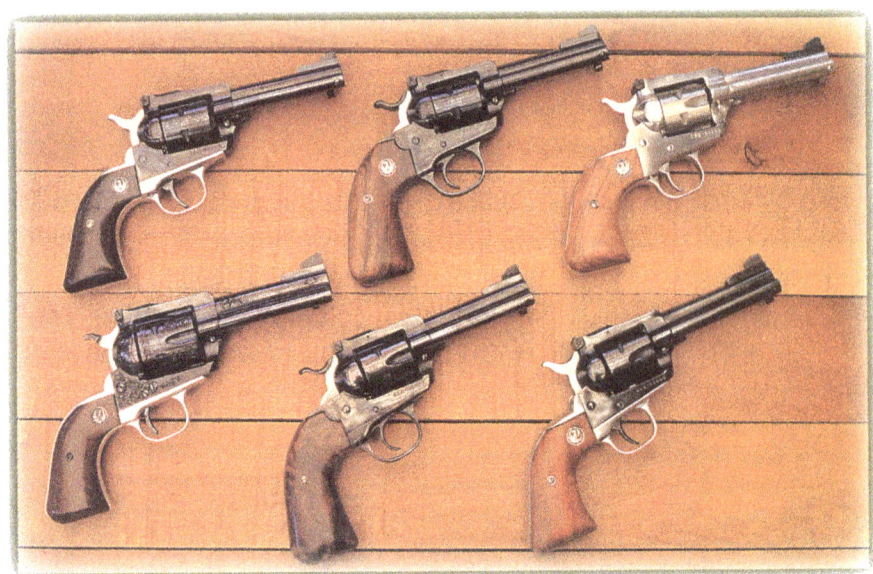

Great Kit Guns! Andy Horvath's round-butted, short barreled Single-Sixes shown with his Old Model 44 Special. They are from top left clockwise: .22 Single-Six, .22 Bisley, .22 stainless steel Single-Six, 32 Magnum Single-Six, 32 Magnum Bisley, and the 44 Special.

Shapel's Gun Shop at what I considered an incredibly low price for such a high-demand Single-Six, as these little adjustable-sighted .32s are extremely hard to find. Horvath also applied one of his beautiful blue finishes after removing the barrel warning. The grip frame, since it is an aluminum alloy as on all the standard Single-Six models, was polished bright, which looks very attractive when mated with the high polish bright blue. The factory grips chosen for this little sixgun were a reddish color and had originally been found on a stainless steel Vaquero. The bright blue, the polished aluminum, and the refinished reddish colored stocks all come together to make a very attractive sixgun portrait. Someday, perhaps half a century from now, one of my great grandkids will still be using these little sixguns.

HAMILTON BOWEN

It's impossible to discuss custom sixguns without mentioning Hamilton Bowen. We often say of someone who is at the top of his field, "He wrote the book on...." Hamilton Bowen really did write the book on custom sixguns, appropriately titled *The Custom Revolver*. It is not a how-to book but rather a what-do-we-do book on custom sixguns. Anyone contemplating having a custom single action sixgun built should read this book for two reasons. First, it just may possibly give some excellent ideas on which direction to take, and more importantly, anyone having a custom revolver built will understand exactly why they cost a lot more than factory-produced revolvers.

As we have seen, Bowen also does extensive customizing on New Model Rugers. His Long Hunter starts as a standard Model Super Blackhawk or Bisley Model. A custom round barrel with a recoil-proof ejector rod housing is installed along with a Bowen Custom front sight. He can also supply the Bowen rear sight and install a Bisley hammer on a Super Blackhawk or Blackhawk. Calibers available are 41 and 44 Magnums, 45 Colt, 50 Special, and 50 Action Express. A Lightweight version is also available on a standard Blackhawk frame with a tapered 4-inch barrel, metal removed from the recoil shield and loading gate, and fitted with aluminum ejector rod housing and grip frame. Needless to say, recoil can be very fierce in such a lightweight sixgun.

Bowen also offers The Nimrod, a 5-1/2-inch sixgun with an integral band around the barrel in front of the ejector rod housing that secures it under heavy recoil. A post front sight is pinned to the express front sight base, while the rear sight is a Bowen Custom. Calibers available are 41 Magnum, 44 Magnum, 45 Colt, 454 Casull, 50 Action Express, 475 Linebaugh, and 500 Linebaugh. Single action sixguns simply do not get any better than this!

Bowen also offers action tuning, trigger adjustments, polished cylinder notch lead-ins, freewheeling cylinders, half-cock conversions, oversize locking cylinder base pins, regulation of barrel/cylinder gaps, headspace setting, honing and reaming of cylinder chambers, and several versions of custom front sights. Custom barrels of course are available and standard Blackhawks can be converted to Bisley Models. If it is possible and if it is safe when it comes to converting single action Rugers, Hamilton Bowen can accomplish it.

Even before Ruger offered Sheriff's Model Vaqueros, these two, a 45 Colt and a 44-40, were built up by David Clements on standard Vaqueros using QPR grip frames.

DAVID CLEMENTS

One of Bowen's contemporaries, David Clements, is also renowned for fine work. Several years ago I had David (of Clements Custom Guns) build me two Ruger Vaquero "Sheriff's Models" long before they were offered by Ruger as a factory production sixgun. Starting with two New Model round butt grip frames from QPR, I installed them on a 7-1/2-inch 45 and a 5-1/2-inch 44-40, which were then both shipped off to CCG to have the barrels shortened, new sights fitted, and grip frames and grips fitted. Clements was able to trim the barrels to 3-7/8 inches by altering the head of the base pin to allow the ejector rod to do its work of shucking fired brass. Two steel ejector rods with crescent heads and two steel ejector rod housings, also all from QPR, were sent to Clements, and these were also cut to fit the short barrels. Both the Vaqueros, one in 45 Colt and the other in 44-40, had chambers that were much too tight for the best accuracy with cast bullets and the factory barrels, so Clements opened the .45-caliber chamber mouths to .453" and those of the 44-40 to .429". The result is two very easy to pack sixguns capable of handling heavy loads easily. Such loads exhibit much less felt recoil because of their QPR round-butted grip frames.

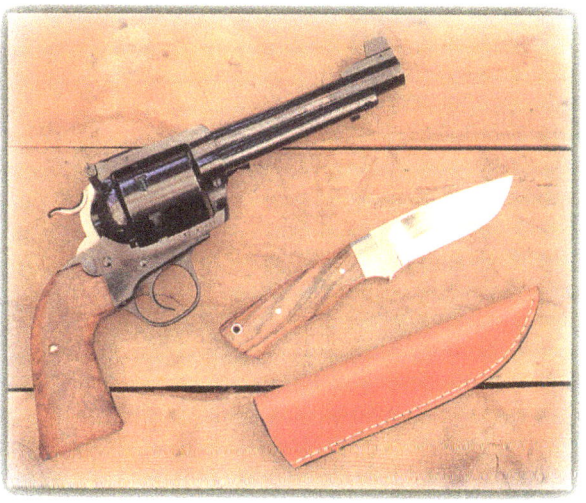

In the early 1980s this was a 10-1/2-inch Super Blackhawk used for long-range silhouetting; now it has been converted into a 5-1/2-inch Bisley Model 44 Magnum better suited for easy packin' by David Clements.

A 5-1/2-inch 44 Magnum Super Blackhawk was made into a much easier shooting sixgun with a Bisley grip frame, hammer and trigger. This sixgun started life as my 10-1/2-inch .44 silhouette revolver, but it was transformed into a Packin' Pistol when I found a Ruger factory "Liberty"-marked barrel at Shapel's Gun Shop. It was installed on the Super Blackhawk New Model and cut to 5-1/2 inches, making a sixgun that would cut one-hole groups at 25 yards with BRP's 295-gr. Keith bullet over 21.5 grains of H110. Clements finished the project with the addition of Bisley parts.

Single Action Sixguns | 227

Chapter 33 | Customizing The New Model Ruger

This beautiful custom stainless steel Vaquero by David Clements features Bisley Model hammer, trigger, and round butted grip frame with scrimshawed grips. Photo courtesy of Lloyd Smale.

Color case hardening sets off this custom Bisley Model, with special front sight having gold bars inlaid for shooting at different ranges, built by David Clements. Photo courtesy of Mark Cassill.

Clements Custom Guns offers a full line of special features for Ruger's New Models single actions. Custom barrels can be the factory contour, straight bull barrel, octagon, ovate rib, even round with full-length rib. Several styles of front sights are also offered including express, post, and a modified post with a 20-degree forward slant. All barrels are fitted with an 11-degree forcing cone. Cylinder-to-barrel gaps mike .002" - 003", and cylinders are line-bored. Customers have a choice of six-shot cylinders in 44 Special, 44-40, 41 Magnum, 45 Colt, 44 Magnum and even semi-automatic chamberings such as 10 mm, 40 S&W, and 45 ACP. Five-shot conversions utilize an oversized unfluted cylinder, recessed case heads, oversized base pin, steel ejector rod housing, interchangeable post front sight, freewheeling cylinder, and .800" bull barrel. Calibers available are 45 Colt, 454 Casull, 480 Ruger, 475 Linebaugh, and the 500 S&W shortened to 1.4 inches. Two very special conversions are the Ruger Old Army to 50 caliber (see Chapter 23) and the .22 New Model Single Six fitted with a match grade cylinder, oversized base pin, and custom barrel.

BEN FORKIN

It has been my good fortune to shoot many of the custom Rugers, both single and double action, crafted by Ben Forkin of Forkin Arms. Ben worked for Hamilton Bowen before moving to Montana and he is also a fellow Shootist, which gave me the opportunity to try out many of his big bore single actions at the annual Shootists Holiday. But for some reason, I had never had him actually build a custom revolver for me. That changed all because of a hunting trip to the Penn Baggett Ranch outside of Ozona Texas as related in Chapter 27. Penn's revolver was a custom Ruger, a Long Range Ruger, by Ben Forkin. Forkin had started with a Ruger 357 Maximum, rechambered it to 445 SuperMag, fitted it with a 10-inch bull barrel, and incorporated Bisley Model parts, grip frame, hammer, and trigger. Ruger's 357 Maximum had originally been aimed at the silhouetting crowd using a longer frame and cylinder to house the 1.600" 357 Maximum case as compared to the original 357 Magnum at 1.300".

Accurate, powerful, and relatively easy shooting: a custom .445 on a Ruger Maximum frame by Ben Forkin with stocks by Scott Kolar.

I put the Forkin .445 on paper that afternoon using Penn's handloads with 265-gr. Hornady flat-points and was well satisfied with the accuracy of the load. A 357 Maximum was found and shipped off to Ben with the orders to make me a sixgun just like Penn's .445 Ruger. As expected, Forkin performed all the action niceties such as action and trigger job, total tightening, post front sight mated up with a Bowen rear sight, and a beautiful deep blue finish. After receiving it back from Forkin, I added a pair of exotic burl mesquite grips from SK Custom. Whether shooting jacketed or cast bullets it performs to my highest expectations and is able to do with 300-gr. bullets what my three 44 Magnum Long Range Rugers provide with 250-gr. bullets

Ben Forkin does just about anything anyone could want to a New Model Ruger including action tuning, setting endshake, setting the proper barrel/cylinder gap, installing Belt Mountain base pins and Bowen rear sight, shortening existing barrels or installing new barrels, installing steel grip frames, and providing five-shot cylinders. His brochure says, "Pride in workmanship is evident in every job we turn out." He is not exaggerating.

JOHN LINEBAUGH

Linebaugh's philosophy of handguns is found in the following quote: "We are a custom sixgun shop dedicated to the old school sixgunner. We follow the theories of Elmer Keith and John (Pondoro) Taylor. Theirs was one of big bullets; so is ours. Bullet weight and caliber are constants in external ballistics; velocity is a constantly diminishing variable. I believe high velocity to be a superb killer if placed with exact precision, and if it reaches the inside of the animal. But without exact placement, it lacks the penetrating qualities and thus it wastes its energy in flesh wounds. The big bullet does not have these

Truly Big-Bore Sixguns are these custom-built .475 and .500s by John Linebaugh.

Chapter 33 | Customizing The New Model Ruger

shortcomings. It will penetrate fully from any angle, thus letting the hunter take shots with confidence that he would otherwise pass up with a 'little gun.' I for one do not like big guns, just big bullets. With this in mind we offer models and ideas to the old school sixgunner. Remember, old school to us is powerful, practical, and packable."

John builds everything from heavy-duty six-shot and five-shot 45 Colt sixguns, through his most well-known cartridges, the 475 and 500 Linebaugh. Even before the advent of the 500 S&W Magnum, John was building long-cylindered and long-framed custom sixguns chambered in three 1.610" Linebaugh Long cartridges, the 44LL, the 475LL, and the 500LL, made from 30-40, 45-70, and 348 Winchester brass respectively. Linebaugh uses the Bisley grip frame almost exclusively, calling it superior for accuracy and comfort. I certainly agree with that!

As far as I know, John Linebaugh was the pioneer when it came to building really powerful sixguns starting with his full-house 45 Colt loads, then the 500 Linebaugh, followed by the 475 Linebaugh, all with free-spinning cylinders that rotate in either direction. This is especially useful if a bullet jumps the crimp and protrudes far enough forward that the cylinder will not rotate in one direction. A free-spinning cylinder can be rotated backward and the offending round removed. We have a lot of excellent sixgunsmiths turning out high-quality custom single actions sixguns today. In fact the best gunsmiths of all time are plying their trade today. John Linebaugh was not only among the first of these modern-era artists, but certainly one of the greatest, too.

MILT MORRISON

Milt Morrison of Qualite Pistol & Revolver (QPR) has long been known for custom Rugers and some of the finest bluing imaginable. Milt's latest project is the Chameleon. A chameleon is a little fellow with the ability to change colors to suit his surroundings, and while QPR's Chameleon is no little fellow by any means, it offers shooters four quick change options as to caliber and all on the same customer-supplied Ruger Blackhawk mainframe/grip frame. While the original chameleon changes colors right before your eyes, the Chameleon from QPR is literally the gun that changes calibers right before your eyes! The change is made quickly and easily and if I can do it, anybody can.

QPR's prototype Chameleon consists of a New Model Ruger fitted with a 7-1/2-inch 45 Colt Douglas barrel and corresponding cylinder, a 7-inch Apex 44 Magnum barrel and cylinder, a 5-inch Shilen 41 Magnum barrel and cylinder; and finally, a 5-3/4-inch Shilen .357 barrel and cylinder. All barrels are marked on the barrel ring for caliber and each cylinder is marked on the rim end of the cylinder. Later Chameleons will have the caliber markings etched with bold numbers on the barrels and on two sides of the cylinders.

One concern with any multi-caliber systems such as this is that of getting a large-caliber cylinder matched up with a small caliber barrel. This is impossible with the Chameleon as the tolerances are such that it is impossible to match a large caliber cylinder with a small caliber barrel. They simply will not fit together, but it is possible for someone who is not paying attention to match a small caliber cylinder with a large caliber barrel. However if this happens no harm would be done.

The QPR barrel ring is in the patent pending stage. It is this barrel ring that makes everything work. The barrel ring is forward of the threads and butts up against the mainframe as the barrel is screwed into place. This ring has two holes, one to accept the base pin and the other for the ejector rod. To put everything together properly, the Chameleon comes with a barrel wrench with an adjustable stop and a sleeve that goes into the ejector rod hole. It is this sleeve and the base pin that keep the barrel in the proper position after they have been screwed into the frame with the proper torque.

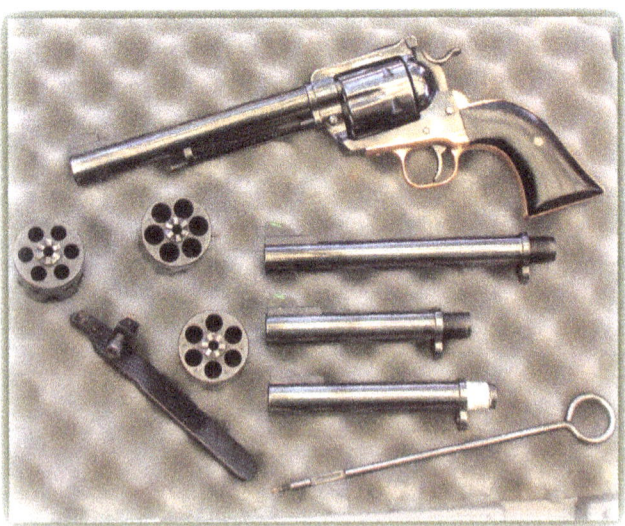

Milt Morrison's QPR Chameleon is four guns in one with a quick-change feature that allows a choice of shooting 45 Colt, 357, 41, or 44 Magnums.

QPR says of the Chameleon: "This conversion allows the shooter to change calibers on the same gun. It is designed to exchange barrel & cylinder with ease in the field. This allows your trigger pull and general feel of the gun to remain the same regardless of the activity being performed (i.e. hunting varmints vs. big game vs. target shooting)."

As I have said, if I can use the system anyone can. To assemble one particular caliber, the barrel is screwed on hand tight. The barrel wrench is then used to tighten the barrel until the stop on the wrench touches the frame. One can also see and feel the barrel ring line up properly with the frame. The check on proper alignment is whether or not the base pin can be inserted easily. If it will not, the barrel and mainframe alignment must be adjusted. Once this has been accomplished, the extractor rod sleeve easily enters its hole in the frame. If both the sleeve and the base pin are easily inserted in the alignment is correct. All this takes more time to explain that it does to accomplish.

Once the alignment is correct the cylinder is installed with the base pin, and using the provided combination cleaning rod and base pin extractor, the ejector rod housing sleeve is seated into the ejector rod housing hole. The ejector rod housing, ejector rod and spring as one unit are installed and secured with the ejector rod housing screw. The Chameleon itself, including all barrels and cylinders and the mainframe, are beautifully bright blued as only QPR can do it. The grip frame is one of QPR's brass versions fitted with black micarta grip panels. The hammer is a modified Bisley-style and looks very attractive on the standard Blackhawk frame and grip frame and is also extremely functional. All barrels have black ramp-style front sights, with two barrels having green inserts. This is a high-quality and extremely good-looking sixgun.

The Chameleon has several advantages. One would be the ability to carry what are basically four separate revolvers with a minimum of weight. For those shooters who happened to live under a regime limiting the number of handguns, The Chameleon allows one to have four revolvers counting as only one. However, the main advantage is pride of ownership and a high quality conversion kit from a high-quality gunsmith.

This may very well be the ultimate sixgun for the backpacker: Gary Reeder's ultralightweight 45 Colt Backpacker.

GARY REEDER

If there ever was a supermarket of custom sixguns, it is Gary Reeder Custom Guns. Reeder not only offers dozens upon dozens of custom New Model Rugers on Blackhawks, Bisleys, and Vaqueros, but he can also tune and embellish customer's guns. For example, my wife, Diamond Dot, has had all of her cowboy action shooting sixguns tuned and fancied up by Gary Reeder.

Diamond Dot's competition sixguns: a pair of stainless steel .357 Blackhawks polished and engraved by Gary Reeder with grips scrimshawed by Twylla Taylor.

Her Modern Class sixguns, a pair of stainless steel 4-5/8-inch New Model .357 Blackhawks, have been highly polished and decorated with engraving. Gary uses standard patterns and machine engraving to allow fancying up sixguns without depleting the customer's wallet. Diamond Dot's Traditional Class CAS sixguns are a pair of consecutive serial numbered 5-1/2-inch stainless-steel Vaqueros, which have also been polished and covered with cattle brands. Then just to make them a little different and since Dot uses full-house 38 Specials in all of her sixguns, they have been marked in script with "38 Special."

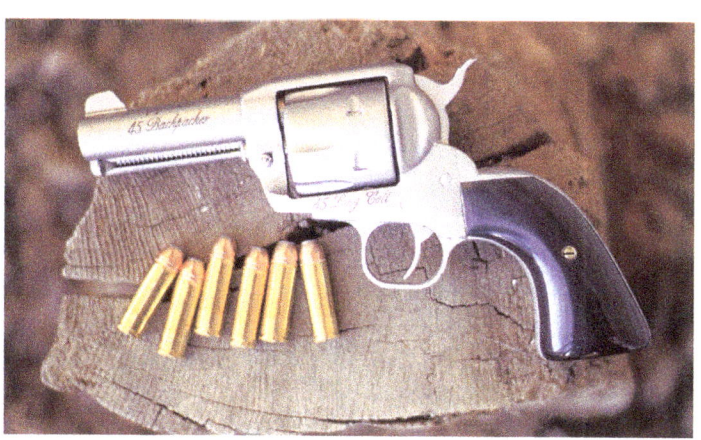

Chapter 33 | Customizing The New Model Ruger

This Bisley Model 357 Magnum has been beautifully refinished and fitted with a second cylinder in 356GNR by Gary Reeder.

Elmer Keith's #5 lives again with this totally custom-built Keith #5 by Gary Reeder.

Gary Reeder's version of Keith's #5 features the #5 SAA grip frame Keith preferred; however, it is made slightly longer to better fit most shooters' hands.

One of my favorite long-range sixguns is the Ruger stainless-steel 10-1/2-inch Super Blackhawk. Reeder tuned this 44 Magnum, gave it a bead-blasted finish, and placed "John Taffin The Shootists" in script on the left side of the barrel. When I came up with an extra .357 New Model cylinder it was sent off to Gary Reeder with my Bisley Model 357 Magnum. Reeder removed the sharp edges at the front and back edges of the butt, converted the extra cylinder to his 356 GNR, and finished everything in high polished blue embellished with gold. A most beautiful .357 sixgun with an extra boost in power using the 356 GNR, which is based on the 41 Magnum necked to .357.

Reeder offers the African Hunter in either 475 or 500 Linebaugh on a Bisley Model complete with Express sights and built-in muzzle brake; and the Long Colt Hunter, a stainless-steel 45 Colt with Bisley grip frame, hammer, and trigger, custom front sight, and ebony grips on a slightly rounded grip frame. The Vaquero is a grand platform for such sixguns as the Doc Holliday Classic in 45 Colt with a 3-1/2-inch barrel and round butt grip frame; the Tombstone Classic, another 3-1/2-inch 45 Colt, this time with a bird's head grip frame; the Gambler's Classic .45 with a 2-1/2-inch barrel without an ejector rod; and we could go on and on. Every Reeder custom offering is embellished with the appropriate engraving. All are very attractive, easy packin' sixguns.

One of the slickest handling and easiest packin' sixguns from Gary Reeder is his .45 Backpacker. He starts with a stainless-steel Vaquero, shortens the barrel to 3-1/2 inches, re-crowns the muzzle with a deeply concave crown, fits a foreword-sloping Colt-style front sight and then fits a shortened aluminum alloy ejector rod housing. To match the weight-saving advantage of the alloy ejector rod housing, the steel grip frame is also replaced by an aluminum frame slightly rounded with all sharp edges removed. Metal is removed from the loading gate and recoil shield to further remove weight, and the hammer and trigger are also re-contoured to remove as much weight as possible. The result is a 30-ounce Backpacker capable of handling heavy 45 Colt loads.

At the other end of the spectrum, one of Reeder's latest custom sixguns is the 510 GNR 7-1/2-inch Hunter

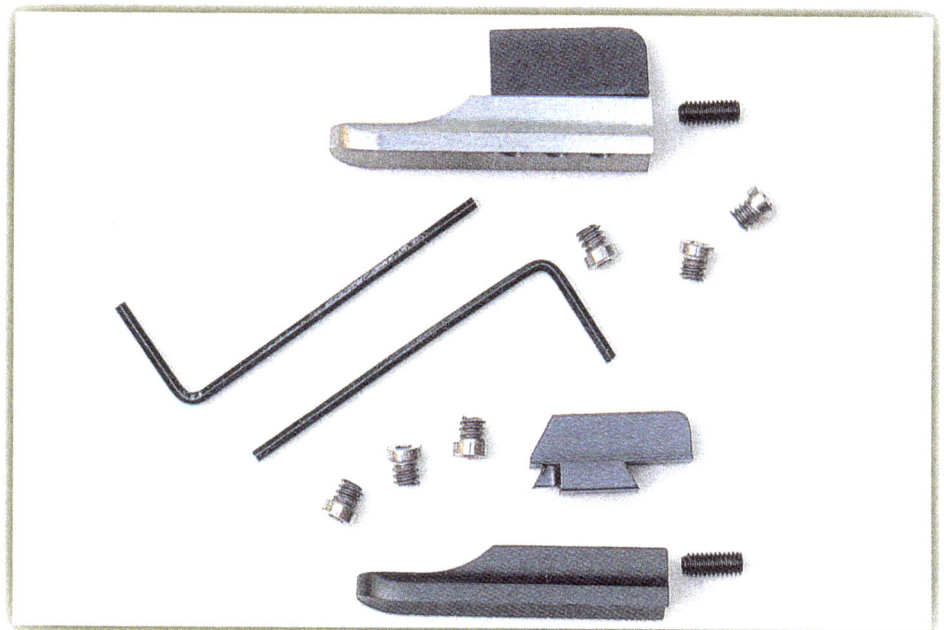

Jim Stroh's interchangeable sight system is firmly attached to the barrel with three screws and fourth Allen screw entering from the front to secure the sight blade.

Model. Three loads are available for this truly big bore sixgun: the 510 GNR 350-gr. Short at 1250 fps, the 510 GNR 350-gr. Long at 1360 fps, and the 510 GNR 435-gr. Long at 1310 fps. As one might expect, this sixgun is made for the heaviest and most dangerous big game.

One of the all-time classic single action sixguns is Elmer Keith's #5 SAA with its grip frame formed by combining a Colt Bisley Model backstrap with Colt Single Action Army trigger guard. This design goes all the way back to the late 1920s and for short time was offered on the Texas Longhorn Arms Improved Number Five. Now Gary Reeder is offering fully custom single actions built on a standard frame or large frame with a slightly longer #5 SAA grip frame to better fit most shooter' hands. Reeder is also producing his own frames and will be offering several different sixguns. One will be called the #5 and will be his recreation of Elmer Keith's #5 SAA in both blue and stainless steel and chambered in 44 Special and 45 Colt. Reeder's #6 will have a larger frame with New Model style lockwork and will be chambered in 44 and 41 Magnums with six-shot cylinders and in 454 with a five-shot cylinder; and finally something I have been wanting for nearly a half century, the Frontier Classic. This will be a blending of the Colt single action and Three Screw Ruger. It will also be available in both 44 Special and 45 Colt and in blue or stainless steel. All sixguns will be deluxe-grade and also available with custom stocks, engraving, and octagonal barrels.

JIM STROH

Last, but definitely and certainly not least, we come to Jim Stroh of Alpha Precision. While I prefer to convert Old Model .357 Blackhawks to the much-used, respected, and loved 44 Special, the larger framed Ruger Super Blackhawk is larger than necessary for a 44 Special but is a perfect platform for full-house 45 Colt loads. So when I wanted a custom 45 Colt single action sixgun, a Ruger New Model Super Blackhawk was sent off to Alpha Precision.

Cylinder, barrel, hammer, trigger and grip frame of the original Super Blackhawk were all replaced. Stroh used one of his custom five-shot cylinders matched up with a 5-1/2-inch barrel with one of his interchangeable front

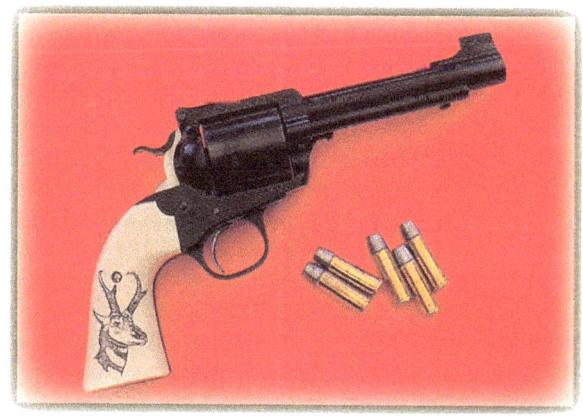

For a combination of easy packin' and portable power, it would be hard to beat this five-shot 45 Colt Bisley Model by Jim Stroh with custom stocks by Charles Able.

Single Action Sixguns | 233

Chapter 33 | Customizing The New Model Ruger

Starting life as a fixed-sight Vaquero, this stainless-steel Ruger has now been fitted with a S&W adjustable rear sight and a ramp front sight resulting in a very trim single action sixgun, all by Jim Stroh.

Ruger's Bearcat should have been fitted with adjustable sights from the very beginning; since it hasn't been, Jim Stroh offers this highly desirable custom feature.

Jim Stroh's interchangeable front sight system fitted on a stainless-steel Ruger New Model allows a shooter to change sights to accommodate every possible load.

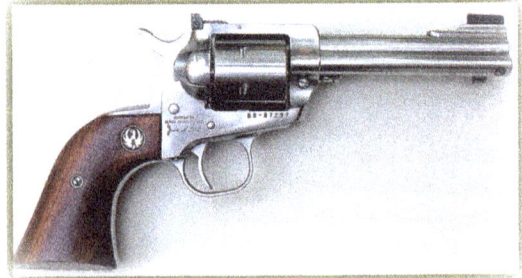

Ruger's Single-Six can be easily upgraded with tuning by Jim Stroh as well as custom sights.

sight systems. The action was totally tuned and precisely fitted so there's absolutely no endshake or side-to-side movement of the cylinder. The steel ejector rod housing was fitted precisely and securely using Jim's double dowel method. This system consists of two small steel dowels fitted behind the ejector rod screw hole on the barrel and two corresponding holes in the ejector rod housing. Standard ejector rod housings held on with one screw will normally shear the screw with the recoil from heavy loads. Stroh's system takes all the pressure off the screw and prevents the housing from moving when the sixgun is fired.

Alpha Precision offers many options for the Ruger Blackhawk such as custom cylinders that are lined-bored by having each chamber locked in line with the bore as it is chambered, total action jobs including hardening of the hammer notch and trigger sear, free spinning cylinders with added half-cock notches, full-length cylinder pin bushings fitted along with an oversized base pin, new custom oversized bolts for precise fitting of the cylinder, special contoured ramp front sight bases with interchangeable blades, and even the fitting of S&W adjustable rear sights to the fixed sighted Vaquero and flat-topping of New Model frames.

Stroh's Best Grade Ruger New Models are built with custom cylinders and premium quality match barrels, free-spinning cylinders allowing rotation in either direction, a full-length cylinder pin bushing and matching oversized base pin, chambers held to minimum dimensions and lined-bored, Stroh front sight fitted with interchangeable blades, a Bowen adjustable rear sight, a steel ejector rod housing fitted using the double dowel system, hammer spur checkered, and special barrel crown and forcing cone cut. The final finish is high polish blue or stainless with "Best Grade" marked on the top of the frame. Again, we have a custom single action built as well as it is possible for a master craftsman to accomplish.

Everything at Alpha Precision is not big bore. At the other end of the spectrum, Stroh fits S&W adjustable rear sights and a corresponding front sight to the little .22 Bearcat, resulting in a single action kit gun capable of being precisely sighted in. Stroh also offers a Best Grade stainless steel Ruger Single-Six .22 converted to 32 Magnum with a custom oversized cylinder and a flat-topped frame with an Alpha Precision front sight. Stroh's sixguns are works of art and as such he is recognized by his fellow gunsmiths of the American Pistolsmiths Guild as a master artist when it comes to working with steel.

Ruger makes an excellent basic single action sixgun. In today's world it is one of the premier shooting bargains available. Any of these talented artisans can start with a Ruger New Model and turn it into a total work of sixgun art that not only looks beautiful, but also performs the same way.

–Chapter 34–

SINGLE ACTION GRIPS AND GRIP FRAMES

Single action sixgun grips and grip frames have been around since Sam Colt introduced the first successful single action sixgun, the Paterson, in 1836. Colt made many modifications on their grip frames over the years as did other single action manufacturers, including Smith & Wesson and Remington in the nineteenth century, as well as Ruger in the twentieth. Even as this is written, Gary Reeder Custom Guns is working on introducing two levels of single action sixguns both wearing modifications of the Harold Croft/Elmer Keith #5 SAA, which itself came about with these two gentlemen and their gunsmiths modifying then-existing Colt grip frames.

Why so many different grip frames? The size and weight of each particular model has some bearing as the bigger and heavier the sixgun, the larger the grip/grip frame needs to be. Shooting comfort is another driving force as a grip that was comfortable on a mild-shooting percussion revolver did not always work with the switch to cartridge firing sixguns that were much more powerful. For many decades the classic Colt Single Action Army was considered just about perfect. It fits the most hands and also allows the grip to naturally roll in the hand under recoil. This worked fine with such standard loads as the 45 Colt, 44 Special, 44-40, 38-40, and even the 357 Magnum.

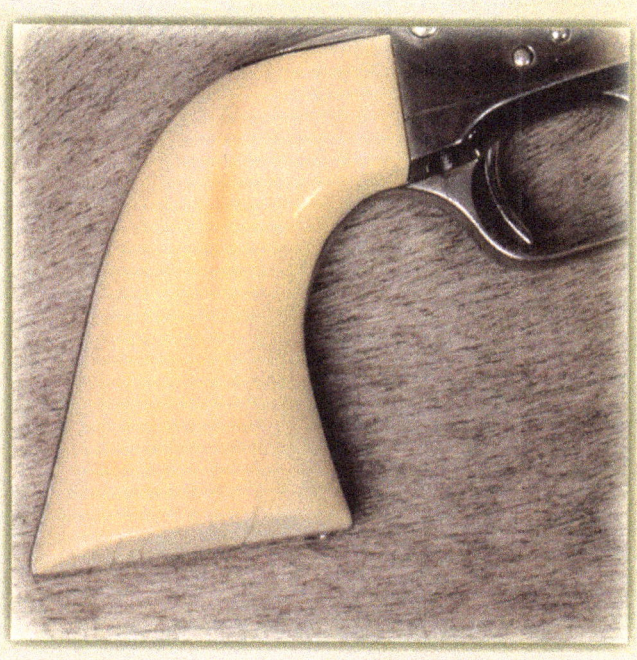

The beauty of one-piece ivory stocks on a Colt SAA cannot be surpassed.

Then something happened and that something was the 44 Magnum. Suddenly the classic grip frame was no longer the answer. Since the advent of the 44 Magnum and even more powerful cartridges the search has been for the most comfortable grip frame possible. It is not possible to make a comfortable grip frame for such cartridges as the 454 Casull, 475 and 500 Linebaughs, but rather the search is for the most control and least discomfort possible.

Along with the changes in grip frame sizes and shapes have also come many choices as to material. The first grips on Colts were one-piece walnut. It was not long before Colt switched to gutta percha, or rubber, and other options were offered such as ivory, pearl, and staghorn. Today we have all of these as well as micarta, bone from such creatures as buffalo and giraffe, ram's horn, and a virtually endless supply of varied exotic woods. We can also add in the many synthetic grips offered with old-time designs molded into the grip itself. The installation of custom grips is one of the easiest ways to personalize a single action sixgun.

Single Action Sixguns | 235

Chapter 34 | Single Action Grips and Grip Frames

The evolution of the Colt single action grip frame from 1836 to 1860 is shown on these replicas: 1836 Paterson, 1847 Walker, Third Model Dragoon, 1851 Navy, 1860 Army.

COLT SINGLE ACTION GRIP FRAMES

From 1836 and the Colt Paterson until the adoption of the 1873 Colt Single Action Army, Colt used five basic grip frames on their full-sized single actions. The grip frame of the Paterson was relatively small, but that of the 1847 Walker was huge to accommodate the 4-1/2-lb. sixgun. One year later, the Walker was downsized slightly to the Dragoon. For the first time, Colt now used a 90-degree cut at the top of the frame instead of the somewhat oval shape of the Paterson and Walker. The three grip frames and grip shapes of the First, Second, and Third Model Dragoons were the same except that the square-back triggerguard was dropped on the Third Model.

The Dragoons were still very large, weighing 4 lbs. and having correspondingly large grips and grip frames, but when the Colt Navy was adopted in 1851, Sam Colt came up with what has been considered the ideal single action grip frame for more than 150 years. This same grip frame would be used on the Single Action Army. The SAA has been produced over three generations, 1873 - 1941, 1956-1974, and 1976 to the present. All grip frames are basically the same size and shape and the bolt pattern is the same for all three. That is, a First Generation grip frame can be attached easily to a Third Generation mainframe as well as any other combination. However problems arise when it comes to the generations of grips themselves. First Generation grips are slightly smaller and there are subtle differences between the Second and Third Generation grips. Add to this the changing tolerances of the grip frames themselves including the location of the grip pin, and quite often some fitting is needed to swap grips even when staying in the same generation. Once in a while we get lucky and a Third Generation grip frame accepts a Second Generation grip panel, but this is rare.

What about the replicas? All of the copycat Colts, whether from Uberti or Armi San Marco, basically have the same size and shape grip frame as the original, but once again we run into the differences in tolerances. Since most of these grips are one-piece wood, they have been fitted to a particular frame and it is difficult to find a match when swapping. Usually the grip frames themselves can be swapped from gun to gun as the bolt patterns will line up. I have fitted Colt grips to replica single actions. Some have required the grips to be made slightly smaller, while others required removing metal on the backstrap to fit it to the Colt two-piece wooden grips.

The grip frame found on the 1860 Army is longer and better suited for most people for heavy loads. The Cimarron .45 on the left has a standard Single Action Army grip frame while the three single actions on the right, in 44 Special, 45 Colt, and 44-40, all wear 1860 Army grip frames.

There is very little difference in the grip frames of these First, Second and Third Generation Colt single actions, but the Bisley Model sits radically apart from the rest.

The Great Western single actions of the 1950s and 1960s were a very close copy of the Colt Single Action Army, but the grips were not only slightly smaller, but the angle at the top of the frame was not a true 90 degrees. Colt grip panels can be altered to fit, but Great Western grips do not generally fit any Colt single actions.

In between the 1851 Navy and the 1873 SAA came the 1860 Army. When William Mason set about designing the Colt 1873, he skipped over one of the best grip frames for single actions, that being the longer frame of the 1860 Army. The standard Colt grip frame is near perfect and has served for many years for 250- to 260-gr. .44 and .45 bullets up to around 1200 fps, so it works fine for most loads used in standard-size single actions. In fact Colt did supply the 1860 Army grip frame on both their cartridge conversions and their 1871-72 Open-Tops, but when the Model P arrived in 1873 it wore the smaller grip frame of the 1851 Navy. I do not know of any factory-built First Generation Colt single actions made from 1873 to 1941 being issued with 1860 grip frames.

I have now installed 1860 grip frames on three 7-1/2-inch Uberti-manufactured single actions chambered in 44 Special, 44-40, and 45 Colt. The 1860 grip frame is not as natural pointing as the original, nor is it is easy to reach the hammer, but it is more comfortable for prolonged shooting. So where does one get 1860 grip frames? With two of these guns, I just switched straight across with a pair of Uberti 1860 Army replicas. It is an easy switch for anyone able to disassemble and reassemble a Colt-pattern single action. The triggers must also be swapped out, as the 1860 trigger is slightly shorter than the 1873 trigger, which will not fit in the 1860 trigger guard.

For the third swap I went to VTI Replica Gun Parts and ordered a complete 1860 Uberti grip frame assembly consisting of steel back strap, brass trigger guard, and one-piece wooden stocks all finished and ready to bolt on. If parts are ordered separately, one has a choice of brass or steel back strap, and brass or steel trigger guard. The all-steel parts are found listed under the Richards Conversion and Open-Top. A new backstrap-to-triggerguard screw must also be ordered as it is larger than normal.

In 1896 Colt came out with a target shooting grip frame, the Bisley Model. This grip frame is longer than the standard Single Action; it comes up higher along the backstrap and also behind the trigger guard, which is also larger; and it requires the use of a different hammer and trigger. Bisley Model mainframes are also slightly different from the standard SAA frame as they are longer where the back strap bolts on. The conversion of Bisley Model grip frame to an SAA grip frame requires some gunsmithing to accomplish.

Elmer Keith's ideal grip frame in the late 1920s was his #5, here duplicated by Gordon Marts on a 44 Special Bisley Model.

Single Action Sixguns | 237

Chapter 34 | Single Action Grips and Grip Frames

Stag is very hard to obtain now, but it looks exceptionally good on a stainless-steel single action sixgun such as this Ruger Vaquero.

RUGER SINGLE ACTION GRIP FRAMES

When Bill Ruger introduced the Single-Six in 1953 he used same basic size and shape for the grip frame as the Colt Single Action Army. This same grip frame would be used on the .357 and .44 Blackhawks. Subtle changes that seemed radical to many sixgunners were made to the Blackhawk line in 1963. The grip frame shape was changed ever so slightly to allow about one-fourth of an inch more room between the front strap and the back of the trigger guard with the result that the Colt Single Action feel was gone. The grip frames from the original Ruger Flat-Tops of 1953-1962 are marked XR3, while the Old Model grip frames are XR3-RED inscribed. Bolt patterns are the same and the grip frames will interchange. I have installed several XR3 grip frames and grips to Old Model Rugers with no fitting required.

The Old Army uses the XR3-RED shaped grip frame, which will generally bolt on to any Flat-Top or Old Model Ruger. All of these grip frames have a hole behind the trigger to accept the trigger return spring. This was changed with the advent of the New Model Rugers in 1972. These frames are the same shape as the Old Model and Old Army grip frames and they have been marked XR3-RED for many years. However, due to differences in the actions it takes considerable alteration to fit a NM grip frame to an OM mainframe or vice versa. To add to the confusion, Ruger grip frames are now marked XR3. For those wanting a grip frame the same size and shape as the Colt Single Action Army, Power Custom now offers a steel two-piece grip frame to fit Ruger mainframes and they are not only the same size and shape as those of the Colt Single Action Army, they will also accept one-piece style grips. These grip frames are available for both Old Model and New Model Rugers.

Within three years of introducing the 44 Magnum Blackhawk, Ruger, in an effort to help tame felt recoil, increased the weight slightly with the use of a non-fluted cylinder and a steel grip frame to replace the alloy grip frame of the first three Ruger single actions. Instead of the standard Colt-style grip frame copied from the 1851 Navy and 1873 Peacemaker and used on the first Rugers, Bill Ruger reached farther back in time to 1848 and the larger, square-backed trigger guard of the Colt Dragoon. Most sixgunners praised the grip frame of the new Super Blackhawk, but I find it to be more punishing to my hand than the original. Ruger Super Blackhawk

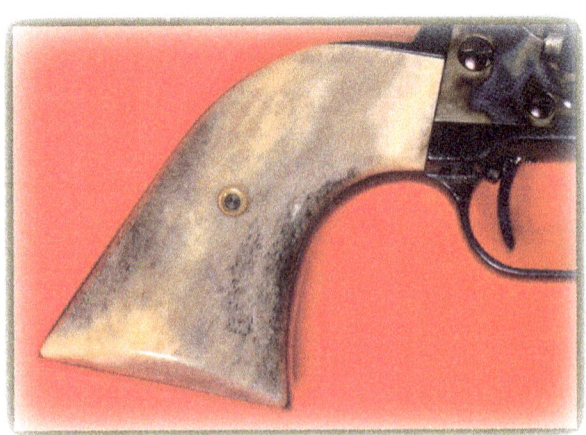

A material having a most beautiful and unusual look is buffalo bone as found on this Ruger Old Model.

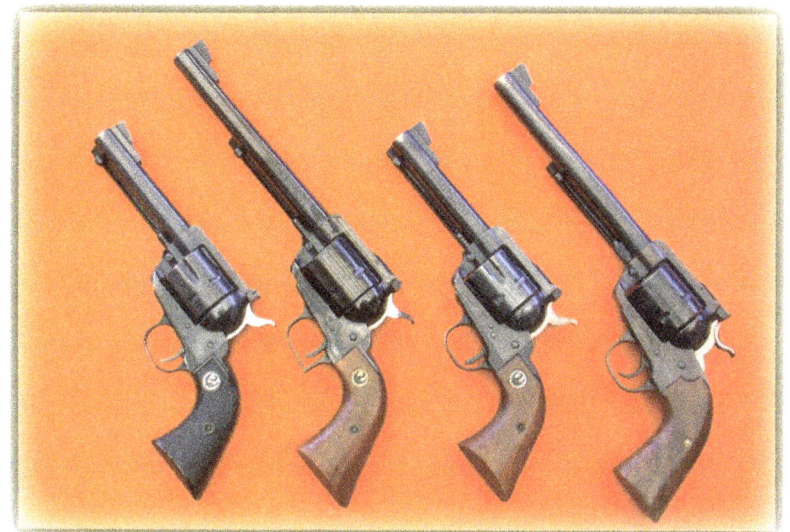

Ruger grip frames have also evolved over the years. The Colt-style frame first appeared on the Blackhawk in 1955, the Super Blackhawk arrived in 1959, the Old Model Blackhawk in 1963, and the Bisley Model in 1986.

grip frames, triggers, and hammers can generally be installed in standard Blackhawk models and vice versa. Of course we are talking Old Model to Old Model and New Model to New Model.

It would not be until the advent of the Bisley Model from Ruger that I would find a Ruger grip frame that would decrease felt recoil of heavy loads considerably for my hands. The Colt Bisley grip frame was designed for target shooting whereas the Ruger Bisley is made to handle heavy loads. It is absolutely mandatory, at least for me, on custom Rugers chambered for the 475 and 500 Linebaugh, and heavy 45 Colt as well. The Ruger Bisley grip frame is not the same as the Colt Bisley grip frame and it does not come up as high behind the trigger guard as does the Colt version. Bisley Model grip frames are all New Model style. Bolt patterns are the same, but the Bisley Model mainframe, as the Colt Bisley was more than one hundred years ago, is slightly taller. Until recently it required altering the Bisley Model grip frame to fit a New Model Ruger.

Currently there are two fairly easy ways to turn a standard Ruger New Model into a Bisley Model. If one starts with the Bisley Model Vaquero and any New Model Blackhawk, it is generally a straight swap of the Bisley grip frame, hammer, trigger, grips, and back strap screws. With a couple hours' work I was able to swap two Bisley Vaquero and two Blackhawk grip frames and corresponding parts with no required fitting. Both Brownell's and Ruger now offer Bisley Model grip frame kits, both blue and stainless steel, with all needed parts to convert the Blackhawk to a Bisley Model. Expect some fitting to be required.

The great difference in non-Colt single actions can be seen here with stocks from TLA's Improved Number Five, Colt Bisley Model, Ruger Super Blackhawk, and Ruger Bisley Model.

Single Action Sixguns | 239

Chapter 34 | Single Action Grips and Grip Frames

Ivory is highly valued for its beauty as shown in the one-piece grips on a Second Generation 44 Special and a First Generation 45 Colt.

GRIPS

Why custom single action grips? There are a number of reasons. Personal taste in material is a large factor: exotic woods, ivory, staghorn, ram's horn, micarta, just to name a few. A look at famous sixguns used by several Texas Rangers and Southwestern lawmen reveals their preference for pearl or ivory as their grip material. Another reason for custom stocks is for a better fit, and with some grips the shape or checkering adds greatly to security of handling when shooting. At one time many of the grips found on single action sixguns were excellent. Over the years they have become more flared at the bottom, resulting in a grip that, for me, accentuates recoil. Check a Flat-top Ruger .357 or .44 against a New Model Ruger in any caliber and notice the great difference in the feel of the grips. Grips should have great aesthetic appeal, feel good to the hand, and help with security and/or recoil. As single action sixgunners we are blessed with a relatively large number of single action grip makers, both custom fit and aftermarket. In a book this size we cannot cover everyone, but I offer the following as sources for great grips.

> "A look at famous sixguns used by several Texas Rangers and Southwestern lawmen reveals their preference for pearl or ivory as their grip material."

BluMagnum is best known for Skeeter Skelton-style grips on double action Smith & Wessons, but they also offer beautifully fitted and finished single action stocks. From the top right clockwise, fancy walnut on a Bowen 41 Special Flat-Top Blackhawk, mesquite on a Clements Bisley Model, and one-piece ivory on a Texas Longhorn Arms 44 Special Ruger.

BLUMAGNUM/TEDD ADAMOVICH

BluMagnum's specialty is single action grips of exotic woods such as maple, rosewood, kingwood, ebony, and fancy walnut, with both two-piece and one-piece grips being offered. Genuine ivory as well as black and ivory micarta also are available along with genuine stag when available. For all single actions, stocks are made in the standard two-piece style, or in the case of Colt or replicas thereof one-piece style grips are offered. The original grips for the Colt SAA in 1873 were actually one piece of walnut that were grooved out to accept the backstrap and trigger guard, and were installed by removing the backstrap, sliding on the grip and then reattaching with three screws. This style gives a very smooth look to a single action sixgun. With today's epoxies, these one-piece grips can actually be made by using two grip panels and a middle spacer all glued together. BluMagnum must have the grip frame in their possession for Rugers, or the backstrap and trigger guard for Colts, for fitting of custom grips.

Long-barreled single action sixguns such as the 10-1/2-inch Ruger 357 Maximum and Freedom Arms 44 Magnum are more easily controlled with BluMagnum's filler grips.

Chapter 34 | Single Action Grips and Grip Frames

Master gripmaker Roy Fishpaw takes a break in his stockmaking shop.

If these don't stir your single action sixgunnin' spirit, you have none! This Old Model Ruger wears French walnut stocks by the master himself, Roy Fishpaw.

ROY FISHPAW/ROY'S CUSTOM GRIPS

Fishpaw is well known as both a craftsman and a complete gripmaker with a line of grip materials that includes exotic woods, aged elephant ivory, even mastodon ivory, and the very rare ram's horn. I have Fishpaw grips in figured walnut on a Ruger Blackhawk, the very unusual snakewood on a Colt Single Action, Dall sheep horn on a Texas Longhorn Arms Improved #5 45 Colt, big horn sheep on a USFA 44 Special, and ivory on a Colt single action. Fishpaw is one of the few sources for not only ivory but the almost mythical ram's horn as well. The latter makes into yellowish colored stocks that almost seem to be translucent, and it is highly prized and extremely beautiful.

Fishpaw has a perfect feel for what a sixgun grip should be and his work is absolutely flawless and as close to perfect fit as is humanly possible. He achieves this by fitting each pair to the individual gun frame, and also dealing with each customer as an individual. He is normally back-logged. Each customer is put on a list and when the customer's name comes up, Roy asks that the customer send him the frame. It would be impossible to find better grips anywhere than from the Master Gripmaker himself!

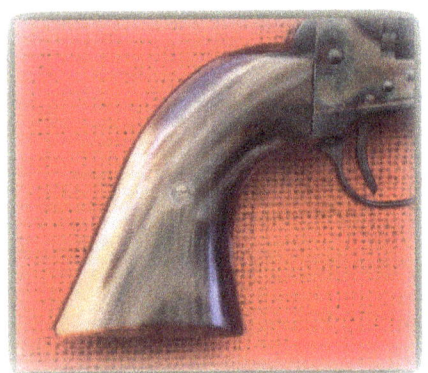

One material that can challenge ivory is desert bighorn as found on these stocks by Roy Fishpaw on a USFA 44 Special.

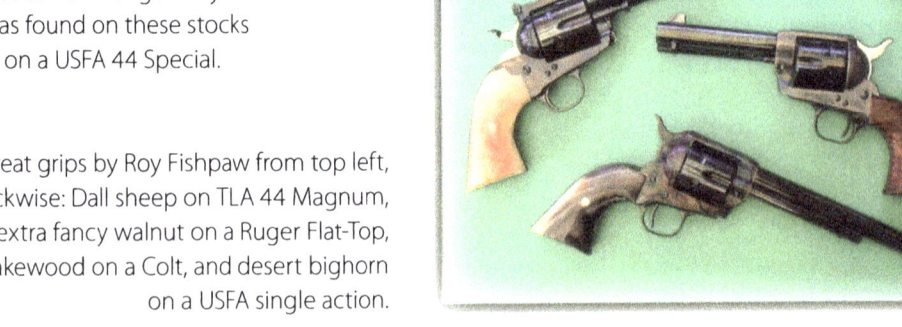

Great grips by Roy Fishpaw from top left, clockwise: Dall sheep on TLA 44 Magnum, extra fancy walnut on a Ruger Flat-Top, snakewood on a Colt, and desert bighorn on a USFA single action.

Mouthwatering wood was used for these exotic wood grips by Scott Kolar on a pair of Bisleys.

SCOTT KOLAR/SK CUSTOM GRIPS

I first encountered Kolar over the net when he posted that he would refinish any Ruger stocks with a two-for-one offer. For anyone who would send in two pair, he would refinish one pair and keep the other pair as payment. I took him up on this offer, sending him four pairs of Bisley and two pairs of Vaquero stocks. The three pairs returned were beautifully finished, so much so that except for the factory medallions one would doubt that they were original grips.

The grips found on replica single actions are the right shape and are well fitted, but their finish leaves a lot to be desired and often gives them away as replicas. Grips were pulled from Patersons, Walkers, Dragoons, 1851s, 1860s, and both Remington and Colt single action replicas. Some were refinished in walnut, others with an ebony color. The change in the personality of the sixgun was dramatic. Scott even managed to find some decent wood under some of the cherry-colored Italian stain.

SK Custom Grips also offers custom-made grips in some of the most beautiful wood available such as flame-grained maple and burl mesquite. The color and figure in the latter definitely falls into the category of having to be seen to be believed. He has done several pair for me for Ruger's Bisley Model both in burl mesquite and maple. Somehow he manages to come up with the most exotic of exotic woods. There is considerable variation in grip frames, so the frame must be sent to him for a matching fit.

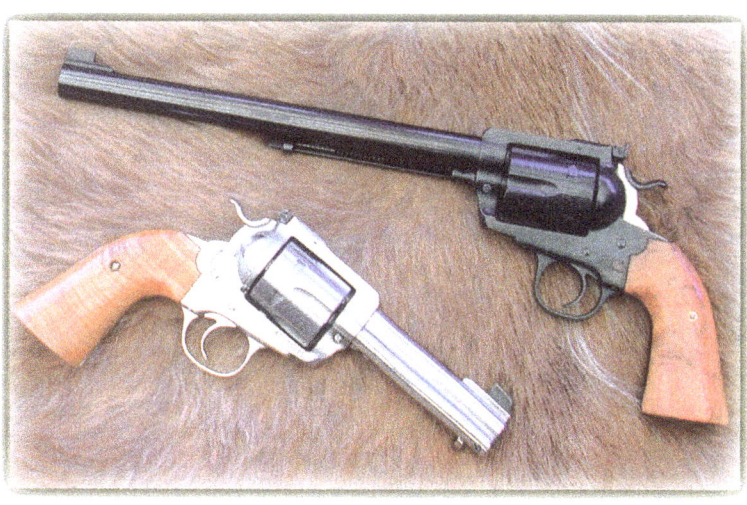

Maple stocks by Scott Kolar greatly add to the beauty of custom sixguns such as this 445 Ruger by Ben Forkin and a stainless-steel Bisley Model put together by Taffin.

Chapter 34 | Single Action Grips and Grip Frames

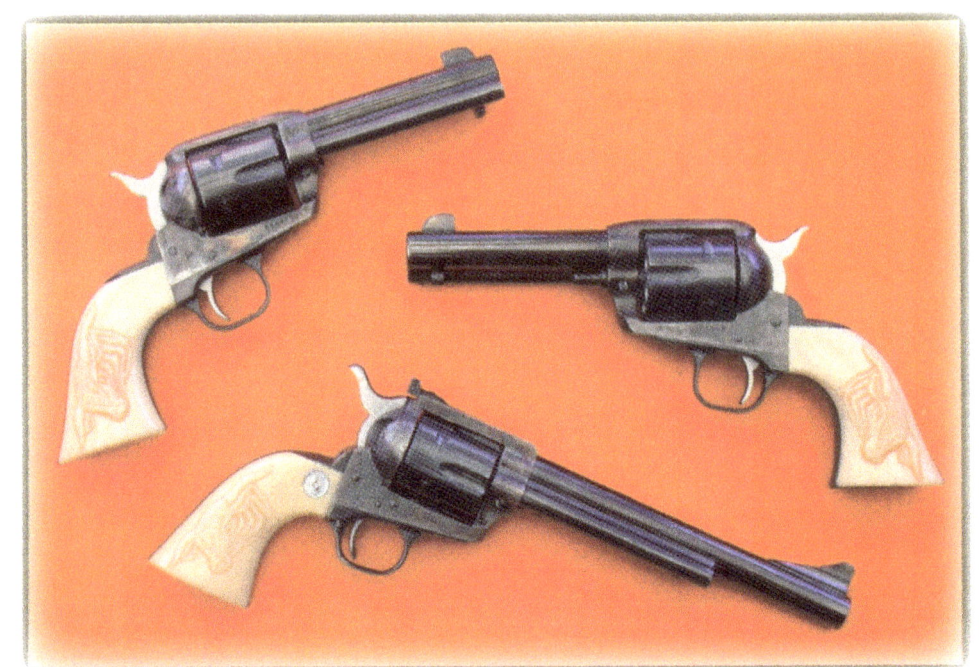

Bob Leskovec duplicated Elmer Keith's single action Colt stocks in ivory polymer for this pair of .45 Ruger Vaqueros and a 45 Colt New Frontier.

"Have Gun, Will Travel" lives again with these custom stocks by Bob Leskovec.

A favorite single action sixgun for hunting can be customized with silver inlays such as this Cape buffalo in fancy walnut by Bob Leskovec.

BOB LESKOVEC/PRECISION PRO GRIPS

Bob Leskovec of Precision Pro Grips works with several media including exotic woods, silver inlays, ivory, and acrylics, with both of the latter being offered in carved motifs. I grew up reading Elmer Keith and always admired his ivory-stocked single actions and even more so after I got to see, feel, touch, and experience them in person. Leskovec was commissioned to carry out a pair of Keith's favorite ivory grips with a carved steerhead in ivory polymer for heavy-duty use. These now reside on a Colt New Frontier .45. I also had Precision Pro Grips do the same pattern to stock a pair of Ruger .45 Vaqueros with one sixgun carved on the right panel and the matching gun on the left panel. The carved steerhead not only looks great but also provides a non-slip surface for one-handed shooting.

Leskovec can also copy any of the old-style carved ivory stocks and reproduce them in a tougher acrylic that looks much like ivory. Precision Pro has their version of the B Western imitation stag grip carried out in ivory acrylic with the stag lines carved into the material. They are more eye-pleasing than the plastic imitation stag, less expensive than genuine stag, and are available now.

This First Generation Colt Frontier Six-Shooter deserves these beautiful bone grips fashioned by Jim Martin. Photo courtesy of Richard Talacek.

A sixgun that fairly reeks of history is this First Generation 4-3/4-inch 44-40 Colt SAA with stag stocks by Jim Martin. Photo courtesy of Richard Talacek.

JIM MARTIN

Martin is long-time single action gunsmith, fast draw shooter, trick shooter, and instructor of movie cowboys on the use of the single action sixgun as well as a master gripmaker. Way back in the 1950s Great Western not only offered completed sixguns but kits as well. As a young man, Jim Martin purchased Great Western kits, assembled them and sold them, using the money to buy more kits. Today Martin offers his single action sixgun tuning skills for Colts, Great Westerns, and all replica single actions. He also offers beautifully finished and fitted custom one-piece stocks of exotic woods, including mesquite, and, when available, staghorn and bone.

Most grip makers taper the bottom of the grip panels for single action sixguns, resulting in a smaller grip. For those with larger than normal hands, Martin goes the other way and actually extends the grip panels 1/4 inch beyond the bottom of the grip frame and then tapers the insides of the grip panels to me the bottom of the grip frame. One-fourth of an inch may not sound like an awful lot but it makes a huge difference for those with larger hands. Many of the single action sixguns pictured throughout this book are fitted with custom stocks by Jim Martin.

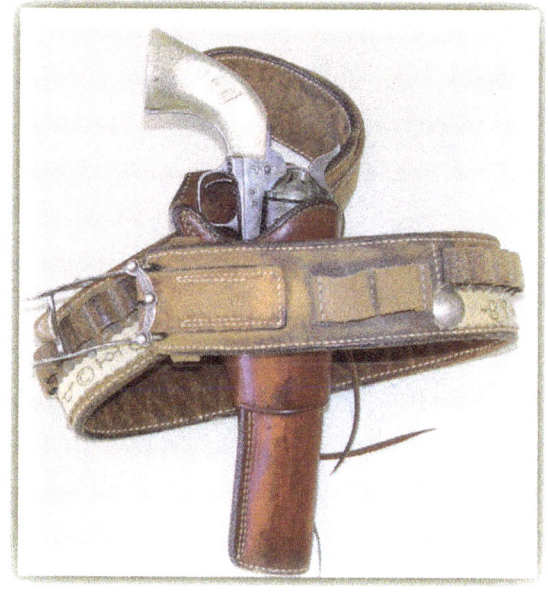

Pistolero Jim Martin is known for his long association with fast draw, gun spinning, custom action jobs, and custom grips as shown on one of his favorite sixguns, a 7-1/2-inch 44 Colt SAA. Photo courtesy of Richard Talacek.

Chapter 34 | Single Action Grips and Grip Frames

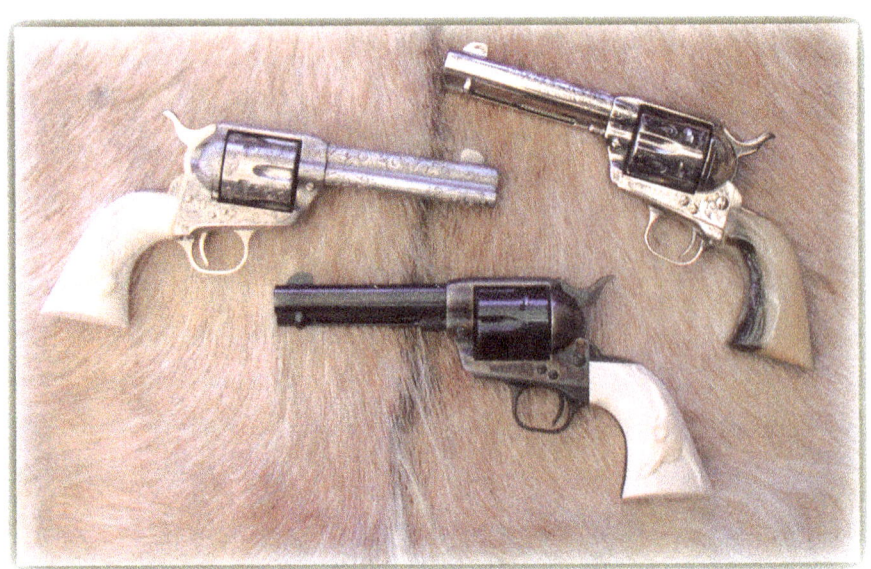

Life is too short to spend it with an ugly gun, and beautiful sixguns need special stocks. From top right clockwise, Dale Miller engraved 44-40 with bighorn sheep stocks by Paul Persinger; another Dale Miller sixgun, a 38-40 with Eagle's carved Ultra Ivory stocks; and the Jim Riggs engraved .45 also has been stocked by Paul Persinger, this time with carved ivory.

PAUL PERSINGER

The Colt Single Action Army is one of the few factory sixguns that come with stocks that fit my hand. The only reason to replace them is to come up with a more exotic material than black rubber eagle grips or the extremely plain walnut stocks found on Third Generation Colts. Paul Persinger is an artist of tremendous talent in several mediums. His drawings are unbelievable; he can duplicate any of the carved ivory stocks offered by Colt on their cap and ball presentation pieces and any of several well-known carvings found on Single Action Armies. He can work from a picture or sketch.

Persinger offers a full line of old-style carvings such as that Mexican eagle, American eagle, Hickok and Patton eagles, buffalo and longhorn skulls, and just about anything else desired. Carved longhorn steer skulls not only look good, but they also naturally fill in the crease in my shooting hand making it much easier to control the recoiling sixgun with heavier than standard loads and to keep the sixgun from shifting in my hands. Persinger carries out carving to perfection, and most importantly, the raw material he starts with is of extremely high quality with lots of marbled milk showing. Tony Kojis, who fits grips for me often, looked at Persinger's work, studied it, removed the backstrap to look closer, and said, "This guy is the best I have ever seen!" Paul Persinger is a true Western artist working in ivory.

Paul Persinger is a true artist working in carved ivory, as seen on these matching longhorn steer skulls on a pair of 45 Colts.

Persinger's carving and fitting, as well as his shaping of each grip, are all nearly perfect. In addition to ivory, Persinger also supplies grips of ivory micarta, ebony, and rosewood with either two-piece or one-piece styling as well as the material that rivals (some would say surpasses) ivory, ram's horn from the bighorn sheep. My two engraved 4-3/4-inch Colt Single Actions are very special sixguns to me that will be passed on to two of my grandsons. Both have been appropriately stocked to compliment their nickel finish, with the Jim Riggs engraved .45 fitted with Persinger carved ivory while the other, a 44-40 engraved by Dale Miller, carries Persinger grips of ram's horn.

KIRK RATAJESAK

I recently had the occasion to have a pair of my custom one-piece Colt Single Action Army grips carved by a master artisan by the name of Kirk Ratajesak. Ratajesak is a man who performs an amazing job of superb craftsmanship. Each grip panel contains seven carved maple leaves complete with vines and all the background design. They are absolutely beautiful. Special grips belong on a special sixgun. Two years ago a very special friend of mine, Ron Elerick aka the Kilted Preacher, passed away suddenly and totally unexpectedly. I now have his 5-1/2-inch Third Generation 45 Colt. This Colt is a standard blued and case colored single action that has now gone close to the head of the line of my favorite custom sixguns. The addition of these carved grips by Kirk Ratajesak turned it into what is one of the most attractive sixguns I have ever seen.

BluMagnum made the one-piece maple stocks, which were then carved by Kirk Ratajesak. This 45 Colt belonged to Ron Elerick, the Kilted Preacher.

ROGER WARMUSKERKEN

A new source for stag grips is found in the work of Roger Warmuskerken. Genuine staghorn has been in very short supply for several years and, when found, is quite expensive, in fact getting very close to the price of ivory. This situation exists due to an export embargo being placed on Indian sambar stag antlers. Roger offers an excellent and reasonably priced alternative by using antlers from the red stag.

Roger is a pastor who supplements his income by crafting custom stocks. The material used from the red stag has a lot of bark and color but the surface is quite smooth in spite of this. Roger has built two pair of red stag antler grips for my use on Ruger New Model single actions. One pair went on a custom round butted Vaquero built up utilizing a Qualite Pistol & Revolver stainless-steel frame, while the other is on a 38-40 Blackhawk that has been fitted with a Ruger standard stainless-steel grip frame. Workmanship on both pairs is of exceptionally high quality with both pairs of grips not only fitting perfectly to the grip frame but also mating up exquisitely with my shooting hand. Warmuskerken's grips are offered at a surprisingly reasonable price. Currently, grips are offered only for those one-piece grip frames as found on Ruger and Freedom Arms sixguns. The grip frame only must be sent for fitting as Warmuskerken is not set up to accept firearms.

Today Sambar stag is virtually impossible to find, but Roger Warmuskerken offers an excellent substitute with stocks from the antlers of the red deer as found on these Rugers, a 38-40 Blackhawk with stainless steel grip frame, and Vaquero with stainless steel bird's head grip frame from QPR.

Single Action Sixguns | 247

Chapter 34 | Single Action Grips and Grip Frames

Buffalo Brothers offers a full assortment of antique style grips for nineteenth-century sixguns such as, from top left clockwise, cracked ivory and Mexican eagle on a pair of Remingtons, checkered star on an 1875 Remington, and imitation stag on an 1861 Colt Navy.

BUFFALO BROTHERS

I first met Buffalo Brothers at the SHOT Show several years ago and was most impressed with the look and feel of their line of molded old-style grips. A few weeks later at Winter Range I stopped by the Buffalo Brothers tent on Sutler's Row and wound up purchasing a Second Generation 45 Colt with the coveted 4-3/4-inch barrel. It had been totally tuned by American Frontier Firearms. Since it had to be shipped FFL to FFL, I made arrangements to have Buffalo Brothers first fit it with a pair of one-piece style checkered grips with a Texas Star in the middle. They look like old bone and the color in the butt is particularly striking.

Since that time Buffalo Brothers have greatly expanded their line and have stag, bone, checkered, carved old style patterns: almost anything anyone could want for a single action sixgun. I have now fitted their stag, bone, carved, and checkered grips to several replica single action sixguns, greatly enhancing their appearance. All grips, whether one or two-piece style, need to be fitted to each individual sixgun. They are usually oversized but once in awhile a pair of undersized grips will be encountered. Simply return them for replacements.

Stainless steel .45 Model Ps from Cimarron benefit greatly, aesthetically speaking, with longhorn skull and Mexican eagle grips from Buffalo Brothers.

EAGLE GRIPS

To fill in the void caused by the shortage of ivory, and to also supply a grip at a much lower cost than the real thing, Eagle developed a new synthetic that is the closest to the genuine article I have ever seen. Most imitation ivory has a flat plastic look. Not so with Eagle's Ultra Ivory. Not only does it not look cheap, it also has a wavy, milky pattern throughout such as one finds in real ivory. This milky pattern really shows up in strong sunlight. These grips are offered in three single action versions: plain smooth, carved, and checkered. I have had Ultra Ivory fitted to several single action sixguns. First was a Second Generation 7-1/2-inch Colt SAA 44 Special that I had totally rebuilt from a 38 Special by Eddie Janis at Peacemaker Specialists; then came a custom Ruger 44 Magnum with a 4-5/8-inch barrel and standard grip frame built by Mag-Na-Port on a Three Screw Super Blackhawk with a stainless steel looking finish and utilizing a grip frame from the Ruger Old Army grip; and finally a 4-5/8-inch Colt SAA 38-40 now wears a pair of Ultra Ivories with a carved steerhead on the right panel.

With the shortage of real staghorn, several companies have been looking for viable alternatives. Eagle's answer has been elk horn. It looks exceptionally good on the blued Vaqueros and polishing brings out a lot of color not present in the staghorn grips from the antlers of the Sambar stag. These are an excellent alternative for those who prefer genuine stag. In addition to the elkhorn grips, Eagle also offers genuine mother of pearl grips – and yes, I know what General Patton (one of my all-time heroes) said about pearl grips. However, many of the old time Texas Rangers preferred pearl grips on their Colt single actions and Tom Threepersons always carried a nickel-plated, 4-51/2-inch Colt single action with real pearl grips. No one ever dared accuse him of anything.

Eagle's answer for a secure shaped grip for competition is the Gun Fighter featuring a narrow butt portion and a wider top portion with a obvious shelf that serves to keep the sixgun from rotating upward in the hand, allowing faster recovery between shots. I have these grips in checkered buffalo horn on a pair of 5-1/2-inch Ruger Old Army sixguns that are used with black powder in either the original percussion cylinders or with black powder loads in a pair of R&D 45 Colt cylinders; and also on Diamond Dot's stainless-steel Vaqueros.

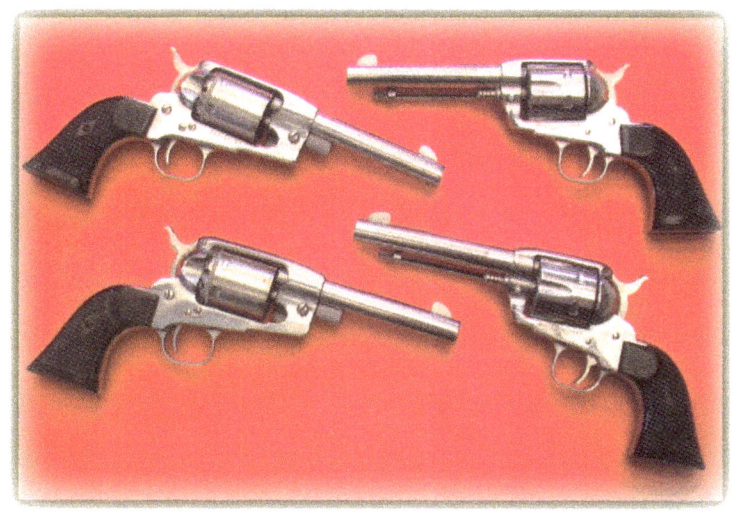

Black powder sixguns, or any used in cowboy action shooting, benefit by the security offered by checkered Gunfighter grips from Eagle Grips as shown on a pair of Ruger Old Armies with R&D conversion cylinders and Belt Mountain base pins, and .357 Vaqueros.

Having the look and feel of carved ivory at a much lower cost are these one-piece Ultra Ivory grips from Eagle Grips.

Royal grips from Eagle Grips include elkhorn on a .45 Vaquero and mother of pearl and Ultra Ivory on Colt Single Actions.

Single Action Sixguns | 249

Chapter 34 | Single Action Grips and Grip Frames

The Navy Arms Model #3 Russian and Smith & Wesson Model 2000 Schofield have been stocked with Ultra Ivory by Eagle Grips; the leather is by Back Hills Leather.

GRIPMAKER

Not finished grips but rather a do-it-yourself kit, all of these grips are of ivory urethane and Larry Little of Gripmaker says they will age just like original ivory. Gripmaker's grips, which must be hand fitted by the purchaser, are offered for almost every single action sixgun imaginable from the 1848 and 1849 Pocket Colts through the 1851, 1860, and 1861 Colt cap-n-balls, the Colt Single Action Army and Bisley, all for both original and replica. The imports, Remington cap-n-ball and 1875, the New Thunderer and Lightning, the S&W Schofield and Model #3, and all of the Ruger Single Actions are also provided for.

In addition to a plain synthetic ivory, Gripmaker offers well over a dozen carved designs which are copied from Frontier versions such as the Hickok eagle, the Mexican eagle, the Texas star, and the Liberty head. Of course, all carvings are not available for all grip shapes. I have had a pair of 7-1/2-inch Cimarron 38-40s fitted with one-piece staghorn grips from Larry and then colored them to my taste using orange and brown leather dye. I have also been able to fit Gripmaker's grips myself to a pair of 1860 Armies with a few hours' work and the use of a Moto-Tool. Panels were first fitted fairly closely to the frames and then epoxied together to make a one-piece grip. For this operation the frame was heavily coated with Vaseline to prevent the panels being glued to the grip frame. Using the spacer provided by Gripmaker, the panels and the spacer were both given a light coating of glue, then placed on the sixguns, rubber banded in place, then left to dry overnight. The next day they were ready for final fitting. Carefully. If I can do it anyone can!

Gripmaker offers antique-style Colt and Remington grips that can easily be colored using leather die to add a century-old look.

LARRY CAUDILL

My latest "discovery" when it comes to custom grips is Larry Caudill. Actually, Larry has been around a long time making beautiful custom rifle stocks as well as handgun stocks with leftover pieces of wood. When I recently had David Clements build a 44 Special/44-40 on an Old Model Ruger 357 Magnum Blackhawk, Larry he suggested walnut for the grips. Larry sent pictures of several blanks of circassian walnut so I could select exactly what I wanted. In addition to expertly fitting the grips to the frame he also flat-filed the frame behind the trigger and also removed the built-in flare at the heel of the grip frame. His grips also have a blind screw, that is instead of drilling completely through two-piece stocks, the nut is hidden behind the right hand panel so grips appear to be one-piece. His work is outstanding.

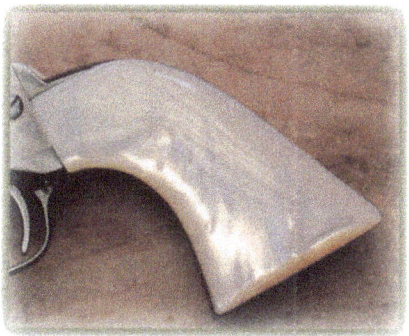

General Patton didn't like it, but Tom Threepersons and many Texas Rangers preferred mother of pearl for their single action stocks.

Larry Caudill can flat file Ruger grip frames before fitting custom grips in order to give a better feel.

General George S. Patton, Theodore Roosevelt, Tom Threepersons, Hopalong Cassidy, Tom Mix, Buck Jones, Tim McCoy, Elmer Keith, and Skeeter Skelton all had two things in common. At one time in my life or another they have all been my personal heroes, and they all personalized their single action sixguns with custom stocks. I prefer to join their select company.

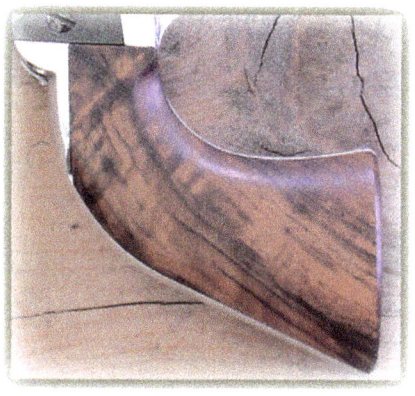

David Clements had Larry Caudill fashion the beautiful circassian walnut stocks for a custom Old Model Ruger.

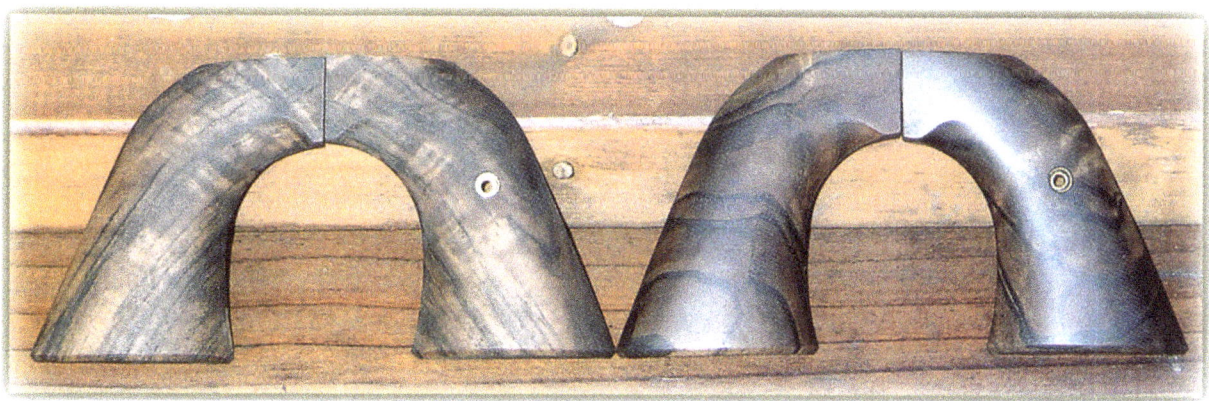

Notice there is only one hole in the two-piece grips by Larry Caudill. The secret is a nut fitted inside the grip, allowing a one-piece look.

Single Action Sixguns | 251

–Chapter 35–

TIPS FOR HANDLING THE SINGLE ACTION SIXGUN

All traditional single action sixguns, such as these, from top left clockwise, Colt SAA, Colt New Frontier, Old Model Ruger Blackhawk, and replica Model P, MUST be carried with only five rounds and the hammer down on an empty chamber.

The handling of any firearm, and especially any traditional single action sixgun, should not be approached lightly. From 1836 to 1973, except for a few models of percussion revolvers offering a notch between cylinder chambers to accept the lowered hammer, all single action sixguns were actually five-shooters as safety required the hammer to be lowered on an empty chamber for carrying. Those foolish enough to carry six rounds with the hammer down on a cap or primer could easily wind up shooting themselves or someone else if the hammer were struck by a heavy object, such as a stirrup thrown over the saddle while tightening the cinch, or by dropping the sixgun. Ruger introduced the transfer safety bar with the New Model Blackhawk in 1973, which made single actions thus equipped safe to carry fully loaded. All traditional single actions such as Colt, USFA, modern Great Western Italian replicas, and Rugers made prior to 1973 MUST be carried with the hammer down on an empty chamber.

We now agree the proper way to carry a loaded traditional single action six-shooter is with one empty chamber under the hammer, but how do we do it safely? Many times I have seen a shooter load five rounds and then look down the front of the cylinder to find the empty chamber. Looking down the front end of loaded sixgun in someone else's hands, or my own, is not something I care to do.

To properly and safely load a traditional single action, open the loading gate, pull the hammer back to the half cock notch, load one round, rotate the cylinder skipping the next chamber, and then load four more cartridges. The cylinder now contains five loaded and one empty chamber. The next step is to safely rotate the cylinder so that the empty is under the hammer. If the load-one-skip-one-load-four procedure has been done correctly, one then simply pulls the hammer back to the full cock notch and then carefully lowers it while releasing the trigger. The hammer will then be resting on an empty chamber.

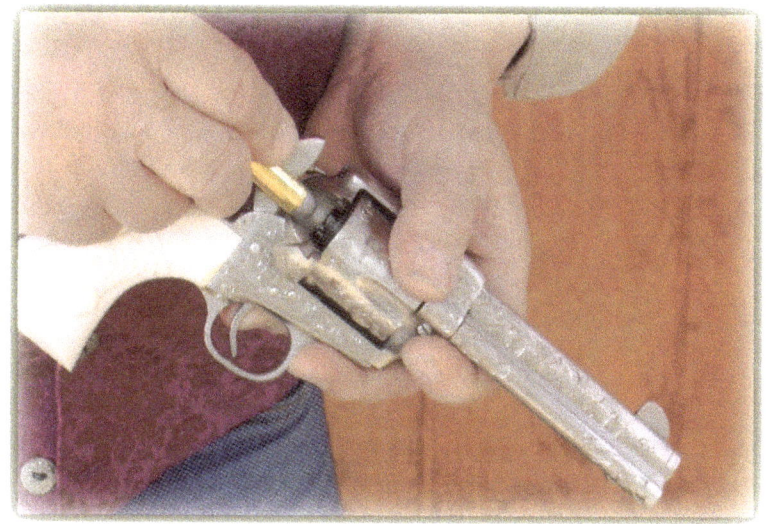

To reload, the sixgun is still in the left hand that rotates the cylinder as the right hand loads new cartridges.

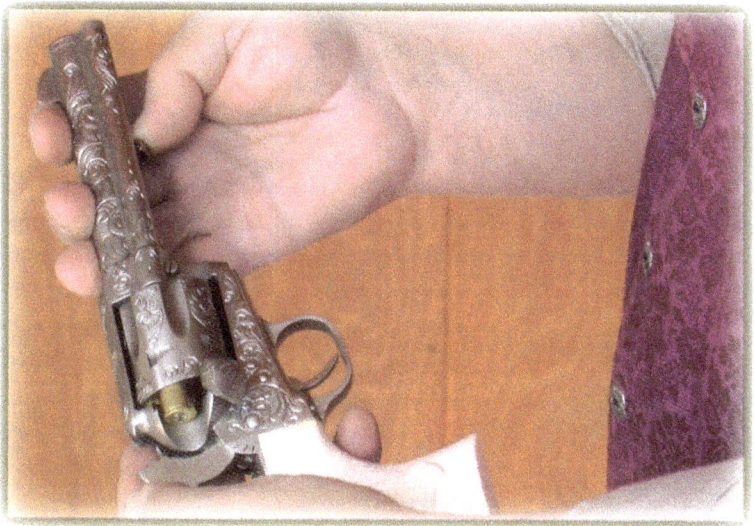

Taffin's method of emptying a single action sixgun is to place the grip in the cupped left hand as the right hand works the ejector rod dropping the empties into the left hand.

Taffin's friend and Fellow Shootist, Brian Pearce of *Handloader* magazine, shows his method for loading a single action sixgun, keeping it in his right hand and rotating the cylinder with his thumb.

This should be practiced diligently with DUMMY cartridges until it can be accomplished perfectly. If one is not a reloader or doesn't have access to dummy cartridges, it should not be very difficult to find a reloader that can provide five dummy cartridges. Note the hammer is never let down from the half cock notch but is brought back to the full cock notch before lowering. One of the best ways to lock up any traditional single action is to lower the hammer from the half cock. The internal parts will not be in the right place and the single action revolver will sometimes lock up when this is done.

To unload a single action, I have found that placing the sixgun in my left hand, after the loading gate is opened and the hammer is brought back to the half cock notch, cradles the tip of the hammer and the backstrap in my hand. Then with my right hand, I work the ejector rod with the barrel pointed downrange and slightly upwards. This drops all of the empties into my cradled left hand.

Single Action Sixguns | 253

Chapter 35 | Tips For Handling The Single Action Sixgun

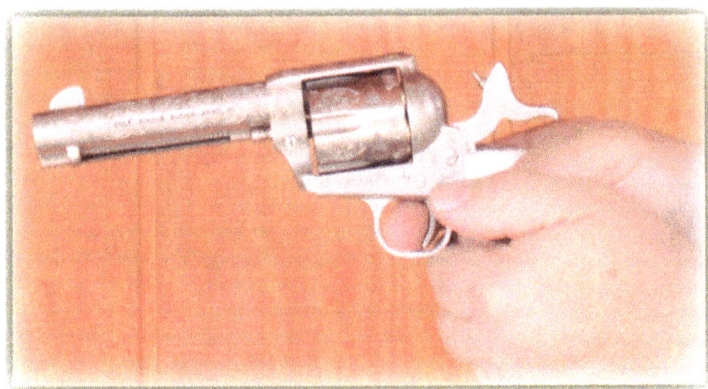

Taffin's two-handed hold is basically the same as the one-handed hold except the right hand is cupped by the left hand.

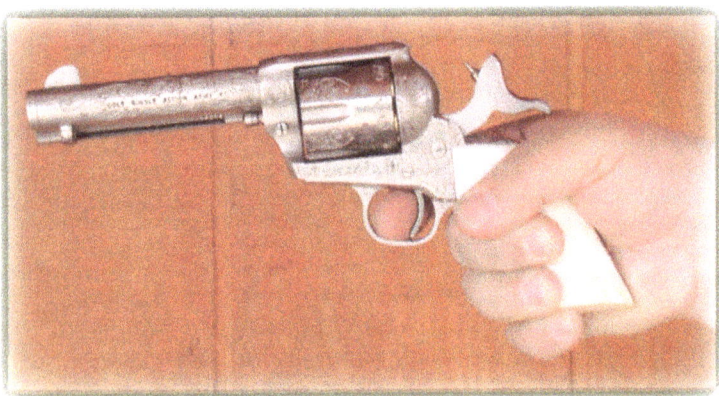

Taffin's one-handed hold on a single action sixgun, two fingers around the grip, little finger under the butt, thumb wrapped around to the middle finger. Some shooters prefer to place the thumb at the back of the recoil shield.

How one holds a single action is quite subjective, as everyone's hands are not the same size and shape. I've tried several different ways with the traditional single action revolver with a Colt-style grip, including all generations of the Colt Single Action Army, all replicas thereof, and Ruger Blackhawks. The grip that works best for me is two fingers wrapped around the grip, the little finger under the butt, and the thumb curled around so it makes contact with the middle finger. When using this style of grip it is absolutely necessary to not allow the little finger to contact a hard surface or a sharp pain and tears in the eyes will result. When shooting with two hands, I simply bring the left hand over and form a cup for the last three fingers of my shooting hand.

Some shooters prefer placing the index finger of the offhand in front of the trigger guard, but I have found using all fingers in the cupping method works best for me. When you're shooting, follow-through is very important. As the gun is fired, you must continue to press the trigger rearward while maintaining a rock-steady grip. The easiest way to practice this is to have someone else load the revolver with three or four live rounds and one or two dummy cartridges so the shooter does not know when the hammer will drop on a live round. Any movement at all when a dummy round is encountered calls for increased practice and concentration.

Taffin's single action sixgun grip shown from the front: notice the trigger finger is not pushed all the way through the trigger guard but rather the tip of the finger is used to actuate the trigger.

Sequence photos for handling a single action sixgun safely with live ammunition:

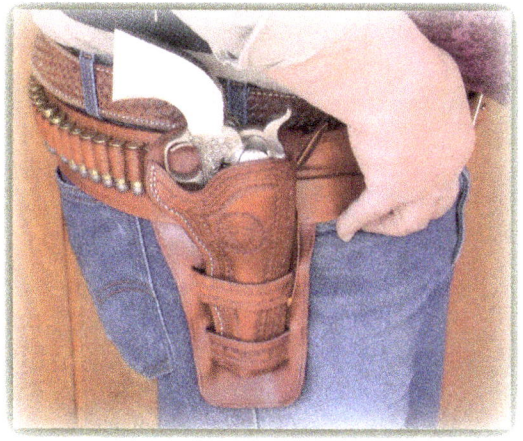

1. The loaded single action rests securely in the holster, the hand is off the gun.

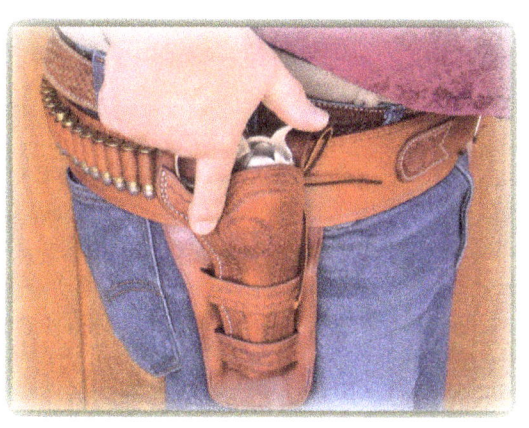

2. The hand moves grasping the sixgun securely, the thumb is on the hammer, the finger is off the trigger.

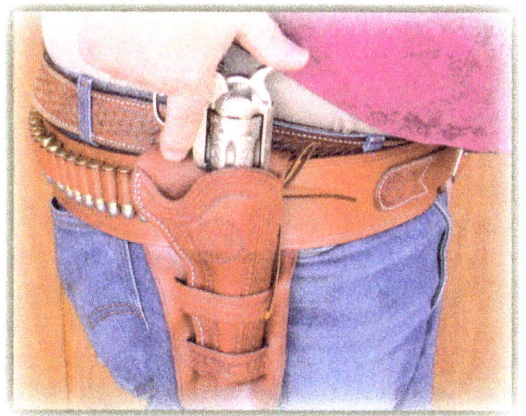

3. The draw begins, thumb is on hammer, and the finger is off the trigger.

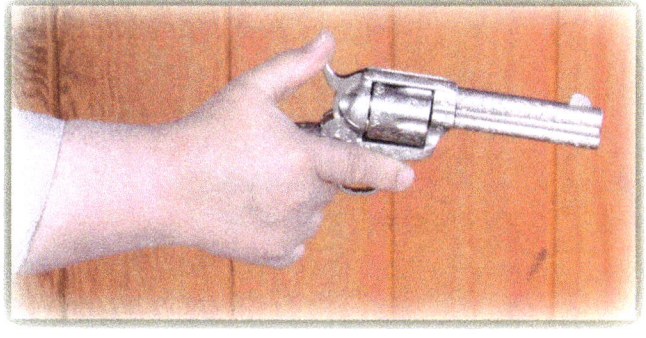

4. The draw is complete, the single action is well in front of the body, the finger is still off the trigger, the hammer is not yet cocked.

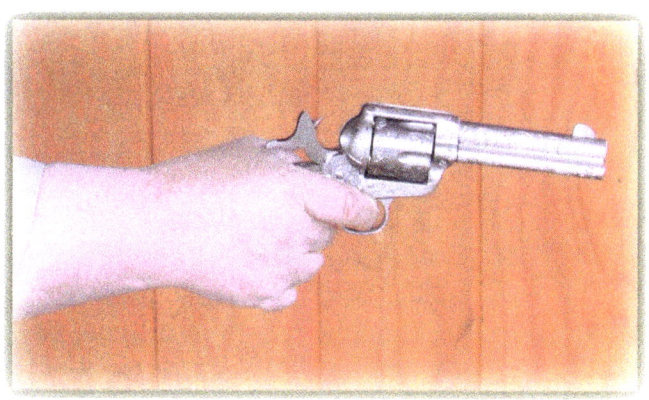

5. The sixgun is on target, the hammer is cocked, the trigger is ready to be squeezed.

The safest handguns to draw from leather are a double action sixgun or a semi-auto with the safety on. A single action can be just as safe but first we must forget everything we have ever seen in the movies. In fact, that goes for handling all firearms as they are routinely handled unsafely on TV and in the movies. If it weren't so dangerous, what they do would be almost laughable. What works with blanks and movie cameras not only does not work in real-life; moreover, it is absolutely dangerous. A single action revolver MUST NEVER BE COCKED IN THE HOLSTER! The proper method is to grasp the butt with the normal shooting grip, trigger finger alongside the trigger guard, and the thumb on the hammer. Once the revolver is pointed at the target, then, and only then, is the hammer to be cocked and the trigger finger placed upon the trigger.

Single Action Sixguns | 255

Chapter 35 | Tips For Handling The Single Action Sixgun

Before attempting to file down a front sight, the barrel should be wrapped with protective tape. Not using the tape is a guarantee the file will slip.

Most fixed-sight single action sixguns are made with high front sights designed to be dialed in by each individual shooter with the use of a file. If a sixgun shoots low but is on for windage it is necessary to lower the front sight to raise the impact of the bullet on target. To bring the point of impact up, the top of the front sight is filed until the bullet strikes exactly where desired. Several cautions here: first wrap the sixgun with tape just in case the file slips and hits the barrel. Murphy's Law will certainly kick in if the barrel is not taped. Every file stroke is most important as it takes very little metal removed from the top of the front sight to change the impact of the bullet on target drastically. Ruger steel is much harder than Italian steel, which files down very quickly. It is also necessary to choose the load that will be used with each particular sixgun and file the front sight for that load. With care and by moving slowly, the top of the front sight can be filed parallel to the barrel.

Another caution is necessary here. If the sixgun is shot from a rest using two hands for sighting in, and then in actual use (i.e., fired from a standing position using one hand), chances are very good that the point of impact will be different. For myself, the point of impact is higher from a standing one-handed position. The stance that will be used for most shooting should also be used as the front sight is filed in.

If the sixgun in question shoots to the right or left I do not recommend attempting to bend the front sight as it can result in the front sight becoming detached from the barrel. The best way is to seek the services of a gunsmith with the proper barrel vise to turn the barrel. A gun that shoots left, needs the front sight moved the opposite of the direction that one would move the rear sight to change point of impact. This means the barrel is turned to the left to move point of impact of a sixgun that shoots left to center. For most sixguns the barrel is simply turned in tighter to move the impact and loosened slightly if the sixgun shoots to the right.

The basic design goes back only to 1836, but the traditional single action is still a classic and is still a pleasure to shoot if handled safely.

Better gunsmiths are set up with a barrel vise that will not scratch the surface of the barrel. I have had numerous barrels turned by the gunsmiths at our local gunshop, Shapel's, with excellent results. I carefully shoot a target and take it into the gunsmith and he proceeds accordingly. A sixgun that is off as to both windage and elevation should be adjusted for windage first as turning the barrel for windage will also effect elevation. If the change needed is minor, say one inch right or left, or a couple of inches up and down, it may be possible, with a little experimentation with bullets, powder types, and charges, to move the point of impact enough to bring the sixgun to point-of-aim impact. I have been able to do this with several sixguns with very little time and trouble. Generally, to lower the point-of-impact use a lighter or faster bullet or both; to raise the point of impact use heavier bullets, or slower velocities, or both. Differences in powder and velocity will often move the impact right or left.

Most single actions are assembled but not tuned, so they may be slightly out of time. This results in significant travel when cocking the hammer, which continues to move backwards after the locking bolt has found its place in the locking notch on the cylinder; or the opposite scenario in which the hammer has reached the full-length of its travel before the cylinder locks up. In either case, an expert in tuning single actions should be consulted. There are many excellent single action sixgunsmiths out there. Any of the custom sixgunsmiths mentioned in this book can make a single action sit up and sing. Their work is absolutely A+. They are the ones to call on when serious problems exist or when one simply desires a super smooth action and specific trigger pull.

There are a few simple things that I am able to accomplish myself and if I can do it, anyone can. Many mainsprings are heavier than they need to be. The simple solution on a Ruger is to cut a coil or two from the mainspring. To do this, consult a Ruger manual on how to disassemble the revolver and follow the directions for capturing the mainspring. It can then be carefully removed from the strut and shortened no more than one coil at a time.

> "There are many excellent single action sixgunsmiths out there. Any of the custom sixgunsmiths mentioned in this book can make a single action sit up and sing."

Single Action Sixguns

Chapter 35 | Tips For Handling The Single Action Sixgun

Taffin uses a relaxed stance shooting a Colt single action 44-40 offhand.

Fanning a sixgun may look spectacular, especially in the movies, but as Skeeter Skelton has said, it may be a quick way to empty an alley but is awfully hard on interior parts.

When shooting a single action sixgun one-handed, the stance is rigid yet relaxed.

True hip shooting is normally a waste of ammunition; the sixgun should be well out in front of the body before being fired.

Single Action Sixguns | 259

Chapter 35 | Tips For Handling The Single Action Sixgun

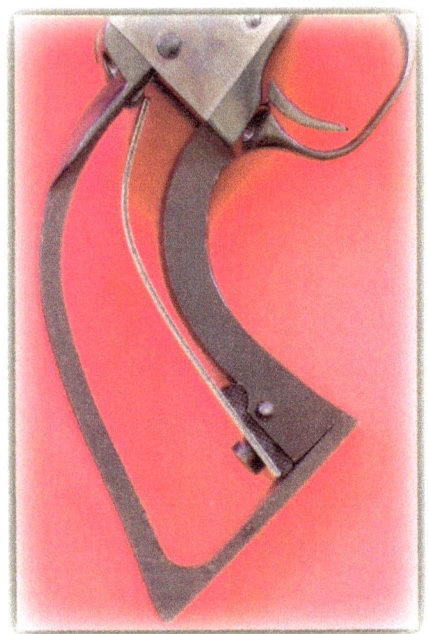

An easy method for lightening a heavy mainspring on a traditional single action sixgun is to place a leather or rubber spacer between the back of the spring and the frame.

With Colt-style revolvers I have been padding the mainspring since 1957. Some gunsmiths say this is perfectly OK and others will tell you never to do it. However, it works for me. The three screws fastening the back strap to the mainframe are removed, the mainspring screw is removed, and a rubber or leather washer is placed under the mainspring and the spring replaced. This will lighten the hammer pull significantly. However, for handgun used for hunting I prefer a full power factory, or even heavier, mainspring. The last thing I want is to have a mad hog coming at me while I'm holding a sixgun that won't fire!

Several companies also now offer lighter mainsprings and bolt springs for Colt and Colt-style single actions. Be careful when using lightened springs as they may throw off the geometry of the action. Smoothing is better than light springs. Brownell's offers several of these all of which are very easy to install, and they also have a stoning kit for smoothing up the inside surfaces in the frame. This also works very easily. Unless one is an expert, the trigger/hammer engagement services should not be touched.

Cylinders from single actions do not always fit the base pin correctly, exhibiting a lot of play. This is an easy fix thanks to Belt Mountain Enterprises. This outfit specializes in slightly oversize base pins of several styles including larger knurled heads and also those styled after the base pin found on both Elmer Keith's famous #5 SAA as well as the Texas Longhorn Arms Improved #5. Not only do these pins provide a tighter cylinder fit, many of them also have a locking screw to keep them in place under recoil.

There are several must tools for anyone to have to do any basic work or even cleaning of a single action sixgun. Base pins can be very stubborn when one tries to remove them. Brownells offers a base pin

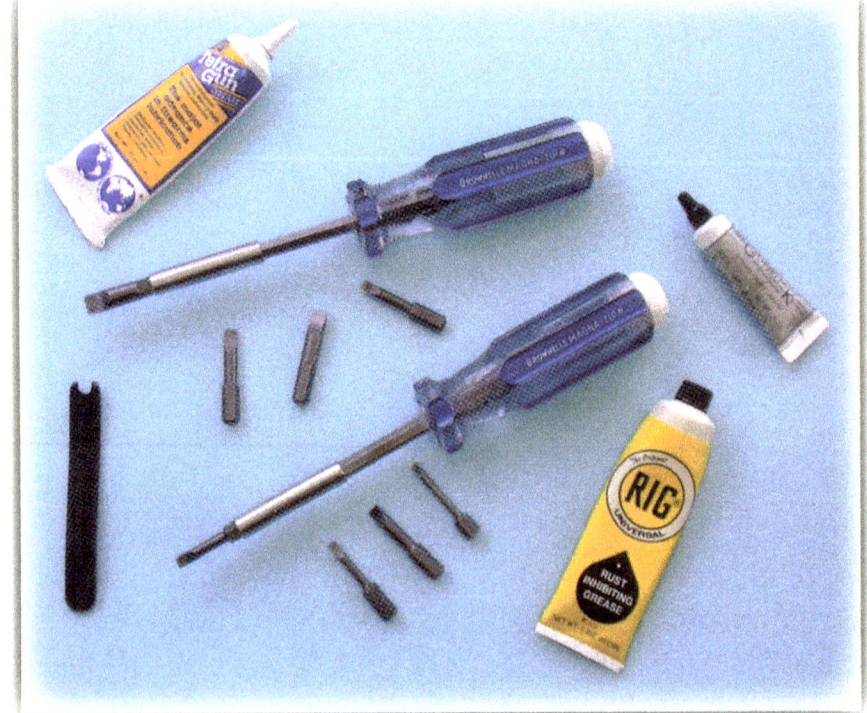

Necessary items, all available from Brownells, for any single action sixgunner: high-quality gun grease, a base pin puller, and screwdrivers with specially selected bits for use on Colts and Ruger Blackhawk.

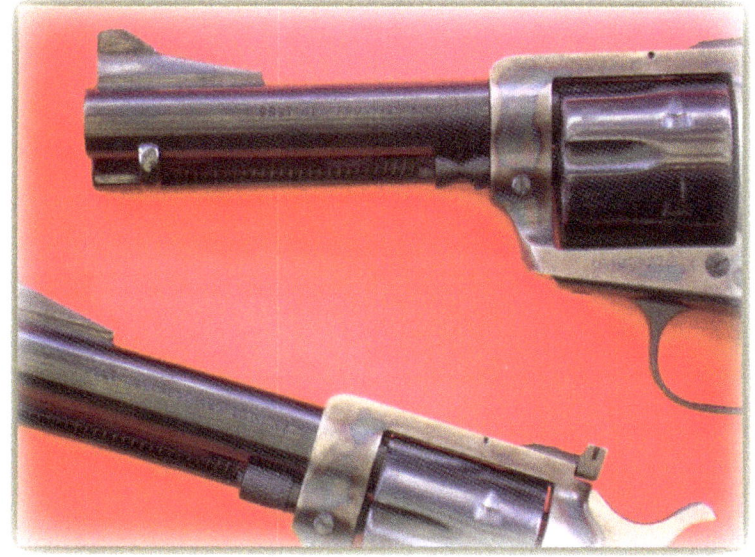

Belt Mountain base pins are available in a variety of configurations and do an excellent job of both tightening the cylinder and securing the base pin. The #5 and large knurled-head versions are shown on a pair of Colt New Frontiers.

puller with a small lever that fits into the notch on the head of the base pin giving the necessary leverage to remove it easily. While the base pin is out I prefer to grease the pin with something like Tetra Gun Grease, Rig, or Gunslick, whichever happens to be on the bench at the time, and also to place a spot of grease at the front and rear contact points on the cylinder itself. This not only aids functioning but also provides for longer life for these parts. Brownells also has two special screwdriver offerings for single action users. Both of these have removable tips of the proper size and number to fit all the screws on either a Colt single action or a Ruger Blackhawk. Buggered-up screw heads are the mark of a rank amateur. These special screwdriver kits have the proper tips to fit all single action screws correctly and keep screw heads in factory-new shape.

A good single action sixgun properly handled will always be safe and not only last a lifetime but can be handed down to several generations. If a single action sixgun is chosen for self-defense use, there are other considerations, which we shall look at in the next chapter.

KABOOM! This is what happens when ammunition of an unknown quality is purchased for a bargain price at a gun show or when careless reloading makes itself known.

Single Action Sixguns | 261

–Chapter 36–

SINGLE ACTION SIXGUNS FOR DEFENSIVE USE?

Is the single action still viable as a defensive sixgun? Many of the Texas Rangers, including Frank Hamer, carried a single action long after it was made "obsolete" by double action revolvers and semi-automatics.

Should a single action sixgun be used for defensive use or concealed carry? For more than seventy years the single action was state-of-the art when it came to self-defense, with double action revolvers reaching perfection with the Smith & Wesson Triple-Lock of 1907 while semi-autos arrived at the same state in 1911 with Colt's Government Model 45 ACP. Modern as the new handguns were, many lawmen including the Texas Rangers held onto their single action sixguns well into the twentieth century; and anyone old enough to remember WWII, or who now has the History Channel, has seen the famous 45 Colt SAA on the hip of General Patton.

Realistically, I would rate the double action revolver as the first choice for most who seek a self-defense handgun, followed by a carefully selected semi-automatic, and finally the single action sixgun. I will neither encourage nor discourage anyone as to picking a single action as his or her concealed weapon of choice. However, if it is chosen we must forget anything ever seen in the movies concerning the use of single actions and start all over again. Gun handling in the movies is about as far removed from reality as it possibly can be. If one chooses a single action, one must be competent in its loading, shooting, unloading, and reloading. Any handgun carried for self-defense purposes should be used for regular practice, and this is even more important if the choice is a single action revolver.

Three times in my life I have had to draw a sixgun for self-defensive purposes against something other than four-legged animals. Twice my family was with me and the 44 Special double action sixgun was very comforting. The other time, simply the sight of a 7-1/2-inch Colt Single Action Army was enough to immediately deter those seeking trouble. Four men thought they had a young teenager at their mercy. They did not know I was armed but the sight of that long-barreled Colt altered their perceptions very quickly. In fact, they decided they had urgent business elsewhere. Had I had to resort to its use I do not feel that I would have been at any great disadvantage with five 255-gr. 45 Colt loads.

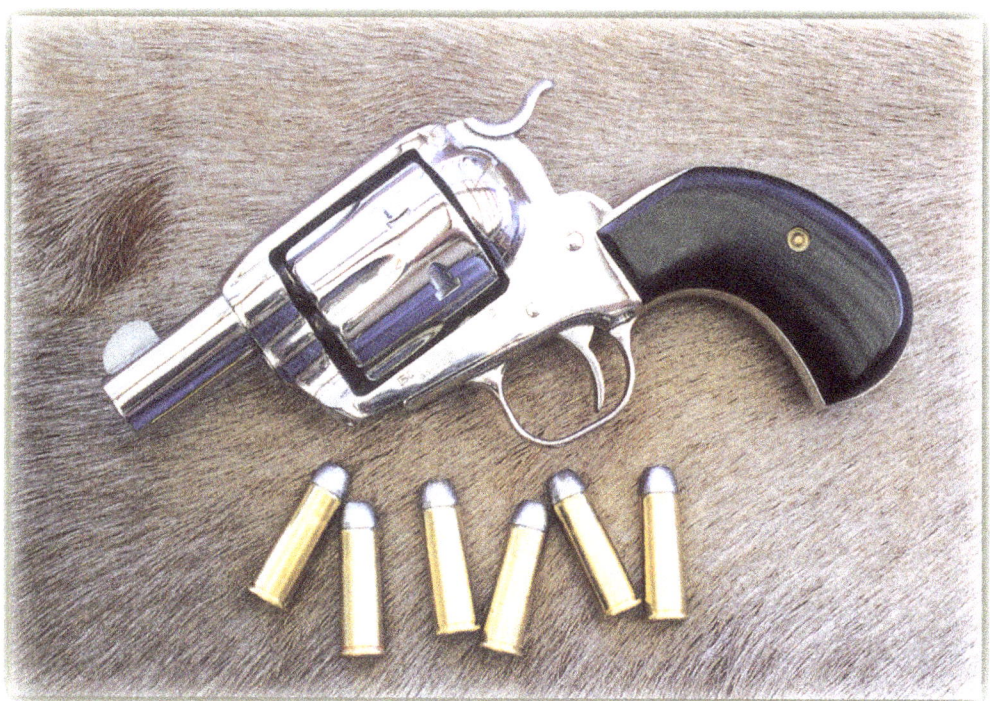

Call this the ultimate single action belly gun: a truly concealable custom Ruger by Milt Morrison of Qualite Pistol & Revolver.

Is the single action sixgun the best choice for self-defense? Of course not! Over the years, the double action sixgun, the single action semi-automatics such as the 1911 Government Model and the Browning Hi-Power, and today the new wave of double action semi-autos have all been better choices. This is not because they are so much better but simply because their use is so much easier to master than a single action.

As mentioned, I would rate the double action revolver as the first choice for most who seek a self defense handgun, followed by the double action semi-automatic, the standard single action 1911-style semi-automatic, and finally the single action sixgun. The order of rating is based on simplicity and mastery of operation. For the first two it is simply a matter of drawing the gun and firing. The double action sixgun with a smoothed-up action will give the same feel with every pull of the trigger while the double action semi-automatic, at least most models, can be operated double action on the first shot and then go to a single action mode for subsequent shots. This means the first shot will have a trigger pull that is markedly different from the first shot.

With the 1911-style semi-automatic, the slide must be worked to jack a round into the chamber. If it is carried with a round in the chamber, in cocked-and-locked mode with the safety on, the safety must be operated before the gun can be fired. Finally with the single action, the hammer must be cocked before the gun can be fired and then cocked for each subsequent firing.

Is the single action slowest to get into operation? Is it too slow for repeat shots? Is it too slow for reloading? One might think the double action sixgun or semi-automatic of either style would be eons faster than the old single action. Not so! The key point is not the type of firearm used but the training involved. No handgun is any faster for the first shot from leather than the single action. We are talking an aimed shot not

> "No handgun is any faster for the first shot from leather than the single action."

Single Action Sixguns | 263

Chapter 36 | Single Action Sixguns For Defensive Use?

For a lightweight, easy to carry, sixgun on the trail that could be used for defense against large wild animals, Gary Reeder offers the .45 Backpacker.

just clearing leather fast draw and blasting away. There is no practical difference between the action styles for that first shot from leather. At my age, with my reflexes, I can SAFELY draw a single action from the leather, cock the hammer, fire a shot and HIT the center of the FBI silhouette target at seven yards in less than one second using a 7-1/2-inch single action.

When it comes to self-defense, there are really two separate and distinct categories: wild animals and human animals. For those working or traveling in areas where attack by wild animals is a possibility, the single action is certainly the number one choice as it is the easiest to pack, the most portable, and chambered for such powerful cartridges such as the 454 Casull, 475 and 500 Linebaugh. With animals of lesser size and gentler temperament than the big bears, such as mountain lions and black bears, the need for such power does not exist. These critters are much easier to stop and the 44 Magnum, 45 Colt, and 44 Special, even the 45 ACP, all properly loaded will do just fine.

When it comes to carrying any gun for self-defense no matter what the choice of action type, I again issue a reminder to forget anything that has ever been seen on the silver screen. Gun handling in movies is about as far removed from reality as it is possible to be; in many cases it is exceedingly dangerous. Just about everything the movies teach about guns is unsafe and virtually impossible. Every time I see a movie-type walking around with a cocked revolver I wonder how many gun accidents are really the fault of what someone has seen in the movies? The decision to carry a gun is one of the most important decisions in life and it must not be entered into matter-of-factly, and every handgun that is carried for self-defense purposes should be used for regular practice. One would think that would go without saying but were I a betting man I would be willing to wager that more aren't than are! Practice should not only include shooting but drawing from the carry position and reloading. This is even more imperative with single actions than with the other types.

Most fights are stopped with fewer than two shots. When it comes to self-defense many believe that the only answer is a semi-auto with a high-capacity magazine with several backup magazines. Statistics do not support this. Unless one is in law enforcement, the possibility of needing so many rounds is probably somewhat less than the probability of hitting the lottery. However, if one does find oneself needing more than two rounds, or even more than the five normally carried in a single action, how and how fast can a reload be accomplished?

When it comes to normal reloads, the Colt SAA is always going to come in last, as a new magazine can be inserted in a very short time, and the double action sixgun using a full moon clip is also much faster than punching out the empties from a single action's cylinder and then reloading them one at a time. However, what if the reload isn't normal? What if one doesn't have a spare magazine or loses the extra magazine? It is quicker to load the cylinder of a single action than to insert cartridges into the one magazine at hand. For that matter, catch an empty cartridge case under the extractor star of a double action and see how slow the reloads become.

Safety is a prime concern when carrying any handgun, with the single action having special considerations in this area. Heroes and bad guys of the movies may run around with cocked single action in hand but this is definitely a disaster waiting to happen. In every training course I have taken as well as police qualification courses I have been invited to participate in, one of the scenarios requires covering a suspect with the handgun until help arrives. With a double action sixgun or semi-auto this is no problem as it take quite a deliberate pull of the trigger to fire the gun. With a 1911-style semi-auto the gun can be cocked and ready to fire with the safety on, so again there is no problem, but with single action sixguns what do we do? If the gun is cocked, usually very little pressure is required to fire the weapon. In this case it would be very wise to not cock it but rather leave the single action hammer at rest until the gun is to be fired. It's a good idea to practice cocking and firing with as much speed and steadiness as possible.

One other aspect of safety arises with a single action sixgun: if the hammer is cocked and one decides not to fire, then what? With the old-style single actions such as the Colt Single Action Army, the Ruger Flat-Tops and Old Models and the replica imports – all carried with an empty under the hammer – once the gun is cocked the cylinder rotates. If the hammer is let down it now rests on a loaded round. This is very dangerous. Letting the hammer down must be done so that it doesn't rest on a loaded round but rather back on the empty chamber. And it must be done in the midst of a stressful situation. In real life it is extremely hazardous. So how do we handle it without looking down the front of the cylinder to find the empty chamber? This is something that should be practiced until it can be done perfectly and, as with loading and unloading, even in the dark.

The hammer has been cocked on a loaded single action and the decision is made not to fire. Now what? Anyone who carries a traditional single action must learn how to safely de-cock it.

The method is actually very simple. The hammer has been cocked, a live round is under that hammer, and it is necessary to place the revolver in a safe condition without firing it. To do this, the hammer is VERY CAREFULLY lowered. Remember, there's a live round under that hammer! The hammer is now brought back to the half cock notch, and the cylinder is rotated as one listens to 1, 2, 3, 4 clicks. Draw the hammer all the back to the full cock notch and carefully lower it all the way. If this is done correctly the empty chamber is now back under the hammer. This drill should be practiced with dummy cartridges until it is mastered perfectly. Practice in the dark; practice blindfolded. It actually sounds harder to do than it is to accomplish.

If a traditional single action is chosen for self-defense, one should also be careful about the leather that is used to house it. Again forget everything the movies teach. What is needed is a compact and secure holster that allows the single action in question to be carried concealed. Texas Ranger Tom Threepersons designed the single action sixgun holster known as the Threepersons. He cut away all excess leather from the designs of the time, and came up with the most popular single or double action sixgun holster of the better part of the twentieth century.

Chapter 36 | Single Action Sixguns For Defensive Use?

Perhaps equaled, but certainly never bettered, is the original Tom Threepersons holster. Everything about it speaks of speed with no leather to interfere with the draw or reaching the hammer. This re-creation by Walt Ostin is totally faithful to the original design.

The most used and copied single action sixgun holster is the Tom Threepersons here shown as offered by El Paso Saddlery.

Threepersons' original holster was crafted by S.D. "Tio Sam" Myres in his El Paso shop. Over the past eight decades the Threepersons holster has been produced by virtually every leather maker including Bianchi and George Lawrence. El Paso Saddlery offers it beautifully crafted as the #1920 in plain, roughout, border stamped, basket stamped and with full floral carving, all fully lined and the choice of a hammer thong or safety strap.

The original Threepersons holster is pictured in several books including R. L. Wilson's *The Peacemakers*, John Bianchi's *Blue Steel & Gunleather*, and the leather connoisseur's bible, *Packing Iron* by Richard Rattenbury. I often refer to these books to study leather designs, not the least of which is the original Tom Threepersons. As a collector of quality leather I have Threepersons-style holsters from the three companies mentioned above and have seen the original holster and sixgun used by Tom himself.

Texas Ranger Lee Trimble designed this rig as the most practicable for carrying a single action sixgun. It is offered as the #1930 Austin by El Paso Saddlery.

A single action carried for defense requires a special holster; these concealable rigs are by Walt Ostin.

These currently offered, beautifully crafted renditions are not exact duplicates of the original. For that we turn to Walt Ostin of Custom Leather. His rendition of Threepersons' holster would certainly be considered perfection by the old lawman himself. Everything is here: the right slant, the heavy-duty single weight leather, no safety strap or excess leather, a tight belt loop, and as a great added bonus, full carving exactly as Threepersons' has.

Thad Rybka offers a full line of concealment holsters. The Speed Scabbard is his version of the Tom Threepersons. Straight draw, crossdraw, or muzzle to the rear slant are all available on this model as well as plain roughout or fully carved. A favorite of mine is the M81 Crossdraw featuring a high-riding design that rides in close to the body with the front half of the trigger guard covered. There is no better choice than Rybka's design for a single action inside the pants holster that is made of roughout leather so the holster itself will cling to the clothing and not move.

Thad Rybka is known for offering extremely practical single action sixgun holsters such is these easy for packing concealed models.

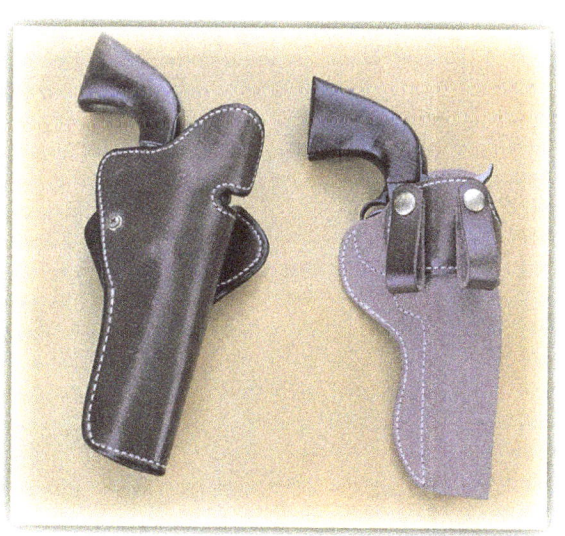

Milt Sparks Leather offers a large line of concealable leather for both double action revolvers and semi automatics, but they have not forgotten the single action user as shown by their 200AW and Inside The Pants versions.

Single Action Sixguns | 267

Chapter 36 | Single Action Sixguns For Defensive Use?

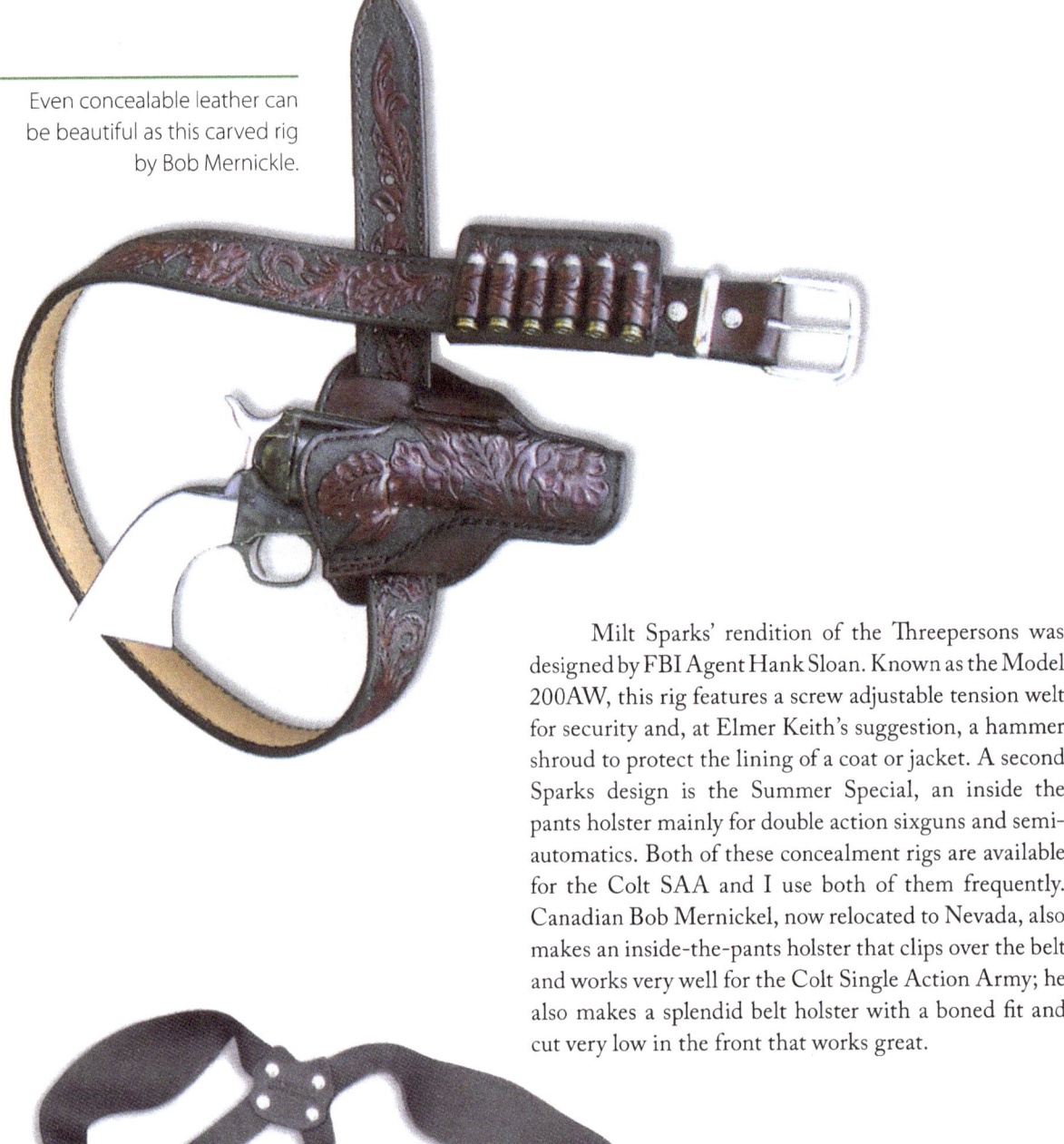

Even concealable leather can be beautiful as this carved rig by Bob Mernickle.

Milt Sparks' rendition of the Threepersons was designed by FBI Agent Hank Sloan. Known as the Model 200AW, this rig features a screw adjustable tension welt for security and, at Elmer Keith's suggestion, a hammer shroud to protect the lining of a coat or jacket. A second Sparks design is the Summer Special, an inside the pants holster mainly for double action sixguns and semi-automatics. Both of these concealment rigs are available for the Colt SAA and I use both of them frequently. Canadian Bob Mernickel, now relocated to Nevada, also makes an inside-the-pants holster that clips over the belt and works very well for the Colt Single Action Army; he also makes a splendid belt holster with a boned fit and cut very low in the front that works great.

Sometimes the best choice for concealment leather is a shoulder rig such as this version by Bob Mernickle.

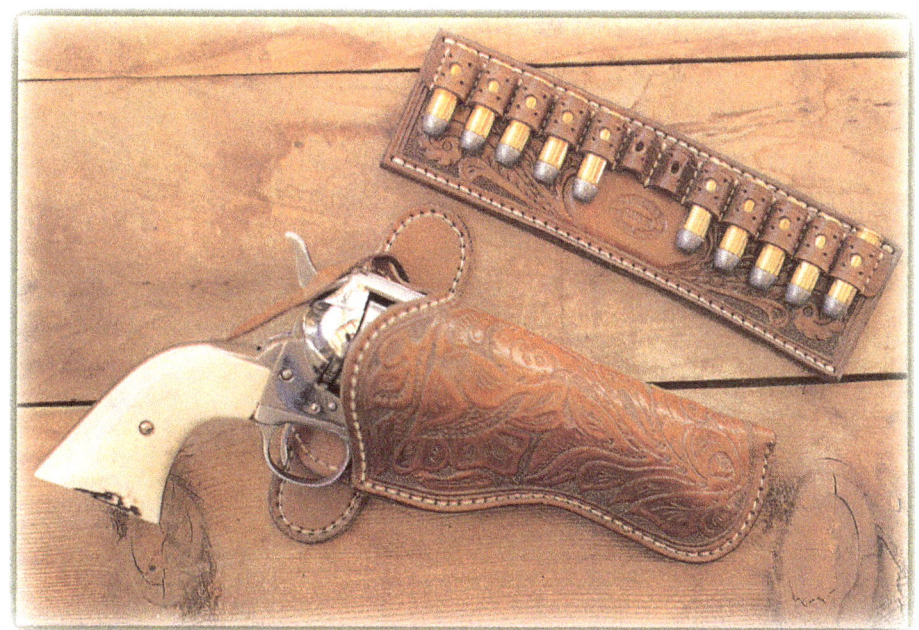

Jim Lockwood's "Billy Old" is a highly practical holster for packing a single action, especially when mated up with his cartridge slide.

Jim Lockwood of Legends in Leather offers a unique concealment or open carry holster fully lined, floral carved, and made to hang straight. As with the Tom Threepersons design, it uses a minimum of leather, but it rides slightly lower and also features a low-cut out in the front below the hammer for an easier draw and easy one-handed return. Rather than being sewn to the holster, the belt loop is secured with two Chicago screws, and the loop also has two stabilizing ears that ride behind the belt. To match the holster, Lockwood supplies a floral carved cartridge slide holding 12 rounds. Normally such a slide would be too stiff to ride comfortably on a pants belt, but Lockwood cuts a large slot in the back of the slide so it easily conforms to the body and also allows positioning of the pants belt loop in the middle of the slide.

Rusty Sherrick works in horsehide and exotic leather and has come up with a high-riding concealment rig for a 3-1/2-inch New Thunderer in 45 Colt. Being of horsehide, it maintains its shape without being bulky and also holds the gun without the need for a safety strap. The holster is formed to the contours of the single action and is basically a belt slide with a holster body incorporated. It rides high and tight and is easily concealed.

Derry Gallagher specializes in concealment holsters for semi-automatics, double action sixguns, and single action sixguns. Derry crafts his holsters from horsehide, which is not only lighter in weight but also tougher than cowhide. Each holster is hand finished, and formed to the exact shape of the sixgun it will carry, then dyed or left natural and waxed. The wax minimizes any transfer of dye to the clothing. With the formed fit, no safety strap is necessary.

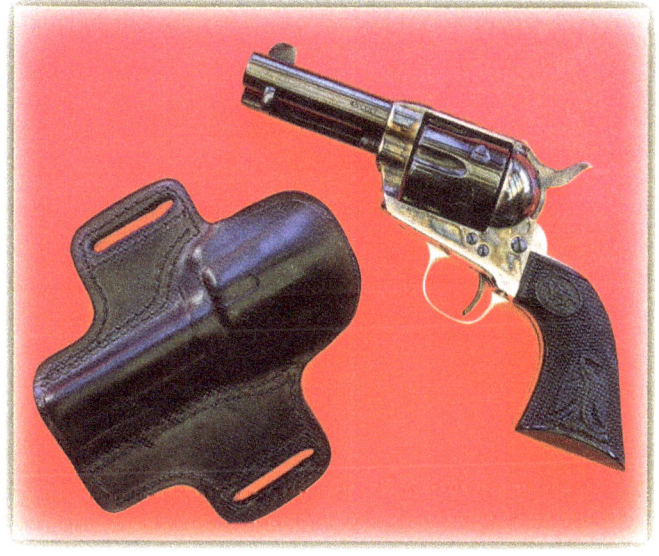

This custom straight draw concealable holster constructed of horsehide is by C. Rusty Sherrick for a 3-1/2-inch Cimarron 45 Colt Model P.

Chapter 36 | Single Action Sixguns For Defensive Use?

Three different variations on the same theme of carrying a single action sixgun for defensive purposes: quality leather by Jim Lockwood, Bob Mernickle, and Derry Gallagher.

At the Shootists Holiday in 1986, I watched two well-known single action pistoleros – Jim Taylor, the Pistol Packin' Preacher, and my colleague Mike Venturino – shoot bowling pins with single actions against an accomplished action shooter with a $2000 semi-auto and competition holster. Venturino stood on the left and used an old Colt Single Action 38-40 with a 7-1/2-inch barrel and a traditional 1880s style holster. Taylor, on the right, used a Ruger 45 Colt, also with a 7-1/2-inch barrel and a 20 year-old homemade holster. At the signal, both would draw, fire and take the pin before the action shooter had a chance. Who says single actions are slow into action?

Forgetting the games and looking at the serious side of life, is the person who packs a single action at a great disadvantage? In the vast majority of cases I do not believe so and I pack a single action as often as not and almost always when the hardware is packed openly. When I am out testing a double action or semi-automatic, more often than not I will be wearing a single action. They just seem to holster and pack so much easier than other types. The first shot is fast. Subsequent shots may be slower, but the big bore single action can be depended upon to deliver five or six shots from a gun whose balance and portability has never been equaled. In the areas I frequent the most – the mountains, foothills, forests, and deserts of Idaho – the chances of needing anything faster than a big-bore single action for the first shot and subsequent shots is about as close as we can get to zero. The single action not only fits my hand just fine, I cannot hit a target as easy from the hip with a either a double action or semi-auto as well as I can with a single action. It just points the way a sixgun should.

Yes, I realize packin' a single action in the twenty-first century could be looked on as more tradition than practicality, but given my choice as to a big-bore single action sixgun or a high capacity nine I would pick the single action every time. By "big-bore" I refer to the 250- to 300-gr. bullets from the 41 and 44 Special, the 41 and 44 Magnum, the 45 Colt and the 454 Casull, or even heavier bullets from the 475 and 500 Linebaugh. Of course, I am not speaking from the standpoint of a large city peace officer by any means. If I had to go into the daily jungles that many peace officers must face every working day I would want a 100 percent reliable semi-automatic, preferably chambered in 45 ACP or at the very least, a Smith & Wesson K-frame 357 or big-bore N-frame.

The traditional single action Single Action Army is a classic, pure and simple. So are the 1911 Government Model and the Smith & Wesson Models 19 (357 Magnum), 27 (357 Magnum) and 29 (44 Magnum). There are semi-automatics being manufactured today that will probably be labeled classics in the future. I like 'em all. But first and foremost I always have been a single action sixgunner and always will be.

–Chapter 37–

LONG RANGE SINGLE ACTION SIXGUNS

I do not like summer! I would gladly trade every July and August for one great October. This particular long hot summer had been worst than most; actually there had been three painful summers in a row. The only way to survive summers with any semblance of a good attitude remaining is plenty of time for shooting, camping, hiking, and outdoor activities with the family. However, my last three had been spent sitting in a non-air conditioned graduate school classroom at the University of Montana working on my Master's degree. Like most things, good or bad, the time passed and it was finally over. I had survived. I had my degree. I deserved a reward.

A stop at the Gunhaus revealed the appropriate specimen. My wife graciously agreed and I had my first long range single action sixgun. At the time I felt $150 was a lot of money to spend for a Ruger single action, but it was unlike any Ruger 44 Magnum I had ever seen and the stocks, although factory, were made of beautifully grained fancy walnut. What made this Ruger .44 Flat-Top different is the fact it was one of the very rare 10-inch sixguns made in the early 1960s. My wife insisted that we could afford it and she has proven to be far more perceptive than I am as that Flat-Top Ruger is now worth at least six times what we paid for it.

For hunting, the Ruger was matched up with one of the Al Goerg shoulder holsters of the time. I would hate to have to retrace all the miles the Ruger, shoulder holster, and I made together. When Ruger dropped the Flat-Top Model in favor of the Old Models in 1963, the longest barrel offered was the 7-1/2-inch Super Blackhawk. With the debut of the New Model Super Blackhawk 44 Magnum in 1973, the barrel length stayed at 7-1/2 inches. As a mate to my 10-inch Flat-Top, I had Trapper Gun build me a custom New Model 44 Magnum with a 10-inch barrel and a satin nickel finish. That sixgun is marked "Trapper Long Range" on the left side of the barrel and has also been used for many hunting trips both with iron sights and a scope for more than 25 years.

The most accurate long-range revolver of any kind Taffin has ever experienced is Freedom Arms 41 Magnum. It is capable of staying well under one inch for five shots at 100 yards.

Single Action Sixguns | 271

Chapter 37 | Long Range Single Action Sixguns

She doesn't weigh much more than her Freedom Arms single action, but Rosetta Sleeva has no trouble hitting at long-range.

Dick Casull prefers the sitting position when shooting the 454 at long-range.

My wife and I both were early participants and eventually settled on a pair of long range single actions for Revolver Category when Ruger finally brought out 10-1/2-inch 44 Magnum Super Blackhawks for the silhouette shooters. Both of those sixguns were magnificently accurate, but even they were runner-ups to Ruger's next long-range sixgun, the 10-1/2-inch stainless Ruger Super Blackhawk. They shot well; this one really shoots very well!

Elmer Keith, writing in *Sixguns* (1955), said, "During the Indian campaigns on the plains, quite a few cavalry officers who had learned to shoot a sixgun during the Civil War became very expert at long-range revolver shooting. Many a time with their horses shot out from under them, they were able to keep enemies out at long rifle range and completely out of bowshot with the old 7-1/2-inch Peacemaker. A good revolver shot with a long barrel gun and accurate heavy ammunition, can, and they frequently did, make it hot for enemy horsemen out to 400 or 500 yards. When the shooting was over dry, dusty plains or over water where the strike of the bullet could be located, they could hold accordingly and soon walked their shots onto the target."

Twenty-five years earlier, Keith – writing about long-range sixguns in two articles in the *American Rifleman* (September 1928 and April 1929) – told of a visit from Harold Croft and the long-range shooting at 700 yards they did on Keith's little cattle ranch out of Durkee, Oregon. Keith would follow these articles with one in November 1930 showing pictures of custom Flat-Topped Colt Single Actions and Bisley Models looking much like the current Ruger Blackhawks and Bisley Blackhawks. Want to bet a young teenager by the name of Bill Ruger saw and mentally preserved those old articles? In an article written in May of 1939, Keith mentions earlier proponents of long-range shooting such as Chauncey Thomas, E.A. Price, and Ashley Haines, all well-established writers and editors when Keith was a young man.

B-Western cowboys always shot one-handed and there is a faction of the cowboy shooting game who wants to see only one-handed shooting, claiming two-handed shooting is a recent arrival with Jack Weaver and his ilk. But no one knows who the first pistolero to practice long-range sixgunning was. I would guess it goes back at least to the Walker Colt of 1847. We do know that the Colt Walker was advertised as being effective on both man and horse out to 200 yards. To hit at this range one needs a solid rest or two hands. Early in his writing career Elmer Keith began talking about sixguns that were more than a short range proposition, and after being guided by Keith on a pack trip, Zane Grey wrote the novel *Thunder Mountain* featuring the use of a sixgun at long-range.

Keith often talked of shooting his sixguns at ranges of 500 and 600 yards using such targets as rocks and stumps. At no time did he ever advocate taking such long-range shots at big game. For Keith and men like him from his era, the big bore sixgun, be it 44 Special, 45 Colt, or the later 44 and 41 Magnums, was a tool of convenience that was belted on in the morning and not taken off until bedtime, at which time it probably went under the pillow or bedroll to spend the night within easy reach.

Watch out for that recoil! Jim Taylor shooting his 454 at 700 yards during the Shootist Holiday in Cody Wyoming.

The sport of long range silhouetting certainly proved all of these men were correct in their assessment of the use of revolvers for long-range shooting. Several shooters have managed to shoot perfect scores taking down all 40 targets – 10 each at 50, 100, 150, and 200 meters – with a revolver. I never achieved perfection but did come close, shooting a score of 38 with my single action 10-1/2-inch Ruger 357 Maximum and leaving one turkey and one ram standing. That remains, and will always remain, a local club record as the club has disbanded and the rails removed. The Maximum came after the 10-1/2-inch Ruger 44 Magnum Super Blackhawks my wife and I both used, and later came the Freedom Arms 10-1/2-incher in 454 Casull and 44 Magnum and the most accurate sixgun I have ever experienced, the Model 83 41 Magnum.

A good sixgun, such as the USA's stainless steel 375 SuperMag, is capable of excellent 200 meter accuracy. This group was shot from the Creedmore position by a much younger author.

Single Action Sixguns

Chapter 37 | Long Range Single Action Sixguns

The first long range sixgun was the 1847 Colt Walker; Sam Walker himself said it was good on man or beast out to 200 yards. A lone man armed with pair of Walkers would be able to hold off pursuers for a great distance.

I decided to find out for myself if Sam Walker and Keith were correct in that it was possible that someone caught in the open could actually survive against a large group of hostiles with nothing more than a Colt Single Action Army US-issue 7-1/2-inch 45 Colt. No, I did not shoot a horse to use for cover and a rest, but the sixgun used was an original circa 1881 US-marked 7-1/2-inch Colt Single Action Army chambered in 45 Colt. Instead of modern square sights with a square rear notch matched up with an equally square front sight, this old sixgun has a very shallow "V" rear sight and a very thin tapered front sight. With black powder loads, the only loads that should be used in an old sixgun such as this one, I knew it would keep five shots in one inch at 50 feet. I used the same load, a 255-gr. conical bullet over 40 grains of black powder in old style balloon-head brass: the original loading of the 45 Colt. Shooting two-handed and using a solid rest such as the saddle on a downed horse would be, I discovered several things.

Standard man silhouette targets were set up at 50, 100, and 200 yards and the old 45 Colt and I went to work with two cylinders fired at each target. At 50 yards that old sixgun and I could be counted on to deliver head shots. At 100 yards, we could consistently place our shots all in the body. Moving out to 200 yards changed things considerably. Sighting at this distance with those 125-year-old sights, and my not-quite-as-old eyes, made it very difficult. I never did hit the outlined body of the target silhouette, but I did hit the paper several times and those shots that did miss the paper were so close that any enemy at that distance would think very carefully before moving from any cover he had.

Sometimes it really is possible to find a "bench rest" in the field. This bench isn't going to wobble!

Taffin's favorite class of sixguns is a 7-1/2-inch single action combining long-range accuracy with portability. Some favorite sixguns, beginning at top left clockwise: Ruger 45 Colt Old Model, Colt New Frontier 45 Colt, Colt New Frontier 44 Special, Ruger 44 Magnum Super Blackhawk, and Ruger 44 Magnum Flat-Top. All would benefit with a flat post front sight, but they are easier to holster with the ramp front sight.

Long-ranging shooting, like plinking, has no rules, no required stances, no maximum sight radius, and no caliber restrictions. I prefer big bore calibers, .44 and up, because the bigger and heavier the bullet is, the easier it is to see it hit. Longer barrels, 7-1/2 to 10 inches are my favorite for shooting at long distances. I can shoot as far away as I can see and also shoot safely.

This is fun shooting, not hunting! The longest revolver shot I ever made at a big game animal was 125 yards on a Texas whitetail buck. The revolver was a Freedom Arms Model 83 7-1/2-inch 44 Magnum with a 2X Leupold scope, a revolver that had been shot extensively during many whitetail hunts and always used with the same ammunition (Black Hills 240-gr. jacketed hollowpoint). I knew the sixgun, I knew the ammunition, and I knew what I was capable of doing when shooting from a solid rest. I had a solid rest, the whitetail standing perfectly broadside and presenting me with my kind of shot. The results were perfect. One shot, one deer whose only movement was straight down.

We have no restrictions placed upon us when long-range shooting with iron-sighted sixguns at inanimate objects except the responsibility of a safe place to shoot with a backstop for any shots we fire. Whether we miss or hit has no great consequences. No prizes are awarded if we hit, no animal suffers needlessly if we have a near miss. If so inclined we can count only the hits and forget the misses if we also learn in the process. It is very unlikely we will ever have to hold off a half dozen pursuers while waiting for help to come – but it is mighty reassuring to know if we had to we could.

Both of these custom Rugers were put together by Taffin for long-range shooting. The top sixgun is a 357 Maximum rechambered and rebarreled to 445 Maximum by Ben Forkin; bottom, Flat-Top .357 Blackhawk has been fitted with a 10-1/2-inch 357 Maximum barrel by Mike Rainey and re-finished by Gary Reeder.

Rocks and old tree stumps make excellent targets, but any safe target is acceptable, with a large safe backstop being absolutely necessary. It should go without saying that signs, utility poles, etc., are totally out of the question. As our country becomes more and more urbanized with housing developments packed closer and closer together, it is imperative we know where are bullets are going to finally come to rest. Many of the barren areas I used for long-range shooting 35 years ago are now places of habitation.

Single Action Sixguns | 275

Chapter 37 | Long Range Single Action Sixguns

Taffin selected these 44 Magnum sixguns especially for long-range shooting. The 10-1/2-inch barrels, undercut post front sights, and BluMagnum stocks filling in behind the trigger guard all combine to make shooting with the Ruger Super Blackhawk and Freedom Arms Model 83 relatively easy.

My pistol packin' preacher friend and Brother, Jim Taylor, and I were shooting above the Gray's River in Wyoming during a Shootists Holiday in the late 1980s. Our targets were long-abandoned log cabins constructed of logs six to eight inches in diameter, and our sixguns were quite similar. Jim and I were both using 7-1/2-inch Rugers, his a first-year 45 Colt Blackhawk and mine an even older 44 Magnum Flat-Top. Our loads were also much alike, both of us using 300-gr. bullets, his at 1200 fps, mine slightly over 1300 fps. Sitting down on the hillside with a right knee drawn up and used as a rest, neither one of us had any problems hitting those cabins; even at 700 yards they were fairly large targets.

What is of significance is the fact those bullets had enough energy left at that distance to penetrate the front wall and exit the back. Once heavyweight bullets get moving they are very difficult to stop. After Elmer Keith told of his now-famous 600 yard shot on a mule deer wounded by another hunter, Col. Charles Askins said he would stand out at 600 yards and catch any 44 Magnum bullets fired from a sixgun in a catcher's mitt. He would have needed a mitt made of heavy-duty steel!

The next year again in Wyoming, outside of Cody this time, we set up a two-foot square section of metal painted bright orange and propped up against some sagebrush on the side of the hill. The distance was 700 to 800 yards this time and it looked awfully small out there in the sagebrush over fixed sights. This time shooting the same 45 Colt load in a 4-5/8-inch Freedom Arms and standing using both hands, I was able to hit that target several times before my box of 100 rounds was gone. Normally shooting long-range we do not hold over the target but rather raise the front sight in the rear notch with the target perched on top of the front sight just as Elmer Keith had always taught. This target was so far away I had to aim at a sagebrush bush way above it.

As mentioned earlier my preferred sixgun set-up for shooting long-range is a 7-1/2- to 10-inch single action big bore revolver and I prefer to have large, square, black sights. For my eyes the choice is a black front post without a white outline rear sight. An undercut post is even better but it wreaks havoc with the interior of leather holsters. Ramp style front sights tend to get lost, at least for me, in bright sunlight and the same is true of colored inserts.

Taffin's two-handed standing position consists of cupping the right hand in the left hand and the left foot slightly forward. That big sixgun is Gary Reeder's 510 GNR.

Long range silhouetting proved the old-time sixgunners' claim about the possibility of shooting sixguns way, way out past 25 yards. The most popular position for shooting was Creedmore, which is nearly as steady as a bench rest.

What is the best shooting position? This is purely subjective. One of the most practical is that of standing on your hind legs, almost squarely facing the target with the shooting side leg slightly forward, and using two hands with the off hand used to support the shooting hand. I like to exert a slight push-pull action with the shooting and supporting hand. It is the easiest position to assume, the quickest, and also the most comfortable. If a backrest is available it can be used to excellent advantage from the sitting position with both elbows resting inside the drawn up knees and once again shooting two-handed. The downside here is the fact that your pants (or even worse, the contents of your pants) can be burned by the hot gases exiting from the gap between barrel and cylinder. The worst position for me is prone. I have no neck but rather my head just sits upon my shoulders. There is no way I can hold my head back enough to shoot prone whether with a handgun or rifle.

There are three ways to shoot one-handed. One of the toughest is the classic bullseye stance with the shooting arm extended straight, the body slightly turned, the foot on the gun side forward, and the off hand at the side tucked in a pants pocket or with the thumb tucked in the belt. Long-range silhouetters used and still use the modified Creedmore position. This is assumed by lying on one's back, placing the offside arm under the back of the head, drawing up the shooting-side knee and resting the shooting hand on the outside of the knee with the elbow on the ground. Some shooters are able to place their off hand on the ground behind their head, but I always had to forcibly hold my head up due to the no-neck situation. If any extended amount of shooting is to be done, this position requires some sort of a blast shield to protect the leg from the hot gases coming from the barrel-cylinder gap of a revolver.

It is almost as good as a bench rest. Elmer Keith may or may not have been the first sixgunner to use this position for long range shooting but he was certainly the man who spread the word of its use.

Chapter 37 | Long Range Single Action Sixguns

It works even better with a back rest but sometimes there is nothing available to lean against, so draw up the knees and shoot steady.

The best one-handed position for me, perhaps the best position period, is the classic Keith position. This is shot from sitting, leaning back on the off-hand elbow, drawing in the knee of the shooting side with the shooting hand placed upon that knee for support. With a little practice this position becomes very stable and also capable of allowing us to shoot very accurately. With a little practice, a long-range sixgunner soon finds it fairly easy to outshoot the average rifle shooter.

For the most part, long range shooting with a sixgun is a game, a most pleasant way to spend an afternoon especially if one can shoot in an area that has plenty of different sized targets. There are no rules; there are no minimum caliber requirements; there is no required shooting position, either sitting, standing, kneeling, or prone; and barrel length can be anything desired. Actually all one needs is an accurate sixgun with a good trigger and a good set of sights. With a little practice, one finds that hits come much more frequently, and even near misses are exciting as there are no five shot or six shot groups to be measured. Some shooters prefer gold bars inlaid in the front sight blade to compensate for different distances, but I am past the age of seeing them well enough to make any difference.

If you've always been a close range paper puncher find an area preferably with dry, dusty ground that will easily show point of impact and prepare to enjoy yourself with a different kind of shooting. The result will be enjoyment and in all probability better "scores" than expected.

–Chapter 38–

SINGLE ACTION SIXGUNS AND AUXILIARY CYLINDERS

Bill Ruger was not only a firearms design genius, but he also understood quite well what the public feeling was for firearms. Consider all of the sixguns ever offered by Ruger over the last 50-plus years and how many of them were dropped for lack of demand. The list is very short, if it even exists at all, as the 357 Maximum was actually killed off by those not understanding its true purpose, and the 256 Hawkeye was simply ahead of its time and should be resurrected.

To give shooters a chance to shoot the 22 Magnum rimfire without having to buy a sixgun that would only accept that relatively expensive cartridge, Ruger simply offered a convertible. Sixgun, that is. Beginning in 1961 shooters could purchase a .22 Single-Six with the extra magnum cylinder and for many years now all Single-Sixes have come with two cylinders. We've all seen the commercial, over and over and over again, with the lovely twins singing, "Double your pleasure, double your fun," and although they are selling Doublemint chewing gum they could just as well be selling convertible sixguns.

Single actions with extra cylinders make a lot of sense, allowing us to shoot several cartridges from the same sixguns. One rarely encounters a double action with an extra cylinder, as it requires not only an extra cylinder but a crane assembly as well. With the single action it is a simple matter of pulling the base pin, removing one cylinder, replacing it with another, and returning the base pin.

Since my .22 Single-Six was one of the original flatgates from the 1950s it would be nearly 10 years before I would ever personally encounter a convertible Ruger. At the time I was in graduate school, which has to be one of the worst ways to spend a summer. I was married with three kids home for the summer from grade school and I was 500 miles away from home going to graduate school. I was almost convinced it would pay large dividends in the future, and of course it did, but the day-by-day drudgery was beating me down to the point where I needed inspiration and also had to take several quick trips home on weekends. One weekend while staying in the college town I found a little gun shop and wandered in simply to kill time with no thought of finding anything and especially not the great sixgun awaiting me. There in the glass case was a 7-1/2-inch Ruger Blackhawk unlike any I had never seen before.

Only five sixguns, but 12 combinations of cartridges can be used. From top left clockwise: Freedom Arms 454 with extra cylinders in 45 Colt and 45 ACP; Ruger Blackhawk 38-40 and 10mm; Ruger 45 Colt and 45 ACP; 7-1/2-inch Colt New Frontier 44 Special and 44-40; and 4-3/4-inch 45 Colt New Frontier with an auxiliary cylinder chambered in 45 Auto Rim/45 ACP.

Single Action Sixguns | 279

Chapter 38 | Single Action Sixguns & Auxiliary Cylinders

Ruger started the trend toward dual cylinder sixguns with their Convertible Model Single-Six nearly a half-century ago. These custom Ruger Single-Sixes by Andy Horvath all shoot 22 Long Rifles and came with a red bag containing a 22 Magnum cylinder.

It was not a Super Blackhawk, nor was it one of the rare 7-1/2-inch 44 Magnum Flat-Tops that had been dropped from production in 1963. What was before me was probably the first 45 Colt Blackhawk to reach the northwest. Up to this point I didn't even know Ruger would at last be chambering the Blackhawk for the 45 Colt.

Since I lived in Idaho while attending graduate school in Montana I had to make the proper arrangements under the GCA' 68 law to purchase that first Ruger 45 Colt. It came with a little red bag containing an extra cylinder chambered in 45 ACP, and my first thought was "what in the world for?" In those days I never really expected to use that cylinder, but in a weak moment I slipped it into the Blackhawk, loaded five rounds of government surplus .45 hardball, tacked up a lid from a Mason jar, backed off 25 yards, and proceeded to put all five rounds, offhand, in the center of that small target. I was sold on extra cylinders.

Ruger convertible sixguns are now cataloged in 22 LR/22 Magnum, 357 Magnum/9mm, and 45 Colt/45 ACP. In the past Ruger has offered at least three limited runs of convertible sixguns. Two special runs offered through the defunct Buckeye Sports Supply were Blackhawks in 30 Carbine/32 H&R Magnum and 38-40/10mm, and the third was a Super Blackhawk combination of 44 Magnum and 44-40. From time to time distributors offer special runs of Vaqueros with two cylinders in 45 Colt and 45 ACP and even 38-40/40 S&W. I've never shot one of the newer 38-40 Vaqueros, but the 38-40/10mm Blackhawk is a particularly good shooting combination. With the 38-40 cylinder in place, it's probably one of the most accurate guns ever in that chambering.

The 38-40 was the third most popular chambering of the pre-war Colt single actions. It lives again as a convertible model in this custom 38-40/401 PowerMag by Hamilton Bowen and Ruger's limited edition 38-40/10mm Blackhawk.

280 Part 7

The Freedom Arms Model 83 chambered in 454 Casull becomes exceptionally versatile with factory cylinders added for 45 Colt, 45 ACP, and 45 WinMag.

When I came up with an New Model auxiliary 9mm cylinder for a 7-1/2-inch Bisley Model .357, it was not to shoot surplus ammo through but rather to have Gary Reeder re-chamber it to his wildcat 356 GNR, a 41 Magnum necked down to .357. While Reeder had the Bisley for fitting the extra cylinder, I also had him take the sharp edges off the grip frame, fits stag grips, inscribe my name in gold on the barrel, and finish off the whole project in a high bright blue. The result is a beautiful custom sixgun that handles the 357 Magnum as well as the 356 GNR, which gives 357 Maximum performance in a standard-length cylinder.

In the mid-1980s I first encountered Freedom Arms, and since I was deeply involved in long-range shooting at the time, I ordered an early silhouette pistol, a 10-1/2-inch 454 Casull set up with BoMar sights for competition. When I stopped shooting silhouettes in the early 1990s, that long barreled 454 was turned into a hunting single action and has been wearing a 4X Leupold Long Eye Relief scope instead of iron sights ever. It is the rare person who can stop at just one Freedom Arms single action sixgun, and the more I shot the long barreled 454 Casull, the more I knew I would have to have another one. This time instead of a long-barreled 454 it would have to be a real honest-to-goodness Packin' Pistol and the choice was easy: a 4-3/4-inch adjustable-sight with a Freedom Arms action job and ivory micarta grips.

This gun from Freedom Arms was about as close as anyone could get to having a Perfect Packin' Pistol. I used both 454 loads and heavy 45 Colt loads in it, and I must admit to using more 45 Colt loads than 454 loads as I did not always need the full power afforded by the heavy loaded 454s. One of my favorite 45 Colt loads is the BRP 300-gr. cast gas-checked Casull bullet over 21.5 grains of WW296. This is an 1100 fps load from a 4-3/4-inch barrel, but it is very accurate and continues to be so at long ranges. I have used it to 700 to 800 yards, shooting at two foot square targets, and have actually managed to hit them once in awhile by watching the bullets strike in dry dusty dirt.

> "It is the rare person who can stop at just one Freedom Arms single action sixgun, and the more I shot the long barreled 454 Casull, the more I knew I would have to have another one."

Single Action Sixguns | 281

Chapter 38 | Single Action Sixguns & Auxiliary Cylinders

Whether for close range hunting or simply to serve as a Packin' Pistol, it would be very difficult to beat these combinations: Freedom Arms Model 83s in 454/45 Colt and 475 Linebaugh/480 Ruger.

"With a single action revolver, both rimmed and rimless brass all extract the same way."

I was shooting more 45 Colt loads than 454s. If the 454 cylinder is not carefully and meticulously scrubbed out after using 45 Colt loads, a ring can develop in the cylinder at the end of the case mouth, which could then interfere with the use of full-house 454 loads. So the Packin' Pistol 454 was returned to the factory to have a 45 Colt cylinder installed. Now I had the best of two worlds. However, the 4-3/4-inch Freedom Arms sixgun was not finished yet.

While the 45 Colt cylinder was being fitted, a third cylinder was also added as the Freedom Arms was made even more versatile with the addition of an auxiliary cylinder in 45 ACP. Now why would anyone want a 45 ACP cylinder for a 454 Casull? Simple. I for one have hundreds, probably thousands, of rounds of various persuasions of 45 ACP loads sitting around. When used in the Casull single action, they make for an extremely pleasant shooting outing and I do not have to chase brass all over Idaho nor do I have to mess with full or half-moon clips. With a single action revolver, both rimmed and rimless brass all extract the same way. Shoot'em. Tumble 'em. Load 'em. Start all over again.

The 4-3/4-inch 454 was returned to the factory one last time to be fitted with cylinder number four, this one chambered in 45 Winchester Magnum. Normally I would not consider chambering a sixgun for the WinMag, but I had come into a large quantity of 45 WinMag brass and ammunition, and what better sixgun to run it through than the Freedom Arms Model 83?

Although not quite as versatile as the four-cylindered Model 83 that started life as a 454, a second Perfect Packin' Pistol candidate from Freedom Arms is the same basic sixgun chambered in 475 Linebaugh. What extra cylinder does this one take? Why, the 480 Ruger of course, which uses the same bullets at somewhat slower muzzle velocities. This was my choice for my first American bison hunt. Using Buffalo Bore's 480 Ruger load with an LBT hard-cast bullet at 1100 fps from the auxiliary cylinder in the 4-3/4-inch Freedom Arms 475 Linebaugh, I took a magnificent big bull at 35 yards. The Buffalo Bore 480 Ruger gave total penetration, in one side and out the other.

One of the few 44 Specials also able to handle the 44 Magnum is the Texas Longhorn Arms West Texas Flat-Top Target 44 Special. With extra cylinders in 44-40 and 44 Magnum it becomes a triple-threat hunting handgun.

Not long after introducing the Model 97 in a six-shot 357 Magnum, Freedom Arms began offering auxiliary cylinders in 38 Special. The latter can be used for cowboy action shooting or just general plinking with the 357 Magnum cylinder returned for more serious uses like Texas turkeys. The Model 97 has been such a selling success that two more small bore auxiliary cylinder versions are now offered, one in 22 Long Rifle/22 Magnum, and the other a 32 Magnum/32-20 version. A third cylinder is offered for the .22 Model 97, that being a match chambered cylinder. However, the standard cylinder and the Magnum cylinder both shoot so well I don't know how a special match chambered cylinder could improve things.

The second chambering offered in the Model 97 was the legendary 45 Colt, a five-shot 45 Colt, and the most compact single action 45 Colt ever factory produced. The 45 Colt Model 97 from Freedom Arms is one ounce lighter than a 5-1/2-inch Colt SAA at 38 ounces, two ounces lighter than the same barrel length in the Colt New Frontier. It also has the same natural feel and pointability as the Colt. This is an accurate sixgun that packs easily all day with a 5-1/2-inch barrel with adjustable sights. The Model 97 is made even more versatile with the addition of the 45 ACP cylinder, allowing a whole range of target and defensive loads. With its interchangeable front sight system on the adjustable sighted models including the large-frame models, the height of the front blade can be easily changed as one goes from 185-gr. JHP 45 ACPs to 260-gr. hard-cast 45 Colt loads.

My favorite single action sixgun is a 7-1/2-inch .44 or .45 preferably with adjustable sights, and one of my favorite sixguns in this category is a Texas Longhorn Arms West Texas Flat-Top Target. This started out as one of the late Bill Grover's personal sixguns. However, when he sent it to me for testing I told him he might as well give me a price as I would not going to send it back. He quoted a price high enough he figured I wouldn't take it, but I did, and then he felt so bad he offered to build extra cylinders for it. So for the price of one sixgun I really wound up with a 44 Special/44-40/44 Magnum/44 Russian. When the 44 Colt was resurrected, Grover offered to build me a fifth cylinder, but before I got around to shipping the Flat-Top Target back to Texas Longhorn Arms, they had gone out of business. Now Bill has passed away so that fifth cylinder will probably never become a reality.

I have used this sixgun with every cylinder except the 44 Russian to take deer-sized game. I also recently used this sixgun with the 44 Special cylinder in place to take two large feral boars, one weighing in at 500 pounds and the other over 600 pounds. My load was the standard Keith 44 Special load using a hollow-pointed Lyman #429421 Keith bullet at 1200 fps. The load performed superbly and I now have over 600 pounds of pork in my daughter's chest freezer. We are just finishing up the last of a buffalo taken with a 45 Colt and are now ready to spend the next year eating pork.

At one time Christie Gun Works offered several auxiliary cylinders for the different calibers and somewhere along the line I picked up one in 45 Auto Rim.

Chapter 38 | Single Action Sixguns & Auxiliary Cylinders

The 45 Colt and 45 ACP can be fired from the same single action sixguns; all it takes is a change of cylinders. The 4-3/4-inch Colt New Frontier and Ruger have extra cylinders from Christy and Ruger respectively. Notice that the auxiliary cylinder for the Colt accepts both 45 ACP and 45 Auto Rim cartridges.

I decided to try it out in a Second Generation 4-3/4-inch Colt New Frontier 45 Colt, not really expecting it to work. It installed easily, locked up perfectly and turned the New Frontier into a double-duty sixgun. The New Frontier 44 Special is too small to be chambered to 44 Magnum, but Third Generation examples can be fitted with an extra 44-40 cylinder, and if one feels nostalgia, Hamilton Bowen can re-chamber a 357 Magnum to 44 Russian for a sixgun that shoots all three .44s.

Starting around 1870, cartridge conversions began to appear as cap and ball revolvers were converted to the new fixed ammunition. Today auxiliary cylinders are available to convert Colt, Remington, and Ruger percussion revolvers to cartridge firing and it is perfectly legal to do so. The Kirst Cartridge Konverter for percussion revolving pistols consists of a replacement cylinder and a conversion ring and is offered as a six-shot 45 Colt for the Ruger, a six-shot 45 ACP for the Remington, and a five-shot Safety Cylinder in 45 Colt also for the Remington. This latter cylinder has a safe area for the hammer to rest on. Both Colt and Remington 38 cylinders are offered as six-shooters.

All Kirst cylinders are basically used the same way. To load, the hammer is placed in the half-cock position, the old cylinder is removed, cartridges are loaded in the new cylinder, and the Konverter Ring is placed on the back of the cylinder. The Conversion cylinder is now installed in the revolver with an empty chamber or the safety area under the hammer. In the case of the Colt 1851 or 1861 Navy revolvers the barrel assembly must be removed before replacing the cylinder and then reinstalled. Walt Kirst now offers a six-shot 45 Colt cylinder for the Ruger Old Army which turns the 7-1/2-inch adjustable-sighted Old Army into a real tack-drivin' .45.

If one so desires, the Colt Navy revolvers can be modified by cutting a loading port in the recoil shield to allow the insertion of cartridges and removal of fired brass without removing the cylinder. This requires something to serve as an ejector rod as there is no such rod on the Navy revolvers. I

Since 1878 Colt has been building single action .44s, first in 44-40, then 44 Russian, followed by 44 Special; three cylinders allow this 7-1/2-inch New Frontier to fire all three.

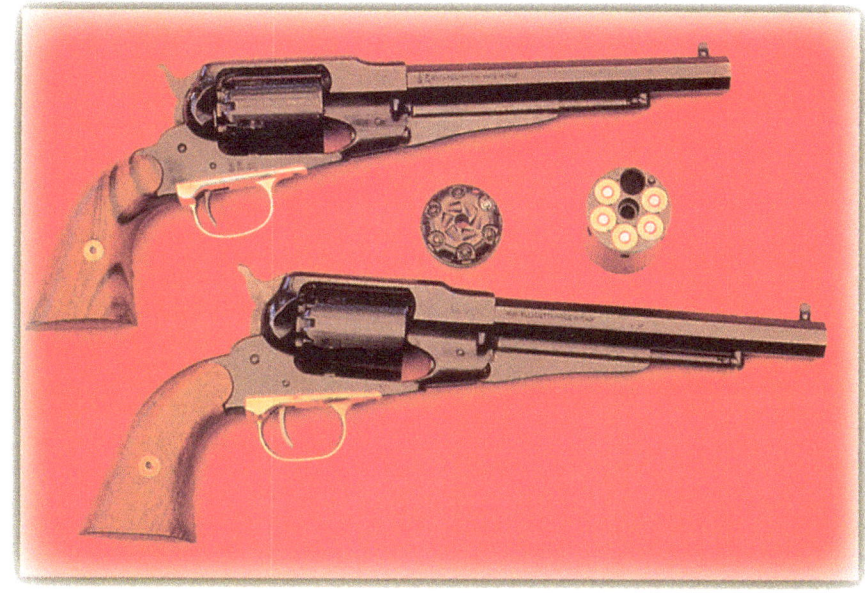

Auxiliary cylinders from Kirst allow Remington percussion pistols to be converted to standard-load-only 45 Colt or 45 ACP.

find a very small screwdriver works fine. Both the 1858 Remington .36 and the 1851 and 1861 Navy Colts have barrels that are oversized, disallowing the use of regular .38-caliber bullets. Instead it is necessary to use hollow base bullets that will expand to fit the rifling. The 148-gr. swaged lead hollow base wadcutter bullets as offered by Hornady and Speer normally used for 38 Special target loads will work fine. Close parameters exist when loading cartridges for use in either the 1858 Remington .36 or the Navy Colts, and loads must be black powder or held to black powder levels

At about the same time that Ruger announced the 5-1/2-inch Old Army, Taylor's & Co. took over distributorship of the R&D conversion cylinders for percussion revolvers, offering six-shot 45 Colt cylinders for both Remington and Ruger cap and ball sixguns. My original plan was to acquire a pair of stainless steel 44 Remington New Model Army revolvers and fit them with nickel-plated R&D cylinders from Taylor's. Before this happened I saw the 5-1/2-inch Old Armies. A pair of test Rugers was obtained from Ruger and at the same time, an order was placed for two nickel-plated R&D Ruger cylinders chambered in 45 Colt. These cylinders are not cheap, but they exhibit excellent workmanship and are well worth the going price. They are a two-piece affair with a typical bored-through cylinder with a removable back plate. This back plate has six firing pins that look like percussion nipples, and a hole in the back plate lines up with a pin on the back of the cylinder to lock the plate in place after five cartridges are loaded in the cylinder. One of the firing pins is a different color so it is always easy to locate the empty chamber. Once the cylinder is loaded and the back plate replaced, it is then placed carefully into the Ruger frame, the base pin replaced, and the percussion revolver is now ready to be fired with metallic cartridges.

I've been doing everything I could over the past 15 years to let everyone know what a great sixgun a 357 Magnum Flat-Top or Old Model Blackhawk converted to 44 Special makes. My last conversion by David Clements on a Three Screw Ruger has an extra cylinder, as David did a 44 Special/44-40 convertible. Both cylinders shoot exceptionally well. "Double your pleasure, double your fun. . . ."

Taylor's & Co. now offers 45 Colt chambered cylinders from R&D for the Ruger Old Army. The removal of the loading lever assembly and the addition of a Belt Mountain base pin simplify the removal of the cylinder for reloading.

Single Action Sixguns | 285

–Chapter 39–

HUNTING WITH THE SINGLE ACTION SIXGUN

Is hunting with a single action sixgun really different from hunting with a rifle? I quote from an article I wrote for the November, 2004 issue of *Guns Magazine*: "It was one of those afternoons that can only occur in the late fall days known as Indian summer and especially only in the mountains of Southern Idaho. The type of day that one feels so lucky to be alive. Crisp cool mornings with a touch of frost, the welcoming of the sun as it rises to remove the chill in the air, and the arrival of a day that allows one to hunt in comfort wearing nothing more than regular clothes, long sleeve shirt, jeans, Stetson, and loggers, all topped off with a down vest. I'm sure others will try to tell me that such beautiful days are also found in their part of the country, and I will accept that, but I will never believe that anything, anywhere, could be better than this.

"Even the down vest proved to be more than I needed as I worked my way from the creek bottom to the top of the canyon. It was time to rest and cool down. An old log, the folded up vest for a pillow, and I had a perfect resting place that no amount of money could purchase. As I lay there very close to a short nap while contemplating the joys of life, I looked across the canyon and there he was. I didn't need binoculars to see this was not just a mule deer, but a very large buck, and the sunlight glistening off his antlers caused my heart to skip a beat or two. He was a long ways off from me, and if I were careful I could slowly roll off the log, move behind it, use my down vest as a rest for the long-range scope sighted rifle that the situation demanded, and with one well placed shot I would have winter meat and a nice trophy as a bonus; all very simple except for one thing. I didn't have a rifle.

"Yes, I was hunting, and yes I did have a gun, but it was the wrong gun for this situation. Years before I had replaced my scope sighted 30-06 Remington 700 with a sixgun, an iron-sighted Ruger 10-inch Flat-Top Blackhawk 44 Magnum sixgun, which now rode very comfortably and securely in its Goerg shoulder holster. I did not get excited when I saw the buck. I did not reach for my 44 Magnum, even though it was certainly capable of downing any mule deer. I did not try

There are no shooting benches in the hunting fields, but it is often possible to improvise.

For a 10-1/2-inch single action sixgun such as the Freedom Arms Model 83, a sling can be much more convenient than a holster.

to move behind the log. I simply savored the moment like a good steak, enjoying every morsel of it. I knew the muley was at least six times farther away than I would feel comfortable shooting with an iron-sighted sixgun even with a solid rest. I knew he was too far away for me to get to him by dark even if he did allow it. I did not feel cheated. I did not feel handicapped. The choice was mine and once I decided to be a handgun hunter, my attitude had to change. There would be no long shots. There would be no regrets. There would be an honest appraisal of my ability to not simply hit game, but to precisely place my bullet. There would be a lot of days such as this in which I was simply a spectator. It is part of the real picture for a handgun hunter."

The above selection captures the essence of what it means to be a handgun hunter. Once the choice is made to leave the rifle at home, our attitude must continue to change; and the right attitude demands we are honest in what we can accomplish with a handgun. There are very few natural anythings in this world. Those that look the most natural are probably those that practice the most, and I've never heard of a musician or athlete arriving at a time when they no longer felt practice was necessary. I must admit I am somewhat bothered by the rifle hunters who never shoot during the year except to go out and sight in just prior to going hunting. Perhaps rifle shooters can get away with this; handgun hunters cannot.

To become a good shot with a sixgun, and one does not have to be an exceptionable shot to be a handgun hunter, requires practice which in turn is required to maintain the acquired skills. It is one thing to be able to connect on an inanimate target at a known distance from a solid target shooting position with a single action sixgun. It is quite another to be able to the same thing on a live animal at an unknown distance when one is slightly out of breath and the adrenaline is pumping. An honest assessment of my ability tells me that what I could do at 200 meters with everything perfect (such as in a long range silhouette match) would shrink to what I could do at 50 yards in the not so perfect game fields.

One of the best ways to assess, really honestly assess, one's abilities to connect is to practice using paper plates, or even better, proper-sized Shoot-N-See targets. A simple paper plate is about the size of the kill zone on most big game animals. There are no shooting benches found in the foothills, forests, or mountains where most of us hunt; there are bushes, tree limbs, rocks, and backpacks that can be used as a rest. Sometimes even these are not available, so it is necessary to also practice shooting two-handed standing on our own two legs.

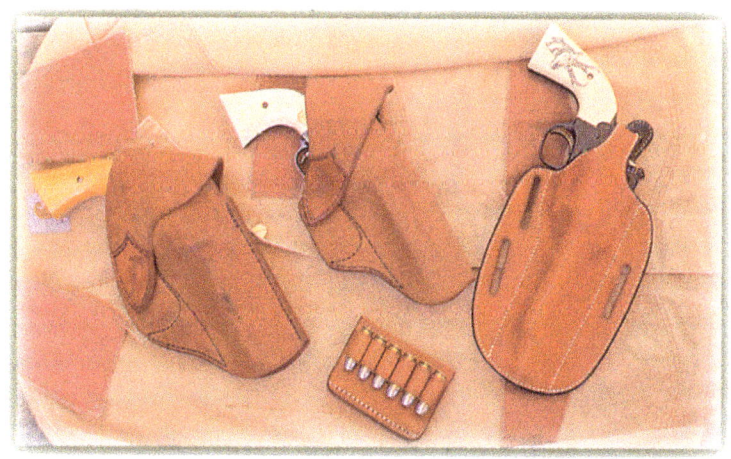

Thad Rybka's Tomahawk half flap and Von Ringler's Pancake are excellent holster choices for large bore handguns.

Single Action Sixguns | 287

Chapter 39 | Hunting With The Single Action Sixgun

Shoulder holsters, such as this Idaho Leather Model 44, are a good choice for handgun hunting.

Von Ringler specializes in trim holsters and cartridge slides for carrying big bore hunting handguns.

Practice with the makeshift rests and shooting offhand will give us a clear picture of our ability to place a bullet if we are not excited, if we are not out of breath, if our hands are not cold, if our glasses are not fogged up, and if we don't suffer from buck fever. There is no magic in the game fields. If the paper plate cannot be hit consistently, we will not somehow become magically proficient when game appears. I will pass up a shot rather than shoot when I am out of breath, and I am very fortunate in that my excitement ends once I see the intended animal target. Buck fever does not exist for me.

If one plans to use iron sights, one should determine the distance at which, with 99+ percent reliability, shots can be placed on that paper plate; if the scope sighted handgun is used, the same thing must be known. For myself I have determined that 50 to 75 yards is my absolute maximum distance for an iron-sighted sixgun, but I prefer 50 yards or even less. Twenty-five yards is ideal; perhaps 50 yards farther than that with a scoped sixgun if all conditions are perfect.

Every state game commission sets hunting regulations independent of all other states. Some states, such as my home state of Idaho, allow any centerfire handgun for big game while others regulate both the muzzle energy and barrel length of handguns that may be used. It is therefore necessary to check with each separate game commission for any state in which one plans to hunt with a single action sixgun. For most of us, deer are the number one handgun hunting quarry, but again it is necessary to check state regulations. Many states also have large populations of feral hogs, which can often be hunted at any time of the year. A check of the regulations is required here also. Hunting big mean hogs with an iron-sighted sixgun is about as exciting as it gets. I've been "charged" several times and the sixgun, rather a well-placed heavy hard-cast slug from the sixgun, stopped things before they got out of hand. I say "charged" because I'm not sure the boar was charging me or just trying to run away and came in my direction.

Any single action sixgun, no matter what the caliber or chambering, is suitable for handgun hunting if it is accurate, has good sights, and possesses a decent trigger. It is simply a matter of matching the game to the gun. Sixguns chambered in 22 Long Rifle, 22 Magnum, 32 Magnum, 32-20, and 38 Special are normally reserved for small game and varmints; a 357 Magnum also fits in here as well as being adequate for small deer; the 38-40, 44-40, 44 Special, and 41 Magnum, all property loaded, will also do for close range shooting of deer and deer-sized game. For truly big game, we start at the 44 Magnum and go up through the heavy 45 Colt, 454 Casull, 475 Linebaugh, 480 Ruger, and 500 Linebaugh. The 44 Magnum was the first factory produced big bore handgun round for big game hunting and it is still the cartridge by which all others are judged. I have used every cartridge mentioned, but my most reached-for hunting handgun continues to be a 7-1/2-inch Freedom Arms Model 83 44 Magnum with a 2X Leupold scope. There are those who say scopes do not belong on handguns. I agree, given a perfect world. However, this world is far from perfect, and a scope sight helps us to precisely place our bullet, resulting in a quick and humane kill, which is what every hunter should strive for.

El Paso Saddlery's #1920 makes a convenient handgun hunting holster for long barreled single action sixguns in the crossdraw version.

Brian Pearce of *Handloader* magazine with an Idaho mountain lion taken with the Hamilton Bowen-built 44 Special #5 SAA.

Chapter 39 | Hunting With The Single Action Sixgun

Taffin's favorite hunting holster for the scoped Freedom Arms M83 is Freedom Arms' "shoulder holster"; it rides low but comfortable.

One great advantage of a single action sixgun over a rifle is the fact it is so much easier to carry a sixgun in a proper holster than an eight-pound rifle on a sling. Thad Rybka learned long ago that crossdraw holsters were very suitable for hunting use. Most of his designs are offered in crossdraw persuasion with a favorite of hunters and woodsbummers alike being the Tomahawk. Originally designed for a Mag-Na-Port Custom Predator 44 Magnum Ruger Blackhawk with a 4-5/8-inch barrel, I use Tomahawks for the Ruger as well as a short-barreled Freedom Arms 454. The 2/3 flap holds the sixgun safely and securely while allowing easy access.

Von Ringler offers a modified Threepersons design known as The Linebaugh to carry the big custom sixguns of John Linebaugh as well as those offered by Freedom Arms. This is a very sturdy holster, lined, with a safety strap, and its main seam, unlike the Threepersons design, features a curve as it travels downward from the trigger guard to the end of the mainframe and then into the barrel profile. Ringler also offers an excellent Pancake design for the big single action sixguns as well as compact cartridge slides. All these from Ringler are designed with a handgun hunter in mind.

When the weather is really crummy or the going is tough I reach for a nylon shoulder holster from Idaho Leather. This is a true shoulder holster in that it rides under the armpit, and unlike other nylon holsters this one is lined with suede leather. It accepts a 6-inch Freedom Arms sixgun and this is the rig and revolver I used when making my way up a mountain in waist deep snow to get my mountain lion. Idaho Leather also offers an excellent leather spring clip shoulder holster, the Model 44, covering everything but the grip frame. Made of the best leather obtainable, this rig helps distribute the weight by the use of a cartridge holder on the off side strap. This wide flat piece of leather holds two vertical rows of 12 cartridge loops each.

Cast bullet expert Glen Fryxell took this large feral boar on the Clover Creek Ranch in Oregon using a custom Ruger 45 Colt with a 335-gr. bullet.

John Linebaugh was a pioneer in building sixguns to handle full-house 45 Colt loads. Ross Seyfried successfully tested one of John's early 45 Colts on Cape buffalo.

Three of my favorite hunting handguns are all scoped 7-1/2-inch Freedom Arms Model 83s in 357 Magnum, 44 Magnum, and 454 Casull. Which caliber I choose depends on what I'm after. In either case I grab the shoulder holster that Freedom Arms offers for their scoped revolvers. Perhaps it is not correct to call this a shoulder holster as it really rides across the front of the body. Whether walking, standing, sitting, or riding, this holster works! I wear it so my pants belt enters the loop on the back of the holster, which takes much of the weight off the shoulder straps. This works out very comfortably and perfectly secure.

When I first started hunting with handgun, the only suitable single action sixgun choices were the Ruger 357 and 44 Magnum Flat-Top Blackhawks. The 10-inch 44 Flat-Top mentioned at the beginning of this chapter was carried in an Al Goerg holster. Goerg was a true handgun hunting pioneer and offered an excellent lightweight shoulder holster for sixguns. After the Flat-Tops came the 44 Magnum Super Blackhawk and the Colt New Frontiers in 44 Special and 45 Colt, all followed by the first real heavy duty 45 Colt sixgun, the Ruger Blackhawk of 1971. In 1983 Freedom Arms began offering the 454 Casull and now also chambers the same Model 83 in 44 Magnum, 41 Magnum, 357 Magnum, 475 Linebaugh, and 50 Action Express.

The 1980s also saw Ruger's Bisley Model arrive chambered in 357 Magnum, 41 Magnum, 44 Magnum, and 45 Colt. Ruger further improved the Super Blackhawk in the 1990s with the Hunter Models and this excellent heavy-barreled, scope-ready 7-1/2-inch single action sixgun handgun is now also offered as a Bisley Model and even a .22 Single-Six version. Magnum Research's BFR is a proven, accurate and dependable single action sixgun available in 454 Casull, 475 Linebaugh, 500 S&W Magnum, and even 45-70 and Marlin's 444 and 450. What all this means is today's single action sixgunner has a veritable supermarket of single action sixguns to choose from for hunting. Whatever the choice heed carefully the words of Robert Ruark: "Use Enough Gun!"

Before all of these sixguns arrived on the scene there was the 44 Special. Until the 44 Magnum appeared in 1956, the handloaded heavy 44 Special was the only game in town. My first 44 Special, an

"When I first started hunting with handgun, the only suitable single action sixgun choices were the Ruger 357 and 44 Magnum Flat-Top Blackhawks."

Chapter 39 | Hunting With The Single Action Sixgun

Look at the tusks on this wild boar taken in Michigan by Al Anderson using a 500 Linebaugh!

S&W 1950 Target, was given to me by my wife on the occasion of our first Christmas together in 1959. Colt would introduce the single action 44 Special New Frontier with adjustable sights in 1962. Very few Texas Longhorn Arms West Texas Flat-Top Targets were built in 44 Special in the late 1980s.

When it comes to hunting I have been blessed being able to hunt in many states as well as Africa. With single actions sixgun from Colt, Freedom Arms, Ruger and Texas Longhorn Arms I have taken deer, bear, buffalo, wart hog, feral pigs, and numerous exotic species using the 357 Magnum, 41 Magnum, 44 Magnum, 45 Colt, 454 Casull, 475 Linebaugh, 480 Ruger, and 50 Action Express. I am neither an expert hunter nor a tremendous shot. I am a good shot, very careful, patient enough to wait for my shot, and relaxed enough to pass up bad shots; and in every case with every sixgun and load I have followed the three most important things to remember when handgun hunting: bullet placement, bullet placement, and bullet placement.

For my latest hunt after feral hogs I chose the 44 Special loaded with a hollowpoint cast bullet, Lyman's #429421 Keith, at 1200 fps muzzle velocity from the 7-1/2-inch 44 Special Texas Longhorn Arms West Texas Flat-Top Target. On the first pig the bullet went in right behind the upper part of the front leg and, as we found out later, came out on the other side right through the center of the upper part of the leg on the off side. Now this was a 500-pound pig and a hollowpoint cast bullet at 1200 fps gave total penetration! At the shot he stumbled and looked like he was going to run. I did not hesitate but put a second shot in him. He went over with all four feet in the air and proceeded to tumble over and over and down the hill. He accommodated us by coming to a stop on the dirt road.

That was to be the end of it is far as I was concerned. There were two pigs there; I intended to take one pig and be on my way. His big buddy would have none of that. By now he was up on his feet and using his snout moving that 500-pound pig. He was not about to leave. He gave me my perfect shot broadside. At the shot he turned around, started to run, and I put a second shot in him and down he went. The smaller pig had four-inch tusks, while this 650-pounder had tusks curling around for six inches. We would later find out the 44 Special hollow point had gone through the heart of the second boar, the second shot was only two inches away from the first shot, and the bullet was perfectly mushroomed and lodged under the hide on the far side. In both cases the 44 Special cast hollowpoint bullets did everything a sixgun, load, and bullet combination are supposed to do.

The 44 Special still works! This 500-lb. boar with 4-inch tusks was taken with the Texas Longhorn Arms West Texas Flat-Top Target 44 Special with the Keith load.

–Chapter 40–

SINGLE ACTION SIXGUN GAMES

All firearms, including single action sixguns, have a serious side such as hunting and self-defense. However, this is just a small part of firearms usage, probably less than 1 percent. The vast majority of the time firearms are used for fun activities, great times with family and friends, just generally enjoying life with a firearm as part of the picture. As an extra-added bonus, most of these, but certainly not all, fun activities help to train as they prepare us for the serious side of sixguns. Let's have some fun!

Western Movies

Anyone growing up in the 1930s and 1940s spent much of their time in the front row of the neighborhood theater with a large bag of popcorn, an equally large pop to wash it down with, and a double feature with Roy Rogers, Gene Autry, Hopalong Cassidy, Johnny Mack Brown, the Three Mesquiteers, and on and on with a nearly endless list of cowboy heroes. By the 1950s the switch had been made to television, and the same B movies came around once again with a whole list of new heroes added from TV productions. Matt Dillon, Paladin, Maverick, the Cartwrights, all galloped across the little box giving everyone a vicarious experience with single action sixguns.

Westerns, whether they were big screen movies or came from the corner of our living room, had common attributes. They were fun. Good always triumphed over Evil, there was no doubt who the hero was, and we always left the theater on Saturday afternoon feeling inspired and uplifted, almost like coming from a religious service. We would be pumped up through the weekend, and then a weeklong schedule of school would drain us, and we would have to return the following Saturday for new inspiration. The heroes and bad guys alike, but especially the heroes, accomplished the impossible with their single action sixguns. The shooting, especially on the part of a hero, was incredible but perfectly believable to any eight-year-old. The down side to both movie and television westerns was, and is, the unsafe handling of firearms, especially single actions. Thousands upon thousands of times, thousands upon thousands of impressionable youngsters received

Possibly the best-known of Fast Draw rigs is the Paladin rig as used by Richard Boone in *Have Gun, Will Travel*. This rare rig was produced by Arvo Ojala. Photo courtesy of Bob Arganbright.

Single Action Sixguns | 293

Chapter 40 | Single Action Sixgun Games

their first "training" in handling firearms from the movies. Hopefully, by the time they reached adulthood, the same youngsters realized the difference between fantasy and reality and approached all firearms with the proper attitude. Unfortunately, not all were able to make the transition, which resulted in firearms "accidents" – in reality, for the most part, nothing more than negligent and unsafe handling practices.

Plinking

The grandest of all single action sixgun sports is plinking. There are no rules except those addressing safe practices and also cleaning up any mess created. The number one plinking target is the lowly pop can and at no time under any circumstances should glass targets ever be used. One of the best targets for plinking is charcoal briquets. They are cheap, large enough to hit, and biodegradable so there's no cleanup required. The number one caliber for plinking is the 22 Long Rifle and the number one single action sixgun, at least since 1953, has been the Ruger Single-Six.

In the late 1950s, Saturday afternoons were reserved for good friends, the Ruger Single-Six, and my companion Marlin Mountie. Plinking builds many pleasant memories that never leave, no matter how many years have passed. The powder smoke and the smell of Hoppe's #9 still remain a half-century later and memories are rekindled as I regularly plink these days with my grandkids. The old friends are long gone, but the grandkids are now building their own memories.

Johnny Mack Brown not only made very many enjoyable movies for kids in the 1930s and 1940s, he was also an accomplished gun spinner. Photo courtesy of Walt Ostin.

Richard Boone as Paladin bought a new attribute of the gunfighter to the screen by drawing his Colt only as a last resort. Photo courtesy of Jim Lockwood.

It wasn't very realistic, but when the Peaceable Man, Gordon "Wild Bill" Elliott, drew his sixgun and threw bullets at the bad guys it at least looked good. Photo courtesy of Walt Ostin.

Fast Draw

The sport of fast draw was directly responsible for the tremendous improvement in leather belts and holster taking place in the 1950s/1960s. I started shooting fast draw in the late 1950s, first using a double rig built by Ray Howser of the Pony Express Shop in California and then later a single Arvo Ojala Hollywood rig. The Ojala was soon seen in all the Western movies and TV westerns as Paladin, Matt Dillon, Cheyenne, Bret Maverick, and virtually every other Western star of the time frame used an Ojala rig. This rig featured a steel-lined, low-riding holster with a steel-reinforced shank, all to provide a solid platform that would not move and would also allow cocking in the holster when using blanks or wax bullets only. The 1960s saw a new style of holster emerge as Andy Anderson, a former employee of Arvo Ojala, opened his own shop to sell his Gunfighter line of fast draw leather. Instead of the low riding holster, Anderson brought his holster up on the belt with a marked muzzle forward slant and called the design the Walk-n-Draw. This is the style holster normally seen on the hips of Clint Eastwood in his spaghetti westerns and James Drury as the Virginian.

Cowboy action shooting also has the Gunfighter class, shooting two sixguns in sequence as demonstrated by Ray Walters.

Ray Walters shooting Traditional Class in cowboy action shooting with a two-handed hold.

Single Action Sixguns

Chapter 40 | Single Action Sixgun Games

The Winners Circle at Winter Range: Handlebar Doc, Frederick Jackson Turner, Billy Boots, and Long Hunter all won their individual classes.

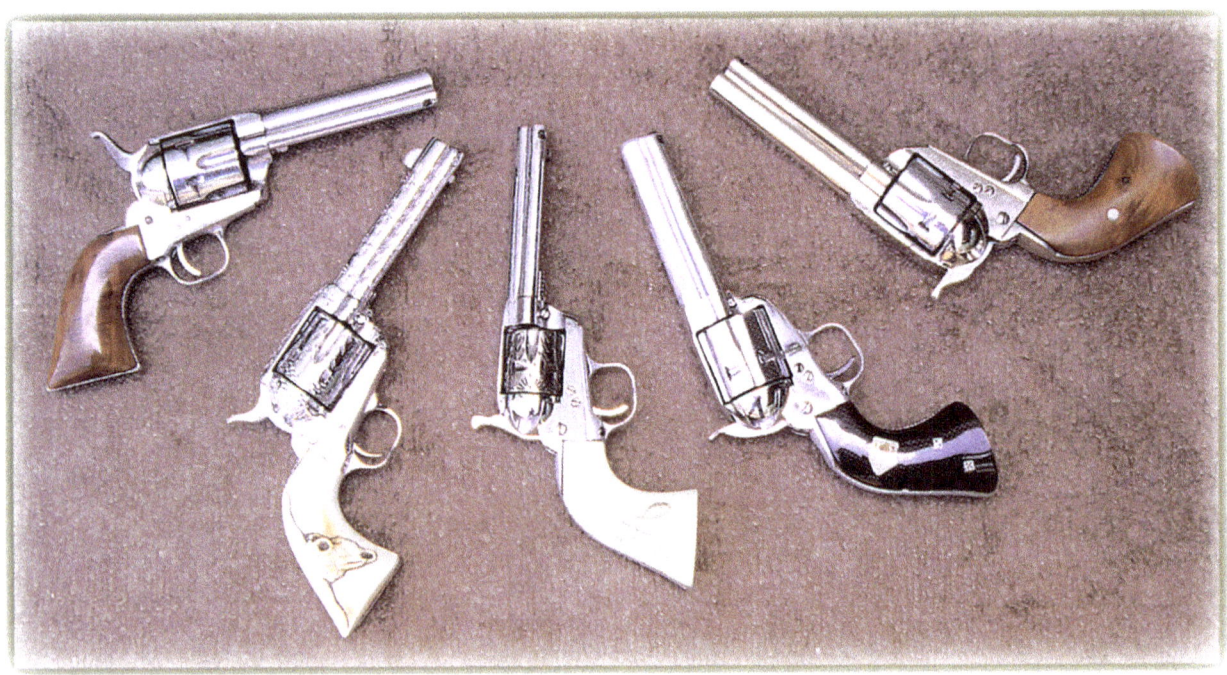

Customized Fast Draw single actions: early black powder Colt with no front sight and hammer extended for fanning; Colt First Generation engraved by Joe Bowman; Ruger 22-38 with 38 barrel and cylinder for .22 rimfire blanks; Ruger .357 converted to 45 Colt and set up for fanning; another .357 Ruger converted to 45 Colt. Photo courtesy of Bob Arganbright.

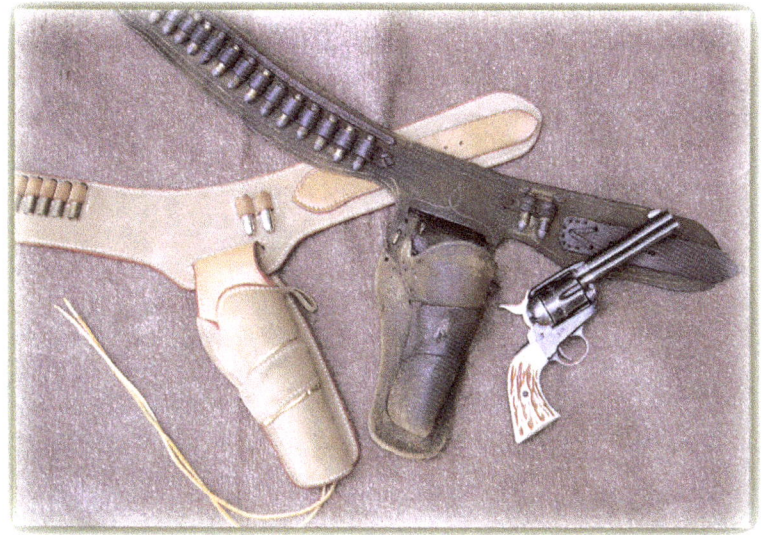

Rodd Redwing, movie gun coach, made his own Fast Draw rigs using corset stays in the holster to allow the cylinder to spin freely. The well-used rig is one of Redwing's while the light-colored rig was produced by Andy Anderson. This style rig was used by Glenn Ford in many of his movies. Photo courtesy of Bob Arganbright.

The favorite sixguns for fast draw back then were 4-3/4-inch Colt SAA and Great Western sixguns chambered in 45 Colt. Great Western offered specially-tuned fast draw 45s and Colt sponsored many fast draw contests. The only revolvers I ever used in fast draw were 7-1/2-inch Colts; if that barrel length was good enough for Paladin, Matt Dillon, Chris Colt of Colt .45, and Clay Hollister of Tombstone Territory, it was certainly good enough for me!

Most fast draw contests, whether with blanks or wax bullets, were set up with a timer giving the shooter a light or sound signal to go for his sixgun. Rules required the hand to be at least six-inches away from the gun butt before the signal was given. Top shooters then, and now, could get their times down well below a half-second to react, grip the sixgun, cock the hammer, and, in the case of wax bullets, hit the target. In the glory days of fast draw there were clubs all over the country as well as many major contests. Fast draw still exists, though on a much smaller scale.

Dee Woolem is known as the Father of Fast Draw. The top rig is one of his personal holsters, while the bottom is from a kit offered by Tandy Leather. Photo courtesy of Bob Arganbright.

Single Action Sixguns | 297

Chapter 40 | Single Action Sixgun Games

Cowboy Action Shooting

Cowboy action shooting is a large enough topic for a whole book and several have been written, including my own *Action Shooting Cowboy Style* by KP Books. CAS came out of southern California with the Wild Bunch, a group of single action shooters who got together for informal competition. It has now spread to the entire country and beyond, with the Wild Bunch forming SASS (Single Action Shooting Society) as the main governing body for this great sport. Simply put, cowboy action shooting attempts to capture the spirit of the Old West by having shooters dressing in frontier period clothes using frontier period single action sixguns, leverguns, and double barreled shotguns in fast-paced competition. It has proven to not only be great fun but also a major force in attracting new shooters. It is without a doubt the fastest-growing shooting sport with well over 70,000 current registered members with SASS and at least an equal number of non-member shooters.

To compete, a cowboy shooter needs two single action sixguns, a levergun, and a period-style double barrel or pump shotgun. By period-style we mean prior to 1899 with the use of original guns of the time or replicas thereof. The single action sixguns of cowboy action shooting fall into three major classification: real sixguns (originals produced before 1899 such as First Generation Colt Single Action Armies); the thoroughly modern coil spring-operated Ruger single actions; and replica sixguns, both cartridge-firing and cap-n-ball.

Competition consists of several stages, usually five or six at the local level, and 12 or more at regional and national competitions. Each stage normally requires two single action sixguns, each loaded with five rounds; a lever action rifle chambered in a pistol cartridge and holding 10 rounds; and several rounds from the shotgun. Targets are normally made of metal and are big and set close. The score is determined by the time for each stage plus five seconds for each target missed.

There are two basic classes of cowboy action competitors: those who approach it mainly as a speed shooting game and use low-recoiling loads to shoot as fast as possible; and another larger group who just like to shoot the old-style sixguns with loads comparable to those of the 1880s. There is the vast difference in recovery time between a minimum velocity 38 Special with a light bullet and a full-house 45 Colt black powder load. No matter how one wishes to compete or shoot, safety is the number one rule, followed closely by fun.

Cowboy shooting clubs offer many classes of competition covering all types of single action sixguns. Whatever the class entered, all loads must be lead bullets only with a muzzle velocity from a sixgun under 1000

Cowboy Mounted Shooting requires exceptional sixgun skill, but more importantly an excellent horse. Competitors shoot balloons with .45 black powder blanks over a prescribed course of fire. It is a spectacular spectator event. Photos by Mr. Quigley courtesy of *Shoot!* Magazine.

fps. Modern class is for any .32 or larger single action sixgun with adjustable sights, e.g., the Ruger Blackhawk. Traditional class is for the use of fixed-sighted sixguns such as the Colt SAA, the Ruger Vaquero, and Smith and Wesson and Remington single actions, original or replicas. This class allows the use of smokeless or black powder loads, as well as cap and ball sixguns.

There are several classes that are offshoots of the Traditional class. Frontier Cartridge allows black powder or black powder substitute loads only; Duelist class requires the single action sixgun to be cocked and fired one-handed only; Gunfighter is shot double duelist, that is, one shoots a sixgun in each hand; and Frontiersman class requires percussion revolvers. The most recent class is Classic Cowboy, which requires sixguns of .40 caliber or higher, and in the case of percussion revolvers, .36 or larger. This class is designed to be historically correct, so the shotgun must be a double-barreled version with outside hammers, while the rifle must be a design from 1873 or earlier. There are also age- and gender-based categories, all resulting in such a very large umbrella that virtually anyone interested in shooting single action sixguns is able to participate.

One aspect of cowboy action shooting is Mounted Shooting. This game requires two single action sixguns and a good horse. The course of fire consists of balloons on sticks and the competitor must be able to guide his or her horse through the course while shooting 45 Colt blanks at the balloons. The blanks, of course, are for safety, but it still requires a great deal of skill to be able to control the horse and shoot at the same time. Obviously, the most important item in this game is the horse! Said horse must be able to travel the course speedily and safely and at the same time put up with the noise.

Single Action Sixguns | 299

Chapter 40 | Single Action Sixgun Games

The latest single action sixgun game is Cowboy Fast Draw shot man-to-man using wax bullets over a small charge of black powder.

Cowboy Fast Draw

The latest single action sixgun game is Cowboy Fast Draw, which differs from the original Fast Draw in several ways. Steel-lined holsters are not permitted and the top of the holster must be no lower than three inches from the top of the belt. The rules state the holster must be of the Slim Jim or Mexican pattern. Competitors start with their hands on their gun and draw and fire when the light in the center of the target comes on.

Targets are steel discs 24 inches in diameter and are set anywhere from 15 to 21 feet in front of the shooters. Single action sixguns must be chambered in 45 Colt as the ammunition, which consists of a wax bullet and approximately 6.0 grains of black powder, is provided to the shooter. Competition is man-to-man or woman-to-woman with the best three out of five times the winner. Most competitors use 4-3/4-inch Colts, Colt replicas, or Ruger Vaqueros. I'm still using my 7-1/2-inch SAA in an El Paso Saddlery 1897 Sweetwater Mexican loop holster.

Long Range Silhouettes

The sport that tells us more about our shooting ability and also the capability of our single action sixgun than any other is long-range silhouetting. The sport goes back to the 1970s and really grew in the 1980s, when it peaked. At one time there were organized silhouette clubs all over the country, but the interest today is nowhere near when it was in the late 1980s. On a cold, wet, rainy, snowy, windswept day in February in the early 1980s we had 132 sign-ups. This is not total shooters, as some shooters shot two or three times, but it does show how popular the sport was. Now the club is gone, the target rails have been removed from the range, and the closest club is 150 miles away.

Throughout this book mention had been made of single action sixguns for long-range shooting. The Long Range Silhouette course of fire consists of 10 each of metal chickens, pigs, turkeys, and rams set at 50, 100, 150, and 200 meters. While I was competing I used several 10-1/2-inch barreled single action sixguns including the Ruger 44 Magnum Blackhawk and 357 Maximum, the U.S. Sporting Arms 375 SuperMag, and the Freedom Arms Model 83 in 454 Casull, 44 Magnum, and 357 Magnum. All great sixguns, all superbly accurate sixguns, but the most accurate long-range sixgun I ever found was the Freedom Arms Model 83 chambered in 41 Magnum.

Shooting should be fun for the most part, and all of these activities simply add to the enjoyment of life, especially our sixgunnin' life. Plinking can take place anywhere there's a safe backstop, and organized competitions are now so widespread that one or more should be within a short driving distance of everyone.

–Chapter 41–

PERFECT PACKIN' PISTOLS, SINGLE ACTION STYLE

It has been around for more than 125 years, but the 4-3/4-inch 45 Colt SAA is still a viable and dependable Packin' Pistol. Tom Threepersons holster by Walt Ostin, snakewood stocks by Roy Fishpaw and pearl grips by Eagle grips.

Single action sixguns have many uses: plinking, fast draw, cowboy action shooting, hunting, long-range shooting, self-defense, silhouette shooting, and most assuredly as a Packin' Pistol. Regular readers of my articles and columns in *American Handgunner* and *Guns Magazine* know immediately what I mean by a Packin' Pistol as I have written several times of the search for it. Here is my definition of what a Packin' Pistol should be: "Packin' Pistol: (pak´-in pis´-tol): *n* a revolver, normally a big-bore sixgun, relatively light in weight, having a barrel length of not less than 4 inches or more than 5-1/2 inches, easy to holster, and chambered in a caliber which can be depended upon to do any job or task encountered. It may operate single action or double action and can be chambered in any caliber from 32 Magnum to 500 Linebaugh. However, most Packin' Pistols fall into the .44 - .45 category." (*Taffin's Unabridged Dictionary of Big-Bore Sixguns*)

Notice that the definition includes both single action and double action sixguns, but in this book we're concerned only with single actions. The best double action Packin' Pistols do definitely come from Smith and Wesson going back to the .357 Magnum of 1935, through a long line of K-and N-frames, and right up to today's Mountain Guns.

There are numerous best quality single action Packin' Pistols available both new and used as well as many custom offerings. Most single action sixguns will fit in several categories of use, and the same is true of Packin' Pistols. They can be used for hunting, self-defense, plinking, and long-range shooting, but their number one asset is that of a go-almost-anywhere and do-almost-anything sixgun. They are the best answer for the largest number of situations, not necessarily the best choice for hunting or long-range shooting or self-defense, but rather the jack-of-all-trades of the single action scene. They are most usually packed openly in a high-riding, sturdy but compact holster threaded on a cartridge belt, and they also slide easily under a pillow or beside one's bedroll at night. If a man could have only one single action sixgun, and I can't imagine such a dreary situation, the most useful sixgun would be a Packin' Pistol.

Single Action Sixguns | 301

Chapter 41 | Perfect Packin' Pistols Single Action Style

Ruger has been providing great Packin' Pistols since 1955. Here we have three 4-5/8-inch examples: a .357 Blackhawk with grips by BluMagnum; a Three-Screw .44 Super Blackhawk customized by Mag-Na-Port; and in the Bianchi Lawman holster, a 44 Magnum Flat-Top with stocks by Roy Fishpaw.

I have previously mentioned the first Packin' Pistol I ever encountered found in an old *American Rifleman* dated April, 1929. In this piece Elmer Keith unveiled his idea of the perfect sixgun in an article entitled "The Last Word" as he described his #5 SAA which as it turns out definitely fits the definition of Perfect Packin' Pistol. This custom sixgun, incorporating the ideas of Elmer Keith and his friend Harold Croft, started as a standard fixed-sighted Single Action Army or perhaps a Bisley Model. The grip frame was made by mating a cut-down Bisley backstrap with an SAA trigger guard. The mainframe was flat-topped, adjustable sights were added, the barrel length was an easy packin' 5-1/2 inches, the caliber was 44 Special, and the entire sixgun was fully engraved and fitted with carved ivory stocks.

Keith offered his design to Colt as he tried to interest them in improving the standard Single Action Army; no one in Hartford would listen to him. A little over a quarter-century later, a much improved single action sixgun would surface, not from Colt, but from the new company known as Sturm, Ruger. That first factory produced single action sixgun vying for the title of Perfect Packin' Pistol was the 4-5/8-inch 357 Magnum Blackhawk of 1955. At the time it was chambered for the most powerful sixgun cartridge available, and with its adjustable sights, Colt Single Action Army grip frame, and virtually indestructible coil spring action, it was the perfect outdoorsman's sixgun.

One year after the introduction of the 357 Flat-Top, Ruger brought out the 44 Magnum Blackhawk, but it was never offered in either a 4-5/8- or 5-1/2-inch barrel length; and when the 44 Magnum Super Blackhawk came forth in 1959 it was offered only with a 7-1/2-inch barrel. A whole lot of sixgunners, myself included, turned both models into Perfect Packin' Pistols by having the barrels cut to 4-5/8 inch.

Thirty-five years of 4-5/8-inch Ruger Packin' Pistols: blue and stainless Bisley Model .45s, with stocks by Lett and Scott Kolar, are flanked by a stag-gripped Three Screw 41 Magnum Blackhawk, and in the homemade holster, a Three Screw 45 Colt Blackhawk with ivories.

These two sixguns started life as 10-1/2-inch Ruger 44 Magnum Super Blackhawks used by Taffin and his wife, Diamond Dot, for long range silhouetting. They are now 5-1/2-inch Packin' Pistols with Bisley grip frames. Top, six-shot 44 Magnum by David Clements; bottom, five-shot 45 Colt by Jim Stroh.

The first big bore Packin' Pistol to come from Ruger would be the 4-5/8-inch barreled 41 Magnum in 1965. With the coming of the Old Model Rugers in 1963, Ruger not only added the 41 Magnum chambering to their catalog, but they also introduced the 45 Colt Blackhawk in 1971 as an easy packin' 4-5/8-inch heavy duty sixgun. Today, Ruger offers short-barreled stainless-steel New Model Perfect Packin' Pistols in 357 Magnum, 44 Magnum, and 45 Colt. With the barrel shortened to 4-5/8 inches, the Bisley Model also makes an excellent Packin' Pistol.

Colt did not listen to Elmer Keith but they did bring out a fine Packin' Pistol in 1962 with the introduction of the adjustable sighted, flat-topped New Frontier. They would be made through the Second Generation production, probably some of the best single action sixguns ever to be offered by Colt, and also in the Third Generation version. The earlier guns were offered in 44 Special and 45 Colt and are very hard to find and quite pricey when they are located. The Third Generation New Frontiers are much more numerous and can usually be picked up for less than the price of a standard Single Action Army. These can be found in 44 Special, 45 Colt, and also 44-40 in both 4-3/4-inch and 5-1/2-inch barrel lengths.

The Ultimate Big Bore Packin' Pistol size-wise: John Linebaugh's 500 built on a Ruger New Model frame with a 5-1/2-inch barrel and ivory micarta grips.

Single Action Sixguns | 303

Chapter 41 | Perfect Packin' Pistols Single Action Style

Taffin takes a rest break across the fence with one of his favorite Packin' Pistols, the Freedom Arms Model 83.

The last New Frontiers came off the assembly line in 1984. I cannot understand why Colt has not resurrected this beautiful sixgun; it simply makes no sense to me. A Colt New Frontier with an expert tune-up and trigger job and a pair of custom stocks of ivory, staghorn, or fancy walnut is right at the top of the list of Perfect Packin' Pistols.

Freedom Arms makes the finest single action sixguns ever to come from a factory, so it is obvious they qualify as Perfect Packin' Pistols. The Model 83 with a 4-3/4-inch barrel in 454 Casull with an extra cylinder chambered in 45 Colt, the same sixgun in 475 Linebaugh with an extra cylinder for the 480 Ruger, or the same simply chambered in 44 Magnum, is tough to beat as the Perfect Packin' Pistol. For those whose idea of big bore is a little smaller, it even comes in 357 Magnum and 41 Magnum.

With these three Freedom Arms Model 83 Perfect Packin' Pistols and Heavy Duty ammunition from Buffalo Bore, any outdoor situation can be handled. Sixguns include from the left counterclockwise: 6-inch 44 Magnum, 4-3/4-inch 454 Casull, and 4-3/4-inch 475 Linebaugh.

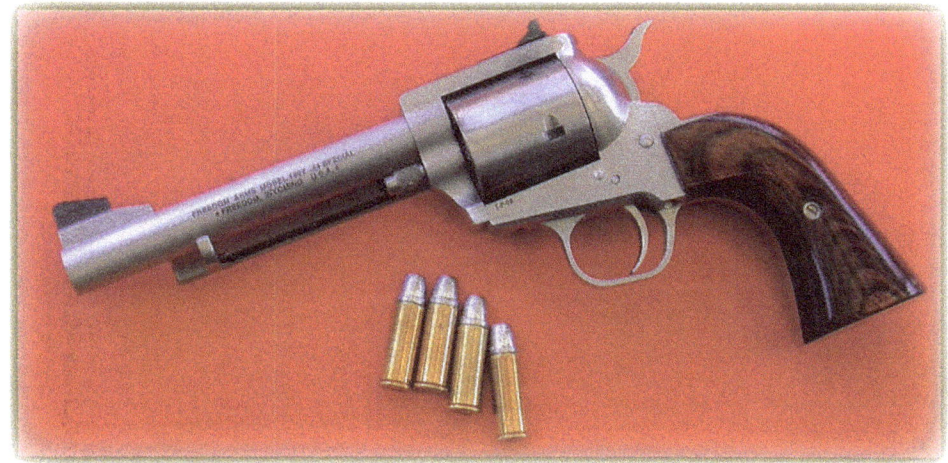

Since before World War I the 44 Special has been found in excellent Packin' Pistols; there is no finer example than this Freedom Arms Model 97 44 Special.

The easiest to pack Perfect Packin' Pistols are the Freedom Arms Model 97s. These little sixguns, slightly smaller than a standard size Colt Single Action Army with a 5-1/2-inch barrel, are available as five-shooters in 45 Colt, 44 Special, 41 Magnum, and as a six-shot 357 Magnum. If one wishes they can be special ordered with a 4-1/4-inch barrel; however, I find the 5-1/2-inch length suits me just fine.

Texas Longhorn Arms' Improved Number Five was a salute to Elmer Keith and his original #5 SAA. The Improved Number Five from Texas Longhorn Arms managed to maintain the flavor of the original while being stronger and replacing Keith's favorite cartridge of the 1920s-1950s with his choice from 1955 on, the 44 Magnum. Even with its larger frame and cylinder, the TLA Number Five still maintains Colt-style balance rather than seeming overly large.

All TLA sixguns have the ejector rod housing and loading gate on the left side for natural use by right-handed shooters, meaning that a right-handed shooter did not have to switch hands to unload or load as the ejector rod and loading gate were on the left side. Other features of the Improved Number Five include a rounded trigger guard with a shotgun style trigger sitting as far back in the trigger guard as possible and also one that moves very little as the hammer is cocked. The hammer spur rides low and is wide for easy cocking, and the top strap is of the flat-top style fitted with a Micro-style adjustable rear sight that is matched up with a Patridge front sight.

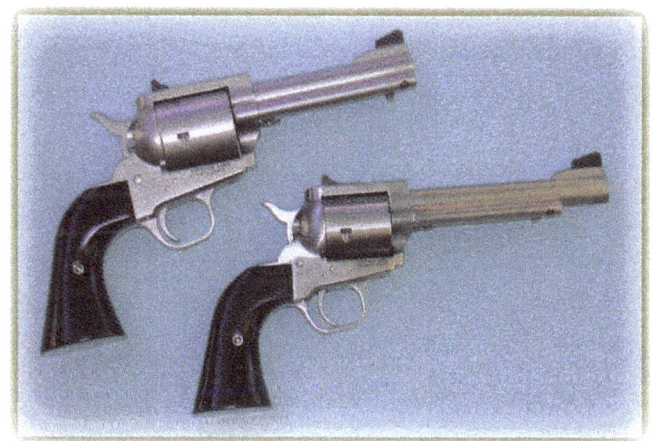

For the serious devotee of Perfect Packin' Pistols, Freedom Arms offers two frame sizes: the Model 83, top, in 454 Casull, 44 Magnum, and 475 Linebaugh; and the smaller Model 97 in 45 Colt, 44 Special, and 357 and 41 Magnum.

In comparing the Keith #5 SAA with the Grover Improved Number Five we find both identical features and improved features. The former includes the grip frame, the cylinder base pin latch release, and a 5-1/2-inch barrel. Differences are the right hand/left hand features already described, the one-piece style grip, a larger frame with a double heat treated cylinder, chambering in 44 Magnum, 4140 aircraft steel construction, coil springs, rounded trigger guard, frame mounted firing pin, improved adjustable sights, a larger ejector rod head, and no frame screws protruding to the left side of the sixgun.

Chapter 41 | Perfect Packin' Pistols Single Action Style

Superb 5-1/2-inch Packin' Pistols: Colt New Frontiers chambered in 45 Colt and 44 Special, a 44 Magnum TLA #5, and in the Lawrence holster, a 45 Colt TLA #5 with Dall sheep grips by Roy Fishpaw.

With one of these Perfect Packin' Pistols a sixgunner is ready for anything! From the top: 5-1/2-inch 500 Linebaugh; 4-3/4-inch Freedom Arms Model 83s in 475 and 454; 5-1/2-inch five-shot 45 Colt by Jim Stroh; and 5-1/2-inch 44 Magnum by David Clements. The last two have both been fitted with Bisley Model grip frames, hammers, and triggers.

Grover's original plans were to build 1200 Improved Number Fives in 44 Magnum as well as some in 45 Colt. The plan of 1200 44 Magnums never materialized, very few 45 Colts were ever produced, and Texas Longhorn Arms closed their doors in the late 1990s. However the guns remain excellent candidates for the "Triple P" title and are well worth searching for at gun shows, in gun shops, and even over the internet.

If I am going to shoot long-range, I will chose a 10-1/2-inch single action sixgun; for hunting it is normally a 7-1/2-inch big bore single action with iron sights or a scope; and for self-defense single action style, the choice would normally be a fixed sighted Colt Single Action Army. But for an everyday sixgun capable of doing anything I ask of it no matter where, no matter what, I'll take a Packin' Pistol.

–Chapter 42–

SINGLE ACTION SIXGUN LEATHER

The early .44-caliber Colt sixguns of the 1840s, the 4-1/2-lb. Walker and the 4-lb. Dragoons, were too heavy to be comfortably carried in a leather holster worn on a belt around the waist; instead, they were normally carried in pommel holsters draped over the front of the saddle, forcing the horse to carry the weight. In the middle of the nineteenth century both the much easier to pack Colt 1851 Navy .36 and Slim Jim holster appeared. The '51 Navy Colt at 2-1/2 lbs. was a viable packing pistol and could be carried high around the waist out of the way but still readily, and it was relatively quickly accessible from quality leather. The Slim Jim rode high in either the crossdraw position or for a twist draw on the strong side. Those claiming a fast draw was not possible with old-style holsters need to go back to take a closer look at authentic Old West leather.

When Ruger introduced the 5-1/2-inch Old Army, Taffin ordered Gunfighter grips from Eagle Grips and this custom high-ride double rig by Bob Mernickle.

The next step forward in leather design for packin' a sixgun was the Mexican, or Cheyenne, loop holster. From the time of the Civil War until after World War I, this was the most common holster in use. In this style of holster the back flap is an integral part of the holster having one, too, or three loops that accept the main body of the bolster. When made of quality leather that is not overly bulky, the Mexican loop still serves well today as an everyday open-carry holster. I am nowhere near as fast as I was as a teenager, not even close, but using a 7-1/2-inch Colt .45 in an El Paso Saddlery 1897 Sweetwater Mexican loop holster, I can draw, cock the hammer, level the sixgun on target, and hit the center of a silhouette target at seven yards with an elapsed time, including reaction time, of eight-tenths of a second. Imagine how fast some of the old-time gunfighters would be with the same equipment! Don't tell me a fast draw was not possible until the invention of the Hollywood steel-lined holster.

Rawhide Walt Ostin engages in some sixgun handling at a Cowboy Action shoot with none other than the Lone Ranger. Photo courtesy of Walt Ostin.

Ever since my three kids were very young, and that goes back a long way, my wife and I have shared responsibilities and household chores. For example I have done all the grocery shopping and we share the cooking; she is the bargainer in the family and it is her job to get the best prices on any major purchases. She is a great asset at a gun show and when my youngest daughter

The most popular holster of the second half of the nineteenth century was the Mexican loop a.k.a. the Cheyenne. This old holster by an unknown maker carries a Colt Bisley securely with maximum protection while still offering a reasonably fast draw.

Single Action Sixguns | 307

Chapter 42 | Single Action Sixgun Leather

Master Leather Craftsman Walt Ostin displays a completed custom rig. Photo courtesy of Walt Ostin.

bought her first car she took Mom along. After the deal was closed the salesman paid Dot the ultimate bargaining compliment by telling my daughter if she ever came in again to buy a car to leave her mother at home. Dot also shops and bargains for her own cars and she does better than most men when it comes to picking a dependable vehicle.

I typically don't haggle but go for quality, rather than low price, whenever I can. There are bargain holsters and there are cheap holsters; the latter should be avoided at all costs. My leather makers are as important to me as my doctors and my gunsmiths. Sixguns are expensive and they deserve the best care when taken afield and that care will be delivered by a well-designed holster made of the best available materials and crafted by experts who understand what a holster should do and what it must not do. Probably even more important than the protection given by the proper leather is the fact that a well-designed holster will not only be the most comfortable for carrying a sixgun, but it will also provide security and the easiest possible access.

Our choice of holsters – like spouses, friends, vehicles, dogs, and firearms – is highly subjective. When it was time for me to choose my first commercial holster, it was relatively simple. The three big manufacturers were George Lawrence, S.D. Myres, and H.H. Heiser, with all representing the best quality it was possible to obtain. However, my local dealer handled only George Lawrence. The Lawrence #120 I purchased for a Ruger .44 Blackhawk in 1957 is still in service today. It has scratches and blemishes after nearly a half century, but it is still in excellent using shape. Good leather properly cared for will last a lifetime and then some. My choice was limited, but today's shooters have a much more difficult time. All three of the 1950's major purveyors of leather are gone, but there are dozens upon dozens of excellent leather craftsman out there with everything from one-man shops to mom-and-pop operations to large companies. Many of these crafters advertise their products in magazines and on the net, so access to them is relatively easy.

Sixgun leather is found throughout this book with concealed carry leather being covered in Chapter 36 and hunting leather in the Chapter 39. What follows herein is just a short glimpse of some of the other great leather available – some of the leather that I have used successfully for many years for hiking, backpacking, camping, or just plain old fashioned woods bumming. Different situations will require different sixguns and different holsters, but the need always remains the same. The holster must provide comfort, security, and most of the time, easy accessibility.

Our choice of sixgun leather will largely depend upon how we are moving about, be it on foot, by horseback, or in a vehicle. A right-handed person may have difficulty driving with a long-barreled sixgun in a hip holster on the strong side, but will be fine with either a crossdraw or shoulder holster. A southpaw can handle the shoulder holster or strong side hip holster, while the cross draw may interfere with seating in the vehicle. Switch to the passenger side and just the opposite is true. If one is going to drive some time and be the co-pilot other times, this should be taken into consideration when selecting a holster.

One of the best designs for carrying a single action sixgun came from Texas Ranger Lee Trimble and is now offered by El Paso Saddlery. Basket stamped and floral carved #1930 Austins carry a pair of Colt .45 New Frontiers.

For security, holsters normally require some sort of retaining device or at the very least fit tightly. A pleasant trip in the field can be ruined as one watches a prized sixgun bouncing off the rocks. The best retaining device is what is known as a safety strap. It consists of sturdy piece of leather that goes over the hammer and then fastens to the front of the holster with a dot snap. It is easily unfastened and can be folded behind the belt when its use is not necessary. I also like the hammer thong for single action sixguns, but it can be hard to release in cold or wet weather with equally cold fingers. Not using the safety strap can be disastrous to a hunting trip. When in Africa I shot a Warthog early on, placed my scoped Freedom Arms in its shoulder holster, leaving it un-snapped. When I bent over to look for the bullet that had exited the Warthog and plowed into the mud, my sixgun slipped out of its holster and the scope hit the only large rock around. Fortunately I had backups.

Cheyenne loop holsters normally hold single action sixguns securely except for the most vigorous activity without the use of a safety strap or hammer thong. This design may be nearly 150 years old, but it is still a practical holster for outdoor use. A good holster deserves an equally good belt. Some holsters such as crossdraws and pancakes ride well on the pants belt if it is a sturdy lined belt of sufficient width and if one also wears suspenders to help distribute the weight. When it comes to cartridge belts, I prefer the folded-over money style belt made of soft leather that conforms to the body shape. For years I felt the belt had to have a full row of cartridges. I have changed completely on this. When out for a day's shooting, a full cartridge loop belt may be appropriate, but mostly I now go with 12-15 cartridge loops on the belt or a cartridge slide that holds 6 or 12 rounds. When going with a shoulder holster I use the same suspenders and I also hope that the weather is at least cool enough to wear a heavy shirt that helps pad the straps of the shoulder holster rig.

The Slim Jim of the 1850s and the Cheyenne of the 1860s and 1870s bring us to the third important holster developments. I use the plural as two men, conferring together, came up with two similar great designs. In 1920 Texas Ranger Lee Trimble and former Northwest Mounted Policeman Tom Threepersons met around a campfire, enjoyed the calm of the night, and discussed sixguns and leather. At the time both were using Mexican loop holsters and put their heads together to design a new holster that would work much better than the Mexican loop style when riding in automobiles, which by that time had mostly replaced the horse. Threepersons removed all excess leather, which included the back flap and that part enclosing the trigger guard, raised the gun as high as possible by having the exposed trigger guard riding on a heavy welt at the back of the holster and also folding over enough leather to sew a very tight belt loop on the back of the holster. The sixgun now rode very high on the belt so the holster was slanted with the muzzle to the rear to allow the sixgun to be drawn quickly.

Trimble was apparently a little more traditional than Threepersons and although he used the same basic design, his holster maintained an abbreviated back flap and rode about one-inch lower than Threeperson's design while maintaining the same angle.

Chapter 42 | Single Action Sixgun Leather

El Paso Saddlery's version of The Cheyenne is shown with this pair, floral carved, carrying a pair of nickel-plated, stag-gripped .45 single actions.

Now it was time to find leathermakers to bring the designs to fruition. Tom Threepersons took his design to S.D. Myres in El Paso while Trimble went to A. W. Brill in Austin. The basic Tom Threepersons has been made by virtually every holster maker with George Lawrence offering it as the #120 Keith and Bianchi as the #1 Lawman. Today both of the original designs are available from El Paso Saddlery and they make excellent packin' holsters. Available in plain, basket stamped, border stamped, and floral carving, the #1920 Threepersons and the #1930 Austin are both fully lined and can be had equipped with or without a safety strap or hammer thong. Both the #1920 and #1930 represent the epitome of leather crafting and the artist who does the floral carving is without equal. I have excellent holsters from the 1950s bearing both the Lawrence and Myres brand that reveal that holsters from El Paso Saddlery are of even a higher quality.

Authentic old West designs from El Paso include the Mexican loop style Rio Grande, Cheyenne, 1880 Ranger, 1890 Original, Dodge City, and the 1897 Sweetwater of S. D. Myers. Going back even farther we have the Californian and Slim Jim, which were originally designed for percussion revolvers. As mentioned earlier, the Slim Jim was probably the first revolver holster to allow a relatively fast draw. For all of these original designs, cartridge belts are offered of standard style and folded over money belt style, all with any combination of cartridge loops desired. All holsters feature a full-leather lining which is also available for cartridge belts. For further treatment of El Paso Saddlery leather, in fact a full chapter, see my previous book *Big Bore Handguns*, published by KP Books.

Anyone over the age of 50 surely recognizes this King of the Cowboys rig as worn by Roy Rogers and duplicated by Jim Lockwood. Photo courtesy of Jim Lockwood.

Another category of holsters is those based upon B-movie and TV western movie rigs. Two of the top craftsmen offering such rigs are Jim Lockwood of Legends In Leather and Walt Ostin of Custom Gunleather. Jim Lockwood is an expert on holster history and especially

One of the all-time great westerns was *Shane*; the belt and holster worn by Alan Ladd as the gunfighter are shown here as re-created by Jim Lockwood of Legends in Leather. Photo courtesy of Jim Lockwood.

western movie leather. Lockwood was a student of Bob Brown and specializes in replicas of the rigs Brown created for many of the B movies of the 1930s and 1940s. Col Tim McCoy, Wild Bill Elliott, Hopalong Cassidy, and Roy Rogers are not just the names of Western movie heroes of days gone by; they are also names of just a few of the intricate holster and belt combinations worked out in the tiniest detail from Legends in Leather.

Lockwood works with the thin leather that was used by the creators of the B movie rigs, which though fully lined are lightweight, thin, and most importantly very comfortable to wear. Comfort went south with the arrival of the heavy-duty rigs with long drop loops and metal linings arriving in the 1950s and it must have been real chore for movie cowboys to wear them while sitting at a table or riding a horse. John Wayne's last movie was made in 1976, and yet he was one of the few movie cowboys who never, ever used the Hollywood fast draw style of cowboy leather. Instead, the Duke spent most of his career after the mid-1940s wearing a comfortable soft belt with a high-riding holster. Jim Lockwood's belts fit the curve of the body rather than the other way around and will not wear one down during a long day afield.

Lockwood says of his leather crafting: "...I had the great fortune to become friends with perhaps the greatest leather artist of all time, Mr. Bob Brown. Back in the 1930s Hollywood, Bob's genius helped mold and embellish the developing tradition of the Western by designing and handcrafting the gunleather for many of the famous Western stars of that golden era. Among Bob's credits are the rigs worn by Bill Boyd as Hopalong

Another Jim Lockwood re-creation is The Red Ryder as worn by Wild Bill Elliott as Fred Harman's Red Ryder. Photo courtesy of Jim Lockwood.

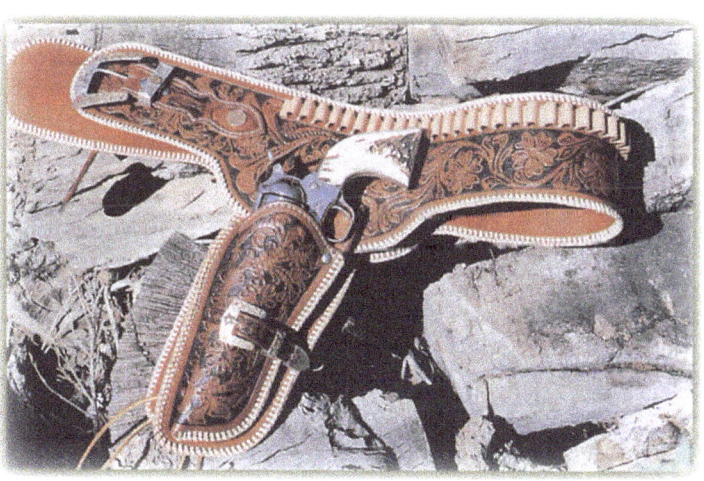

The Three Mesquiteers were a very popular trio in the 1930s and 1940s B movies. Jim Lockwood re-created this rig as worn by Crash Corrigan in the role of Tucson Smith. Photo courtesy of Jim Lockwood.

Single Action Sixguns | 311

Chapter 42 | Single Action Sixgun Leather

Another great Western was *The Angel and the Badman* with John Wayne as gunfighter Quirt Evans tamed by the lovely Quaker girl portrayed by Gail Russell. Jim Lockwood calls this rig Angel and the Badman. Photo courtesy of Jim Lockwood.

Cassidy, Charles Starrett as the Durango Kid, Bill Elliott, Lash LaRue, Sunset Carson, Buck Jones, Rex Allen, and even John Wayne's outfit in *Red River*. Bob has generously given me permission to use many of his original patterns and carving designs, which I've used to produce many rigs. By carefully researching old movies and videos, movie books, and stills; by exploring the many Western museums and taking pictures; and by visiting with the stars of the era, I have developed a library of my own patterns that duplicate the personal rigs of most of the popular Western heroes and heroines. My rigs are high quality, fully-lined, carefully handcrafted replicas in the appropriate colors, plain or carved, sewn or laced, just like the originals." He's right.

Anyone who grew up watching westerns on TV, or even now in re-runs, should recognize Ben Cartright's belt and holster as built by Jim Lockwood. Photo courtesy of Jim Lockwood.

Everyone should recognize this rig as that worn by John Wayne in so many movies and re-created by Walt Ostin. Photo courtesy of Walt Ostin.

Walt Ostin of Custom Gun Leather offers authentic Old West styles, fancy silver screen hero B Western rigs, or TV cowboy patterns, mostly of the Fast Draw style. He makes some of the best renditions of the various Lone Ranger rigs found anywhere. Custom Gun Leather provides several variations of the Mexican loop style of holster include the Cheyenne, the Russell, the Montanan, the Kansas, the Utah, the Colorado, and the Texas. Every local leather maker of the nineteenth century had his own technique and special rendition of the basic Southwestern Mexican loop holster design by using one or two loops, wide or slim loops, and more or less trigger guard exposed.

One of my favorite rigs is Ostin's Colorado, consisting of a single weight belt with cartridge loops and a holster that allows the sixgun to ride deeply and securely in its basic Mexican loop design. The uniqueness of this outfit comes from the stamping pattern. In addition to the border stamping, Ostin uses a stamp that is neither basket weave nor fish scale but rather his own design that combines a little bit of each. The result is striking. Walt can also provide excellent concealment leather and makes the best replica of the original Tom Threepersons I have ever seen. In fact the old lawman would surely be pleased to wear a rig from Walt Ostin.

Not too many movies allowed the hero to wear two different rigs. This Walt Ostin holster and belt is patterned after that worn by Charles Starrett, the Durango Kid, when he was Steve instead of the Kid. Photo courtesy of Walt Ostin.

This beautiful re-creation by Walt Ostin is reminiscent of the two-gun heroes of the silver screen. Photo courtesy of Walt Ostin.

I was just getting heavily involved in the shooting of single action sixguns when Fast Draw arrived. I had both a double rig from Ray Howser and a single Hollywood Fast Draw single rig from Arvo Ojala, both made for 7-1/2-inch Colt SAAs. In the early 1960s, Andy Anderson, who had been working under Ojala, went out on his own with his Gunfighter line of fast draw holsters. Unfortunately I never purchased one of Anderson's Walk and Draw rigs. Today they are very

Chapter 42 | Single Action Sixgun Leather

A most practical holster for everyday use is this Walt Ostin rig allowing the sixgun to be carried high and securely. Note the unusual stamping pattern on the holster body.

difficult to find, but Walt Ostin offers a perfect recreation of Anderson's Walk and Draw outfit. Made to carry a 7-1/2-inch Colt, Walt's rig incorporates all of Andy's ideas including no back flap on the holster, six cartridge loops on the offside, a special Gunfighter buckle, and the decorative Gunfighter stitching on the belt.

One of my favorite old movies is *The Plainsman* starring Gary Cooper as Wild Bill Hickok. I always enjoyed Cooper westerns, but for me the real star of this movie was his belt and holsters. Never mind that Coop carried stag-gripped 5-1/2-inch Colt SAAs instead of Hickok's ivory-stocked 1851 Navies – how he carried them was what was important to me. Some Hollywood leatherworker had taken the basic Slim Jim design and added a drop loop. They were worn butts to the front and radically slanted backwards. They looked good but did flop around quite a bit. From the first time I saw this movie as a kid I knew that someday I would have a rig like this but modified to remove the sloppiness.

Another rig everyone should recognize is this Walt Ostin double set as worn by the Lone Ranger. A true work of art carried out in leather. Photo courtesy of Walt Ostin.

The design may be 150 years old, but the Mexican double loop holster for a 7-1/2-inch single action is still a good choice; holster and belt by Walt Ostin. Photo courtesy of Walt Ostin.

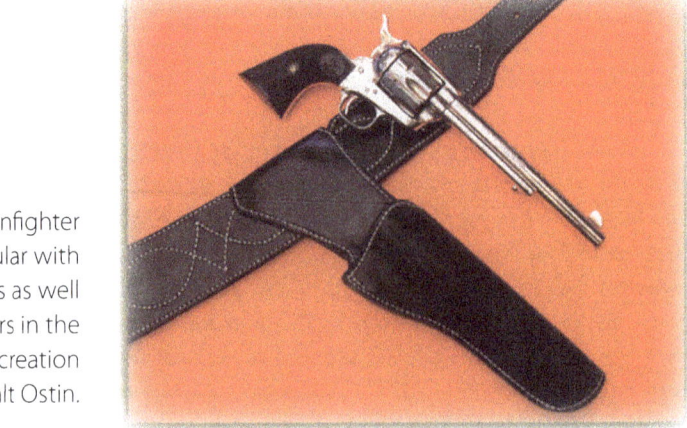

Andy Anderson's Gunfighter rig was very popular with Fast Draw shooters as well as many Western stars in the 1960s. This faithful recreation is by Walt Ostin.

Bart Ballew patterned this holster after that worn by Gary Cooper as Wild Bill Hickok in *The Plainsman*. The carving was beautifully done by Marty Overstreet.

Forty years passed and someday never arrived. Then I ran into Bart Ballew of Circle Bar T Leatherworks. As we were talking, I mentioned Cooper's rig and my desire to have a modified version. It sounded like a great idea to Bart so we came up with the idea of a fully lined belt and two drop-loop Slim Jim holsters made to hang straight. I ordered them to fit an 8-inch Colt Single Action. The extra half-inch over standard was to allow the use of not only 7-1/2-inch Colt SAAs but also 1860 Armies, cartridge conversions, and 1871-72 Open-Tops as well.

I turned Bart loose as to whatever design he wished to put on the holsters and the belt with the only stipulation that there be no cartridge loops because I wished to use this rig with sixguns of several chamberings as well as percussion revolvers. I was overwhelmed with the beauty of the custom rig that resulted. Marty Overstreet of Circle Bar T, an absolute master craftsman, performed the custom carving, covering the belt and both holsters with a floral design and a most attractive stamped background that gives the whole rig an antique look. The entire rig is black except for the floral carving, which is a dark brown. This allows the carving to stand out from the background. Both the belt and holsters are fully lined and everything is sewn together with a double row of stitching. Both billets feature a silver rhombus with a gold border, and the final touch was a great surprise to me as the engraved silver plated buckle is inscribed SIXGUNNER across the top in gold plating. Great leather.

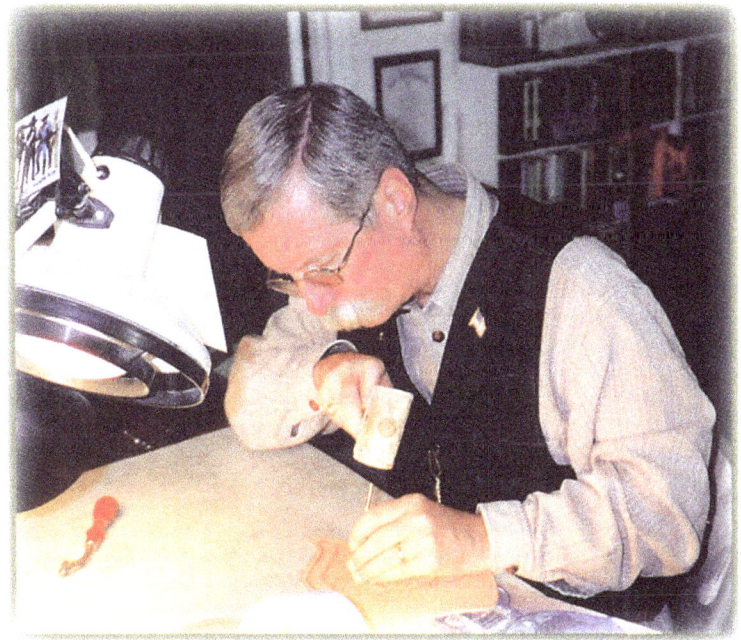

Master craftsman Jim Lockwood of Legends in Leather is shown at his leather working bench stamping a pattern on a custom holster. Photo courtesy of Jim Lockwood.

Single Action Sixguns | 315

Chapter 42 | Single Action Sixgun Leather

For cowboy action shooters, or anyone else preferring two straight drop holsters, Bob Mernickle offers this handsomely tailored black outfit with silver embellishments. Photo courtesy of Bob Mernickle.

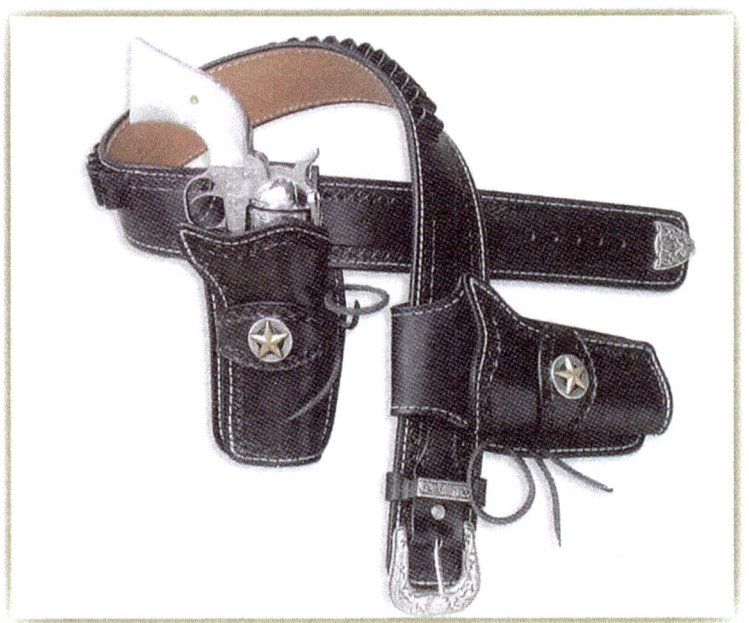

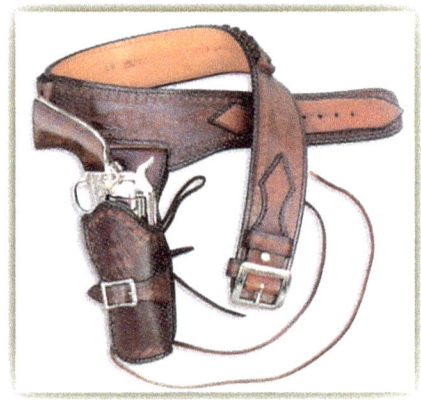

Bob Mernickle is one of the top Fast Draw shooters as well as a Master craftsman. This steel-lined holster is cut low in the front for the utmost in speed. Photo courtesy of Bob Mernickle.

Bob Mernickle, recently of Canada and now settled into Nevada, offers a complete line of custom leather especially for Fast Draw and Cowboy Fast Draw as he is one of the top participants in both. He does it all: plain, stamped, carved, extra fancy, whatever the shooter desires. I have been using his PS-6 concealment rig for a Colt Single Action for several years now; it is crafted of minimum leather, is secure, and yet offers immediate access to the sixgun without any retaining device to get in the way.

When Ruger announced the 5-1/2-inch stainless steel Old Army, I ordered a pair for cowboy action shooting, added Eagle's buffalo horn Gunfighter grips, a pair of R&D 45 Colt conversion cylinders from Taylor's & Co., and a double rig from Bob Mernickle. Bob crafted a lined belt and two holsters patterned after the Slim Jim but made to hang straight and very high on both sides. They are finished in a very dark brown, almost black, with gunfighter stitching on both holsters and belt: a very high-quality, well-designed rig.

This beautifully patterned double rig by Bob Mernickle carries a pair of 1890 Remingtons for cowboy action shooting. Photo courtesy of Bob Mernickle.

Many cowboy action shooters prefer a strong side holster and a cross draw holster. This custom rig fully carved with silver embellishments and buckle is by Bob Mernickle. Photo courtesy of Bob Mernickle.

Andy Anderson designed it and Clint Eastwood made it popular. David Cox of Cedar Ridge Saddlery built this rough-out "Eastwood" for a 7-1/2-inch Colt. The carved ivory stocks are by Paul Persinger.

The newest leathercrafter I have discovered is David Cox of Cedar Ridge Saddlery. David was one of the vendors at the first National Cowboy Fast Draw Championships held in Idaho, and I was immediately struck by the beauty, quality, and craftsmanship exhibited in the holsters and belts he had on display. David specializes in Mexican loop style holsters as well as Andy Anderson's style in plain, full floral carved, or roughout. When I saw his leather displayed I immediately recognized the chance to purchase something very special for Diamond Dot.

David's carving is exceptionally beautiful, so a full floral carved belt with two matching holsters was made to fit her 5-1/2-inch Ruger Vaqueros was secretly ordered with room left on the back of the belt for me to apply 1-inch silver letters spelling out her alias. David added a special touch to the belt as instead of leaving the back plain he did a background carving consisting of a Diamond Dot pattern, diamonds with dots at each corner. Belt and holsters are both fully lined and the carving is absolutely exquisite. What I didn't know at the time I ordered the items for Dot was that she had also ordered a rig for me, proving once again that great minds really do run in the same channel. My rig is the Eastwood, patterned after the Andy Anderson rig worn by Clint Eastwood in so many spaghetti westerns. It is tailored for Cowboy Fast Draw competition, rough out, made to hang straight, and to carry a 7-1/2-inch Colt. Like Dot's outfit, it also has a beautiful silver buckle.

David Cox of Arizona is an extremely talented leather worker. The carved holsters carry a pair of 5-1/2-inch Colt Single Actions, while the rough-out rig packs a 7-1/2-inch Colt .45 with carved ivory stocks by Paul Persinger.

Single Action Sixguns

Chapter 42 | Single Action Sixgun Leather

The Leather Arsenal offers a complete line of single action holsters such as this very fast holster cut extra low in the front for speed and finished off with a custom silver belt buckle.

Elmer McElroy of the Leather Arsenal, former employee of the master leather crafter Milt Sparks, has been building concealment leather for several decades and recently branched out offering top quality, double leather rigs for the Western enthusiast and cowboy action shooter. All of his rigs are high quality, double leather, plain or border stamped, and built to last a lifetime of shooting.

Some shooters simply consider sixguns as a tool; I consider them works of art. As such they deserve to be carried in well-designed, exceptionally-crafted, high-quality leather.

A pair of 5-1/2-inch Colt single action 44 Specials match up well with this rig by the Leather Arsenal.

–Chapter 43–

CRAFTING YOUR OWN SINGLE ACTION SIXGUN LEATHER

When I purchased my first single action, in fact my first sixgun, a .22 Ruger Single-Six, I found myself with the pleasant decision of choosing a belt and holster for it. The two premium holster makers in those days were S.D. Myres and George Lawrence, and since my local dealer used the second supplier I chose a #120 Keith holster with a matching belt. I wanted a full floral-carved, fully-lined, laced-edge fancy rig, but my wallet dictated the plain-black, single-weight outfit. It served me well. I don't have the slightest idea whatever happened to it, but I wish I had it back.

Will Ghormley put together this packet of Cheyenne Holster patterns for the home craftsman to be able to make his own leather.

A few months later my first Colt Single Action arrived, a 38-40 from the very early 1900s. I felt really fortunate to have such a fine Colt, but the price difference between a box of .22s and 38-40s was an enormous chasm. In those pre-reloading days the .22 still served for most of my shooting and I rationed a box of factory 38-40s. The first leather rig for this 4-3/4-inch Colt 38-40 was totally handmade for the simple reason I was now in debt and certainly did not have enough money buy the Lawrence rig I really wanted. The only answer was to make my own. I had not yet discovered Tandy Leather and their catalog sales, and there was no leather store in my area, so I did the next best thing and went to the local belting supplier. For a very little amount of cash I was able to buy a three-inch wide piece of belting for the belt and another wider piece leather to make the holster.

This was very heavy-duty leather and after drawing the holster pattern I cut it out with a razor blade box cutter. The belt was easy; I simply cut it to length, riveted a buckle billet at one end and the corresponding billet with holes at the other end, and I had a belt. The holster was folded over, formed around the sixgun, had holes drilled along the edge, and was then fastened together with a rawhide thong. A slot was cut in the belt to accept the back flap, which was folded over and then fastened to the holster proper with a strip of leather also riveted to the back flap. It wasn't the prettiest outfit ever seen but it was definitely serviceable and exceptionally sturdy. Again, I don't know whatever happened to this one, and as an example of my first journey into leatherworking, I wish I had it back also.

Single Action Sixguns | 319

Chapter 43 | Crafting Your Own Single Action Sixgun Leather

With a little practice, it is possible for the hobby leather maker to use Will Ghormley's patterns to build these Cheyenne holsters.

In addition to the holster pattern packet, Will Ghormley's Old West Collection also provides three other packets for belts, cuffs, and spur straps. All packets are offered by Tandy Leather.

George Lawrence and the original S.D. Myres are now long gone, but Myres has been revived by a fellow down in Texas, and El Paso Saddlery offers many of the old-style S.D. Myres patterns. Today there are dozens of leather manufacturers and leather crafters offering just about anything anyone could desire. However, I have never lost the inclination to make my own even though I do own some of the best rigs put together by some of the finest leather artisans who ever lived. I learned by doing, by observing, and by trial and error. Over the decades various leather companies have offered holster patterns, but most of these were not very good. One notable exception is the excellent book by Al Stohlman, *How To Make Holsters*. Even though it is nearly a half-century old it is still viable and available in reprinted form from Tandy Leather.

In the 1950s Chic Gaylord ran a one-man leather shop in New York City specializing in concealed leather for law enforcement officers. In fact, he is the father of modern concealed carry leather. All of his concealed carry holsters used minimum leather and were hand-fitted and boned to fit a particular sixgun or semi automatic. Federal officers and undercover agent were regular customers to his small shop. Gaylord published a book in 1960, *Handgunner's Guide*, covering speed shooting and holster design. This book, which has also been reprinted, contains an excellent section on making a Missouri Skin-Tite holster for a single action sixgun. Two other excellent books for studying holster styles are John Bianchi's *Blue Steel and Gunleather* and Richard Rattenbury's *Packing Iron*.

In addition to the Cheyenne Holster and Cartridge Belts packet, Will Ghormley has now added Dodge City Holster, Forty-Niner Holster, and Law Dog Holster packets to the Old West Collection line found at Tandy Leather.

One of the easiest holsters to make is the Tom Threepersons, a design that features no excess leather whatsoever. Until Threepersons arrived on the sixgun leather scene, most holsters were of the Mexican style with a wide back flap. Threepersons removed the back flap and replaced it by a piece of trim leather that is folded over and sewn to the back to the holster to provide the belt loop. The front of the trigger guard rides on a heavy leather welt along the back of the holster. Although later modifications would offer safety straps or leather hammer thongs, the Threepersons design called for heavy saddle skirting that was perfectly wet formed to the outline of the exact sixgun it was to carry. To make such a holster one simply folded over enough leather to make a belt loop, sewed it to the back of the holster, and then folded over the body proper of the holster and sowed it along the edge. I have found the easiest way for me to sew leather is to first drill holes with a small drill bit in a MotoTool and then use two needles, one at each end of the waxed linen thread to form double stitching.

Will Ghormley is not only one of the top leather crafters in the business, but he is now sharing his expertise with the rest of us. Will says: "Everything I craft is hand-made for my customers. I cut each item from the hide when it's ordered. It's worked and tooled right here at my bench. I dye and oil it and clamp it in my stitching pony to sew by hand. I started crafting leather over 30 years ago. I don't do it because it's easy. I don't do it because I'm smart. I fact, I only stick with it because I'm stubborn and I love the work I do.

You can get store-bought leather most anywhere, but during my lifetime I'm only going to be able to craft so many rigs bearing my name. I make 'em like the pioneer craftsmen made them over a hundred years ago."

I have several Ghormley rigs. Ghormley is a student of western history and truly authentic designs, so all of his leather work comes from studying old examples of the Frontier period. His true love being cap-n-ball sixguns, he sent along two true period pieces for two of the most popular of the percussion pistols. For the 1851 Navy came a Slim Jim style that he calls the Pistolero, with matching belt. The belt is border stamped while the holster, which completely covers the trigger guard and hammer, is carved in the old-time incised style that was found on frontier leather of the mid-nineteenth century. For the 1860 Army .44, Ghormley crafted an authentically styled holster, the West Texas, with a half back flap and the hammer and trigger guard slightly exposed.

A matched pair of Cheyennes, which carry a pair of Colt single actions, is lined with red leather. The holster itself is of the Mexican style with two holster loops and fully carved with a darkly dyed background. The matching cartridge belt also features leather rosettes with a red background and nickel spots. It is authentically styled a fitting rig for a pair of 5-1/2-inch Colts.

Will discovered leatherworking in a high school shop class and that changed his life's direction. Leatherworking for him is not just a job but a very important part of his life. I learned by gathering information from a wide variety of sources over a period

Single Action Sixguns | 321

Chapter 43 | Crafting Your Own Single Action Sixgun Leather

Taffin made all of these heavy duty field holsters with safety straps to pack 4-3/4-inch Colt single actions and a 7-1/2-inch Ruger Vaquero securely and comfortably.

of more than four decades. Today it is much simpler as Ghormley now provides access to truly authentic nineteenth century professional leather patterns as well as carving and stamping designs.

Will has come up with four packets of patterns covering four types of leather accoutrements, all of which are available from both Tandy Leather and the Leather Factory. All packets are complete with patterns for each project including the leather needed and a list of all required materials and tools. These are not basic instructions on how to actually produce a holster or other leather goods. For this valuable information both Will and I highly recommend *How To Make Holsters* by Al Stohlman.

Will's Cheyenne Holster Packet is, as its name signifies, designed for crafting an authentic nineteenth century holster. The Cheyenne or Mexican Loop holster was the most popular and practical holster available in the late 1800s. This packet contains tooling patterns, lining holsters, adapting patterns for left-handed or cross draw use, all for the following sixguns: Colt SAA, Bisley, Thunderer and Lightning, in 4-5/8-, 5-1/2- and 7-1/2-inch barrel lengths; Colt 1851 Navy; Colt 1860 Army; Remington 1858; Ruger Vaquero and Bisley Vaquero, 4-5/8-, 5-1/2- and 7-1/2-inch barrel lengths; and the Smith & Wesson Schofield. Holsters can also be easily modified to fit the cartridge conversions and the 1871-72 Open-Top.

A good holster needs a good belt, so we have the Cartridge Belts Packet. In addition to the materials and required tools list, this packet contains cutting and measuring patterns for two money belts, two Ranger belts, and two Scout belts. The latter belt is lighter and trimmer than either the money belt or Ranger style.

Instructions are also given on installing cartridge loops and buckles.

Okay. You have decided to make your own holster. As a minimum you'll need heavyweight paper to make a pattern (I like posterboard), a very sharp knife or single edged razor blade, two needles, some heavyweight waxed linen thread, and of course, some leather. You will find you can turn out very serviceable rigs with this equipment. For less than the cost of one good holster, you can purchase all the equipment needed to make top-quality holsters. I would also suggest the following: a pair of heavy-duty leather scissors, a supply of needles and waxed linen thread, a can of leather cement, a stitching groover, a stitching spacer wheel, an edge beveler, a supply of dot fasteners for safety straps, and a setter for same. If you want to lace holsters instead of sewing them, you'll need Florentine lacing and special needles. The only expensive item in this list is the scissors. Later on, you may wish to add decorating stamping tools, basket weave stamps, or even floral carving tools.

Tandy's Leather has stores in many areas as well as a mail-order catalog, and a subscription to the *Leather Craftsman* magazine gives access to a long list of suppliers of leather and tools. Belly leather is absolutely worthless for holsters either because of its quality or thickness. Only the back of a cowhide is suitable for making holsters and belts. Leather is sold by thickness with one ounce equal to 1/64-inch in thickness. Usually 10 to 12 ounces is the best for making holsters. Saddle skirting is also very good, but it is very thick and very hard to work with.

Here are the basic steps for crafting a simple holster such as the Tom Threepersons: Using the heavyweight paper, make a pattern to fit the individual

Gordon Marts made this holster patterned after the Tom Threepersons using the tools pictured. Photo courtesy of Gordon Marts.

sixgun, allowing at least one inch at the bottom and along the edges where it will be sewn together. Don't forget the belt loop. The pattern is traced on the leather, and then the rough holster is cut out and folded around the sixgun to check for fit. Before sewing, the edge beveler is used to bevel all edges except those that will be sewn together.

A stitching groover is used to make a channel for the thread to lie in and a stitching spacer wheel spaces the holes evenly. I use a very small drill bit and drill my holes before sewing, being careful to keep the drill perpendicular to the leather. If a safety strap is installed, this is done before folding the belt loop over and sewing. At the same time, the male end of a safety snap is carefully installed on the holster proper so it will not rub against the sixgun on the interior of the holster. Before sewing the holster together, cement a welt about one-half inch in width and the same thickness as the leather used for the holster along the entire length of the edge on the inside back part of the holster. I also like to add another welt about three inches long in the trigger guard area.

The entire center area of the holster where it folds around the sixgun should be wet down with water. (I just hold it under the faucet.) The holster is then folded over and the two edges cemented together. Holes are drilled carefully and the holster is sewn together using two needles, one at each end of the waxed linen thread, and with each hole is entered from both sides. Approximately 16 times the length of the holster is needed in thread. I prefer to start at the trigger guard area about four holes down, go up and then backstitch down again. This gives extra strength in the trigger guard area. When I reach the toe of the holster I backstitch about four holes and cut the thread off flush. Sandpaper or a sanding wheel is used to smooth-finish the edge of the holster, and it is then rubbed vigorously with a round piece of hardwood.

Before applying any finish it is necessary to perform the most important step. The holster is immersed in water and then removed and the excess water shaken off. The intended sixgun is shoved into the holster and carefully set correctly. Fingers or a small piece of hardwood are used to shape the holster around the sixgun. The sixgun is removed, dried off, and oiled, while the holster is set aside to dry for 24 hours. The snap on the safety strap should not be set until the holster has dried thoroughly. The final step is to apply edge dressing if desired and then oil or die the holster. I prefer a neatsfoot oil finish, applying with a small brush and hand rubbing to the desired color. If the holster is going to be worn concealed, instead of oil a natural wax should be used to prevent staining clothes.

This chapter has not been a total how to do it piece but rather an encouragement to try it. I have made hundreds of holsters for myself and a few friends, and I can't begin to rival any of the professional holster makers. But then I don't have to. All I have to do is please myself.

–Chapter 44–

SINGLE ACTION SIXGUN LOADS

Single action sixgunners have a wide range of cartridges to choose from including 357 Magnum, 41 Magnum, 44 Special, 44 Magnum, 45 Colt, 454 Casull, and the 475 and 500 Linebaughs.

Life was so much simpler, but certainly much harder, in the 1870s and 1880s. Just imagine a life without airport security, or even airplanes, television and an endless supply of mindless programming, cell phones, gasoline engines, freeways, the IRS, and thousands upon thousands of rules and regulations, which now intrude into all facets of our life. At least from this end of history, travel by rail looks a whole lot more appealing than by airplanes or automobiles. Of course, the great advantage of looking back is the fact we can look through rose-colored glasses and everything looks much better than it probably was. At least we can dream and wonder if these are the best of times or those days were.

When it came to sixgun ammunition, things were definitely much simpler. Whether your single action sixgun was chambered for 44 Russian, 38-40, 44-40, or 45 Colt, it was simply necessary to ask for a box of cartridges as they were all black powder and pretty standardized as to bullet weight. The one fellow that had to be careful was he who had a 45 Schofield. He had to make sure he had the shorter 45 S&W ammunition rather than the 45 "Long" Colt.

Today there are all levels of sixguns strength-wise and ammunition loaded with either smokeless or black powder; heavy-duty hunting loads with standard and heavyweight bullets; and reloading information that must be tailored to a specific sixgun. For example, the old 45 Colt is offered in many single action sixguns that are not all equal when it comes to strength. At the bottom end, strengthwise, we have the replica single actions including the top-break Smith & Wesson copies, and then we work our way up with the Colt Single Action Army, the Colt New Frontier, the USFA Single Action with its slightly larger cylinder, the Ruger Blackhawk, the Freedom Arms Model 97, custom five-shot single actions, and finally the Freedom Arms Model 83 454 with an extra cylinder chambered in 45 Colt. Even with the 38-40 and 44-40 there are two different levels, with the Colt-style single action sixguns being nowhere near as strong as the Ruger Blackhawks and Vaqueros; all of this means that care should be used in selecting any single action sixgun ammunition, be it factory produced or reloaded.

Big bore sixguns do not always have to be run full bore; enjoyable easy shooting loads can be assembled with Bullseye or Unique.

Over the years, I've settled on some favored sixgun loads, both those I refer to as everyday working loads and heavy duty hunting loads. Sometimes these overlap, for example my EWL for the old 44 Magnum Flat-Top Rugers also serves well as a hunting load. There was a time in my life in which I thought everything had to be loaded pedal to the metal. In those days, I loaded for the 45 Colt, 44 Magnum, 44 Special, and 38 Special. Although I had 357 Magnum-chambered sixguns at the time, they were normally fed heavy 38 Special loads. I never marked the boxes as I used the standard Keith load for everything. I was missing one of the main advantages of loading my own, which is tailoring loads for specific situations and specific sixguns. I've learned over the years and reload much smarter these days.

Everyday working loads are standard loads capable of doing just about anything short of hunting our largest big game. The original black powder loads for 45 Colt, 44-40, and 38-40 used 255-, 200-, and 180-gr. bullets respectively at muzzle velocities of 850 to 1000 fps from a sixgun. These are the same levels I set for my everyday working loads. Years ago all my bullets were carefully cast, sized, and lubricated to fit a particular sixgun. These days my time is at a much greater premium and I find myself turning more and more to commercial cast bullets and using my own home-cast bullets for much less than 50 percent of my shooting chores.

For sizing 38-40 and 44-40 cartridges, a spray lube works very well and allows them to be loaded on an RCBS Progressive Model 2000 Press.

For standard 38 Special loads I long ago settled on 5.0 grains of Unique. Used with Oregon Trail's 158-gr. SWC, this is about an 850 fps load and safe in any Colt Single Action-style full-sized sixgun chambered for the 38 Special or for any 357 Magnum. Before +P 38 Special loads there was the 38/44 loading originally made for Smith & Wesson's Heavy Duty N-frame 38 Special in 1930. I still stay with Keith's Lyman #358429, a hard-cast bullet of around 168 grains weight, but I have dropped his 13.5 grains load to 11.5 grains of #2400 for right at 1100 fps. For my use this load goes only into sixguns marked 357 Magnum or in large-framed 38 Specials such as original 38 Specials from Colt and Great Western, or the current USFA 38 Special single action.

Single Action Sixguns | 325

Chapter 44 | Single Action Sixgun Loads

Some sixguns do their best with gas-checked bullets such as these excellent designs by Ray Thompson from Lyman, 156 grain #358156, 215-gr. #429215, 255 grain #431244; and 260 grain #452490.

Two superb 357 Magnum bullets for everyday use are Elmer Keith's #358429 and Ray Thompson's #358156.

For three decades the best cartridge/bullet combination for the handgun hunter was the 250-gr. hard-cast Keith loaded in the 44 Special at 1,200 fps.

My favorite everyday working load for the 357 Magnum in the Ruger Blackhawk has pretty much remained the same over several decades. Since the late 1950s my load of choice for the 357 Magnum has been 14.5 to 15.5 grains of 2400 under the Lyman/Thompson #358156GC bullet. This is still a favorite and it has been joined by 13.0 grains of WW296 or H110 with Cast Performance Bullet Co.'s 187-gr. flat-nosed, gas-checked, hard-cast bullet. This load is just under 1300 fps from a special 357 Flat-Top Blackhawk I had fitted with a 10-1/2-inch barrel from a Ruger .357 Maximum.

I have pretty much standardized my everyday working loads for the 45 Colt, 44-40, and 38-40 using the same powder charge. My most used load with all three is 8.0 grains of Unique with bullets from Oregon Trail Bullet Co. With the RCBS Pro 2000 Progressive Press, I have found I can use the same shell plate for all three cartridges and it takes less than 15 seconds to change the die plate, the powder measure is stationary, and all three take the same primer, all going together to make the assembly of everyday working loads very easy. Bullet weights and styles are 250-gr. RNFP and 255-gr. SWC for the 45 Colt, 200- and 225-gr. RNFPs for the 44-40, and 180-gr. RNFP for the 38-40 respectively. These are not only great everyday working loads in Colt Single Actions and replicas, they place very little stress on either sixgun or sixgunner. In a short, easy to pack 4-3/4-inch sixgun muzzle velocities are around 850 fps with the 45 Colt, 900 to 950 fps with the 44-40, and right at 1000 fps with the 38-40. These are black powder level loads without the black powder smoke and necessary cleanup.

I used to think it was pretty close to blasphemy to load the 44 Special with anything but the original Keith bullet. After many years of carefully casting, lubing, and sizing my own bullets I discovered that Oregon Trail's 240-gr. SWC not only shot just as good as my bullets but often even better. Much of my casting time is now put to better use as about 90 percent of my 44 Special loads are assembled with Oregon Trail's 240-gr. SWC bullet. A very easy shooting load that duplicates the original pre-World War I load is 6.0 grains of Unique for around 750 fps from a short-barreled Colt Single Action, Great Western Frontier, or 44 Special conversion on an old Model 357 Blackhawk. A more powerful everyday working load is 7.5 grains of Unique for around 950 fps.

Oregon Trail's 240-gr. SWC also works exceptionally well in the 44 Magnum. To duplicate Keith's heavy 44 Special load in Magnum brass, I use 10.0 grains of Unique for 1180 fps in a 7-1/2-inch 44 Magnum Ruger Flat-Top Blackhawk. To duplicate my everyday

There are many excellent bullets offered for the loading of the 44 Magnum or 44 Special including the 250-gr. Keith SWC, 215- and 255-gr. gas checked designs by Ray Thompson, Oregon Trail's 240 SWC, and Speer's 240 and 200 Gold Dot jacketed bullets.

Whether chambered in 44 Special or 45 Colt, the Colt single action runs very well using 250 to 260 hard cast bullets loaded over Unique, 2400, or H4227.

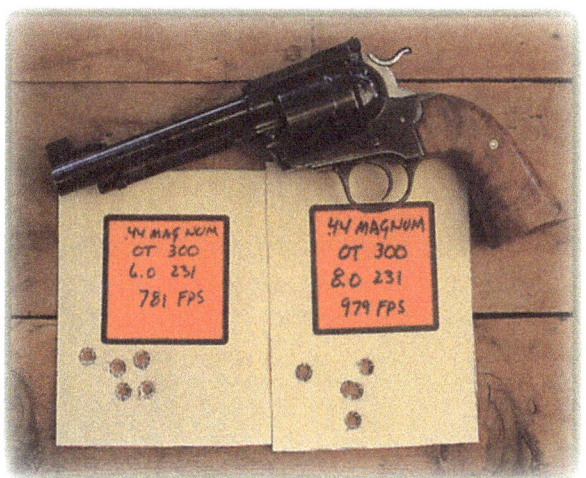

Easy shooting loads for the 44 Magnum using Oregon Trail's 300 grain bullet are assembled with Winchester's WW231.

The 45 Colt is easy on a shooter using Oregon Trail's 300 grains bullet with WW231, Universal, or HS-6.

working load for the 44 Special in the 44 Magnum, I use the same bullet with 8.5 grains of Unique. I still like to use the Keith bullet in the 44 Magnum, as well as the 44 Special, 45 Colt and 38 Special. Dry Creek Bullet Works offers authentic Keith bullets in all of these calibers. For easy shooting loads in the 44 Magnum with a 300-gr. bullet I go with Oregon Trail's 300FN over 6.0 to 8.0 grains of WW231 for 725 to 975 fps.

I have already mentioned the 45 Colt with the 38-40 and 44-40 and the fact my most used load with the 45 Colt these days is 8.0 grains of Unique and Oregon Trail's 250-gr. RNFP or their 255-gr. SWC. When I do cast my own, the same charge goes under the RCBS #45-270 SWC, an excellent Keith design weighing 275 to 280 grains, depending upon alloy used, that clocks out at 900+ fps and shoots superbly. For easy shooting with heavy bullets, I again go with Oregon Trail's 300-gr. FN over 7.0 grains of Universal or 10.0 grains of HS-6 for around 850 fps, and 8.0 grains of WW231 for around 975 fps. One load that I always keep on hand, simply because it works when others may fail, is the original Lyman Keith bullet #454424 over 20.0 grains of H4227 for a little over 1000 fps. This is my all-time favorite load in a special 4-3/4-inch 45 Colt New Frontier – in fact, it is the only load that will group all the shots in one hole from this little sixgun.

Single Action Sixguns | 327

Chapter 44 | Single Action Sixgun Loads

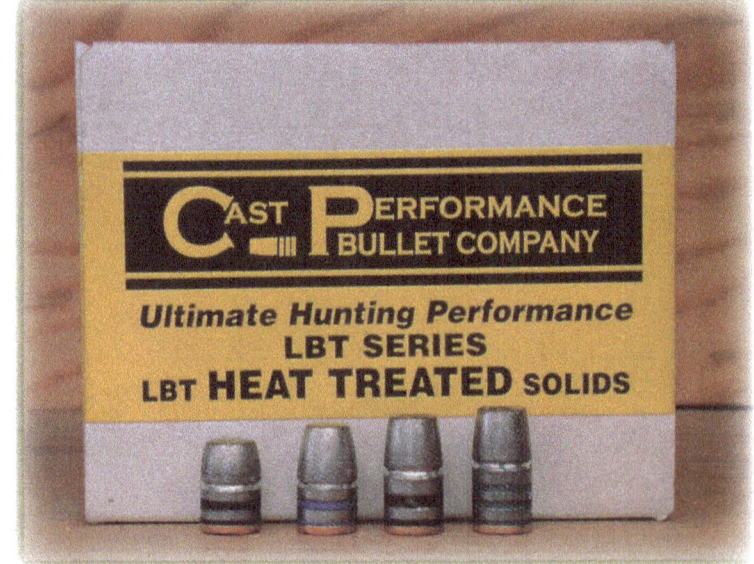

Cast Performance Bullet Company offers a full line of LBT designs in both Wide Flat Nose and Long Flat Nose versions with gas checks for assembling full power hunting loads.

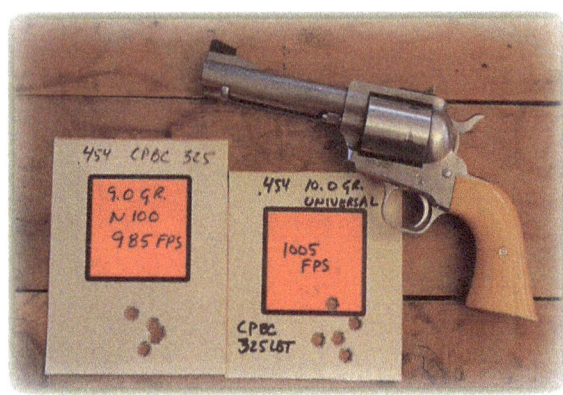

The 454 Casull made its reputation with full bore loads, but it is much more pleasant to shoot with Cast Performance Bullet Co.'s 325 grain LBT at 1000 fps.

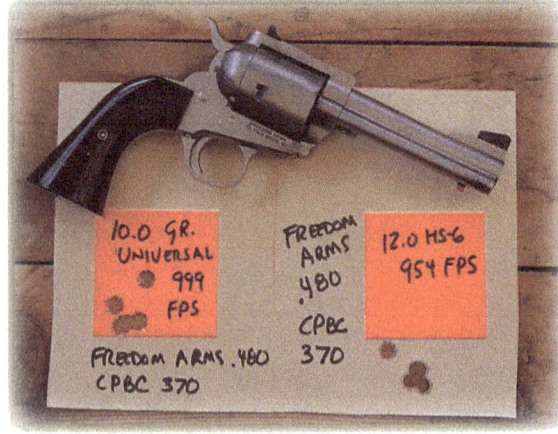

The 480 Ruger is another big bore sixgun that is much easier to shoot using Cast Performance Bullet Co.'s 370 bullets at 950 to 1000 fps.

I would hate to try to tally the number of full power loads, which have gone down the barrels of a Freedom Arms 454 Casulls. The sixguns came through unscathed; however my wrists and hands demand lighter loads be used as everyday working loads, so I now use 10.0 grains of HS-6 and either Oregon Trail's 300-gr. FP or my own hard-cast NEI 325-gr. Keith-style bullets. Muzzle velocity is right at a very pleasant-shooting 900 fps. With Cast Performance Bullet Co.'s 325-gr. LBT, I like 10.0 grains of Universal or 9.0 grains of AA N-100 for around 1000 fps.

You have probably noticed that most of my everyday working loads are in the 900 to 1000 fps range no matter what the bullet weight. This holds true for the 480 Ruger. Cast Performance Bullet Co. offers a full range of bullet weights for the 480 Ruger. For use in a 4-3/4-inch Freedom Arms Model 83 I choose the CPBC 370-gr. LBT over 20.0 grains of H4227, 12.0 grains of HS-6, or 10.0 grains of Universal for 950 to 1,000 fps or their 425-gr. LBT with 18.0 grains of H4227 for 925 fps.

For the 475 Linebaugh-chambered 4-3/4-inch Freedom Arms Model 83 I move up a bit above the 480, which is used in the same sixgun. For an everyday working load with the 475 Linebaugh, I once again go with a CPBC LBT bullet, the same 425-gr. bullet used in the 480 Ruger. However, the powder charge of H4427 is bumped up to 23.0 grains for right at 1100 fps from a 4-3/4-inch barrel. With this load we are beginning to move out of the pleasant shooting range and entering the realm of heavy duty hunting loads. An easy shooting, and exceptionally accurate, load for the 475 is CPBC's 390-gr. LBT over 8.0 grains of Unique and 825 fps.

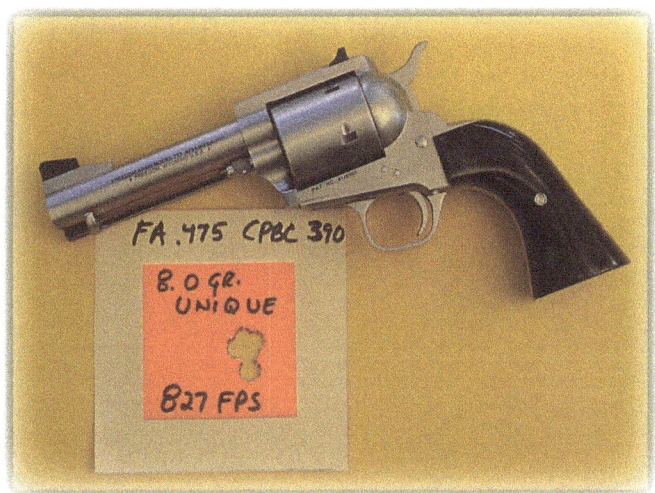

Is the .475 a target pistol? It can be, using Cast Performance Bullet Co.'s 390 grain LBT over 8.0 grains of Unique.

We can't forget the 500 Linebaugh, which, while known for power, does not always have to be run full throttle. CPBC's 410-gr. LBT over 12.0 grains of Unique does 900 fps and will surely take care of any deer at close range even though it is relatively easy shooting. For an even milder load, 13.0 grains of HS-6 does 775 fps and is very easy on the shooter.

My heavy duty hunting loads begin with the 357 Magnum although I do not normally recommend it for hunting big game. However I have taken several animals with the 357 Magnum and all of them were one-shot instantaneous kills. I stacked the deck in my favor by taking only animals that weighed 150 pounds or less and with standing broadside shots. Actually, standing broadside shots is what I want in every situation with any animal and any sixgun load. Hornady's 158-gr. XTP-JHP is my bullet of choice using either 15.5 grains of 2400 or 17.5 grains of WW296 for around 1350 fps from a 7-1/2-inch Ruger Bisley. It will do the job cleanly if the animals are reasonably small and distances kept reasonably short.

My favorite hunting load for the 41 Magnum, again in the 7-1/2-inch Ruger Bisley, is Lyman's 220-gr. #410459 SWC over 19.5 grains of 2400 for about 1450 fps, making it plenty potent for deer and black bear. Freedom Arms opened new parameters on the 41 Magnum by chambering their Model 83 for the smallest of the true big bores. The 10-1/2-inch Model 83 41 Magnum is not only the most accurate 41 Magnum I have ever fired; it is also the most accurate centerfire revolver I have ever experienced. My load of choice, which is only for use in the Model 83, is Hornady's 210-gr. XTP over 22.0 grains of Accurate Arm's AA#9 for 1750 fps and the capability of placing three shots in 5/8 inch at 100 yards. If I had to pick a sixgun/load combination for shooting deer at 100 yards or a bit more, this would be my choice. We are, of course, talking about using a scope sight, not iron sights, and a solid rest.

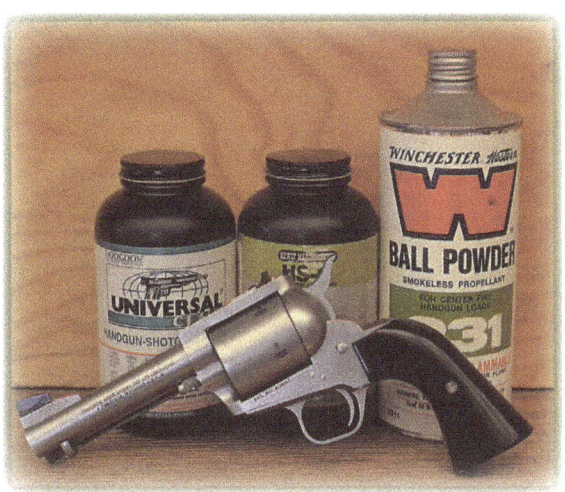

The barrel may say 475 Linebaugh but that doesn't always mean heavy horsepower loads; life is much more enjoyable using loads assembled with Universal, HS-6, and WW231.

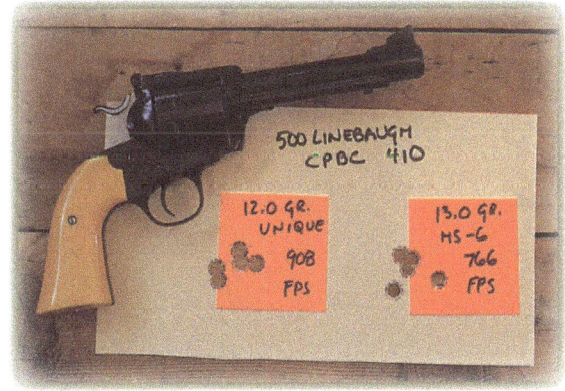

John Linebaugh's .500 delivers excellent accuracy when downloaded to 750 to 900 fps. Even at these moderate speeds the 410 Cast Performance Bullet Co. bullet still delivers enough power for most situations.

Single Action Sixguns

Chapter 44 | Single Action Sixgun Loads

The Keith Bullets: They have been around long enough to be called Classic, but they are still excellent bullets; they are Lyman's #358429, #429421, and #454424.

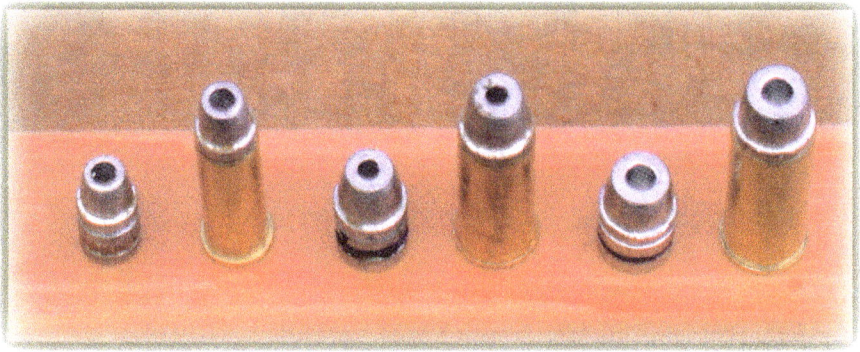

Long before there were jacketed bullets there were cast hollow points. Those shown here are Keith bullets loaded in 38 Special, 44 Special, and 45 Colt.

The 44 Special is fast approaching its one hundredth anniversary. It is still an excellent cartridge, especially in the Colt New Frontier, when loaded with Unique, #2400, or Hodgdon's 4227.

For use as a heavy duty hunting load in the 44 Special I still like the 250-gr. hard-cast Keith bullet over 17.0 grains of 2400 for 1200 fps or 18.5 grains of H4227 for 1160 fps from 7-1/2-inch sixguns. However a better choice, for me at least, is Speer's copper-cupped, lead-core 225-gr. JHP over 16.5 grains of 2400 for 1150 fps. I related in the chapter on hunting handguns of the use of the hollow point version of the Keith bullet over 17.0 grains of 2400 to successfully and quickly take two very large feral boars. If I were to take nothing the rest of my handgun hunting life except deer-sized animals at 50 yards or less I could get by quite famously with the 44 Special. However, be warned, all of these 44 Special loads are in the 25,000 to 30,000 psi range and should be approached with the mandatory caution warning of starting well below the listed loads and working upwards.

Great bullets for single action sixguns: for the 45 Colt or 454, the 260 Keith, 270 Scovill/RCBS, 300 Freedom Arms, 340 SSK; for the 44 Magnum, 290 BRP and 310 SSK.

With the 44 Magnum we enter the bottom rung of the ladder marked True Big-Bore Sixguns, those which are adequate for taking large boned, tough, heavily muscled animals where deep penetration is needed. My favorite heavy-duty 44 Magnum load is BRP's 290-gr. Keith-style gas-checked hardcast bullet over 21.5 grains of either WW296 or H110 for right at 1350 to 1400 fps from a long-barreled sixgun. For those who prefer to cast their own bullets this is NEI's #295.429. I do not use this load on deer-sized game, but instead prefer Hornady's 240-gr. XTP over 25.0 grains of H110 for around 1350 fps. This duplicates the Black Hills 44 Magnum load, which is absolutely deadly on deer-sized game.

For use in my Ruger 45 Colts, be they Blackhawks or Bisley Blackhawks, my favorite heavy duty load is BRP's 305-gr. FNGC (flat-nosed gas check) over 21.5 grains of either WW296 or H110 for 1200 fps from a 7-1/2-inch barrel. Others push these sixguns further, but I see no reason to do so as this load is more than adequate for my use with the 45 Colt. Besides, I have the 454 Casull if I want to go further with a .45-caliber bullet.

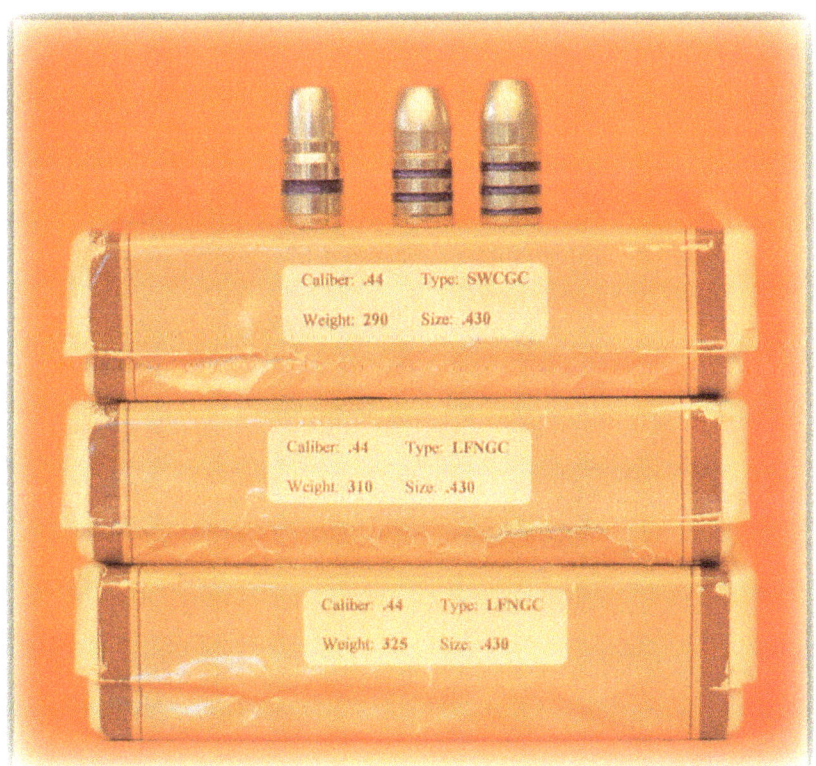

BRP offers excellent, hard cast, gas checked bullets for big bore sixguns.

Single Action Sixguns | 331

Chapter 44 | Single Action Sixgun Loads

These .45s will handle just about anything: 45 Colt loaded with 255 and 310 SWC bullets; Lyman #454424, NEI #310.451 and #325.451; the 454 Casull loaded with a 300-gr. FN; the Freedom Arms 300-gr. gas check and the J.D. Jones-designed 340 FN.

Garrett Cartridges offers heavy-duty hunting loads for just one cartridge, the great 44 Magnum with 310- and 330-gr. HammerHeads at 1300 fps. The 310s are for the Super Blackhawk and similar sized-single actions.

The same bullet mentioned as a favorite with the 45 Colt is also my number one choice for the 454 Casull; in fact BRP's 305-gr. FNGC was originally designed by Dick Casull for the 454 Casull. It is superbly accurate in either the 45 Colt or the 454 Casull. In the bigger .45, I use the same bullet and powders as with the 45 Colt, but the powder charge is increased to 32.0 grains for 1700 fps. This is an extremely powerful and flat-shooting load.

The 480 Ruger is simply the 475 Linebaugh trimmed back, so I normally treat it as I would the 44 Special when compared to the 44 Magnum, i.e., in the 1200 fps range. Favorite loads include the Cast Performance Bullet Company 370-gr. LBT over 22.0 grains of Lil' Gun for 1216 fps, and 19.0 grains of Lil' Gun or 21.0 grains of H110 for right at 1125 fps with Cast Performance Bullet Company's 390-gr. LBT. Do not take these comparatively mild muzzle velocities for granted. I took my first American bison with a 420-gr. hard-cast bullet at 1100 fps in the 480 Ruger from the Freedom Arms 4-3/4-inch Model 83. At 35 yards, the bullet gave complete penetration, in one side and out the other.

My bullets of choice for the 475 Linebaugh from CPBC are the 370-gr. LBT over 26.0 grains of Lil' Gun for 1450 fps; the 420-gr. LBT and 23.0 grains of Lil' Gun for 1350 fps; and the 440-gr. LBT with the same powder cut back to 22.0 grains for 1300 fps. These bullets are all designed for the deepest possible penetration of the toughest animals that walk.

There was a time when it was impossible to find true hunting loads for sixguns. All that has changed and we have many factory heavy duty hunting Loads to choose from. Several years ago Randy Garrett of Garrett Cartridges began offering serious heavy duty hunting loads for the 44 Magnum using 280-gr. and 310-gr. Keith-style hard-cast semi-wadcutters. This great 44 ammunition has been dropped from production and replaced by two new loads that have proven to be even more accurate and to also give more penetration on big, tough critters.

The newest .44 loads from Garrett are known as the Hammerheads. They feature 310-gr. and 330-gr. LBT hard cast bullets rated at 1300 fps. The heavier-bulleted load is designed to be used only in the Ruger

Buffalo Bore offer serious hunting loads in all the big bore calibers.

Redhawk and Super Redhawk with their longer than normal cylinders. I was pleasantly surprised to find both loads would chamber in my Freedom Arms 44 Magnum. The former Garrett loads with Keith-style bullets would not work in this revolver. Test firing the Garrett loads at 50 yards was accomplished with a Freedom Arms .44 with a 7-1/2-inch barrel and Leupold 2x LER scope. The 310-gr. and 330-gr. Hammerheads both came in at 1400 fps with 1-3/8-inch 50-yard groups in the Freedom Arms. Garrett Cartridges offers these 44 Magnum loads as their only handgun load, and they are for serious handgun hunters who desire power and superior penetration.

Buffalo Bore's motto is Strictly Big Bore, Strictly Business and they mean exactly that as they offer only heavy duty hunting loads, Until very recently the smallest bore they offered was the 41 Magnum, followed by all the other big bore sixgun loadings. They have now added a 170-gr. JHP and a 180-gr. hard-cast load for the 357 Magnum.

All of Buffalo Bore's 45 Colt loads are advertised as heavy and are for use only in modern heavy duty 45 Colt sixguns. There are three standard offerings: for maximum penetration, a hard-cast 325-gr. LBT-LFN at 1325 fps; for penetration combined with expansion, a 300-gr. Speer PSP (Plated Soft Point) at 1300 fps; and for smaller critters where expansion is more important than deep penetration, a 260-gr. jacketed hollow point at 1450 fps. The fourth offering from Buffalo Bore was designed with the mid-framed Freedom Arms Model 97 45 Colt in mind and is a 300-gr. Speer PSP at 1200 fps.

Buffalo Bore has not forgotten the ancient 45 Colt offering Heavy 45 Colt loads for strong sixguns such as this five-shot Ruger by Jim Stroh.

Chapter 44 | Single Action Sixgun Loads

Kelye Schlepp of Belt Mountain base pins has come up with another fine idea, Punch Bullets, which are designed for maximum penetration without deforming for big game hunting. Shown are bullets for the 44 Magnum, 45 Colt/454, 480/475, and 500 Linebaugh. The fired .500 on the right could be loaded and fired again.

Buffalo Bore's 44 Magnum loads consist of three heavy 44 Magnum offerings. First there is the 270-gr. Speer Gold Dot loaded to 1450 fps; then a 300-gr. Speer PSP (Plated Soft Point) at 1300 fps; and finally, for maximum penetration, a 305-gr. hard-cast LBT-LFN (Long Flat Nose) rated at 1325 fps.

Buffalo Bore, as far as I know, is the only company offering heavy-duty 41 Magnum hunting loads. Their standard weight bullet is a 170-gr. JHP at 1650 fps, which is joined by two hard-cast bulleted loads: a 230-gr. Keith bullet rated at 1450 fps, and for maximum penetration there is the 265-gr. LWN (Long Wide Nose) at 1350 fps. As with most Keith-bulleted rounds, the Buffalo Bore 230-gr. bullet will not fit the tight chambers of the Freedom Arms Model 83.

Buffalo Bore offers two hard-cast and one jacketed bullet load for the 454 Casull. The jacketed version consists of Freedom Arms' 300-gr. jacketed flat nose at 1625 fps, while the two hard-cast bullet loads are a 325-gr. LBT-LFN at 1525 fps and a 360-gr. LBT-WFN (Wide Flat Nose) at 1425 fps. These loads are made to handle big, mean critters.

John Linebaugh's first wildcat is well represented by custom five-shot revolvers from John Linebaugh as well as other sixgunsmiths including Hamilton Bowen, David Clements, Jack Huntington, Gary Reeder, and Jim Stroh. The only factory loads available are those from Buffalo Bore. There are three hard-cast LBT designs: a 435-gr. LFN at an easy shootin' 950 fps; the same bullet at a full-bore 1300 fps; and a 440-gr. WFN for maximum shocking power combined with penetration at 1250 fps. All of these are joined by a 400-gr. jacketed hollow point at 1400 feet per second. A 435-gr. LFN at 950 fps may be easy shootin' compared to the others, but it would certainly do the job on a deer or feral pigs.

John Linebaugh's original 475 was made by trimming 45-70 brass to length, resulting in a cartridge with a large rim that will fit in custom five-shot cylinders fitted to Ruger frames. However, there is not enough room for the same rounds to fit in a Freedom Arms cylinder as the rims would overlap as well as interfere with the ratchet. When Buffalo Bore began offering 475 Linebaugh ammunition as a factory chambering, the rims were trimmed to fit in the Freedom Arms-sized cylinders. So we now have the excellent Model 83 offered in 475 Linebaugh in all standard barrel lengths, as well as six versions of 475 ammunition from Buffalo Bore.

First comes an easy shootin' loading, deer and pig load of a 420-gr. LBT-LFN at 950 fps; next comes the two heavy-duty cast bullet loads, both at 1350 fps and both weighing in at 420 grains, one an LBT-LFN for maximum penetration and the other an LBT-WFN (Wide Flat Nose) for maximum shocking power. For those preferring jacketed bullets, there is a 400-gr. JSP at 1400 fps and finally two loadings of a 350-gr. JHP at 1500 fps and a 440-gr. LBT-WFN at 1325 fps.

The 480 Ruger is simply the 1.400" 475 Linebaugh cut back to 1.275" and loaded by Buffalo Bore to be easier handling than the bigger brother. For practice, or for deer hunting as well, there is the 370-gr. LFN at an easy shooting 1000 fps; the same bullet loaded to a full 1300 fps; and my choice for bison, the 420-gr. WFN that clocks out at 1200 fps from a 7-1/2-inch barrel.

During all the years Elmer Keith was trying to get ammunition companies to offer his 1200 fps Keith load, he also asked if they could at least load it to 1000 fps. Ammo manufacturers were concerned about his heavy load in older guns so he suggested this compromise. It never happened until now. Buffalo Bore offers a true 255-gr. hard-cast Keith bullet rated at an even 1000 fps. This load should do fine for close-range operations on small deer.

Bullets for hunting have been mentioned throughout this book and we now have a new style of bullet offered to us for deep penetration on big game by Kelye Schlepp of Belt Mountain base pins. Kelye's latest offering is Punch Bullets, bullets turned from brass on a lathe with a solid lead core. He currently offers heavyweight Belt Mountain Punch Bullets for the 44 Magnum, 45 Colt/454 Casull, 457 Linebaugh/480 Ruger, and the 500 Linebaugh. They not only offer deep penetration; they also shoot very well. Thus far my loads have been as follows:

45 Colt in a Ruger 4-5/8-inch Blackhawk:
320-gr. bullet over 22.0 grains of H4227 for 1169 fps.

454 Freedom Arms 4-3/4-inch Model 83:
320-gr. bullet with 26.0 grains of H4227 for 1326 fps.

475 Linebaugh in a Freedom Arms 4-3/4-inch M83:
388-gr. bullet, 25.0 grains of H4227 for 1175 fps.

480 Ruger in a Freedom Arms 4-3/4-inch M83:
388-gr. bullet and 25.0 grains of H4227 for 1010 fps.

500 Linebaugh in a custom five-shot Linebaugh 5-1/2-inch Bisley:
458-gr. Punch Bullet with 24.0 grains of H4227
for an easy shootin' but deep penetrating 939 fps.

> "Buffalo Bore offers a true 255-gr. hard-cast Keith bullet rated at an even 1000 fps."

Single Actions Sixgunners gather at a Shootists Holiday in Colorado. From left: Tedd Adamovich of BluMagnum Grips; John Taffin, Sr., Field Editor for *Guns* and *American Handgunner*; Hal Swiggett, the Dean of single action sixgunners; Blackie Sleeva, one of the top single action pistoleros; and Jim Wilson, former Sheriff of Crockett County, Tex., and Handgun Editor for *Shooting Times*.

FINIS

My first thought when starting any work like this is always how will I ever fill the allotted pages? That soon changes as the problem shifts from finding enough material to trying to figure out what must be left out. The pictures in this book represent less than one-tenth of the total pictures, both personal and those provided by several single action sixgunners, I had to choose from. For those providing both pictures and information, I wish to express a very sincere thank you to all, and especially to Jim Martin, who went more than the extra mile.

It has been 50 years since I fired my first single action sixgun. Over this one half-century I have been privileged to fire almost every model of single action ever produced in this great country. I've never had the pleasure of shooting a Mikkenger or a Merwin-Hulbert, but at least 50 percent of this will be solved shortly as I have a 99.9% condition, nickel-plated, 44-40 Merwin Hulbert dating back to the last quarter of the nineteenth century on layaway at Shapel's. I never, ever, thought I would ever spend this much money for a single action, but then again in 50 years of shooting I've only rarely ever encountered a Merwin-Hulbert and never in like new condition. I still look forward to the day I find a Great Western Deputy Model chambered in 44 Special. There has to be one out there somewhere.

I started shooting just at the right time. I saw the beginning of the Great Western and the return of the Colt Single Action; I grew up with Ruger single actions, especially the original Blackhawks; I witnessed the beginning of Freedom Arms and have been able to shoot all of their models and calibers, hunting with many of them; I was privileged to be the first writer to shine the spotlight on Texas Longhorn Arms, Cimarron Firearms, and Hartford Armory; I've seen United States Patent Firearms go from a company producing Italian replicas to become United States Firearms with a totally American-made single action; and I have happily watched the progression of replica single actions from the spaghetti western days to the very authentic reproductions we now have.

All of the single actions have provided enormous pleasure over this past half-century, but this pales in comparison to the wonderful men I have met who also have the same love for single action sixguns I do. In 1986, I invited a dozen men to meet me in Wyoming and basically to shoot single action sixguns. That was the beginning of the Shootists and our annual Holiday. We got together with a common interest in single actions and found something much deeper. Over the years solid friendships have been formed: friendships that have helped each other over the hard times. One of the toughest things we do each year is have a memorial service in the mountains for those who have passed away. There's something very special about firing a single action sixgun salute to fallen comrades as seven men each fire three rounds from a single action sixgun and hear the reverberating echo coming back from the rocks.

We live in what seems to be a semi-automatic era and yet the single action sixgun survives; it always will. Not only is it a most practical sidearm, but it also takes us back to what in many ways was a much better time. May it always be so.

About the author . . .

John Taffin has been a handgun writer for the past 50+ years and a staff writer for the *American Handgunner* and *Guns* for the past 36+ years assigned to do feature articles as well as regular columns, "Taffin Tests", "The Sixgunner", "Handloading", and "Campfire Tales". He has also contributed regular columns and features to *Shoot!Magazine*, *The Freedom Arms Collectors Journal*, and *Handgun Hunters International* as well as the *Digest Annuals* from Krause Publications. His main interests are big bore sixguns, lever action rifles, and single-shot rifles and pistols, and he has hunted extensively with handguns in America and Africa.

Taffin is also the founder, 1986, and first chairman of The Shootists and past chairman of the Outstanding American Handgunner Awards Foundation. He has also served on the board of the Handgun Hunters Chapter of SCI, and is a NRA Life Member. He considers only five things in this life to be important, namely, Faith, Family, Friends, Firearms, and most assuredly Freedom.

Author of eight books and more than 2,000 articles, Taffin and his wife Dot have three children and 14 grandchildren and reside in Idaho. The kids are all grown-up and on their own, however, Taffin's constant companions during his writing chores are Chloe, a Pomeranian, and Molly, a Shih Tzu, who also serve as doorbells and watchdogs. He still misses his two Malamutes, Red and Wolf.

Other Titles from *John Taffin* You May Enjoy

Action Shooting Cowboy Style
Grab your handgun, take aim and pull the trigger as John Taffin brings the wild west to the era of modern shooting. In this in-depth guide, he explains America's hottest game for shooters of all levels—with a cowboy twist. Whether you're brand new or a seasoned competitor, this book shows you all the guns, loads and accessories you'll need.

HARDCOVER ISBN 978-1-63561-683-5

Big Bore Handguns
From his beloved Colt Single Action to Freedom Arms and Taurus pistols, acclaimed expert John Taffin is armed with facts about the biggest six-guns around. In this must-have guide, he discusses the ins and outs of shooting, hunting and competing with high caliber handguns. Included are hundreds of photos and honest reviews.

HARDCOVER ISBN 978-1-63561-689-7

Big Bore Sixguns
In this comprehensive guide, firearms expert John Taffin follows the development of big bores from 1870 to today. His fascinating model to model review includes more than 300 photos and fine details about the pioneering sixguns, as well as the influence those guns have had on each other and the field of competitive shooting.

HARDCOVER ISBN 978-1-63561-690-3

Our books may be ordered from any bookstore or online purveyor of books, or directly through our Web site, www.echopointbooks.com. Or visit our retail store, located in Brattleboro, Vermont.

www.ingramcontent.com/pod-product-compliance
Lightning Source LLC
Chambersburg PA
CBHW061747290426
44108CB00028B/2913